S0-BWX-019

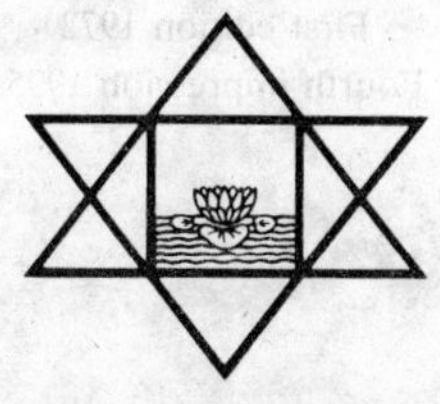

SRI AUROBINDO

BANDE MATARAM

EARLY POLITICAL WRITINGS

SRI AUROBINDO ASHRAM
PONDICHERRY

First edition 1972
Fourth impression 1995

ISBN 81-7058-416-7

Published by Sri Aurobindo Ashram Publication Department
Printed at Sri Aurobindo Ashram Press, Pondicherry
PRINTED IN INDIA

Contents

CONTENTS

CONTENTS

CONTENTS

CONTENTS

CONTENTS

CONTENTS

CONTENTS

CONTENTS

NOTE: The dates marked with asterisks denote only probable dates.

EARLY POLITICAL WRITINGS

From 1890 to May 1908

NOTE

The articles in this Volume are not an index of Sri Aurobindo's later views on the leading problems of the day. His views had undergone a great change with the development of his consciousness and knowledge.

The latest views of Sri Aurobindo on these problems appear in Volume 15 : "Social and Political Thought".

1890 - 1905

India Renascent*

THE patriot who offers advice to a great nation in an era of change and turmoil, should be very confident that he has something worth saying before he ventures to speak; but if he can really put some new aspect on a momentous question or emphasise any side of it that has not been clearly understood, it is his bounden duty, however obscure he may be, to ventilate it.

*

It is time that an Indian who has devoted his best thoughts and aspirations to the service of his country, should have in his turn a patient hearing.

* Notes found in Sri Aurobindo's earliest available manuscripts, dated 1890-92, his student days in England.

NEW LAMPS FOR OLD

The facts about the articles in the *Indu Prakash* were these. They were begun at the instance of K. G. Deshpande, Aurobindo's Cambridge friend who was editor of the paper, but the first two articles made a sensation and frightened Ranade and other Congress leaders. Ranade warned the proprietor of the paper that, if this went on, he would surely be prosecuted for sedition. Accordingly the original plan of the series had to be dropped at the proprietor's instance. Deshpande requested Sri Aurobindo to continue in a modified tone and he reluctantly consented, but felt no farther interest and the articles were published at long intervals and finally dropped of themselves altogther.

*

The title refers to Congress politics. It is not used in the sense of the Aladdin story, but was intended to imply the offering of new lights to replace the old and faint reformist lights of the Congress.

From notes and letters of Sri Aurobindo

New Lamps for Old - 1

IF THE blind lead the blind, shall they not both fall into a ditch? So or nearly so runs an apopthegm of the Galilean prophet, whose name has run over the four quarters of the globe. Of all those pithy comments on human life, which more than anything else made his teaching effective, this is perhaps the one which goes home deepest and admits of the most frequent use. But very few Indians will be found to admit — certainly I myself two years ago would not have admitted, — that it can truthfully be applied to the National Congress. Yet that it can be so applied, — nay, that no judicious mind can honestly pronounce any other verdict on its action, — is the first thing I must prove, if these articles are to have any *raison d'être*. I am quite aware that in doing this my motive and my prudence may be called into question. I am not ignorant that I am about to censure a body which to many of my countrymen seems the mightiest outcome of our new national life; to some a precious urn in which are guarded our brightest and noblest hopes; to others a guiding star which shall lead us through the encircling gloom to a far distant paradise: and if I were not fully confident that this fixed idea of ours is a snare and a delusion, likely to have the most pernicious effects, I should simply have suppressed my own doubts and remained silent. As it is, I am fully confident, and even hope to bring over one or two of my countrymen to my own way of thinking, or, if that be not possible, at any rate to induce them to think a little more deeply than they have done.

I know also that I shall stir the bile of those good people who are so enamoured of the British Constitution, that they cannot like any one who is not a partisan. "What!" they will say, "you pretend to be a patriot yourself, and you set yourself with a light heart to attack a body of patriots, which has no reason at all for existing except patriotism, — nay, which is the efflorescence, the crown, the summit and coping-stone of patriotism? How wickedly inconsistent all this is! If you are really a friend to New India, why do you go about to break up our splendid unanimity? The Congress has not yet existed for two lustres; and in that brief space of time has achieved miracles. And even if it has faults, as every institution however excellent it may be, must have its faults, have you any plausible reason for telling our weakness in the streets of Gath, and so taking our enemies into the secret?" Now, if I were a strong and self-reliant man, I should of course go in the way I had chosen without paying much attention to these murmurers, but being, as I am, exceedingly nervous and afraid of offending any one, I wish to stand well, even with those who admire the British Constitution. I shall therefore find it necessary to explain at some length the attitude which I should like all thinking men to adopt towards the Congress.

And first, let me say that I am not much moved by one argument which may possibly be urged against me. The Congress, it will be said, has achieved miracles, and in common gratitude we ought not to express [towards] it any sort of harsh or malevolent criticism. Let us grant for the moment that the Congress has achieved miracles for us. Certainly, if it has done that, we ought to hold it for ever in our grateful memory; but if our gratitude goes beyond this, it at once incurs the charge of fatuity. This is the difference between a man and an institution; a great man who has done great things for his country, demands from us our reverence, and however he may fall short in his after-life, a great and high-hearted nation — and no nation was ever justly called great that was not high-hearted — will not lay rude hands on him to dethrone him from his place in their hearts. But an institution is a very different thing. It was made for the use and not at all for the worship of man, and it can only lay claim to respect so long as its beneficent action remains not a memory of the past, but a thing of the present. We cannot afford to raise any institution to the rank of a fetish. To do so would be simply to become the slaves of our own machinery. However I will at once admit that if an institution has really done miracles for us — and miracles which are not mere conjuring tricks, but of a deep and solemn import to the nation, — and if it is still doing and likely yet to do miracles for us, then without doubt it may lay claim to a certain immunity from criticism. But I am not disposed to admit that all this is true of the Congress.

It is within the recollection of most of us to how giddy an eminence this body was raised, on how prodigious a wave of enthusiasm, against how immense a weight of resisting winds. So sudden was it all that it must have been difficult, I may almost say impossible, even for a strong man to keep his head and not follow with the shouting crowd. How shall we find words vivid enough to describe the fervour of those morning hopes, the April splendour of that wonderful enthusiasm? The Congress was to us all that is to man most dear, most high and most sacred; a well of living water in deserts more than Saharan, a proud banner in the battle of Liberty, and a holy temple of concord where the races met and mingled. It was certainly the nucleus or thrice-distilled essence of the novel modes of thought among us; and if we took it for more than it really was, — if we took it for our pillar of cloud by day and pillar of fire by night; if we worshipped it as the morning-star of our liberty; if we thought of old myths, of the trumpets that shook down Jericho or the brazen serpent that healed the plague, and nourished fond and secret hopes that the Congress would prove all this and more than this; — surely our infatuation is to be passed by gently as inevitable in that environment rather than censured as unnatural or presuming.

If then any one tells me that the Congress was itself a miracle, if in nothing else, at any rate in the enthusiasm of which it was the centre, I do not know that I shall take the trouble to disagree with him; but if he goes on and tells me that the Congress has achieved miracles, I shall certainly take leave to deny the truth of his statement. It appears to me that the most signal successes of this body were not miracles at all, but simply the natural outcome of its constitution and policy. I suppose that in the sphere of active politics its greatest success is to be found in the enlargement of the Legislative Councils. Well, that was perhaps a miracle in its way. In England a very common trick is to put one ring under a hat and produce in another part of the room what appears to be the same ring and is really one exactly like it — except perhaps for the superscription. Just such a miracle is this which the Congress has so triumphantly achieved. Another conjuring trick, and perhaps a cleverer one, was the snatch vote about Simultaneous Examinations, which owed its success to the sentimentalism of a few members of Parliament, the self-seeking of others and the carelessness of the rest. But these, however much we may praise them for cleverness, are, as I hope to show later on, of no really deep and solemn import to the nation, but simply conjuring tricks and nothing more. Over the rest of our political action the only epitaph we can write is "Failure". Even in the first flush of enthusiasm the more deep-thinking among us were perhaps a little troubled by certain small things about the Congress, which did not seem altogether right. The bare-faced hypocrisy of our enthusiasm for the Queen-Empress, — an old lady so called by way of courtesy, but about whom few Indians can really know or care anything — could serve no purpose but to expose us to the derision of our ill-wishers. There was too a little too much talk about the blessings of British rule, and the inscrutable Providence which has laid us in the maternal, or more properly the step-maternal bosom of just and benevolent England. Yet more appalling was the general timidity of the Congress, its glossing over of hard names, its disinclination to tell the direct truth, its fear of too deeply displeasing our masters. But in our then state of mind we were disposed to pass over all this as amiable weaknesses which would wear off with time. Two still grosser errors were pardoned as natural and almost inadvertent mistakes. It was true that we went out of our way to flatter Mr. Gladstone, a statesman who is not only quite unprincipled and in no way to be relied upon, but whose intervention in an Indian debate has always been of the worst omen to our cause. But then, we argued, people who had not been to England could not be expected to discern the character of this astute and plausible man. We did more than flatter Mr. Gladstone; we actually condescended to flatter "General" Booth, a vulgar imposter, a convicted charlatan, who has enriched himself by trading on the sentimental emotions of the English middle class. But here too, we thought, the Congress has perhaps made the common mistake of confounding wealth with merit, and has really taken the "General" for quite a respectable person. In the first flush of enthusiasm, I say, such excuses and such toleration were possible and even natural, but in the moment of disillusionment it will not do for us to flatter ourselves in this way any longer. Those amiable weaknesses we were then disposed to pass over very lightly, have not at all worn off with time, but have rather grown into an ingrained habit; and the tendency to grosser errors has grown not only into a habit, but into a policy. In its broader aspects the failure of the Congress is still clearer. The walls of the Anglo-Indian Jericho stand yet without a breach, and the dark spectre of Penury draws her robe over the land in greater volume and with an ampler sweep.

Indu Prakash, August 7, 1893

New Lamps for Old - 2

BUT after all my present business is not with negative criticism. I want rather to ascertain what the Congress has really done, and whether it is so much as to condemn all patriots to an Eleusinian silence about its faults. My own genuine opinion was expressed, perhaps with too much exuberance of diction,—but then the ghost of ancient enthusiasm was nudging my elbow—when I described the Congress as a well of living water, a standard in the battle, and a holy temple of concord. It is a well of living water in the sense that we drink from it assurance of a living political energy in the country, and without that assurance perhaps the most advanced among us might not have been so advanced: for it is only one or two strong and individual minds, who can flourish without a sympathetic environment. I am therefore justified in describing the Congress as a well of living water; but I have also described it as the standard under which we have fought; and by that I mean a living emblem of our cause the tired and war-worn soldier in the mellay can look up to and draw from it from time to time fresh funds of hope and vigour: such, and such only, is the purpose of a banner. One does not like to say that what must surely be apparent even to a rude intelligence, has been beyond the reach of intellects trained at our Universities and in the liberal professions. Yet it is a fact that we have entirely ignored what a casual inspection ought at once to have told us, that the Congress is altogether too unwieldy a body for any sort of executive work, and must solely be regarded as a convenient alembic, in which the formulae of our aspirations may be refined into clear and accurate expression. Not content with using a banner as a banner, we have actually caught up the staff of it with a view of breaking our enemy's heads. So blind a misuse must take away at least a third part of its virtue from the Congress, and if we are at all to recover the loss, we must recognise the limits of its utility as well as emend the device upon it.

The Congress has been, then, a well of living water and a

standard in the battle of liberty; but besides these it has been something, which is very much better than either of them, good as they too undoubtedly are; it has been to our divergent races and creeds a temple, or perhaps I should be more correct in saying a school of concord. In other words the necessities of the political movement initiated by the Congress have brought into one place and for a common purpose all sorts and conditions of men, and so by smoothing away the harsher discrepancies between them has created a certain modicum of sympathy between classes that were more or less at variance. Here, and not in its political action, must we look for any direct and really important achievement; and even here the actual advance has as a rule been absurdly exaggerated. Popular orators like Mr. Pherozshah Mehta, who carry the methods of the bar into politics, are very fond of telling people that the Congress has habituated us to act together. Well, that is not quite correct; there is not the slightest evidence to show that we have at all learned to act together; the one lesson we have learned is to talk together, and that is a rather different thing. Here then we have in my opinion the sum of all these capacities, in which the Congress has to any appreciable extent promoted the really high and intimate interests of the country. Can it then be said that on these lines the Congress has had such entirely beneficial effects as to put the gag on all harsher criticism? I do not think that it can be properly so said. I admit that the Congress has promoted a certain modicum of concord among us; but I am not prepared to admit that on this line of action its outcome has been at all complete and satisfying. Not only has the concord it tends to create been very partial, but the sort of people who have been included in its beneficent action, do not extend beyond certain fixed and narrow limits. The great mass of the people have not been appreciably touched by that healing principle, which to do the Congress justice, has very widely permeated the middle class. All this would still leave us without sufficient grounds to censure the Congress at all severely, if only it were clear that its present line of action was tending to increase the force and scope of its beneficence; but in fact the very contrary appears. We need no soothsayer to augur that, unless its entire policy be remodelled, its power for good, even in the narrow circle of its present influence, will prove to have been already exploited. One sphere still remains to it; it is still our only grand assurance of a living political energy in the country: but even this well of living water must in the end be poisoned or dried up, if the inner political energy, of which it is the outward assurance remains as poor and bounded as we now find it to be. If then it is true that the action of the Congress has only been of really high import on one or two lines, that even on those lines the actual result has been petty and imperfect, and that in all its other aspects we can pronounce no verdict on it but failure, then it is quite clear that we shall get no good by big talk about the splendid unanimity at the back of the Congress. A splendid unanimity in failure may be a very magnificent thing in its way, but in our present exigencies it is an unanimity really not worth having. But perhaps the Congress enthusiast will take refuge in stinging reproaches about my readiness to publish our weakness to the enemy. Well, even if he does, I can assure him, that however stinging his reproaches may be, I shall not feel at all stung by them. I leave that for those honest people who imagine that when they have got the Civil Service and other lucrative posts for themselves, the Indian question will be satisfactorily settled. Our actual enemy is not any force exterior to ourselves, but our own crying weaknesses, our cowardice, our selfishness, our hypocrisy, our purblind sentimentalism. I really cannot see why we should rage so furiously against the Anglo-Indians and call them by all manner of opprobrious epithets. I grant that they are rude and arrogant, that they govern badly, that they are devoid of any great or generous emotion, that their conduct is that of a small coterie of masters surrounded by a nation of Helots. But to say all this is simply to say that they are very commonplace men put into a quite unique position. Certainly it would be very grand and noble, if they were to smother all thought of their own peculiar interests, and aim henceforth, not at their own promotion, not at their own enrichment, but at the sole good of the Indian people. But such conduct is what we have no right to expect save from men of the most exalted and chivalrous character; and the sort of people England sends out to us are not as a rule exalted and chivalrous, but are usually the very reverse of that. They are really very ordinary men, — and not only ordinary men, but ordinary Englishmen — types of the middle class or Philistines, in the graphic English phrase, with the narrow hearts and commercial habit of mind peculiar to that sort of people. It is something very like folly to quarrel with them for not transgressing the law of their own nature. If we were not so dazzled by the artificial glare of English prestige, we should at once acknowledge that these men are really not worth being angry with: and if it is idle to be angry with them, it is still more unprofitable to rate their opinion of us at more than a straw's value. Our appeal, the appeal of every high-souled and self-respecting nation, ought not to be to the opinion of the Anglo-Indians, no, nor yet to the British sense of justice, but to our own reviving sense of manhood, to our own sincere fellow-feeling — so far as it can be called sincere — with the silent and suffering people of India. I am sure that eventually the nobler part of us will prevail, — that when we no longer obey the dictates of a veiled self-interest, but return to the profession of a large and genuine patriotism, when we cease to hanker after the soiled crumbs which England may cast to us from her table then it will be to that sense of manhood, to that sincere fellow-feeling that we shall finally and forcibly appeal. All this, it will be said, may be very true or very plausible, but it is after all made up of unsupported assertions. I quite admit that it is more or less so, nor did I at all intend that it should be otherwise; the proof and support of those assertions is a matter for patient development and wholly beside my present purpose. I have been thus elaborate with one sole end in view. I wish even the blindest enthusiast to recognise that I have not ventured to speak without carefully weighing those important considerations that might have induced me to remain silent. I trust that after this laboured preface even those most hostile to my views will not accuse me of having undertaken anything lightly or rashly. In my own opinion I should not have been to blame even if I had spoken without this painful hesitation. If the Congress cannot really face the light of a free and serious criticism, then the sooner it hides its face the better. For nine years it has been exempt from the ordeal; we have been content to worship it with that implicit trust which all religions demand, but which sooner or later leads them to disaster and defeat. Certainly we had this excuse that the stress of battle is not the time when a soldier can stop to criticise his weapon: he has simply to turn it to the best use of which it is capable. So long as India rang with turbulent voices of complaint and agitation, so long as the air was filled with the turmoil of an angry controversy between governors and governed, so long we could have little leisure or quiet thought and reflection. But now all is different; the necessity for conflict is no longer so urgent and has even given place to a noticeable languor and passivity, varied only by perfunctory public meetings. Now therefore, while the great agitation that once filled this vast peninsula with rumours of change, is content to occupy an obscure corner of English politics it will be well for all of us who are capable of reflection, to sit down for a moment and think. The hour seems to have come when the Congress must encounter that searching criticism which sooner or later arrives to all mortal things; and if it is so, to keep our eyes shut will be worse than idle. The only good we shall get by it is to point with a fresh example the aphorism with which I set out. "If the blind lead the blind, shall they not both fall into a ditch?"

Indu Prakash, August 21, 1893

New Lamps for Old - 3

"Thou art weighed in the balance and found wanting."

"The little that is done seems nothing when we look forward and see how much we have yet to do."

Thus far I have been making a circuit, in my disinclination to collide too abruptly with the prepossessions of my countrymen and now that I am compelled to handle my subject more intimately and with a firmer grasp, nothing but my deliberate conviction that it is quite imperative for someone to speak out, has at all persuaded me to continue. I have at the very outset to make distinct the grounds on which I charge the Congress with inadequacy. In the process I find myself bound to say many things that cannot fail to draw obloquy upon me: I shall be compelled to outrage many susceptibilities; compelled to advance many unacceptable ideas; compelled, — worst of all, — to stroke the wrong way many powerful persons, who are wont to be pampered with unstinted flattery and worship. But at all risks the thing must be done, and since it is on me that the choice has fallen, I can only proceed in the best fashion at my command and with what boldness I may. I say, of the Congress, then, this, — that its aims are mistaken, that the spirit in which it proceeds towards their accomplishment is not a spirit of sincerity and whole-heartedness, and that the methods it has chosen are not the right methods, and the leaders in whom it trusts, not the right sort of men to be leaders; — in brief, that we are at present the blind led, if not by the blind, at any rate by the one-eyed.

To begin with, I should a little while ago have had no hesitation in saying that the National Congress was not really national and had not in any way attempted to become *national*. But that was before I became a student of Mr. Pherozshah Mehta's speeches. Now to deal with this vexed subject, one must tread on very burning ground, and I shall make no apology for treading with great care and circumspection. The subject is wrapped in so thick a dust of controversy, and legal wits have been so busy drawing subtle distinctions about it, that a word which was once perfectly straightforward and simple, has become almost as difficult as the Law itself. It is therefore incumbent on me to explain what I wish to imply, when I say that the Congress is not really national. Now I do not at all mean to re-echo the Anglo-Indian catchword about the Hindus and Mahomedans. Like most catchwords it is without much force, and has been still further stripped of meaning by the policy of the Congress. The Mahomedans have been as largely represented on that body as any reasonable community could desire, and their susceptibilities, far from being denied respect, have always been most assiduously soothed and flattered. It is entirely futile then to take up the Anglo-Indian refrain; but this at least I should have imagined, that in an era when democracy and similar big words slide so glibly from our tongues, a body like the Congress, which represents not the mass of the population, but a single and very limited class, could not honestly be called national. It is perfectly true that the House of Commons represents not the English nation, but simply the English aristocracy and middle class and yet is none the less national. But the House of Commons is a body legally constituted and empowered to speak and act for the nation, while the Congress is self-created: and it is not justifiable for a self-created body representing only a single and limited class to call itself national. It would be just as absurd if the Liberal Party, because it allows within its limits all sorts and conditions of men, were to hold annual meetings and call itself the English National Congress. When therefore I said that the Congress was not really national, I simply meant that it did not represent the mass of the population.

But Mr. Pherozshah Mehta will have nothing to do with this sense of the word. In his very remarkable and instructive Presidential address at Calcutta, he argued that the Congress could justly arrogate this epithet without having any direct support from the proletariate; and he went on to explain his argument with the profound subtlety expected from an experienced advocate. "It is because the masses are still unable to articulate definite political demands that the functions and duty devolve upon their educated and enlightened compatriots to feel, to understand and to interpret their grievances and requirements, and to suggest and indicate how these can best be redressed and met."

This formidable sentence is, by the way, typical of Mr. Mehta's style and reveals the secret of his oratory, which like all great inventions is exceedingly simple: it is merely to say the same thing twice over in different words. But its more noteworthy feature is the idea implied that because the Congress professes to discharge this duty, it may justly call itself national. Nor is this all; Calcutta comes to the help of Bombay in the person of Mr. Manmohan Ghose, who repeats and elucidates Mr. Mehta's idea. The Congress, he says, asserting the rights of that body to speak for the masses, represents the thinking portion of the Indian people, whose duty it is to guide the ignorant, and this in his opinion sufficiently justifies the Congress in calling itself national. To differ from a successful barrister and citizen, a man held in high honour by every graduate in India, and above all a future member of the Viceroy's Council, would never have been a very easy task for a timid man like myself. But when he is reinforced by so respectable and weighty a citizen as Mr. Manmohan Ghose, I really cannot find the courage to persevere. I shall therefore amend the obnoxious phrase and declare that the National Congress may be as national as you please, but it is not a popular body and has not in any way attempted to become a popular body.

But at this point some one a little less learned than Mr. Pherozshah Mehta may interfere and ask how it can be true that the Congress is not a popular body. I can only point his attention to a previous statement of mine that the Congress represents not the mass of the population, but a single and limited class. No doubt the Congress tried very hard in the beginning to believe that it really represented the mass of the population, but if it has not already abandoned, it ought now at least to abandon the pretension as quite untenable. And indeed when Mr. Pherozshah Mehta and Mr. Manmohan Ghose have admitted this patent fact — not as delegates only, but as officials of the Congress — and have even gone so far as to explain the fact away, it is hardly requisite for me to combat the fallacy. But perhaps the enquirer, not yet satisfied, may go on to ask what is that single and limited class which I imagine the Congress to represent. Here it may be of help to us to refer again to the speeches of the Congress leaders and more especially to the talented men from whom I have already quoted. In his able official address Mr. Manmohan Ghose asks himself this very question and answers that the Congress represents the thinking portion of the Indian people. "The delegates present here today," he goes on, "are the chosen representatives of that section of the Indian people who have learnt to think, and whose number is daily increasing with marvellous rapidity." Perhaps Mr. Ghose is a little too facile in his use of the word "thinking". So much at the mercy of their instincts and prejudices are the generality of mankind, that we hazard a very high estimate when we call even one man out of ten thousand a thinking man. But evidently by the thinking portion Mr. Ghose would like to indicate the class to which he himself belongs; I mean those of us who have got some little idea of the machinery of English politics and are eager to import it into India along with cheap Liverpool cloths, shoddy Brummagem wares, and other useful and necessary things which have killed the fine and genuine textures. If this is a true interpretation he is perfectly correct in what he says. For it is really from this class that the Congress movement draws its origin, its support and its most enthusiastic votaries. And if I were asked to describe their class by a single name, I should not hesitate to call it our new middle class. For here too English goods have driven out native goods: our society has lost its old landmarks and is being demarcated on the English model. But of all the brand new articles we have imported, inconceivably the most important is that large class of people — journalists, barristers, doctors, officials, graduates and traders — who have grown up and are increasing with prurient rapidity under the aegis of the British rule: and this class I call the middle class: for, when we are so proud of our imported English goods, it would be absurd, when we want labels for them, not to import their English names as well. Besides this name which I have chosen is really a more accurate description than phrases like "thinking men" or "the educated class" which are merely expressions of our own boundless vanity and self-conceit. However largely we may choose to indulge in vague rhetoric about the all-pervading influence of the Congress, no one can honestly doubt that here is the constituency from which it is really empowered. There is indeed a small contingent of aristocrats and a smaller contingent of the more well-to-do ryots: but these are only two flying-wheels in the great middle-class machine. The fetish-worshipper may declare as loudly as he pleases that it represents all sorts and conditions of people, just as the Anglo-Indians used to insist that it represented no one but the Bengali Babu. Facts have been too strong for the Anglo-Indian and they will be too strong in the end for the fetish-worshipper. Partisans on either side can in no way alter the clear and immutable truth — these words were put on paper long before the recent disturbances in Bombay and certainly without any suspicion that the prophecy I then hazarded would be fortified by so apt and striking a comment. Facts are already beginning to speak in a very clear and unambiguous voice. How long will the Congress sit like careless Belshazzar, at the feast of mutual admiration? Already the decree has gone out against it; already even the eyes that are dim can discern, — for has it not been written in blood? — the first pregnant phrase of the handwriting upon the wall. "God has numbered the kingdom and finished it." Surely after so rough a lesson, we shall not wait to unseal our eyes and unstop our ears, until the unseen finger moves on and writes the second and sterner sentence: "Thou art weighed in the balance and found wanting." Or must we sit idle with folded hands and only bestir ourselves when the short hour of grace is past and the kingdom given to another more worthy than we?

Indu Prakash, August 28, 1893

New Lamps for Old - 4

I REPEAT then with renewed confidence, but still with a strong desire to conciliate Mr. Pherozshah Mehta, that the Congress fails, because it has never been, and has made no honest endeavour to be, a popular body empowered by the fiat of the Indian people in its entirety. But for all that I have not managed to bring my view into coincidence with Mr. Mehta's. It is true he is not invincibly reluctant to concede the limits, which hedge in the Congress action and restrict its output of energy; but he is quite averse to the dictum that by not transgressing the middle-class pale the Congress has condemned itself, as a saving power, to insignificance and ultimate sterility. The bounded scope of its potency and the subdued tone which it affects, are, he opines, precisely what our actual emergencies of the moment imperatively demand; wider activity and a more intense emphasis would be in his view highly unadvisable and even injurious and besides it does not at all signify whether we are fortified by popular sympathy or are not; for is not Mr. Pherozshah Mehta there with all the enlightenment of India at his back to plead temperately — temperately, mind you; we are nothing if not temperate — for just and remedial legislation on behalf of a patient and suffering people? In plain words a line of argument is adopted amounting to this: — "The Congress movement is nothing if not a grand suit-at-law, best described as the case of India *vs.* Anglo-India, in which the ultimate tribunal is the British sense of justice, and Pherozshah Mehta, Mr. Umesh Chandra Bonerji and the other eminent leaders of the bar are counsel for the complainant. Well, then, when so many experienced advocates have bound themselves to find pleas for him, would it not be highly rash and inopportune for the client to insist on conducting his own complaint?" Now it is abundantly clear that, judged as it stands, this line of argument, though adroit beyond cavil and instinct with legal ingenuity, will nevertheless not answer. I am not going to deny that Mr. Pherozshah Mehta and the enlightenment of India, such as it is, are pleading, undoubtedly with temperance and perhaps with sincerity, for something or other, which for want of a more exact description, we may call remedial legislation. But so far there has been nothing at all to prevent me from denying that the analogy of the law-court holds; this sort of vicarious effort may be highly advantageous in judicial matters, but it is not, I would submit, at all adequate to express the reviving energies of a great people. The argument, I say, is not complete in itself, or to use a vernacular phrase, it will not walk; it badly wants a crutch to lean upon. Mr. Mehta is clever enough to see that and his legal acumen has taken him exactly to the very store where or not at all he must discover an efficient crutch. So he goes straight to history, correctly surmising that the experience of European races is all that we, a people new to modern problems, can find to warn or counsel us, and he tells us that this sort of vicarious effort has invariably been the original step towards progress: or, to put it in his own rhetorical way, "History teaches us that such has been the law of widening progress in all ages and all countries, notably in England itself." Here then is the argument complete, crutch and all; and so adroit is it that in Congress propaganda it has become a phrase of common parlance, and is now in fact the stereotyped line of defence. Certainly, if he is accurate in his historical data, Mr. Mehta has amply proved his case; but in spite of all his adroitness, I suspect that his trend towards double-shotted phrases has led him into a serious difficulty. "In all ages and all countries" is a very big expression, and Mr. Mehta will be exceedingly lucky if it will stand a close scrutiny. But Mr. Manmohan Ghose at least is a sober speaker; and if we have deserted his smooth but perhaps rather tedious manner for a more brilliant style of oratory, now at any rate, when the specious orator fails us, we may well return to the rational disputant. But we shall be agreeably disappointed to find that this vivid statement about the teaching of history is Mr. Ghose's own legitimate offspring and not the coinage of Mr. Mehta's heated fancy: indeed, the latter has done nothing but convey it bodily into his own address. "History teaches us," says Mr. Ghose, "that in all ages and all countries it is the thinking classes who have led the unthinking, and in the present state of our society we are bound not only to think for ourselves, but also to think for those who are still too ignorant to exercise that important function." When we find the intellectual princes of the nation light-heartedly propagating such gross inaccuracies, we are really tempted to inquire if high education is after all of any use. History teaches us! Why, these gentlemen can never have studied any history at all except that of England. Would they be ignorant otherwise that mainly to that country, if not to that country alone, their statement applies, but that about most ages and most countries it is hopelessly inaccurate? Absurd as the statement is, its career has been neither limited nor obscure. Shot in the first instance from Mr. Ghose's regulation smooth-bore, it then served as a bullet in Mr. Pherozshah Mehta's patent new double-barrelled rifle, and has ultimately turned out the stock ammunition of the Congress against that particular line upon which I have initially ventured. Here then the argument has culminated in a most important issue; for supposing this line of defence to be adequate, the gravest indictment I have to urge against the Congress goes at once to the ground. It will therefore be advisable to scrutinise Mr. Ghose's light-hearted statement; and if the policy he advocates is actually stamped with the genuine consensus of all peoples in all ages, then we shall very readily admit that there is no reason why the masses should not be left in their political apathy. But if it is quite otherwise and we cannot discover more than one precedent of importance, then Mr. Ghose and the Congress chairman will not make us dance to their music, charm they never so wisely, and we shall be slow to admit even the one precedent we have got without a very narrow scrutiny. If then we are bent upon adopting England as our exemplar, we shall certainly imitate the progress of the glacier rather than the progress of the torrent. From Runnymede to the Hull riots is a far cry; yet these seven centuries have done less to change partially the political and social exterior of England, than five short years to change entirely the political and social exterior of her immediate neighbour. But if Mr. Ghose's dogmatic utterance is true of England, I imagine it does not apply with equal force to other climes and other eras. For example, is it at all true of France? Rather we know that the first step of that fortunate country towards progress was not through any decent and orderly expansion, but through a purification by blood and fire. It was not a convocation of respectable citizens, but the vast and ignorant proletariate, that emerged from a prolonged and almost coeval apathy and blotted out in five terrible years the accumulated oppression of thirteen centuries. And if the example of France is not sufficient to deprive Mr. Ghose's statement of force, let us divert our eyes to Ireland where the ancient and world-wide quarrel between Celt and Teuton is still pending. Is it at all true that the initiators of Irish resistance to England were a body of successful lawyers, remarkable only for a power of shallow rhetoric, and deputed by the sort of men that are turned out at Trinity College, Dublin? At any rate that is not what History tells us. We do not read that the Irish leaders annually assembled to declaim glib orations, eulogistic of British rule and timidly suggestive of certain flaws in its unparalleled excellence, nor did they suggest as a panacea for Irish miseries, that they should be given more posts and an ampler career in the British service. I rather fancy Turlough O'Neill and his compeers were a different sort of men from that. But then it is hardly fair perhaps to cite as an example a disreputable people never prolific of graduates and hence incapable of properly appreciating the extraordinary blessings which British rule gives out so liberally wherever it goes. Certainly men who preferred action to long speeches and appealed, by the only method available in that strenuous epoch, not to the British sense of justice but to their own sense of manhood, are not at all the sort of people we have either the will or the power to imitate. Well then, let us return to our own orderly and eloquent era. But here too, just as the main strength of that ancient strenuous protest resided in the Irish populace led by the princes of their class, so the principal force of the modern subtler protest resides in the Irish peasantry led by the recognised chiefs of an united people. I might go on and cull instances from Italy and America, but to elaborate the matter further would be to insult the understanding of my readers. It will be sufficient to remind them that the two grand instances of ancient history point to an exactly similar conclusion. In Athens and in Rome the first political quarrel is a distinct issue between the man of the people and a limited, perhaps an alien, aristocracy. The force behind Cleisthenes and the constituency that empowered Tiberius Gracchus were not a narrow middle class, but the people with its ancient wrongs and centuries of patient endurance.

If then, as we are compelled to infer, Mr. Mehta's statement is entirely inaccurate of remoter ages and in modern times accurate of one country alone, we shall conclude that whatever other proof he may find for his lame argument, that crutch at least is too large and must go [to] the ground. But Mr. Mehta, too acute and experienced a pleader to be disheartened by any initial failure, will no doubt pick up his crutch again and whittle it down to the appropriate size. It may be quite correct, he will perhaps tell me, that his statement applies with appreciable force to England and to England alone, but when all is said, it does not eventually matter. In allowing that his statement does generally apply to England, I have admitted everything he seriously wants me to admit, for England is after all that country which has best prospered in its aspirations after progress, and must therefore be the grand political examplar of every nation animated by a like spirit, and it must be peculiarly and beyond dispute such for India in her present critical stage of renascence. I am quite aware that in the eyes of that growing community which Mr. Ghose is pleased to call the thinking class, these plausible assertions are only the elementary axioms of political science. But however confidently such statements are put before me, I am not at all sure that they are entirely correct. I have not quite made up my mind that England is indeed that country which has best prospered in its aspirations after progress and I am as yet unconvinced that it will eventually turn out at all a desirable examplar for every nation aspiring to progress, or even for its peculiar pupil, renascent India. I shall therefore feel more disposed to probe the matter to the bottom than to acknowledge a very disputable thesis as in any way self-evident. To this end it is requisite closely to inquire what has actually been the main outcome of English political effort, and whether it is of a nature to justify any implicit reliance on English methods or exact imitation of English models.

Indu Prakash, September 18, 1893

New Lamps for Old - 5

WE HAVE then to appreciate the actual conditions of English progress, in their sound no less than their unsound aspects: and it will be to our convenience to have ready some rough formulae by which we may handle the subject in an intelligible way. To this problem Mr. Surendranath Banerji, a man who with all his striking merits, has never evinced any power of calm and serious thought, proffers a very grandiloquent and heart-stirring solution. "We rely," he has said, "on the liberty-loving instincts of the greatest representative assembly in the world, the palladium of English Liberty, the sanctuary of the free and brave, the British House of Commons" and at this inspiriting discharge of oratory there was, we are told, nor do we wonder at it — a responding volley of loud and protracted applause. Now when Mr. Banerji chooses to lash himself into an oratorical frenzy and stir us with his sounding rhetoric, it is really impracticable for anything human to stand up and oppose him: and though I may hereafter tone down his oriental colouring to something nearer the hue of truth, yet it does not at present serve my purpose to take up arms against a sea of eloquence. I would rather admit at once the grain of sound fact at the core of all this than strip off the costly integuments with which Mr. Banerji's elaborate Fancy chooses to invest it. But when Mr. Banerji's words no longer reverberate in your ears, you may have leisure to listen to a quieter, more serious voice, now unhappily hushed in the grave, — the voice of Matthew Arnold, himself an Englishman and genuine lover of his country, but for all that a man who thought deeply and spoke sanely. And where according to this sane and powerful intellect shall we come across the really noteworthy outcome of English effort? We shall best see it, he tells us, not in any palladium or sanctuary, not in the greatest representative assembly in the world, but in an aristocracy materialised, a middle class vulgarised and a lower class brutalised: and no clear-sighted student of England will be insensible to the just felicity with which he has hit off the social tendencies prevailing in that country. Here then we have ready rough formulae by which we may, at the lowest, baldly outline the duplicate aspect of modern England: for now that we have admitted Mr. Banerji's phrase as symbolic of the healthy outcome creditable to English effort, we can hardly be shy of admitting Matthew Arnold's phrase as symbolic of the morbid outcome discreditable to it. But it is still open to us to evince a reasonable doubt whether there is any way of reconciling two items so mutually destructive: for it does seem paradoxical to rate the produces of institutions so highly lauded and so universally copied at a low grade in the social ladder. But this apparent paradox may easily be a vital truth; and in establishing that, as I hope to establish it, I shall have incidentally to moot another and wider theorem. I would urge that our entire political philosophy is rooted in shallow earth, so much so indeed that without repudiation or radical change we cannot arrive at an attitude of mind healthily conducive to just and clear thinking. I am conscious that the argument has hitherto been rather intangible and moved too largely among wide abstract principles. Such a method is by its nature less keenly attractive to the general readers than a close and lively handling of current politics, but it is required for an adequate development of my case, and I must entreat indulgence a step or two further, before I lay any grasp on the hard concrete details of our actual political effort.

Now the high value at which Mr. Mehta appraises history as our sole available record of human experience in the mass will clearly be endorsed by every thoughtful and judicious mind. But to sustain it at that high level of utility, we must not indulge in hasty deductions based on a very partial scrutiny, but must group correctly and digest in a candid spirit such data as we can bring within our compass. If we observe this precept, we shall not easily coincide with his opinion that European progress has been of a single texture. We shall rather be convinced that there run through it two principles of motion distinct in nature and adverse in event, the trend of whose divergence may be roundly expressed as advance in one direction through political methods and in another direction through social methods. But as the use of these time-worn epithets might well promote misconception and drag us into side-issues, I will attempt a more delicate handling and solicit that close attention without which so remote and elusive a subject cannot come home to the mind with proper force and clearness.

In bringing abstractions home to the human intelligence, it is perhaps best to dispel by means of near and concrete specimens that sense of remoteness which we shrink from in what is at all intangible. Hence I shall attempt to differentiate by living instances the two principles which I suggest as the main motors of progress. The broadcast of national thought in England prevalent from very early times, may not inappropriately stand for the sort of progress that runs after a political prize. The striking fact of English history — the fact that dwarfs all others — is, without doubt, the regular development from certain primordial seeds and the continuous branching out, foliation and efflorescence of the institution which Mr. Banerji has justly termed the greatest representative assembly in the world. This is highly typical of the English school of thought and the exaggerated emphasis it lays on the mould and working of institutions. However supreme in the domain of practical life, however gifted with commercial vigour and expansive energy, the English mind with its short range of vision, its too little of delicacy and exactness, its inability to go beyond what it actually sees, is wholly unfit for any nice appraisal of cause and effect. It is without vision, logic, the spirit of curiosity, and hence it has not any habit of entertaining clear and high ideals, any audacity of experiment, any power of finding just methods nicely adopted to produce the exact effect intended: — it is without speculative temerity and the scientific spirit, and hence it cannot project great political theories nor argue justly from effect to cause. All these incapacities have forced the English mind into a certain mould of thought and expression. Limited to the visible and material, they have put their whole force into mechanical invention; void of curiosity, they have hazarded just so much experiment and no more, as was necessary to suit existing institutions to their immediate wants; inexact, they have never cared in these alterations to get at more than an approximation to the exact effect intended; illogical and without subtlety, they have trusted implicitly to the political machines for whose invention they have a peculiar genius, and never cared to utilise mightier forces and a subtler method. Nor is this all: in their defect of speculative imagination, they are unable to get beyond what they themselves have experienced, what they themselves have effected. Hence, being unscientific and apt to impute every power to machinery, they compare certain sets of machines, and postulating certain effects from them, argue that as this of their own invention has been attended by results of the highest value, it is therefore of an unique excellence and conserves in any and every climate its efficiency and durability. And they do not simply flaunt this opinion in the face of reason, but, by their stupendous material success and vast expansion, they have managed to convince a world apt to be impressed by externals, that it is correct, and even obviously correct. Yet it is quite clear that this opinion, carefully analysed, reduces itself to a logical absurdity. By its rigid emphasising of a single element it slurs over others of equal or superior importance: it takes no account of a high or low quality in the raw material, of variant circumstances, of incompatibilities arising from national temperament, and other forces which no philosophical observer will omit from his calculations. In fact it reduces itself to the statement, that, given good machinery, then no matter what quality of materials is passed through it, the eventual fabric will be infallibly of the most superior sort. If the Indian intellect had been nourished on any but English food, I should be content with stating the idea in this its simplest form, and spare myself a laborious exegesis; but I do not forget that I am addressing minds formed by purely English influences and therefore capable of admitting the rooted English prejudice that what is logically absurd, may be practically true. At present however I will simply state the motive principle of progress exemplified by England as a careful requisition and high appraisal of sound machinery in preference to a scientific social development.

But if we carry our glance across the English Channel, we shall witness a very different and more animating spectacle. Gifted with a lighter, subtler and clearer mind than their insular neighbours, the French people have moved irresistibly towards a social and not a political development. It is true that French orators and statesmen, incapacitated by their national character from originating fit political ideals, have adopted a set of institutions curiously blended from English and American manufactures; but the best blood, the highest thought, the real grandeur of the nation does not reside in the Senate or in the Chamber of Deputies; it resides in the artistic and municipal forces of Parisian life, in the firm settled executive, in the great vehement heart of the French populace — and that has ever beaten most highly in unison with the grand ideas of Equality and Fraternity, since they were first enounced on the banner of the great and terrible Republic. Hence though by the indiscreet choice of a machine, they have been compelled to copy the working of English machinery and concede an undue importance to politics, yet the ideals which have genuinely influenced the spirit which has most deeply permeated their national life are widely different from that alien spirit, from those borrowed ideals. I have said that the French mind is clearer, subtler, lighter than the English. In that clarity they have discerned that without high qualities in the raw material excellence of machinery will not suffice to create a sound and durable national character, — that it may indeed develop a strong, energetic and capable temper, but that the fabric will not combine fineness with strength, will not resist permanently the wear and tear of time and the rending force of social problems: — through that subtlety they divined that not by the mechanic working of institutions, but by the delicate and almost unseen moulding of a fine, lucid and invigorating atmosphere, could a robust and highly-wrought social temper be developed: — and through that lightness they chose not the fierce, sharp air of English individualism, but the bright influence of art and letters, of happiness, a wide and liberal culture, and the firm consequent cohesion of their racial and social elements. To put all this briefly, the second school of thought I would indicate to my readers, is the preference of a fine development of social character and a wide diffusion of happiness to the mechanic development of a sound political machinery. Here then as indicated by these grand examples we have our two principal motors of progress; a careful requisition for the sake of evolving an energetic national character and high level of capacity, of a sound political machinery; and the ardent, yet rational pursuit, for its own sake, of a sound and highly-wrought social temper.

It may be worth while here to develop a point I have broadly suggested, that with these distinct lines of feeling accord distinct types of racial character. The social ideal is naturally limited to peoples distinguished by a rare social gift and an unbounded receptivity for novel ideas along with a large amount of practical capacity. The ancient Athenian, pre-eminent for lightness of temper and lucidity of thought, was content with the simplest and most nakedly logical machinery, and principally sought to base political life on equality, a wide diffusion of culture, and a large and just social principle. Moreover, as the subtlest and hence the most efficient way of conserving the high calibre of his national character, he chose the infusion of light, gaiety and happiness into the common life of the people. Clear in thought and felicitous in action, he pursued an ideal strictly consonant with his natural temper and rigidly exclusive of the anomalous: and so highly did he attain, that the quick, shifting, eager Athenian life, with its movement and colour, its happy buoyancy, its rapid genius, or as the Attic poet beautifully phrases it, walking delicately through a fine and lucid air, has become the admiration and envy of posterior ages. The modern Frenchman closely allied by his clear habit of mind to the old Athenian, himself lucid in thought, light in temper and not without a supreme felicity of method in practical things, evinces much the same sentiments, pursues much the same ideals. He too has a happily-adjusted executive machinery, elaborated indeed to fit the needs of a modern community, but pervaded by a thoroughly clear and logical spirit. He also has a passionate craving for equality and a large and just social principle, and prefers to conserve the high calibre of his national character by the infusion of light, gaiety and happiness into the common life of the people. And he too has so far compassed his ideal that a consensus of competent observers have pronounced France certainly the happiest, and, taken in the mass, the most civilised of modern countries. But to the Englishman or American, intellect, lucidity, happiness are not of primary importance:

they strike him in the light of luxuries rather than necessities. It is the useful citizen, the adroit man of business, the laborious worker, whom he commends with the warmest emphasis and copies with the most respectful emulation. Such a cast of mind being entirely incompatible with social success, he directs his whole active powers into the grosser sphere of commerce and politics, where practical energy, unpurified by thought, may struggle forward to some vulgar and limited goal. To put it in a concrete form, Paris may be said to revolve around the Theatre, the Municipal Council and the French Academy, London looks rather to the House of Commons and New York to the Stock Exchange. I trust that I have now clearly elucidated the exact and intimate nature of those two distinct principles on which progress may be said to move. It now remains to gauge the practical effect of either policy as history indicates them to us. We in India, or at any rate those races among us which are in the van of every forward movement, are far more nearly allied to the French and Athenian than to the Anglo-Saxon, but owing to the accident of British domination, our intellects have been carefully nurtured on a purely English diet. Hence we do not care to purchase an outfit of political ideas properly adjusted to our natural temper and urgent requirements, but must eke out our scanty wardrobe with the cast-off rags and thread-bare leavings of our English Masters and this incongruous apparel we display with a pompous self-approval which no unfriendly murmurs, no unkind allusions are allowed to trouble. Absurd as all this is, its visible outcome is clearly a grave misfortune. Prompted by our English instruction we have deputed to a mere machine so arduous a business as the remoulding of our entire destinies, needing as it does patient and delicate manual adjustment and a constant supervising vigilance — and this to a machine not efficient and carefully pieced together but clumsy and made on a rude and cheap model. So long as this temper prevails, we shall never realise how utterly it is beyond the power of even an excellent machine to renovate an effete and impoverished national character and how palpably requisite to commence from within and not depend on any exterior agency. Such a retrospect as I propose will therefore be of peculiar value, if it at all induces us to acknowledge that it is a vital error, simply because we have invented a clumsy machine, to rest on our oars and imagine that expenditure of energy in other directions is at present superfluous.

Indu Prakash, October 30, 1893

New Lamps for Old - 6

THAT this intimate organic treatment of which I speak is really indispensable, will be clearly established by the annals of ancient Rome. The Romans were a nation quite unique in the composition and general style of their character; along with a predilection for practical energy, a purely material habit of mind, and an indifference to orderly and logical methods which suggest a strong affinity to the Anglo-Saxon temperament, they possessed a robust and clear perception, and a strong practical contempt for methods pronounced by hard experience to be ineffectual, which are entirely un-English and allied rather to the clarity and impatience of the Gaul. Moreover their whole character was moulded in a grand style, such as has not been witnessed by any prior or succeeding age — so much so that the striking description by which the Greek ambassador expressed the temper of the Roman Senate, might with equal justice be transferred to the entire people. They were a nation of Kings: that is to say, they possessed the gift of handling the high things of life in a grand and imposing style, and with a success, an astonishing sureness of touch, only possible to a natural tact in government and a just, I may say a royal instinct for affairs. Yet this grand, imperial nation, even while it was most felicitous abroad in the manner and spirit in which it dealt with foreign peoples, was at home convulsed to a surprising extent by the worst forms of internal disorder: — and all for the want of that clear, sane ideal which has so highly promoted the domestic happiness of France and Athens. At first, indeed, the Romans inexpert in political methods, were inclined to repose an implicit trust in machinery, just as the English have been inclined from the primary stages of their development, and just as we are led to do by the contagious influence of the Anglomaniac disease. They hoped by the sole and mechanic action of certain highly lauded institutions to remove the disorders with which the Roman body politic was ailing. And though at Rome no less than among ourselves, the social condition of the poor filled up the reform posters and a consequent amelioration was loudly trumpeted by the popular leaders, yet the genuine force of the movement was disposed, as is the genuine force of the present Congress movement, to the minimising of purely political inequality. But when the coveted institutions were in full swing, a sense gradually dawned on the people that the middle class had the sole enjoyment of any profit accruing from the change, as indeed it is always to the middle class alone that any profit accrues from the elimination of merely political inequality; but the great Roman populace untouched by the change for which they had sacrificed their ease and expended their best and highest energies, felt themselves pushed from misery to misery and broke out again in a wild storm of rebellion. But to maintain a stark persistence in unreason, to repose an unmoved confidence in the bounded potency of a mechanic formula, proved ineffectual by the cogent logic of hard experience; they had no thought, or if they had the thought, they being a genuinely practical race, and not like the English straining after practicality, had not the disposition. Hence that mighty struggle was fought out with perplexed watchwords, amid wild alarms and rumours of battle and in a confused medley of blood, terror and unspeakable desolation. In that horror of great darkness, the Roman world crashed on from ruin to ruin, until the strong hand of Caesar stayed its descent to poise it on the stable foundation of a sane and vigilant policy rigorously enforced by the fixed will of a single despotic ruler. But the grand secret of his success and the success of those puissant autocrats who inherited his genius and his ideals, was the clear perception attained to by them that only by social equality and the healing action of a firm despotism, could the disorders of Rome be permanently eradicated. Maligned as they have been by those who suffered from their astuteness and calm strength of will, the final verdict of posterity will laud in them that terrible intensity of purpose and even that iron indifference to personal suffering, which they evinced in forcing the Caesarian policy to its bitter but salutary end. The main lesson for us however is the pregnant conclusion that the Romans, to whom we cannot deny the supreme rank in the sphere of practical success, by attempting a cure through external and mechanic appliances entailed on themselves untold misery, untold disorder, and only by a thorough organic treatment restored the sanity, peace, settled government and calm felicity of an entire world.

But perhaps Mr. Mehta will tell me "What have we to do with the ancient Romans, we who have an entirely modern environment and suffer from disorders peculiar to ourselves?" Well, the connection is not perhaps so remote as Mr. Mehta imagines: I will not however press that point, but rather appeal to the instance of two great European nations, who also have an entirely modern environment and suffer or have suffered from very similar maladies — and so end my long excursion into the domain of abstract ideas.

As the living instances most nearly suggesting the diversity of impulse and method, which is my present subject, I have had occasion to draw a comparison between these two peoples, whom, by a singular caprice of antithesis, chance has put into close physical proximity, but nature has sundered as far as the poles in genius, temper and ideals. Whatever healthy and conservative effects accrue from the close pursuit of either principle, whatever morbid and deleterious effects accrue from the close pursuit of either principle, will be seen operating to the best advantage in the social and political organism of these two nations. The healthy effects of the one impulse we shall find among those striking English qualities which at once catch the eye, insatiable enterprise, an energetic and pushing spirit, a vigorous tendency towards expansion, a high capacity for political administration, and an orderly process of government; the morbid effects are social degradation and an entire absence of the cohesive principle. The better qualities have no doubt grown by breathing the atmosphere of individualism and been trained up by the habit of working under settled and roughly convenient forms; but after all is said, the original high qualities of the raw material enter very largely into the credit side of the account. Even were it not so, we are not likely, tutored by English instruction, to undervalue or to slur over the successful and imposing aspect of English attainment. Hence it will be more profitable for us, always keeping the bright side in view, to concentrate our attention on the unsounder aspects which we do not care to learn, or if we have learned, are in the habit of carefully forgetting. We may perhaps realise the nature of that unsounder aspect, if we amplify Matthew Arnold's phrase: — an aristocracy no longer possessed of the imposing nobility of mind, the proud sense of honour, the striking pre-eminence of faculty, which are the saving graces — nay, which are the very life-breath of an aristocracy; debased moreover by the pursuit, through concession to all that is gross and ignoble in the English mind, of gross and ignoble ends: — a middle class inaccessible to the influence of high and refining ideas, and prone to rate every thing even in the noblest departments of life, at a commercial valuation: — and a lower class equally without any germ of high ideas, nay, without any ideas high or low; degraded in their worst failure to the crudest forms of vice, pauperism and crime, and in their highest attainment restricted to a life of unintelligent work relieved by brutalising pleasures. And indeed the most alarming symptoms are here; for it may be said of the aristocracy that the workings of the Time-Spirit have made a genuine aristocracy obsolete and impracticable, and of the middle class, that, however successful and confident, it is in fact doomed; its empire is passing away from it; but with the whole trend of humanity shaping towards democracy and socialism, on the calibre and civilisation of the lower class depends the future of the entire race. And we have seen what sort of lower class England, with all her splendid success, has been able to evolve — in calibre debased, in civilisation nil. And after seeing what England has produced by her empiricism, her culture of a raw energy, her exaltation of a political method not founded on reason, we must see what France has produced by her steady, logical pursuit of a fine social ideal: it is the Paris *ouvrier* with his firmness of grasp on affairs, his sanity, his height of mind, his clear, direct ways of life and thought, — it is the French peasant with his ready tact, his power of quiet and sensible conversation, located in an enjoyable corner of life, small it may be, but with plenty of room for wholesome work and plenty of room for refreshing gaiety. There we have the strong side of France, a lucid social atmosphere, a firm executive rationally directed to insure a clearly conceived purpose, a high level of character and refinement pervading all classes and a scheme of society bestowing a fair chance of happiness on the low as well as the high. But if France is strong in the sphere of England's weakness, she is no less weak in the sphere of England's strength. Along with and militating against her social happiness, we have to reckon constant political disorder and instability, an alarming defect of expansive vigour, and entire failure in the handling of general politics. France, unable to conceive and work out a proper political machinery, has been reduced to copy with slight variations the English model and import a set of machinery well suited to the old English temper, but now unsuited even to the English and still more to the vehement French character. Passionate, sensitive, loquacious, fond of dispute and apt to be blown away by gusts of feeling, the Gaul is wholly unfit for that heavy decorum, that orderly process of debate, that power of combining anomalies, which still exist to a great extent in England, but which even there must eventually grow impossible. Hence the vehement French nation after a brief experience of each alien manufacture has grown intensely impatient and shipped it back without superfluous ceremony to its original home. Here is the latent root of that disheartening failure which has attended France in all her brief and feverish attempts to discover a stable basis of political advance, — of that intense consequent disgust, that scornful aversion to politics which has led thinking France to rate it as an indecent harlequin-show in which no serious man will care to meddle. But if this were all, a superficial observer might balance a defect and merit on one side by an answering merit and defect on the other, and conclude that the account was clear; but social status is not the only department of success in which England compares unfavourably with France. There is her fatal incoherency, her want of political cohesion, her want of social cohesion. A Breton, a Basque, a Provençal, though no less alien in blood to the mass of the French people than the Irish, the Welsh, the Scotch to the mass of the English people, would repel with alarm and abhorrence the mere thought of impairing the fine solidarity, the homogeneity of sentiment, which the possession of an agreeable social life has developed in France. And we cannot sufficiently admire the supreme virtue of that fine social development and large diffusion of general happiness, which has conserved for France in the midst of fearful political calamities her splendid cohesiveness as a nation and as a community. In England on the other hand we see the sorry spectacle of a great empire lying at the mercy of disintegrating influences, because the component races have neither been properly merged in the whole nor persuaded by the offer of a high level of happiness to value the benefits of solidarity. And if France by her injudicious choice of mechanism, her political incapacity, her refusal to put her best blood into politics, has involved herself in fearful political calamities, no less has England by her exclusive pursuit of machinery, her social incompetence, her prejudice against a rational equality, her excessive individualism, entered on an era of fearful social calamities. It is a suggestive fact that the alienation of sympathy, the strong antipathetic feelings of Labour towards Capital, are nowhere so marked, the quarrel between them is nowhere so violent, sustained and ferocious as in the two countries which are proudest of their institutions and have most systematically neglected their social development — England and America. It is not therefore unreasonable to conclude — and had I space and leisure, I should be tempted to show that every circumstance tends to fortify the conclusion and convert it into a certainty — that this social neglect is the prime cause of the fearful array of social calamities, whose first impact has already burst on those proud and successful countries. But enough has been said, and to discuss the matter exhaustively would unduly defer the point of more direct importance for ourselves: — I mean the ominous connection which these truths have with the actual conditions of politics and society in India.

Indu Prakash, November 13, 1893

New Lamps for Old - 7

I AM not ignorant that to practical men all I have written will prove beyond measure unpalatable. Strongly inimical as they are to thought in politics, they will detect in it an offensive redolence of dilettantism, perhaps scout it as a foolish waste of power, or if a good thing at all a good thing for a treatise on general politics, a good thing out of place. To what end these remote instances, what pertinence in these political metaphysics? I venture however to suggest that it is just this gleaning from general politics, this survey and digestion of human experience in the mass that we at the present moment most imperatively want. No one will deny, — no one at least in that considerable class to whose address my present remarks are directed, — that for us and even for those of us who have a strong affection for oriental things and believe that there is in them a great deal that is beautiful, a great deal that is serviceable, a great deal that is worth keeping, the most important objective is and must inevitably be the admission into India of occidental ideas, methods and culture: even if we are ambitious to conserve what is sound and beneficial in our indigenous civilisation, we can only do so by assisting very largely the influx of Occidentalism. But at the same time we have a perfect right to insist, and every sagacious man will take pains to insist, that the process of introduction shall not be as hitherto rash and ignorant, that it shall be judicious, discriminating. We are to have what the West can give us, because what the West can give us is just the thing and the only thing that will rescue us from our present appalling condition of intellectual and moral decay, but we are not to take it haphazard and in a lump; rather we shall find it expedient to select the very best that is thought and known in Europe, and to import even that with the changes and reservations which our diverse conditions may be found to dictate. Otherwise instead of a simply ameliorating influence, we shall have chaos annexed to chaos, the vices and calamities of the West superimposed on the vices and calamities of the East.

No one has such advantages, no one is so powerful to discourage, minimise and even to prevent the intrusion of what is mischievous, to encourage, promote and even to ensure the admission of what is salutary, than an educated and vigorous national assembly standing for the best thought and the best energy in the country, and standing for it not in a formal parliamentary way, but by the spontaneous impulse and election of the people. Patrons of the Congress are never tired of giving us to understand that their much lauded idol does stand for all that is best in the country and that it stands for them precisely in the way I have described. If that is so, it is not a little remarkable that far from regulating judiciously the importation of occidental wares we have actually been at pains to import an inferior in preference to a superior quality, and in a condition not the most apt but the most inapt for consumption in India. Yet that this has been so far the net result of our political commerce with the West, will be very apparent to any one who chooses to think. National character being like human nature, maimed and imperfect, it was not surprising, not unnatural that a nation should commit one or other of various errors. We need not marvel if England, overconfident in her material success and the practical value of her institutions has concerned herself too little with social development and set small store by the discreet management of her masses: nor must we hold French judgment cheap because in the pursuit of social felicity and the pride of her magnificent cohesion France has failed in her choice of apparatus and courted political insecurity and disaster. But there are limits even to human fallibility and to combine two errors so distinct would be, one imagines, a miracle of incompetence. Facts however are always giving the lie to our imaginations; and it is a fact that we by a combination of errors so eccentric as almost to savour of felicity, are achieving this prodigious *tour de force.* Servile in imitation with a peculiar Indian servility we have swallowed down in a lump our English diet and especially that singular paradox about the unique value of machinery: but we have not the stuff in us to originate a really effective instrument for ourselves. Hence the Congress, a very reputable body, I hasten to admit, teeming with grave citizens and really quite flush of lawyers, but for all that meagre in the scope of its utility and wholly unequal to the functions it ought to exercise. There we have laid the foundations, as the French laid the foundations, of political incompetence, political failure; and of a more fatal incompetence, a more disastrous failure, because the French have at least originality, thought, resourcefulness, while we are vainglorious, shallow, mentally impotent: and as if this error were not enough for us, we have permitted ourselves to lose all sense of proportion, and to evolve an inordinate self-content, an exaggerated idea of our culture, our capacity, our importance. Hence we choose to rate our own political increase higher than social perfection or the advancement, intellectual and economical, of that vast unhappy proletariate about which everybody talks and nobody cares. We blindly assent when Mr. Pherozshah in the generous heat of his temperate and carefully restricted patriotism, assures us after his genial manner that the awakening of the masses from their ignorance and misery is entirely unimportant and any expenditure of energy in that direction entirely premature. There we have laid the foundation, as England laid the foundation, of social collapse, of social calamities. We have sown the wind and we must not complain if we reap the whirlwind. Under such circumstances it cannot be superfluous or a waste of power to review in the light of the critical reason that part of human experience most nearly connected by its nature with our own immediate difficulties. It is rather our main business and the best occupation not of dilettantes but of minds gifted with insight, seriousness, original power. So much indeed is it our main business that according as it is executed or neglected, we must pronounce a verdict of adequacy or inadequacy on our recent political thought: and we have seen that it is hopelessly inadequate, that all our efforts repose on a body organically infirm to the verge of impotence and are in their scheme as in their practice, selfishly frigid to social development and the awakening of the masses.

Here then we have got a little nearer to just and adequate comprehension. At any rate I hope to have enforced on my readers the precise and intrinsic meaning of that count in my indictment which censures the Congress as a body not popular and not honestly desirous of a popular character — in fact as a middle-class organ selfish and disingenuous in its public action and hollow in its professions of a large and disinterested patriotism. I hope to have convinced them that this is a solid charge and a charge entirely damaging to their character for wisdom and public spirit. Above all I hope to have persuaded Mr. Pherozshah Mehta, or at least the eidolon of that great man, the shadow of him which walks through these pages, that our national effort must contract a social and popular tendency before it can hope to be great or fruitful. But then Mr. Pherozshah is a lawyer: he has, enormously developed in him, that forensic instinct which prompts men to fight out a cause which they know to be unsound, to fight it out to the last gasp, not because it is just or noble but because it is theirs; and in the spirit of that forensic tradition he may conceivably undertake to answer me somewhat as follows. "Material success and a great representative assembly are boons of so immense a magnitude, so stupendous an importance that even if we purchase them at the cost of a more acute disintegration, a more appalling social decadence, the rate will not be any too exorbitant. Let us exactly imitate English success by an exact imitation of English models and then there will be plenty of time to deal with these questions which you invest with fictitious importance." Monstrous as the theorem is, profound as is the mental darkness which pervades it, it summarises not unfairly the defence put forward by the promoters and well-wishers of the Congress.

On us as the self-elected envoys of a new evangel there rests a heavy responsibility, assumed by our own will, but which once assumed we can no longer repudiate or discard; a responsibility which promises us immortal credit, if performed with sincerity and wisdom, but saddled with ignominy to ourselves and disaster to our country, if we discharge it in another spirit and another manner. To meet that responsibility we have no height, no sincerity of character, no depth of emotion, no charity, no seriousness of intellect. Yet it is only a sentimentalist, we are told, who will bid us raise, purify and transform ourselves so that we may be in some measure worthy of the high and solemn duties we have bound ourselves to perform! The proletariate among us is sunk in ignorance and overwhelmed with distress. But with that distressed and ignorant proletariate, — now that the middle class is proved deficient in sincerity, power and judgment, — with that proletariate resides, whether we like it or not, our sole assurance of hope, our sole chance in the future. Yet he is set down as a vain theorist and a dreamy trifler who would raise it from its ignorance and distress. The one thing needful we are to suppose, the one thing worthy of a great and statesmanlike soul is to enlarge the Legislative Councils, until they are big enough to hold Mr. Pherozshah M. Mehta, and other geniuses of an immoderate bulk. To play with baubles is our ambition, not to deal with grave questions in a spirit of serious energy. But while we are playing with baubles, with our Legislative Councils, our Simultaneous Examinations, our ingenious schemes for separating the judicial from the executive functions, — while we, I say, are finessing about trifles, the waters of the great deep are being stirred and that surging chaos of the primitive man over which our civilised societies are superimposed on a thin crust of convention, is being strangely and ominously agitated. Already a red danger-signal has shot up from Prabhas-Patan, and sped across the country, speaking with a rude eloquence of strange things beneath the fair surface of our renascent, enlightened India; yet no sooner was the signal seen than it was forgotten. Perhaps the religious complexion of these occurrences has lulled our fears; but when turbulence has once become habitual in a people, it is only folly that will reckon on its preserving the original complexion. A few more taxes, a few more rash interferences of Government, a few more stages of starvation, and the turbulence that is now religious will become social. I am speaking to that class which Mr. Manmohan Ghose has called the thinking portion of the Indian community: well, let these thinking gentlemen carry their thoughtful intellects a hundred years back. Let them recollect what causes led from the religious madness of St. Bartholomew to the social madness of the Reign of Terror. Let them enumerate if their memory serves them, the salient features and symptoms which the wise man detected many years before the event to be the sure precursors of some terrible catastrophe; and let them discover, if they can, any of those symptoms which are absent from the phenomena of our disease. With us it rests — if indeed it is not too late — with our sincerity, our foresight, our promptness of thought and action, that the hideous parallel shall not be followed up by a sequel as awful, as bloody and more purely disastrous. Theorist, and trifler though I may be called, I again assert as our first and holiest duty, the elevation and enlightenment of the proletariate: I again call on those nobler spirits among us who are working erroneously, it may be, but with incipient or growing sincerity and nobleness of mind, to divert their strenuous effort from the promotion of narrow class interests, from silly squabbles about offices and salaried positions, from a philanthropy laudable in itself and worthy of rational pursuit, but meagre in the range of its benevolence and ineffectual towards promoting the nearest interests of the nation, into that vaster channel through which alone the healing waters may be conducted to the lips of their ailing and tortured country.

Indu Prakash, December 4, 1893

New Lamps for Old - 8

POVERTY of organic conception and unintelligence of the deeper facts of our environment are the inherent vices I have hitherto imputed to the Congress and the burgess-body of which it is the political nucleus. But I have not done enough when I have done that. Perversion or error in the philosophy of our aim does indeed point to a serious defect of the political reason, but it is not incompatible with a nearer apprehension and happier management of surface facts; and if we had been so far apprehensive and dexterous, that would have been an output of native directness and force on which we might reasonably felicitate ourselves. For directness and force are an inalienable ancestral inheritance handed down by vigorous forefathers, and where they are, the political reason which comes of liberal culture and ancient experience, may be waited for with a certain patient hopefulness. But it is to be feared that our performance up to date does not give room for so comforting an assurance. Is it not rather the fact that our whole range of thought and action has been pervaded by a stamp of unreality and helplessness, a straining after achievement for which we have not the proper stamina and an entire misconception of facts as well as of natural laws? To be convinced of this we have only to interrogate recent events, not confiding in their outward face as the shallow and self-contented do, but getting to the heart of them, making sure of their hidden secret, their deeper reality. Indeed it will not hurt any of us to put out of sight for a moment those vain and fantastic chimeras about Simon de Montfort and the gradual evolution of an Indian Parliament, with which certain politicians are fond of amusing us, and look things straight in the face. We must resolutely hold fast to the primary fact that right and effective action can only ensue upon a right understanding of ourselves in relation to our environment. For by reflection or instinct to get a clear insight into our position and by dexterity to make the most of it, that is the whole secret of politics, and that is just what we have failed to do. Let us see whether we cannot get some adequate sense of what our position really is: after that we shall be more in the way to hit closely the exact point at which we have failed.

Whatever theatrical attitude it may suit our vanity to adopt, we are not, as we pretend to be, the embodiment of the country's power, intelligence and worth: neither are we disinterested patriots striving in all purity and unselfishness towards an issue irreproachable before God. These are absurd pretensions which only detract from the moral height of our nature and can serve no great or serious end. We may gain a poor and evanescent advantage by this sort of hypocrisy, but we lose in candour and clearness of intellect, we lose in sincerity which is another name for strength. If we would only indulge less our bias towards moral ostentation and care more to train ourselves in a healthy robustness and simple candour, it would really advantage us not only in character, but in power; and it would have this good effect, that we should no longer throw dust into our own eyes; we should be better fitted to see ourselves as a critic of human society would see us, better able to get that clear insight into our own position, which is one condition of genuine success. No, we are not and cannot be a body of disinterested patriots. Life being, as science tells us, an affirmation of one's self, any aggregate mass of humanity must inevitably strive to emerge and affirm its own essence, must by the law of its own nature aspire towards life, aspire towards expansion, aspire towards perfecting of its potential strength in the free air of political recognition and the full light of political predominance. That is just what has been happening in India. In us the Indian burgess or middle class emerges from obscurity, perhaps from nothingness, and strives between a strong and unfeeling bureaucracy and an inert and imbecile proletariate to possess itself of rank, consideration and power. Against that striving it is futile to protest; one might as well quarrel with the law of gravitation; but though our striving must be inherently selfish, we can at least make some small effort to keep it as little selfish as possible, to make it, as far as may be, run in harness with the grand central interests of the nation at large. So much at least those of us who have a broad human affection for our country as distinct from ourselves, have a right to expect.

Thus emergent, thus ambitious, it was our business by whatever circumstances we were environed, to seize hold of those circumstances and make ourselves masters of them. The initial difficulties were great. A young and just emergent body, without experience of government, without experience even of resistance to government, consequently without inherited tact, needs a teacher or a Messiah to initiate it in the art of politics. In England the burgess was taught almost insensibly by the nobility; in France he found a Messiah in the great Napoleon. We had no Napoleon, but we had a nobility. Europeans, when the spirit moves them to brag of their superiority over us Asiatics, are in the habit of saying that the West is progressive, the East stationary. That is a little too comprehensive. England and France are no doubt eminently progressive but there are other countries of Europe which have not been equally forward. America is a democratic country which has not progressed: Russia is a despotic country which has not progressed: in Italy, Spain, Germany even progress has been factitious and slow. Nevertheless, though the vulgar wording of the boast may be loose and careless, yet it does not express a very real superiority. The nations of the West are not all progressive, true; but they are all in that state which is the first condition of progress, a state, I mean, of fluidity, but of fluidity within limits, fluidity on a stable and normal basis. If no spirit of thought or emotion moves on the face of the waters, they become as foul and stagnant as in the most conservative parts of Asia, but a very slight wind will set them flowing. In most Asiatic countries, — I do not speak of India — one might almost imagine a hurricane blowing without any perceptible effect. Accordingly in Europe the transition of power from the noble to the burgess has been natural and inevitable. In India, just as naturally and inevitably, the administration remained with the noble. The old Hindu mechanism of society and government certainly did prescribe limits, certainly had a basis that was stable and normal; but it was too rigid, too stationary: it bound down the burgess and held him in his place by an iron weight of custom and religious ordinance. The regime that overthrew and succeeded it, the Mussulman regime, was mediaeval in character, fluid certainly, indeed in a perpetual state of flux, but never able to shake off the curse of instability, never in a position to prescribe limits, never stable, never normal. In such a society the qualities which make for survival, are valour, dexterity, initiative, swiftness, a robust immorality, qualities native to an aristocracy and to nations moulded by an aristocracy, native also to certain races, but even in those nations, even in those races, alien to the ordinary spirit of the burgess. His ponderous movements, his fumbling, his cold timidity, his decent scrupulousness have been fatal to his pretensions, at times inimical to his existence. Accordingly in India he has been submerged, scarcely existent. Great affairs and the high qualities they nourish have rested in the hand of the noble. We had then our nobility, our class trained and experienced in government and affairs: but to them unhappily we could not possibly look for guidance or even for co-operation. At the period of our emergence they were lethargic, effete, moribund, partially sunk in themselves; and even if any of the old energy had survived their fall, the world in which they moved was too new and strange, the transition to it had been too sudden and confounding to admit of their assimilating themselves so as to move with ease and success under novel conditions. The old nobility was quite as helpless from decay and dotage, as we from youthful inexperience. It was foreign energy that had pushed aside the old outworn machinery, it was an alien government that had by policy and self-will hurried us into a new and quite unfamiliar world. Would that government, politic and self-willed as it was, help us to an activity that might, nay, that must turn eventually to their personal detriment? Certainly they had the power but quite as certainly they had not the will. No doubt Anglo-Indians have very little right to speak of us as bitterly as they are in the habit of doing. By setting themselves to compel our social elements into a state of fluidity, and for that purpose not only of putting in motion organic forces but bringing direct pressure to bear, by strictly enforcing system and order so as to lay down fixed limits and a normal basis, within which the fluid elements might settle into new forms, they in fact made themselves responsible for us and lost the right to blame anyone but themselves for what might ensue. They are in the unlucky position of responsibility for a state of things which they abhor and certainly had no intention of bringing about. The force which they had in mind to construct was a body of grave, loyal and conservative citizens, educated but without ideas, a body created by and having a stake in the present order, and therefore attached to its continuance, a power in the land certainly, but a power for order, for permanence, not a power for disturbance and unrest. In such an enterprise they were bound to fail and they failed egregiously. Sir Edwin Arnold when he found out that it was a grievous mistake to occidentalise us, forgot, no doubt, for the moment his role as the preacher and poetaster of self-abnegation, and spoke as an ordinary mundane being, the prophet of a worldly and selfish class: but if we accept his words in that sense, there can be no doubt that he was perfectly right. Anglo-Indians had never seriously brought themselves to believe that we are in blood and disposition a genuine Aryan community. They chose to regard our history as a jungle of meaningless facts, and could not understand that we were not malleable dead matter, but men with Occidental impulses in our blood, not virgin material to be wrought into any shape they preferred, but animate beings with a principle of life in us and certain, if subjected to the same causes, placed in the same light and air as European communities, to exhibit effects precisely similar and shape ourselves rather than be shaped. They proposed to construct a tank for their own service and comfort; they did not know that they were breaking up the fountains of the great deep. There, stated shortly, is the whole sense of their policy and conduct. The habit, set in vogue by rhetoricians of Macaulay's type, of making large professions of benevolence invested with an air of high grandiosity, has become so much a second nature with them, that I will not ask if they are sincere when they make them: but it is a rhetorical habit and nothing more. We who are not interested in keeping up the fiction, may just as well pierce through it to the fact. If they had seen things as they really are, they would have been wisely inactive: but they wanted a submissive and attached population, and they thought they had hit on the best way of getting what they wanted. In this confidence, if there was a great deal of delusion, there was also something of truth. But we must not be surprised or indignant if the Anglo-Indians, when they saw their confidence so rudely dashed and themselves confronted, not with submission and attachment but with a body eager, pushing, recriminative, pushing for recognition, pushing for power, covetous above all of that authority which they had come to regard as their private and peculiar possession, — there is no cause for surprise or resentment, if they cared little for the grain of success in their bushelful of failure, and regarded us with those feelings of alarm, distrust and hatred which Frankenstein experienced when having hoped to make a man, he saw a monster. Their conduct was too natural to be censured. I do not say that magnanimity would not have been better, more dignified, more politic. But who expects magnanimity from bureaucracy? The old nobility then were almost extinct and had moreover no power to help us: the bureaucracy had not the will. Yet it was from their ranks that the Messiah came.

Indu Prakash, February 5, 1894

New Lamps for Old - 9

THE Civilian Order, which accounts itself, and no doubt justly, the informing spirit of Anglo-India, is credited in this country with quite an extraordinary degree of ability and merit, so much so that many believe it to have come down to us direct from heaven. And it is perhaps on this basis that in their dealings with Indians, — whom being moulded of a clay entirely terrestrial, one naturally supposes to be an inferior order of creatures, — they permit themselves a very liberal tinge of presumption and arrogance. Without disputing their celestial origin, one may perhaps be suffered to hint that eyes unaffected by the Indian sun, will be hard put to it to discover the pervading soul of magnificence and princeliness in the moral and intellectual style of these demigods. The fact is indeed all the other way. The general run of the Service suffers by being recruited through the medium of Competitive Examination: its tone is a little vulgar, its character a little raw, its achievement a little second-rate. Harsh critics have indeed said more than this; nay, has not one of themselves, has not Mr. Rudyard Kipling, a blameless Anglo-Indian, spoken, and spoken with distressing emphasis to the same effect? They have said that it moves in an atmosphere of unspeakable boorishness and mediocrity. That is certainly strong language and I would not for a moment be thought to endorse it; but there is, as I say, just a small sediment of truth at the bottom which may tend to excuse, if not to justify, this harsh and unfriendly criticism. And when one knows the stuff of which the Service is made, one ceases to wonder at it. A shallow schoolboy stepping from a cramming establishment to the command of high and difficult affairs, can hardly be expected to give us anything magnificent or princely. Still less can it be expected when the sons of small tradesmen are suddenly promoted from the counter to govern great provinces. Not that I have any fastidious prejudice against small tradesmen. I simply mean that the best education men of that class can get in England, does not adequately qualify a raw youth to rule over millions of his fellow-beings. Bad in training, void of culture, in instruction poor, it is in plain truth a sort of education that leaves him with all his original imperfections on his head, unmannerly, uncultivated, unintelligent. But in the Civil Service, with all its vices and shortcomings, one does find, as perhaps one does not find elsewhere, rare and exalted souls detached from the failings of their order, who exhibit the qualities of the race in a very striking way; not geniuses certainly, but swift and robust personalities, rhetorically powerful, direct, forcible, endowed to a surprising extent with the energy and self-confidence which are the heirlooms of their nation; men in short who give us England — and by England I mean the whole Anglo-Celtic race — on her really high and admirable side. Many of these are Irish or Caledonian; others are English gentlemen of good blood and position, trained at the great public schools, who still preserve that fine flavour of character, scholarship and power, which was once a common possession in England, but threatens under the present dispensation to become sparse or extinct. Others again are veterans of the old Anglo-Indian school, moulded in the larger traditions and sounder discipline of a strong and successful art who still keep some vestiges of the grand old Company days, still have something of a great and noble spirit, something of an adequate sense how high are the affairs they have to deal with and how serious the position they are privileged to hold. It was one of these, one endowed with all their good gifts, it was Mr. Allan Hume, a man acute and vigorous, happy in action and in speech persuasive, an ideal leader, who prompted, it may be by his own humane and lofty feelings, it may be by a more earthly desire of present and historic fame, took us by the hand and guided us with astonishing skill on our arduous venture towards pre-eminence and power. Mr. Hume, I have said, had all the qualities that go to make a fine leader in action. If only he had added to these the crowning gifts, reflectiveness, ideas, a comprehensive largeness of vision! Governing force, that splendid distinction inherited by England from her old Norman barons, governing force and the noble gifts that go along with it, are great things in their way, but they are not the whole of politics. Ideas, reflection, the political reason count for quite as much, are quite as essential. But on these, though individual Englishmen, men like Bolingbroke, Arnold, Burke, have had them pre-eminently, the race has always kept a very inadequate hold: and Mr. Hume is distinguished from his countrymen, not by the description of his merits, but by their degree. His original conception, I cannot help thinking, was narrow and impolitic.

He must have known, none better, what immense calamities may often be ripening under a petty and serene outside. He must have been aware, none better, when the fierce pain of hunger and oppression cuts to the bone what awful elemental passions may start to life in the mildest, the most docile proletariates. Yet he chose practically to ignore his knowledge; he conceived it as his business to remove a merely political inequality, and strove to uplift the burgess into a merely isolated predominance. That the burgess should strive towards predominance, nay, that for a brief while he should have it, is only just, only natural: the mischief of it was that in Mr. Hume's formation the proletariate remained for any practical purpose a piece off the board. Yet the proletariate is, as I have striven to show, the real key of the situation. Torpid he is and immobile; he is nothing of an actual force, but he is a very great potential force, and whoever succeeds in understanding and eliciting his strength, becomes by the very fact master of the future. Our situation is indeed complex and difficult beyond any that has ever been imagined by the human intellect; but if there is one thing clear in it, it is that the right and fruitful policy for the burgess, the only policy that has any chance of eventual success, is to base his cause upon an adroit management of the proletariate. He must awaken and organise the entire power of the country and thus multiply infinitely his volume and significance, the better to attain supremacy as much social as political. Thus and thus only will he attain to his legitimate station, not an egoist class living for itself and in itself, but the crown of the nation and its head.

But Mr. Hume saw things in a different light, and let me confess out of hand, that once he had got a clear conception of his business, he proceeded in it with astonishing rapidity, sureness and tact. The clear-cut ease and strong simplicity of his movements were almost Roman; no crude tentatives, no infelicitous bungling, but always a happy trick of hitting the right nail on the head and that at the first blow. Roman too was his principle of advancing to a great object by solid and consecutive gradations. To begin by accustoming the burgess as well as his adversaries to his own corporate reality, to proceed by a definitive statement of his case to the Viceregal government, and for a final throw to make a vehement and powerful appeal to the English parliament, an appeal that should be financed by the entire resources of middle-class India and carried through its stages with an iron heart and an obdurate resolution, expending moreover infinite energy, — so and so only could the dubious road Mr. Hume was treading, lead to anything but bathos and anticlimax. Nothing could be happier than the way in which the initial steps were made out. To be particularly obstreperous about his merits and his wrongs is certainly the likeliest way for a man to get a solid idea of his own importance and make an unpleasant impression on his ill-wishers. And for that purpose, for a blowing of trumpets in concert, for a self-assertion persistent, bold and clamorous, the Congress, however incapable in other directions may be pronounced perfectly competent; nay, it was the ideal thing. The second step was more difficult. He had to frame somehow a wording of our case at once bold and cautious, so as to hit Anglo-India in its weak place, yet properly sauced so as not to offend the palate, grown fastidious and epicurean, of the British House of Commons. Delicate as was the task he managed it with indubitable adroitness and a certain success. We may perhaps get at the inner sense of what happened, if we imagine Mr. Hume giving this sort of ultimatum to the Government. "The Indian burgess for whose education you have provided but whose patrimony you sequestrated and are woefully mismanaging, having now come to years of discretion, demands an account of your stewardship and the future management of his own estate. To compromise, if you are so good as to meet us half-way, we are not unready, but on any other hypothesis our appeal lies at once to the tribunal of the British Parliament. You will observe our process is perfectly constitutional." The sting of the scorpion lay as usual in its tail. Mr. Hume knew well the magic power of that word over Englishmen. With a German garrison it would have been naught; they would quickly have silenced with bayonets and prohibitive decrees any insolence of that sort. With French republicans it would have been naught; they would either have powerfully put it aside or frankly acceded to it. But the English are a nation of political jurists and any claim franked by the epithet "constitutional" they are bound by the very law of their being to respect or at any rate appear to respect. The common run of Anglo-Indians, blinded as selfishness always does blind people, might in their tremulous rage and panic vomit charges of sedition and shout for open war; but a Government of political jurists pledged to an occidentalising policy could not do so without making nonsense of its past. Moreover a Government viceregal in constitution cannot easily forget that it may have to run the gauntlet of adverse comment from authorities at home. But if they could not put us down with the strong hand or meet our delegates with a *non possumus*, they were not therefore going to concede to us any solid fraction of our demands. It is the ineradicable vice of the English nature that it can never be clear or direct. It recoils from simplicity as from a snake. It must shuffle, it must turn in on itself, it must preserve cherished fictions intact. And supposing unpleasant results to be threatened, it escapes from them through a labyrinth of unworthy and transparent subterfuges. Our rulers are unfortunately average Englishmen, Englishmen, that is to say, who are not in the habit of rising superior to themselves; and if they were uncandid, if they were tortuously hostile we may be indignant, but we cannot be surprised. Mr. Hume at any rate saw quite clearly that nothing was to be expected, perhaps he had never seriously expected anything, from that quarter. He had already instituted with really admirable promptitude, the primary stages of his appeal to the British Parliament.

Indu Prakash, March 6, 1894

Unity*

An Open Letter

To Those Who Despair of Their Country

TO THE sons of our mother Bharat who disclaim their sonhood, to the children of languor and selfishness, to the wooers of safety and ease, to the fathers of despair and death — greeting.

To those who impugning the holiness of their Mother refuse to lift her out of danger lest they defile their own spotless hands, to those who call on her to purify herself before they will save her from the imminent and already descending sword of Death, — greeting.

Lastly to those who love and perhaps have striven for her but having now grown themselves faint and hopeless bid others to despair and cease, — to them also greeting.

Brothers, for whether unwise friends or selfish enemies of my Mother, you are still her children, — there is a common voice among you spreading dismay and weakness in the hearts of the people; for you say to each other and to all who would speak to you of their country, "Let us leave these things and look to our daily bread; this nation must perish but let us at least and our children try to live while live we can. We are fallen and depraved and our sins grow upon us day by day; we suffer and are oppressed and oppression increases with every setting of the sun; we are weak and languid and our weakness grows weaker and langour more languid every time the sun rises in the east. We are sick and broken; we are idle and cowardly; we perish every year from famine and plague; disease decimates us, with every decade poverty annihilates family after family; where there were a hundred in one house, there are now ten; where there was once a flourishing village, the leopard and the jackal will soon

* An incomplete piece of writing found among the early manuscripts, probably belonging to a period before 1905.

inhabit. God is adverse to us and ourselves our worst enemies; we are decaying from within and smitten from without. The sword has been taken out of our hands and the bread is being taken out of our mouths. Worst of all we are disunited beyond hope of union and without union we must ere long perish. It may be five decades or it may be ten, but very soon this great and ancient nation will have perished from the face of the earth and the Negro or the Malay will inherit the homes of our fathers and till the fields to glut the pockets and serve the pleasure of the Englishman or the Russian. Meanwhile it is well that the Congress should meet once a year and deceive the country with an appearance of life; that there should be posts for the children of the soil with enough salary to keep a few from starving, that a soulless education should suck the vigour and sweetness of body and heart and brain of our children while flattering them with the vain lie that they are educated and enlightened; for so shall the nation die peacefully of a sort of euthanasia lapped in lies and comforted with delusion and not violently and in a whirlwind of horror and a great darkness of fear and suffering."

With such Siren song do you slay the hearts of those who have still force and courage to strive against Fate and would rescue our Mother out of the hands of destruction. Yet I would willingly believe that matricides though you are, it is in ignorance. Come therefore, let us reason calmly together.

Is it indeed...

(*Incomplete*)

BHAWANI MANDIR

Bhawani Mandir was written by Sri Aurobindo but it was more Barin's idea than his. It was not meant to train people for assassination but for revolutionary preparation of the country. The idea was soon dropped as far as Sri Aurobindo was concerned, but something of the kind was attempted by Barin in the Manicktala Garden...

From notes and letters of Sri Aurobindo

Bhawani Mandir

OM Namas Chandikayai

A TEMPLE is to be erected and consecrated to Bhawani, the Mother, among the hills. To all the children of the Mother the call is sent forth to help in the sacred work.

Who is Bhawani?

Who is Bhawani, the Mother, and why should we erect a temple to her?

Bhawani is the Infinite Energy

In the unending revolutions of the world, as the wheel of the Eternal turns mightily in its courses, the Infinite Energy, which streams forth from the Eternal and sets the wheel to work, looms up in the vision of man in various aspects and infinite forms. Each aspect creates and marks an age. Sometimes She is Love, sometimes She is Knowledge, sometimes She is Renunciation, sometimes She is Pity. This Infinite Energy is Bhawani, She also is Durga, She is Kali, She is Radha the Beloved, She is Lakshmi, She is our Mother and the Creatress of us all.

Bhawani is Shakti

In the present age, the Mother is manifested as the mother of Strength. She is pure Shakti.

The Whole World is Growing Full of the Mother as Shakti

Let us raise our eyes and cast them upon the world around us. Wherever we turn our gaze, huge masses of strength rise before our vision, tremendous, swift and inexorable forces, gigantic figures of energy, terrible sweeping columns of force. All is growing large and strong. The Shakti of war, the Shakti of wealth, the Shakti of Science are tenfold more mighty and colossal, a hundredfold more fierce, rapid and busy in their activity, a thousandfold more prolific in resources, weapons and instruments than ever before in recorded history. Everywhere the Mother is at work; from Her mighty and shaping hands enormous forms of Rakshasas, Asuras, Devas are leaping forth into the arena of the world. We have seen the slow but mighty rise of great empires in the West, we have seen the swift, irresistible and impetuous bounding into life of Japan. Some are Mlechchha Shaktis clouded in their strength, black or blood-crimson with Tamas or Rajas, others are Arya Shaktis, bathed in a pure flame of renunciation and utter self-sacrifice: but all are the Mother in Her new phase, remoulding, creating. She is pouring Her spirit into the old; She is whirling into life the new.

We in India Fail in All Things for Want of Shakti

But in India the breath moves slowly, the afflatus is long in coming. India, the ancient Mother, is indeed striving to be reborn, striving with agony and tears, but she strives in vain. What ails her, she who is after all so vast and might be so strong? There is surely some enormous defect, something vital is wanting in us, nor is it difficult to lay our finger on the spot. We have all things else, but we are empty of strength, void of energy. We have abandoned Shakti and are therefore abandoned by Shakti. The Mother is not in our hearts, in our brains, in our arms.

The wish to be reborn we have in abundance, there is no deficiency there. How many attempts have been made, how many movements have been begun, in religion, in society, in politics! But the same fate has overtaken or is preparing to overtake them all. They flourish for a moment, then the impulse wanes, the fire dies out, and if they endure, it is only as empty shells, forms from which the Brahma has gone or in which it lies overpowered with Tamas and inert. Our beginnings are mighty, but they have neither sequel nor fruit.

Now we are beginning in another direction; we have started

a great industrial movement which is to enrich and regenerate an impoverished land. Untaught by experience, we do not perceive that this movement must go the way of all the others, unless we first seek the one essential thing, unless we acquire strength.

Our Knowledge is a Dead Thing for Want of Shakti

Is it knowledge that is wanting? We Indians, born and bred in a country where Jnana has been stored and accumulated since the race began, bear about in us the inherited gains of many thousands of years. Great giants of knowledge rise among us even today to add to the store. Our capacity has not shrunk, the edge of our intellect has not been dulled or blunted, its receptivity and flexibility are as varied as of old. But it is a dead knowledge, a burden under which we are bowed, a poison which is corroding us, rather than as it should be a staff to support our feet and a weapon in our hands; for this is the nature of all great things that when they are not used or are ill used, they turn upon the bearer and destroy him.

Our knowledge then, weighed down with a heavy load of Tamas, lies under the curse of impotence and inertia. We choose to fancy indeed, nowadays, that if we acquire Science, all will be well. Let us first ask ourselves what we have done with the knowledge we already possess, or what have those who have already acquired Science been able to do for India. Imitative and incapable of initiative, we have striven to copy the methods of England, and we had not the strength; we would now copy the methods of the Japanese, a still more energetic people; are we likely to succeed any better? The mighty force of knowledge which European Science bestows is a weapon for the hands of a giant, it is the mace of Bheemsen; what can a weakling do with it but crush himself in the attempt to wield it?

Our Bhākti cannot Live and Work for Want of Shakti

Is it love, enthusiasm, Bhakti that is wanting? These are ingrained in the Indian nature, but in the absence of Shakti we cannot concentrate, we cannot direct, we cannot even preserve it. Bhakti is the leaping flame, Shakti is the fuel. If the fuel is scanty how long can the fire endure?

When the strong nature, enlightened by knowledge, disciplined and given a giant's strength by Karma, lifts itself up in love and adoration to God, that is the Bhakti which endures and keeps the soul for ever united with the Divine. But the weak nature is too feeble to bear the impetus of so mighty a thing as perfect Bhakti; he is lifted up for a moment, then the flame soars up to Heaven, leaving him behind exhausted and even weaker than before. Every movement of any kind of which enthusiasm and adoration are the life must fail and soon burn itself out so long as the human material from which it proceeds is frail and light in substance.

India therefore Needs Shakti Alone

The deeper we look, the more we shall be convinced that the one thing wanting, which we must strive to acquire before all others, is strength — strength physical, strength mental, strength moral, but above all strength spiritual which is the one inexhaustible and imperishable source of all the others. If we have strength everything else will be added to us easily and naturally. In the absence of strength we are like men in a dream who have hands but cannot seize or strike, who have feet but cannot run.

India, Grown Old and Decrepit in Will, has to be Reborn

Whenever we strive to do anything, after the first rush of enthusiasm is spent a paralysing helplessness seizes upon us. We often see in the cases of old men full of years and experience that the very excess of knowledge seems to have frozen their powers of action and their powers of will. When a great feeling or a great need overtakes them and it is necessary to carry out its promptings in action, they hesitate, ponder, discuss, make tentative efforts and abandon them or wait for the safest and easiest way to suggest itself, instead of taking the most direct; thus the time when it was possible and necessary to act passes away. Our race has grown just such an old man with stores of knowledge, with ability to feel and desire, but paralysed by senile sluggishness, senile timidity, senile feebleness. If India is to survive, she must be made young again. Rushing and billowing streams of energy must be poured into her; her soul must become, as it was in the old times, like the surges, vast, puissant, calm or turbulent at will, an ocean of action or of force.

India can be Reborn

Many of us, utterly overcome by Tamas, the dark and heavy demon of inertia, are saying nowadays that it is impossible, that India is decayed, bloodless and lifeless, too weak ever to recover; that our race is doomed to extinction. It is a foolish and idle saying. No man or nation need be weak unless he chooses, no man or nation need perish unless he deliberately chooses extinction.

What is a Nation? The Shakti of Its Millions

For what is a nation? What is our mother-country? It is not a piece of earth, nor a figure of speech, nor a fiction of the mind. It is a mighty Shakti, composed of the Shaktis of all the millions of units that make up the nation, just as Bhawani Mahisha Mardini sprang into being from the Shakti of all the millions of gods assembled in one mass of force and welded into unity. The Shakti we call India, Bhawani Bharati, is the living unity of the Shaktis of three hundred million people; but she is inactive, imprisoned in the magic circle of Tamas, the self-indulgent inertia and ignorance of her sons. To get rid of Tamas we have but to wake the Brahma within.

It is Our Own Choice whether We Create a Nation or Perish

What is it that so many thousands of holy men, Sadhus and Sannyasis, have preached to us silently by their lives? What was the message that radiated from the personality of Bhagawan Ramakrishna Paramhansa? What was it that formed the kernel of the eloquence with which the lion-like heart of Vivekananda sought to shake the world? It is this, that in every one of these three hundred millions of men, from the Raja on his throne to the coolie at his labour, from the Brahmin absorbed in his Sandhya to the Pariah walking shunned of men, GOD LIVETH. We are all gods and creators, because the energy of God is within us and all life is creation; not only the making of new forms is creation, but preservation is creation, destruction itself is creation. It rests with us what we shall create; for we are not, unless we choose, puppets dominated by Fate and Maya; we are facets and manifestations of Almighty Power.

India must be Reborn, because her Rebirth is Demanded by the Future of the World

India cannot perish, our race cannot become extinct, because among all the divisions of mankind it is to India that is reserved the highest and the most splendid destiny, the most essential to the future of the human race. It is she who must send forth from herself the future religion of the entire world, the Eternal Religion which is to harmonise all religion, science and philosophies and make mankind one soul. In the sphere of morality, likewise, it is her mission to purge barbarism (Mlechchhahood) out of humanity and to Aryanise the world. In order to do this, she must first re-Aryanise herself.

It was to initiate this great work, the greatest and most wonderful work ever given to a race, that Bhagawan Ramakrishna came and Vivekananda preached. If the work does not progress as it once promised to do it is because we have once again allowed the terrible cloud of Tamas to settle down on our souls — fear, doubt, hesitation, sluggishness. We have taken, some of us, the Bhakti which poured forth from the one and the Jnana given us by the other, but from lack of Shakti, from the lack of Karma, we have not been able to make our Bhakti a living thing. May we yet remember that it was Kali, who is Bhawani, Mother of strength whom Ramakrishna worshipped and with whom he became one.

But the destiny of India will not wait on the falterings and failings of individuals; the Mother demands that men shall arise to institute Her worship and make it universal.

To Get Strength We must Adore the Mother of Strength

Strength then and again strength and yet more strength is the need of our race. But if it is strength we desire, how shall we gain it if we do not adore the Mother of Strength? She demands worship not for Her own sake, but in order that She may help us and give Herself to us. This is no fantastic idea, no superstition but the ordinary law of the universe. The gods cannot, if they would, give themselves unasked. Even the Eternal comes not unawares upon men. Every devotee knows by experience that we must turn to Him and desire and adore Him before the Divine Spirit pours in its ineffable beauty and ecstasy upon the soul. What is true of the Eternal is true also of Her who goes forth from Him.

Religion, the True Path

Those who, possessed with Western ideas, look askance at any return to the old sources of energy, may well consider a few fundamental facts.

The Example of Japan

I. There is no instance in history of a more marvellous and sudden up-surging of strength in a nation than modern Japan. All sorts of theories had been started to account for the uprising, but now the intellectual Japanese are telling us what were the fountains of that mighty awakening, the sources of that inexhaustible strength. They were drawn from religion. It was the Vedantic teachings of Oyomei and the recovery of Shintoism with its worship of the national Shakti of Japan in the image and person of the Mikado that enabled the little island empire to wield the stupendous weapons of Western knowledge and science as lightly and invincibly as Arjun wielded the Gandiv.

India's Greater Need of Spiritual Regeneration

II. India's need of drawing from the fountains of religion

is far greater than was ever Japan's; for the Japanese had only to revitalise and perfect a strength that already existed. We have to create strength where it did not exist before; we have to change our natures, and become new men with new hearts, to be born again. There is no scientific process, no machinery for that. Strength can only be created by drawing it from the internal and inexhaustible reservoirs of the Spirit, from that Adya-Shakti of the Eternal which is the fountain of all new existence. To be born again means nothing but to revive the Brahma within us, and that is a spiritual process — no effort of the body or the intellect can compass it.

Religion, the Path Natural to the National Mind

III. All great awakenings in India, all her periods of mightiest and most varied vigour have drawn their vitality from the fountain-heads of some deep religious awakening. Wherever the religious awakening has been complete and grand, the national energy it has created has been gigantic and puissant; wherever the religious movement has been narrow or incomplete, the national movement has been broken, imperfect or temporary. The persistence of this phenomenon is proof that it is ingrained in the temperament of the race. If you try other and foreign methods we shall either gain our end with tedious slowness, painfully and imperfectly, or we shall not attain it at all. Why abandon the plain way which God and the Mother have marked out for you, to choose faint and devious paths of your own treading?

The Spirit within is the True Source of Strength

IV. The Brahma within, the one and indivisible ocean of spiritual force is that from which all life, material and mental, is drawn. This is beginning to be as much recognised by leading Western thinkers as it was from the old days by the East. If it be so, then spiritual energy is the source of all other strength. There are the fathomless fountain-heads, the deep and inexhaustible sources. The shallow surface springs are easier to reach, but they soon run dry. Why not then go deep instead of scratching the surface? The result will repay the labour.

Three Things Needful

We need three things answering to three fundamental laws.

I. Bhakti — the Temple of the Mother

We cannot get strength unless we adore the Mother of Strength.

We will therefore build a temple to the white Bhawani, the Mother of Strength, the Mother of India; and we will build it in a place far from the contamination of modern cities and as yet little trodden by man, in a high and pure air steeped in calm and energy. This temple will be the centre from which Her worship is to flow over the whole country; for there, worshipped among the hills, She will pass like fire into the brains and hearts of Her worshippers. This also is what the Mother has commanded.

II. Karma — A New Order of Brahmacharins

Adoration will be dead and ineffective unless it is transmuted into Karma.

We will therefore have a Math with a new Order of Karma Yogins attached to the temple, men who have renounced all in order to work for the Mother. Some may, if they choose, be complete Sannyasis, most will be Brahmacharins who will return to the Grihasthashram when their allotted work is finished, but all must accept renunciation.

Why? For Reasons:

1. Because it is only in proportion as we put from us the preoccupation of bodily desires and interests, the sensual gratifications, lusts, longings, indolences of the material world, that

we can return to the ocean of spiritual force within us.

2. Because for the development of Shakti, entire concentration is necessary; the mind must be devoted entirely to its aim as a spear is hurled to its mark; if other cares and longings distract the mind, the spear will be carried out from its straight course and miss the target. We need a nucleus of men in whom the Shakti is developed to its uttermost extent, in whom it fills every corner of the personality and overflows to fertilise the earth. These, having the fire of Bhawani in their hearts and brains, will go forth and carry the flame to every nook and cranny of our land.

III. Jnana — the Great Message

Bhakti and Karma cannot be perfect and enduring unless they are based upon Jnana.

The Brahmacharins of the Order will therefore be taught to fill their souls with knowledge and base their work upon it as upon a rock. What shall be the basis of their knowledge? What but the great *so-aham*, the mighty formula of the Vedanta, the ancient gospel which has yet to reach the heart of the nation, the knowledge which when vivified by Karma and Bhakti delivers man out of all fear and all weakness.

The Message of the Mother

When, therefore, you ask who is Bhawani the Mother, She herself answers you, "I am the Infinite Energy which streams forth from the Eternal in the world and the Eternal in yourselves. I am the Mother of the Universe, the Mother of the Worlds, and for you who are children of the Sacred Land, Aryabhumi, made of her clay and reared by her sun and winds, I am Bhawani Bharati, Mother of India."

Then if you ask why we should erect a temple to Bhawani, the Mother, hear Her answer, "Because I have commanded it, and because by making a centre for the future religion you will be furthering the immediate will of the Eternal and storing up merit which will make you strong in this life and great in another. You will be helping to create a nation, to consolidate an age, to Aryanise a world. And that nation is your own, that age is the age of yourselves and your children, that world is no fragment of land bounded by seas and hills, but the whole earth with her teeming millions."

Come then, hearken to the call of the Mother. She is already in our hearts waiting to manifest Herself, waiting to be worshipped, — inactive because the God in us is concealed by Tamas, troubled by Her inactivity, sorrowful because Her children will not call on Her to help them. You who feel Her stirring within you, fling off the black veil of self, break down the imprisoning walls of indolence, help Her each as you feel impelled, with your bodies or with your intellect or with your speech or with your wealth or with your prayers and worship, each man according to his capacity. Draw not back, for against those who were called and heard Her not She may well be wroth in the day of Her coming; but to those who help Her advent even a little, how radiant with beauty and kindness will be the face of their Mother.

Appendix

THE work and rules of the new Order of Sannyasis will be somewhat as follows:

I. General Rules

1. All who undertake the life of Brahmacharya for the Mother will have to vow themselves to Her service for four years, after which they will be free to continue to work or return to family life.

2. All money received by them in the Mother's name will go to the Mother's service. For themselves they will be allowed to receive shelter and their meals, when necessary, and nothing more.

3. Whatever they may earn for themselves, e.g., by the publication of books, etc., they must give at least half of it to the service of the Mother.

4. They will observe entire obedience to the Head of the Order and his one or two assistants in all things connected with the work or with their religious life.

5. They will observe strictly the discipline and rules of Achar and purity, bodily and mental, prescribed by the Heads of the Order.

6. They will be given periods for rest or for religious improvement during which they will stop at the Math, but the greater part of the year they will spend in work outside. This rule will apply to all except the few necessary for the service of the Temple and those required for the central direction of the work.

7. There will be no gradations of rank among the workers, and none must seek for distinction or mere personal fame but practise strength and self-effacement.

II. Work for the People

8. Their chief work will be that of mass instruction and

help to the poor and ignorant.

9. This they will strive to effect in various ways:

1. Lectures and demonstrations suited to an uneducated intelligence.
2. Classes and nightly schools.
3. Religious teachings.
4. Nursing the sick.
5. Conducting works of charity.
6. Whatever other good work their hands may find to do and the Order approves.

III. Works for the Middle Class

10. They will undertake, according as they may be directed, various works of public utility in the big towns and elsewhere connected especially with the education and religious life and instruction of the middle classes, as well as with other public needs.

IV. Work with the Wealthy Classes

11. They will approach the zamindars, landholders and rich men generally, and endeavour —

1. To promote sympathy between the zamindars and the peasants and heal all discords.
2. To create the link of a single and living religious spirit and a common passion for one great ideal between all classes.
3. To turn the minds of rich men to works of public beneficence and charity to those in their neighbourhood independent of the hope of reward and official distinction.

V. General Work for the Country

12. As soon as funds permit, some will be sent to foreign countries to study lucrative arts and manufactures.

13. They will be as Sannyasis during their period of study, never losing hold of their habits of purity and self-abnegation.

14. On their return they will estabilish with the aid of the Order, factories and workshops, still living the life of Sannyasis and devoting all their profits to the sending of more and more such students to foreign countries.

15. Others will be sent to travel through various countries on foot, inspiring by their lives, behaviour and conversation, sympathy and love for the Indian people in the European nations and preparing the way for their acceptance of Aryan ideals.

After the erection and consecration of the Temple, the development of the work of the Order will be pushed on as rapidly as possible or as the support and sympathy of the public allows. With the blessing of the Mother this will not fail us.

An Organisation*...

HAVING in an organisation of this kind a ready and efficient instrument of work, it remains to consider on what lines the energy of the nation may best expend itself. Strength and unity are our objective; ceaseless and self-reliant labour is our motive power; education, organisation and self-help are our road. It is moreover a triple strength we shall have to seek, strength mental, strength material and strength moral. Now it is not the object of this pamphlet to lay down rigidly or in detail the lines on which our movement ought to proceed: that is a question beyond the scope of any single intellect; it is for the united thought of the nation to decide. But the main principles and divergent branches which national energy is bound to take if it would do its work thoroughly may well be very briefly specified. To improve the mental force of the race will be our first object; and for this we need that we ourselves should think, more deeply as well as that we should...

(*Incomplete*)

* The beginning of an article found in early manuscripts.

The Proposed Reconstruction of Bengal*

PARTITION OR ANNIHILATION?

IN THE excitement and clamour that has followed the revolutionary proposal of Lord Curzon's Government to break Bengal into pieces, there is some danger of the new question being treated only in its superficial aspects and the grave and startling national peril for which it is the preparation being either entirely missed or put out of sight. On a perusal of the telegrams which pour in from Eastern Bengal one is struck with the fact that they mainly deal with certain obvious and present results of the measure, not one of which is really vital. The contention repeatedly harped on that Assam is entirely different to us in race, language, manners etc. is in the first place not altogether true, and even if true, is very bad political strategy. In these days when the whole tendency of a reactionary Government is to emphasize old points of divisions and create new ones, it should plainly be the policy of the national movement to ignore points of division and to emphasize old and create new points of contact and union. The Assamese possess the same racial substratum as ourselves though the higher strata may be less profoundly Aryanised and their language is a branch of Bengali which but for an artificial diversion would have merged into the main stream of Bengali speech. Why then should we affront our brothers in Assam and play the game of our opponents by declaring them outcast from our sympathies? The loss by Eastern Bengal of a seat on the Legislative Council is again the loss of a delusion and does not really concern its true national welfare. Even separation from the Calcutta High Court if it should come about, means very little now that the High Court has definitely ceased to protect the liberties of the people and become an informal department of the Government. The dislocation of trade caused by its diversion from Calcutta to Chittagong might be a calamity of the first magnitude to Calcutta but its evil effects

* An incomplete article found among early manuscripts.

on Eastern Bengal would, the enemy might well argue, be of a very temporary character. The transfer of advanced provinces to a backward Government is, no doubt, in itself a vital objection to the measure but can be at once met by elevating the new province to the dignity of a Lieutenant-Governorship with a Legislative Council and a Chief Court. Indeed by this very simple though costly contrivance the Government can meet every practical objection of a political nature that has been urged against their proposal. There are signs which seem to indicate that this is the expedient to which Government will eventually resort and under the cover of it affect an even more extended amputation than it was at first convenient to announce; for Rajshahi as well as Faridpur and Backergunje, are it appears also to be cut away from us. There would remain the violation of Bengali sentiment and the social disturbance and mortal inconvenience to innumerable individuals which must inevitably accompany such a disruption of old ties and interests and severance from the great centre of Bengali life. But our sentiments the Government can very well afford to ignore and the disturbance and inconvenience they may politely regret as deplorable incidents indeed but after all minor and temporary compared with the great and permanent administrative necessities to be satisfied. Will then the people of Eastern Bengal finally, seeing the Government determined pocket the bribe of a separate Lieutenant-Governorship, a Legislative Council and High Court and accept this violent revolution in our national life? Or will Western Bengal submit to lose Eastern Bengal on such terms? If not, then to nerve them for the struggle their refusal will involve they must rely on something deeper than sentiment, something more potent than social and personal interests, they must have a clear and indelible consciousness of the truth that this measure is no mere administrative proposal but a blow straight at the heart of the nation. The failure to voice clearly this, the true and vital side of the question can arise only from want of moral courage or from that fatal inability to pass beyond superficialities and details and understand in their fulness deep truths and grand issues in politics which has made our political life for the last fifty years so miserably barren and ineffective. That it springs largely if not altogether from the latter is evidenced by the amazing apathy which allows Western Bengal to sit with folded hands and allow Eastern Bengal to struggle alone and unaided. Eastern Bengal is menaced with absorption into a backward province and therefore struggles; Western Bengal is menaced with no such calamity and can therefore sit lolling on its pillows, hookah-pipe in hand, waiting to see what happens; this apparently is how the question is envisaged by a race which considers itself the most intelligent and quick-witted in the world. That it is something far other than this, that the danger involved far more urgent and appalling, is what I shall try to point out in this article.

Unfortunately, to do this is impossible without treading on Lord Curzon's corns and indeed on the tenderest of all the crop. We have recently been permitted to know that our great Viceroy particularly objects to the imputation of motives to his Government — and not unnaturally; for Lord Curzon is a vain man loving praise and sensitive to dislike and censure; more than that, he is a statesman of unusual genius who is following a subtle and daring policy on which immense issues hang and it is naturally disturbing him to find that there are wits in India as subtle as his own which can perceive something at least of the goal at which he is aiming. But in this particular instance he has only himself and Mr. Risley to thank, if his motives have been discovered — or let us say, misinterpreted. The extraordinary farrago of discursive ineptitudes which has been put forward...

(*Incomplete*)

BANDE MATARAM

A NOTE ON "BANDE MATARAM"

Bepin Pal started the *Bande Mataram* with Rs. 500 in his pocket. ...He called in my help as assistant editor and I gave it. I called a private meeting of the young Nationalist leaders in Calcutta and they agreed to take up the *Bande Mataram* as their party paper with Subodh and Nirod Mullick as the principal financial supporters. A company was projected and formed, but the paper was financed and kept up meanwhile by Subodh.

*

The new party was at once successful and the *Bande Mataram* paper began to circulate throughout India. On its staff were not only Bepin Pal and Sri Aurobindo but some other very able writers, Shyam Sundar Chakravarty, Hemendra Prasad Ghose and Bejoy Chatterjee. Shyam Sundar and Bejoy were masters of the English language, each with a style of his own; Shyam Sundar caught up something like Sri Aurobindo's way of writing and later on many took his articles for Sri Aurobindo's.... The *Bande Mataram* was almost unique in journalistic history in the influence it exercised in converting the mind of a people and preparing it for revolution. But its weakness was on the financial side; ... So long as Sri Aurobindo was there in active control, he managed with great difficulty... but ...when he was arrested and held in jail for a year, the economic situation of the *Bande Mataram* became desperate: finally, it was decided that the journal should die a glorious death rather than perish by starvation and Bejoy Chatterjee was commissioned to write an article for which the Government would certainly stop the publication of the paper.... The manoeuvre succeeded and the life of the *Bande Mataram* came to an end in Sri Aurobindo's absence.

From notes and letters of Sri Aurobindo

THE DOCTRINE OF PASSIVE RESISTANCE

This series of articles first appeared in the daily *Bande Mataram* under the general title of *New Thought* from April 11 to April 23, 1907. It was brought out in 1948 in book-form. The last article *The Morality of Boycott*, which had been produced as an exhibit in the Alipore Conspiracy Case, was also included in the book.

ONE

Introduction

IN A series of articles, published in this paper soon after the Calcutta session of the Congress, we sought to indicate our view both of the ideal which the Congress had adopted, the ideal of Swaraj or Self-Government as it exists in the United Kingdom or the Colonies, and of the possible lines of policy by which that ideal might be attained. There are, we pointed out, only three possible policies: petitioning, an unprecedented way of attempting a nation's liberty, which cannot possibly succeed except under conditions which have not yet existed among human beings; self-development and self-help; and the old orthodox historical method of organised resistance to the existing form of Government. We acknowledge that the policy of self-development which the New Party had forced to the front, was itself a novel departure under the circumstances of modern India. Self-development of an independent nation is one thing; self-development from a state of servitude under an alien and despotic rule without the forcible or peaceful removal of that rule as an indispensable preliminary, is quite another. No national self-development is possible without the support of *rāja-śakti*, organised political strength, commanding, and whenever necessary compelling general allegiance and obedience. A caste may develop, a particular community may develop, by its own efforts supported by a strong social organisation; a nation cannot. Industrially, socially, educationally, there can be no genuine progress carrying the whole nation forward, unless there is a central force representing either the best thought and energy of the country or else the majority of its citizens and able to enforce the views and decisions of the nation on all its constituent members. Because Japan had such a central authority, she was able in thirty years to face Europe as an equal; because we in India neither had such an authority nor tried to develop it, but supported each tottering step by clinging to the step-motherly apron-strings of a foreign Government, our record of more than seventy years has not been equal to one year of Japan. We have fumbled through the nineteenth century, prattling of enlightenment and national regeneration; and the result has been not national progress, but national confusion and weakness. Individuals here and there might emancipate themselves and come to greatness; particular communities might show a partial and one-sided development, for a time only; but the nation instead of progressing, sank into a very slough of weakness, helplessness and despondency. Political freedom is the life-breath of a nation; to attempt social reform, educational reform, industrial expansion, the moral improvement of the race without aiming first and foremost at political freedom, is the very height of ignorance and futility. Such attempts are foredoomed to disappointment and failure; yet when the disappointment and failure come, we choose to attribute them to some radical defect in the national character; as if the nation were at fault and not its wise men who would not or could not understand the first elementary conditions of success. The primary requisite for national progress, national reform, is the free habit of free and healthy national thought and action which is impossible in a state of servitude. The second is the organisation of the national will in a strong central authority.

How impossible it is to carry out efficiently any large national object in the absence of this authority was shown by the fate of the Boycott in Bengal. It is idle to disguise from ourselves that the Boycott is not as yet effective except spasmodically and in patches. Yet to carry through the Boycott was a solemn national decision which has not been reversed but rather repeatedly confirmed. Never indeed has the national will been so generally and unmistakably declared; but for the want of a central authority to work for the necessary conditions, to support by its ubiquitous presence the weak and irresolute and to coerce the refractory, it has not been properly carried out. For the same reason national education languishes. For the same reason every attempt at large national action has failed. It is idle to talk of self-development unless we first evolve a suitable central authority or Government which all will or must accept. The Japanese perceived this at a very early stage and leaving aside all other matters, devoted their first energies to the creation of such an authority in the person of the Mikado and his Government, holding it cheaply purchased even at the price of temporary internal discord and civil slaughter. We also must develop a central authority, which shall be a popular Government in fact though not in name. But Japan was independent; we have to establish a popular authority which will exist side by side and in rivalry with a despotic foreign bureaucracy — no ordinary rough-riding despotism, but quiet, pervasive and subtle — one that has fastened its grip on every detail of our national life and will not easily be persuaded to let go, even in the least degree, its octopus-like hold. This popular authority will have to dispute every part of our national life and activity, one by one, step by step, with the intruding force to the extreme point of entire emancipation from alien control. This and no less than this is the task before us. A Moderate critic characterised it at the time as an unheroic programme; but to us it seems so heroic that we frankly acknowledge its novelty and audacity and the uncertainty of success. For success depends on the presence of several very rare conditions. It demands in the first place a country for its field of action in which the people are more powerfully swayed by the fear of social excommunication and the general censure of their fellows than by the written law. It demands a country where the capacity for extreme self-denial is part of the national character or for centuries has taken a prominent place in the national discipline. These conditions exist in India. But it requires also an iron endurance, tenacity, doggedness, far above anything that is needed for the more usual military revolt or sanguinary revolution. These qualities we have not as yet developed at least in Bengal; but they are easily generated by suffering and necessity and hardened into permanence by a prolonged struggle with superior power. There is nothing like a strong pressure from above to harden and concentrate what lies below — always provided that the superior pressure is not such as to crush the substance on which it is acting. The last requisite therefore for the success of the policy of self-development against the pressure of foreign rule is that the bureaucracy will so far respect its former traditions and professions as not to interfere finally with any course of action of the popular authority which does not itself try violently to subvert the connection of the British Empire with India. It is extremely doubtful whether this last condition will be satisfied. It is easy to see how the bureaucracy might put a summary end to National Education or an effective check on industrial expansion or do away arbitrarily with popular Arbitration Courts. It is easy to see how the temptation to resort to Russian methods on a much larger and effective scale than that of mere Fullerism might prove too strong for a privileged class which felt power slipping from its hold. We therefore said in our previous articles that we must carry on the attempt at self-development as long as we were permitted. What would be our next resource if it were no longer permitted, it is too early to discuss.

The attempt at self-development by self-help is absolutely necessary for our national salvation, whether we can carry it peacefully to the end or not. In no other way can we get rid of the fatal dependence, passivity and helplessness in which a century of all-pervasive British control has confirmed us. To recover the habit of independent motion and independent action is the first necessity. It was for this reason that after extreme provocation and full conviction of the hopelessness otherwise of inducing any change of policy in the older politicians, the leaders of the New School decided to form an independent party and place their views as an independent programme before the country. Their action, though much blamed at the time, has been thoroughly justified by results. The National Congress has not indeed broken with the old petitioning traditions, but it has admitted the new policy as an essential part of the national programme. Swadeshi and National Education have been recognised, and, in all probability, Arbitration will be given its proper prominence at the next session; Boycott has been admitted as permissible in principle to all parts of India though the recommendation to extend it in practice as an integral part of the national policy was not pressed. It only remained to develop the central authority which will execute the national policy and evolve with time into a popular Government. It was for this object that the

New Party determined not to be satisfied with any further evasion of the constitution question, though they did not press for the adoption of their own particular scheme. It is for this object that a Central National Committee has been formed; that Conferences are being held in various districts and sub-divisions and Committees created; that the Provincial Conferences are expected to appoint a Provincial Committee for all Bengal. The mere creation of these Committees will not provide us with our central authority, nor will they be really effective for the purpose until the new spirit and the new views are paramount in the whole country. But it is the first step which costs and the first step has been taken.

So far, well; but the opposition of the bureaucracy to the national self-development must be taken into account. Opposition, not necessarily final and violent, will undoubtedly be offered; and we have not as yet considered the organisation of any means by which it can be effectually met. Obviously, we shall have to fall back on the third policy of organised resistance, and have only to decide what form the resistance should take, passive or active, defensive or aggressive. It is well known that the New Party long ago formulated and all Bengal has in theory accepted, the doctrine of passive, or, as it might be more comprehensively termed, defensive resistance. We have therefore not only to organise a central authority, not only to take up all branches of our national life into our hands, but, in order to meet bureaucratic opposition and to compel the alien control to remove its hold on us, if not at once, then tentacle by tentacle, we must organise defensive resistance.

TWO

Its Object

ORGANISED resistance to an existing form of government may be undertaken either for the vindication of national liberty, or in order to substitute one form of government for another, or to remove particular objectionable features in the existing system without any entire or radical alteration of the whole, or simply for the redress of particular grievances. Our political agitation in the nineteenth century was entirely confined to the smaller and narrower objects. To replace an oppressive land revenue system by the security of a Permanent Settlement, to mitigate executive tyranny by the separation of judicial from executive functions, to diminish the drain on the country naturally resulting from foreign rule by more liberal employment of Indians in the services — to these half-way houses our wise men and political seers directed our steps, — with this limited ideal they confined the rising hopes and imaginations of a mighty people re-awakening after a great downfall. Their political inexperience prevented them from realising that these measures on which we have misspent half a century of unavailing effort, were not only paltry and partial in their scope but in their nature ineffective. A Permanent Settlement can always be evaded by a spendthrift Government bent on increasing its resources and unchecked by any system of popular control; there is no limit to the possible number of cesses and local taxes by which the Settlement could be practically violated without any direct infringement of its provisions. The mere deprivation of judicial functions will not disarm executive tyranny so long as both executive and judiciary are mainly white and subservient to a central authority irresponsible, alien and bureaucratic; for the central authority can always tighten its grip on the judiciary of which it is the controller and paymaster and habituate it to a consistent support of executive action. Nor will Simultaneous Examinations and the liberal appointment of Indians mend the matter; for an Englishman serves the Government as a member of the same ruling race and can afford to be occasionally independent; but the Indian civilian is a serf masquerading as a heaven-born and can only deserve favour and promotion by his zeal in fastening the yoke heavier upon his fellow-countrymen. As a rule the foreign Government can rely on the "native" civilian to be more zealously oppressive than even the average Anglo-Indian official. Neither would the panacea of Simultaneous Examinations really put an end to the burden of the drain. The Congress insistence on the Home Charges for a long time obscured the real accusation against British rule; for it substituted a particular grievance for a radical and congenital evil implied in the very existence of British control. The huge price India has to pay England for the inestimable privilege of being ruled by Englishmen is a small thing compared with the murderous drain by which we purchase the more exquisite privilege of being exploited by British capital. The diminution of Home Charges will not prevent the gradual death by bleeding of which exploitation is the true and abiding cause. Thus, even for the partial objects they were intended to secure, the measures for which we petitioned and clamoured in the last century were hopelessly ineffective. So was it with all the Congress nostrums; they were palliatives which could not even be counted upon to palliate; the radical evil, uncured, would only be driven from one seat in the body politic to take refuge in others where it would soon declare its presence by equally troublesome symptoms. The only true cure for a bad and oppressive financial system is to give the control over taxation to the people whose money pays for the needs of Government. The only effective way of putting an end to executive tyranny is to make the people and not an irresponsible Government the controller and paymaster of both executive and judiciary. The only possible method of stopping the drain is to establish a popular government which may be relied on to foster and protect Indian commerce and Indian industry conducted by Indian capital and employing Indian labour. This is the object which the new politics, the politics of the twentieth century, places before the people of India in their resistance to the present system of Government, — not tinkerings and palliatives but the substitution for the autocratic bureaucracy, which at present misgoverns us, of a free constitutional and democratic system of Government and the entire removal of foreign control in order to make way for perfect national liberty.

The redress of particular grievances and the reformation of particular objectionable features in a system of Government are sufficient objects for organised resistance only when the Government is indigenous and all classes have a recognised place in the political scheme of the State. They are not and cannot be a sufficient object in countries like Russia and India where the laws are made and administered by a handful of men, and a vast population, educated and uneducated alike, have no political right or duty except the duty of obedience and the right to assist in confirming their own servitude. They are still less a sufficient object when the despotic oligarchy is alien by race and has not even a permanent home in the country, for in that case the Government cannot be relied on to look after the general interest of the country, as in nations ruled by indigenous despotism; on the contrary, they are bound to place the interests of their own country and their own race first and foremost. Organised resistance in subject nations which mean to live and not to die, can have no less an object than an entire and radical change of the system of Government; only by becoming responsible to the people and drawn from the people can the Government be turned into a protector instead of an oppressor. But if the subject nation desires not a provincial existence and a maimed development but the full, vigorous and noble realisation of its national existence, even a change in the system of Government will not be enough; it must aim not only at a national Government responsible to the people but a free national Government unhampered even in the least degree by foreign control.

It is not surprising that our politicians of the nineteenth century could not realise these elementary truths of modern politics. They had no national experience behind them of politics under modern conditions; they had no teachers except English books and English liberal "sympathisers" and "friends of India". Schooled by British patrons, trained to the fixed idea of

English superiority and Indian inferiority, their imaginations could not embrace the idea of national liberty, and perhaps they did not even desire it at heart, preferring the comfortable ease which at that time still seemed possible in a servitude under British protection, to the struggles and sacrifices of a hard and difficult independence. Taught to take their political lessons solely from the example of England and ignoring or not valuing the historical experience of the rest of the world, they could not even conceive of a truly popular and democratic Government in India except as the slow result of the development of centuries, progress broadening down from precedent to precedent. They could not then understand that the experience of an independent nation is not valid to guide a subject nation, unless and until the subject nation throws off the yoke and itself becomes independent. They could not realise that the slow, painful and ultra-cautious development, necessary in mediaeval and semi-mediaeval conditions when no experience of a stable popular Government had been gained, need not be repeated in the days of the steamship, railway and telegraph, when stable democratic systems are part of the world's secured and permanent heritage. The instructive spectacle of Asiatic nations demanding and receiving constitutional and parliamentary government as the price of a few years' struggle and civil turmoil, had not then been offered to the world. But even if the idea of such happenings had occurred to the more sanguine spirits, they would have been prevented from putting it into words by their inability to discover any means towards its fulfilment. Their whole political outlook was bounded by the lessons of English history, and in English history they found only two methods of politics, — the slow method of agitation and the swift decisive method of open struggle and revolt. Unaccustomed to independent political thinking, they did not notice the significant fact that the method of agitation only became effective in England when the people had already gained a powerful voice in the Government. In order to secure that voice they had been compelled to resort no less than three several times to the method of open struggle and revolt. Blind to the significance of this fact, our nineteenth century politicians clung to the method of agitation, obstinately hoping against all experience and reason that it would somehow serve their purpose. From any idea of open struggle with the bureaucracy they shrank with terror and a sense of paralysis. Dominated by the idea of the overwhelming might of Britain and the abject weakness of India, their want of courage and faith in the nation, their rooted distrust of the national character, disbelief in Indian patriotism and blindness to the possibility of true political strength and virtue in the people, precluded them from discovering the rough and narrow way to salvation. Herein lies the superiority of the new school that they have an indomitable courage and faith in the nation and the people. By the strength of that courage and faith they have not only been able to enforce on the mind of the country a higher ideal but perceive an effective means to the realisation of that ideal. By the strength of that courage and faith they have made such immense strides in the course of a few months. By the strength of that courage and faith they will dominate the future.

The new methods were first tried in the great Swadeshi outburst of the last two years, — blindly, crudely, without leading and organisation, but still with amazing results. The moving cause was a particular grievance, the Partition of Bengal; and to the removal of the particular grievance, pettiest and narrowest of all political objects, our old leaders strove hard to confine the use of this new and mighty weapon. But the popular instinct was true to itself and would have none of it. At a bound we passed therefore from mere particular grievances, however serious and intolerable, to the use of passive resistance as a means of cure for the basest and evilest feature of the present system, — the bleeding to death of a country by foreign exploitation. And from that stage we are steadily advancing, under the guidance of such able political thinking as modern India has not before seen and with the rising tide of popular opinion at our back, to the one true object of all resistance, passive or active, aggressive or defensive, — the creation of a free popular Government and the vindication of Indian liberty.

THREE

Its Necessity

WE HAVE defined, so far, the occasion and the ultimate object of the passive resistance we preach. It is the only effective means, except actual armed revolt, by which the organised strength of the nation, gathering to a powerful central authority and guided by the principle of self-development and self-help, can wrest the control of our national life from the grip of an alien bureaucracy, and thus, developing into a free popular Government, naturally replace the bureaucracy it extrudes until the process culminates in a self-governed India, liberated from foreign control. The mere effort at self-development unaided by some kind of resistance, will not materially help us towards our goal. Merely by developing national schools and colleges we shall not induce or force the bureaucracy to give up to us the control of education. Merely by attempting to expand some of our trades and industries, we shall not drive out the British exploiter or take from the British Government its sovereign power of regulating, checking or killing the growth of Swadeshi industries by the imposition of judicious taxes and duties and other methods always open to the controller of a country's finance and legislation. Still less shall we be able by that harmless means to get for ourselves the control of taxation and expenditure. Nor shall we, merely by establishing our own arbitration courts, oblige the alien control to give up the elaborate and lucrative system of Civil and Criminal Judicature which at once emasculates the nation and makes it pay heavily for its own emasculation. In none of these matters is the bureaucracy likely to budge an inch from its secure position unless it is forcibly persuaded. The control of the young mind in its most impressionable period is of vital importance to the continuance of the hypnotic spell by which alone the foreign domination manages to subsist; the exploitation of the country is the chief reason for its existence; the control of the judiciary is one of its chief instruments of repression. None of these things can it yield up without bringing itself nearer to its doom. It is only by organised national resistance, passive or aggressive, that we can make our self-development effectual. For if the self-help movement only succeeds in bringing about some modification of educational methods, some readjustment of the balance of trade, some alleviation of the curse of litigation, then, whatever else it may have succeeded in doing, it will have failed of its main object. The new school at least have not advocated the policy of self-development merely out of a disinterested ardour for moral improvement or under the spur of an inoffensive philanthropic patriotism. This attitude they leave to saints and philosophers, — saints like the editor of the *Indian Mirror* or philosophers like the ardent Indian Liberals who sit at the feet of Mr. John Morley. They for their part speak and write frankly as politicians aiming at a definite and urgent political object by a way which shall be reasonably rapid and yet permanent in its results. We may have our own educational theories; but we advocate national education not as an educational experiment or to subserve any theory, but as the only way to secure truly national and patriotic control and discipline for the mind of the country in its malleable youth. We desire industrial expansion, but Swadeshi without boycott, — non-political Swadeshi, — Lord Minto's "honest" Swadeshi — has no attractions for us; since we know that it can bring no safe and permanent national gain; — that can only be secured by the industrial and fiscal independence of the Indian nation. Our immediate problem as a nation is not how to be intellectual and well-informed or how to be rich and industrious, but how to stave off imminent national death, how to put an end to the white peril, how to assert ourselves and live. It is for this reason that whatever minor differences there may be between different exponents of the new spirit, they are all agreed on the immediate necessity of an organised national resistance to the state of things which is crushing us out of existence as a nation and on the one goal of that resistance, — freedom.

Organised national resistance to existing conditions, whether directed against the system of Government as such or against some particular feature of it, has three courses open to it. It may attempt to make administration under existing conditions impossible by an organised passive resistance. This was the policy initiated by the genius of Parnell when by the plan of campaign he prevented the payment of rents in Ireland and by persistent obstruction hampered the transaction of any but Irish business in Westminster. It may attempt to make administration under existing conditions impossible by an organised aggressive resistance in the shape of an untiring and implacable campaign of assassination and a confused welter of riots, strikes and agrarian risings all over the country. This is the spectacle we have all watched with such eager interest in Russia. We have seen the most absolute autocrat and the most powerful and ruthless bureaucracy in the world still in unimpaired possession of all the most effective means of repression, yet beaten to the knees by the determined resistance of an unarmed nation. It has mistakenly been said that the summoning of the Duma was a triumph for passive resistance. But the series of strikes on a gigantic scale which figured so largely in the final stages of the struggle was only one feature of that widespread, desperate and unappeasable anarchy which led to the first triumph of Russian liberty. Against such an anarchy the mightiest and best-organised Government must necessarily feel helpless; its repression would demand a systematic and prolonged course of massacre on a colossal scale the prospect of which would have paralysed the vigour of the most ruthless and energetic despotism even of mediaeval times. Only by concessions and compromises could such a resistance be overcome. The third course open to an oppressed nation is that of armed revolt, which instead of bringing existing conditions to an end by making their continuance impossible sweeps them bodily out of existence. This is the old time-honoured method which the oppressed or enslaved have always adopted by preference in the past, and will adopt in the future if they see any chance of success; for it is the readiest and swiftest, the most thorough in its results, and demands the least powers of endurance and suffering and the smallest and briefest sacrifices.

The choice by a subject nation of the means it will use for vindicating its liberty, is best determined by the circumstances of its servitude. The present circumstances in India seem to point to passive resistance as our most natural and suitable weapon. We would not for a moment be understood to base this conclusion upon any condemnation of other methods as in all circumstances criminal and unjustifiable. It is the common habit of established Governments and especially those which are themselves oppressors, to brand all violent methods in subject peoples and communities as criminal and wicked. When you have disarmed your slaves and legalised the infliction of bonds, stripes and death on any one of them, man, woman or child, who may dare to speak or to act against you, it is natural and convenient to try and lay a moral as well as a legal ban on any attempt to answer violence by violence, the knout by the revolver, the prison by riot or agrarian rising, the gallows by the dynamite bomb. But no nation yet has listened to the cant of the oppressor when itself put to the test, and the general conscience of humanity approves the refusal. Under certain circumstances a civil struggle becomes in reality a battle and the morality of war is different from the morality of peace. To shrink from bloodshed and violence under such circumstances is a weakness deserving as severe a rebuke as Sri Krishna addressed to Arjuna when he shrank from the colossal civil slaughter on the field of Kurukshetra. Liberty is the life-breath of a nation; and when the life is attacked, when it is sought to suppress all chance of breathing by violent pressure, any and every means of self-preservation becomes right and justifiable, — just as it is lawful for a man who is being strangled to rid himself of the pressure on his throat by any means in his power. It is the nature of the pressure which determines the nature of the resistance. Where, as in Russia, the denial of liberty is enforced by legalised murder and outrage, or, as in Ireland formerly, by brutal coercion, the answer of violence to violence is justified and inevitable. Where the need for immediate liberty is urgent and it is a present question of national life or death on the instant, revolt is the only course. But where the oppression is legal and subtle in its methods and respects life, liberty and property and there is still breathing time, the circumstances demand that we should make the experiment of a method of resolute but peaceful resistance which, while less bold and aggressive than other methods, calls for perhaps as much heroism of a kind and certainly more universal endurance and suffering. In other methods, a daring minority purchase with their blood the freedom of the millions; but for passive resistance it is necessary that all should share in the struggle and the privation.

This peculiar character of passive resistance is one reason why it has found favour with the thinkers of the New Party. There are certain moral qualities necessary to self-government which have become atrophied by long disuse in our people and can only be restored either by the healthy air of a free national life in which alone they can permanently thrive or by their vigorous exercise in the intensity of a national struggle for freedom. If by any possibility the nation can start its career of freedom with a fully developed unity and strength, it will certainly have a better chance of immediate greatness hereafter. Passive resistance affords the best possible training for these qualities. Something also is due to our friends, the enemy. We have ourselves made them reactionary and oppressive and deserved the Government we possess. The reason why even a radical opportunist like Mr. Morley refuses us self-government is not that he does not believe in India's fitness for self-government, but that he does not believe in India's determination to be free; on the contrary, the whole experience of the past shows that we have not been in earnest in our demand for self-government. We should put our determination beyond a doubt and thereby give England a chance of redeeming her ancient promises, made when her rule was still precarious and unstable. For the rest, circumstances still favour the case of passive resistance. In spite of occasional Fullerism, the bureaucracy has not yet made up its mind to a Russian system of repression. It is true that for India also it is now a question of national life or death. Morally and materially she has been brought to the verge of exhaustion and decay by the bureaucratic rule and any farther acquiescence in servitude will result in that death-sleep of centuries from which a nation, if it ever awakes at all, awakes emaciated, feeble and unable to resume its true rank in the list of the peoples. But there is still time to try the effect of an united and unflinching pressure of passive resistance. The resistance, if it is to be of any use, must be united and unflinching. If from any timidity or selfishness or any mistaken ideas of caution and moderation, our Moderate patriots succeed in breaking the unity and weakening the force of the resistance, the movement will fail and India will sink into those last depths of degradation when only desperate remedies will be of any utility. The advocates of self-development and defensive resistance are no extremists but are trying to give the country its last chance of escaping the necessity of extremism. Defensive resistance is the sole alternative to that ordeal of sanguinary violence on both sides through which all other countries, not excepting the Moderates' exemplar England, have been compelled to pass, only at last "embracing Liberty over a heap of corpses".

FOUR

Its Methods

THE essential difference between passive or defensive and active or aggressive resistance is this, that while the method of the aggressive resister is to do something by which he can bring about positive harm to the Government, the method of the passive resister is to abstain from doing something by which he would be helping the Government. The object in both cases is the same, — to force the hands of the Government; the line of attack is different. The passive method is especially suitable to countries where the Government depends mainly for the continuance of its administration on the voluntary help and acquiescence of the subject people. The first principle of passive resistance, therefore, which the new school have placed in the forefront of their programme, is to make administration under present conditions impossible by an organised refusal to do anything which shall help either British commerce in the exploitation of the country or British officialdom in the administration of it, — unless and until the conditions are changed in the manner and to the extent demanded by the people. This attitude is summed up in the one word, Boycott. If we consider the various departments of the administration one by one, we can easily see how administration in each can be rendered impossible by successfully organised refusal of assistance. We are dissatisfied with the fiscal and economical conditions of British rule in India, with the foreign exploitation of the country, the continual bleeding of its resources, the chronic famine and rapid impoverishment which result, the refusal of the Government to protect the people and their industries. Accordingly, we refuse to help the process of exploitation and impoverishment in our capacity as consumers, we refuse henceforth to purchase foreign and especially British goods or to condone their purchase by others. By an organised and relentless boycott of British goods, we propose to render the further exploitation of the country impossible. We are dissatisfied also with the conditions under which education is imparted in this country, its calculated poverty and insufficiency, its anti-national character, its subordination to the Government and the use made of that subordination for the discouragement of patriotism and the inculcation of loyalty. Accordingly we refuse to send our boys to Government schools or to schools aided and controlled by the Government; if this educational boycott is general and well-organised, the educational administration of the country will be rendered impossible and the control of its youthful minds pass out of the hands of the foreigner. We are dissatisfied with the administration of justice, the ruinous costliness of the civil side, the brutal rigour of its criminal penalties and procedure, its partiality, its frequent subordination to political objects. We refuse accordingly to have any resort to the alien courts of justice, and by an organised judicial boycott propose to make the bureaucratic administration of justice impossible while these conditions continue. Finally, we disapprove of the executive administration, its arbitrariness, its meddling and inquisitorial character, its thoroughness of repression, its misuse of the police for the repression instead of the protection of the people. We refuse, accordingly, to go to the executive for help or advice or protection or to tolerate any paternal interference in our public activities, and by an organised boycott of the executive propose to reduce executive control and interference to a mere skeleton of its former self. The bureaucracy depends for the success of its administration on the help of the few and the acquiescence of the many. If the few refused to help, if Indians no longer consented to teach in Government schools or work in Government offices, or serve the alien as police, the administration could not continue for a day. We will suppose the bureaucracy able to fill their places by Eurasians, aliens or traitors; even then the refusal of the many to acquiesce, by the simple process of no longer resorting to Government schools, courts of justice or magistrates' Katcherries, would put an end to administration.

Such is the nature of passive resistance as preached by the

new school in India. It is at once clear that self-development and such a scheme of passive resistance are supplementary and necessary to each other. If we refuse to supply our needs from foreign sources, we must obviously supply them ourselves; we cannot have the industrial boycott without Swadeshi and the expansion of indigenous industries. If we decline to enter the alien courts of justice, we must have arbitration courts of our own to settle our disputes and differences. If we do not send our boys to schools owned or controlled by the Government, we must have schools of our own in which they may receive a thorough and national education. If we do not go for protection to the executive, we must have a system of self-protection and mutual protection of our own. Just as Swadeshi is the natural accompaniment of an industrial boycott, so also arbitration stands in the same relation to a judicial boycott, national education to an educational boycott, a league of mutual defence to an executive boycott. From this close union of self-help with passive resistance it also follows that the new politics do not contemplate the organisation of passive resistance as a temporary measure for partial ends. It is not to be dropped as soon as the Government undertakes the protection of indigenous industries, reforms its system of education, improves its courts of justice and moderates its executive rigour and ubiquity, but only when the control of all these functions is vested in a free, constitutional and popular Government. We have learned by bitter experience that an alien and irresponsible bureaucracy cannot be relied upon to abstain from rescinding its reforms when convenient or to manage even a reformed administration in the interests of the people.

The possibilities of passive resistance are not exhausted by the refusal of assistance to the administration. In Europe its more usual weapon is the refusal to pay taxes. The strenuous political instinct of European races teaches them to aim a direct blow at the most vital part of the administration rather than to undermine it by slower and more gradual means. The payment of taxes is the most direct assistance given by the community to the administration and the most visible symbol of acquiescence and approval. To refuse payment is at once the most emphatic protest possible short of taking up arms, and the sort of attack which the administration will feel immediately and keenly and must therefore parry at once either by conciliation or by methods of repression which will give greater vitality and intensity to the opposition. The refusal to pay taxes is a natural and logical result of the attitude of passive resistance. A boycott of Government schools, for example, may be successful and national schools substituted; but the administration continues to exact from the people a certain amount of revenue for the purposes of education, and is not likely to relinquish its claims; the people will therefore have doubly to tax themselves in order to maintain national education and also to maintain the Government system by which they no longer profit. Under such circumstances the refusal to pay for an education of which they entirely disapprove, comes as a natural consequence. This was the form of resistance offered by the Dissenters in England to the Education Act of the last Conservative Government. The refusal to pay rents was the backbone of the Irish Plan of Campaign. The refusal to pay taxes levied by an Imperial Government in which they had no voice or share, was the last form of resistance offered by the American Colonists previous to taking up arms. Ultimately, in case of the persistent refusal of the administration to listen to reason, the refusal to pay taxes is the strongest and final form of passive resistance.

This stronger sort of passive resistance has not been included by the new party in its immediate programme, and for valid reasons. In the first place, all the precedents for this form of resistance were accompanied by certain conditions which do not as yet obtain in India. In the Irish instance, the refusal was not to pay Government taxes but to pay rents to a landlord class who represented an unjust and impoverishing land system maintained in force by a foreign power against the wishes of the people; but in India the foreign bureaucracy has usurped the functions of the landlord, except in Bengal where a refusal to pay rents would injure not a landlord-class supported by the alien but a section of our own countrymen who have been intolerably harassed, depressed and burdened by bureaucratic policy and bureaucratic exactions and fully sympathise, for the most part, with the national movement. In all other parts of India the refusal to pay rents would be a refusal to pay a Government tax. This, as we have said, is the strongest, the final form of passive resistance, and differs from the method of political boycott which involves no breach of legal obligation or direct defiance of administrative authority. No man can be legally punished for using none but Swadeshi articles or persuading others to follow his example or for sending his boys to a National in preference to a Government school, or for settling his differences with others out of court, or for defending his person and property or helping to defend the person and property of his neighbours against criminal attack. If the administration interferes with the people in the exercise of these legitimate rights, it invites and compels defiance of its authority and for what may follow, the rulers and not the people are responsible. But the refusal to pay taxes is a breach of legal obligation and a direct defiance of administrative authority precisely of that kind which the administration can least afford to neglect and must either conciliate or crush. In a free country, the attempt at repression would probably go no farther than the forcible collection of the payments refused by legal distraint; but in a subject country the bureaucracy, feeling itself vitally threatened, would naturally supplement this legal process by determined prosecution and persecution of the advocates of the policy and its adherents, and, in all probability, by extreme military and police violence. The refusal to pay taxes would, therefore, inevitably bring about the last desperate struggle between the forces of national aspiration and alien repression. It would be in the nature of an ultimatum from the people to the Government.

The case of the English Dissenters, although it was a refusal to pay taxes, differed materially from ours. The object of their passive resistance was not to bring the Government to its knees, but to generate so strong a feeling in the country that the Conservative Government would be ignominiously brushed out of office at the next elections. They had the all-powerful weapon of the vote and could meet and overthrow injustice at the polling-station. In India we are very differently circumstanced. The resistance of the American colonists offers a nearer parallel. Like ourselves the Americans met oppression with the weapon of boycott. They were not wholly dependent on England and had their own legislatures in local affairs; so they had no occasion to extend the boycott to all departments of national life nor to attempt a general policy of national self-development. Their boycott was limited to British goods. They had however to go beyond the boycott and refuse to pay the taxes imposed on them against their will; but when they offered the ultimatum to the mother country, they were prepared to follow it up, if necessary, and did finally follow it up by a declaration of independence, supported by armed revolt. Here again there is a material difference from Indian conditions. An ultimatum should never be presented unless one is prepared to follow it up to its last consequences. Moreover, in a vast country like India, any such general conflict with dominant authority as is involved in a no-taxes policy, needs for its success a close organisation linking province to province and district to district and a powerful central authority representing the single will of the whole nation which could alone fight on equal terms the final struggle of defensive resistance with bureaucratic repression. Such an organisation and authority has not yet been developed. The new politics, therefore, confines itself for the time to the policy of lawful abstention from any kind of co-operation with the Government, — the policy of boycott which is capable of gradual extension, leaving to the bureaucracy the onus of forcing on a more direct, sudden and dangerous struggle. Its principle at present is not "no representation, no taxation," but "no control, no assistance".

FIVE

Its Obligations

IN THE early days of the new movement it was declared, in a very catching phrase, by a politician who has now turned his back on the doctrine which made him famous, that a subject nation has no politics. And it was commonly said that we as a subject nation should altogether ignore the Government and turn our attention to emancipation by self-help and self-development. This was the self-development principle carried to its extreme conclusions, and it is not surprising that phrases so trenchant and absolute should have given rise to some misunderstanding. It was even charged against us by Sir Pherozshah Mehta and other robust exponents of the opposition-cum-cooperation theory that we were advocating non-resistance and submission to political wrong and injustice! Much water has flowed under the bridges since then, and now we are being charged, in deputations to the Viceroy and elsewhere, with the opposite offence of inflaming and fomenting disturbance and rebellion. Yet our policy remains essentially the same, — not to ignore such a patent and very troublesome fact as the alien bureaucracy, for that was never our policy, — but to have nothing to do with it, in the way either of assistance or acquiescence. Far from preaching non-resistance, it has now become abundantly clear that our determination not to submit to political wrong and injustice was far deeper and sterner than that of our critics. The method of opposition differed, of course. The Moderate method of resistance was verbal only — prayer, petition and protest; the method we proposed was practical, — boycott. But, as we have pointed out, our new method, though more concrete, was in itself quite as legal and peaceful as the old. It is no offence by law to abstain from Government schools or Government courts of justice or the help and protection of the fatherly executive or the use of

British goods; nor is it illegal to persuade others to join in our abstention.

At the same time this legality is neither in itself an essential condition of passive resistance generally, nor can we count upon its continuance as an actual condition of passive resistance as it is to be understood and practised in India. The passive resister in other countries has always been prepared to break an unjust and oppressive law whenever necessary and to take the legal consequences, as the non-Conformists in England did when they refused to pay the education rate, or as Hampden did when he refused to pay ship-money. Even under present conditions in India there is at least one direction in which, it appears, many of us are already breaking what Anglo-Indian courts have determined to be the law. The law relating to sedition and the law relating to the offence of causing racial enmity are so admirably vague in their terms that there is nothing which can escape from their capacious embrace. It appears from the *Punjabee* case that it is a crime under bureaucratic rule to say that Europeans hold Indian life cheaply, although this is a fact which case after case has proved, and although British justice has confirmed this cheap valuation of our lives by the leniency of its sentences on European murderers; nay, it is a crime to impute such failings to British justice or to say even that departmental enquiries into "accidents" of this kind cannot be trusted, although this is a conviction in which, as everyone is aware, the whole country is practically unanimous as the result of repeated experiences. All this is not crime indeed when we do it in order to draw the attention of the bureaucracy in the vain hope of getting the grievance redressed. But if our motive is to draw the attention of the people and enlighten them on the actual and inevitable results of irresponsible rule by aliens and the dominance of a single community, we are criminals, we are guilty of breaking the law of the alien. Yet to break the law in this respect is the duty of every self-respecting publicist who is of our way of thinking. It is our duty to drive home to the public mind the congenital and incurable evils of the present system of Government, so that they may insist on its being swept away in order to make room for a more healthy and natural state of things. It is our duty also to press upon the people the hopelessness of appealing to the bureaucracy to reform itself and the uselessness of any partial measures. No publicist of the new school holding such views ought to mar his reputation for candour and honesty by the pretence of drawing the attention of the Government with a view to redress the grievance. If the alien laws have declared it illegal for him to do his duty, unless he lowers himself by covering it with a futile and obvious lie, he must still do his duty, however illegal, in the strength of his manhood; and if the bureaucracy decide to send him to prison for the breach of law, to prison he must willingly and, if he is worth his salt, rejoicingly go. The new spirit will not suffer any individual aspiring to speak or act on behalf of the people to palter with the obligation of high truthfulness and unflinching courage without which no one has a claim to lead or instruct his fellow-countrymen.

If this penalty of sedition is at present the chief danger which the adherent or exponent of passive resistance runs under the law, yet there is no surety that it will continue to be unaccompanied by similar or more serious perils. The making of the laws is at present in the hands of our political adversaries and there is nothing to prevent them from using this power in any way they like, however iniquitous or tyrannical, — nothing except their fear of public reprobation outside and national resistance within India. At present they hope by the seductive allurements of Morleyism to smother the infant strength of the national spirit in its cradle; but as that hope is dissipated and the doctrine of passive resistance takes more and more concrete and organised form, the temptation to use the enormously powerful weapon which the unhampered facility of legislation puts in their hands, will become irresistible. The passive resister must therefore take up his creed with the certainty of having to suffer for it. If, for instance, the bureaucracy should make abstention from Government schools or teaching without Government licence a penal offence, he must continue to abstain or teach and take the legal consequences. Or if they forbid the action of arbitration courts other than those sanctioned by Government, he must yet continue to act on such courts or have recourse to them without considering the peril to which he exposes himself. And so throughout the whole range of action covered by the new politics. A law imposed by a people on itself has a binding force which cannot be ignored except under extreme necessity: a law imposed from outside has no such moral sanction; its claim to obedience must rest on coercive force or on its own equitable and beneficial character and not on the source from which it proceeds. If it is unjust and oppressive, it may become a duty to disobey it and quietly endure the punishment which the law has provided for its violation. For passive resistance aims at making a law unworkable by general and organised disobedience and so procuring its recall; it does not try, like aggressive resistance, to destroy the law by destroying the power which made and supports the law. It is therefore the first canon of passive resistance that to break an unjust coercive law is not only justifiable but, under given circumstances, a duty.

Legislation, however, is not the only weapon in the hands of the bureaucracy. They may try, without legislation, by executive action, to bring opposition under the terms of the law and the lash of its penalties. This may be done either by twisting a perfectly legal act into a criminal offence or misdemeanour with the aid of the ready perjuries of the police or by executive order or ukase making illegal an action which had previously been allowed. We have had plenty of experience of both these contrivances during the course of the Swadeshi movement. To persuade an intending purchaser not to buy British cloth is no offence; but if, between a police employed to put down Swadeshi and a shopkeeper injured by it, enough evidence can be concocted to twist persuasion into compulsion, the boycotter can easily be punished without having committed any offence. Executive orders are an even more easily-handled weapon. The issuing of an ukase asks for no more trouble than the penning of a few lines by a clerk and the more or less illegible signature of a District Magistrate; and hey-presto! that brief magical abracadabra of despotism has turned an action, which five minutes ago was legitimate and inoffensive into a crime or misdemeanour punishable in property or person. Whether it is the simple utterance of 'Bande Mataram' in the streets or an august assemblage of all that is most distinguished, able and respected in the country, one stroke of a mere

District Magistrate's omnipotent pen is enough to make them illegalities and turn the elect of the nation into disorderly and riotous Budmashes to be dispersed by police cudgels. To hope for any legal redress is futile; for the power of the executive to issue ukases is perfectly vague and therefore practically illimitable, and wherever there is a doubt, it can be brought within the one all-sufficient formula, — "It was done by the Magistrate in exercise of the discretion given him for preserving the peace." The formula can cover any ukase or any action, however arbitrary; and what British Judge can refuse his support to a British Magistrate in that preservation of peace which is as necessary to the authority and safety of the Judge as to that of the Magistrate? But equally is it impossible for the representatives of popular aspirations to submit to such paralysing exercise of an irresponsible and unlimited authority. This has been universally recognised in Bengal. Executive authority was defied by all Bengal when its representatives, with Babu Surendranath Banerji at their head, escorted their President through the streets of Barisal with the forbidden cry of 'Bande Mataram'. If the dispersal of the Conference was not resisted, it was not from respect for executive authority but purely for reasons of political strategy. Immediately afterwards the right of public meeting was asserted in defiance of executive ukase by the Moderate leaders near Barisal itself and by prominent politicians of the new school in East Bengal. The second canon of the doctrine of passive resistance has therefore been accepted by politicians of both schools — that to resist an unjust coercive order or interference is not only justifiable but, under given circumstances, a duty.

Finally, we must be prepared for opposition not only from our natural but from unnatural adversaries, — not only from bureaucrat and Anglo-Indian, but from the more self-seeking and treacherous of our own countrymen. In a rebellion such treachery is of small importance, since in the end it is the superior fate or the superior force which triumphs; but in a campaign of passive resistance the evil example, if unpunished, may be disastrous and eat fatally into the enthusiastic passion and serried unity indispensable to such a movement. It is therefore necessary to mete out the heaviest penalty open to us in such cases — the penalty of social excommunication. We are not in favour of this weapon being lightly used; but its employment, where the national will in a vital matter is deliberately disregarded, becomes essential. Such disregard amounts to siding in matters of life and death against your own country and people and helping in their destruction or enslavement, — a crime which in Free States is punished with the extreme penalty due to treason. When, for instance, all Bengal staked its future upon the Boycott and specified three foreign articles, — salt, sugar and cloth, — as to be religiously avoided, anyone purchasing foreign salt or foreign sugar or foreign cloth became guilty of treason to the nation and laid himself open to the penalty of social boycott. Wherever passive resistance has been accepted, the necessity of the social boycott has been recognised as its natural concomitant. "Boycott foreign goods and boycott those who use foreign goods," — the advice of Mr. Subramaniya Aiyar to his countrymen in Madras, — must be accepted by all who are in earnest. For without this boycott of persons the boycott of things cannot be effective; without the social boycott no national authority depending purely on moral pressure can get its decrees effectively executed; and without effective boycott enforced by a strong national authority the new policy cannot succeed. But the only possible alternatives to the new policy are either despotism tempered by petitions or aggressive resistance. We must therefore admit a third canon of the doctrine of passive resistance, that social boycott is legitimate and indispensable as against persons guilty of treason to the nation.

SIX

Its Limits

THE three canons of the doctrine of passive resistance are in reality three necessities which must, whether we like it or not, be accepted in theory and executed in practice, if passive resistance is to have any chance of success. Passive resisters, both as individuals and in the mass, must always be prepared to break an unjust coercive law and take the legal consequence; for if they shrink from this obligation, the bureaucracy can at once make passive resistance impossible simply by adding a few more enactments to their book of statutes. A resistance which can so easily be snuffed out of being is not worth making. For the same reason they must be prepared to disobey an unjust and coercive executive order whether general or particular; for nothing would be simpler than to put down by a few months' coercion a resistance too weak to face the consequences of refusing submission to Government by ukase. They must be prepared to boycott persons guilty of deliberate disobedience to the national will in vital matters because, if they do not, the example of unpunished treason will tend to be repeated and destroy by a kind of dry rot the enthusiastic unity and universality which we have seen to be necessary to the success of passive resistance of the kind we have inaugurated in India. Men in the mass are strong and capable of wonder-working enthusiasms and irresistible movements; but the individual average man is apt to be weak or selfish and, unless he sees that the mass are in deadly earnest and will not tolerate individual treachery, he will usually, after the first enthusiasm, indulge his weakness or selfishness to the detriment of the community. We have seen this happening almost everywhere where the boycott of foreign goods was not enforced by the boycott of persons buying foreign goods. This is one important reason why the boycott which has maintained itself in East Bengal, is in the West becoming more and more of a failure.

The moment these three unavoidable obligations are put into force, the passive resistance movement will lose its character of inoffensive legality and we shall be in the thick of a struggle which may lead us anywhere. Passive resistance, when it is confined — as at present — to lawful abstention from actions which it lies within our choice as subjects to do or not to do, is of the nature of the strategical movements and large manoeuvrings previous to the meeting of armies in the field; but the enforcement of our three canons brings us to the actual shock of battle. Nevertheless our resistance still retains an essential character of passivity. If the right of public meeting is suspended by Magisterial ukase, we confine ourselves to the practical assertion of the right in defiance of the ukase and, so long as the executive also confines itself to the dispersal of the meeting by the arrest of its conveners and other peaceful and legal measures, we offer no active resistance. We submit to the arrest, though not necessarily to the dispersal, and quietly take the legal consequences. Similarly, if the law forbids us to speak or write the truth as we conceive it our duty to speak it, we persist in doing our duty and submit quietly to whatever punishment the law of sedition or any other law coercive ingenuity may devise, can find to inflict on us. In a peaceful way we act against the law or the executive, but we passively accept the legal consequences.

There is a limit however to passive resistance. So long as the action of the executive is peaceful and within the rules of the fight, the passive resister scrupulously maintains his attitude of passivity, but he is not bound to do so a moment beyond. To submit to illegal or violent methods of coercion, to accept outrage and hooliganism as part of the legal procedure of the country is to be guilty of cowardice, and, by dwarfing national manhood, to sin against the divinity within ourselves and the divinity in our motherland. The moment coercion of this kind is attempted, passive resistance ceases and active resistance becomes a duty. If the instruments of the executive choose to disperse our meeting by breaking the heads of those present, the right of self-defence entitles us not merely to defend our heads but to retaliate on those of the head-breakers. For the myrmidons of the law have ceased then to be guardians of the peace and become breakers of the peace, rioters and not instruments of authority, and their uniform is no longer a bar to the right of self-defence. Nor does it make any difference if the instruments of coercion happen to be the recognised and usual instruments or are unofficial hooligans in alliance or sympathy with the forces of coercion. In both cases active resistance becomes a duty and passive resistance is, for that occasion, suspended. But though no longer passive, it is still a defensive resistance. Nor does resistance pass into the aggressive stage so long as it resists coercive violence in its own kind and confines itself to repelling attack. Even if it takes the offensive, it does not by that mere fact become aggressive resistance, unless the amount of aggression exceeds what is necessary to make defence effective. The students of Mymensingh, charged by the police while picketing, kept well within the right of self-defence when they drove the rioters off the field of operations; the gentlemen of Comilla kept well within the rights of self-defence if they attacked either rioters or inciters of riot who either offered, or threatened, or tried to provoke assault. Even the famous shot which woke the authorities from their waking dreams, need not have been an act of aggression if it was fired to save life or a woman's honour or under circumstances of desperation when no other means of defence would have been effective. With the doubtful exception of this shot, supposing it to have been fired unnecessarily, and that other revolver shot which killed Mr. Rand, there has been no instance of aggressive resistance in modern Indian politics.

The new politics, therefore, while it favours passive resistance, does not include meek submission to illegal outrage under that term; it has no intention of overstressing the passivity at the expense of the resistance. Nor is it inclined to be hysterical over a few dozen of broken heads or exalt so simple a matter as a bloody coxcomb into the crown of martyrdom. This sort of hysterical exaggeration was too common in the early days of the movement when everyone who got his crown cracked in a street affray with the police was encouraged to lift up his broken head before the world and cry out, "This is the head of a martyr."

The new politics is a serious doctrine and not, like the old, a thing of shows and political theatricals; it demands real sufferings from its adherents, — imprisonment, worldly ruin, death itself, before it can allow him to assume the rank of a martyr for his country. Passive resistance cannot build up a strong and great nation unless it is masculine, bold and ardent in its spirit and ready at any moment and at the slightest notice to supplement itself with active resistance. We do not want to develop a nation of women who know only how to suffer and not how to strike.

Morever, the new politics must recognise the fact that beyond a certain point passive resistance puts a strain on human endurance which our natures cannot endure. This may come in particular instances where an outrage is too great or the stress of tyranny too unendurable for anyone to stand purely on the defensive; to hit back, to assail and crush the assailant, to vindicate one's manhood becomes an imperious necessity to outraged humanity. Or it may come in the mass when the strain of oppression a whole nation has to meet in its unarmed struggle for liberty, overpasses its powers of endurance. It then becomes the sole choice either to break under the strain and go under or to throw it off with violence. The Spartan soldiers at Plataea endured for some time the missiles of the enemy and saw their comrades falling at their side without any reply because their general had not yet declared it to be the auspicious time for attack; but if the demand on their passive endurance had been too long continued, they must either have broken in disastrous defeat or flung themselves on the enemy in disregard of their leader's orders. The school of politics which we advocate is not based upon abstractions, formulas and dogmas, but on practical necessities and the teaching of political experience, common sense and the world's history. We have not the slightest wish to put forward passive resistance as an inelastic dogma. We preach defensive resistance mainly passive in its methods at present, but active whenever active resistance is needed; but defensive resistance within the limits imposed by human nature and by the demands of self-respect and the militant spirit of true manhood. If at any time the laws obtaining in India or the executive action of the bureaucracy were to become so oppressive as to render a struggle for liberty on the lines we have indicated, impossible; if after a fair trial given to this method, the object with which we undertook it, proved to be as far off as ever; or if passive resistance should turn out either not feasible or necessarily ineffectual under the conditions of this country, we should be the first to recognise that everything must be reconsidered and that the time for new men and new methods had arrived. We recognise no political object of worship except the divinity in our Motherland, no present object of political endeavour except liberty, and no method or action as politically good or evil except as it truly helps or hinders our progress towards national emancipation.

SEVEN

Conclusions

TO SUM up the conclusions at which we have arrived. The object of all our political movements and therefore the sole object with which we advocate passive resistance is Swaraj or national freedom. The latest and most venerable of the older politicians who have sat in the Presidential Chair of the Congress, pronounced from that seat of authority Swaraj as the one object of our political endeavour, — Swaraj as the only remedy for all our ills, — Swaraj as the one demand nothing short of which will satisfy the people of India. Complete self-government as it exists in the United Kingdom or the Colonies, — such was his definition of Swaraj. The Congress has contented itself with demanding self-government as it exists in the Colonies. We of the new school would not pitch our ideal one inch lower than absolute Swaraj, — self-government as it exists in the United Kingdom. We believe that no smaller ideal can inspire national revival or nerve the people of India for the fierce, stubborn and formidable struggle by which alone they can again become a nation. We believe that this newly awakened people, when it has gathered its strength together, neither can nor ought to consent to any relations with England less than that of equals in a confederacy. To be content with the relations of master and dependent or superior and subordinate, would be a mean and pitiful aspiration unworthy of manhood; to strive for anything less than a strong and glorious freedom would be to insult the greatness of our past and the magnificent possibilities of our future.

To the ideal we have at heart there are three paths, possible or impossible. Petitioning, which we have so long followed, we reject as impossible, — the dream of a timid inexperience, the teaching of false friends who hope to keep us in perpetual subjection, foolish to reason, false to experience. Self-development by self-help which we now purpose to follow, is a possible though uncertain path, never yet attempted under such difficulties, but one which must be attempted, if for nothing else yet to get free of the habit of dependence and helplessness, and re-awaken and exercise our half-atrophied powers of self-government. Parallel to this attempt and to be practised simultaneously, the policy of organised resistance to the present system of government forms the old traditional way of nations which we also must tread. It is a vain dream to suppose that what other nations have won by struggle and battle, by suffering and tears of blood, we shall be allowed to accomplish easily, without terrible sacrifices, merely by spending the ink of the journalist and petition-framer and the breath of the orator. Petitioning will not bring us one yard nearer to freedom; self-development will not easily be suffered to advance to its goal. For self-development spells the doom of the ruling bureaucratic despotism, which must therefore oppose our progress with all the art and force of which it is the master; without organised resistance we could not take more than a few faltering steps towards self-emancipation. But resistance may be of many kinds, — armed revolt, or aggressive resistance short of armed revolt, or defensive resistance whether passive or active; the circumstances of the country and the nature of the despotism from which it seeks to escape must determine what form of resistance is best justified and most likely to be effective at the time or finally successful.

The Congress has not formally abandoned the petitioning policy; but it is beginning to fall into discredit and gradual disuse, and time will accelerate its inevitable death by atrophy; for it can no longer even carry the little weight it had, since it has no longer the support of an undivided public opinion at its back. The alternative policy of self-development has received a partial recognition; it has been made an integral part of our political activities, but not in its entirety and purity. Self-help has been accepted as supplementary to the help of the very bureaucracy which it is our declared object to undermine and supplant, — self-development as supplementary to development of the nation by its foreign rulers. Passive resistance has not been accepted as a national policy, but in the form of Boycott it has been declared legitimate under circumstances which apply to all India.

This is a compromise good enough for the moment but in which the new school does not mean to allow the country to rest permanently. We desire to put an end to petitioning until such a strength is created in the country that a petition will only be a courteous form of demand. We wish to kill utterly the pernicious delusion that a foreign and adverse interest can be trusted to develop us to its own detriment, and entirely to do away with the foolish and ignoble hankering after help from our natural adversaries. Our attitude to bureaucratic concession is that of Laocoon: "We fear the Greeks even when they bring us gifts." Our policy is self-development and defensive resistance. But we would extend the policy of self-development to every department of national life; not only Swadeshi and National Education, but national defence, national arbitration courts, sanitation, insurance against famine or relief of famine, — whatever our hands find to do or urgently needs doing, we must attempt ourselves and no longer look to the alien to do it for us. And we would universalise and extend the policy of defensive resistance until it ran parallel on every line with our self-development. We would not only buy our own goods, but boycott British goods; not only have our own schools, but boycott Government institutions; not only erect our own Arbitration Courts, but boycott bureaucratic justice; not only organise our league of defence, but have nothing to do with the bureaucratic Executive except when we cannot avoid it. At present even in Bengal where Boycott is universally accepted, it is confined to the boycott of British goods and is aimed at the British merchant and only indirectly at the British bureaucrat. We would aim it directly both at the British merchant and at the British bureaucrat who stands behind and makes possible exploitation by the merchant.

The double policy we propose has three objects before it:— to develop ourselves into a self-governing nation; to protect ourselves against and repel attack and opposition during the work of development; and to press in upon and extrude the foreign agency in each field of activity and so ultimately supplant it. Our defensive resistance must therefore be mainly passive in the beginning, although with a perpetual readiness to supplement it with active resistance whenever compelled. It must be confined for the present to Boycott, and we must avoid giving battle on the crucial question of taxation for the sole reason that a No-Taxes campaign demands a perfect organisation and an ultimate preparedness from which we are yet far off. We will attack the resources of the bureaucracy whenever we can do so by simple abstention, as in the case of its immoral Abkari revenue; but we do not propose at present to follow European precedents and refuse the payment of taxes legally demanded from us. We desire to keep our resistance within the bounds of law, so long as law does not seek directly to interfere with us and render impossible our progress and the conscientious discharge of our duty to our fellow-countrymen. But if, at any time, laws should be passed with the object of summarily checking our self-development or unduly limiting our rights as men, we must be prepared to break the law and endure the penalty imposed for the breach with the object of making it unworkable as has been done in other countries. We must equally be ready to challenge by our action arbitrary executive coercion, if we do not wish to see our resistance snuffed out by very cheap official extinguishers. Nor must we shrink from boycotting persons as well as things; we must make full though discriminating use of the social boycott against those of our countrymen who seek to baffle the will of the nation in a matter vital to its emancipation, for this is a crime of *lèse-nation* which is far more heinous than the legal offence of *lèse-majesté* and deserves the severest penalty with which the nation can visit traitors.

We advocate, finally, the creation of a strong central authority to carry out the will of the nation, supported by a close and active organisation of village, town, district and province. We desire to build up this organisation from the constitution the necessity of which the Congress has recognised and for which it has provided a meagre and imperfect beginning; but if, owing to Moderate obstruction, this constitution cannot develop or is not allowed to perform its true functions, the organisation and the authority must be built up otherwise by the people itself and, if necessary, outside the Congress.

The double policy of self-development and defensive resistance is the common standing-ground of the new spirit all over India. Some may not wish to go beyond its limits, others may look outside it; but so far all are agreed. For ourselves we avow that we advocate passive resistance without wishing to make a dogma of it. In a subject nationality, to win liberty for one's country is the first duty of all, by whatever means, at whatever sacrifice; and this duty must override all other considerations. The work of national emancipation is a great and holy *yajña* of which Boycott, Swadeshi, National Education and every other activity, great and small, are only major or minor parts. Liberty is the fruit we seek from the sacrifice and the Motherland the goddess to whom we offer it; into the seven leaping tongues of the fire of the *yajña* we must offer all that we are and all that we have, feeding the fire even with our blood and lives and happiness of our nearest and dearest; for the Motherland is a goddess who loves not a maimed and imperfect sacrifice, and freedom was never won from the gods by a grudging giver. But every great *yajña* has its Rakshasas who strive to baffle the sacrifice, to bespatter it with their own dirt or by guile or violence put out the flame. Passive resistance is an attempt to meet such disturbers by peaceful and self-contained *brahmatejas*; but even the greatest Rishis of old could not, when the Rakshasas were fierce and determined, keep up the sacrifice without calling in the bow of the Kshatriya. We should have the bow of the Kshatriya ready for use, though in the background. Politics is especially the business of the Kshatriya, and without Kshatriya strength at its back, all political struggle is unavailing.

Vedantism accepts no distinction of true or false religions, but considers only what will lead more or less surely, more or less quickly to *mokṣa*, spiritual emancipation and the realisation of the Divinity within. Our attitude is a political Vedantism. India, free, one and indivisible, is the divine realisation to which we move, — emancipation our aim; to that end each nation must practise the political creed which is the most suited to its temperament and circumstances; for that is the best for it which leads most surely and completely to national liberty and national self-realisation. But whatever leads only to continued subjection must be spewed out as mere vileness and impurity. Passive resistance may be the final method of salvation in our case or it may be only the preparation for the final *sādhanā*. In either case, the sooner we put it into full and perfect practice, the nearer we shall be to national liberty.

The Morality of Boycott*

AGES ago there was a priest of Baal who thought himself commissioned by the god to kill all who did not bow the knee to him. All men, terrified by the power and ferocity of the priest, bowed down before the idol and pretended to be his servants; and the few who refused had to take refuge in hills and deserts. At last, a deliverer came and slew the priest and the world had rest. The slayer was blamed by those who placed religion in quietude and put passivity forward as the ideal ethics, but the world looked on him as an incarnation of God.

A certain class of mind shrinks from aggressiveness as if it were a sin. Their temperament forbids them to feel the delight of battle and they look on what they cannot understand as something monstrous and sinful. 'Heal hate by love', 'drive out injustice by justice', 'slay sin by righteousness' is their cry. Love is a sacred name, but it is easier to speak of love than to love. The love which drives out hate is a divine quality of which only one man in a thousand is capable. A saint full of love for all mankind possesses it, a philanthropist consumed with a desire to heal the miseries of the race possesses it, but the mass of mankind does not and cannot rise to the height. Politics is concerned with masses of mankind and not with individuals. To ask masses of mankind to act as saints, to rise to the height of divine love and practise it in relation to their adversaries or oppressors is to ignore human nature. It is to set a premium on injustice and violence by paralysing the hand of the deliverer when raised to strike. The Gita is the best answer to those who shrink from battle as a sin, and aggression as a lowering of morality.

A poet of sweetness and love, who has done much to awaken Bengal, has written deprecating the boycott as an act of hate. The saintliness of spirit which he would see brought into politics is the reflex of his own personality colouring the political ideals

* This article was intended for the *Bande Mataram* but could not be published. It was seized by the Police and made an exhibit in the Alipore Conspiracy Case (May, 1908).

of a sattwic race. But in reality the boycott is not an act of hate. It is an act of self-defence, of aggression for the sake of self-preservation. To call it an act of hate is to say that a man who is being slowly murdered, is not justified in striking at his murderer. To tell that man that he must desist from using the first effective weapon that comes to his hand, because the blow would be an act of hate, is precisely on a par with this deprecation of boycott. Doubtless the self-defender is not precisely actuated by a feeling of holy sweetness towards his assailant; but to expect so much from human nature is impracticable. Certain religions demand it, but they have never been practised to the letter by their followers.

Hinduism recognises human nature and makes no such impossible demand. It sets one ideal for the saint, another for the man of action, a third for the trader, a fourth for the serf. To prescribe the same ideal for all is to bring about *varṇasaṅkara*, the confusion of duties, and destroy society and race. If we are content to be serfs, then indeed, boycott is a sin for us, not because it is a violation of love, but because it is a violation of the Sudra's duty of obedience and contentment. Politics is the ideal of the Kshatriya, and the morality of the Kshatriya ought to govern our political actions. To impose in politics the Brahmanical duty of saintly sufferance is to preach *varṇasaṅkara*.

Love has a place in politics, but it is the love of one's country, for one's countrymen, for the glory, greatness and happiness of the race, the divine *ānanda* of self-immolation for one's fellows, the ecstasy of relieving their sufferings, the joy of seeing one's blood flow for country and freedom, the bliss of union in death with the fathers of the race. The feeling of almost physical delight in the touch of the mother-soil, of the winds that blow from Indian seas, of the rivers that stream from Indian hills, in the hearing of Indian speech, music, poetry, in the familiar sights, sounds, habits, dress, manners of our Indian life, this is the physical root of that love. The pride in our past, the pain of our present, the passion for the future are its trunk and branches. Self-sacrifice and self-forgetfulness, great service, high endurance for the country are its fruit. And the sap which keeps it alive is the realisation of the Motherhood of God in the country, the vision of the Mother, the knowledge of the Mother, the perpetual contemplation, adoration and service of the Mother.

Other love than this is foreign to the motives of political action. Between nation and nation there is justice, partiality, chivalry, duty, but not love. All love is either individual or for the self in the race or for the self in mankind. It may exist between individuals of different races, but the love of one race for another is a thing foreign to Nature. When therefore the boycott, as declared by the Indian race against the British, is stigmatised for want of love, the charge is bad psychology as well as bad morality. It is interest warring against interest, and hatred is directed not really against the race, but against the adverse interest. If the British exploitation were to cease tomorrow, the hatred against the British race would disappear in a moment. A partial *adhyāropa* makes the ignorant for the moment see in the exploiters and not in the exploitation the receptacle of the hostile feeling. But like all *māyā*, it is an unreal feeling and sentiment and is not shared by those who think. Not hatred against foreigners, but antipathy to the evils of foreign exploitation is the true root of boycott.

If hatred is demoralising, it is also stimulating. The web of life has been made a mingled strain of good and evil and God works His ends through the evil as well as through the good. Let us discharge our minds of hate, but let us not deprecate a great and necessary movement because, in the inevitable course of human nature, it has engendered feelings of hostility and hatred. If hatred came, it was necessary that it should come as a stimulus, as a means of awakening.

When *tamas*, inertia, torpor have benumbed a nation, the strongest forms of *rajas* are necessary to break the spell; there is no form of *rajas* so strong as hatred. Through *rajas* we rise to *sattva* and for the Indian temperament the transition does not take long. Already the element of hatred is giving place to the clear conception of love for the Mother as the spring of our political actions.

Another question is the use of violence in the furtherance of boycott. This is, in our view, purely a matter of policy and expediency. An act of violence brings us into conflict and may be inexpedient for a race circumstanced like ours. But the moral question does not arise. The argument that to use violence is to interfere with personal liberty involves a singular misunderstanding of the very nature of politics. The whole of politics is an interference with personal liberty. Law is such an interference; protection is such an interference; the rule which makes the will of the majority prevail is such an interference. The right to prevent such use of personal liberty as will injure the interests of the race, is the fundamental law of society. From this point of view the nation is only using its primary rights when it restrains the individual from buying or selling foreign goods.

It may be argued that peaceful compulsion is one thing, and violent compulsion, another. Social boycott may be justifiable, but not the burning or drowning of British goods. The latter method, we reply, is illegal and therefore may be inexpedient, but it is not morally unjustifiable. The morality of the Kshatriya justifies violence in times of war, and boycott is a war. Nobody blames the Americans for throwing British tea into Boston harbour, nor can anybody blame a similar action in India on moral grounds. It is reprehensible from the point of view of law, of social peace and order, not of political morality. It has been eschewed by us because it is unwise and because it carried the battle on to a ground where we are comparatively weak, from a ground where we are strong.

Under other circumstances we might have followed the American precedent, and if we had done so, historians and moralists would have applauded, not censured.

Justice and righteousness are the atmosphere of political morality, but the justice and righteousness of a fighter, not of the priest. Aggression is unjust only when unprovoked; violence, unrighteous when used wantonly or for unrighteous ends. It is a barren philosophy which applies a mechanical rule to all actions, or takes a word and tries to fit all human life into it.

The sword of the warrior is as necessary to the fulfilment of justice and righteousness as the holiness of the saint. Ramdas is not complete without Shivaji. To maintain justice and prevent the strong from despoiling, and the weak from being oppressed, is the function for which the Kshatriya was created. "Therefore," says Sri Krishna in the *Mahabharata*, "God created battle and armour, the sword, the bow and the dagger."

Man is of a less terrestrial mould than some would have him to be. He has an element of the divine which the politician ignores. The practical politician looks to the position at the moment and imagines that he has taken everything into consideration. He has, indeed, studied the surface and the immediate surroundings, but he has missed what lies beyond material vision. He has left out of account the divine, the incalculable in man, that element which upsets the calculations of the schemer and disconcerts the wisdom of the diplomat.

BANDE MATARAM

Daily: August 6, 1906 to October 29, 1908
Weekly: June 2, 1907 to September 27, 1908

Bande Mataram

Darkness in "Light"

We regret to find our contemporary *Light* surpassing the most moderate of the moderatists in the timidity of its aspirations. "What the most ambitious of Indians have dared to hope for is that a day may come, *may be a century hence*, when in the domestic affairs of their country they will enjoy some measure of freedom from autocratic control." Here is an inspiring ideal indeed! Hail, Holy Light! thou art indeed a fit candle to illumine a somnolent constitutionalist's repose!

Our Rip Van Winkles

The development of sounder political ideas and the birth and growth of a new national energy has been so swift and wonderful that it is not surprising to find a number of our older politicians quite left behind by the rising tide. Stranded on their desert islands of antiquated political ideas, they look forlornly over the heaving tumult around them and strive piteously to imagine themselves still in their old carefully sheltered arena of mimic political strife and safe, cheap, and profitable patriotism. But the walls of the arena have been washed away, its very ground is being obliterated, and a new world of stern reality and unsparing struggle is rapidly taking its place. In the fierce heat of that conflict all shams must wither away and all empty dreams be dissolved. The issue has been fairly put between the Indian people and the alien bureaucracy. "Destroy or thou shalt be destroyed", and the issue will have to be fought out, not "it may be a century hence", but now, in the next two or three decades. We cannot leave the problem for posterity to settle nor shift our proper burdens on to the shoulders of our grandchildren. But our Rip Van Winkles persist in talking and writing as if Partition and Boycott and Sir Bampfylde Fuller had never been.

Indians Abroad

India to hand this mail laments the exclusion of Indians from the representative system on which the new constitution in the Transvaal is to be based and plaintively recalls the professions and promises of the British Government at the time of the Boer War. The saintly simplicity of *India* grows daily more and more wearisome to us. Everybody who knew anything at all about politics understood at the time that those professions were merely a diplomatic move and the promises made were never meant to be carried out. We see no reason to lament what was always foreseen. What we do regret and blame is the spirit of Indians in the Transvaal who seek escape from the oppression they suffer under by ignoble methods similar in spirit to those practised by the constitutionalists in this country. The more the Transvaal Indians are kicked and insulted, the more loyal they seem to become. After their splendid services in the Transvaal war had been rewarded by the grossest ingratitude, they had no business to offer their services again in the recent Natal rebellion. By their act they associated themselves with the colonists in their oppression of the natives of the country and have only themselves to thank if they also are oppressed by the same narrow and arrogant colonial spirit. Their eagerness to dissociate themselves from the Africans is shown in Dr. Abdurrahman's letter quoted by *India*. All such methods are as useless as they are unworthy. So long as the Indian nation at home does not build itself into a strong and self-governing people, they can expect nothing from Englishmen in their colonies except oppression and contumely.

Officials on the Fall of Fuller

The seriousness of the blow which has fallen on the bureaucracy by the downfall of Shayesta Khan can be measured by the spite and fury which it has excited in such public organs of officialdom as the *Englishman* and the *Pioneer*. The letter of I.C.S. to the *Pioneer* which we extract in another column is a more direct and very striking indication of the feelings which it has aroused especially among the colleagues of the deposed proconsul. The Anglo-Indian press has for the most part grasped the fact that the resignation of Sir Bampfylde Fuller was a victory for the popular forces in Eastern Bengal. Had the new province allowed itself to be crushed by the repressive fury of Shayesta Khan or answered it only with petitions, like a sheep bleating under the knife of the butcher, bureaucracy would have triumphed. But determined repression met by determined resistance finally made Sir Bampfylde's position untenable. Neither Lord Minto who from the first supported the Fullerian policy nor Mr. Morley who has done his best to shield and protect the petty tyrant in his worst vagaries, deserves the angry recriminations with which they are being assailed. They have both acted in the interests of the bureaucracy and if they have made an error of judgment in throwing Sir Bampfylde to the wolves, it is because the choice put before them was a choice of errors. By maintaining their lieutenant they would have helped the revolutionary forces in the country to grow; by sacrificing him they have given fresh vigour and self-confidence to the people in their resistance to the Partition. There comes a time in all such struggles when whatever the Government may do, it cannot fail to weaken itself and strengthen the people. Such a time has come in India and all the rage of Anglo-India cannot alter the inevitable march of destiny.

Cow-Killing: An Englishman's Amusements in Jalpaiguri

A correspondent writes to us from Jalpaiguri: —

An Englishman, a forester, at Jalpaiguri has shot three cows one of them belonging to the school Head Pandit. The open garden of the forester is near certain bungalows adjoining the school, and it appears that the cows strayed into the garden, whereupon the Saheb calmly proceeded to shoot them. This he did laughing and in spite of the remonstrance of another Englishman, his friend. On the Head Pandit consulting his neighbours, he was told to consider himself lucky that it was the cows and not he whom the Saheb elected to shoot. Perceiving the force of this remark and apprehensive about his service, the Pandit has swallowed and is trying to digest the loss and the mortification. I hear that when the bodies of the cows were being taken away, the Saheb was dancing with exultation.

We publish the above extraordinary story of wanton oppression with reservation, but Anglo-Indian vagaries of the kind are too common for us quite to disbelieve it. If it is a fact, we trust the sufferer will think better of it and seek redress; the fear of swift punishment is the only motive force that can keep these vagaries in check and every Indian who submits is partly guilty of the insults and oppressions inflicted on his fellow countrymen.

Bande Mataram, August 20, 1906

National Education and the Congress

National Education received the seal of approbation from united Bengal at the Barisal Conference. It should be the aim of the nationalists to elicit from the Congress this year a solemn expression of the national will recognising the new movement and recommending it to all India. It is possible that there may be some difficulty in carrying the motion, for the small-minded and faint-hearted figure largely in the Congress ranks. At Benares this element disgraced the nation by excluding Swadeshi, the universal national movement, from the purview of the national assembly. This time there should be no repetition of such pusillanimity. Such exhibitions of moral cowardice are one reason more why the Congress should be reconstituted on a basis sufficiently popular to prevent the sentiment of the people from being outraged or caricatured by self-constituted representatives. If the Congress had not been hopelessly out of date in its form and spirit, it would by this time have organised itself for work, with a department for the organisation of National Education on a basis of voluntary self-taxation figuring prominently in its list of national duties.

Bande Mataram, August 22, 1906

A Pusillanimous Proposal

WE published yesterday the letter of Babu Ananda Chandra Roy of Dacca in which he invites East Bengal to welcome Mr. Hare and establish with the Shillong Government the ordinary relations of kow-towing and petitioning. We characterised the letter as an indefensible production and a second perusal only confirms us in the impulse to give it a yet harsher name. What Babu Ananda Chandra proposes under the cover of lawyer-like arguments and illogical sophistry, is no less than to betray his country.

The whole of Bengal has registered a solemn vow that let Viceroys do what they will and Secretaries of State say what they will, the united Bengali nation refuses and will for ever refuse to acknowledge the Partition. Taxes we may pay, laws we may obey, but beyond that we have no farther relations with the overnment of Shillong. The position is clear, beyond sophistry, above dispute. Whatever differences may exist among us, on this there is one unanimous voice. But Babu Ananda Chandra Roy can no longer bear the deprivation of the fleshpots of Egypt or the strain of self-denial and stern resistance which this resolution implies and wishing himself to recoil from that arduous position, he invites all his countrymen to follow his lead and countenance him in a cowardly surrender.

And why are we to commit this inglorious act of political suicide? In the first place, because Mr. Hare is such a nice gentleman and therefore the "grounds and causes" we had for avoiding that bad bold man Sir Bampfylde no longer exist. We do not know what grounds and causes Ananda Babu had for avoiding Sir B. Fuller — we have a suspicion that it was because public opinion left him no choice; but the one ground and cause that Bengal had for this action was the existence of the Partition, that and nothing else. The Partition exists in full force and the "grounds and causes" exist therefore unabated and unimpaired. The "leadership" which regulates grave political issues according to the personal character and amiability of the ruler for the time being, is a leadership for which India has no longer any use. It is not Hare and Fuller that matter, but our country and the British system and policy which seeks to keep us in perpetual servitude.

Other of Ananda Babu's reasons for submission are that it will enable himself and his friends to enter the Legislative Council of the new province, to act as Honorary Magistrates and visitors of Lunatic Asylums and to get the circulars for the preference of Mahomedans in appointments modified or abrogated. The fossils of the old days of selfish submission are incorrigible. We should have thought otherwise — that to advance such contemptible reasons for acquiescing in the mutilation of one's country would have been regarded as an act of inconceivable shamelessness.

Ananda Babu, however, will not admit that he is counselling acquiescence, for he is quite willing to mention in every address to the new ruler of Shillong that we are weeping for the Partition and will go on weeping inconsolably — on stated public occasion until it is rescinded! The childishness of such a suggestion would be amusing if it were not painful to think that such political ineptitude proceeds from a man who has long been looked up to as a leader and counsellor in our political movements.

Manifestos and utterances of this kind compel us to ask whether some of our "Swadeshi" leaders are sincere in desiring that the Partition should be rescinded. The ugliest feature of the Swadeshi agitation has been the refusal of the members for the East Bengal districts to vacate their seats on the Legislative Council. Ananda Babu's letter is another sign of evil omen. But there is one man among the older leaders whose sincerity cannot be doubted. Babu Surendranath Banerji is the leader of United Bengal; he has just declared himself at Barisal, the high priest of the mother's worship. Will he permit this calm proposal to desecrate her image and perpetuate its mutilation and utter no protest?

Ananda Babu has other proposals equally remarkable. He proposes to beseech the Government to help us in the Swadeshi movement; to smother the Boycott, as an illegtimate child or at least to conceal it as if it were something we were ashamed of; to bow down to the settled fact, as the fiat of the Highest Authority, confusing apparently Mr. John Morley with that Power which undoes the decrees of Statesmen and Princes! And he asks us, "Save and except showing our disapprobation of the Partition what else can we gain by avoiding the new L.-G. ?" That is a question easy to answer. If we persist in the Boycott both of British goods and of British offices and officials, we shall gain, if nothing else, the speedy reversal of the Partition. It is a pity that our leaders understand so little of British politics, otherwise they would understand that it is only in this way that Mr. Morley's game of bluff can be met. The Partition cannot be maintained against a permanently alienated and restless Bengal. But there is one way in which we can perpetuate Lord Curzon's work, and that is to submit, to give up the fight and bow the knee betraying, for individual advantages and temporary gains, our mother.

Bande Mataram, August 25, 1906

BY THE WAY

It is sad to watch the steady intellectual degeneration of our once vigorous contemporary the *Indian Mirror*. Commenting on the formation of Labour Unions, the *Mirror* advises the promoters to make the *suppression* of strikes the principal object of their efforts! Certainly, the strike is the last weapon in the hands of labour and should not be used as the first. But the idea of organising Labour Unions to suppress strikes is a masterpiece of unconscious humour. We shall next hear that Mahomedan Educational Conferences should be organised to discourage Mahomedan education, that the anti-circular laws should make it their chief object to put down picketing, and perhaps that a League is being formed with Babu Narendra Nath Sen at its head to "suppress" the *Indian Mirror*.

*

We do not think the amazing timidity of our political leaders can be paralleled in any other country in the world. Is a National Congress established? Its object, one would think, must be to concentrate the strength of the nation and fight its way to power. Oh, by no means, it is only to advise and assist the Government! Is a national Council of Education instituted? Of course, it has arisen to rival and replace the alien-ruled University. Not at all, not at all; it is meant not to stand in opposition to but to supplement the old University! Does Labour rise in its strength and band itself into formidable combinations? Their work will be, then, to resist the greed and heartlessness of Capital and vindicate the claims of the toiler to just treatment and a man's wages for a man's work. O God indeed! These Unions are rather meant to suppress strikes and establish kindly relations between the employers and the employed! Are we, after all, one wonders sometimes, a nation of cowards and old women?

*

The excuse usually urged for these pitiful insincerities is that it is all diplomacy. The diplomacy of grown-up children! The diplomacy of the ostrich hiding its head in the sand? What a poor idea these "leaders" must have formed of the political intelligence of the British Government and of Englishmen generally, if they think they can be deceived by such puerile evasions. Bureaucracy and Anglo-India take advantage of these professions and laugh in their sleeves. Meanwhile, the country loses the inspiration of great ideals, the exaltation of frank and glorious conflict, the divine impulse that only comes to those who know they are battling bravely and openly for the freedom of their country, not to men who cringe to the enemy and lie and palter with their consciences.

Truth and bold straight dealings we believe to be not only our noblest but our wisest policy in our struggle with the alien. Our leaders have no faith in the nation; they believe it is weak and impotent, and shufflings, evasions and shallow insincerities are the weapons of the weak. We for our part believe in the immense strength of the nation and demand that our leaders shall bring it face to face with the enemy. Still if they must have diplomacy let them give some diplomacy worth the name. If the shades of Cavour and Bismarck have leisure to listen to such senilities, what a smile of immortal contempt must pass over their lips as they watch the "diplomacy" of our leaders.

Bande Mataram, August 27, 1906

The "Mirror" and Mr. Tilak

THE *Indian Mirror*, which is now the chief ally of Government among the Congress organs in Bengal, has chosen, naturally enough, to fall foul of Mr. Tilak. Our contemporary, it appears, has heard that some people propose to put forward Mr. Tilak's name as President of the next Congress, and it hastens to point out how extremely distasteful the idea is to all thoughtful and enlightened men, that is to say, to all whose views agree with the *Mirror*'s. Mr. Tilak, we learn, has seriously offended our contemporary by giving honour to Mr. Bhopatkar on his release from jail; his speeches on the occasion of the Shivaji festival were displeasing to the thoughtful and enlightened men who congregate in the office of the *Indian Mirror*; and to sum up the whole matter, he is a man of extreme views and without "tact". Ergo, he is no fit man for the presidential chair of the Congress.

It is interesting to learn on this unimpeachable authority what are the qualifications which the moderate and loyalist mind demands in a President of the "National" Congress. It is not, apparently, the acknowledged leader of one of the greatest Indian races who can aspire to that post; it is a man of "tact" — one, in other words, who does not like to offend the authorities. It is not the great protagonist and champion of Swadeshi in Western India; it is a man of moderate views, one, let us say, who dare not look Truth in the face and speak out boldly what he thinks. It is not the one man whom the whole Hindu community in Western India delights to honour, from Peshawar to Kolhapur and from Bombay to our own borders; it is one who will not talk about Shivaji and Bhavani — only about Mahatmas. It is not the man who has suffered and denied himself for his country's sake and never abased his courage nor bowed his head under the most crushing persecution; it is one who by refusing to honour a similar courage in others, dishonours the country for which they have suffered.

If this is the creed of our contemporary and those whose opinions it "mirrors", it is not the creed of the country at large. With the exception of a fast-dwindling minority of Anglophiles, the whole of India has learned to honour the name of the great Maratha leader and patriot. His social and religious views may not agree with those of the "enlightened", but we have yet to learn that the Congress platform is sacred to advanced social reformers, that the profession of the Hindu religion is a bar to leadership in its ranks. Mr. Tilak's only other offence is the courage and boldness of his views and his sturdiness in holding by them. He has dared to go to jail and honour those who follow his example, — the bold bad man! And yet we seem to have somehow or other a dim recollection of a venerable Congress leader named Babu Narendra Nath Sen figuring prominently at a meeting in which men and boys who had gone to jail for resisting the Government were honoured and saluted as national heroes. Evidently we have been under an error. Evidently our contemporary is at heart a favourer of the doctrine of self-help and action. It is talking and writing against the Government that he condemns, but to act against the Government, rebellion against constituted authorities has Babu Narendra Nath's full approval. Wearing the outward guise of a loyalist, he is at heart revolutionary. Otherwise would he have presided at the 7th of August celebration and countenanced the raising of the National flag? Now, at last, we understand the policy of the *Mirror*.

Whether loyalism likes it or not, Mr. Tilak is now the leader of the Deccan, a man whom twenty millions look up to as their chief and head. If Mr. Mehta is the "uncrowned King" of Bombay City, Mr. Tilak is the uncrowned King of all Maharashtra. The attempt to exclude such a man from his rightful place and influence in the counsels of the nation can only recoil on its authors.

Leaders in Council

The conference held in the Land-holders Association on Sunday seems to have been very select in its composition, the organisers confining themselves mostly to staunch congress-men or those who might be supposed to hold fast by Congress views. It must have been a disagreeable surprise to them to find that even in this small circle a strong opposition was offered to the renewal of a petitioning policy. Babu Motilal Ghose could not be excluded and the views of this veteran leader on the question of action *versus* resolution are well known. But Babu Motilal was backed up by strong voices from the Mofussil and we understand that it was only by the old plea of its being the very last time that the conference was persuaded to agree to something in the shape of a memorial. We know that "last time" well. It was the very last time on the occasion of the Town Hall; it was the very last time at Barisal; and now again this long-lived old friend of ours crops up like the clown of the pantomime with his eternal smirk and his eternal "Here I am". Our leaders resemble English theatrical managers, when their audiences grow small. They declare that today is the last night of the piece; next day it becomes the very last night; then it is absolutely the last night, and so on till it is absolutely quite the very very last, last night of all. Meanwhile audiences increase and the shillings pour in.

Bande Mataram, August 28, 1906

BY THE WAY

Diogenes in the *Statesman* indulges himself in a paragraph of grave advice to the 'self-constituted' leaders of the Indian labour movement. For a philosopher, our friend takes singularly little trouble to understand the opponents' case. Neither Mr. A. K. Ghose nor Mr. Aswini Banerji nor any of their assistants proposes, so far as we know, to benefit labour by getting rid of English capital. What they do propose is to get rid of the exceedingly unjust conditions under which Indian labour has to sweat in order to enrich alien capitalists. And by the way, as it were, they also propose to get rid of the habit of coarse insult and brutal speech which Englishmen have accustomed themselves to indulge in when dealing with 'low-class' Indians.

Are the leaders of Indian labour self-constituted? One would imagine that men whom Indian workers naturally turn to in difficulty and who can organise in a few weeks so large an affair as the Railway Union have vindicated their claims to be the national leaders of Labour. At any rate, their constitutents have very enthusiastically ratified their 'self-constituted' authority. But perhaps Diogenes has been converted from cynicism to Vedanta, and sees no difference between the self of the railway employees and the self of Mr. A. K. Ghose. Still, the tub from which he holds forth is a small one, and he should not cumber one-sixth of his space with such cumber.

The rift between the Labourites and the Liberals grows daily wider. The alliance was never natural and cannot in its nature be permanent. But official Liberaldom will be foolish indeed if it declares war on Labour at the present juncture. The Socialistic element in England is quite strong enough to turn the Liberal triumph of 1905 into a serious disaster at the next elections. Nor are the Labourites likely to be frightened by Ministerial menaces. Mr. Winston Churchill and the Master of Elibank may thunder from their high official Olympus, but Mr. Keir Hardie will go on his way unscathed and unmoved. He knows that the future is with Socialism and he can afford to despise the temporary and imperfect fruits which a Liberal alliance promises.

For us English politics have small personal interest. From the Conservatives we can expect nothing but open oppression, from the Liberals, nothing but insincere professions and fraudulent concessions, — shadows calling themselves substance. Can we hope better things from Labour? Many whose judgment we respect think that there is a real ally — that the friendship of Labour for India is sincere and disinterested. For the present, yes. But when Labour becomes a power and sits on front benches we fear that it will be as intolerant and oppressive as Conservatism itself. Australia is a Labour Commonwealth, and we know the attitude of the Australian working-man to Indians and Asiatics generally. India's hope lies not in English Liberalism or

Labour, but in her own strong heart and giant limbs. Titaness, who by thy mere attempt to rise can burst these Lilliputian bonds, why shouldst thou clamour feebly for help to these pigmies over the seas?

Bande Mataram, August 30, 1906

Lessons at Jamalpur

THE incidents at Jamalpur are in many ways a sign of the times. They reveal to us, first and foremost, as many incidents of the Swadeshi movement have revealed to us, the great reservoir of potential strength which the Congress movement has for so long a time left untapped. The true policy of the Congress movement should have been from the beginning to gather together under its flag all the elements of strength that exist in this huge country. The Brahman Pandit and the Mahomedan Maulavi, the caste organisation and the trade-union, the labourer and the artisan, the coolie at his work and the peasant in his field, none of these should have been left out of the sphere of our activities. For each is a strength, a unit of force; and in politics the victory is to the side which can marshal the largest and most closely serried number of such units and handle them most skilfully, not to those who can bring forward the best arguments or talk the most eloquently.

But the Congress started from the beginning with a misconception of the most elementary facts of politics and with its eyes turned towards the British Government and away from the people. To flaunt its moderation and reasonableness before approving English eyes, to avoid giving offence to British sentiments, to do nothing that would provoke a real conflict, this was its chief pre-occupation. It concerned itself with such things as Simultaneous Examinations, Exchange Compensation, with the details of administration and the intricacies of finance; it presumed to give the Government advice on its military policy, and it passed omnibus resolutions covering the whole field of Indian affairs. All the time it had nothing behind it that could be called strength, no tangible reason why the British Government should respect and give form to its irresponsible criticisms. The Government on its side took the measure of the Congress and acted accordingly.

Under the stimulus of an intolerable wrong, Bengal in the

fervour of the Swadeshi movement parted company with the old ideals and began to seek for its own strength. It has found it in the people. But the awakening of this strength immediately brought the whole movement into collision with British interests, and the true nature of the Englishman, when his interests are threatened, revealed itself. The Swadeshi threatened British trade and immediately an unholy alliance was formed between the magistracy, the non-officials and the pious missionaries of Christ, to crush the new movement by every form of prosecution and harassment. The Trade Union movement threatens the tyranny of British Capital over Indian Labour, and at once British Capital responds by unprovoked lockouts, illegal dismissals and finally by volleys of gunshot. The struggle is bound to increase in its intensity and the prospect it opens, is one which only the most courageous can face. But for us there is no choice. The faith in British justice has crumbled into the dust. Nothing can again restore it. Go back we cannot, halt we cannot, go on we must. It will be well for us if our leaders recognise the situation and instead of hesitation and timidity which will not help them, meet it with clear eyes and an undaunted spirit.

BY THE WAY

There is a limit to everything. There is also a limit to hero-worship and to self-laudation. It seems to us that limit was passed in the extraordinary proceedings of the Pandits' meeting which deified Babu Surendranath Banerji, and in the undignified effusion of the report which appeared in Babu Surendranath's own paper the *Bengalee*. A regular *abhishek* ceremony seems to have been performed and the assembled Brahmins paid him regal honours as if he had been the just and truthful Yudishthira at the Rajasuya sacrifice. If Babu Surendranath wishes to be the king of independent Bengal, he should surely conquer his kingdom first and then enjoy it. Even Caesar refused the crown thrice; but Surendra Babu has no scruples. He accepted his coronation with effusive tearfulness in the touching language of the *Bengalee*, "his mighty voice shook and he got choky".

*

But the thing passes a joke. Whatever differences of opinion we may have with Babu Surendranath, we have always recognised him as the leader of Bengal, the one man among us whose name is a spell to sway the hearts of millions. We do not like to see him making himself publicly ridiculous, for, by doing so, he makes the whole of Bengal ridiculous. Such performances are rather likely to diminish his prestige than increase it. But ever since the rise of a party which questions his methods and ideals, Surendra Babu has shown an uneasy desire to have his personal leadership proclaimed on the housetops and an almost hysteric tendency towards self-praise. The indecorous comparisons of himself with Christ and Gauranga, the tone of his Barisal speech and this coronation ceremony are indications which make us uneasy for our veteran leader. He should remember the last days of Keshab Chandra Sen and avoid a similar debacle.

*

It is time that public opinion should forbid this habit of self-laudation in our leaders. The Maratha leaders have a much keener sense of the decorum and seriousness which public life demands. Recently a movement was set on foot in the Deccan to celebrate Mr. Tilak's birthday and pay to the great Maratha leader almost the same honours as are paid to the memory of Shivaji in the Shivaji Utsav. The whole of Maharastra prepared to go mad with a frenzy of hero-worship when everything was brought to a sudden end by prompt and imperative prohibition from Mr. Tilak himself. This entire absence of self-seeking and self-advertisement is one of the most characteristic features of Mr. Tilak's public conduct. We hope it will become a more general standard if not of character, at least of public etiquette throughout India.

Bande Mataram, September 1, 1906

BY THE WAY

The *Bengalee* publishes an apologetic explanation of the Kamboliatola ceremony on which we passed a few strictures more in sorrow than in anger the other day. The defence seems to be that Babu Surendranath Banerjee was bediademed neither with a crown of gems nor a crown of thorns, but only a harmless chaplet of flowers. Moreover, the ceremony was not in the nature of an *abhishek* or coronation, but a *Shanti-Sechan* or homage of hearts from Bengal's assembled Pandits. We do not think the explanation betters things in any way. In whatever way we look at it, the whole affair was a piece of childishness which could have no object but to minister to personal vanity.

This same silly chaplet, it appears, represented the crown of success and might be likened to the laurel crown of the ancient Roman. Visions arise before us of our only leader wrapped majestically in an ancient toga and accepting on the Capitol the laurel crown that shall shield his head from the lightnings. But who is the hostile deity against whom the muttered Mantras of the Brahmins were invoked to shield the head of our Surendra Caesar? Sir Jupiter Fuller is gone and no other Thunderer takes his place. We repeat, the whole affair was silly in the extreme and we hope it will not be repeated.

*

Mr. A. K. Ghose has gone to Jamalpur. That is well. Such affairs as the sanguinary outrage at Jamalpur demand that our strongest man should be himself on the spot, and Mr. A. K. Ghose has proved himself a leader of men, the greater because, unaided by supreme powers of oratory, he has by mere honest work and organising power, become the voice and the head of thousands of men.

Bande Mataram, September 3, 1906

English Enterprise and Swadeshi

The Anglo-Indian papers are nowadays repeatedly referring to the Jamalpur Railway workshop as a Swadeshi enterprise. The use of the word throws a good deal of light on the meaning of that Swadeshi which our benevolent Government so unctuously professes. The Jamalpur workshop does nothing for India beyond employing a number of coolies who are ill-paid and therefore underfed and a staff of Bengali clerks. It adds nothing appreciable to Indian wealth, on the contrary, it diminishes it. All that can be said is that instead of taking 100 per cent of the profits out of India, it takes 90 per cent. This is precisely the meaning of Government Swadeshi — to provide a field for English Capital, English skilled work in India and employ Indian labour, not out of desire for India's good, but because it is cheap. If the Government really desired India's good, it would provide for the training of educated Indians so that such work as is done in Jamalpur might be executed by Indian brains and with Indian capital, as well as by Indian hands. But we do not ask the Government to give us such training. It would be foolish to expect a foreign Government to injure the trade of its own nation in India. We must provide for our own training ourselves.

Jamalpur

Our correspondent's report from Jamalpur gives the sober facts of the situation and clears away the mist of misrepresentation and wild rumour with which the Anglo-Indian journals have sought to obscure the incident. From the beginning the English version has been an attempt to throw the whole blame on the workmen by charging them with rioting before the gunshots. Their version has varied from day to day. With the exception of one or two minor details, the opposite version has been throughout clear, consistent and rational. There will, of course, be the usual cases and counter-cases and diametrically opposite statements sworn to in evidence. But we have ceased to take any interest in this futile legal proceedings. An Englishman assaulting an Indian may be innocent or guilty, but, as he cannot be punished, it does not matter an atom whether he is innocent or guilty. The fight has to be fought out to the end and the resort to law is no more than a persistent superstition.

BY THE WAY

The wailings of the *Englishman* for Sir Bampfylde Fuller do not cease. The Rachel of Hare Street mourns for the darling of her heart and will not be comforted. We wish our contemporary would realise that the rest of the world are heartily sick of this daily ululation. Deeply as we sympathise with his grief we cannot help thinking that it is indecently prolonged. Rest, rest, perturbed spirit, rest!

*

The *Englishman* makes, after his fashion a curious use of the severe criticisms on Babu Surendranath's *Shanti-Sechan* which have appeared in the Bengali press. He thinks that it means the "repudiation" of Surendra Babu and the abandonment of the Partition Agitation. Prodigious! Apparently the *Englishman* has yet to learn that the movement in Bengal was not created by any single man and does not depend on any single man. It is a great natural upheaval and the leaders are no more than so many corks tossing on the surface of a whirlpool. If one or more goes down, what does it matter to the whirlpool?

*

It is amusing to find Babu Bepin Chandra Pal represented as a fanatical worshipper of Surendra Babu. "When Babu Bepin Chandra finds it in his heart to condemn the editor of the *Bengalee*," cries the *Englishman*, "then indeed all is over." Shabash! The humours of Hare Street are mending.

*

There is another kind of humour which pervades the columns of the *Indian Mirror*, but it is not so pleasing as the

Englishman's. The *Mirror* poses as a Nationalist organ, but its paragraphs and articles often breathe Anglo-Indian inspiration. Its comments on the official verdict of the Shantipur case are an instance. It even goes so far as to call on the Railway authorities to punish the "Bengali Stationmaster" because Mr. Carlyle complains of his conduct in the matter. We had to look twice at the top of the sheet before we could persuade ourselves that it was not an Anglo-Indian sheet we were reading.

*

Still worse is the paragraph on the Jamalpur affair. The *Mirror* calls on the promoters of the Railway Union not to do anything which will provoke the feelings of the workmen to a white heat. We had thought it was the gunshots of the European railway officials which had done that work. But no: in the eyes of the *Mirror* that seems to have been a harmless act. It is Mr. A. K. Ghose and Babu Premtosh Bose who are to blame. Yet the editor of this paper is one of our "leaders".

*

The *Mirror* farther gives hospitality to an amusing utterance of Kumar Kshitendra Deb, that renowned statesman who is standing for the Bengal Legislative Council. This Kumar first carefully differentiates true Swadeshi from false, the true being the kind of Swadeshi which allows Kumars and others to become Legislative Councillors, the false the kind of Swadeshi which doesn't. All this is to prevent misunderstanding about his views, which he innocently imagines that the public are anxious to learn. We think our Kumar is rather ungrateful to the "false" Swadeshi, but for which he would have had rather less chance of becoming Legislative Councillor than the man in the moon. The worthy Kumar has no sympathy with martyrs, naturally enough. We want, apparently, not martyrs but men who are determined to attain a position. No, thank you, Kumar, we have had too many of that kind already; the little change to martyrs will do no harm.

Bande Mataram, September 4, 1906

The Times on Congress Reforms

THE pronouncement of the *Times* on the proposal of the Congress for a further reform and expansion of the Indian Councils is significant for the thoroughness with which the futility and impossibility of the entire Congress ideal is exposed by the writer. Mr. Gokhale took great pains last year in his address as President of the Congress to point out, in detail, how the present Council of the Indian Viceroy might be remodelled, without disturbing the present position of the Government. His idea is that the elected members of the Viceregal Council may well be increased from five to twelve, of whom two shall be elected by the Chamber of Commerce and the representative of some important industry, and ten by the different Provinces. The two representatives of Commerce and Industry will, Mr. Gokhale opined, be Europeans, as there shall be 10 Indian members elected to the Council, out of 25, the total strength of that body; and even if they voted together they would be in a permanent and absolute minority; and the only effect of any vote they might give against the Government would be a moral effect. This is Mr. Gokhale's position and programme; and neither the *Times* nor, we are afraid, anybody else outside the ranks of those who hold that everything that is unreal and moderate is the product of sound statesmanship, clearly sees what the gain either to the people or to the Government will be from the acceptance of this wise and cautious counsel. The ten Indian members will form H.M.'s permanent Opposition in India: that is all; but a permanent Opposition has all the evils of irresponsible criticism without the advantages of a real Opposition which can some day hope to be the Government, and whom this possibility always makes sober and responsible. "The policy proposed by the Congress," says the *Times*, "is a policy for bringing the Government into disrepute without the safeguards which all popular constitutions provide; it is a policy for generating steam without the precaution of supplying safety-valves;" and the justice of this criticism cannot be honestly denied.

If Mr. Gokhale's programme does not guarantee any benefit to the Government, neither is it likely to confer any benefit on the people except, of course, on a handful of men who shall enjoy the luxury of being Hon'bles and get enlarged opportunities of recommending their friends, relatives and protégés for office under the Government. The people will take little interest in these Council-elections, because they will soon find out — as they have already done in Bengal, that the elected members cannot carry any popular measure successfully through the Council or oppose effectively even the most mischievous ones. Mr. Gokhale is not only anxious to keep the elected members perpetually in the minority, but though he wants them to be vested with the right of moving amendments on the Budget, the Viceroy must have the right of vetoing them even if they are carried. The fact is, there is absolutely no seriousness about the whole thing. It is all to be a mere child's play. Or, Mr. Gokhale thinks, perhaps, that by gradually securing these so-called rights, he will ultimately get real constitutional rights and privileges from his British masters, but he forgets that these masters have never in the past done anything that has directly affected their interests and status as a sovereign power, nor will they do any such thing in the future, unless, of course, they are compelled to do it, by apprehensions of some great loss or danger. As for the idea that this so-called reform in the Legislative Council will, in any way, make for popular freedom by educating the people, that also is evidently without any reasonable justification for its success; for, as the *Times* very justly points out, Mr. Gokhale's programme has no room for any real political education for the people. To quote it in full: —

"Nor is the policy one which offers any substantial advantage to the people of India; it gives them increased opportunities of criticism but no increase of responsibility; it does nothing to give the people that education in politics which is essential if... they are now for the first time to have some share in the management of their own affairs. By the scheme under consideration the leaders of Indian opinion would not acquire that sense of responsibility which necessarily comes to men who expect that they will shortly be in power themselves; they are to have opportunities for finding fault with the Government but they will never have to make their words good; they can with a light heart demand a reduction of taxation or denounce the Government for not putting a stop to famines, because they know that they can never themselves be called upon to prove that these reforms are practicable. It is the prospect of office which sobers and restrains a European Opposition! Is it wise to assume that Indian politicians will be moderate and without this restraint?"

And the justice of this criticism who will deny? Mr. Gokhale's programme if accepted by Government, can have only one effect on the growth of public opinion and political life in India: it will prove the utter futility of any half-measures like these to secure real and substantial rights for the people. Such an education through failure was needed twenty-five years ago, when people still had faith in British shibboleths or had confidence in British character and British policy; it is absolutely needless and involves sheer waste of time and energy that have much greater calls on them for more substantial and urgent work now,— today when the people have already commenced to realise that their future must be shaped by themselves, without any help from their British masters, and indeed in spite of the most violent opposition that will, naturally, be offered by them. Mr. Gokhale's creed and his policy are anachronisms in the India of 1906; the one stands absolutely discredited with the people, the other is declared unwise and impracticable by the Government. The Congress must give these up, or continue as an effete anachronism in the country, or probably turn by the logic of this creed and this policy, into a loyalist opposition to all true and forceful popular movement and propaganda in India. Can we afford to allow an institution that we have all served so faithfully all these years, and that may at once become an organised institution of popular deliberation and effective public life, to grow effete and useless? Much less can we afford to place it in the hands of the enemies of popular freedom. That is the question before the country now. The coming Congress in Calcutta will perhaps decide this question. Friends of popular freedom should understand this and gather their forces accordingly for saving the Congress from both these calamities.

BY THE WAY

The *Mirror* complains piteously that the country is in the hands of extremists on one side and ultra-moderates on the other, while the voices of sitters on the fence, like the *Indian Mirror*, go totally unheard. It is hard on our contemporary. But he should realise that a time has come in the history of the nation when men must take one side or the other, if they wish to count for anything in the making of the future. To preside at a boycott meeting and disparage the boycott is a course which the politician concerned may reconcile with his own conscience, but it is not likely to increase the weight of his influence with his countrymen.

*

We are surprised to see the *Pioneer* join in the extraordinary *can-can* which the *Englishman* has been performing ever since the Fuller dismissal. We were accustomed to regard the *Pioneer* as a sober and well-conducted journal, though its political views are no less pernicious than the *Englishman*'s; but it is surpassing Hare Street itself in journalistic high-kicks. "Beware, beware, Bengalis," it shouts, "if you rebel, we will exterminate you with fire and sword, we will outdo the atrocities we committed during the Mutiny; we are tigers, we are tigers! Look at our claws." All this is very bloody indeed and paints the *Pioneer* one red. But it does seem as if Anglo-India had gone clean mad. Such a pitiful exhibition will not increase the respect of the subject race for its rulers.

*

The *Indian Mirror* comes out with an article on the selfishness of Indian patriots. According to this self-satisfied critic Mr. T. Palit and the *Indian Mirror* are the only unselfish men in Bengal. Raja Subodh Mullick and Brajendra Kishore of Gauripore are notoriety-hunters who have chosen to pay heavily in cash and land for the titles of Raja and Maharaja. Babu Shishir Kumar Ghose is a humbug who poses as an Avatar; Babu Surendranath Banerji is a humbug who poses as a Martyr; there is a third patriotic humbug somewhere who poses as a Hero,— we cannot fix this gentleman at present. The country does not want these gentlemen at all; it wants people who can dare and die for their country. Whether this dying is to come about by fire and sword, and the claws of the British tiger, as the *Pioneer* threatens, or by influenza, cholera or fright, is not clear. We gather, however, that Mr. Palit and Babu Narendranath Sen have entered into a league to dare and die for their country, and we rejoice to hear it. While waiting for this glorious consummation, we would suggest to the latter that he might expect his martyrdom with more meekness and, secondly, that if he has to attack people, he might just as well cross his t's and dot his i's instead of employing the method of half-veiled allusions. It is a method which some people might call cowardly.

The *Englishman* still pegs away at his portentous discovery of a secret society with the romantic name. His knowledge about it increases every day. It is not a Chinsurah society, it appears, but a Calcutta affair which is especially active in Mymensingh. This ubiquitous monster seems to be under the direction of Tibetans: probably the Tashi Lama formed it when he came to Calcutta. For it appears that the word "Golden" is a piece of Oriental symbolism and is employed by the Tibetans to signify men who are sworn to die for this or that purpose. As a matter of fact, the word *Sonar* is an ordinary Bengali term of pride and affection no more mystic or symbolic than Shakespeare's "golden lads and girls". The *Englishman* seems determined to supply the absence of a good comic paper in Calcutta. Apparently its descent to anna-price has not increased its circulation.

Bande Mataram, September 8, 1906

The "Sanjibani" on Mr. Tilak

The *Sanjibani* pronounces in its last issue against Mr. Tilak, on the ground that he is unpopular. But unpopular with whom? With a certain section of the old Congress leaders. Is then unpopularity with a section to be a bar against filling the Presidential chair? If so, the circle of choice will become extremely limited; for just as there are some leaders who are unpopular with the ultra-moderate section, there are others who are unpopular with the advanced section. Mr. Gokhale, for instance, is by no means popular in his own country, the Deccan, especially since his notorious apology. His support of the boycott, qualified though it be, has somewhat rehabilitated him in the eyes of many, but he is still strongly distrusted by great numbers. Yet none dreamed of opposing his selection to the Presidential chair, on the mere ground of a partial unpopularity. If, however, the Congress leaders are going to publicly proclaim such a principle, it will be applied freely on both sides and the treasured "unanimity" of the Congress will disappear.

Secret Tactics

The telegram from our correspondent in Mymensingh, which we publish in another column, is extremely significant. It is now an open secret throughout the country that the Swadeshi movement has developed two distinct parties in the country. One of these desires to use Boycott as a political weapon merely in order to force on the annulment of the Partition and there finish; its quarrel with the bureaucracy is a passing quarrel and it is ready to be again hand in glove with the Government as soon as its turn is served; it still desires to sit on the Legislative Councils, figure on the Municipalities, and carry on politics by meetings and petitions. The other party will be satisfied with nothing less than absolute control over our own affairs and is not willing to help the Government to put off the inevitable day when that demand must be conceded; it is therefore opposed to any co-operation with the Government or to the adoption of a suppliant attitude in our relations to the Government; it desires the Boycott as a necessary part of our economic self-development and by no means to be relinquished even if the Partition be rescinded. Here are definite issues which have to be fought out until some definite settlement is reached. We desire the issue to be fought out on a fair field, each party seeking the suffrages of the country and attempting to educate the great mass of public opinion to its views. Unfortunately, the Leaders of the older school are not willing to give this fair field. They prefer to adopt a Machiavellian strategy and work in the darkness and by diplomatic strokes and secret *coup d'état*. They do not wish to work with the prominent and most militant members of the new school on the Reception Committee, they will not admit the country to their councils for fear the strength of the new school might increase, and they attempt to follow the example of the Fuller Government, to prevent them from holding public meetings. Recently the new school have put forward Mr. Tilak as the fittest name for the Presidentship, and the country has already begun to respond to the suggestion. The old leaders cannot publicly confess their reasons for not desiring Mr. Tilak, but they seem to be attempting cleverly to get out of the difficulty by bringing Mr. Dadabhai Naoroji over from England. We should have thought the Grand Old Man of India was a name too universally revered to be made the stalking-horse of a party move. But quite apart from this aspect of the question, we would draw attention to the indecorous and backstairs manner in which this important step is being made. It is the work of the Reception Committee to propose a President for the Congress; but the old leaders have been carefully avoiding any meeting of the Reception Committee and are meanwhile making all arrangements for the Congress and Exhibition secretly, unconstitutionally, and among a small clique. Had the name of Mr. Dadabhai Naoroji been proposed constitutionally in the Reception Committee, all would have been well; as it is, the most venerable name in India is in danger of being associated with a party stratagem carried through by unconstitutional means. Meanwhile, there is no reason why the meetings for Mr. Tilak's Presidentship should not be proceeded with; until the Reception Committee meets and Mr. Naoroji accepts an invitation from them, the question remains open. But the attitude of the old leaders shows a settled determination to exclude the new school from public life. If that be so, the present year will mark a struggle for the support of the country, and the control of the Congress which, however long it may last, can only have one end.

BY THE WAY

The *Indian Mirror* sympathises with the strikers, but is quite opposed to the strike. Workmen should not combine to get their rights; they must, like good slaves, appeal to the gracious generosity of their masters! The spirit of the serf which governed our agitation in pre-Swadeshi days, still disports itself in the columns of the *Mirror*, naked and unashamed.

*

We confess the pother the Anglo-Indian press has raised over the matter has surprised us. A certain amount of ridicule we expected, but that the Kamboliatola affair should be magnified into sedition and by people calling themselves sane! We are informed, though we can hardly credit it, that Hare Street has been at the expense of telegraphing columns of matter on the subject to England, apparently in order to convince the British public that Bengal has revolted and chosen a King. Verily, the dog-star rages.

*

Hare Street, having failed to impress the public with that fire-breathing seditious monster of Chinsurah, "Golden Bengal", turns sniffing round, nose to earth, for a fresh trail, and finds it in our own columns. We also, it appears, no less than Babu Surendranath and "Golden Bengal" have declared "open war" against King Edward VII; we wish to get rid of "British control". Beside this the manifesto of "Golden Bengal" fades into insignificance. That Indians should openly express their aspiration to govern themselves and yet remain out of jail is a clear sign that the British Empire is coming to an end.

*

The *Statesman* has at last come to the rescue anent the moral belabouring of Babu Surendranath Banerji for his *Shanti-Sechana* indiscretion. The *Statesman* sees two dangers looming through the dust which has been kicked up over the affair. One is that the ignorant peasantry may imagine a King has been crowned in India to whom they must give their allegiance. We confess this alarming idea never occurred to us; and when we spoke of Surendra Babu as King of independent Bengal, we thought we were indulging in a harmless jest. The *Statesman* has opened our eyes. It is an alluring idea and captivates our imagination. But what has happened to our sober-minded contemporary? Has the madness of the *Englishman* infested even him that he should see such alarming visions?

*

The other danger is that the Anglo-Indian Journals in their wild career may discredit constitutional agitation and play into the hands of the extremists. The extraordinary demoralisation of the Anglo-Indian press has indeed been painfully evident throughout the affair; but the *Statesman* does not see his friend's point of view. To Hare Street Babu Surendranath Banerji is not a moderate and constitutional leader, but a dangerous and fiery red revolutionist charging full tilt at British supremacy in India, with other revolutionists more or less scarlet in colour rushing on before or behind him. Hare Street has gone mad and, as is natural to a distracted John Bull, sees everything red. Sedition to right of him, sedition to left of him, sedition before and behind him, and through it all the *Englishman* like a heroic Light Brigade, charges in for King and Motherland.

Bande Mataram, September 10, 1906

The Question of the Hour

There is every sign that the issue on which the future of the national movement depends, will soon become very acute. Babu Bhupendranath Bose has put it with great frankness when he says that we must act in association with and not in opposition to the Government. In other words, the whole spirit which has governed the national movement, must be changed and we must go back to the policy of pre-Swadeshi days. This then is the issue before us. We declared a war of passive resistance against the bureaucracy on the 7th of August; and we understood that the struggle was not to end — till such a regime as Lord Curzon's should be rendered for ever impossible in the future. Are we now to declare peace and alliance with the bureaucracy and blot out the last twelve months from our history? Babu Ananda Chandra Ray made the proposal a little while ago; a much more considerable politician makes it today. It is for the country to judge.

A Criticism

Babu Naresh Chandra Sen Gupta, at a meeting of the Students' Union, made certain remarks upon the new party and the old. The spirit of the remarks was good, but the information on which they were based seems to be remarkably one-sided. He said, for instance: "The old leaders never forgot to take counsel with the new party; but the new party had spurned the old men." When, may we ask, except at Barisal where the new school was in a majority, did the old leaders take counsel with the new? Since then it has been the deliberate policy of the old leaders to exclude the new party from their counsels, and some influential men among them have even declared that they will not work with the principal men of that party. We do not pretend to dictate to the old leaders or to the Congress, or to any other public body; we wish to have an opportunity of pressing our views on the Congress as the views of increasing numbers in the country.

The future is ours and we are content to conquer it by degrees. But the determination of the old leaders is to give us no foothold on the present. A great and growing school of politics cannot consent to be treated in such cavalier fashion.

Bande Mataram, September 11, 1906

The Old Policy and the New

BABU Bhupendranath Bose has issued a manifesto of his views in the *Bengalee*, in which he explains his letter to the Secretary of the People's Association at Comilla. That document, it seems, was a private letter, although it was obviously intended to produce a public effect, *viz.* to prevent the nomination of Mr. Tilak and to counteract the effect of Babu Bepin Chandra Pal's meeting and speeches in Comilla. However, we have now an authoritative statement of Babu Bhupendranath's "policy", and no further misunderstanding is possible. This policy is precisely what we expected; it might have been penned in the pre-Partition and pre-Swadeshi days and amounts simply to the old Congress programme. We are to solicit Government help and favours as before, to oppose its measures when they are bad and, when they are very bad, to support this opposition "with the vital energy of the entire nation". But we are not to attempt to stand apart from the Government; we are not fit (because we have castes!) to stand among the self-governing countries of the world. We must therefore accept our subjection and wait for the golden days when we are thoroughly Europeanised, before we make any attempt to assert our national existence. At the same time, we may work out our own salvation in industrial matters, by such enterprises as the Banga Lakshmi Mill, in social matters by the abolition of caste, and even in educational matters by — but no, Babu Bhupendranath Bose has never been a friend of the National University idea. Such, when stripped of all verbiage, is the programme which Babu Bhupendranath sets before us, and since, in spite of his modest disclaimer, he has a commanding influence in determining the active policy of our leaders, his programme may be taken as the ultimate programme of his party.

We should like to know what Babu Bhupendranath precisely means by opposition to Government schemes. Except in extreme cases, so far as we understand him, he is opposed to bringing the vital energy of the nation to bear on the Government; and the only alternative policy is one of prayer and petition. It has been demonstrated repeatedly that prayer and petition have no appreciable influence on the British Government and that whatever slight influence it might have once had, has faded into nullity. It is only when the nation, finding its prayers and petitions rejected, begins to manifest its strength that the British Government inclines its ear and is graciously pleased to withdraw a circular, to dismiss a Fuller or to consider whether it can unsettle a settled fact. But Babu Bhupendranath argues that we cannot bring "the vital energies of the nation" to support opposition to any and every measure of Government. We are quite at one with him; but we cannot follow him in the strangely illogical conclusion he draws from this premise. He concludes from it that our right course is to trust to the broken weapon of remonstrance and futile petition in all but exceptional cases like the Partition. We conclude that our right course is not to waste unnecessary time over smaller matters, but to go to the root of the matter, the control over finance and legislation which is the basis of self-government and the first step towards autonomy.

The proposal of the old party is to use the great outburst of national strength which the Partition has evoked, in order to get the Partition rescinded, and then to put it back in the cupboard until again wanted. Such a policy will be absolutely suicidal. These outbursts can only come once or twice in a century, they cannot be evoked and ruled at the will of any leader, be he Surendranath Banerji or even a greater than Surendranath. Nor would such frequent outbursts benefit the country, but would rather, like frequent occasions of fever, weaken the nation and render it finally listless and strengthless. The problem for statesmanship at this moment is to organise and utilise the energy which has been awakened for an object of the first importance to our national development. The withdrawal of the Partition by itself will not improve the position of our race with regard to its rulers nor leave it one whit better than before Lord Curzon's regime. Even if the present Government were overflowing with liberal kindness, it cannot last for ever, and there is nothing to prevent another Imperialist Viceroy backed up by an Imperialist Government from perpetrating measures as injurious to the interests and sentiments of the nation. The only genuine guarantee against this contingency is the control by the nation of its own destinies, and to secure an effective instalment of this control should be the first aim of all our political action. No British Government will willingly concede anything in the nature of effective control. It can only be wrested from them by concentrating "the vital energies of the entire nation" into opposition to the Government and admitting of no truce until the desired end is secured. This is the kernel of the new party's policy and it differs entirely from Babu Bhupendranath's meaningless and futile programme.

Is a Conflict Necessary?

The old leaders are now telling the country that there is no need of a conflict as their ideals are identical with those of the new party, and it is only the latter who are heating themselves into a passion about nothing. The other day, Babu Naresh Chandra Sen Gupta in perfect good faith accepted this statement and declared it to the assembled students. But yesterday we learned that Babu Bhupendranath Bose insists on our working in association with the Government and not in opposition! This is emphatically not the ideal of the new party, for we are opposed to any accommodation with the Government which precedes or dispenses with the concession of effective self-government to the Indian people. We shall shortly make a succinct and definitive statement of our programme and demands; and if there is really no difference of ideals, if the whole quarrel is a misunderstanding and the old leaders are prepared not only to profess but to carry out those ideals in co-operation with the new party, the conflict will die a natural death. But it should be realised that without sincerity and frank openness no attempt at an understanding can be successful or worth making.

The Charge of Vilification

A charge which is being freely hurled against the new party is that they, or at least an active section of them, indulge in "vile abuse" of the old leaders. We do not care to deny that some of our writers and speakers are unsparing and outspoken in their attacks on individual leaders and that sometimes the bounds are passed. But this is a common incident of any political controversy under modern conditions. Both sides are guilty of such excesses. The correspondence to which the *Bengalee* has been recently giving a large part of its space is often of a poisonous virulence and an almost absurd violence of misrepresentation and the chief vernacular organ of the old party has no better claims to "respectability" in this respect than the most outspoken exponent of a more extreme policy. It is merely party passion which tries to ascribe all the violence and vilification to one side. These are inevitable concomitants of a party conflict and it will not do for either side to affect a sanctimonious spotlessness of demeanour; for the affectation will not bear scrutiny.

Autocratic Trickery

It is announced that Mr. Dadabhai Naoroji has accepted Babu Bhupendranath's offer of the Presidentship of the National Congress at Calcutta. No one was likely to oppose Mr. Naoroji as a President and had the proposal been brought forward constitutionally in the Reception Committee, the supporters of Mr. Tilak would have consented to postpone his name till the next year. But the Secret Cabal which is managing affairs in defiance of all rule and practice, were determined to score a party success and to use Mr. Naoroji, without his knowledge, as a tool for their ignoble purpose. They would face the supporters of Mr. Tilak with an accomplished fact, which they must either accept or incur the odium of opposing an universally respected name. They have followed a similar method with regard to the Exhibition which they have practically sold to the Government for a price. In this way, the Reception Committee is being turned into a farce and when they allow it to meet, it will find itself without occupation as all its functions have been performed for it behind its back. It becomes therefore the imperative duty of all who have any desire for national control over the national assembly to demand a settled elective constitution not only for the Congress but for every Congress body and law for its procedure which the leaders shall not be allowed to violate unless they are prepared to face a public impeachment from the platform of the Congress.

The Bhagalpur Meeting

The *Englishman* is very glad that Mr. Dadabhai Naoroji and not Mr. Tilak is going to preside at the National Congress, but it is also very glad of anything that can discredit Babu Surendranath Banerji. Its statement that the Bhagalpur meeting was very scantily attended while the *Bengalee* reckons 6,000 may be compared with the previous attempt of a correspondent in the *Bengalee* to prove that the population of Chittagong district was about the same as the computed audience of Babu Bepin Chandra Pal's mass meeting! Just as a Mymensingh adherent of petitionary politics declares that none of the leading men attended Bepin Babu's meeting at Mymensingh, so the *Englishman* declares that the Behari gentry and even the leading Bengalis held aloof from Babu Surendranath's Bhagalpur meeting. The *Bengalee* against the "extremists" and the *Englishman* against Mr. Banerji seem to be wonderfully unanimous! There is, however, one statement of the *Englishman*'s which is significant: "Some Behari students apparently taking the cue set by Calcutta, it alleges, created a disturbance, protesting against the proceedings. They intend, we learn, to call an indignation meeting." There is no breath of all this in the *Bengalee* which represents the meeting as crowded, enthusiastic and unanimous. We have seen some recent Calcutta meetings, very sparsely attended, which have been represented as numbering thousands. It is about time that some rein should be placed on the arithmetical imagination of reporters; otherwise we shall justify Lord Curzon's infamous attack by growing into a nation of exaggerators. We wish to know also whether there is any truth in the *Englishman*'s report of opposition. If there is opposition in Behar, it is better to know its extent and reasons than to burke it by a disingenuous silence.

BY THE WAY

The *Englishman* has been making all sorts of remarkable discoveries recently; its activity in this field is stupendous. Recently, it discovered the respectability of the Congress. Yesterday, it suddenly found out that Mr. Dadabhai Naoroji is an angel. A comparative angel, of course, but still an angel. He is pardoned all his wild and whirling speeches, his fiery denunciations of British rule, his immeasured expressions of condemnation; for will he not keep out Mr. Tilak from the Presidential Chair of the Calcutta Congress? Why is it that the very name of this man, with his quiet manner of speech, his unobtrusive simplicity and integrity, his absence of noisy and pushing "patriotism", is such a terror to Moderate and Anglo-Indian alike? Far more tactful and measured in speech than Mr. Naoroji, the idea of him yet causes them an ague. It is because he is the one man among us who sees clearly and acts. The man of action in the Presidential Chair of the Congress! The Anglo-Indian envisages the idea and sees in it the very image of his doom. Of course, it is the appearance of that wild new species, the "extremist", that is responsible for Mr. Naoroji's angelic transfiguration. There is a delightful flexibility about this word "extremist". It is imbued with a thoroughly progressive spirit and never stands still. Once quite within the memory of man, Babu Surendranath Banerji was an "extremist" but his scarlet coat is growing quite a dull and faded pink in these latter times. Mr. Dadabhai Naoroji was once denounced as a blatant extremist — that was the day before yesterday. But now that Mr. Shyamji Krishnavarma and his Home Rulers raise their wild heads above the terrified horizon, Mr. Naoroji is on a fair way to being admitted into the sacred fold of the "statesman-like" and "moderate". A still worse species of fire-breathing monster has recently turned up in the Bengal extremist. And we look forward with blissful hope to the day when the *Englishman* will learn to respect the "notorious Bepin Chandra Pal" and embrace him tearfully as the sole remaining bulwark against more anarchic monsters than himself. The upshot is that India progresses.

Bande Mataram, September 12, 1906

Strange Speculations

The *Statesman*, not content with lecturing the Bengali leaders, opens its news columns to curious speculations about the President of the next Congress. It is apparently not quite satisfied with Mr. Naoroji — a natural sentiment, since, whatever the moderates profess, Mr. Naoroji is not one of them, though he may not go the whole way with the advanced school. Accordingly, the name of Nawab Sayyed Mohammed is thrust forward — because he is a Mahomedan. The idea that the election of a Mahomedan President will conciliate the anti-Congress Mahomedans is a futility which has been repeatedly exposed by experience. Mr. Rasul's presidentship at Barisal has not conciliated the following of the Nawab of Dacca; such nominations can only gratify those Mahomedans who are already for the Congress. The question this year for the Congress is Swadeshi or no Swadeshi, Boycott or no Boycott, and no minor considerations can be admitted. A still more extraordinary piece of information is that Punjab will put up Lala Lajpat Rai against Mr. Tilak! We know, on the contrary, that Punjab is for Mr. Tilak and that Lala Lajpat Rai is the last man to countenance opposition to Mr. Tilak. In itself the candidature of Lala Lajpat Rai would not be unwelcome to the new party. He is one of those men who act, more than they talk, a man with a splendid record of solid patriotic work behind him and to him above all other belongs the credit of building up the Arya Samaj into the most powerful and practically effective organisation in the country. Were both Mr. Tilak and Mr. Naoroji to decline the Presidentship, Lala Lajpat Rai's would be the only other possible candidature.

The "Statesman" under Inspiration

An obviously inspired article appears in the *Statesman* in which a gallant attempt is made to misrepresent the issues before the country. It tries to convey the idea that the "extremists" have set up Mr. Tilak in opposition to Mr. Dadabhai Naoroji. As everybody is aware, it was not until Mr. Tilak's name was already put prominently before the country that the "moderate section", seeing no other way of avoiding the issue, bethought themselves of Mr. Naoroji. On the issue of representation or no representation our contemporary affects to be in doubt as to the position of the new party, and it discovers that the Bengali people are no longer unanimous against the Partition. How then can Mr. Morley reconsider the question? Need we inform the *Statesman* that the Bengali people are as unanimous against the Partition as they ever were and always will be? We do not doubt Mr. Morley's ability to find excuses for evading a concession which he has never meant to yield, unless his hand is forced. But the movement for a new representation is not only a contravention of the understanding which had existed among all parties since the last Town Hall meeting, but it was hatched in secret and engineered in secret. The country was not taken into confidence as to the motives or justification for this important departure. Had the old leaders acted straightforwardly in the matter and shown overwhelmingly strong reasons for the step, the leaders of the new party, although opposed on principle to the submission of new prayers and entreaties, might not have refused to countenance a strong and dignified representation which did not sacrifice in any degree the policy of Swadeshi and Boycott. Since they would not adopt this straightforward course, it is fair to conclude that the case for a new representation was too weak to be publicly presented. We have therefore every right to appeal to the country to maintain the policy hitherto successful. Tighten the grip of the Boycott, let both parties unite to give a new impetus to the Swadeshi; paralyse the two-headed administration of Bengal by every legitimate means of passive resistance — and the Partition will inevitably be rescinded or modified.

Bande Mataram, September 13, 1906

A Disingenuous Defence

The strictures which the extraordinary announcement made at Bhagalpur by Babu Surendranath Banerji has aroused, have compelled the *Bengalee* to offer a sort of apology or explanation for the unconstitutional action of the leaders. It was distinctly stated at Bhagalpur that Mr. Dadabhai Naoroji had accepted the Presidentship of the Congress. It follows, therefore, that the Presidentship was unconstitutionally offered to Mr. Naoroji by one or two individuals behind the back of the Reception Committee. It is now explained that Mr. Naoroji simply wired his willingness to accept the Presidentship offered to him. On this theory the offer was a private suggestion of individuals and the individuals made a public announcement of their private suggestion and its private acceptance, in order to compromise the Reception Committee and force its hands. The explanation therefore does not exculpate the authors of this stratagem; it only makes their action more disingenuous and tricky. No individual has any right to take privately the consent of Mr. Naoroji or another, as if the Presidentship depended on his choice. Until the Reception Committee has decided to whom it will offer the function, all that individuals, be they never so much leaders, have the authority to do is to put forward name or names for recommendation by the Committee. It is only after the Committee has made its decision that the person selected can be asked whether he is willing to accept the offer. If it is thought necessary to make sure of this beforehand, that also can only be done with the sanction or by the direction of the Committee. The fact that the *Bengalee* should have advanced such a puerile quibble to justify the conduct of Babu Bhupendranath is a proof that these "constitutional" leaders have no conception whatever of what constitutional action means. The plea that it had long been known Mr. Naoroji was coming to India and it was therefore thought fit to ask him to preside at the Congress, is one which will command no credit. When did this "fitness" occur to men who were proposing Harram Singh and Mudholkar and everybody and anybody, but never Mr. Naoroji; although it was known that he was coming to India? Not until Mr. Tilak's name was before the country and they saw that none of the mediocrities they had suggested could weigh in the scale with the great Maratha leader. Not by these sophisms will the Calcutta autocrats escape the discredit of their actions.

Bande Mataram, September, 14 1906

The Friend Found Out

Our frank criticism of the political ideals in regard to India, of the Anglo-Indian leaders of the Congress has revealed the old "Friend of India" in his true colour. This friend who could not in the last century brook the thought that there was anything worthy of reverence in the spiritual ideals of the Hindu and fell foul of Rammohan Roy for his advocacy of rational and spiritual Hinduism cannot now be patient with those who claim the common right of humanity to manage its own affairs and realise its own divinely appointed destiny without foreign interference and control. We have long ceased to believe in the sincerity of the sympathy of the British middle class who thrives upon our serfdom, with our civic and economic needs and aspirations. The *Statesman*'s ill-tempered attack on us comes not therefore as a surprise and if it acts as an eye-opener to our infatuated "moderate" friends, we shall feel ourselves more than amply compensated for the hysterical and violent attack inspired by a nervous anticipation of the inevitable. But perhaps we are misjudging our friend, for though the hand is the hand of Jacob, the voice is the voice of Esau.

"An open foe may prove a curse,
But a pretended friend is worse."

Stopgap Won't Do

Even *India* has sometimes a ray of light in the midst of its twilight obscurity and crass lack of insight. Thus saith the organ of the Cottons and Wedderburns: "Mr. Morley will not be Secretary of

State for India for ever and a day. So long as he is at the helm, the prow of the ship will be set in the right direction. But what will happen when his controlling hand is removed?" Precisely so, Mr. Morley may set the prow in the right direction, but it is perfectly evident from his public statements that he is not prepared to travel fast or far; on the contrary he is utterly against any decision and effective treatment of the intolerable situation in India. He is simply going to repeat an experiment which has failed and is out of date. We shall therefore gain little during his lease of power — and afterwards? Who shall secure us against another Curzonian reaction? We therefore say that an instalment of effective self-government is the one thing which the Congress should insist on because it is the one thing which will make reaction impossible. We farther contend that an effective instalment of self-government not only ought to be but must inevitably be the first step towards complete autonomy. For the statement of these plain and indisputable truths we must, forsooth, be dubbed "seditionists" and "extremists", not only by Anglo-Indian papers for whose opinion we do not care a straw, but by Indian Journals professing to be nationalist. There could not be a greater evidence of the dull servility of attitude, the fear of truth and the unworthy timidity which has become ingrained in our habits of mind by long acquiescence in servitude. If these things are sedition, then we are undoubtedly seditious and will persist in our sedition till the end of the chapter.

BY THE WAY

The *Bengalee* came out on Sunday with an extraordinary leader in which it appeals to its opponents to sink all personal differences and unite in one common cause. The better to further this desirable end it kicks them severely all round so as to bring them into a reasonable state of mind. The opponents of the *Bengalee* are all actuated by base personal motives; their organs of opinion are upstart journals trying to create a sensation; their championing of advanced political principles is a trick of the trade, etc. etc. And *therefore* the *Bengalee* appeals to them to be friendly, toe the line and follow faithfully in the wake of Babu Surendranath Banerji. Does our contemporary really think that this is the sort of appeal which is likely to heal the breach?

*

The praise and approval of the Anglo-Indian papers, says the *Bengalee* wisely, is a sure sign that we are on the wrong road. Let the galled jade wince, our withers are unwrung. On this principle, we ought to go on our way rejoicing. If there is one pleasing feature of the present situation, it is the remarkable unanimity with which the Anglo-Indian Press has greeted our appearance in the field with a shriek of denunciation and called on Heaven and Earth and the Government and the Moderates to league together and crush us out of existence. *Statesman* and *Englishman*, *Times* and *Pioneer*, all their discordant notes meet in one concord on this grand swelling theme. The "moderate" papers of all shades, pro-Government or advocates of association with Government or advocates of association-cum-opposition, have all risen to the call. The *Hindu Patriot* rejoices at our lack of influence, the *Mirror* threatens us with the prison and the scaffold, the *Bengalee* mutters about upstart journals and warns people against the morass which is the inevitable goal, in its opinion, of a forward policy. Well, well, well! Here is an extraordinary and most inexplicable clamour about an upstart journal and a party without influence or following in the country.

*

The *Statesman* is taking its cue from the *Mirror* and is growing very truculent and minatory. It is not going to give us any quarter, this merciless "Friend of India", but will abolish, expunge and blot us out of existence in no time. It will not consent to support Indian aspirations unless we consent to perform *hara-kiri*. It will advise its friend Mr. Morley to make no concession, no, not even increase the number of our Legislative Honourables, until even the very scent of a "sedition" can no longer be sniffed in the Indian breezes.

Bande Mataram, September 17, 1906

Is Mendicancy Successful?

An apologia for the mendicant policy has recently appeared in the columns of the *Bengalee*. The heads of the defence practically reduce themselves to two or three arguments.

1. The policy of petitioning was recommended by Raja Rammohan Roy, has been pursued consistently since then, and has been eminently successful — at least whatever political gains have been ours in the last century, have been won by this policy.

2. Supposing this contention to be lost, there remains another. There petitioning is bad, but when the petition is backed by the will of the community, resolved to gain its object by every legitimate means, it is not mendicancy but an assertion of a natural right.

3. Even if a petitioning policy be bad in principle, politics has nothing to do with principles, but must be governed by expediency, and not only general expediency, but the expediency of particular cases.

4. Then there is the *argumentum ad hominem*. The Dumaists petition, the Irish petition, why should not we?

We believe this is a fair summary of our contemporary's contentions.

We are not concerned to deny the antiquity of the petitioning policy, nor its illustrious origin. Raja Rammohan Roy was a great man in the first rank of active genius and set flowing a stream of tendencies which have transformed our national life. But what was the only possible policy for him in his times and without a century of experience behind him, is neither the only policy nor the best policy for us at the present juncture. We join issue with our contemporary on his contention that whatever we have gained politically has been due to petitioning. It appears to us to show a shallow appreciation of political forces and an entire inability to understand the fundamental facts which underlie outward appearances. When the sepoys had conquered

India for the English, choice lay before the British, either to hold the country by force and repression or to keep it as long as possible by purchasing the co-operation of a small class of the people who would be educated so entirely on Western lines as to lose their separate individuality and their sympathy with the mass of the nation. An essential part of this policy which became dominant owing to the strong personalities of Macaulay, Bentinck and others, was to yield certain minor rights to the small educated class, and concede the larger rights as slowly as possible and only in answer to growing pressure. This policy was not undertaken as the result of our petitions or our wishes, but deliberately and on strong grounds. India was a huge country with a huge people strange and unknown to their rulers. To hold it for ever was then considered by most statesmen a chimerical idea; even to govern it and keep it tranquil for a time was not feasible without the sympathy and co-operation of the people themselves. It was therefore the potential strength of the people and not the wishes of a few educated men, which was the true determining cause of the scanty political gains we so much delight in. Since then the spirit of the British people and their statesmen has entirely changed — so changed that even a Radical statesman like Mr. Morley brushes aside the expressed "will of the community" with a few abrupt and cavalier phrases. Why is this? Precisely because we have been foolish enough to follow a purely mendicant policy and to betray our own weakness. If we had not instituted the National Congress, we might have continued in the old way for some time longer, getting small and mutilated privileges whenever a strong Liberal Viceroy happened to come over. But the singularly ineffective policy and inert nature of the Congress revealed to British statesmen — or so they thought — the imbecility and impotence of our nation. A period of repression, ever increasing in its insolence and cynical contempt for our feelings, has been the result. And now that a Liberal Government of unprecedented strength comes into power, we find that the gains we can expect will be of the most unsubstantial and illusory kind and that we are not to get any guarantee against their being withdrawn by another reactionary Viceroy after a few years. It is perfectly clear therefore that the policy of mendicancy will no longer serve. After all, cries the *Bengalee*, we have only failed in the case of the Partition. We have failed in everything of importance for these many years, measure after measure has been driven over our prostrate heads and the longed-for Liberal Government flouts us with a few grudging concessions in mere symptomatic cases of oppression. The long black list of reactionary measures remains and will remain unrepealed. We do not care to deny that in small matters petitioning may bring us a trivial concession here or a slight abatement of oppression there, even there we shall fail in nine cases and win in one. But nothing important, nothing lasting, nothing affecting the vital questions which most closely concern us, can be hoped for from mere mendicancy. To the contention of antiquity and success, therefore, our answer is that this antique policy has not succeeded in the long run, but utterly failed, and that the time has come for a stronger and more effective policy to take its place. To the other contentions of the *Bengalee* we shall reply in their proper order. This which is the true basis of the petitionary philosophy has neither reason nor fact to support it.

BY THE WAY

The *Englishman* is at it again. His fiery imagination has winged its way over rivers and hills and is now disporting itself on airy pinions over far Sylhet. We learn from our contemporary that the British Government has been subverted in Sylhet, which is now being governed by a number of schoolboys who — horrible to relate — are learning the use of deadly *lathi*. This startling resolution is the result of Babu Bepin Chandra Pal's recent visit to Sylhet. To crown these calamities, it appears that Golden Bengal is circulating its seditious pamphlets broadcast. Its irrepressible emissaries seem not to have despaired even of converting the Magistrate to their views, for even he is in possession of a copy. We have, however, news later than the *Englishman*'s. We have been informed from a reliable source that the Sylhet

Republic has been declared and that Babu Bepin Chandra Pal is to be its first President.

*

The *Englishman* graciously accedes to the request of a correspondent who prays this "much-esteemed journal to accommodate the following lines". There are some gems from the delicious production which the accommodating *Englishman* has accommodated. "We should always beg the Government and not fight it for favours." Fighting for favours is distinctly good; but there is better behind. "It is impossible for us to obtain rights and privileges by fulminating acrimonious invectives on the Government and making the Anglo-Indian rulers the butt-end of mendacious persiflage and anathema." Shade of Jabberjee! The junior members of the Bar Library will enjoy this elegant description of themselves. "For ought I know most of the educated men are opposed to the despicable spread-eagleism of a coterie of raw youths, who having adopted European costumes and rendered their upper lips destitute of "knightly growth" give themselves all the airs of a learned Theban and range themselves against the British Government." This is a sentence which we would not willingly let die and we would suggest to the raw youths with the destitute upper lips that they might sit in council and devise means to preserve a literary gem which will immortalise them no less than the brilliant author. How infinitely superior is the true Jabberjee to the mock imitation. Even the author of the letter to Mr. Morley must hide his diminished head before this outburst.

*

This attitude of the Extremists merely exposes their Boeotian stupidity. Let them lay to it, that if they do not yet refrain from the obnoxious procedure, they are sure to come to grief. We will lay to it, S.M. After such a scintillation of Attic wit and rumbling of Homeric thunder, our Boeotian stupidity finds itself irremediably reduced to Laconic silence. Truly, there seems to be some fearful and wonderful wild fowl in the ranks of the moderationists.

Bande Mataram, September 18, 1906

Mischievous Writings

The leading article in last Tuesday's *Mirror*, reproduced in another column, shows the peculiar frame of mind that finds safety both from bold thoughts and brave sacrifices, in its professions of friendship and loyalty to the foreigner. The *Indian Mirror* gives an assurance to his Anglo-Indian friends that there is no danger to the Empire from the insignificant band of "extremists" who preach the pernicious doctrines of national autonomy and popular freedom; and we hope, it will give rest and sleep to the Chowringee paper. The *Mirror* says: —

"To say that educated India desires to be absolutely free of the British control is absolutely idiotic, and we are sure every thoughtful and cultured Indian will *resent* such a suggestion with the utmost *indignation*."

But why *resent*, my brother? And where is there any room for indignation here, either? It may be idiotic, we admit, for we are sure that the *Indian Mirror* with all its conceits would not dare to claim an absolute monopoly of this virtue for itself and those who think with it. But this indignation is difficult to understand unless the Ophelia of old has taken to play the part of Godiva with the whole lot of British friends as his spouse, in his old age. Go on, thou brave queen, ride in all thy nudeness through the country, and we shall close our doors, put down our blinds, and desert every thoroughfare until thou comest to thy journey's end.

A Luminous Line

There is, however, one sentence in this lengthy leader of the *Mirror* which is, after all, very reassuring even to the extremists.

Our amiable contemporary unconsciously admits that *absolute* autonomy is not an absolutely sinful ideal even for the people of this country, who are head over ears burdened with a debt immense of endless gratitude to their British rulers; — only, we must first of all be fit for it.

"We have not as yet gone through our preliminary training and such a thing as *absolute* autonomy would *just now* be an evil rather than a blessing to us."

So says the *Mirror*, and it shows us how slowness of thought and understanding may exist in some minds, with a lightning-swiftness of fearful imagination. Take heart, dear friend, we do not propose to procure a *decree nisi* now and at once, and set you free immediately. What we say is that for this preliminary training, which even you would not object to, a clear perception of the end is necessary, in both trainer and trained; the one needs it for right guidance, and the other for diligent pursuit of the goal. Fear not, soft soul, we are not so heartless as to disturb your sweet slumber so soon!

BY THE WAY

The *Statesman* and the *Indian Mirror* appear to have entered into a Holy Alliance for the suppression of the extremists. The basis of this great political combination seems to be mutual admiration of the most effusive and affectionate kind. *Mirror* assures *Statesman* that he is a noble Anglo-Indian and a true and tried Friend of India; *Statesman* quotes *Mirror*'s solemn lucubrations by the yard. It only needs the *Hindu Patriot* to join the league and complete the Triple Alliance. An Anglo-Indian paper, a Government journal masking under the disguise of an Indian daily, and the exponent of the most pale and watery school of "patriotism", would make a beautiful symphony in whites and greys. Such an alliance is most desirable: it would be a thing of artistic beauty and a joy forever — and it would not hurt the new party.

*

We were a little surprised to find the *Bengalee* lending itself to the campaign. It chooses to insinuate that while the methods of the old party are extremely proper, sober and legal, those of the new party are outside the bounds of the law. In what respect, pray? We advocate boycott and picketing, but that is a gospel of which Babu Surendranath Banerji has constituted himself in the past the chief Panda. We advocate abstention from Legislative Councils and other Government bodies, but so do the old leaders strongly recommend it — to East Bengal. We advocate the assertion by the people of their right to carry on the agitation in every lawful way — but so did the old leaders at Barisal. We advocate abstention from all association with the Government, but such abstention has not yet been forbidden by law. We advocate the substitution of Indian agency and Indian energy in every department of life for our old state of dependence on foreign agency and energy. We advocate an organised system of self-development guided by a Council with regard to Bengal and an open democratic constitution for the Congress instead of the secret unconstitutional manipulations of a few leaders. We advocate finally, autonomy as the ideal and goal of our endeavours. Where is the illegality, if you please?

*

To listen to these excited people one would imagine we were calling on the teeming millions of India to rise in their wrath, fall upon the noble Anglo-Indian friends of the *Mirror* and with teeth, nails and claws, drive them pell-mell into the Indian Ocean. All these imputations have, of course, a definite object and the excitement is a calculated passion. On one side to discredit the party with the timid and cautious, on the other to draw the attention of the bureaucracy and secure for us free lodgings from a paternal Government, seems to be the objective. Of neither contingency are we afraid; the new policy is not for those who tremble or who prefer their own safety and ease to the service of their country, and the fear of the Government we renounced long ago and have forgotten what it means. It is no use trying to awaken that dead feeling in our nature. We shall go on our way steadily and persistently, careless of defeat or victory, indifferent to attack or suffering, until we have built up such a nucleus of force and courage in India as will compel both moderate and official to yield to the demands of the people. But always within the bounds of the law, if you please, our friend of Colootola. We are a law-abiding people, even when we are extremists.

*

We have been severely attacked more than once for splitting up the country into factions and thus marring the majestic unity of the national movement. We have already given our answer to that charge. Already before the Swadeshi movement the divergence of ideals had begun to declare itself and in several parts of India strong sections had grown up who were already dissatisfied with mendicancy and with the haphazard formation and methods of the Congress. Until recently the only course which seemed left to men of this persuasion was to hold entirely aloof from the Congress or else to attend it without taking any prominent part in its deliberations. But at the present time the aspect of things has greatly changed. The party predominates in the Deccan, is extremely strong in the Punjab and a force to be reckoned with in Bengal. It numbers among its leaders and adherents many men of ability, energy and culture some of whom have done good service in the past and others are obviously among the chief workers of the future. They have a definite ideal which is not the ideal of the older leaders and definite methods by which they hope to arrive at their ideal. It is idle to expect that a party so constituted will any longer consent to be excluded from political life or from the deliberations of the Congress through which it may exercise a general influence over the country. The old party is anxious that we should take up the position of an insignificant "extremist" party, tolerated perhaps and sometimes made use of to frighten the Government into concessions, but not recognised. "Exist, if you please, but do not interfere with or oppose us," is their cry, "and do not try to assert yourselves in the Congress." Such a demand is ridiculous in the extreme. When there is a definite difference as to ideals and methods, it is too much to expect of any growing party that it shall not use every means to educate the people to their views and organise such opinion as has declared itself on their side. Nor is it reasonable to demand a considerable part of the educated community to banish itself from Congress or only attend as a mute and inert element. If the Congress is really a national body, it must admit all opinions and give them free facility for expressing their views and urging their measures. If, on the other hand, it is merely a gathering of moderates, it has no right to pose as a national body. The argument usually urged that the Congress has been built up by a certain class of people and with certain ideas and that therefore it should remain in the same hands and under the domination of the same ideas, is one which has no value whatever, unless we are to accept the Congress merely as a society for the cultivation of good relations with the Government. If it is a national assembly, it must answer to changes of national feeling and progress with the progress of the nation. We shall therefore persist in disseminating our ideas with the utmost energy of which we are capable and in organising the opinion of the country wherever we have turned it in the desired direction, for action and for the prevalence of our ideals. The only question that remains, is the question of united action. It is certainly desirable, if it can be brought about, that the action of the whole country in certain important matters should be united. But the very first condition of such unity is that all important sections of opinion should have the chance of expressing its views and championing its own proposals, before the united action to be taken is decided by a majority. It is for this reason that we demand an elective constitution and a Council honestly representing all sections, so that real unity may be possible and not the false unity which is all the old party clamours for. Their plan for united action is simply to boycott the new party and impose silence on it under penalty of "suppression". So long as they persist in that spirit, united action will remain impossible.

Bande Mataram, September 20, 1906

BY THE WAY

To the onlooker the duel between the *Statesman* and the *Englishman* is extremely amusing. The interests of Anglo-India are safe in the hands of both; only they differ as to the extent to which the alien yoke should be made light. The *Englishman* advocates an open and straightforward course — to make the Indians feel that they are a conquered people — as helpless in the hands of the conquerors as was the dwarf of the story in the iron grip of the giant. The *Statesman*, on the other hand, wants to cover the heels of British boots with soft velvet. We for ourselves prefer an open course to a crooked policy.

*

The fun of the thing is that from consideration of methods they have descended to personalities. The *Englishman* credits the *Statesman* with the instinct to follow Mr. Surendranath Banerji with doglike fidelity. To this the *Statesman* replies — "Strange as it may appear to the *Englishman*, we are in the habit of forming our own opinions and of expressing them without any extraneous assistance — even from the Bar Library, or elsewhere. Mr. Banerji has certainly not done us the honour of tendering his help, nor have we found it necessary to invite it." We take our contemporary at his word. But we may be permitted to ask our contemporary if the paragraph about the *New India* to which we referred the other day was not written under some extraneous inspiration, — white or brown? Next, our Chowringhee contemporary boasts of his independent policy and fearless proclamation of it. "In order," says our contemporary, "to attain a wide circulation and a position of influence, it is not enough to follow the example which this journal set a quarter of a century ago by reducing its price to an anna. If the *Englishman* is ever again to become a force in journalism, it must copy the *Statesman* in matters of greater importance than the mere cost of its daily issue. It must learn to have an honest and independent policy and to proclaim it fearlessly." And our contemporary seems to think that man's lapses like their civil claims are barred by limitation, or he has a very conveniently short memory, or how could he otherwise so soon forget the dangerous position he was placed in at the time of the Rent Bill controversy and the way out he found by removing Mr. Riach, the responsible editor?

*

After all we do not despair. There is yet some hope left for our contemporary, for he can still understand that — "it is possible for a newspaper, as for an individual, to err at times and honestly to advocate views which may be mistaken."

*

The *Indian Mirror* has, after all, found one good point in the armour of the "extremists"; they will not stand any humbug, says our ancient contemporary, and no one will dare question the truth of his opinion, for he speaks clearly from personal experience.

*

Babu Surendranath Banerji is reported to have advised the youthful students of Bally — "to keep themselves within the limits of law and never, in their excitement, run into excesses but always to serve their motherland with unflinching devotion, through *good report and evil*", and the old leader is right, because the latest experience shows that Indian publicists and patriots have good reason to stand in fear of reports.

*

The *Indian Mirror* is surprised that we are resting on our oars when the Congress-bark should be fast sailing. The light that the *Mirror* is reflecting is both dim and antiquated in these days of radium and X-rays. Our information is that the "recognised" leaders are making arrangements for the Congress though even the *Mirror* has not been taken into their confidence.

*

The old saw was that a mountain in labour produced a mouse. But the modern saw is that the Indian politicians in labour produce speeches and interviews. Somehow the information has leaked out that the Hon'ble Mr. Gokhale's recent visit to England has not been much of a success. Now Sir William Wedderburn comes to the rescue of the Bombay patriot and says that the Hon'ble gentleman had a series of interviews with eminent British politicians from the Prime Minister down to 150 pro-Indian M.P's. Achievement indeed!

*

"Star to star vibrates light" — is there also a similar responsiveness between mind and matter, or else why should there be so fearful a tremor in mother earth, keeping time, as it were, to the nervous tremours of the bold British and the timid Indian heart, at the present unrest in Bengal caused by *Sonar Bangla* and the *Shanti-Sechan*?

Bande Mataram, October 1, 1906

BY THE WAY

Mr. Gopal Krishna Gokhale is a mathematician and these mathematicians are a wonderful people. They can prove anything they please. If Mr. Gokhale's political opponents are numerous, he applies the qualitative test, and shakes his head — "no good"; if they are not many, he applies the quantitative test and turns his nose up at — "too poor!" Anyhow, what was required to be demonstrated has been demonstrated, Q.E.D.

*

Is Narendranath Sen among the boycotters? — enquires the *Englishman*, else how has he put his name on the Rakhi-Circular, which asks people to renew their boycott vow on the Rakhi-Day? Will Babu Narendranath send a copy of his *Subliminal Consciousness* (sic) to his Hare Street brother to illumine the situation? That, or the *Isis Unveiled*, will explain all.

*

The *Bengalee* is in mortal agony because of the prolonged "tension between the rulers and the ruled". Love's quarrels never last long, we know. But how to make these up? The traditional Dooti must be called in, and Morley and Minto must play Brinda and get about a re-union between the forlorn *Bengalee* and their discarded Lords. "Call them back, for old love's sake, or we cannot live — outside the Council Chambers," — cries the widowed *Bengalee*. The Rakhi-Day is coming, and love-bands will be distributed to all the world, except only to him whose association makes the world sweet! Oh the bitterness of it!

*

"The demonstrations of last year passed off without any excesses of any kind and without any breaches of the law. The same temper animates us now. The triumphs of constitutionalism are writ large on the pages of the year's history." Thus perorates the *Bengalee* in its appeal for the coming Rakhi-celebrations. "The triumphs of constitutionalism!" but of whose constitution: of the *Bengalee* or of the British?

*

Empire Portents — Following the portentous tremors of mother earth came, says the *Empire*, the capture of "a huge Boal fish at the Haldi river. It measured six feet and was unusually swollen." What was swollen, the editor does not say — the feet, the tail, or the fish itself? When cut open, however, a dead jackal was found inside! When doors are "crossed", and trees are marked, and jackals are found inside greedy Boal fish, and there is the murderous cry of *Bande Mataram* all over the land, judgment cannot, surely, be far away.

*

Many things, the world knows, have saving power, but that a striking metaphor could save a Conference was not known to us before. But this seems actually to have happened recently at Umballa. When the Legislative Council Resolution came up for discussion, there suddenly developed a rift in the lute. Everybody agreed to the view that "the Punjab Council as at present constituted serves no useful purpose". The New Party, with their acknowledged partiality for inconvenient logic, wanted to add, "and it may as well be abolished". The logic of it was dreadfully strong, and the amendment was pressed on the Conference and debated upon. But the situation was saved by a "statesmanly metaphor" from Lala Murlidhar, the well-known poet-politician of Umballa. "Do men cut down a tree because its fruit is unripe or happens *to be bitter* or worm-eaten? Do men raze to the ground a house that leaks?" After this, the amendment was bound to be negatived and the Resolution carried. Lala Murlidhar has discovered the art evidently of making sunshine out of cucumber, and pressing sweet honey out of bitter almond!

*

An additional proof of the tremendous work the "Moderates" have been doing in the country was found by the last Provincial Conference at Umballa. It passed a number of Resolutions asking the Government to *do* this and *undo* that thing; but when it was proposed that a Committee or Association should be started "to establish and help District Associations," the Conference left it, we are told, "*untouched*".

*

Mr. Gokhale resolves the complexities of the present problem in Bengal into "private quarrels and personal jealousies" — Burke was right when he said that he had known great statesmen with the intellect of pedlars; yet Burke did not know us of modern India.

*

Is Mr. Gokhale also among the extremists? He advises the Bengalis to agitate "in statesmanlike and reasonable manner" and explaining these terms, says —

The Boers have got self-government by fighting manfully. The Irish will get self-government within a year or so. We must keep their examples before our eyes. And everything will be easy, he adds, if we imitate their ways — and perhaps finish with an object — but our policy interdicts all personalities.

Bande Mataram, October 10, 1906

BY THE WAY

Emerson and original sin have never as yet gone together. But Principal Herambachandra Moitra has achieved the impossible. Lecturing to a Bombay congregation on a Wednesday he solemnly declared that "even children themselves are not free from sin," and on the following Sunday discoursed on "Emerson". Poor sage of Concord!

*

Calcutta is going to have a *Tower of Silence* — for the Parsis. The *Patrika* would, however, seem to hold that it is more needed by our own patriots. They evidently permit writing in that dreadful place.

*

A "veteran" laments the decay of manners among the people of this country, in the hospitable columns of the *Pioneer*. There was a time, only forty years ago, when on the approach of a European, Indian lads would cry — "Gora ata Gora ata" — and skid. When the same class of lads now "pass a European with a cigarette between their lips and stare him calmly in the face," and a "large number of natives salaam with their left hands" — the world or the British Empire, which means the same thing, must be nearing its end.

*

Bengal politicians seem determined to maintain the ancient reputation of the nation for its logical acumen and subtlety. The Barisal Conference resolved *not* to send any prayer or petition to Government; when the Conference was forcibly dispersed, the leaders sent a wire to the Viceroy on the ground that a telegram was surely not a petition. They have resolved not to approach the Lieutenant-Governor of the partitioned Province with any prayer or address, but may still draw their Honours' "serious attention" to various matters, public and personal, including the gift of a Deputy Magistracy to their sons. Surely a cosy place in the Executive Service is *not* a membership of the Legislative Council.

*

There is considerable indignation among the true "Friends of India", both in England and in this country, at the "political oration" delivered by Mr. Manmatha Chandra Mullik at the recent Tyabji memorial meeting in London. After this we shall be told that it would be sinful to discourse on religion at a commemoration service in honour of Lord Bishop of Canterbury, or to speak on science at a memorial meeting of a President of the British Association. We think at the recent Tyabji Bose meeting in London, Babu Romesh Chandra Dutta must have discoursed, therefore, on the greatness of Islam, and Sir Henry Cotton on the saving grace of Brahmo-Theology. We anxiously await full reports of their speeches.

Bande Mataram, October 11, 1906

The Coming Congress

WITH the usual practice of frail humanity to give a dog a bad name, and then hang him, some of our up-country contemporaries, of the so-called Moderate Party, have been trying to make it out that the New Party is responsible for all the sins of omission and commission that are found in this part of the country in regard to the work of the coming session of the Congress. A Reception Committee was organised many months ago, but no meeting of it has as yet been held, and the New Party must be responsible for it, even if it be a fact that not one of the Secretaries of the Committee, who alone are competent to convene a meeting of that body, belongs to their ranks. The Executive Committee of the Reception Committee have not yet been elected, and who must be blamed for this except the dreadful Extremists? The work of the Congress, the construction of the Pandal, the raising of funds, and a thousand other things upon which the success of the show will depend, and which require timely preparation, have not yet been taken in hand; and for this also, these mischievous men are responsible. This is the summary verdict of our honourable friends both here and elsewhere.

And in one sense, and only in one, they are right. The difficulty is due to us, — to our presence in the country, even though it may not be to our interference or obstruction. The old leaders would like to do everything according to their sweet will and pleasure, outraging at every point whatever constitution the Congress has. But the New Party will not be likely to permit these autocratic ways even in the Congress; and that is the difficulty. The Executive Committee has not been formed because of the fear lest any strong complement of these "Extremists" should get in there. No meeting of the Reception Committee has been called, lest the New Party get a chance of having their views and ideas inconveniently impressed upon the sacred functions of the Congress. They are *not* wanted: but they cannot by a mere pious wish, be got rid of either. Hence all this trouble.

And this being so, what, we ask, would the *Hindu* or the *Madras Standard*, or even the *Indian Mirror* want us to do? Do our contemporaries want us to commit *hara-kiri* so that their Moderate friends might be in undisputed possession of the Congress and arrange its work and programme, in accordance with their sweet will and pleasure? They might consider this act of suicide on our part as a noble sacrifice for the country's cause. But we have not, unfortunately, risen as yet to that height of theosophic unity, where Babus Bhupendranath and Surendranath might symbolise Bengal, Messrs. Mehta and Watcha Bombay, and about half a dozen Moderates and Loyal Patriots India.

The fact, really, is that not the New Party but the old one is responsible for the confusion in which Congress-matters seem to stand just now in Calcutta. All that we want is that the constitution of the Congress, its unwritten laws and traditions, should be faithfully observed and obeyed. If this is done, there will be no difficulty, even if we should fail to carry our particular views or programme through the Reception Committee. We have repeatedly said this from the press and the platform alike. But some people have a wonderful knack of not understanding things that place them in awkward positions.

The *Madras Standard* does us scant justice when it puts into our mouth that "if any man of whose nomination to the Congress Presidency" we "cannot approve is chosen for the office," our Party will signify "their disapproval of the same in the form of an amendment to the resolution formally voting the President to the chair." This is not our position. Whomsoever the Reception Committee may, in consultation with the Congress Committees of the other presidencies, where such Committees really exist, elect, will be accepted by us, if the election is properly and constitutionally made. If, however, any attempt is made to spring an Anglo-Indian or British President on the Reception Committee at the last moment, and the nomination is carried by any *coup d'état*, then, we shall have to reserve to ourselves the right of moving an amendment, upon a question of principle, even as we shall be bound to do, if the Subjects Committee should accept any Resolution against which we may have any fundamental objection.

But why, indeed, should it be thought so outrageous on the part of a delegate to move such an amendment, when any popular man is kept, — by a small cabal — out of the Presidential Chair? Mr. Tilak's name has been presented to the Reception Committee: if the Reception Committee reject it, on the ground that Bombay, *i.e.*, Mr. Mehta and Mr. Watcha and Mr. Gokhale do not wish to have him, or that Bengal, *i.e.*, Babus Surendranath and Bhupendranath and Krishnakumar consider him to be unsafe, or that a few Moderates in Madras feel nervous about him, — then, why should it be so wrong for those who are not within the charmed circle of Mr. Gokhale's "responsible leaders", to demand an open poll at the Congress itself? That the President-elect is formally proposed and seconded and elected by a vote of the delegates, gives itself the right to any delegate to oppose the motion or move an amendment to it. If such a thing has not yet happened in the Congress, it is because so long there were not two Parties in the Congress with two distinct policies and programmes. There has, of late grown two such Parties at least, and if not this year, the next, or the year after, some day — either of them will seek to make the Congress an organ of their own opinions. Politics and patriotism have ceased to be pastimes with us; and the amenities of the playground cannot be expected in the field of vital conflicts and competitions. But the possibility of such conflicts need cause no nervousness in any quarter, for these will not kill, but rather breathe life and reality into the movement.

We want Mr. Tilak, as any other Congress-man or any other section or party of the Congress might desire to have another person for the Congress Presidency. Babus Bhupendranath and Surendranath stole a march upon us by asking Mr. Naoroji if he would come, in case he was duly elected by the Reception Committee. They did not play fair, but still if Dadabhai Naoroji comes, we will raise no difficulty, provided the Reception Committee formally elects him. Our attitude will be the same with regard to any other man also. But if any name is suddenly sprung upon us at the last moment, if the opinions of the other Provinces are taken in an underhand way, if names are passed at meetings due notice of which was not given — then every delegate will have just grounds to publicly oppose such an unauthorised and unconstitutional nomination for the Congress Presidency. Will the *Hindu* or the *Standard* refuse him this right?

But, after all, we still think there is no cause for anxiety. It does not take long to make such preparations as may have to be made for the Congress, in a City like Calcutta, and everything will be all right in due time, whatever the *Indian Mirror*, when sorely pressed for "copy" might write or print on the subject.

Bande Mataram, October 13, 1906

Statesman's Sympathy Brand

The design of the extended New Market was an achievement on which Mr. MacCabe, the Chief Engineer of the Corporation was congratulated by an Anglo-Indian contemporary. But Mr. MacCabe wrote to say that he was an engineer and not an architect and the credit of the design should be given not to him but to his Indian Assistant, Mr. Cavasjee. No sooner was the fact revealed that the work was done by an Indian than the *Statesman* recognised that the design was a replica which had for its original the Crawford Market in Bombay. This startling revelation has consoled our sympathetic contemporary and repaired the wounded vanity of Anglo-India. We cannot sufficiently admire the connoisseurs who delight in the peculiar flavour of the *Statesman*'s friendly sympathy towards Indians.

BY THE WAY

News from Nowhere
(From our correspondent)

The Punjab journal, *Light*, has suggested that in order to safeguard the Congress the Standing Committee should be empowered to expel from the Congress ranks any uncomfortable and undesirable delegate, by three-fourths majority and with reasons given. This statesmanlike proposal has attracted great attention in Bombay and a meeting was held in Mr. D. E. Watcha's office yesterday to consider and give effect to it. Sir Pherozshah Mehta, resplendent with eternal youth, took the chair. After some discussion the proposal was passed and declared, on the spot, a fundamental law of the Congress constitution. It was decided, however, that the Bombay Committee alone should enjoy the power, Sir Pherozshah pointing out that Bombay was the only safe, loyal and moderate city in India and would remain so as long as he (Sir Pherozshah) was its uncrowned King. It was suggested, but timidly and in an awestruck whisper, that even Sir Pherozshah might not live forever but the great man answered, "*L'État, c'est moi*" and "*après moi le déluge*" (The State? I am the State, and after me, the deluge). As no one present happened to know French, this argument was considered unanswerable. An amendment to the effect that Madras and the United Provinces might also be given the power, under proper safeguards and restrictions, was overwhelmingly defeated, the majority being composed of Sir Pherozshah Mehta and the minority of all the other members present. It was next proposed that Mr. B. G. Tilak should be the first person declared disqualified from becoming a Congress delegate. A member present had the temerity to suggest that this proceeding would hurt the Congress and not Mr. Tilak. He was augustly commanded by the chairman to shut up, but as he still persisted the members rose in a body, hustled him out of the room, propelled him downstairs and then returned to their seats fatigued but with a consciousness of duty done. After this the proscription of Lala Lajpat Rai was proposed and carried *nem. con.* Babu Bepin Chandra Pal was the last name suggested and carried uproariously, the members voting twice in their enthusiasm. The reasons alleged for these proscriptions have not been fully ascertained. Mr. Tilak was disqualified because he has been to jail and has no tact, Babu Bepin Chandra Pal because he is Babu Bepin Chandra Pal; I am unable to discover the precise reason alleged in Lala Lajpat Rai's case, but I believe it was because he was not Mr. Alfred Nundy. After the other members had left, Sir Pherozshah and

Mr. Watcha constituted themselves into a public meeting, reconstituted the Standing Committee and elected fifty delegates for the Calcutta Congress.

*

There is little other fresh news from this quarter. The announcement of Mr. Morley's intended reforms in the *Pioneer* has created great excitement and it is understood that several petitions have reached Lord Minto protesting against the selection of a Gurkha prince and suggesting the petitioners' superior claims. Nawabzada Nasurullah Khan of Sachin and Nawab Salimullah of Dacca are among the claimants. It is also understood that Mr. K. G. Gupta has sent in his pretensions through the Bengal Government, but for this I cannot vouch. Much alarm has been created in royalist and moderate circles by the persistent attempts of Mr. Tilak to bring the merchants and mill-owners into the Swadeshi Movement. The weather here is sultry but not thunderous. Fireworks are frequent.

Bande Mataram, October 29, 1906

The Man of the Past and the Man of the Future

Two men of the moment stand conspicuously before the eyes of the public in connection with the present session of the National Congress. The advent of these two men close upon each other is full of meaning for us at the present juncture. Both of them are sincere patriots, both have done what work lay in them for their people and for the land that bore them; both are men of indomitable perseverance and high ability; but there the resemblance ends. One of them worn and aged, bowed down with the burden of half a century's toils and labours, comes to us as the man of the past, reminding us of a generation that is passing away, ideals that have lost their charm, methods that have been found to be futile, an energy and hope once buoyant and full of life but which now live on only in a wearied and decrepit old age phantom-like, still babbling exploded generalities and dead formulas. The other comes with his face to the morning, a giant of strength and courage bearing on his unbowed shoulders the mighty burden of our future. We do not know yet what will be the nature of Mr. Dadabhai's Presidential speech; it may contain Pisgah sights of the future, to a great extent it is likely to be the swan song of the dying past. From Mr. Tilak we expect no great speech and no sensational pronouncement, his very presence is more powerful than the greatest declamations; for it is not as an orator he stands prominent in spite of his clear incisive utterances, nor as a writer in spite of the immense influence which as the editor of the *Kesari* he exercises on the political ideal of Maharashtra, but as the man who knows what has to be done and does it, knows what has to be organised and organises it, knows what has to be resisted and resists it. He is pre-eminently the man who acts, and action is to be the note of our future political energies.

Mr. Dadabhai, on the other hand, is the man who remonstrates; all his life has been spent in one energetic and unceasing remonstrance through books, through public speeches, through letters and writings in public print. Remonstrance, not action, was the note of our political energies in the past. Action was, according to the old gospel, the prerogative of the Government whether in India or in Great Britain, and our only duty was to urge them to act justly and not unjustly, in our interests and not in their own. We expected them to be angels and remonstrated with them when they proved to be merely men; this spur of that remonstrance, it was hoped, would prick them or at least the home-bred of Englishmen to justify the angelic hues in which they had painted themselves, for our benefit. To the young generation these hopes nowadays seem so incredibly futile that they are tempted to wonder how men of ability and education — many of them had studied something at least of history — could ever have cherished them. But when Mr. Naoroji began his career, nothing more real and solid was possible. The falling in pieces of the Maratha Confederacy and the overthrow of the Sikh power had left the Punjab and the Deccan stupefied and apathetic; the rest of India was politically exhausted and inert. In such circumstances it was inevitable that the task of reviving the life of the nation should fall into the hands of a small class of men educated in English Schools and in English ways of thinking. It was the one great service these men did to our country, that they accustomed us to hope once more and live politically. It was our misfortune rather than their fault that the hopes they proclaimed were delusive and the life they imparted meagre and superficial. Destitute of political experience, they could not avoid basing their political creed on theories and ideals rather than upon facts; without any education but what the rulers chose to impart, they had no choice but to borrow their theories and ideas from their English teachers; confined to English books and influence, cut off from the wide wholesome atmosphere of the world's culture, they were obliged to accept Englishmen at their own valuation. They were for the most part men of talent and ability; and it requires more than talent and ability; it needs the eye of genius to dispense with the necessity of experience and see truth with a single intuitive glance.

The ideas on which our agitation in the nineteenth century proceeded were therefore fantastic and unfounded; its methods were unsuited to the realities of political life in this country, its spirit and aim were so purely Westernised as to preclude the possibility of seizing on the whole people and creating a new national life. The energy expended on it was therefore small, limited both in intensity and area; and the results it brought about were not even commensurate with the little energy expended. But two things were gained — the renewal of political activity in the country and of political experience. A renewed life might have been brought about in other ways and with greater power and reality; but for experience that long wandering in the desert of unrealities and futilities was probably indispensable. However that may be, Mr. Naoroji was among the small knot of able men who first set in motion the new political activities of the country. And one thing distinguished him above most of his fellows that while they wasted themselves on things petty and unreal, he seized on one great fact and enforced it in season and out of season on all who could be got to listen, — the terrible poverty of India and its rapid increase under British rule. It was necessary that a persistent voice should din this into the ears of the people; for what with the incessant pratings about British peace, British justice and the blessings of British rule on the one side and the clamour for Legislative Councils, Simultaneous Examinations, High Education and similar shams on the other.... This one central all-important reality was in danger of being smothered out of sight. It was necessary for the nation but to realise its increasing poverty under British rule; only then could it take the next step and take to heart the fact that British rule and increasing poverty stood in the relation of cause and effect; last of all comes the inevitable conclusion that the effect could only be cured by the removal of the cause, in other words, by the substitution of autonomy in place of a British or British-controlled Government. Mr. Naoroji's was the persistent voice that compelled the nation to realise the first two of these fundamental truths; Mr. Romesh Dutt and others powerfully assisted the result, but it was Mr. Naoroji who first forced the question of Indian poverty into prominence, and for this India owes him a debt of gratitude deeper than that due to any other of our older politicians dead or living. It is true that he has not been able to proclaim the third of the three connected truths consistently and frankly; especially have those of his utterances, which were meant for purely Indian consumption, been marred by the desire to qualify, moderate and even conceal a plain fact, which, though it was necessary, it might yet be dangerous to proclaim. Nevertheless it is something that a man of his age and traditions should at least have frankly declared that freedom from foreign rule must needs be the only governing ideal of Indian politics. The man who is responsible for that declaration ought to be no Moderate. His heart at least should be with us. That in India and in the Presidential chair of the Congress his voice also will be for us we cannot so confidently forecast. If it is, his venerable sanction will be a support to our efforts; if not, his reticence or opposition will be no hindrance to our final triumph. For that which Time and Fate intend, no utterances of individuals however venerable or esteemed, can delay or alter.

Bande Mataram, December 26, 1906

The Results of the Congress

THE great Calcutta Congress, the centre of so many hopes and fears, is over. Of the various antagonistic or contending forces which are now being hurled together into that Medea's cauldron of confused and ever fiercer struggle out of which a free and regenerated India is to arise, each one had its own acute fears and fervent hopes for the results of this year's Congress. Anglo-India and Tory England feared that the Extremists might capture the assembly, they hoped that a split would be created, and, as a result, the Congress either come to an end and land itself in the limbo of forgotten and abortive things or else, by the expulsion of the new life and the new spirit from its midst, sink into the condition of a dead-alive ineffectual body associated with the Government and opposing it now and then only for form's sake. Liberal England represented by the Cottons and Wedderburns hoped that the unsustaining and empty concessions Mr. Morley is dangling before the eyes of the Moderate leaders might bring back the Congress entirely into its old paths and the new spirit be killed by the show of kindness. It feared that the National Assembly might see through the deception and publicly demand that there should be either substantial concessions or none at all. In India itself the Moderates feared that the forward party in Bengal might force through the Congress strong resolutions on Boycott and other alarming matters or else avenge their failure by wrecking the Congress itself, but they hoped that by an imposing show of ex-Presidents on the platform, by the reverence due to the age and services of Mr. Dadabhai Naoroji, by the dominant personality of the lion of the Bombay Corporation, by the strong contingents from Bombay city, Gujerat and other provinces still unswept by new brooms, by the use of tactics and straining in their favour all the advantages of an indefinite and nebulous constitution, they would quell the Extremists, prevent the bringing forward of the Boycott and keep absolute control of the Congress. The forward party hoped to leave the impress of the new thought and life on the Congress of 1906, to get entire Self-Government recognised as the ideal of the Congress and Swadeshi and Boycott as the means, and to obtain a public recognition of the new ideas in the Presidential address, but they feared that the realisation of such considerable results would be too much to hope for in a single year and a fierce and prolonged struggle would be needed to overcome the combined forces of conservatism, timidity, self-distrust and self-interest, which have amalgamated into the loyalist Moderate Party. Such was the state of mind of the conflicting parties when the Calcutta Congress was opened on the 26th.

Today on the 30th, we can look back and count our gains and losses. The hopes of Anglo-India have been utterly falsified and the Anglo-Indian journals cannot conceal their rage and disappointment. The loudest in fury is our dear old perfervid *Englishman* which cries out in hollow tones of menace that if the Congress tolerates Boycott, the Congress itself will not be tolerated. The hopes and fears of Liberal England have been only partially fulfilled and partially falsified; the Congress has definitely demanded Colonial Self-Government and it has accepted the offered concessions of Mr. Morley only as steps towards that irreducible demand; the new spirit, instead of being killed by kindness, has declared in no uncertain voice its determination to live. The fears of the Moderates have been falsified; no strongly worded resolutions have been passed: neither has the Congress been wrecked by the rapid development of contending parties in our midst. Their hopes too have been falsified. Nothing was more remarkable in the present Congress than its anti-autocratic temper and the fiery energy with which it repudiated any attempt to be dictated to by the authority of recognised leaders. Charges of want of reverence and of rowdyism have been freely brought against this year's Congress. To the first charge we answer that the reverence has been transferred from persons to the ideal of the motherland; it is no longer Pherozshah Mehta or even Mr. Dadabhai Naoroji who can impose silence and acquiescence on the delegates of the nation by their presence and authority, for the delegates feel that they owe a deeper reverence and a higher duty to their country. Henceforth the leaders can only deserve reverence by acting in the spirit of the chief servants of their country and not in the spirit of masters and dictators. This change is one of the most genuine signs of political progress which we have observed in our midst. The charge of rowdyism merely means that the Congress, instead of a dead unanimity and mechanical cheers, has this time shown lively signs of real interest and real feeling. It is ridiculous to contend that in a national assembly the members should confine themselves to signs of approval only and conceal their disapproval; in no public assembly in the world, having a political nature, is any such rule observed; and the mother of Parliaments itself is in the habit of expressing its disapproval with far greater vehemence than was done in this year's Congress. It was due to this growth of deep feeling and of the spirit of independence that the spells on which the Moderate leaders had depended, failed of their power to charm. The lion of the Bombay Corporation found that a mightier lion than himself had been aroused in Bengal, — the people.

For ourselves, what have we to reckon as lost or gained? No strongly worded resolutions have been pressed and we are glad that none have been passed, for we believe in strong action and not in strong words. But our hopes have been realised, our contentions recognised if not always precisely in the form we desired or with as much clearness and precision as we ourselves would have used, yet definitely enough for all practical purposes. The Congress has declared Self-Government on Colonial lines to be its demand from the British Government and this is only a somewhat meaningless paraphrase of autonomy or complete self-government. The Congress has recognised the legitimacy of the Boycott movement as practical in Bengal without limitation or reservation and in such terms that any other province which feels itself called upon to resort to this weapon in order to vindicate its rights, need not hesitate to take it up. The Congress has recognised the Swadeshi movement in its entirety including the adoption of a system of self-protection by the people; within the scope of its resolution it has found room for the idea of self-help, the principle of self-sacrifice and the policy of the gradual exclusion of foreign goods. The Congress has recognised the necessity of National Education. The Congress has recognised the necessity of a Constitution and adopted one as a tentative measure for a year, which, crude, meagre and imperfect as it is, depends only on our own efforts to develop by degrees into a working constitution worthy of a national assembly. All that the forward party has fought for, has in substance been conceded, except only the practice of recommending certain measures which depend on the Government for their realisation; but this was not a reform on which we laid any stress for this particular session. We were prepared to give the old weakness of the Congress plenty of time to die out if we could get realities recognised. Only in one particular have we been disappointed and that is the President's address. But even here the closing address with which Mr. Naoroji dissolved the Congress, has made amends for the deficiencies of his opening speech. He once more declared Self-Government, Swaraj, as in an inspired moment he termed it, to be our one ideal and called upon the young men to achieve it. The work of the older men had been done in preparing a generation which were determined to have this great ideal and nothing less; the work of making the ideal a reality, lies with us. We accept Mr. Naoroji's call and to carry out his last injunctions will devote our lives and, if necessary, sacrifice them.

Bande Mataram, December 31, 1906

Yet There is Method in It

THE "Moderate" Indian politician aspires to be an Imperial citizen. His ambition has at last been screwed up to the point of seeking equality with his "colonial brother". His loyalty draws him towards the Empire and his politics draws him towards self-government and the resultant is self-government within the Empire. Colonies have been granted self-government within the Empire and it logically follows that if the Indians try, try, and try again, they too will gain their end because nothing is impossible to perseverance. Thus two birds will be killed with one stone. The ruling people, whose immense power can be turned against us any moment if they happen to be irritated, will be pleased with our desire not to break away from the Empire and, at the same time the spirit of independence which is constantly urging us to demand a greater and greater measure of self-government will have its full play. Such a compromise, such a smooth scheme of accommodating comprehensiveness is being welcomed everywhere as suddenly revealed to a political prophet who is going the round of the country with the inviting message: "Come to me, all ye that are heavy-laden, and I shall give rest unto you."

The talk of this Colonial Self-Government or self-government within the Empire at a time they are going to have an Imperial conference of the Colonial Prime Ministers and have condescended to admit a representative of India to the same may very well entrap the unwary, especially when it comes from a personage who is said to have explained to the Secretary of State all that India needs in a five-minute interview. But the pretension of the frog to rank as a quadruped of the elephant class with the mere expression of a pious wish should receive a heavy shock on learning from Reuter that either Mr. Morley or his nominee will represent India at the coming Colonial Conference. This is quite in keeping with the system of representation that India enjoys.

This is a further extension of the sham which we see here in the local Legislative Councils. This is but the continuation of the farce which is known as the Local Board or Municipal Board representation.

It is a favourable sign that when some leading moderate politicians are trying fresh and big doses of poppy on our people for the offence of giving a slight indication of self-consciousness, these smart shocks for regaining self-possession are coming of themselves. The spurious politics that has so long lived only on the delusion of the people has very nearly been found out and thus elaborate preparations are going on to give it a fresh lease of life. But when the gods want to destroy a thing no human efforts can avail. Mendicancy is no longer consistent with the stand-up position the Indians have taken up. The beggar knows only begging and bullying but his day-dreams surpass even those of Alanschar. The imposing ideal of self-government within the Empire with which begging politics has been making its last attempt to catch the fancy of the people will hardly survive such disenchanting strokes as the representation of India on the Colonial Conference by the Secretary of State himself or his own nominee.

If India is to be India, if her civilisation is to retain a distinctive stamp and extend its spiritual conquests for the benefit of the world at large, it must be propped up with the strength of her own people.

To include India in a federation of colonies and the motherland is madness without method. The patriotism that wishes the country to lose itself within an Empire which justifies its name by its conquest — the colonies being no portion of the Empire in its strict sense — is also madness without method. But to talk of absolute independence and autonomy — though this be madness, yet there is method in it.

Bande Mataram, February 25, 1907

Mr. GOKHALE'S DISLOYALTY

Dear Bande Mataram,

You may reasonably ask me where I had been so long. My answer is that seeing the Extremists fare very well at the last Congress, I thought I had some claim to a well-earned repose. When all India kindly took to my views and fought for them in the National Assembly, I thought I could suspend my activity for a time.

But with Mr. Gokhale stumping the country to recover the lost ground and the *Bengalee* taking the brief of the all-powerful executive, I cannot be a silent spectator of the cold-blooded deposition of Demos.

The Aga Khan too has entered the lists. Alarmed at the Extremists' talk of freedom from British control, the combined wit and wisdom of the country is making a dead set at this crazy class so that prudence and good sense may once more prevail in the land. The normal calm and the much-coveted peace has, to a certain extent, been restored to the country and what little of unrest still exists will pass away as soon as Mr. Gokhale will say "Amen".

Unlike the grave-diggers of Ophelia, Mr. Gokhale wants to make the extinction of British autocracy in India quite an unchristian procedure. Here lies the Empire, good; here stands India, good; if India goes to this Empire and prays for its death, it is will she nill she, she prays for something bad but if the Empire comes to her and kills itself, she kills not the Empire: argal, she is not guilty of disloyalty.

The Extremists want to bring the Empire to themselves, and not themselves to go to the Empire. What is more Christian and loyal? To make the Empire part with us as friends, or to provoke it with childish demands of colonial self-government or self-government within the Empire?

Besides, does not Mr. Gokhale know the fable that by mere buzzing about the head of a Bull or even settling himself upon his head, the gnat cannot at all inconvenience him, but though small it is by stinging only that he can arouse his attention.

In vain is Mr. Gokhale trying conclusions with people who have tried their remedies times without number and found them wanting.

Mr. Gokhale's patriotism is based on truth — he paints us as we are and warns us against the danger of too strong a stimulus in this our exceptionally weak condition.

Here is he like a wise physician who knows his patient.

But Mr. Gokhale, being such an educated and enlightened reformer, with supreme contempt for Indian prejudices, superstitions and idolatry, should be the last man to trust to mere prayer and petition for the recovery of his patient.

When the Scotch asked the King of England to appoint a day of prayer and fasting for abating the fury of cholera when it raged there a few years back, the authorities in England pooh-poohed the idea and told them to attend to the recommendations of sanitary science.

Should not Mr. Gokhale be true to himself and ask the people to attend to the recommendations of political science excluding altogether from their programme the superstition of prayer? More in my next.

Yours sincerely,
By The Way

Bande Mataram, February 28, 1907

The Comilla Incident

THE Comilla affair remains, after everybody has said his say, obscured by the usual tangle of contradictions. The Hindu version presents a number of allegations, — specific, detailed and categorical — of attacks on Hindus, making up in the mass a serious picture of a mofussil town given over for days to an outbreak of brutal lawlessness on the part of one section of the Mahomedan community, a Magistrate quiescent and sympathetically tolerant of the rioters, and the final resort by the Hindu community to drastic measures of self-defence on the continued refusal of British authority to do its duty as the guardian of law and order. A Mahomedan report belittled the accounts of Mahomedan violence and presented picturesque and vivid details of Hindu aggressiveness; but as this version has since been repudiated we have to turn to the official account for the other side of the picture. But the official account — well, the value of official statements is an understood thing all the world over. Is it not a political byword in England itself that no rumour or irresponsible statement should be believed until it had been officially denied? The official version of the Comilla incident published on the 9th March is hard to beat as a specimen of its class — it is a most amazingly unskilful production over which suppression of truth and suggestion of falsehood are written large and palpable; but it presents a beautiful and artistic picture of wanton and murderous Hindu violence, comparative Mahomedan moderation, and fatherly British care brooding dove-eyed and maternal-winged over its irreconcilably quarrelsome step-children.

If anyone should think our characterisation of this historical document too sweeping, we invite him to a careful study both of what it says and what it does not say. It commences with the statement that "a series of anti-Partition meetings were recently held here *without incident* and on 6th March Nawab Salimullah arrived from Dacca to hold counter-meetings". The insertion of the words "without incident" is admirable. It implies that there was violent irritation between Hindus and Mahomedans on the Partition question and the latter might have been expected to show their irritation by "incidents", — especially when the "inflammatory" speeches of Babu Bepin Chandra Pal and other firebrands are taken into account, — but they very considerately refrained. Thus Mahomedan moderation is contrasted with the Hindu aggressiveness which is presently to be related, and the way paved for throwing the whole responsibility on the anti-Partition agitation and aggressive Swadeshism. Then we are informed as a positive fact that a brick was thrown at the Nawab's procession and brooms held up in derision. "This led to some disturbance and a cloth shop was *entered* but not looted and two prostitutes' houses robbed." Let us pause over this delightful sentence. The outrageous assaults by the rioters which the Hindu accounts carefully specify, are all hidden away and glossed over under the mild and gentlemanly phrase "some disturbance"; the only specific instances which the Commissioner will acknowledge are the cloth-shop "incident" and the "incident" of the two prostitutes. But after all, what occurred in the cloth-shop? It was merely "entered", — admirable word! the rioters were far too polite, honourable and considerate to loot it. They simply entered for the sheer joy of entering and perhaps of gazing ecstatically on bales of Swadeshi cloth! They also "entered" the houses of two prostitutes, but in this instance, indemnified themselves for their trouble; still, the people robbed were merely prostitutes! It is thus suggested that the disturbance was of the most trifling character and the only sufferers a shopkeeper and two prostitutes; in fact, the whole thing was little more than an amiable frolic. Of the violent maltreatment not only of students and shopkeepers but of pleaders and other respectable citizens, of the forcible invasion of private houses and the attempts to break into or, let us say, "enter" women's apartments, there is not a word.

After this day of "entries" there is a blank in the official record until the next evening when "the Nawab's Secretary, a Parsi was attacked *while walking alone* and severely beaten with lathis by some Hindus". The provocation alleged to have been given by Mr. Cursetji is carefully omitted, and we are asked to believe that an inoffensive Parsi gentleman out for an innocent and healthful evening walk was waylaid, when alone, and severely beaten because he happened to be the Nawab's Private Secretary. And the evening and the morning were the second day. On the third all was again quiet till that dangerous time, the evening, when an "unlicensed Mahomedan procession", greatly daring, took the air like Mr. Cursetji before them, apparently with the innocuous object of relieving their feelings and exercising their lungs shouting Allah-ho-Akbar. This explains a great deal; evidently the bands of hooligans ranging the streets and attacking people and "entering" houses were in reality "no such matter" except in vivid Hindu imaginations; they were merely "unlicensed Mahomedan processions" on innocent shouting intent. Some unknown person, however, fired upon this procession and killed a Mahomedan baker; and there, inexplicably enough, matters ended for the day. The shot, however, had a powerful effect upon the authorities; it seems to have stirred them up to some faint remembrance of the elementary duties of a civilised administration. Accordingly our martial Commissioner telegraphed, like Kuropatkin, for "reinforcements", and pending their arrival, sent for the Mahomedan Sardars and Mullahs and "enlisted" their influence to keep the peace. In the name of reason and logic, why? The account shows that all the violence and lawlessness, if we except the trifling affairs of the unlooted shop and the looted prostitutes, proceeded from the Hindus. The Mahomedans, it seems, kept perfectly quiet until the night of this third day, when the only incidents were again of a trifling character; a man riding on the step of a carriage was "struck"; a Hindu peon was "struck", nothing more. We are ourselves "struck" by the mildness of the methods employed by these rioters; they do not break into houses, they merely "enter" them; they do not severely beat any one as Mr. Cursetji was "severely beaten" by the Hindus; they merely "strike" a man or two in playful sort. Under the circumstances it is surely the leaders of the Hindu community who should have been enlisted "to keep the peace" — say, as special constables. However, in the end, the reinforcements arrived and the Commissioner busied himself in the fatherly British way, "inquiring personally into all allegations and endeavouring to bring the leaders of both parties together". On this touching scene the official curtain falls. Who shall say after this that "divide and rule" is the policy of the British bureaucracy in India?

We have said enough to expose thoroughly this ridiculous account of a very serious affair. It is the production not of an impartial official keeping the peace between two communities, but of a partisan in a political fight who looks upon the anti-Swadeshi Mahomedans as allies "enlisted" on the side of the bureaucracy. In order to understand the affair we have to read into the official account all that it carefully omits; and for this we must fall back on the Hindu version of the incident. What seems to have happened is clear enough in outline, whatever doubt there may be as to details. The popular cause was making immense strides in Comilla and the magnificent success of the District Conference had afforded a proof which could not be ignored. The redoubtable Nawab Salimullah of Dacca considered it his duty to his patron, the Assam Government, to stem the tide of nationalism in Tipperah. Accordingly he marched Comillawards with his lieutenants and entered the town in conquering pomp. That he ordered the sack of the conquered city is probably no more than the suspicion natural to excited imaginations; but it is certain that his coming was immediately responsible for the riots. His whole history, since he was shoved into prominence by his Anglo-Indian patrons, has been one long campaign against the Hindus with attempts to excite the passions and class selfishness of the Mahomedans and inflame them into permanent hostility to their Hindu fellow-countrymen. It is only within the territorial limits of the Nawab's influence that there has been any serious friction between Hindus and Mahomedans on the Swadeshi and Partition questions; but so far as it has gone, its immediate results have been not only friction but outbreaks of violence and lawlessness either on a small, as at Serajgunge or on a large scale as at Mymensingh. It is not therefore surprising that while the Conference at Comilla and the recent Swadeshi meetings came off without "incident", the Nawab should no sooner have set his foot in Comilla than a reign of violence and lawlessness began. At the same time it is probable that the suddenness of the outbreak was due to some immediate exciting cause. The brick story bears a suspicious resemblance to the incident which set Sir Bampfylde and his Gurkhas rioting officially at Barisal; but it is likely enough that a few individuals may have shown their feelings towards the Nawab in an offensive way. However that may be, it seems certain that the more rowdy elements of the Mahomedan population broke into lawless riot, attacked Hindus wherever they found them, broke into shops and private houses and brutally assaulted students, pleaders and other respectable Hindus, attempting even in some cases to enter the women's apartments.

Once begun, the affair followed familiar lines. As in Mymensingh, it commenced with an orgy of lawlessness on the part of ignorant low-class Mahomedans inflamed by the Nawab's anti-Hindu campaign. As in Mymensingh, local authorities would not at first interfere, although appealed to by Hindu gentlemen, and confined themselves to academic arguments as to the genesis of the outrages. As in Mymensingh, the Hindus, taken by surprise and denied the protection of the law, fell first into a panic and only afterwards rallied and began to organise self-defence. At Comilla, however, they seemed to have acted with greater promptitude and energy. The disturbances continued for three days at least; but by that time the Hindus had picked themselves together, the women were removed to a safe place where they could be guarded by bands of volunteers and the whole community stood on the defensive. Two or three collisions seem to have taken place in one of which, possibly, Mr. Cursetji was roughly handled, in another a Mahomedan shot dead. By this time, the Commissioner had realised that the policy of non-interference adopted by the British authorities, was leading to serious results which they cannot have anticipated. The military police were telegraphed for and other measures taken which came at least three days too late, since the mischief had been thoroughly done.

Divested of exaggeration and rumour, we fancy the actual facts will be found to amount to something like the above. We do not for a moment believe that the Hindus took aggressive action without serious and even unbearable provocation, any more than we believe that the riot was planned or ordered beforehand by the anti-Swadeshi section of the Mahomedans. We trust that the usual mistake of instituting cases and counter-cases will be avoided. If the Comilla nationalists wish the facts of the case to be known let them draw up a statement of their version with the evidence of the persons assaulted for the enlightenment of public opinion. The time ought to be now past, in Eastern Bengal at least, when appeal to the British courts could be either a remedy or a solace.

Bande Mataram, March 15, 1907

British Protection or Self-Protection

THERE are two superstitions which have driven such deep root into the mind of our people that even where the new spirit is strongest, they still hold their own. One is the habit of appealing to British courts of justice; the other is the reliance upon the British executive for our protection. The frequent recurrence of incidents such as the Mymensingh and Comilla disturbances will have its use if it drives into our minds the truth that in the struggle we have begun we cannot and ought not to expect protection from our natural adversaries. It is perfectly true that one of the main preoccupations of the executive mind has been the maintenance of order and quiet in the country, because a certain kind of tranquillity was essential to the preservation of an alien bureaucratic control. This was the secret of the barbarous system of punishments which make the Indian Penal Code a triumph of civilised savagery; of the license and the blind support allowed by the Magistracy to a phenomenally corrupt and oppressive Police; of the doctrine of no conviction no promotion, which is the gospel of the Anglo-Indian executive, holding it better that a hundred innocent should suffer than one crime be recorded as unpunished. This was the reason of the severity with which turbulent offences have always been repressed, of the iniquitous and oppressive system of punitive Police and of the undeclared but well-understood Police rule that any villager of strong physique, skill with weapons and active habits should be entered in the list of bad characters. By a rigid application of these principles the bureaucracy have succeeded in creating the kind of tranquillity they require. The Romans created a desert and called the result peace; the British in India have destroyed the spirit and manhood of the people and call the result law and order. It is true, on the other hand, that there have been exceptions to the promptness and severity with which turbulence of any kind is usually dealt with; and the most notable is the supineness and dilatoriness, habitually shown by the authorities, in dealing with outbreaks of Mahomedan fanaticism and the gingerly fashion in which repression in such cases is enforced. Fear is undoubtedly at the root of this weakness. The bureaucracy are never tired of impressing the irresistible might of British supremacy on the subject populations, but in their own hearts they are aware that that supremacy is insecure and without root in the soil; the general upheaval of any deep-seated and elemental passion in the hearts of the people might easily shatter that supremacy as so many others have been shattered before it. The one passion which in past times has been proved capable of so upheaving the national consciousness in India is religious feeling; and outraged religious feeling is therefore the one thing which the bureaucracy dreads and the slightest sign of which turns their courage into nervousness or panic and their strength into paralysed weakness. The alarm which the Swadeshi movement created was due to this abiding terror; for in the Swadeshi movement, for the first time patriotism became a national religion, the name of the motherland was invested with divine sacredness and her service espoused with religious fervour and enthusiasm. In its alarm Anglo-India turned for help to that turbulent Mahomedan fanaticism which they had so dreaded; hoping to drive out poison by poison, they menaced the insurgent religion of patriotism with the arming of Mahomedan prejudices against what its enemies declared to be an essentially Hindu movement. The first fruits of this policy we have seen at Mymensingh, Serajgunge and Comilla. It was a desperate and dangerous, and might easily prove a fatal, expedient; but with panic-stricken men the fear of the lesser danger is easily swallowed in the terror of the greater.

It should not therefore be difficult to see that the demand for official protection in such affairs as the Comilla riots is as unpractical as it is illogical. The object of modern civilised Governments in preserving tranquillity is to protect the citizen not only in the peaceful pursuit of his legitimate occupations but in the public activities and ambitions natural to a free people; the Government exists for the citizen, not the citizen for the Government. But the bureaucracy in India is only half-modern and semi-civilised. In India the individual, — for there is no citizen, — exists for the Government; and the object in preserving tranquillity is not the protection of the citizen but the security of the Government. The security of the individual, such as it is, is only a result and not an object. But the security of the Government, if by Government we understand the present irresponsible bureaucratic control, is directly threatened by the Swadeshi movement; for the declared object of that movement is Swaraj, which means the entire elimination of that control. To ask the bureaucracy, therefore, to protect us in our struggle for Swaraj is to ask it to assist in its own destruction.

This plain truth is obviously recognised by the officials of the Shillong Government. The attitude taken up by the Magistrates of Mymensingh and Comilla was identically the same; they saw no necessity for interfering; the Hindus by their Swadeshi agitation had brought the Mahomedan storm upon themselves and must take the consequences. The unexpressed inference is plain enough. The bureaucratic "constitution", under which we are asked to carry on "constitutional" Government, assures us British peace and security only so long as we are not Swadeshi. The moment we become Swadeshi, British peace and security, so far as we are concerned, automatically come to an end, and we are liable to have our heads broken, our men assaulted, our women insulted and our property plundered without there being any call for British authority to interfere. The same logic underlies the imputation of the responsibility for the riot to Babu Bepin Chandra Pal's inflammatory eloquence, which was made, we believe, in both instances and in this last has received the support of the loyalist press. Whom or what did Bepin Babu inflame? Not the Mahomedans to attack the Hindus certainly, — that would be too preposterous a statement for even an Anglo-Indian Magistrate to make, — but all Indians, Hindus and Mahomedans alike, to work enthusiastically for Swadeshi and Swaraj. By raising the cry of Swadeshi and Swaraj, then, we forfeit the protection of the law.

Stated so nakedly, the reasoning sounds absurd; but, in the light of certain practical considerations we can perfectly appreciate the standpoint of these bureaucrats. Arguing as philosophers, they would be wrong; but arguing as bureaucrats and rulers of a subject people, their position is practical and logical. The establishment of Swaraj means the elimination of the British bureaucrat. Can we ask the British bureaucrat to make it safe and easy for us to eliminate him? Swadeshi is a direct attack on that exploitation of India by the British merchant which is the first and principal reason of the obstinate maintenance of bureaucratic control. The trade came to India as the pioneer of the flag; and the bureaucrat may reasonably fear that if the trade is driven out, the flag will leave in the wake of the trade. With that fear in his mind, even apart from his natural racial sympathies, can we ask him to facilitate the expulsion of the trade? On the contrary, the official representative of the British shop-keeper is morally bound, be he Viceroy, Lieutenant-Governor, Secretary of State or be he a mere common District Magistrate, to put down Swadeshi by the best means in his power. Sir Bampfylde thought violence and intimidation, Gurkha Police and Regulation lathis the very best means; Mr. Morley believes Swadeshi can be more easily smothered with soft pillows than banged to death with a hard cudgel. The means differ; the end is the same. At present the bureaucracy have two strings to their bow — general Morleyism with the aid of the loyalist Mehtaite element among the Parsis and Hindus; and occasional Fullerism with the aid of the Salimullahi Party among the Mahomedans. With the growth of the new spirit and the disappearance of a few antiquated but still commanding personalities, the former will lose its natural support and the latter will be left in possession of the field. But we know by this time that Salimullahism means a repetition of the outbreaks of Mymensingh, Serajgunge and Comilla, and the attitude of the Comilla heaven-born will be the attitude of most heaven-borns wherever these outbreaks recur. It is urgently necessary therefore that we should shake off the superstitious habit of praying for protection to the British authorities and look for help to the only true, political divinity, the national strength which is within ourselves. If we are to do this effectually, we must organise physical education all over the country and train up the rising generation not only in the moral strength and courage for which Swadeshism has given us the materials, but in physical strength and courage and the habit of rising immediately and boldly to the height of even the greatest emergency. That strength we must train in every citizen of the newly-created nation so that for our private protection we may not be at the mercy of a Police efficient only for harassment, whose appearance on the scene after a crime means only a fresh and worse calamity to the peaceful householder; but each household may be a protection to itself and when help is needed, be able to count on its neighbour. And the strength of the individuals we must carefully organise for purposes of national defence, so that there may be no further fear of Comilla tumults or official Gurkha riots disturbing our steady and rapid advance to national freedom. It is high time we abandoned the fat and comfortable selfish middle-class training we give to our youth and make a nearer approach to the physical and moral education of our old Kshatriyas or the Japanese Samurai.

Bande Mataram, March 18, 1907

BY THE WAY

Says the *Englishman*: —

It is interesting and to the man with a wicked sense of the ludicrous not unamusing to see the heroism with which various Bengali papers call upon the nations of India to arise, fling out the Feringhee, and establish vast secretariats replete with fat billets in which, secured by the warlike races, sixty million sons of the Lower Provinces will dream and scribble for the benefit of the sixty million. "Motherland" is sadly of opinion that but for the system of education forced upon India, and the presence of Indians in Government Service, foreign dominion in India would be impossible and the "male family members" of its editor's tribe would all be Togos and Kurokis. *Bande Mataram* has "found out the natural antagonism between a handful of aliens and the oppressed and down-trodden children of the soil", and yearning heroically for the inevitable struggle to come, sniffing the battle afar off snorts, "if the aliens are determined to preserve their own superiority, let them make a fresh attempt and see how events turn out". Other papers look back with regret upon the glorious deeds of the Spartan warriors who, Heraclidae and Bayards all, filled Bengal before the recreant English, in coward fashion seduced the people to the paths of peace. All express ardent longings for the coming of the day of Armageddon when the strong man armed will wake from his poppied sleep and a wave 400 million strong will blot out the white specks who think that they govern India. In the meanwhile, we would commend to the attention of our militant friends of the perfervidly patriot press the moral to be drawn from the little drama in Market Street on Sunday. The lads became possessed of a loaded double-barrelled pistol — they may have borrowed it from the armoury of some hopeful patriot. They took it to a tinsmith, and he got playing with it. It went off and a woman was shot in the back. A crowd collected and one man picked up the weapon which went off again and shattered his hand. There was nearly a panic and at length a string was tied to the pistol butt, and it was dragged to the police station. The two boys who had brought the pistol ran away. There is no need to labour the moral, but revolutions are more dangerous than loaded pistols and none can tell who will get badly hurt. All that can be predicted with safety is that the real authors of the trouble will get away early.

"The wicked sense of the ludicrous" has become a little too keen in the *Englishman*. It is no doubt ludicrous that anybody should question the *Englishman*'s natural right to hold down others. It is no doubt ludicrous that two Bengali boys in their teens, only lads according to the *Englishman*'s own version, should not know the use of a loaded double-barreled pistol. It is far more ludicrous that a Bengali crowd should not know what a gun is like when the benign Government has made it penal even for respectable gentlemen to be in possession of that formidable weapon. It is still more ludicrous that the Bengalis should fail to be heroes when the *Englishman* has advised the Government not to give them any offensive weapon lest their naked valour should suffer. It is ludicrous indeed that the Bengalis do not rise to their full height notwithstanding the faculties which the *Englishman*'s countrymen have provided for them. There is no cowardice in emasculating a man in every way and then twitting him with his symptoms of weakness.

The *Englishman* is making capital out of the Market Street incident. He thinks he has scored a point against the Revolutionists who, when their ignorant crowd get dazed at the going off of a pistol, "call upon the nations of India to arise and fling out the Feringhees". We have been further told that revolutions are more dangerous than loaded pistols; and if the worst comes to happen the real authors of the trouble will get away early.

We are glad the *Englishman* has dissipated our ignorance. Till now, we were under the impression that revolutions were far easier than quill-driving in a Chowringhee office, under the electric fan attended by a thousand liveried servants. We have yet to learn that all Englishmen are Heraclidae and Bayards and there is none amongst them whom even our demoralised crowd would put to shame. Every stick is good enough to beat the dog with; and the Market Street incident has very rightly been pounced upon by the *Englishman* to pooh-pooh the aspirations of the perfervidly patriotic press. It is rather late in the day to smile the New Spirit away. The perfervid press have by this time learnt that two and two makes four and can be spared the *Englishman*'s enlightenment as to what revolution is like. The Bengalis are quick-witted and only a day's experience, we believe, has befitted the Market Street crowd to take part in a revolution, if the *Englishman* can bring about any. The real truth is that so many gun-shot incidents are ominous to the *Englishman*.

Bande Mataram, March 21, 1907

The Berhampur Conference

THE Conference which meets at Berhampur tomorrow is the most important that has been yet held in Bengal, for its deliberations are fraught with issues of supreme importance to the future of the country. A heavy responsibility rests upon the delegates who have been sent to Berhampur from all parts of Bengal. For this is the first Provincial Conference after the historic twenty-second session of the Congress at Calcutta. At that session the policy of self-development and self-help was incorporated as an integral part of the political programme by the representatives of the whole nation, the policy of passive resistance was declared legitimate under circumstances which cover the whole of India, and it was decided that a constitution or working organisation should be created for the promotion throughout the year of the programme fixed by the Congress for the whole nation and by the Provinces for themselves. It rests upon the Berhampur Conference to see that proper provision is made for this executive work. We expect the delegates to realise the seriousness of the task that has been put in their hands and to appoint a Provincial Council which will command the confidence of the whole of Bengal and prove by its very composition that an earnest attempt will be made to harmonise all parties in working out so much of the national programme as has been assented to by all. Swadeshi, Boycott, National Education — these are the three planks upon which all can take their stand. We do not disguise from ourselves the fact that on the last two of these questions there are very serious differences of opinion between the two schools now dividing public opinion. In the matter of Boycott, the difference has been one of greater or less thoroughness in practice and of the ultimate goal; but the necessity of Boycott has been recognised by all and there is no reason why any section should refuse to take part in the measures by which it can be made effective. National Education is regarded by one school as an educational experiment to be carried on side by side with Government education, — by the other as a great national cause, the progress of which is to culminate in a truly national system replacing or absorbing the Government schools and colleges. Nevertheless, the spread of the movement has been recognised as desirable by all and there is therefore no reason why measures with that view should not be concerted with general approval. We trust therefore that the delegates at Berhampur will give a mandate to the newly-formed council to organise Swadeshi and Boycott in a practical manner and devise means by which they can be rendered stringent and effective and to see that national schools be established in every district and national support be given to the Council of Education. If they fail to do this, they will have done considerably less than their duty.

But the duty of the delegates does not begin and end with arranging for the execution of the national programme as laid down by the Congress. The Congress deals only with accomplished facts. It set its seal of sanction on National Education and Swadeshi and legitimised the Boycott for all India in recognition of work which had already been commenced in Bengal. But there are other fields in which self-development and self-help are urgently necessary; and it remains for each province to initiate action in each of them successively according to its own circumstances and under the pressure of its own needs. Both the policy of self-help and the Boycott policy have taken shape as a national policy in Bengal as a result of the exceptional trend of events in our province. They are now travelling all over India. Swadeshi has been universally recognised, Boycott is a fact in Maharashtra as well as in Bengal, and is now being publicly advocated in the North and in Madras. But Bengal cannot pause till the rest of India comes up with her, — she must still lead the way even if it be many miles in front. The very initiative she has taken will inevitably sweep her on, whether she wills it or not; for that exceptional trend of events which has carried her along is nothing but the impulsion of a Divine Hand which is shaping through her the way of salvation for all India. That impulsion is not likely to cease; it is already pointing us to fresh departures. Since the Congress met, three new necessities have presented themselves for Bengal, — the necessity of National Arbitration Courts, the necessity of Organised Self-protection and the necessity of Prevention of Famine by self-help. The second of these is the one which we should, in our opinion, take immediately in hand; for it is likely to be urgently needed in the near future and in its absence the national movement will remain deficient in the first element of strength and its defencelessness will perpetually invite attack. If we are to proceed with the work of the nation in peace, we must immediately turn our attention to organising self-protection all over Bengal. The immediate need of the prevention of famine may be met by the suspension of grain-export of which the *Bangabasi* has made itself the champion; but this policy will have to be supplemented and regulated by permanent measures of a far-reaching kind. At present a Resolution approving of export suspension as a temporary measure urgently needed, ought to be sufficient. We do not suppose we need apprehend much difference of opinion on this head. The anti-national superstition of free trade ought to have perished out of Bengal by this time; for a subject nation self-preservation must be the first and dominating principle of its political economy. Neither should there be any opposition to the proposal for Arbitration Courts. Arbitration as a means of diminishing the curse of litigation has been advocated by the Congress and the only difference now is that instead of asking for it from an alien Government which fattens upon the very litigation that impoverishes us, we resolve to establish it for ourselves. We fear, however, that there may be serious difficulty in getting the all-important proposal of self-protection accepted. The attitude of the Moderate leaders in the Comilla matter was of evil omen.

We hope nevertheless that the delegates of the new school will strain every nerve to get these necessary items added to the working programme for the year. By choosing a place where the New Spirit has not made headway and by fixing a date which will make it difficult for the East Bengal delegates to arrive in time, the managers of the Conference will probably have secured a large Moderate majority. We are not sorry that this should be so; for it will give us an opportunity of observing how the advantage gained by this tactical trickery will be used. The present Conference will decide whether the two parties can still hope to work together on the basis of the compromise arrived at in December, or whether, as in Japan, a determined fight for the possession of the national mind and guidance of national action is to precede the great work of emancipation. We shall willingly accept either alternative. If we can work together the work will be more rapid in the beginning and smoother; if, on the contrary, we have to settle our differences first, the work will be more energetic and more rapid in the end. Whatever the result, the forward party stands to win.

Bande Mataram, March 29, 1907

The President of the Berhampur Conference

When the Moderate caucus which arranges our Congresses and Conferences selected Srijut Deepnarain Singh to preside at Berhampur, they thought, no doubt, that they had hit upon a doubly suitable choice. As a young man and one known to be an ardent patriot he would not disgust Bengal by an ultra-moderate pronouncement; as a Zemindar he might be expected to have the fear of the Government before his eyes and to avoid giving open support to the ideas and programme of the New School. It was this latter apprehension, we believe, that lay at the root of the dissatisfaction expressed by some of ourselves at the choice. For our part, we shared neither the hopes of the Moderates nor the fears of our own party. We happen to know something of Srijut Deepnarain Singh by report when he was in England, and we could not believe that so much fire, sincerity and ardour had been quenched in so short a time or even subdued by his position as a rich man and a Zemindar. We confidently expected from him a pronouncement worthy of the occasion, and we have not been disappointed. The spirit of true nationalism underlies his address, as reported in substance; the programme of the New School, so far as it has yet taken concrete shape either in practice or in immediate urgency, has been accepted and the declaration for Boycott is satisfactorily clear and unmistakable. By bringing Srijut Deepnarain forward, it is probable that the real service will have been done to Bihar, which is in bad need of men who can understand the drift of the times and direct the political activities of the province towards the future instead of trying to keep them clamped to a dead and rotting past. Bihar has a future of its own as a Hindi-speaking sub-race of our nationality; and in that United States of India, which the prophetic vision of the President has forecast, it will have its individual station. But in order to carry weight in that Union Bihar must take up its destinies and become an active force in the general movement towards independence. Whether the Biharees are wise in desiring administrative separation from Bengal under the present bureaucracy, it is difficult to say. For our own part, we are inclined to doubt whether Bihar is as yet quite strong enough to stand by itself unassociated with Bengal or the United Provinces in resistance to a bureaucratic oppression; but if the Biharees generally think themselves strong enough and desire to stand apart, we should be the last, professing the principles we do, to oppose the idea. Administrative arrangements have ceased to be of vital importance. But the attempt which has been made in recent times to estrange the Biharees from the Bengalis in spirit is a more serious matter. There can be no ground of quarrel between the two peoples except such as arises from the unholy passion for Government service, places and favours; and this ignoble cause of dissension the new spirit will, we hope, destroy before long by making place and service a brand of dishonour rather than of distinction. Judging from Srijut Deepnarain's address we seem to have in him a Biharee of spirit, judgment and intellectual ability who has already grasped the future in anticipation and is likely to model the activities of his province in accordance with that larger vision and not under the stress of petty and evanescent interests. No province can advance under a more unerring guide or shape its activities to the demands of a more infallible ideal than this vision of an India united in its variety. Regional and communal individualities and activities cannot be blotted out from this vast country, but they can be harmonised into a dominating unity.

For the rest, it is curious to note how invariably the manoeuvres of the Moderates turned against themselves. This is indeed inevitable, for when Fate is against men, their likeliest measures and best-concerted combinations act to their own detriment. Dadabhai Naoroji was made President in order to dish the Extremists; yet it was this Moderate President who gave us the cry of Swaraj which the Extremists have made their own and which is stirring the blood of the nation to great actions and great ideals. Madras and the United Provinces were declared to be unanimous against Boycott in order to prevent the Boycott

Resolution from passing through the Congress; but the only result has been to raise a storm of Extremism in South and North alike, and set the cry of Boycott ringing from one end of India to the other. The shamelessly arbitrary action of the Moderate caucus at Allahabad has done more to kill the old and help the new than the free admission of the Boycotters could possibly have done. The selection at the last moment of Srijut Deepnarain as President in the hope of a "safe" address, — just as Berhampur was selected as a "safe" place — only resulted in a fresh testimony to the growth of the new ideas. How long will you try with these two-penny half-penny brooms of party manoeuvring to sweep back the ocean?

Bande Mataram, April 2, 1907

Peace and the Autocrats

EVER since the differences of opinion which are now agitating the whole country declared themselves in the formation of two distinct parties in Bengal, there has been a class of politicians among us who are never tired of ingeminating peace, peace, deploring every collision between the contending schools and entreating all to lay aside their differences and work for the country. It is all very plausible to the ear and easily imposes on the average unthinking mind. Union, concord, work for the country are all moving and sacred words and must command respect—when they are not misused. But what is it that these politicians ask us to do in the name of union, concord and work for the country? They ask us to sacrifice or stifle our convictions and silence the promptings of conscience in order to follow leaders whom we believe to have lost touch with the spirit of the times and "work together unitedly" in a line of action which we believe to be ruinous to the country. The demand has been made quite nakedly by enthusiastic adherents of Babu Surendranath Banerji that we should all follow the leaders blindly even when we disapprove of what they think, say and do. A more presumptuous demand or one *more destructive of all political morality and honesty could not be made. There is such a thing as a political conscience, even if its existence is not recognised* by the Editor of the *Bengalee*; and expediency is not what that veracious journal declares it to be, the sole god of politics, but a subordinate guide, itself determined by higher considerations.

Of course, many of those who cry out for peace at any price, do not perceive all that is implied in their demand. Is it not possible, they argue, to have differences of opinion and yet work together? We should be the last to deny it. The whole system of party politics, for example, depends on the subordination of minor differences by those who are agreed on main and vital points. So long therefore as the differences are minor and either essentially or for the moment immaterial, there is no reason why there should not be complete unity for all practical purposes; but the moment vital differences arise, parties and party struggle become inevitable. The men of peace and unity are never weary of throwing Japan and England in our faces; but they seem not to have read the history of the countries which they offer us as our examples. Have they never heard of the struggle between Federalists and Imperialists in Japan or of the civil strife between Federalists and Unionists which preceded and made the way clear for her marvellous development? It was the time when American guns had broken open the gates of the country and she was in considerable danger from foreign aggression; yet this was the moment chosen by the most patriotic Japanese for a bitter party struggle attended by mutual assassination and ending in civil slaughter. And what was the point at issue? Simply, whether Shogun or Mikado should be leader and sovereign in Japan. Our wise men would have advised the Japanese to give up their differences and work together under the Shogun because he was "the recognised leader"; but the patriots of Japan knew that the question of Shogun or Mikado involved vital issues which must be settled at any cost; so with one hand they fended off the common enemy while with the other they fought out the question among themselves. This is the only solution to the difficulty which has arisen in India — to present an united front to bureaucratic attacks while fighting out the question among ourselves. For this amount of concord one condition is absolutely required, that neither party shall call in the common enemy to injure or crush the other. There must be no suppression of telegrams defending a leader of one party from official imputations, no attempt by editorial paragraphs to implicate him as an instigator of disorder, no assistance at viceregal interviews in which the bureaucracy is invited to take strong measures against his propaganda.

If it is argued that the differences dividing us are not vital, we entirely disagree. We are all agreed on one point, that the continuance of unmitigated bureaucratic despotism is ruinous to the country and a change is required; but beyond this point there is more difference than agreement. The new party is composed of various elements and there are minor differences of opinion and even of method among them; but they are all agreed in one unanimous determination to put an end to despotism, mitigated or unmitigated, and replace it by a free, modern and national Government. The old party is also composed of various elements, — ultra-loyalist, loyalist, ultra-moderate, moderate, and even semi-demi-extremist; but they are all agreed on this main attitude, that while they aspire to colonial self-government they will put up with mitigated despotism for another century or two if vigorous petitioning will bring them nothing better. Here is a vital difference of ideal, aim and spirit; and it is necessarily accompanied by a vital difference in method. The new party is agreed on a policy of self-help and the organisation at least of passive resistance. The old party is agreed upon nothing except the sacred right of petitioning. Sir Pherozshah Mehta and the Bombay Moderates would confine our politics within those holy limits. Pundit Madan Mohan and the United Provinces Moderates are willing to add a moderate and inoffensive spice of self-help; Babu Surendranath and the Bengal Moderates will even admit passive resistance within narrow limits and for a special and temporary purpose. But the difference of all from the new party remains.

Where there are such serious differences and men wish to follow different paths, no lasting composition is possible. The party struggle must go on until the country has definitely accepted one or other of the alternative ideals and methods. Temporary working compromises are alone possible, and the soundness of even such compromises is conditional, firstly, on the candour and whole-heartedness with which they are undertaken on both sides, and secondly, on the carrying on of the party struggle strictly within the rules of the game. The present bitterness of the struggle is largely due to the disregard of these elementary conditions. National Education is an accepted part of the political programme in Bengal; yet all the best known and most influential of the Moderate leaders are either practically indifferent or passively hostile to the progress of the movement. Boycott is the cry of both parties within Bengal; yet the Moderate leaders did not hesitate to stultify the Boycott movement by the support they gave to the Swadeshi-Bideshi Exhibition. Moreover, our experience has hitherto been that the Moderates look on any compromise in the light of a clever manoeuvre to dish the Extremists or a temporary convenience to stave off unpleasant opposition for the moment.

The second condition is equally disregarded. So long as it is sought to suppress the new spirit by autocratic methods of dishonest manoeuvres, there can be no talk of peace or unity. The conduct of Pundit Madan Mohan Malaviya and his caucus at Allahabad has been both autocratic and dishonest. The delegates elected at the Railway Theatre were elected according to methods that have always been held valid by the Congress and there has never before been any question of the right of gentlemen nominated by a large public meeting to sit in Congress or Conference. Yet the Pundit and his crew chose by autocratic Resolutions of a temporary Committee which had received no power to alter the Congress constitution, to disallow the nominees of the Railway Theatre meeting! Even the British bureaucracy itself would have blushed to perpetrate so cynical and shameless a piece of autocracy. But these autocratic democrats had not even the courage of their autocracy. They tried first to exclude the elected of the people on the ridiculous plea that Mayo Hall would only hold a certain number and therefore — mark the logic of Moderatism! — this certain number must be composed of Malaviya Moderates and the Railway Theatre Forwards excluded; but they found that this trick would not serve. They then bolstered up their autocracy by the excuse that Allahabad must not be over-represented at the Conference. This excuse was a palpable trick since under the present rules it is impossible to prevent the place of the Conference from being over-represented. As a matter of fact among the few delegates who attended, Allahabad had an overwhelming majority. No sane man can expect concord and compromise between the parties while such trickery is considered a legitimate party manoeuvre. The penalty this time has been the failure of the

Allahabad Conference. The penalty next time, unless the caucus learn wisdom, may be open war and the holding of two separate Conferences in the same province.

Bande Mataram, April 3, 1907

Many Delusions

IN A country where subjection has long become a habit of the public mind, there will always be a tendency to shrink from the realities of the position and to hunt for roundabout, safe and peaceful paths to national regeneration. Servitude is painful and intolerable, — servitude is killing the nation by inches, — servitude must be got rid of, true; but the pains and evils of servitude seem almost more tolerable to a good many people than the sharp, salutary pangs of a resolute struggle for liberty. Hence the not uncommon cry, — "The violent and frequently bloody methods followed by other nations are not suited to a gentle, spiritual and law-abiding people; we will vindicate our intellectual originality and spiritual superiority by inventing new methods of regeneration much more gentlemanly and civilised." The result is a hydra-brood of delusions, — two springing up where one is killed. The old gospel of salvation by prayer was based on the belief in the spiritual superiority of the British people, — an illusion which future generations will look back upon with an amazed incredulity. God answers prayers and the British people are god-like in their nature; so why should we despair? Even now there are prominent politicians who say and perhaps believe that although there is no historical example of a nation liberated by petition and prayer, yet the book of history is not closed and there is no reason why so liberal and noble a nation as the British should not open a new and unprecedented chapter, — a miracle which never happened before in the world's records may very well be worked for the sole and particular benefit of India! The petitionary delusion, however, though not yet killed, has been scotched; its lease of life is not for long.

Another delusion of which Babu Narendranath Sen of the *Indian Mirror*, and the cultured and eloquent lady whom the Mahatmas have placed at the head of the new Theosophist

Church, are the principal exponents, asks us to seek our regeneration through religion, — only when we have become religiously and morally fit, can we hope to be politically free. In spite of the confusion of ideas which underlies this theory, it is one which has a natural charm for a religiously-minded people. Nevertheless it is as much a thing in the air as the petitionary delusion. If by religion is meant the *nivṛtti mārga* it is an absurdity to talk of politics and religion in the same breath; for it is the path of the few, — the saints and the elect — to whom there is no I nor thou, no mine or thine, and therefore no my country or thy country. But if we are asked to perfect our religious development in the *pravṛtti mārga*, then it is obvious that politics is as much a part of *pravṛtti mārga* as any other activity, and there is no rationality in asking us to practise religion and morality first and politics afterwards; for politics is itself a large part of religion and morality. We acknowledge that nothing is likely to become a universal and master impulse in India which is not identified with religion. The obvious course is to recognise that politics is religion and infuse it with the spirit of religion; for that is the true patriotism which sees God as the Mother in our country, God as *śakti* in the mass of our countrymen, and religiously devotes itself to their service and their liberation from present sufferings and servitude. We do not acknowledge that a nation of slaves who acquiesce in their subjection can become morally fit for freedom; one day of slavery robs a man of half his manhood, and while the yoke remains, he cannot compass a perfect and rounded moral development. Under a light and qualified subjection, he may indeed develop in certain directions; but in what direction are we asked to develop? In the morality of the slave, the Shudra, whose *dharma* is humility, contentment, service, obedience? In the morality of the merchant whose *dharma* is to amass riches by honesty and enterprise and spend them with liberal philanthropy? In the morality of the Brahmin whose *dharma* is to prepare himself for the *nivṛtti mārga* by learning and holy exercises, to forgive injuries and accept honour or insult, wrong and injustice, with a calm and untroubled mind? It is obvious that we may develop far on these lines without coming at all nearer to moral fitness for freedom. Politics is the work of the Kshatriya and it is the virtues of the Kshatriya we must develop if we are to be morally fit for freedom. But the first virtue of the Kshatriya is not to bow his neck to an unjust yoke but to protect his weak and suffering countrymen against the oppressor and welcome death in a just and righteous battle.

A third delusion to which the over-intellectualised are subject is the belief in salvation by industrialism. One great danger of the commercial aspect of the Swadeshi movement is that many of our young men may be misled into thinking that their true mission is to go abroad, study industries and return to enrich themselves and their country. We would warn them against this pernicious error. This work is an admirable work and a necessary part of the great national *yajña* which we have instituted; but it is only a part and not even the chief part. Those who have never studied Japanese history, are fond of telling our young men that Japan owes her greatness to her commercial and industrial expansion and call on them to go and do likewise. Commercial and industrial expansion are often accompaniments and results of political liberty and greatness, — never their cause. Yet the opposite belief is held by many who should have been capable of wiser discrimination. We find it in the truly marvellous address of Srinath Pal Rai Bahadur at Berhampur; — there is a wonderful contrast between the canine gospel of submissive loyalty preached in the first part of the address and the rampageously self-assertive gospel of economic independence preached in its tail-end. "Whatever the advantages of political advancement, they sink into insignificance when compared with the blessings which industrial prosperity brings in its train," — such is the gospel according to Srinath Pal Rai Bahadur. It is so far shared by many less loyal people that they consider industrial prosperity as prior to and the cause of political advancement. The idea is that we must be rich before we can struggle for freedom. History does not bear out this peculiar delusion. It is the poor peoples who have been most passionately attached to liberty, while there are many examples to show that nothing more easily leads to national death and decay than a prosperous servitude. We are particularly thankful that British rule has not, like the Roman, given us industrial prosperity in exchange for political independence; for in that case our fate would have been that of the ancient peoples of Gaul and Britain who, buying civilisation and prosperity with the loss of their freemanhood, fell a prey to the Goth and Saxon and entered into a long helotage from which it took them a thousand years to escape. We must strive indeed for economic independence, because the despotism that rules us is half-mercantile, half-military, and by mortally wounding the lower mercantile half we may considerably disable the upper; at least we shall remove half the inducement England now has for keeping us in absolute subjection. But we should never forget that politics is a work for the Kshatriya and it is not by the virtues and methods of the Vaishya that we shall finally win our independence.

Bande Mataram, April 5, 1907

Omissions and Commissions at Berhampur

THE spirit of mendicancy has not been given much play in the proceedings of the Berhampur Conference and so far this year marks a distinctive advance. Last year's Conference was totally exceptional; and there could be no certainty that the victory then won for reason and patriotism, would be permanent, for the mendicant spirit fled from the Conference Pandal before Kemp's cudgels and the triumph of the gospel of self-help was accomplished in an atmosphere of such excitement that even the chill blood of a Legislative Councillor was heated into seditious utterance. The very moment after the dispersal of the Conference the mendicant nature reasserted itself, justifying the maxim of the ancients, "Drive out Nature with a pitchfork (or a regulation lathi), yet it will come back at the gallop." But since then Nationalist sentiment in Bengal has grown immensely in volume; and although the Conference was held in a Moderate centre, in the peaceful and untroubled atmosphere of West Bengal, no positive mendicancy was permitted. There were, indeed, certain features of the Conference which we cannot view with approval. Last year the right of raising the cry of the Motherland wherever even two or three of her sons might meet, whether in public places or private, was asserted by the whole body of delegates in spite of police cudgels; this year the right was surrendered because Babu Baikunthanath Sen had pledged his personal honour to a foreign bureaucrat that there would be no breach of the peace. Since this plea was accepted by the delegates, we must take it that all Bengal has acknowledged the shouting of "Bande Mataram" in the streets to be a breach of the peace! Here is a victory for the bureaucracy. And yet the Chairman of the Reception Committee was not ashamed to include in his rotund rhetorical phrases congratulations on our triumph and our scars of victory. The private and personal honour of Babu Baikunthanath was set in the balance against the public honour of the delegates of Bengal, and the latter kicked the beam. It will be said that the position of Babu Baikunthanath as host precluded the delegates from doing anything which would compromise that estimable gentleman. We deny that Babu Baikunthanath stood in the position of host to the Conference, whatever may have been his relation to individual delegates; in any case the representatives of Bengal went to Berhampur not to eat good dinners and interchange kindly social courtesies, but simply and solely to do their duty by the country. We deny the right of any individual, whatever his position, to pledge a whole nation to a course inconsistent with courage and with honour. But the leaders seem to have accepted the plea with alacrity as a good excuse for avoiding a repetition of Barisal. "For such another field they dreaded worse than death." The incident shows the persistence of that want of backbone which is still the curse of our politics. In any other country the very fact that the delegates had been assaulted at one Conference for asserting a right, would have been held an imperative reason for re-asserting that right at every succeeding Conference, till it was admitted. Unless we can show the same firmness, we may as well give up the idea of passive resistance for good and all.

Several of the Resolutions seem to us unnecessary in substance and others invertebrate in phrasing. We have no faith whatever in the Judicial and Executive separation nostrum; we do not believe that it will really remedy the evil which it is designed to meet. So long as the executive and judiciary are both in the pay of the same irresponsible and despotic authority, they will for the most part be actuated by the same spirit and act in unison; the relief given will only be in individual cases. Even that much relief we cannot be sure of; for the moment the functions are separated, it will become an imperious need for the bureaucracy to tighten their hold on the judiciary and, with all the power in their hands, they will not find the task difficult. Already the High Court itself has long ceased to be the "palladium of justice and liberty" against bureaucratic vagaries, and the unanimity of the two Services is likely to be intensified by the so-called reform. It is quite possible that the separation will make things worse rather than better. One reform and one alone can secure us from executive oppression and that is to make the people of this country paymasters and controllers of both executive and judiciary. No patchwork in any direction will be of any avail. What for instance is the use of clamouring about the Road-Cess when we know perfectly well that it was levied not for roads and other district purposes but as a plausible means of circumventing the Permanent Settlement? No one can deny that it is admirably fulfilling the purpose for which it was levied. It is absurd to think that the bureaucracy will be anxious to open out the country any farther than is necessary for military and administrative purposes and for the greater facility of exploitation by the foreign trader and capitalist. The needs and convenience of the people are not and can never be a determining factor in their expenditure. For the same reason they cannot be expected to look to sanitation beyond the limit necessary in order to safeguard the health of Europeans and avoid in the world's eyes manifest self-betrayal as an inefficient, reactionary and uncivilised administration. Really to secure the public health and effectually combat the plagues that are rapidly destroying our vitality, swelling the death-rate and diminishing the birth-rate would demand an amount of cooperation with the people for which they will never be willing to pay the price.

With the exception of these minor triflings and of one glaring omission beside which all its omissions and commissions fade into insignificance, the work of the Conference has on the whole been satisfactory. It is well that it has sanctioned the taking up of sanitation measures by popular agency; it is well that it has dealt with the question of arbitration and that it has approved of measures for grappling with the urgent question of scarcity and famine. But in failing utterly to understand and meet the situation created by the disturbances in East Bengal, the Conference has shown a want of courage and statesmanship which is without excuse, — we wish we could say that it was without parallel. We shall deal with this subject separately as its importance demands.

Bande Mataram, April 6, 1907

The Writing on the Wall

WHEN things violent or fearful take place let no one be alarmed or discouraged — they also are "His goings forth". That there will be only the piping time of peace and we shall sing of the cuckoo and the spring is expecting something unnatural. An individial or a nation cannot rise to its full height except through trouble and stress. The stone block patiently submits to hammering, cutting and chiselling to be made into the statue which pleases the eye and gladdens the soul. If it could feel, it certainly would say, "How dearly I have to pay for the beautiful transformation." This is the inexorable law of nature. Nature has not yet been known to relent in this respect. If you want to get anything grand and beautiful out of her, you must go through the process through which a piece of stone passes before it is endowed with shape, beauty and meaning. The fertilising river rolls down stones, breaks through the impediments, rends asunder the surface of the earth before it bears on its bosom the argosies and crowns the bordering lands with plenty. Those who cannot look this sternness of nature in the face are not destined for things good, noble and high. If you want to grovel in the dust, indolence, ease and ignoble peace may do, but if climbing up the heights of glory is your ambition learn to encounter difficulties and dangers manfully. This is apt to be ignored and ridiculed as a copybook maxim. But it bears repetition times without number and when either an individual or a nation sets about anything earnestly it should start fully impressed with the truth of this copybook commonplace. The truth cannot be confirmed enough and thus the threats of the Anglo-Indian Press have hardly any terror for us.

The Anglo-Indian Press whenever they find that their arguments are seen through, that what is at the back of their minds is at once discovered, that their professions and protestations are taken at their worth, fall to using threats and throw out dark hints as if the people do not know that they cannot regain their independence without a fearful struggle. The Anglo-Indian Press are really nervous at our getting at the truth about political salvation and their arguments about our weakness and incompetency backed by the opinion of the moderate school of politicians in the country are systematically alternated with the arguments of fire and sword. When they cannot coax us into acquiescing in servitude, they want to argue us into it and failing that too, they brandish the sword. The *London Times*, its namesake in Bombay, the *Pioneer*, the *Englishman*, all tried to win over the Congress suddenly changing their attitude of supreme contempt towards the National Assembly of a quarter of a century's standing. But as soon as the news that the extremist programme found favour with the 22nd National Congress was flashed across the seas, the "Thunderer" at once cabled to us that India was won by the sword and will in the last resort be held by the sword. Since then these Anglo-Indian Journals are trying both mild and violent ways. The more the desire for independence seems to be in evidence, the more the signs of the times point to that direction, the more they gnash their teeth, tear their hair and beat their breast. At every fresh proof of reawakening more blood is sent to their eyes and head. Their conduct gives the lie direct to the vaunted profession — that the English people are everywhere the upholders, the representatives, the leaders of the two great interests of a people — Freedom and Justice. The demand of the Egyptian General Assembly has only provoked their laughter. The granting of a constitution to Persia is according to them a move in the wrong direction. They have given the Amir a taste of the flirtation of Western civilisation. They want to retain their spell over those whom they have already enthralled and are ever in quest of fresh victims. Surrender your life, your liberty, your birth-rights to the English nation, go on ministering to their comforts and pleasures and you are credited with common sense, prudence, intelligence and all other mental equipments. But if you think of making any strides in the direction of manhood — if you take it into your head to hold your own in the conflict of interests — if you show the least sign of walking with your head erect you are damned wretches fit for the jail and gallows because it has been settled once for all in the wise dispensations of Providence, that you are to sow and they are to reap, that you are to buy and they are to sell, that you are to be killed and they are to kill, that you are to be deprived of arms while they are to be in their full possession, that you will use arms for nefarious purposes while they will wield them to defend themselves. What else can these ridiculous effusions of the Calcutta *Englishman* mean?:

"Diligent students of newspapers in this part of the world can hardly fail to have been struck by the fact that firearms are now being frequently used in the commission of crime. They have been produced in the case of riots, and within a few days no less than three cases have been reported of persons shot dead by others who ordinarily should not have been in the possession of rifles or guns. When a Maharaja, *particularly a friend of Europeans and officials*, is shot from behind a hedge and the Police Superintendent of a District has a bullet whistling over his head, the time has come to enquire by what means criminal or fanatical persons on this side of India manage to possess themselves of fire-arms. Recent cases in the Police Court show that it is by no means impossible for transfers of revolver and the like to take place by private sale. Any unscrupulous or indigent European can sell a weapon to an Indian without the police being aware of the fact (how can they be aware?) and the question arises whether the punishment for a breach of this kind of the Arms Act should not be made absolutely deterrent. Further, as witness the case at Garden Reach, burglars and thieves are learning when they break into a house, that the most valuable property in it are not jewels or money, but guns, rifles, and revolvers. The latter have even been stolen from so secure a place as Fort William. All this points to the fact that a demand for weapons has suddenly arisen in Bengal. One would naturally like to know why. Some people will find no hesitation in accepting the reply that the demand has been caused by those Bengali newspapers and other preachers of sedition who proclaim that the people of this country ought to perfect themselves in military exercises and the use of arms. *Bande Mataram* yesterday boldly said that Indians must develop the virtues of the Kshatriya, the warrior caste. 'The first virtue of the Kshatriya is not to bow his neck to an unjust yoke but to protect his weak and suffering countrymen against the oppressor and welcome death in a just and righteous battle.' This kind of stuff, of course, is often harmless; but when we consider the lengths to which the boycotters have already gone, is it too much to suppose that some fanatics will go to some trouble in providing themselves with arms even if their courage halts there?"

But we reiterate with all the emphasis we can command that the Kshatriya of old must again take his rightful position in our social polity to discharge the first and foremost duty of defending its interests. The brain is impotent without the right arm of strength. India is now conscious of this long-forgotten truth. And the hand must hold up-to-date arms. And where the arms cannot be procured in a fair way, people are driven to underhand methods, not to kill their own men as the *Englishman* designedly insinuates, but to protect their life and limb, home and hearth, as they had to do at Comilla, as they will shortly have to do at Mymensingh. An awakened nation consults its necessity and proceeds to the invention. The song that nerves the nation's heart is in itself a deed. That song may lead to persecution but as the *Punjabee* has said, "Today we are in the firing line, but our recruits are at our back — ready to take our places the moment we drop down." This music can no longer be silenced and keeping time with it the coming Kshatriya is forging his thunder regardless of the fretting and fuming of the *Englishman*. The writings on the wall are getting distinct and the *Englishman* knows no peace.

Bande Mataram, April 8, 1907

A Nil-admirari Admirer

The splendid speech of Srinath Pal has at last found an admirer in the Nil-admirari Editor of the *Indian Nation*. What is more wonderful still is that the veteran cynic who had up to now directed all his energies in running down Surendranath has now suddenly discovered that "Surendranath is the most prominent man on this side of the country".

The poor President of the Conference who committed the unpardonable sin of differing from the omniscient Editor of the *Indian Nation* in his ideas of nationalism, has come in for a liberal share of abuse. He does not understand the difference in the ideals of the two parties; he fails to find wherein Mr. Tilak's nationalism differs from that of Mr. Gokhale. He fancies he had been cherishing and nursing the national spirit — and this disgust at the very name of the nation is the result. Even Homer nods; and the wise Editor of the *Indian Nation* and his other compatriots have to be told that the supreme test of nationalism is a belief in the future of the nation and a love for it — with all its weaknesses.

As for the scurrility of the New Party organs, we beg to remind this English scholar that even the genial smile of Addison cut the offending section of the public to the bone.

Bande Mataram, April 9, 1907

Pherozshahi at Surat

THE methods of Moderate autocrats are as instructive as they are peculiar. The account of the characteristic proceedings of Sir Pherozshah Mehta at the Surat Conference, which we published in yesterday's correspondence columns, bears a strong family likeness to the ways of the Provincial Congress autocrats all India over. The selection of a subservient President who will call white black at dictatorial bidding; the open scorn of public opinion; the disregard of justice, of fair play, of constitutional practice and procedure, of equality of all before recognised law and rule, and of every other principle essential to a self-governing body; the arrogant claim on account of past "services" to assert private wishes, opinions, conveniences, as superior to the wishes, opinions and conveniences of the people's delegates; these are common and universal characteristics in the procedure of our autocratic democrats. The difference is merely in personal temperament and manner of expression. "The State? I am the State," cried Louis XIV. "The country? I am the country!" cries Sir Pherozshah Mehta or Pundit Madan Mohan Malaviya or Mr. Krishnaswamy Aiyar, as the case may be. Only, as his personality is more robust, so is Sir Pherozshah's dictatorial arrogance more public, open and contemptuous than that of his compeers in less favoured Provinces. If the popular cause is to make any progress, if we are to show ourselves worthy of the self-government we claim, this strong-handed autocracy must itself be put down with the strong hand. As Mr. Tilak pointed out at Kolahpur, the object of the national movement is not to replace foreign autocrats by the Swadeshi article, but to replace an irresponsible bureaucracy by popular self-government.

The most extraordinary of Sir Pherozshah's freaks at Surat was not his treatment of Sir Bhalchandra as if the President of the Conference were his tame cat, — for what else was the Knight of the Umbrella, pushed into a position to which he has no claims of any kind? Nor was it his exclusion of the Aundh Commission from consideration by the Conference; it is part of the orthodox Congress "nationalism" to exclude the Princes and Chiefs of India from consideration as if they were not an important part of the nation, and to leave them without sympathy or support to the tender mercies of the Foreign Office. Nor was it his turning the Conference into a tool for ventilating his personal grievances against Bombay officialdom. It was his action with regard to the question of National Education.

Let us consider one by one the pleas by which he managed to exclude this all-important Resolution from the deliberations of the Conference. They show the peculiar mental texture of our leaders and their crude notions of the politics which they profess. The first plea is that the Resolutions of the Congress are not binding upon the Conference. What then is the necessity or purpose of the Congress? As we understand it, the Resolutions of the Congress embody the opinions and aspirations of the united people of India; they put forward the minimum reforms which that people are agreed to demand from the Government or to effect for themselves. A Provincial Conference can go beyond these minimum reforms if the circumstances of the Province or the general opinion of the public demand it; it cannot diminish, ignore or go behind them without dissociating itself from the programme approved by the nation and breaking up all chances of an united advance. If these are not the relations of Congress and Conference, will Sir Pherozshah inform us what are the true relations? If the Conference does not exist in order to carry forward the national programme with whatever additions the Province may find necessary for its own purposes, does it then exist only in order to record the decrees and opinions of a few Provincial leaders?

The second plea was that Sir Pherozshah Mehta could not understand the meaning of National Education. At Ahmedabad, we remember, the Swadeshi Resolution was disallowed in the Subjects Committee because Sir Pherozshah Mehta would not know where he could get his broadcloth, if it were passed! The nation was not to resolve on helping forward its commercial independence, because Sir Pherozshah Mehta preferred broadcloth to any other wear. And now the people of Bombay are not to educate themselves on national lines because Sir Pherozshah Mehta does not know what a nation means nor what nationalism means nor, in fact, anything except what Sir Pherozshah Mehta means.

When, on a vote of the Subjects Committee, the Resolution was declared by the President to be lost, it seems to have been the opinion of a large body of the delegates that this was a misdeclaration. The obvious course was, under such circumstances, a count of votes by tellers on each side. But Sir Pherozshah was ready with his third plea that this would be to question the veracity of the President. We cannot too strongly insist that politics is not a social drawing-room for the interchange of courtly amenities. Where there is a question of constitutional right, to bring in personal arguments of this kind is to show that you have not grasped the elementary principles of democratic politics. The very first of these principles is that law rules and not persons, — the person is only an instrument of the law. The President or Chairman of a body sits there to keep order and see that law and rule are observed, — he does not sit there to make his own will the law. If therefore there is any question of a miscount, it is his bounden duty to see that immediate measures are taken to satisfy both parties as to its correctness and it is the natural right of the members to demand such a count. That right ought not to be waived in deference to the tender delicacy of a Chairman's self-love, nor has he or his friends any right to talk nonsense about his veracity being questioned or himself being insulted. Such mouthings show either a guilty conscience which cannot face public scrutiny or an entire moral unfitness for leadership in any constitutional proceedings.

We regret that the delegates at Surat did not insist on their rights. Sir Pherozshah Mehta came to Calcutta, prepared to do at the Congress precisely what he has now been doing at the Conference; but he found a spirit awakened in Bengal before which a hundred Pherozshahs are as mere chaff before the wind. It is a spirit which will tolerate no dictation except from the nation and from the laws which the nation imposes on itself.

The progress of the National cause depends on the awakening of that spirit throughout India. Let there be only one dictator — the People.

Bande Mataram, April 10, 1907

The Situation in East Bengal

WHILE commenting on the proceedings of the Berhampur Conference, we expressed our opinion that the leaders had been guilty of the most serious deficiency in statesmanship and courage in failing to understand and meet the situation created by the occurrences in Tipperah. Leadership in this country has hitherto gone with the fluent tongue, the sonorous voice, skill in dialectics and acute adroitness in legal draftsmanship. The leader has not been called upon to understand the great and urgent national needs or to meet the calls of a dangerous crisis. In the opposition-cum-cooperation theory these were functions of the alien Government, and the only duty of the popular leaders was to advise or remonstrate and look on at the results. The present position in Bengal is full of the uncertainty and confusion of a transition period when circumstances have changed and demand new qualities, new ideas and a new spirit in the people's chiefs; but the leadership still remains in the hands of the old type of politicians. This would not have mattered if the old leaders had been men of genius gifted with the adaptability to suit themselves to the new circumstances, — the vision to grasp them and the courage to act. But none of these qualities seems to be possessed either by Babu Surendranath, the one man of genius among the older leaders, or by Mr. Gokhale, the one man of real political ability, — much less by the lesser heads. The country has still to seek for leaders who shall be worthy of the new age.

The Comilla affair has revealed beyond all possible doubt the heart of the new situation. It ought now to be plain to the meanest intelligence that a struggle has begun between two great forces which must go on till one or the other is crushed or driven to surrender. Any attempt to disguise the fact is the merest futility. Our Moderate leaders thought when Fuller had been driven out of the country and Morley had taken up the reins of

Government, the struggle need no longer be a struggle and could again be reduced to the proportions of a public debate between the Congress and the Government. Now again, they thought, a pleasant reversion to the old opposition-cum-cooperation politics may be gradually engineered. But the forces of reaction, opposed to us, understand politics better; they have seen that the fire of the new spirit is not a momentary blaze to be kindled and quenched at the will of individuals, but the beginning of an immense conflagration. Their policy is as astute as might be expected in such past masters of the art of politics. It is evidently to isolate the struggle and fight it out in East Bengal; to oppose and put down the new spirit after it had taken hold of the whole nation would be a task so difficult as to be a practical impossibility; to meet it in a single part of the country and crush it before it had time to spread effectively over all India, is obviously the wisest course. It is part of the policy also to attack it by localities even in the affected area and not as a whole, to destroy it before the defence has organised itself; and to use as instruments the Sallimullahi sect of Mahomedans, while the Police confine themselves to keeping the ring.

The leaders may say that they thought the Comilla incident an unwelcome and deplorable outbreak which had happily been closed whether by the "secret" efforts of Babu Surendranath Banerji or by other less miraculous means. That they did think so, is probable and nothing could more damningly convict them of want of insight and even the smallest measure of political wisdom than such an inexcusable blunder. It was perfectly obvious that, as Comilla had not been the first incident of the kind, so also it would not be the last. Before the Conference met the disturbance at Mogra Hat was already in full course; and that details, reported in Babu Surendranath Banerji's own paper, were of the most glaringly unmistakable character. At Comilla there had been an outbreak of anti-national hooliganism coincident with the Nawab's visit; the authorities had practically refused to help the Hindus and had only interfered when the Hindus were getting the upper hand; and even then, the arrest and punishment of a few rioters was so casually and lightly done as to be absolutely useless for any deterrent effect while the might of the bureaucracy was centred upon the prosecution of alleged Hindu culprits in the shooting case.

Nevertheless, the Comilla incident ended in a national victory. At Mogra Hat measures were taken to prevent a repetition of that victory. A Mahomedan Police official seems to have acted practically as the captain of the rioters; the Subdivisional Officer tried to deprive the Hindus of the means of self-defence; attempts were made to prevent organisation of defence by volunteers; a Police force held the station to exclude help from outside for the Hindus, leaving the Mahomedan rioters a clear field for their operations. Finally when in spite of all these obstructions the Hindus were again getting the upper hand, the higher authorities appeared on the scene, the disturbance was quelled, and arrests and prosecutions of Hindus are now in full swing. This is the substance of the account given by the correspondents of the *Bengalee* and the *Patrika*, and not yet denied. If after this the leaders are still unable to understand the situation, the sooner they give up their leadership and attend to their spiritual salvation, the better for themselves and the country.

The situation in East Bengal puts three important questions to any intelligent leadership. Is East Bengal to be left alone to fight out the battle of nationalism while the rest of the country looks calmly on? Is reaction to be allowed to persecute local and disorganised forces of nationalism or is mutual defence to be organised? What measures are to be taken to prevent the efforts of the officials to give the matter the appearance of a Hindu-Mahomedan quarrel? What answer have the leaders to give to these questions? At Berhampur two measures only were taken, — an empty and halting Resolution of "sympathy" and a flamboyant call for a Defence Fund, to be utilised for we know not what purpose. It is not money that East Bengal needs, but practical assistance, guidance and leadership. These the leaders have proved themselves unable or unwilling to give. They will say perhaps that they have secured the "sympathy" of Lord Minto as well as of the Conference, and nothing further is necessary! It does not matter a jot whether the local officials are or are not acting on their own initiative in their singular attitude in

East Bengal. The sympathy of Lord Minto has not prevented the repetition of the disturbances, and we have no confidence that it will prevent further repetitions which are now threatening. For effectiveness it seems to be on a par with the sympathy of the Berhampur Conference. The people can expect no protection from the alien bureaucracy which is interested in the extinction of nationalism. They can expect, it appears, neither help nor guidance from their own leaders. They are left alone to find out their own salvation. Be it so, then. Ourselves we will protect ourselves: unled and unassisted pave for the country its hope and its future.

Bande Mataram, April 11, 1907

The Proverbial Offspring

The great Mr. Morley has received the Viceroy's dispatch on the question of widening the powers of the Legislative Council. It is long and important and requires his mature consideration, and he cannot therefore have it discussed in the Parliament. It has been prepared in secret, will be matured in secret, and then the official Minerva will see the light of the day and panoply. It will be born a settled fact. Rejoice ye Moderates, the millennium is drawing nigh. The heart of Mr. Gokhale must be beating a little faster in anxious expectation. The tiresome voyages across the seas, his fervent appeals to the British public by day, and his luminous conversations with Mr. Morley by night, are about to bear fruit. The mountain is in labour and will in due course produce the proverbial offspring.

Bande Mataram, April 12, 1907

BY THE WAY

Adversity brings us strange bedfellows, says the poet, but surely it never played as strange a freak as when it brought Babu Surendranath Banerji and Mr. N. N. Ghose under the same political counterpane. Time was when the cryptic sneering self-worshipper of Metropolitan College and the flamboyant, brazen-throated Tribune of the people were polls apart in their politics. The *Tribune* ignored with a splendid scorn the armchair prosings of the Cynic and the unsuccessful Cynic was always digging his fang of cultured envy into the successful Tribune. How all has changed! Adversity has come upon both; the floods of extremism are washing over the political world; and the literary recluse who would fain pose as a politician holds out his arm of succour from the select little Ararat to the great man in difficulties. The mouse protecting the lion and Mr. N. N. Ghose championing the great Surendranath against the attacks of Extremists form companion pictures in freaks of natural history. Whatever else Babu Surendranath may be, he is a great man, an orator, a genius, a personality which will live in history. And for him to be protected by Mr. N. N. Ghose! Really, really! Of all the humiliations to have recently overtaken our famous Tribune, this is surely the worst.

*

If Mr. N. N. Ghose reminds us of the mouse that saved the lion, he still more forcibly recalls Satan reproving sin. We cull a few choice epithets from this gentle and cultured critic in which he described the new party with his usual sweet and courteous reasonableness. "The men who glorify themselves and singularly enough are glorified by others." "The new school has scarcely anything to distinguish itself except scurrility and factiousness." "Its politics are of the do-nothing sort." "It is moved by the dog-in-the-manger spirit." "It seeks to thrust itself into notoriety by abusing prominent men." "In the new school personal malice often did duty for patriotism." It is amazing with what accuracy the sentences characterise the political attitude of Mr. N. N. Ghose through all the years that he has been trying in vain to get the country to take him seriously as a politician. Irresponsible, captious criticism, abuse of everyone more successful than himself, a do-nothing, fault-finding, factious dog-in-the-manger spirit, self-glorification as the one wise man in India, — this is the compound labelled Mr. N. N. Ghose. Surely, those whom he now turns round to rend may well cry, "Physician, heal thyself."

We can well understand why he has transferred his attentions from Babu Surendranath to the new party. Envy of others' success is the Alpha and Omega of Mr. N. N. Ghose's politics. When the new party was still struggling for recognition, he extended to it a sort of contemptuous patronage; now that it is recognised as a force he cannot contain his bitterness and venom.

*

Mr. Ghose is in raptures over Rai Srinath Pal Bahadur's pompous and wordy address — the Rai Bahadur was not successful in commanding approval and respect by the speech, so our only N. N. stands forth as his solitary admirer. Sj. Deepnarain's splendid address revealed a new personality in our midst, — a man with a brain and a heart, not a cold and shallow joiner of choice literary sentences; it commanded the admiration of all Bengal without distinction of parties. After that it was inevitable that Mr. N. N. Ghose should be unable to find in it anything but words. Again we see the ruling passion at work.

*

But Mr. Ghose has another cause of quarrel with Srijut Deepnarain. Has he not dared to talk of the recent birth of Indian Nationalism in Bengal? What can he mean? Has not Mr. Ghose been editing the *Indian Nation* for years past? What then is this new Indian Nation of which Mr. N. N. Ghose knows nothing or this new nationalism which for the life of him Mr. N. N. Ghose cannot understand? Quite right, O sapient critic! Before you can understand it you must change your nature and get what you never possessed — a *heart* that can feel for the sufferings of your fellow countrymen and beat higher at the prospect of making great sacrifices and facing strong perils for their deliverance.

*

We are really struck by the infinite capacity for not understanding which Mr. Ghose possesses. This is his idea of the new politics. "They have nothing to do. As they mean to ignore the Government, they will not discuss its measures or care to suggest reforms. They are waiting for that political millennium, Swaraj. When Swaraj comes, they will assume functions; in the meantime they must only preach and abuse. A comfortable programme of patriotism." Hardly so comfortable as the armchair from which do-nothing critics criticise do-nothingness. Whether the new school is doing something or nothing, is not for him to judge but for the future. He thinks that national schools and colleges are nothing, that the boycott is worse than nothing, that to awake a new heart and a new spirit in a great and fallen nation is nothing; that to restore the habit of self-dependence and self-defence is nothing. What then is something in the eyes of this great man of action? To do something is to discuss Government measures and "suggest" reforms. We are overwhelmed! We can only apostrophise the editor of the *Nation* as the Greek General apostrophised his victorious adversary, "O thou man of mighty activity!"

Bande Mataram, April 12, 1907

BY THE WAY

An old and venerable friend of *our* old and venerable friend the *Indian Mirror*, weeps bitter tears over Raja Subodh Mallik. Subodh Mallik is a large-hearted and generous man, laments our friend's friend; but he is doing immense harm to himself and his country. Is he not partly responsible for the publication of that pernicious sheet, *Bande Mataram*, which attacks old and venerable gentlemen and old and venerable journals and refuses to regard politics as a school for society manners? Has he not given a lakh of rupees to the National Council — an institution for which the *Indian Mirror* cherishes a lively want of sympathy? We call on the young gentleman to repent of his sins, fall weeping on the capacious bosom of the *Indian Mirror* and devote the rest of his possessions to founding a Society for the Prevention of Cruelty to obsolete papers and out-of-date politicians.

We will admit that much that was said and done at Berhampur on both sides was petulant and wanting in dignity. But was it worse than what happens in European Parliaments and political meetings when men are heated by conflict and passions run high? We trow not. Let us try to be perfectly courteous and superior to other nations by all means; but if we cannot, there is no reason for disingenuous concealment and a mere Pharisaic *pretence* of superiority. The Japanese have an excellent habit of keeping anger out of their speech and reserving all their strength for acts; they will express their disapproval of you with great plainness, indeed, but also with wonderful calmness and politeness. The Samurai used to rip up his enemy very mercilessly, but also very politely; he did it as a duty, not out of passion. But of our emotional, sentimental race, so long accustomed to find its outlet in speech, nothing so heroic can be expected.

*

Still we think the young men of the New Party would do well to follow the example of the Japanese as far as possible. We should be absolutely unsparing in our attack on whatever obstructs the growth of the nation, and never be afraid to call a spade a spade. Excessive good nature, *chakshu lajja* (the desire to be always pleasant and polite), will never do in serious politics. Respect of persons must always give place to truth and conscience; and the demand that we should be silent because of the age or past services of our opponents, is politically immoral and unsound. Open attack, unsparing criticism, the severest satire, the most wounding irony, are all methods perfectly justifiable and indispensable in politics. We have strong things to say; let us say them strongly; we have stern things to do; let us do them sternly. But there is always a danger of strength degenerating into violence and sternness into ferocity, and that should be avoided so far as it is humanly possible.

*

Babu Bhupendranath Bose got little by his attempt to frown down the Government of Bengal in their own den over the bureaucratic temper of their replies to his interpolations. It is to be feared that the Government have little appreciation for the opposition-cum-cooperation gospel which their loyal subject not only preaches but practises with such fidelity and vigour. They like their water without salutary bitters. Babu Bhupendranath, however, insists on dealing with Sir Andrew Fraser like a father, and when he makes wry faces at the medicine, treats him to a painful and public spanking, — whereupon Sir Andrew responds with a backhander in Bhupen Babu's fatherly face. The whole affair was most exquisitely ludicrous and futile, but Sir Andrew's was a nasty and stinging backhander!

"The Hon'ble member himself has not infrequently, either on my invitation or of his own motion, discussed with me privately the propriety or wisdom of certain courses of action which he has followed. I have frankly given him my advice. He has sometimes taken it and he has sometimes rejected it. I should have considered it a grave breach of confidence, if, in either case, he had published it and had attributed his line of action to me."

So it appears that often when we have been hanging on the wise words of the popular and democratic leader, the influential adviser of Surendranath, the secret dictator of the Moderate caucus, it was really the Lieutenant-Governor of Bengal to whom we listened and by whose counsel we were guided. The voice was the voice of Bhupen, but the thought was the thought of Andrew. These be thy gods, O Israel!

Bande Mataram, April 13, 1907

The Old Year

THERE are periods in the history of the world when the unseen Power that guides its destinies seems to be filled with a consuming passion for change and a strong impatience of the old. The Great Mother, the Adya Shakti, has resolved to take the nations into Her hand and shape them anew. These are periods of rapid destruction and energetic creation, filled with the sound of cannon and the trampling of armies, the crash of great downfalls, and the turmoil of swift and violent revolutions; the world is thrown into the smelting pot and comes out in a new shape and with new features. They are periods when the wisdom of the wise is confounded and the prudence of the prudent turned into a laughing-stock; for it is the day of the prophet, the dreamer, the fanatic and the crusader, — the time of divine revelation when Avatars are born and miracles happen. Such a period was the end of the eighteenth century and the beginning of the nineteenth; in such a period we find ourselves at the dawn of this twentieth century the years of whose infancy have witnessed such wonderful happenings. The result of the earlier disturbance was the birth of a new Europe and the modernisation of the Western world; we are assisting now at the birth of a new Asia and the modernisation of the East. The current started then from distant America but the centre of disturbance was Western and Central Europe. This time there have been three currents, — insurgent nationalism starting from South Africa, Asiatic revival starting from Japan, Eastern democracy starting from Russia; and the centre of disturbance covers a huge zone, all Eastern, Southern and Western Asia, Northern or Asiaticised Africa and Russia which form the semi-Asiatic element in Europe. As the pace of the revolution grows swifter, each new year becomes more eventful than the last and marks a large advance to the final consummation. No year of the new century has been more full of events than 1906-07, our year 1313.

If we look abroad, we find the whole affected zone in agitation and new births everywhere. In the Far East the year has not been marked by astonishing events, but the total results have been immense. Within these twelve months China has been educating, training and arming herself with a speed of which the outside world has a very meagre conception. She has sent out a Commission of Observation to the West and decided to develop constitutional Government within the next ten years. She has pushed forward the work of revolutionising her system of education and bringing it into line with modern requirements. She has taken resolutely in hand the task of liberating herself from the curse of opium which has benumbed the energies of her people. She has sent her young men outside in thousands, chiefly to Japan, to be trained for the great work of development. With the help of Japanese instructors she is training herself quietly in war, and science, has made an immense advance in the organisation of a disciplined army, and is now busy laying the foundations of an effective navy. In spite of the arrogant protests of British merchants, she has taken her enormous customs revenue into her own hands for national purposes. By her successful diplomacy she has deprived England of the fruits of the unscrupulous, piratical attack upon Tibet and is maintaining her hold on that outpost of the Mongolian world.

Japan during this year has been vigorously pushing on her industrial expansion at home and abroad; she has practically effected the commercial conquest of Manchuria and begun in good earnest the struggle with European trade and her manufactures are invading Europe and America. Her army reorganisation has been so large and thorough as to make the island Empire invincible in her own sphere of activity. A little cloud has sprung up between herself and America, but she has conducted herself with her usual *sang froid*, moderation and calm firmness; and, however far the difficulty may go, we may be sure that she will not come out of it either morally or materially a loser.

In other parts of the Far East there have only been slight indications of coming movements. The troubles in the Philippines are over and America has restored to the inhabitants a certain measure of self-government, which, if used by the Filipinos with energy and discretion, may be turned into an instrument for the recovery of complete independence. Siam has purchased release from humiliating restrictions on her internal sovereignty at the heavy price of a large cession of territory to intruding France; but she is beginning to pay more attention to her naval and military development and it will be well if this means that she has realised the only way to preserve her independence. At present Siam is the one weak point in Mongolian Asia. Otherwise the events of this year show that by the terrible blow she struck at Russia, Japan has arrested the process of European absorption in the Far East.

But the most remarkable feature of the past year is the awakening of the Mahomedan world. In Afghanistan it has seen the inception of a great scheme of National Education which may lay the basis of a State, strong in itself, organised on modern lines and equipped with scientific knowledge and training. Amir Abdur Rahman consolidated Afghanistan; it is evidently the mission of Habibullah, who seems not inferior in statesmanship to his great father, to modernise it. In Persia the year has brought about a peaceful revolution, — the granting of Parliamentary Government by an Asiatic king to his subjects under the mildest passive pressure and the return of national life to Iran. In Egypt it has confronted the usurping role of England with a nationalist movement, not only stronger and more instructed than that of Arabi Pasha but led by the rightful sovereign of the country. The exhibition of cold-blooded British ferocity at Denshawi has defeated its object, and, instead of appalling the Egyptians into submission, made them more determined and united. It is now only a question of time for this awakening to affect the rest of Islam and check the European as effectually in Western Asia as he has been checked in the East.

In this universal Asiatic movement what part has India to play? What has she done during the year 1313? In India too there has been an immense advance, — an advance so great that we shall not be able to appreciate it properly until its results have worked themselves out. The year began with Barisal; it closes with Comilla. The growing intensity of the struggle in Eastern Bengal can be measured by this single transition, and its meaning is far deeper than appears on the surface. It means that the two forces which must contend for the possession of India's future, — the British bureaucracy and the Indian people, — have at last clashed in actual conflict. Barisal meant passive, martyr-like endurance; Comilla means active, courageous resistance. The fighting is at present only on the far eastern fringe of this great country; but it must, as it grows in intensity, spread westwards. Sparks of the growing conflagration will set fire to Western Bengal, and India is now far too united for the bureaucracy to succeed long in isolating the struggle.

.The second feature of the year has been the rapid growth of the Nationalist Party. It has in a few months absorbed Eastern Bengal, set Allahabad and the North on fire, and is stirring Madras to its depths. In Bengal it has become a distinct and recognised force so powerful in its moral influence that petitioning is practically dead and the whole nation stands committed to a policy of self-development and passive resistance. The Press a few months ago was, with the exception of a few Marathi weeklies, one journal in the Punjab, and the *Sandhya* and *New India* in Calcutta, almost entirely Moderate. The increase of Nationalist journals such as the *Balbharat* and *Andhra Keshari* in Madras, the *Aftab* in the North and ourselves in Calcutta, the appearance of local papers filled with the new spirit, the sudden popularity of a paper like the *Yugantar* and the extent to which the new ideas are infecting journals not avowedly of the new school, are indices of the rapidity with which Nationalism is formulating itself and taking pόssession of the country.

A third feature of the year has been the growth of National Education. The Bengal National College has not only become an established fact but is rapidly increasing in numbers and has begun to build the foundations of a better system of education. The schools at Rungpore and Dacca already existed at the commencement of the year; but immediately after the Barisal outrage, fresh schools at Mymensingh, Kishoregunj, Comilla, Chandpur and Dinajpur were established. Since then there have been further additions, — the Magura School, another in the Jessore District, another at Jalpaiguri, as well as a free primary school at Mogra. We understand that there is also a probability of a National School at Chittagong and Noakhali. No mean record for a single year. As was to be expected, most of these schools have grown up in the great centre of Nationalism, East Bengal.

Such is the record of Nationalist advance in India in 1313. It is a record of steady and rapid growth; and the year closes with the starting of a tremendous issue which may carry us far beyond the stage of mere beginnings and preparations. Long ago we heard it prophesied that the year 1907 would see the beginning of the actual struggle for national liberty in India. It would almost seem as if in the turmoil in Tipperah the first blow had been struck.

Bande Mataram, April 16, 1907

A Vilifier on Vilification

Our Bombay contemporary, the *Indu Prakash*, is very wroth with the Nationalist Party for their want of sweet reasonableness. He accuses them of rowdyism "which would put the East End rowdy to shame", and adds, — "Their forte seems to be abuse, vilification, impertinence and superlative silliness, and these are exhibited alternately." It strikes us that the *Indu Prakash* has been guilty of "abuse, vilification, impertinence and superlative silliness" not alternately, but in a lump within the brief space of these two sentences. This sort of phraseology is, however, part of the ordinary Moderate rhetoric which is usually the reverse of moderate in its temper. Unable to meet the Nationalists in argument, they make up for it in invective, denouncing them as "maniacs", "rowdies", "mere school boys". We have already answered the charge of rowdyness and we will only add here that violent personal attack is not confined to one party. But the moderates have their own methods. They attack individual members of our party behind their backs or else in meetings in which the public are not admitted, like those of the Subjects committee, but not usually in public. They vilify them in the correspondence columns of their papers and ignore them or only abuse the party generally in the leading articles. Then they call this the decency and "high dignity of public life". We prefer to call it want of straightforwardness and courage. The *Indu* thinks that personal attacks and violent outbreaks of temper have no part in English politics. This is indeed a holy simplicity; and it is not for nothing that the Bombay journal calls itself *Indu Prakash*, "moonshine". It is true, of course, that English politicians do not carry their political wranglings and acerbities into social life to anything like the extent that the Continental peoples do or we do in India; and this is a most praiseworthy feature of English public life. We do not agree with the *Indu* that the differences which divide us are smaller than those which exist between English parties; but small or great, we agree that they should not generate hatred, if it can be avoided. But if the moderates are so anxious to avoid the acerbation of feelings, why should they not set the example? Let them avoid autocracy and caucus tactics, frankly recognise the Nationalists as a party whose opinions must be consulted, be conciliatory and constitutional in their procedure; and what the *Indu* misterms "Extremist rowdyism" will die a natural death.

BY THE WAY

A Mouse in a Flutter

Poor N. N. Ghose! When we dealt with him faithfully in our "By the Way" column, we did so in the belief that it would do him good; the wounds given by a friend are wholesome, though painful. We expected that if we printed him in his true colours, he would recognise the picture, grow ashamed and reform; but it is possible we did wrong to pluck out so cruelly the heart of our Sankaritola Hamlet's mystery. Certainly we did not anticipate that the sight of his own moral lineaments would drive him into such an exhibition of shrieking and gesticulating fury as disfigures the *Indian Nation* of the 15th April. Such self-degradation by a cultured and respectable literary gentleman is very distressing and we apologise to the public for being the cause of this shocking spectacle. We will devote our column today to soothing down his ruffled plumes. By the way, we assure Mr.

Ghose that when we talk of his ruffled plumes, we are not thinking of him in his capacity as a mouse at all. We are for a moment imagining him to be a feathered biped — say, a pelican solitary in the wilderness or else, if he prefers it, a turtle-dove cooing to his newly-found mate in Colootola.

What is it that Mr. Ghose lays to our charge? In the first place, he accuses us of having turned him into a mouse. In the second place, he complains that after turning him into a mouse, we should still treat him as a human being. "I am a mouse," he complains; "how can I have an arm of succour or a fully organised heart? I am a mouse, ergo I am neither a politician nor a cynic." We plead not guilty to both charges. We do not profess to have any magical power whatever and when we casually compared our revered contemporary to the mouse in the fable, we had not the least idea that we were using a powerful *mantra* which could double the number of Mr. Ghose's legs and change him into a furtive "rodent". The rest of our remarks we made under the impression that he was still a human being; why he should so indignantly resent being spoken of as a human being, we fail to understand. No, when we made the allusion, we did not mean to turn Mr. Ghose into a mouse any more than when we compared him to Satan reproving sin, we intended to turn him into the devil. But the Principal of the Metropolitan College seems as skilful in mixing other people's metaphors as in mixing his own.

If, after this explanation, he still persists in his "mouse I am and mouse I remain" attitude we cannot help it. The worthy publicist seems to have had mice on his brain recently. The other day he discovered a winged or fluttering species of the rodent; now the mere mention of a mouse has engendered the delusion that he is one himself. We do not believe in the existence of fluttering mice, — but after Mr. Ghose's recent exhibition we can well believe in the existence of a mouse in a flutter. This time he seems to have discovered a new species which he calls "rhodents"! There was much discussion in our office as to this new animal. Some thought it a brilliant invention of the printer's devil; others opined that in his wild excitement the editor's cockney-made pen had dropped an "h"; others held that our

Calcutta Hamlet, unlike the Shakespearian, cannot distinguish between a mouse and a rhododendron. A learned Government Professor assured us, however, that *rhodon* is Greek for a rose and that Mr. Ghose has found a new species of mouse that not only flutters but flowers, — of which he believes himself to be the only surviving specimen. However that may be, we have learned our lesson and will never compare him to a "rhodent" again. A rose by another name will smell as sweet and a mouse by any other name will gnaw as hard.

Bande Mataram, April 17, 1907

Simple, not Rigorous

The finale of the *Punjabee* case has converted a tragedy into a farce. The bureaucracy started to crush the New Spirit in Punjab by making a severe example of its leading exponent in the Press. They have ended by acerbating public feeling in the Punjab and creating racial hostility — the very offence for which, ostensibly, the *Punjabee* is punished, — without gaining their ends. The ferocious severity of the sentence passed on Srijut Jaswant Rai has defeated its own object. Reduced in length from two years to six months in the Sessions Court, it has in the final appeal been reduced in its nature from rigorous to simple imprisonment. The upshot is that the Government enjoys the honour of entertaining two patriotic Nationalists with an unsolicited hospitality for the next six months. Meanwhile, the tone of the Nationalist Press will not be lowered by one note nor its determination to speak the truth without fear or favour affected even in the smallest degree. But the memory of the original sentence will remain; the gulf between the aliens and the people yawns yet wider. Incidentally the *Punjabee* has been endeared to all India by its boldness and readiness to suffer for the cause; its circulation has been largely increased and its influence more than doubled. Well done, most simple and rigorous bureaucracy!

British Interests and British Conscience

"The demand for popular self-government must be resisted in the interests of Egypt" — this is the *Pioneer*'s verdict on the National Movement in that unhappy land. We can understand why Egyptian aspirations must be stifled in the interests of the "protectors" of Egypt; but to say that this must be done in the interests of the children of the soil is indeed monstrous. The inordinate self-conceit of Englishmen very often betrays them into ludicrous absurdities. The Britisher fancies himself the Heaven-appointed ruler of the universe; and whoever ventures to stand in his way must be a nuisance, a rebel, a traitor. The whole history of Britain is a long struggle for liberty; and even the other day the British Premier could not help exclaiming, "The Duma is dead; long live the Duma." But whenever it is a question of Egypt or India where British interests are at stake, British greed overpowers British conscience and all sorts of monstrous arguments are fabricated to justify the suppression of popular movements. But the history of the British occupation of Egypt which began as a temporary measure and perpetuated itself as a piece of expediency, is quite well known and the world can no longer be deceived by journalistic falsehoods.

A Recommendation

The *Englishman* has arrogated to itself the office of Press-censor and has commenced to issue certificates of good conduct to our moderate contemporaries. Those that have not the good fortune to see with it eye to eye are branded as seditious. This is what it wrote in its yesterday's issue: —

"We regret that in a recent issue we confounded the two papers *Swadesh* and *Swaraj*, identifying the politics of the former with those of *Bande Mataram* and other journals of the same bilious tinge. As a matter of fact, *Swadesh* is conducted with moderation and ability and is by no means to be confused with the seditious sheets which are doing so much mischief in this country."

A critic who confounds the names of journals on which he sits in judgment, is a sight for Gods and men; and we congratulate our *Swadesh* friend on the testimonial secured from so high a quarter. But is it solicited or unsolicited? The seditious rags may now envy the distinction. But will they be tempted to mend their ways? We would suggest a kaisar-i-Hind for meritorious journals and recommend the *Indian Mirror* and the *Indian Nation* for the first two medals.

Bande Mataram, April 18, 1907

An Ineffectual Sedition Clause

WE commented yesterday on the folly of the Punjab Government in prosecuting the *Punjabee* and the ridiculous and unenviable position in which the practical collapse of that prosecution has landed them. The absolute lack of courage, insight and statesmanship in the Indian government has been always a subject of wonder to us. The English are an exceedingly able and practical nation, well versed in the art of keeping down subject races at the least expense and with the greatest advantage to themselves. It is passing strange to see such a race floundering about and hopelessly at sea in dealing with the new situation in India. There are three possible policies by which it could be met. We could understand a policy of Russian repression, making full use of the means of coercion their despotic laws and practice keep ready to their hand in order to stamp out the fire of nationalism before it had spread. We could understand a policy of firm repression of disorder and maintenance of British supremacy, coupled with full and generous concessions in the sphere of local and municipal self-government. We could understand a frank association of the people in the government with provincial Home Rule as its eventual goal. The first policy would be strong and courageous but unwise; for, its only effect on a nation which has a past and remembers it would be to expedite the advent of its future. The second, if immediately undertaken, might be temporarily effective but could not for long satisfy national aspirations. The third is a counsel of perfection to which, fortunately for India's future greatness, Mr. Blair will hardly get his countrymen to listen. Nevertheless, any of these three would be a rational and sensible policy; but the present attitude of the Government is neither. It is an impossible mixture of timid and flabby coercion with insincere, grudging and dilatory conciliation. The Government looses a Fuller on the people and then at the first check withdraws him. It promises a reform and then hesitates and repents and cannot make up its mind to give it either promptly or frankly. It has stored up any number of legal *brahmāstras* and *nāga-pāśas* to bind down and destroy opposition, but it has not the courage to use them. It would like to crush the people, but it dare not; it feels it necessary to make concessions, but it will not. This is the way Empires are lost. The only instance of a coherent policy is in East Bengal where the bureaucracy has envisaged the situation as an unarmed rebellion and is treating it on the military principle of isolating the insurgent forces and crushing them with the help of local allies before the opposition can become organised and universal. It is an acute and skilful policy but it needs for its success two conditions — weakness, vacillation and cowardice on the part of the Calcutta leaders, and want of tenacity in the strong men of East Bengal. But the situation in East Bengal is only a local symptom. In dealing with the general disease, the Government policy is mere confusion.

We may take its treatment of sedition as an instance. The clause dealing with sedition in the Penal Code is a monument of legal ferocity, but at present, of futile ferocity. The offence is that of exciting contempt and hatred against the Government. The Government means the bureaucracy collectively and individually. Anything therefore in the nature of plain statement and strong comment on any foolish or arbitrary conduct on the part of an official or on any unwise or oppressive policy on the part of the Government, Viceregal or Provincial, or on any absurd or odious feature in the bureaucratic system, or any attempt to prove that the present administration is responsible for distress and suffering in India or that bureaucratic rule is doing material and moral injury to the people and the country, falls within the scope of this insane provision. For, such statements, comments and attempts must inevitably provoke contempt and "want of affection" in the people; and the writer cannot help knowing that they will have that effect. Yet these are things that fall within the natural duty of the journalist in every country which is not still in the Dark Ages.

The alternative punishments — the minor, running to two years' rigorous imprisonment, the major, to the utmost penalty short of the gallows, — are of a Russian ferocity. Yet this terrible sword is hung in vain over the head of the Indian journalists; for, mere imprisonment has no longer any terrors for Indian patriotism and really crushing penalties can only be imposed at the risk of driving the people to secret conspiracy and nihilistic forms of protest. The lower grades of the executive and judiciary are not affected by scruples, for they are neither called upon to consider ultimate consequences or exposed to external censure; but the higher one rises in the official scale, the greater is the deterrent effect of the fear of consequences and the fear of the world's censure. This is the reason why ferocious sentences like that on the *Punjabee* are minimised in successive appeals — a phenomenon an Anglo-Indian contemporary notices with great disgust. The clauses 124A and 153A are therefore weapons which the Government cannot effectually utilise and to employ them ineffectually is worse than useless. If the journalist is acquitted, it is a popular victory; if lightly sentenced, public feeling is irritated, not intimidated; if rigorously dealt with, a great impulse is given to the tide of nationalism which will sweep onward till this place of civilised savagery ceases to pollute the statute-books of a revolutionised and modernised administration.

The "Englishman" as a Statesman

The *Englishman* has a confused and wordy article in yesterday's issue which it considers especially fit "for such a time as this"; but the meaning is a little difficult to disentangle. Our contemporary has a dim perception that there is a "crisis" in the country, the nature of which it is unable to determine; but it is a very terrible sort of crisis, anyway, — a monster horrible, shapeless and huge. "When it matures, influences may be shot forth into the country, and possibly also in Asia, if not also back into Europe through Russia, whose final issues no man can foresee." It acknowledges that there "are some hopes" in the hearts of the people "which it would be fatuous to mock, madness to ignore." So far as we can make out, the *Englishman* has discovered a very original way of respecting and recognising these hopes. It proposes to satisfy them by appointing a large number of non-official Europeans in Mr. Morley's new Legislative Council along with the Nawab of Dacca and any other equally rare specimens bureaucratic research can discover among the "manlier races of the North who, if they grew turbulent, might prove more troublesome than populations of another class from further South, who, if more effeminate, are also more contented". The meaning of this extraordinarily slip-shod rigmarole is that the *Englishman* has been frightened by the disturbances in Lahore which followed on the final conviction of the *Punjabee* and is also a little uneasy at the prospect of unwelcome changes in the Legislative Councils. Hence its unusual and unsuccessful attempt to overcome its customary "fatuity" and "madness". For our part, we prefer the *Englishman* fatuous and mad to the *Englishman* trying in vain to be sensible. In its natural state, it is at least intelligible.

Bande Mataram, April 19, 1907

The Gospel according to Surendranath

THE appearance of Babu Surendranath Banerji as an exponent of the "New Nationalism" is a phenomenon which shows the spread of the new spirit, but, we fear, nothing more. We congratulate Babu Surendranath on his conversion to the New Nationalism, but we are not sure that we can congratulate the New Nationalism on its convert. Nationalism is, after all, primarily an emotion of the heart and a spiritual attitude and only secondarily an intellectual conviction. Its very foundation is the worship of national liberty as the one political deity and the readiness to consider all things well lost if only freedom is won. "Let my name be blasted," cried Danton, "but let France be saved." "Let my name, life, possessions all go," cries the true Nationalist, "let all that is dear to me perish, but let my country be free." But Babu Surendranath is not prepared to consider the world well lost for liberty. He wishes to drive bargains with God, to buy liberty from Him in the cheapest market, at the smallest possible price. Until now he was the leader of those who desired to reach a qualified liberty by safe and comfortable means. He is now for an unqualified liberty; and since the way to absolute liberty cannot be perfectly safe and comfortable, he wants to make it as safe and comfortable as he can. It is evident that his conversion to the new creed is only a half and half conversion. He has acknowledged the deity, but he is not prepared for the sacrifice. It is always a danger to a new religion when it receives converts from among strong adherents of the old, for they are likely to bring in with them the spirit of the outworn creed and corrupt with it the purity of the new tenets. If leaders of the old school wish to be accepted as exponents of the New Nationalism, they must bring to it not only intellectual assent, but a new and changed heart — a new heart of courage and enthusiastic self-sacrifice, to replace the old heart of selfish timidity and distrust of the national strength.

In the leading article of last Friday's *Bengalee* some very important admissions are made. The unlimited possibilities of the organised national strength of India are acknowledged without reservation. "There is no limit to what they can do. We at any rate would set no limits to their ambition.... We want our country to be as great in its own way as other countries are in theirs. And we are determined to secure our rightful place in the federation of humanity by methods which are least wasteful in their nature and would *soonest bring us to the assured destination.*" The federation of humanity is one of those sounding phrases, dear to Babu Surendranath, which have no relation to actualities; but the rightful place of India among the nations, federated or unfederated, is one which cannot admit of any the least restriction on her liberty. And the description of the methods to be used at least rules petitioning out of court, for petitioning is certainly wasteful in its nature and would not bring us soonest, — nor, indeed, at all — to our assured destination. There is more behind. "*Where is the room for compromise in spiritual life?* Nobody has a right to tell us in regard to a question like this, thus far you shall go and no farther. National expansion and self-realisation is a sacred duty which we cannot lay aside at the bidding of any authority above or below. The charter here is a charter from on high and no mundane authority has a right to undo it." All this is admirable. It is true that the writer in the next breath says, "We have no quarrel with anybody who does not stand in our way," — an obvious truism, — and invites the Government "not to block the way", promising it as a reward "a happy and not inglorious transformation at no distant date". But the bureaucracy knows, as well as the writer knows, that transformation is only an euphemism for translation to a better world, and there is not the slightest chance of its listening to this bland invitation. However, the fact stands out that Babu Surendranath has declared for absolute autonomy to be arrived at by methods which among other things *would soonest bring us to the assured destination.*

Unfortunately the rest of the article is devoted to carefully undoing the effect of the first half. It is practically an attempt to controvert the position which we have taken up in this journal. Our position is that it is imperatively necessary for this nation to enter into an immediate struggle for national liberty which we must win at any cost; that in this struggle we must be inspired and guided by the teachings of history and those glorious examples which show how even nations degraded, enslaved and internally disunited, can rapidly attain to freedom and unity; and that for this purpose the great necessity is to awake in the nation a burning, an irresistible, an unanimous will, to be free. The *Bengalee* denies all these positions. We must win liberty, it holds, not by an immediate struggle but by a long and weary journey; not by heavy sacrifices, but in the spirit of a Banya by grudging, limited and carefully-calculated sacrifices. We are not to be guided by the concrete lessons of history, but by vague and intangible rhetorical generalisations about "our increased knowledge and wisdom, our enlarged affections and interests of the present day". We are to curb our will to be free by a "trained intelligence" which teaches us that we are not a homogenous nation and must therefore tolerate differences.

We will content ourselves at present with pointing out that the *Bengalee*'s answer to us is neither objective nor self-consistent. We have tried to establish our position by definite arguments and appeals to well-known facts of human nature and human experience; the *Bengalee* simply denies our conclusions in general terms without advancing a single definite argument. We can only conclude that our contemporary has no definite arguments to advance. The confusion of his ideas is appalling. We are to choose for the attainment of liberty the method which will bring us soonest to our destination; but we must at the same time insist on making it a long and weary journey. We must have the determination to get liberty "at any cost"; but we must not carry out that determination in practice; no, in practice we must get it not at any cost but at the smallest cost possible. We must really ask the *Bengalee* to clear up this tangle of ideas and discover some definite arguments before it again asks the Nationalists to confine themselves to realising their ideas in practice and to abstain from "quarrelling with everybody who differs from them". It would be no doubt very gratifying to the *Bengalee* not to be quarrelled with, in other words, to escape from the annoyance of finding its intellectual positions and its methods assailed; but we cannot gratify it. So far as possible, our ideas are being realised in practice wherever Nationalism is strong; but for their full effectiveness they need the whole nation at their back and it is therefore our first duty to convince the nation by exposing pseudo-Nationalism in all its workings.

We shall meet the *Bengalee*'s positions one by one hereafter. Meanwhile we take the liberty of offering one suggestion to Babu Surendranath Banerji. This veteran leader is a declared opportunist, who believes, as he has himself said, in expediency more than in principles. He seeks to lead the nation not by instructing it but by watching its moods and making use of them. Well and good; but even an opportunist leader must keep pace with public opinion, if he does not even go half a step in front of it; he must know which way it is going to leap before the leap is taken, and not follow halting some paces behind. The nation moves forward with rapidity; Babu Surendranath pants ineffectually after it. It is not by such hesitating pronouncements that he can retain the national leadership. The times are revolutionary, and revolutionary times demand men who know their own mind and are determined to make it the mind of the nation.

Bande Mataram, April 22, 1907

A Man of Second Sight

THE tendency not to mince matters is in itself a virtue seldom appreciated by people who in consequence of long subjection cannot rate boldness in any form at its proper value. But to awaken boldness in a nation which has lost the sense of honour and self-respect, has always been the first engrossing effort of those political thinkers who meant to do their duty by the country honestly and sincerely. The capacity to look facts in the face and support a true grasp of the situation by a programme at once bold and heroic, has always met with a belated recognition when fallen nations have begun their first struggle towards emancipation. The charge of being wild and mischievous dreamers, cursed satanic perversity and a rash haste to mislead and destroy, has invariably been laid at the door of people who tried to initiate great national revivals. The outburst of indignation with which the new school propaganda is being received in some quarters, is therefore perfectly natural. But it is not these unbelievers whom we want to reach and influence. The Pharisees and Philistines will ever dog our footsteps and try their best to dissuade us and to defeat us. They will even try to bring about the persecution of the true patriots; but this too none need fear; for suffering only makes men stronger to bring about the redemption of their country. Timidity at such times is dignified with the name of prudence, moderation and humanitarianism; but it is mere scum and dross which bubbles to the surface; meanwhile the true metal is being purified for use below. The process of purification is always accompanied by such surface impurities, but they only serve to bring truth and sincerity into bold relief. These politicians are intoxicated with the ideal of a prosperous serfdom and cannot realise how it eats into the very vitals of a nation. It is largely because the honour and emoluments of a selfish few, whom the alien bureaucracy seek to humour for victimising the rest, are brought into jeopardy that we hear such hysterical denunciations of the straightforward and fearless efforts of the Nationalists. "Let their conduct be such as not to savour of ingratitude to the benefactors. When we find so many broad-minded Englishmen fighting our cause in and out of Parliament, when we see a Viceroy showing every consideration to our feeling and sentiments, when we see a Secretary of State openly sympathising with our aspirations, when we see the administration of the country shaping itself to modern needs, when we see all these and many more signs of the bright future awaiting us — we should take heart to abandon petty querulous feelings and set ourselves earnestly to the task of self-preparation. Before we aspire to govern our country we must learn to govern our own selves."

Such are the ratiocinations and exhortations of the prophet of the *Indian Mirror*. His powers of vision evidently excel the ability of common men and amount to something more than second sight. He sees Englishmen fighting our cause in and out of Parliament, where the ordinary eye can only see a number of insignificant Members of the Parliament asking questions which lead to nothing and advising an oppressed nation to wait in patience for a far-off millennium. He sees a Viceroy showing every consideration to our feeling and sentiments where common beings can only see a policy of insincerity. He sees a Secretary of State openly sympathising with our aspirations where others can only see a Radical Minister professing liberalism and practising hide-bound conservatism. He sees the administration shaping itself to modern needs where we poor mortals can only see an out-of-date and semi-civilized system, refusing to be modernized and reformed. This it is to be an occultist and dabble in white magic! And what does it all come to? That some slight and ineffectual reforms have been vaguely promised, whose only result will be to give a few more individuals the chance of getting name and fame at the expense of the country. The *Mirror* is in terror of losing this chance because of the spread of Nationalism; hence its hysterical appeals and chidings. The country is not likely to be diverted by these selfish and narrow-minded considerations from the mighty movement into which it is casting itself or held back from the great goal of national autonomy.

Passive Resistance in The Punjab

We are glad to find that Passive Resistance is being boldly carried into effect in the Punjab. The recent demonstrations at Lahore which followed the *Punjabee* conviction have evidently come as a shock upon the white population. So long as the political ferment created by the new spirit was mainly confined to Bengal, Anglo-India comforted itself by saying that the Bengalis were an unwarlike race unlikely to cause real trouble. Their main uneasiness was lest the agitation should spread to the martial races of whom alone they are afraid and whom they lose no opportunity of flattering and trying to separate from the Bengalis. Englishmen respect and fear those only who can strike and, being a race without imagination or foresight, they are unable to realise that national character is not immutable or that the Bengalis, who could once fight both on sea and land, might possibly revert to the ancient type and put behind them their acquired timidity and love of ease. Now, however, their fears are being realised. Anglo-Indian journals had already begun to perceive the truth that there is a real unity in India and that "Lahore has become a political suburb of Calcutta". The Lahore demonstrations have carried the conviction home. Accordingly we find the *Englishman* groping about in an intellectual fog in search of such novelties as concession and reform, while in the Punjab itself the panic is taking the form of incipient terrorism. Sirdar Ajit Singh of the Lahore Patriot's Association has been doing admirable work among the masses. His most recent success has been to induce the Jat peasantry to boycott the Government canals as a protest against an iniquitous water-tax. As a result the Deputy Commissioner in imitation of the Fuller Administration, published this remarkable order, — "Ajit Singh of Lahore is forbidden to address any public meeting in Multan district. If he disobeys, he will be arrested." The only result was that Sirdar Ajit Singh addressed a meeting of 15,000 men in defiance of this ukase and the police stood helplessly by. We pointed out in our last article on Passive Resistance that Government by ukase would always be one of the methods the government must instinctively resort to in order to snuff out our resistance and that it was the imperative duty of every patriot to resist such arbitrary orders. We are glad to see that the Punjab has promptly taken up the challenge thrown down by the bureaucrat.

Bande Mataram, April 23, 1907

BY THE WAY

The *Englishman* and Mr. N. N. Ghose, faithful brothers in arms, were beside themselves with joy last week. What had happened? Had Nationalism by some divine miracle been suddently blotted out of the land? Had the spirit of Nobokissen appeared to his devotee and admirer and prophesied the eternal continuance of the British domination in India? Or had Mr. N. N. Ghose been at last elected to the Legislative Council? No, but happy signs and omens, prophetic of these desirable events, have appeared in the political heavens. Hence this war-dance of victory in Hare Street and Sankaritola. The great Twin Brethren, the black Aswin and the white, the two heavenly physicians of our political maladies, have laid a joint finger on the national pulse and discovered that the fever of Nationalism is passing away and the patient returning to a healthy state of loyalty and contented servitude.

*

The epoch-making pronouncement of the *Indian Mirror* is the chief source of joy and comfort to these allied powers. The Mahatma of Mott's Lane has waved his wonder-working hand and Nationalism is no more. Narendranath has spoken; the British Empire is saved. It is not surprising that the discoveries made by the *Indian Mirror* should have awakened admiring wonder and delight in Hare Street, for they are certainly such discoveries as are only made once or twice in the course of the ages. The *Mirror* has discovered that all is for the best in the best of all possible Governments. It has detected libralism in Mr. Morley's Indian policy and a passionate desire for reform in Anglo-India. And to crown all, it has found out that the Extremists,

— those bold, bad, dangerous men, — represent a party which consists only of themselves. This is a discovery worthy of Newton or Kepler, and it has naturally filled Hare Street with delighted awe. An ordinary man might ask, of whom else should the party consist? But such criticism would be profane in the face of so much occult knowledge.

*

The *Englishman* sits at the feet of Babu Narendranath Sen like a pupil, with lifted eyes full of childlike wonder and admiration. Mr. N. N. Ghose welcomes his neighbour on equal terms as a fellow-loyalist and fellow-discoverer. For Mr. N. N. Ghose has also been industriously discovering things, not only in natural history, but in political science. The other day he discovered the surprising fact that Mr. Tilak and Lala Lajpat Rai do not belong to the new school of politics — a discovery which will certainly edify and astonish both the hearers of Lala Lajpat Rai's speeches and the readers of the *Kesari*. He has discovered too that the new school have no "constructive programme" and are do-nothing politicians. Unhappily, this is a discovery which Mr. N. N. Ghose is in the habit of making about his opponents and critics ever since he attacked Shambhunath Mukherji, in language of astonishing coarseness, so it lacks the charm of novelty.

*

The *Amrita Bazar Patrika* has also become an object of Mr. N. N. Ghose's scientific investigations. He has discovered that this great organ of public opinion is returning to light, — in other words, that it was mad and is becoming sane. We do not precisely know why. The passages quoted from the *Amrita Bazar Patrika* merely report views which it has been insisting on for a long time past and the programme which it sets before the public is one in which the *Amrita Bazar* and the new school are in entire agreement. In the opinion of Mr. Ghose, however, this programme shows an insufficiently broad view, and he holds out an ominous threat of broadening Srijut Motilal Ghose's intelligence. For the present, however, "we reserve our suggestions" and the *Amrita Bazar* is spared this painful operation. In passing, Mr. Ghose informs a startled world that in regard to constructive works he has his own ideas. Evidently he has a constructive programme up his sleeve and is awaiting the dramatic moment for dazzling the world by its appearance. But for how long will he condemn us to hold our breath in awed expectation?

*

The *Amrita Bazar* finds occasion to condemn such effusive receptions as Babu Surendranath received at Rajashahi, and, in doing so, disclaims the charge of envy and jealousy which is usually brought against it when it criticises the moderate leader. Immediately the *Indian Nation* falls on its neck and weeps joyfully, "I too have been accused. Embrace me, my fellow-martyr." We doubt whether our contemporary will quite relish being put on a level with Mr. N. N. Ghose and the *Indian Nation*. Its editor is a recognised political leader and his paper has from early days been a power in the land, read and relished in all parts of India and even in England; but Mr. N. N. Ghose is only Mr. N. N. Ghose and the circulation of his weekly is — well, let us say, confined to the elect.

*

The Hare Street journal has undergone a startling transformation. It is trying to write sympathetically and pretending to have political ideas. This is rather hard on the unfortunate people who are compelled to read its outpourings; for the attempt to make some sense out of its leaders involves an agonising intellectual strain, which one naturally resents because it is not in the day's work. If our contemporary goes on much longer in this strain, we shall all have to go on strike and either petition the Government to pass prohibitive legislation or else organise passive resistance. As a sort of anti-popular Red Indian in warpaint and on the war-path, brandished tomahawk in hand and yelling wild and weird war cries, the *Englishman* is picturesque and amusing. But its new departure makes neither for instruction nor for entertainment.

*

It followed up its great pronouncement. "For such a Time as this" with an almost equally fog-bound leader on "Swaraj". This document begins by entreating us to give up our political aspirations out of respect for the lamented memory of Professor Huxley. After paralysing our wits with this stroke of pathos, the *Englishman*, not to be outdone by the *Mirror* or the *Nation*, announces a political discovery of its own. Our moderate friends, it appears, have been labouring under a serious delusion. The Liberal Party cannot give us reform, even if it would, but there is one who can and will, and it is — the Government of India! Codlin's the friend, not Snort. We congratulate our moderate friends on the delightful choice that is open to them. Minto's the sympathiser, not Morley — Minto will give you Swaraj, — the *Englishman* stands guarantee for it. But after bidding us kowtow to the Government of India because it alone can help or harm us, our contemporary with light-hearted inconsistency declares that our habit of kowtowing to those who can help or harm us, is the chief reason of our unfitness for Swaraj. It seems, on the other hand, that our behaviour is very disrespectful towards those who cannot help or harm us, e.g., Tommies, coolies and the *Englishman*. The Anglo-Indian rules India because of his paternal kindness to the coolie; until we too learn to enquire habitually into the state of the coolie's spleen with our boots and overwhelm him with vigorous and lurid terms of endearment in season and out of season, we shall not be fit for self-government. No wonder the *Mirror* asks us solemnly to lay our hand on our hearts and declare truthfully whether we are morally, mentally and physically fit for self-government. If this is the loyalist test, we answer sorrowfully, "No."

Political discoverers are not confined to this side of India. The *Indu* of Bombay is full of impotent wrath against Mr. Morley for prolonging Lord Kitchener's term and gives him a severe journalistic whipping for his misconduct. The *Indu* is extremely anxious, as a good moderate should be, for the safety of the British possessions in India; it has discovered that Lord Kitchener is not a good general and is capable of nothing more heroic than digging up dead Mahdis, so it clamours for a better general who will defend the British Empire more effectively and spend less over it. Poor Mr. Morley! Even the *Indu* has found him out at last. We cannot expect our contemporary to realise that only in a free and prosperous India can defence be both effective and inexpensive. The present Government has to provide both against aggression from outside and discontent from within, and this means a double expenditure. But what is the use of the *Indu*'s shaking its moony fist in Mr. Morley's face and calling the darling of moderatism bad names? Much better were it done to send a petition with two lakhs of signatures for Lord Kitchener's recall, and, having done that, — sit content.

Bande Mataram, April 24, 1907

Bureaucracy at Jamalpur

THE most recent accounts of the Jamalpur outrage emphasise the sinister nature of the occurrence and the defects in our own organisation which we must labour to remove. The most disgraceful feature of the riots has been the conduct of the British local official who seems to have deceived and betrayed the Hindus into the hands of the Mahomedan Goondas. The nature of the attack, its suddenness and completeness, show beyond doubt that it had been carefully planned beforehand and was no casual outbreak either of fanaticism or rowdyism. It is impossible to believe that the Joint Magistrate, responsible for the peace of the country, was totally uninformed of the likelihood of an organised attack which was generally apprehended by the Hindus. Yet it is reported that the local official induced the Hindus to be present at the Mela by a distinct pledge that they had nothing to fear from the Mahomedans, and then, in violation of his pledge, left them utterly unprotected for brutality and sacrilege to work their will upon them. If he had any inkling of the outbreak which was then in preparation, his action amounted to cynical treachery. Even if he was so imbecile as to be unaware of what was going on in his own jurisdiction, his failure to provide against the possibility of his pledge coming to nothing lays him open to the worst constructions. At the very least he showed a light-hearted disregard for his official obligations and his personal honour. His subsequent action was equally extraordinary. All the accounts agree in saying that the police were quite inactive until the anti-Swadeshists had their fill of plunder and violence and were making for the station. Even then, they confined themselves to depriving them of their lathis, — the mischief being done and further violence superfluous, — and with a paternal indulgence dismissed them to their homes unarrested. The only people arrested were a few of the Hindus who, if they were guilty of anything, can have only been guilty of self-defence. The accounts on which we base these comments are unanimous and have not up to the present moment met with any denial. We can only conclude therefore that, as at Comilla, the local officials looked with sympathy on the rioters as allies in the repression of Swadeshism, and acted accordingly. To stand by while the Mahomedans carry out that violent repression of Swadeshism which the sham Liberalism of the present Government policy forbids them to undertake themselves; to clinch this illegal repression by legal repression in the form of prosecution of respectable Hindus for the crime of self-defence; to strain every nerve to prevent outside help coming to the distressed and maltreated Swadeshists, and finally to save appearances by sending a few of the Mahomedan rioters to prison — a punishment which has no terrors for them, since they are all hooligans and some of them old jail birds: — such has been the consistent attitude of the local officials. The only new circumstance in the Jamalpur incident has been the assurance given by the local official which amounted to a promise of protection, and which alone made the outrage possible. For the last century the British have been dinning into our ears the legend of British justice, British honour, British truth. The belief in the justice of the British nation or of British Magistrates is dead. Generated by liberal professions it has been killed by reactionary practice. The belief in the personal honour and truth of individual Englishmen has somehow managed to survive; but it will not stand such shocks as the East Bengal bureaucrats have managed to administer to it. We would earnestly press upon the people of East Bengal the unwisdom of trusting to official promises or to anything but their own combination, organisation and the strong arm for their protection. We have already pointed out more than once what the Comilla officials took some pains to point out to those who applied to them for protection, that it is folly to raise the cry of Swadeshi and Swaraj and yet to expect protection from the bureaucrats whose monopoly of power the movement threatens.

Is This Your Lion of Bengal?

It is painful to see how utterly helpless and at sea the "recognised leaders" of Bengal are showing themselves in face of the growing acuteness of the crisis in East Bengal. The *Bengalee*'s comments on the Jamalpur outrage are, we are compelled to say, a model of cold timidity and heartless over-caution. The *Bengalee* declares that the whole Hindu community in Calcutta is intensely excited over the outrage done to their community in Jamalpur. It hints and insinuates that the connivance of the British officials is mainly responsible for these outrages; but even these vague insinuations it defends with a triple line of "*ifs*". It threatens dim and terrible consequences if the Government do not take proper measures. But in the meantime what does our contemporary, voicing as it does the mind of the most famous politician in Bengal, propose in order to meet the emergency? It proposes to hold a mass meeting in order to devise steps to minimise the evils of the situation, and, having held a meeting, it proposes to wait and do nothing. Or at least, if anything is to be done, it is merely to boast of our superiority to "lowly passions" and to wait patiently to see what the Government *might* do! These superior and enlightened journals cannot be expected to yield to such "lowly passions" as indignation against oppression, active sympathy with our outraged fellow-countrymen, and the desire to avenge their wrongs. We are sick to death of this false mealy-mouthed affectation of moral blamelessness which is merely an excuse for pusillanimity. Nero fiddled and Rome burned. Jamalpur is in a state of siege, the town held by Goorkhas, succour from outside excluded; one man lies dead and others wounded, some, it is said, fatally; the broken image of Durga, the outraged sanctity of religion, the blood of our kindred, the offended honour of our cause and country, — all cry out for succour and vindication. Yet the *Bengalee* finds time to fiddle about its superiority to "lowly passions". Such is the leading Bengal finds in the crisis of her destinies. Oh, the pity of it!

Anglo-Indian Blunderers

The *Englishman* has its own standing suggestion for the treatment of incidents like the Jamalpur disturbance. The theory is, the riots are the result of Mahomedan indignation at the Swadeshi Boycott; therefore, Swadeshi is the cause of the whole trouble; therefore, put down Swadeshi with the strong hand. No one knows better than the *Englishman* that the disturbances have been caused by the sinister alliance of Anglo-India with the Nawab of Dacca and his following contracted to put down Swadeshi by fair means or foul. For our part we should welcome open oppression by the bureaucracy; it would be more honourable at least than local connivance at violence and brutal lawlessness, and it would be a pleasure to meet an open and straightforward opponent. But open or secret, direct or indirect, no measures whatsoever will succeed in crushing the insurgent national spirit. We wonder whether these complacent bureaucrats and exploiters have any idea of the growing mass of silent exasperation to which the present policy is rapidly giving shape and substance. Possibly, the idea is to force the exasperation to a head and crush it when it breaks into overt action, the old policy of the English in Ireland. But we would remind these blundering Anglo-Saxon Machiavellis that India is not Ireland; it is easier to unchain the tempest than to decree to it what course it shall take and what it shall spare or what destroy.

Bande Mataram, April 25, 1907

The Leverage of Faith

IT IS said of Guru Nanak that on the eve of his departure from the body he was asked to name a successor to his *gadi*. A great storm was raging at the time — the disturbance of Nature synchronising with the passing away of a great spirit. Nanak was then sitting under a tree surrounded by his disciples. It was evening and the Guru perceiving that his Chelas badly needed food and drink, asked his sons Shrichand and Lakshichand to go in quest of food. But the sons inherited none of the spiritual qualities of their father; they thought him to be no better than a maniac and were not inclined to take his request seriously; rather, they mocked at the idea of a search for food when none could stir out of doors for the wild rain and storm without. Nanak then turned to a devoted disciple, who simply enquired where he should go for food, and he was told that he had only to ask of the tree under which they were then sitting and it would give them all they required. The disciple did Nanak's bidding and, as the story goes, was rewarded with sufficiency of sweetmeats. Nanak went afterwards with his disciples to the riverside, and when, on the way, they came across a dead body, he bade his sons partake of this strange food. His sons took the command as conclusive proof of their father's lunacy, but the disciple was prepared to obey unquestioningly and only paused to ask where to begin, whether from the head or from the foot. Nanak, entirely satisfied with the steadfast faith of his disciple, named him the successor to his *gadi* in preference to his own sons.

It is not given to all to possess this heroic spiritual faith which all religious teachers have insisted on as the first preliminary to any difficult *sādhan*; but the moral underlying it is one which all experience justifies. Faith is the first condition of success in every great undertaking. It is no exaggeration to say that faith removes mountains. It is faith that makes the men of will and thought persevere in spite of apparently insurmountable difficulties. They start with a strong confidence in the ultimate success of a noble undertaking, and are therefore never daunted by difficulties, however formidable. Faith is the one predominating characteristic of all great souls. The vision of faith penetrates into the remote future and turns the impossible into the possible. In the region of politics faith is the result of imagination working in the light of history; it takes its stand on reason and experience and aspires into the future from the firm ground of the past. Other nations have risen from the lowest depths of degradation — the weaknesses which prevent us from trying bold and effective remedies were common to all subject nations before us. It is by nerving the nation's heart with inspiring literature and inciting it to struggle for emancipation that freedom has been recovered. For a subject people there is no royal road to emancipation. They must wade to it through struggle, sacrifice, slaughter, if necessary. History suggests no short-cut. Why should it then involve a strain on our faith to believe that if we are only prepared for the necessary sacrifice, we also shall gain the end? Other nations also were weak, disunited and denationalised like ourselves. It is the rallying cry of freedom that combined their scattered units, drawing them together with a compelling and magical attraction. Those who would win freedom, must first imbue the people with an overpowering conviction that freedom is the one thing needful. Without a great ideal there can be no great movement. Small baits of material advantages will not nerve them to high endeavour and heroic self-sacrifice; it is only the idea of national freedom and national greatness that has that overmastering appeal. We must not bend the knee to others but try to be worthy of our past — here is an ideal which, if set forth with conviction and power, cannot fail to inspire self-sacrificing action. We need faith above all things, faith in ourselves, faith in the nation, faith in India's destiny. A dozen men rendered invincible by a strong faith in their future, have in other times, spread the contagion of nationalism to the remotest corner of vast countries. Unbelief is blind — it does not see far ahead, neither stimulates strength nor inspires action. The lack of this faith has kept our moderate politicians tied down to a worn-out ideal which has lost its credibility. No man can lead a rising nation unless he has this faith first of all, that what other great men have done before him, he also can do as well, if not better, — that the freedom other nations have won, we also can win, if only we have the faith, the will.

Bande Mataram, April 25, 1907

Graduated Boycott

THE opponents of the New Spirit have discovered that boycott is an illusion. An entire and sweeping boycott, they say, is a moral and physical impossibility; and their infallible economic authority, Mr. Gokhale, has found out that a graduated boycott is an economic impossibility. They point to the failure of the thorough-going boycott in Bengal as a proof of the first assertion; the second, they think, requires no proof, for how can what Mr. Gokhale has said be wrong? This assertion of the impossibility of a graduated boycott is an answer to the reasoning by which Mr. Tilak has supported the movement in Maharashtra. In the first days of the movement Mr. Tilak published a series of vigorous and thoughtful articles in the *Kesari* on Boycott as a political Yoga. He advocated the entire exclusion of British goods, the preference of Swadeshi goods at a sacrifice when they were attainable, and, when unattainable, the preference of any foreign goods not produced in the British Empire. To the argument that this programme was not immediately practicable in its completeness, he replied that as in Yoga, so in the boycott, "even a little of this *dharma* saves us from a mighty peril". The mighty peril is the entire starvation of the country by foreign exploiters and its complete and hopeless dependence on aliens for almost all articles of common use. Even a slight immediate diminution of this dependence would be a great national gain and could by degrees be extended until the full boycott policy became an accomplished fact. Mr. Tilak, with his shrewd practical insight, was able to see clearly that immediate and complete success of a thorough-going boycott was not possible in India, but that a gradually efficacious boycott would naturally result from a thorough-going boycott campaign. What Mr. Tilak foresaw, is precisely what is happening.

The entire exclusion of British-made goods is the political aspect of the Boycott with which we do not deal in this article.

Is it a fact that as an economic weapon a graduated boycott is impossible? Boycott may be graduated in several ways. First, by the gradual growth of the idea of excluding foreign goods a steadily increasing check may be put on the import of particular foreign articles and a corresponding impulse given to the use of the same articles produced in India. A Government by imposing a gradually increasing duty on an import in successive tariffs may kill it by degrees instead of immediately imposing a prohibitive rate; the growth of the boycott sentiment may automatically exercise the same kind of increasing check. The growth of the sentiment will help on the production of the indigenous article and the increased production of the indigenous article will help on the growth of the sentiment. Thus mutually stimulated, Swadeshi and Boycott will advance with equal and ever more rapid steps, until the shrinkage of the foreign import reaches the point where it is no longer profitable to import it. The process can only be checked by the insufficiency of capital in the country available or willing to invest itself in Swadeshi manufacture. But the growth of the boycott sentiment will of itself encourage and is encouraging capital to invest in this direction; for so much boycott means so much *sure market* for Swadeshi articles and therefore an increase of capital willing to invest in Swadeshi manufacture. The increased production of the Swadeshi article in its turn means more money in the hands of the mercantile class and of investors in Swadeshi Companies and therefore more capital *available* for investment in Swadeshi manufacture. We fail to see how in this sense an automatically graduated boycott is impossible; on the contrary, it seems to us economically inevitable, provided only the boycott sentiment is increasingly embraced by the people.

Boycott may be graduated in another way. When the boycott was declared in Bengal, it was declared specially against cloth, sugar and salt, and only generally against other articles. It is therefore the imports of English piece-goods, Liverpool salt and, though only to a slight extent, of foreign sugar into Bengal which have suffered. When this specific boycott has been proved effective, it may be extended to other articles. Thus the boycott may be graduated not only in its incidence on particular articles, but in its extent and range. The graduation of a specific boycott may be partly artificial and partly automatic. It is artificial when the leaders of the people preach an economic Jehad against particular foreign goods and the people accept their decision. But this artificial boycott can only succeed when there is already an incipient industry in the corresponding Swadeshi article or some existing means of supply however partial, which may be stimulated or extended by the boycott. Liverpool salt has been affected because 'Karkach' is available; British piece-goods have been affected because there was already a mill-industry and a handloom industry which have been enormously stimulated by the boycott, as is shown by the wholesale return of the weaver class to their trade in Bengal and by the increase in the number of weaving mills and the splendid dividends which the existing concerns are paying. On the other hand the campaign against foreign sugar has not been successful, because the proper substitute is not available. Yarns have not been affected because the spinning industry in India is a negligible quantity while the demand for yarn has enormously increased. In time a Jehad against foreign yarn will become feasible. But the specific boycott may also be automatic when the general sentiment of boycott attacks a particular article for which a substitute exists in the country. To take a small instance, the market for steel trunks sent ready-manufactured from England is decreasing to such an extent that failures of dealers in steel trunks are beginning to be recorded. Here again, we fail to see the impossibility of a graduated boycott. It is quite true that in the very beginning the increase of the stimulated Swadeshi article may not be sufficient to blot out entirely the increase in the import, and the superficial and hasty may proclaim the failure of the boycott. But by the growth of the boycott the increase of the Swadeshi article must progressively swell and the increase of the import must progressively shrink until it is turned into an actual decrease. The fact that the success of the boycott is progressive and not miraculous, need not frighten or disappoint any sensible and determined boycotter. It is true also that the growth of Swadeshi may actually stimulate for a time the import of particular foreign articles, such as machinery or yarns; but the stimulation is temporary and, as soon as part of our growing capital is free and willing to invest in new fields, the graduated boycott will naturally extend itself in these directions sooner than in others.

The theory therefore that a graduated boycott is impossible, seems to us to have no foundation either of facts or of reasoning. Whatever the fate of its use as a political weapon, its success as an economical weapon depends solely on the zeal with which it is preached and the readiness with which it is received by the people.

Instinctive Loyalty

The *Indian Mirror* reflects nothing but its own self when it says, — "Nobody in the country, howsoever absorbed in the dreams of an Indian autonomy, wishes to see the British connection severed and the country left to her fate. This instinctive clinging to some sort of relation with England, in other words, this loyalty to the Crown of England, affords the best ground for optimism about a material improvement in the attitude of the Indian peoples toward their British rulers." There are more things in heaven and earth than are dreamt of in the *Mirror*'s philosophy. That a country cannot prosper in the true sense of the term unless it be left to its own fate is a truism with all right-thinking men. The publicists of the *Indian Mirror* type have a comfortable gospel of their own revealed to them by a study of their own needs rather than those of the country. No political thinker has as yet sought to convert the truth that liberty is the essential condition of all-round progress in a nation. Prison life after some time comes to be life as a matter of habit, — the jailor comes to be respected out of fear of the rod. But to describe such diseased and abnormal sentiments as normal and instinctive is to mistake a slave for a man. It is highly prejudicial to our returning sense of self-respect that papers like the *Indian Mirror* should still be able to preach the gospel of servility.

Bande Mataram, April 26, 1907

Nationalism not Extremism

IT IS a curious fact that even after so many months of sustained propaganda and the most clear and definite statements of the New Politics, there should still be so much confusion as to the attitude of the Nationalist Party and the elementary issues they have raised. This confusion is to some extent due to wilful distortion and deliberate evasion of the true issues. The ultra-loyalist publicists especially, Indian or Anglo-Indian, are obliged to ignore the true position of the party, misnamed Extremists, because they are unable to meet its trenchant and irresistible logic and common sense. But with the great majority of Indian politicians, the misapprehension is genuine. The political teaching of the New School is so novel and disturbing to their settled political ideas, — or rather the conventional, abstract, second-hand formulas which take the place of ideas — that they cannot even grasp its true nature and turn from it with repugnance before they have given themselves time to understand it. The most obstinate of these misapprehensions is the idea that the New Politics is a counsel of despair, a mad revolutionary fury induced by Curzonian reaction. We can afford to pass over this misapprehension with contempt, when it is put forward by foolish, prejudiced or conceited critics who are merely trying to bring odium on the movement or to express their enlightened superiority over younger politicians. But when a fair and scrupulous opponent honestly trying to understand the nationalist position falls into the same error, we are bound to meet it and once more clear our position beyond misapprehension or doubt.

Some friends of ours have thought that we were unnecessarily harsh and even unjust in our criticism of Dr. Rash Behari Ghose's speech in the Supreme Legislative Council. They urge that Dr. Ghose at least presented the Extremist position with great energy, clearness, courage, and did it with the greater effect as one who himself stood outside our party. We have every respect for Dr. Rash Behari Ghose personally; he is perhaps the foremost jurist in India, a scholar and master of the English tongue, a mine of literature in possession of a style of his own, too rich and scholarly to be turned to such everyday uses as a Legislative Council speech. But eminence in law and literature do not necessarily bring with them a grasp of politics. Dr. Ghose has only recently turned his attention to this field and has not been long enough in touch with the actualities of politics to get a real grasp of them. It is therefore natural that he should be misled by names instead of penetrating beyond names to the true aspects of current politics. The ordinary nick-names of Moderate and Extremist do not properly describe the parties which they are used to label; and they are largely responsible for much confusion of ideas as to the real difference between the two schools. Dr. Ghose evidently labours, like many others, under the obsession of the word Extremist. He imagines that the essential difference between the parties is a difference in attitude and in the intensity of feeling. The Extremists, in his view, are men embittered by oppression which makes even wise men mad; full of passionate repining at their "more than Egyptian bondage", exasperated by bureaucratic reaction, despairing of redress at the hands of the British Government or the British nation, they are advocating an extreme attitude and extreme methods in a spirit of desperate impatience. The Extremist propaganda is, therefore, a protest against misgovernment and a movement of despair driving towards revolt. We are unable to accept this statement of the nationalist position. On the contrary, it so successfully represents the new politics to be what they are not, that we choose it as a starting-point for our explanation of what they are.

The new movement is not primarily a protest against bad Government — it is a protest against the continuance of British control; whether that control is used well or ill, justly or injustly, is a minor and unessential consideration. It is not born of a disappointed expectation of admission to British citizenship, — it is born of a conviction that the time has come when India can, should and will become a great, free and united nation. It is not a negative current of destruction, but a positive, constructive impulse towards the making of modern India. It is not a cry of revolt and despair, but a gospel of national faith and hope. Its true description is not Extremism, but Democratic Nationalism.

These are the real issues. There are at present not two parties in India, but three, — the Loyalists, the Moderates and the Nationalists. The Loyalists would be satisfied with good Government by British rulers and a limited share in the administration; the Moderates desire self-government within the British Empire, but are willing to wait for it indefinitely; the Nationalists would be satisfied with nothing less than independence whether within the Empire, if that be possible, or outside it; they believe that the nation cannot and ought not to wait, but must bestir itself immediately, if it is not to perish as a nation. The Loyalists believe that Indians have not the capacities and qualities necessary for freedom and even if they succeed in developing the necessary fitness, they would do better for themselves and mankind by remaining as a province of the British Empire; any attempt at freedom will, they think, be a revolt against Providence and can bring nothing but disaster on the country. The Loyalist view is that India cannot, should not and will not be a free, great and united nation. The Moderates believe the nation to be too weak and disunited to aim at freedom; they would welcome independence if it came, but they are not convinced that we have or shall have in the measurable future the means or strength to win it or keep it if won. They therefore put forward Colonial Self-Government as their aim and are unwilling to attempt any methods which presuppose strength and cohesion in the nation. The Moderate view is that India may eventually be united, self-governing within limits and prosperous, but not free and great. The Nationalists hold that Indians are as capable of freedom as any subject nation can be and their defects are the result of servitude and can only be removed by the struggle for freedom; that they have the strength, and, if they get the will, can create the means to win independence. They hold that the choice is not between autonomy and provincial Home Rule or between freedom and dependence, but between freedom and national decay and death. They hold, finally, that the past history of our country and the present circumstances are of such a kind that the great unifying tendencies hitherto baffled by insuperable obstacles have at last found the right conditions for success. They believe that the fated hour for Indian unification and freedom has arrived. In brief, they are convinced that India should strive to be free, that she can be free and that she will, by the impulse of her past and present, be inevitably driven to the attempt and the attainment of national self-realisation. The Nationalist creed is a gospel of faith and hope.

Bande Mataram, April 26, 1907

Shall India be Free?

THE LOYALIST GOSPEL

LIBERTY is the first requisite for the sound health and vigorous life of a nation. A foreign despotism is in itself an unnatural condition and if permitted, must bring about other unhealthy and unnatural conditions in the subject people which will lead to fatal decay and disorganisation. Foreign rule cannot build up a nation — only the resistance to foreign rule can weld the discordant elements of a people into an indivisible unity. When a people, predestined to unity, cannot accomplish its destiny, foreign rule is a provision of Nature by which the necessary compelling pressure is applied to drive its jarring parts into concord. The unnatural condition of foreign rule is brought in for a time in order to cure the previous unnatural condition of insufficient cohesiveness; but this can only be done by the resistance of the subject people; for the incentive to unity given by the alien domination consists precisely in the desire to get rid of it; and if this desire is absent, if the people acquiesce, there can be no force making for unity. Foreign rule was therefore made to be resisted; and to acquiesce in it is to defeat the very intention with which Nature created it.

These considerations are not abstract ideas, but the undeniable teaching of history which is the record of the world's experience. Nationalism takes its stand upon this experience and calls upon the people of India not to allow themselves to fall into the acquiescence in subjection which is the death-sleep of nations, but to make that use of the alien domination which Nature intended, — to struggle against it and throw it off for unity, for self-realisation, as an independent national organism. In this country, however, there is a class of wise men who regard the rule of the British bureaucracy as a dispensation of Providence, not only to create unity but to preserve it. They preach therefore a gospel of faith in the foreigner, distrust of our countrymen and acquiescence in alien rule as a godsend from on high and an indispensable condition for peace and prosperity. Even those whose hearts rebel against a doctrine so servile, are intellectually so much dominated by it that they cannot embrace Nationalism with their whole heart and try to arrive at a compromise between subjection and independence, — a half-way house between life and death. Their ingenuity discovers an intermediate condition in which the blessings of freedom will be harmoniously wedded with the blessings of subjection; and to this palace in fairyland they have given the name of Colonial Self-Government. If it were not for the existence of this Moderate opinion and its strange parti-coloured delusions, we would not have thought it worth while to go back to first principles and show the falsity of the Loyalist gospel of acquiescence. But the Moderate delusion is really a by-product of the Loyalist delusion; and the parent error must be demolished first, before its offspring can be corrected. The Moderates are a hybrid species, emotionally nationalist, intellectually loyalist. It is owing to this double nature that their delusions acquire an infinite power for mischief. People listen to them because they claim to be Nationalist and because a sincere Nationalist feeling not infrequently breaks through the false Loyalist reasoning. Moreover by associating themselves with the Moderates on the same platform the Loyalists are enabled to exercise an influence on public opinion which would otherwise not be accorded to them. The gospel according to Sir Pherozshah Mehta would not have such power for harm if it were not allowed to represent itself as one and the same with the gospel according to Mr. Gokhale.

What then are the original ideas from which the Loyalist gospel proceeds? It has a triple foundation of error. First comes the postulate that disunion and weakness are ingrained characteristics of the Indian people and an outside power is necessary in order to arbitrate, to keep the peace and to protect the country from the menace of the mightier nations that ring us in. Proceeding from this view and supporting it, is the second postulate that there must be an entire levelling down and sweeping away of all differences, aristocrat and peasant, Brahmin and Sudra, Bengali, Punjabee and Maratha, all must efface their characteristics and differences before any resistance to foreign domination can be attempted, even if such resistance were desirable. The third postulate is that a healthy development is possible under foreign domination and that this healthy development must be first effected before we can dream of freedom or even of becoming a nation. If these three postulates are granted, then the Loyalist creed is unassailable; if they are proved unsound, not only the Loyalist creed but the standpoint of the Moderates ceases to have any basis of firm ground and becomes a thing in the air. The Nationalist contention is that all these three postulates are monuments of political unreason and have no firm foundation either in historical experience or in the facts we see around us or in the nature of things. They are inconsistent with the fundamental nature of foreign domination; they ignore the experience of all other subject nations; they disregard human nature and the conditions of human development in communities. The Loyalist gospel is as untrue as it is ignoble.

The Mask is Off

The Anglo-Indian journals are trying to assure the public that everything is quiet in Jamalpur under the shadow of the British sword. The accounts that are appearing in various Indian journals put a very different complexion on the situation. It appears, to begin with, that the Gurkhas who were called in to preserve the peace are being allowed in cooperation with local hooligans to break it. The case of image-breaking is being deliberately put off and the whole energy of the executive is devoted to terrorising the Hindus. Several pleaders, a Muktear, a Naib of Ramgopalpur and a Superintendent of the Gauripur estate, along with other leading gentlemen of Jamalpur have been arrested. "The number of Mahomedan arrests," writes one correspondent, "is simply *nil*". Comment is hardly necessary. The alliance of the British bureaucracy with hooliganism stands confessed. To take advantage of Mahomedan riots in order to further terrorise by legal proceedings the assaulted Hindus, is the first preoccupation of the local magistrates. We have pointed out already that the procedure is to give scope and room enough for anti-Swadeshi violence and pillage and then to punish the Swadeshists for the crime of self-defence or even simply for the crime of being assaulted. The mask is off.

A Loyalist in a Panic

Not only the *Englishman* but the *Indian Mirror* has been seriously frightened by the course of events in the Punjab. No wonder. The lion spirit of the Punjab was not burned on the pyre with Runjit Singh; it only went to sleep for a while after Chilianwala and is now again awake. The *Mirror* is uneasy for the safety of the Empire. The *Mirror* does not mind very much what may happen in East Bengal, but if discontent spreads to the Punjab, it may affect the Sikhs, and then what would become of the British Empire and the *Indian Mirror*? The remedy proposed by our senile contemporary is that we should stop all political agitation by putting off all public meetings until the country is quiet and that Babu Bepin Chandra Pal should not go about stirring up the people of Southern India "as regards Swadeshi, Boycott, Swaraj and other things". Sir Denzil Ibbertson is also advised to cure the evil by kindness, — a wise counsel to which, no doubt, he will incline his patient ear; for where can he find a better well-wisher than the *Indian Mirror*? It appears that the meetings addressed by Srijut Bepin Chandra "are not likely to lessen the political unrest; on the contrary, they are decidedly adding fuel to the fire". Well, what else should be their object? To lull the country back into sleep and submission? The *Mirror* reminds us of a venerable old woman awakened at night by the noise of burglars in the house and recommending everybody to turn over and sleep or pretend to sleep until the house is quiet, — and the burglars, unopposed, have done their business. But we thought that the *Mirror* had discovered the Extremists to be a small and insignificant party without any following in the country. What does it matter what such a party is or is not doing? The country, the *Mirror* declared, is at the back of the Moderate Party. Has that comforting belief so soon gone to pieces?

Bande Mataram, April 27, 1907

Shall India be Free?

NATIONAL DEVELOPMENT AND FOREIGN RULE

IN DEALING with the Loyalist creed it will be convenient to examine first the general postulate before we can come to those which apply particularly to the conditions of India. The contention is that a healthy development is possible under foreign domination. In this view national independence is a thing of no moment or at least its importance has been grossly exaggerated. Nations can very well do without it; provided they have a good government which keeps the people happy and contented and allows them to develop their economic activities and moral virtues, they need not repine at being ruled by others. For certain nations in certain periods of their development liberty would be disastrous and subjection to foreign rule is the most healthy condition. India, argue the Loyalists, is an example of such a nation in such a period. The first business of its people is to develop their commerce, become educated and enlightened, reform their society and their manners and to grow more and more fit for self-government. In proportion as they become more civilised and more fit, they will receive from their sympathetic, just and discerning rulers an ever-increasing share in the administration of the country until with entire fitness will come entire possession of the status of British citizenship. The idea is that foreign rule is a Providential dispensation or a provision of Nature for training an imperfectly developed people in the methods of civilisation and the arts of self-government. This theory is a modern invention. Ancient and mediaeval Imperialism frankly acknowledged the principle of might is right; the conquering nation considered that its military superiority was in itself a proof that it was meant to rule and the subject nation to obey; liberty, being denied by Providence to the latter, could not be good for it and there was no call on the ruler to concede it either now or hereafter. This was the spirit in which England conquered and governed Ireland by the same methods of cynical treachery and ruthless massacre which in modern times are usually considered to be the monopoly of despotisms like Turkey and Russia. But by the time that England had fastened its hold on India, a change had come over the modern world. The Greek ideas of freedom and democracy had penetrated the European mind and created the great impulse of democratic Nationalism which dominated Europe in the 19th century. The idea that despotism of any kind was an offence against humanity, had crystallised into an instinctive feeling, and modern morality and sentiment revolted against the enslavement of nation by nation, of class by class or of man by man. Imperialism had to justify itself to this modern sentiment and could only do so by pretending to be a trustee of liberty, commissioned from on high to civilise the uncivilised and train the untrained until the time had come when the benevolent conqueror had done his work and could unselfishly retire. Such were the professions with which England justified her usurpation of the heritage of the Moghul and dazzled us into acquiescence in servitude by the splendour of her uprightness and generosity. Such was the pretence with which she veiled her annexation of Egypt. These Pharisaic pretensions were especially necessary to British Imperialism because in England the Puritanic middle class had risen to power and imparted to the English temperament a sanctimonious self-righteousness which refused to indulge in injustice and selfish spoliation except under a cloak of virtue, benevolence and unselfish altruism. The genesis of the Loyalist gospel can be found in the need of British Imperialism to justify itself to the liberalised sentiment of the 19th century and to the Puritanic middle-class element in the British nation.

The question then arises, has this theory any firmer root? Is it anything more than a convenient theory? Has it any relations with actual facts or with human experience? To answer this question it is necessary to distinguish between three kinds of liberty which are generally confused together. There is a national liberty of freedom from foreign control; there is an internal liberty or that freedom from the despotism of an individual, a class or a combination of classes to which the name of self-government is properly given; and there is individual liberty or the freedom of the individual from unnecessary and arbitrary restrictions imposed on him either by the society of which he is a part or by the Government, whether that Government be monarchical, democratic, oligarchic or bureaucratic. The question at issue is, then, which, if any, of these three kinds of liberty is essential to the healthy development of national life; or, can there be such development without any liberty at all?

The object of national existence, of the formation of men into groups and their tacit agreement to allow themselves to be ruled by an organised instrument of administration which is called the Government, is nothing else than human development in the individual and in the group. The individual, standing alone, cannot develop; he depends on the support and assistance of the group to which he belongs. The group itself cannot develop unless it has an organisation by means of which it not only secures internal peace and order and protection from external attack but also proper conditions which will give free play for the development of its activities and capacities — physical, moral, intellectual. The nation or group is not like the individual who can specialise his development and throw all his energies into one line. The nation must develop military and political greatness and activity, intellectual and aesthetic greatness and activity, commercial greatness and activity, moral sanity and vigour; it cannot sacrifice any of these functions of the organism without making itself unfit for the struggle for life and finally succumbing and perishing under the pressure of more highly organised nations. The purely commercial State like Carthage is broken in the shock with a nation which has developed the military and political as well as the commercial energies. A purely military state like Sparta cannot stand against rivals which to equal military efficiency unite a greater science, intellectual energy and political ability. A purely aesthetic and intellectual state like the Greek colonies in Italy or a purely moral and spiritual community like the empire of Peru are blotted out of existence in the clash with ruder but more vigorous and many-sided organisms. No government, therefore, can really be good for a nation or serve the purposes of national life and development which does not give full scope for the development of all the national activities, capacities and energies. Foreign rule is unnatural and fatal to a nation precisely because by its very nature it throws itself upon these activities and capacities and crushes them down in the interests of its own continued existence. Even when it does not crush them down violently, it obstructs their growth passively by its very presence. The subject nation becomes dependent, disorganised and loses its powers by atrophy. For this reason national independence is absolutely necessary to national growth. There can be no national development without national liberty.

Individual liberty is necessary to national development, because, if the individual is unduly hampered, the richness of national life suffers and is impoverished. If the individual is given free room to realise himself, to perfect, specialise and enrich his particular powers and attain the full height of his manhood, the variety and rapidity of national progress is immensely increased. In so far as he is fettered and denied scope, the development of the nation is cramped and retarded. A Government which denies scope and liberty to the individual, as all foreign governments must to a considerable extent deny it, helps to cramp the healthy development of the nation and not to forward it. The development of the individual is and must be an embarrassment to the intruding power unless the numbers are so few that they can be bribed into acquiescence and support by the receipt of honours, employment or other personal advantages. For development creates ambition and nothing is more fatal to the continuance of foreign rule than the growth of ambitions in the subject race which it cannot satisfy. The action of Lord Curzon in introducing the Universities Act was for the British domination in India an act of inevitable necessity, which had to be done some time or other. Its only defect from the Imperialist point of view was that it came too late.

Just as individual liberty is necessary for the richness and variety of national development, so self-government is necessary for its completeness and the full deployment of national strength. If certain classes are dominant and others depressed, the result is that the potential strength of the depressed classes is so much valuable force lost to the sum of national strength. The dominant classes may undoubtedly show a splendid development and may make the nation great and famous in history; but when all is said the strength of the nation is then only the sum of the strength of a few privileged classes. The great weakness of India in the past has been the political depression and nullity of the mass of the population. It was not from the people of India that India was won by Moghul or Briton, but from a small privileged class. On the other hand, the strength and success of the Marathas and Sikhs in the 18th century was due to the policy of Shivaji and Guru Govinda which called the whole nation into the fighting line. They failed only because the Marathas could not preserve the cohesion which Shivaji gave to their national strength or the Sikhs the discipline which Guru Govinda gave to the Khalsa. Is it credible that a foreign rule would either knowingly foster or allow the growth of that universal political consciousness in the subject nation which self-government implies? It is obvious that foreign rule can only endure so long as political consciousness can be either stifled by violence or hypnotised into inactivity. The moment the nation becomes politically self-conscious, the doom of the alien predominance is sealed. The bureaucracy which rules us, is not only foreign in origin but external to us, — it holds and draws nourishing sustenance for itself from the subject organism by means of tentacles and feelers thrust out from its body thousands of miles away. Its type in natural history is not the parasite, but the octopus. Self-government would mean the removal of the tentacles and the cessation both of the grip and the sustenance. Foreign rule is naturally opposed to the development of the subject nation as a separate organism, to the growth of its capacity for and practice in self-government, to the development of capacity and ambition of its individuals. To think that a foreign rule would deliberately train us for independence or allow us to train ourselves is to suppose a miracle in nature.

Bande Mataram, April 29, 1907

Shall India be Free?

WE ARE arguing the impossibility of a healthy national development under foreign rule, — except by reaction against that rule. The foreign domination naturally interferes with and obstructs the functioning of the native organs of development. It is therefore in itself an unnatural and unhealthy condition, — a wound, a disease, which must result, unless arrested, in the mortification and rotting to death of the indigenous body politic. If a nation were an artificial product which could be made, then it might be possible for one nation to make another. But a nation cannot be made, — it is an organism which grows under the stress of a principle of life within. We speak indeed of nation-building and of the makers of a nation, but these are only convenient metaphors. The nation-builder, Cavour or Bismarck, is merely the incarnation of a national force which has found its hour and its opportunity, — of an inner will which has awakened under the stress of shaping circumstances. A nation is indeed the outward expression of a community of sentiment, whether it be the sentiment of a common blood or the sentiment of a common religion or the sentiment of a common interest or any or all of these sentiments combined. Once this sentiment grows strong enough to develop into a will towards unity and to conquer obstacles and make full use of favouring circumstances, the development of the nation becomes inevitable and there is no power which can ultimately triumph against it. But the process, however rapid it may be, is one of growth and not of manufacture. The first impulse of the developing nation is to provide itself with a centre, a means of self-expression and united actions, a chief organ or national nerve-centre with subsidiary organs acting under and in harmony with it, if the need of self-protection is its first overpowering need. The organisation may be military or semi-military under a single chief or a warlike ruling class; if the pressure from outside is not overpowering or the need of internal development strongly felt, it may take the shape of some form of partial or complete self-government. In either case the community becomes a nation or organic State.

What, then, is the place of foreign rule in such an organic development? The invasion of the body politic by a foreign element must result either in the merging of the alien into the indigenous nationality or in his superimposition on the latter in a precarious position which can only be maintained by coercion or by hypnotising the subject people into passivity. If the alien and the native-born population are akin in blood and in religion, the fusion will be easy. Even if they are not, yet if the former settles down in the conquered country and makes it his motherland, community of interests will in the end inevitably bring about union. The foreigners become sons of the country by adoption and the sentiment of a common motherland is always a sufficient substitute for the sentiment of a common race-origin. The difficulty of religion may be solved by the conversion of the foreigner to the religion of the people he has conquered, as happened with the ancient invaders of India, or by the conversion of the conquered people to the religion of their rulers, as happened in Persia and other countries conquered by the Arabs. Even if no such general change of creed can be effected, yet the two religions may become habituated to each other and mutually tolerant, or the sentiment of a common interest and a common sonhood of one motherland may overcome the consciousness of religious differences. In all these contingencies there is a fusion, complete or partial; and the nation, though it may be profoundly affected for good or evil, need not be disorganised or lose the power of development. India under Mahomedan rule, though greatly disturbed and thrown into continual ferment and revolution, did not lose its power of organic readjustment and development. Even the final anarchy which preceded the British domination, was not a process of disorganisation but an acute crisis, — the attempt of Nature to effect an organic readjustment in the body politic.

Unfortunately the crisis was complicated by the presence and final domination of a foreign body, foreign in blood, foreign in religion, foreign in interest. This body remains superimposed on the native-born population, without any roots in the soil. Its presence, so long as it is neither merged in the nation nor dislodged, must make for the disorganisation and decay of the subject people. It is possible for a foreign body differing in blood, religion and interest, to amalgamate with the native organism but only on one of two conditions; either the foreign body must cut itself off from its origin and take up its home in the conquered country, — a course which is obviously impossible in the present problem, — or it must assimilate the subject State into the paramount State by the removal of all differences, inequalities, and conflicting interests. We shall point out the insuperable difficulties in the way of any such arrangement which will at once preserve British supremacy and give a free scope to Indian national development. At present there is no likelihood of the intruding force submitting easily to the immense sacrifices which such an assimilation would involve. Yet if no such assimilation takes place, the position of the British bureaucracy in India in no way differs from the position of the Turkish despotism as it existed with regard to the Christian populations of the Balkans previous to their independence or of the Austrians in Lombardy before the Italian Revolution. It is a position which endangers, demoralises and eventually weakens the ruling nation as Austria and Turkey were demoralised and weakened, and which disorganises and degrades the subject people. A very brief consideration of the effects of British rule in India will carry this truth home.

Bande Mataram, April 30, 1907

Moonshine for Bombay Consumption

The Calcutta correspondent of the *Indu Prakash* seems to be an adept in fitting his news to the likings of the clientele. He has discovered that the old party and the new are united not against the Government but against the Mahomedans. All are looking to the Government with a reverent expectation of justice from that immaculate source. We do not know who this anti-Mahomedan and pro-Government Calcutta correspondent may be; but we hope the Bombay public will not be deceived by his inventions. If there is one overmastering feeling in Bengal it is indignation with the Government for allowing or countenancing the outrages in the Eastern districts. Even the Loyalist organs are full of expressions of uneasiness and perturbed wonder at the inaction of the authorities while Moderate organs like the *Bengalee* and Moderate leaders like Babu Surendranath Banerji have expressed plainly an adverse view of the action and spirit of the Government. There is no doubt considerable resentment against men like Nawab Salimullah for fomenting the disturbances; but there is no deep-seated resentment against the low-class Mahomedans who are merely the tools of men who themselves keep safely under cover. The fight is not a fight between Hindus and Mahomedans but between the bureaucrats and Swadeshists.

The "Reformer" on Moderation

The *Indian Social Reformer* has discovered that the Moderate programme needs revision. Moderation is defined by this authority as a desire to preserve the British Raj until social reform has accomplished itself, for the reason that an indigenous Government is not likely to favour social reform so much as the present rulers do. The *Reformer* would therefore like the Moderate programme to be modified in order to tally with its own definition of moderation. We presume that, in its view, the Congress instead of demanding Legislative Councils should ask for the forcible marriage of Hindu widows; instead of the separation of the judicial and executive, the separation of reformed wives from unreformed husbands or *vice versa*; instead of the repeal of the Arms Act, the abolition of the Hindu religion. This introduction of social details into a political programme is a fad of a few enthusiasts and is contrary to all reason. The alteration of the social system to suit present needs is a matter for the general sense of the community and the efforts of individuals. To mix it up with politics in which men of all religious views and various social opinions can join is to confuse issues hopelessly. It is not true that by removing the defects of our social structure we shall automatically become a nation and fit for freedom. If it were so, Burma would be a free nation at present. Nor can we believe that the present system is favourable to social reconstruction or that self-government would be fatal to it. The reverse is the case. Of course, if social reform means the destruction of everything old or Hindu because it is old or Hindu, the continuance of the present political and mental dependence on England and English ideals is much to be desired by the social reformers; for it is gradually destroying all that was good as well as much that was defective in the old society. With the programme of becoming a nation by denationalisation we have no sympathy. But if a healthy social development be aimed at, it is more likely to occur in a free India when the national needs will bring about a natural evolution. Society is not an artificial manufacture to be moulded and remodelled at will, but a growth. If it is to be healthy and strong it must have healthy surroundings and a free atmosphere.

Bande Mataram, May 1, 1907

Shall India be Free?

UNITY AND BRITISH RULE

It is a common cry in this country that we should effect the unity of its people before we try to be free. There is no cry which is more plausible, none which is more hollow. What is it that we mean when we talk of the necessity of unity? Unity does not mean uniformity and the removal of all differences. There are some people who talk as if unity in religion, for instance, could not be accomplished except by uniformity. But uniformity of religion is a psychical impossibility forbidden by the very nature of the human mind. So long as men differ in intellect, in temperament, in spiritual development, there must be different religions and different sects of the same religion. The Brahmo Samaj was set on foot in India by Rammohan Roy with the belief that this would be the one religion of India which would replace and unite the innumerable sects now dividing our spiritual consciousness. But in a short time this uniting religion was itself rent into three discordant sects, two of which show signs of internal fissure even within their narrow limits; and all these divisions rest not on anything essential but on differences of intellectual constitution, variety of temperament, divergence of the lines of spiritual development. The unity of the Hindu religion cannot be attained by the destruction of the present sects and the substitution of a religion based on the common truths of Hinduism. It can only be effected if there is, first, a common feeling that the sectarian differences are of subordinate importance compared with the community of spiritual truths and discipline as distinct from the spiritual truths and discipline of other religions, and, secondly, a common agreement in valuing and cherishing the Hindu religion in its entirety as a sacred and inalienable possession. This is what fundamentally constitutes the sentiment of unity, whether it be religious, political or social. There must be the sense of a community in something dear and precious which others do not possess; there must be an acute sense of difference from other communities which have no share in our common possession; there must be a supreme determination to cherish, assert and preserve our common possession from disparagement and destruction. But the sentiment of unity is not sufficient to create unity; we require also the practice of unity. Where the sentiment of unity exists and the practice does not, the latter can only be acquired by a common effort to accomplish one great, common and all-absorbing object.

The first question we have to answer is — can this practical unity be accomplished by acquiescence in foreign rule? Certainly, under foreign rule a peculiar kind of uniformity of condition is attained. Brahmin and Sudra, aristocrat and peasant, Hindu and Mahomedan, all are brought to a certain level of equality by equal inferiority to the ruling class. The differences between them are trifling compared with the enormous difference between all of them and the white race at the top. But this uniformity is of no value for the purposes of national unity, except in so far as the sense of a common inferiority excites a common desire to revolt against and get rid of it. If the foreign superiority is acquiesced in, the result is that the mind becomes taken up with the minor differences and instead of getting nearer to unity disunion is exaggerated. This is precisely what has happened in India under British rule. The sentiment of unity has grown, but in practice we are both socially and politically far more disunited and disorganised than before the British occupation. In the anarchy that followed the decline of the Moghul, the struggle was between the peoples of various localities scrambling for the inheritance of Akbar and Shahjahan. This was not a vital and permanent element of disunion. But the present disorganisation is internal and therefore more likely to reach the vitals of the community.

This disorganisation is the natural and inevitable result of foreign rule. A state which is created by a common descent, real or fictitious, by a common religion or by common interests welding together into one a great number of men or group of men, is a natural organism which so long as it exists has always within it the natural power of revival and development. But as political science has pointed out, a state created by the encampment of a foreign race among a conquered population and supported in the last resort not by any section of the people but by external force, is an inorganic state. The subject population, it has been said, inevitably becomes a disorganised crowd. Consciously or unconsciously the tendency of the intruding body is to break down all the existing organs of national life and to engross all power in itself. The Moghul rule had not this tendency because it immediately naturalised itself in India. British rule has and is forced to have this tendency because it must persist in being an external and intruding presence encamped in the country and not belonging to it. It is doubtful whether there is any example in history of an alien domination which has been so monstrously ubiquitous, inquisitorial and intolerant of any centre of strength in the country other than itself as the British bureaucracy. There were three actual centres of organised strength in pre-British India — the supreme ruler, Peshwa or Raja or Nawab reposing his strength on the Zemindars or Jagirdars; the Zemindar in his own domain reposing his strength on his retinue and tenants; and the village community independent and self-existent. The first result of the British occupation was to reduce to a nullity the supreme ruler, and this was often done, as in Bengal, by the help of the Zemindars. The next result was the disorganisation of the village community. The third was the steady breaking-up of the power of the Zemindar with the help of a new class which the foreigners created for their own purposes — the bourgeois or middle class. Unfortunately for the British bureaucracy it had in order to get the support and assistance of the middle class to pamper the latter and allow it to grow into a strength and develop organs of its own, such as the Press, the Bar, the University, the Municipalities, District Boards, etc. Finally the situation with which British statesmen had to deal was this: — the natural sovereigns of the land helpless and disorganised, the landed aristocracy helpless and disorganised, the peasantry helpless and disorganised, but a middle class growing in strength, pretensions and organisation. British statesmanship following the instinctive and inevitable trend of an alien domination, set about breaking down the power it had established in order to destroy the sole remaining centre of national strength and possible revival. If this could be done, if the middle class could be either tamed, bribed or limited in its expansion, the disorganisation would be complete. Nothing would be left of the people of India except a disorganised crowd with no centre of strength or means of resistance.

It was in Bengal that the middle class was most developed and self-conscious; and it was in Bengal therefore that a quick succession of shrewd and dangerous blows was dealt at the once useful but now obnoxious class. The last effort to bribe it into quietude was the administration of Lord Ripon. It was now sought to cripple the organs through which this strength was beginning slowly to feel and develop its organic life. The Press was intimidated, the Municipalities officialised, the University officialised and its expansion limited. Finally the Partition sought with one blow to kill the poor remnants of the Zemindar's power and to influence and to weaken the middle class of Bengal by dividing it. The suppression of the middle class was the recognised policy of Lord Curzon. After Mr. Morley came to power, it was, we believe, intended to recognise and officialise the Congress itself if possible. Even now it is quite conceivable, in view of the upheaval in Bengal and the Punjab, that an expanded Legislature with the appearance of a representative body but the reality of official control, may be given not as a concession but as a tactical move. The organs of middle class political life can only be dangerous so long as they are independent. By taking away their independence they become fresh sources of strength for the Government — of weakness for the class which strives to find in them its growth and self-expression.

The Partition opened the eyes of the threatened class to the nature of the attack that was being made on it; and the result was a widespread and passionate revolt which has now spread from Bengal to the Punjab and threatens to break out all over India. The struggle is now a struggle for life and death. If the bureaucracy conquers, the middle class will be broken, shattered perhaps blotted out of existence; if the middle class conquers, the bureaucracy are not for long in the land. Everything depends on the success or failure of the middle class in getting the people to follow it for a common salvation. They may get this support by taking their natural place as awakeners and leaders of the nation; they may get it by the energy and success with which they wage their battle with the bureaucracy. In Eastern Bengal, for instance, the aid of a few Mahomedan aristocrats has enabled the bureaucracy to turn a large section of the Mahomedan masses against the Hiṇdu middle class, and the educated community is fighting with its back to the wall for its very existence. If it succeeds under such desperate circumstances, even the Mahomedan masses will eventually follow its leading.

This process of political disorganisation is not so much a deliberate policy on the part of the foreign bureaucracy, as an instinctive action which it can no more help than the sea can help flowing. The dissolution of the subject organisation into a disorganised crowd is the inevitable working of an alien despotism.

Bande Mataram, May 2, 1907

Extremism in the "Bengalee"

THE *Bengalee*, excited by the news of a second outrage on the Hindu religion at Ambariya in Mymensingh, came out yesterday with a frankly extremist issue. We only wish that we could look on this as anything more than a fit of passing excitement; but the *Bengalee* is hot today and cold tomorrow. Nevertheless, what it says is true, and it is well and pointedly expressed: —

"Fifty years ago, such a revolting outrage, committed upon the religious susceptibilities of Hindus, would have resulted in grave complications and Government would have left no stone unturned to propitiate the Hindu Chiefs and the Hindu population, and last, though not the least, the Hindu section of the Native Army. Today Government officials openly side, presumably with the approval of the head of the Provincial Administration, with those who break Hindu images, desecrate Hindu temples, plunder the houses and shops of Hindus and ravish Hindu women.

"Is this the sum total of our progress after a century and a half of British rule? Have we, Bengali Hindus, become so cravenhearted, so utterly incapable of self-defence, that the Government no longer thinks it necessary to avoid wounding our tenderest feelings or even to keep up appearances? Verily, a nation gets precisely the kind of treatment it deserves; and it appears that in the opinion of Mr. Hare — so far tacitly endorsed by Lord Minto — a nation of weeping and shrieking women as the Bengalis are regarded by their rulers, deserves only to be trampled underfoot. And recent happenings in the district of Mymensingh show that the Government has taken an exact measure of the Hindus of Bengal. For are they not the embodiment of patience and — propriety? They are too highly educated and reflective, you know, to do anything rashly and the native hue of their resolution is most reasonably and naturally and speedily sicklied o'er with the pale cast of thought. They may be quite right from their personal standpoint; but national heroes are not usually made of such stuff nor are national interests promoted by the wearers of soft raiment. The worship of Motherland is the sole privilege of those choice spirits who have the heart to incur sacrifice, the hand to execute the mandate of conscience, and the recklessness to hang propriety and prudence."

And the *Bengalee* complains that we do not even lift our little finger to protect our temples, our holy images and even our women from defilement and dishonour. All this is surprising enough in a Moderate organ; if set before anyone without any clue as to its source, it might all be taken as a verbatim extract from the editorial columns of the *Bande Mataram*.

"Is this the sum total of our progress after a century and a half of British rule?" — asks the *Bengalee*. This precisely and nothing else than this is the one inevitable result of British rule. Has it taken our contemporary so long to discover that foreign rule, and especially such a rule as that of the British bureaucracy which demands entire subordination and dependence in the subject people, can have no other effect than to emasculate and degrade? Loyalists may enumerate a hundred blessings of British rule — though, when closely looked at, they turn out to be apples of the Dead Sea which turn to dust and cinders when tasted, — none of them can compensate for the one radical and indispensable loss which accompanies them, the loss of our manhood, of our courage, of our self-respect and habit of initiative. When these are gone, merely the shadow of a man is left; and neither the veneer of Western culture, nor enlightenment, nor position, nor British peace, nor railways, nor telegraphs nor anything else that God can give or man bestow can compensate for the loss of the very basis of individual and national strength and character. Social reform? What reform can there be of a society of lay figures who pretend to be men? Industrial progress? What will be the use of riches which may be taken from us at any time by the strong hand? Moral and religious improvement? What truth or value have these phrases to men who see their religion outraged before their eyes and whose wives are never safe from dishonour? Get strength first, get independence and all these things will be added unto you. But persist in your foolish moderation, your unseasonable and unreasonable prudence; and another fifty years will find you more degraded than ever, a nation of Greeks with polished intellects and debased souls, body and soul helplessly at the mercy of alien masters.

The *Bengalee* in these fiery paragraphs denounces for the moment prudence and moderation as mere weakness and cowardice. It recommends recklessness and asks us to lift our hands in defence of our temples, our holy images and the honour of our women. This is probably no more than a rhetorical outburst to relieve overcharged feelings. But if there is any seriousness at all in our contemporary's wrath, let him seriously consider what his appeal means. We are to rush to the defence of our temples, our holy images, the honour of our women. But who are "we"? Not surely the people of Eastern Bengal and Northern Bengal who, outnumbered, overwhelmed, are struggling against overwhelming odds and, in spite of weak points like Jamalpur, are not acquitting themselves ill. In West Bengal the Hindus are in overwhelming majority; in West Bengal there is a sturdy Hindu lower class; there are thousands of students who throng to Swadeshi meetings and parade at Swadeshi Jatras and festivals. But West Bengal is under the spell of Babu Surendranath and his Moderate colleagues. Will Babu Surendranath give the word? Is he prepared to speed the fiery cross? Shall West Bengal pour into the East and North to help our kinsmen, to protect "our temples, our holy images and our women from defilement and dishonour"? If not, this momentary boldness and manliness is no more than a fire of straw which had better not have been kindled. To quote our contemporary, — "The worship of Motherland is the sole privilege of those choice spirits who have the heart to incur sacrifice, the hand to execute the mandate of conscience and the recklessness to hang propriety and prudence."

Hare or Another

Our Moderate contemporaries seem unable to understand that the misgovernment in Eastern Bengal is a natural result of British policy, or rather of the peculiar position of the bureaucracy in

India. That position can only be maintained either by hypnotising the people or terrorising them. The new spirit is unsealing the eyes of the people and breaking the hypnotic spell of the last century; especially in East Bengal the process of disillusionment has been fairly thorough. The bureaucracy is therefore compelled to fall back on the only other alternative, terrorism. But our Moderate friends will persist in believing that the policy in East Bengal is only the policy of individuals. They are therefore "demanding" the recall of Mr. Hare. "He has eclipsed," says the *Bengalee*, "the record of Aurangzeb as a persecutor of Hindus, without Aurangzeb's excuse of religious zeal.... He has made every Hindu hate British rule in the privacy of his heart." But will the recall of Mr. Hare be of any more effect than the recall of Bampfylde Fuller? For our part we had never any illusions on the point. We knew that what Sir Bampfylde began in his fury and heat of rage, Mr. Hare would pursue in cold blood and with silent calculation. Supposing the wish of the *Bengalee*'s heart gratified and Mr. Hare sent home to the enjoyment of his well-earned pension, what then? A third man will come who will carry out the same policy in a different way. It is not Hare or Fuller who determines the policy of the Shillong Government, but the inexorable necessity of the bureaucratic position which drives them into a line of action insane but inevitable. They must either crush the Swadeshi movement or give up their powers wholly or in part to the people; and to the latter course they cannot be persuaded by any means which we have yet employed.

Bande Mataram, May 3, 1907

Look on this Picture, then on That

BRITAIN, the benevolent, Britain, the mother of Parliaments, Britain, the champion of liberty, Britain, the deliverer of the slave, — such was the sanctified and legendary figure which we have been trained to keep before our eyes from the earliest years of our childhood. Our minds imbued through and through with the colours of that legend, we cherished a faith in the justice and benevolence of Britain more profound, more implicit, more a very part of our beings than the faith of the Christian in Christ or of the Mahomedan in his Prophet. Officials might be oppressive, Viceroys and Lieutenant-Governors reactionary, the Secretary, of State obdurate, Parliament indifferent, the British public careless, but our faith was not to be shaken. If Anglo-India was unkind, we wooed the British people in India itself. If the British people failed us, we said that it was because the Conservatives were in power. If a Liberal Secretary showed himself no less obdurate, we set it down to his personal failings and confidently awaited justice from a Liberal Government in which he should have no part. If the most Radical of Radical Secretaries condemned us to age-long subjection to a paternal and absolute bureaucracy, we whispered to the people, 'Wait, wait, Britain, the true Britain, the generous, the benevolent, the lover, the giver of freedom, is only sleeping; she shall awake again and we shall see her angelic and transfigured beauty'. Where precisely was this Britain we believed in, no man could say, but we would not give up our faith. *Credo quia impossibile*; — I believe because it is impossible, had become our political creed. Other countries might be selfish, violent, greedy, tyrannical, unjust; in other countries politics might be a continual readjustment of conflicting interests and clashing strengths. But Britain, the Britain of our dreams, was guided only by the light of truth and justice and reason; high ideals, noble impulses, liberal instincts, these were the sole guides of her political actions, — by the lustre of these bright moral fires she guided her mighty steps through an admiring and worshipping world. That was the dream; and so deeply had it lodged in our imaginations that not only the professed Loyalists, the men of moderation, but even the leading Nationalists, those branded as Extremists, could not altogether shake off its influence. Only recently Srijut Bepin Chandra Pal at Rajamundry told his hearers that those who thought the British Government would crush us if we tried by passive resistance to make administration impossible, held too low an opinion of British character and British civilisation. We fancy Srijut Bepin Chandra watching from the south the welter of official anarchy in East Bengal and the Punjab must have modified to a certain extent his trust in the bearing-power of British high-mindedness. We ourselves, though we had our own views about British character and civilisation, have allowed ourselves to speculate whether it was not just possible that the Birtish bureaucracy might be sufficiently tender of their reputation to avoid extreme, violent and arbitrary measures.

That was the dream. The reality to which we awake is Rawalpindi and Jamalpur. The events in the Punjab are an instructive lesson in the nature of bureaucratic rule. The Punjab has, since the Mutiny, been a quiet, loyal and patient province; whatever burdens have been laid on it, its people have borne without complaint; whatever oppression might go on, it gave rise to no such clamour and agitation as the least arbitrary act would be met with in Bengal. How have the bureaucracy treated this loyal and quiet people? What fruit have they reaped from their loyalty, the men who saved the British Empire in 1857? Intolerable burdens, insolent treatment, rude oppression. The Anglo-Indian cry is that disloyal Bengal has infected loyal Punjab with the virus of sedition. Undoubtedly, the new spirit which has gone out like a mighty fire from Bengal lighting up the whole of India, has found its most favourable ground in the Punjab; but a fire does not burn without fuel, and where there is the most revolutionary spirit, there, we can always be sure, has been the most oppression. The water tax, the land laws, the Colonisation Act legalising the oppressions and illegalities under which the Punjab landholders and peasantry have groaned, had generated the feeling of an intolerable burden, and when a few fearless men brought to the people the message of self-help, the good tidings that in their own hands lay their own salvation, the men of the Punjab found again their ancient spirit and determined to stand upright in the strength of their manhood. They committed no act of violence, they broke no law. They confined themselves to sending in a statement of their grievances to the Government and passively abstaining from the use of the Canal water so that the bureaucracy might not benefit by an iniquitous tax. The rulers of India know well that if passive resistance is permitted, the artificial fabric of bureaucratic despotism will fall down like the walls of Jericho before mere sound, with the mere breath of a people's revolution. To save the situation, they resorted to the usual device of stifling the voice of the people into silence. On a frivolous pretext they struck at the *Punjabee.* The only result was that the calm resolution of the people received its first tinge of fierce indignation. Then the bureaucracy hurriedly resolved to lop off the tall heads — the policy of the tyrant Tarquin which is always the resort of men without judgment or statesmanship. Lala Hansraj, one of the most revered and beloved of the Punjab leaders, a man grown grey in the quiet and selfless service of his country, Ajit Singh, the nationalist orator, and other men of repute and leading were publicly threatened with prosecution and imprisonment as criminals and an enquiry begun with great pomp and circumstance. Then followed a phenomenon unprecedented, we think, in recent Indian history. For the first time the man in the workshop and the man in the street have risen in revolt for purely political reasons in anger at an attack on purely political leaders. The distinction, which Anglo-India has striven to draw between the 'Babu class' and the people, has in the Punjab ceased to exist. It was probably the panic at this alarming phenomenon which hurried the Punjab Government into an extraordinary *coup d'état*, also unprecedented in recent Indian history. The result is that we have a strange companion picture to that dream of a benevolent and angelic Britain, — a city of unarmed men terrorised by the military, the leaders of the people hurried from their daily avocations to prison, siege-guns pointed at the town, police rifles ready to fire on any group of five men or more to be seen in the streets, bail refused to respectable pleaders and barristers from sheer terror of their influence. Look on this picture, then on that!

And what next? It is too early to say. This much only is certain that a new stage begins in the struggle between democracy and bureaucracy, a new chapter opens in the history of the progress of Indian Nationalism.

Bande Mataram, May 6, 1907

Curzonism for the University

AT LAST the *brahmāstra* which Lord Curzon forged for the stifling of patriotism through the instrumentality of the University, is to be utilised, and utilised to its full capacity. We all remember the particular skirmish in the first Swadeshi struggle in which Sir Bampfylde Fuller fell. Sir Bampfylde insisted on the disaffiliation of the Serajgunge Schools because the teachers and students were publicly taking part in politics. Lord Minto's Government refused to support him in this action becuse it was inadvisable, having regard to the troubled nature of the times, and Sir Bampfylde had to resign. Whatever stronger motives were behind Lord Minto's action, this was the ostensible occasion for a resignation which practically amounted to a dismissal. Now we find the same Government and the same Lord Minto out-fullering Fuller and threatening in much more troubled times against all Government or aided or affiliated Colleges and Schools the action which Sir Bampfylde contemplated against only two.

The circular letter issued to the local Governments "with the object of protecting Higher Education in India" from any connection with politics, is an awkward and clumsily worded document such as we would not have expected from the pen of Sir H. Risley, but it manages to make its object and methods pretty clear. The object is to put a stop to the system of National Volunteers which is growing up throughout Bengal, to use the Universities as an instrument for stifling the growth of political life and incidentally to prevent men of ability and influence in the educational line from becoming a political power. This is how Lord Minto, presumably with the approval of Mr. John Morley, proposes to bring about these objects. The objects of their benevolent and high-minded attention are divided into four classes, schoolboys, college students, school masters, professors, and for each a scientifically varied treatment is carefully prescribed.

For students in high schools, "In the interest of the boys themselves, it is clearly undesirable that they should be distracted from their work by attending political meetings or engaging in any form of political agitation. In the event of such misconduct being persisted in and encouraged or permitted by masters or managing authorities, the offending school can after due warning be dealt with — (a) by the local Government, which has the power of withdrawing any grant-in-aid and of withholding the privilege of competing for scholarships and of receiving scholarship-holders; (b) by the University, which can withdraw recognition from the school, the effect of which is to prevent it from sending up pupils as candidates for matriculation examination." Students in high school are therefore to be debarred from all political education and brought up on an exclusive diet of Lee Warner and Empire Day. Attending political meetings, outside school hours mind you, and, it may be, with the full consent of the guardians, is to be reckoned as misconduct coming within the scope of school discipline. It is to be punished by the disciplining, that is to say, the flogging or expulsion of the boys. But what if the teachers or the managing authorities remember that they are men and not dogs who for a little food from the Government are ready to do its will just or unjust? What if they decline to do the Government's dirty work for it? Then the local magistrate appears on the scene and takes away the grant-in-aid and the privilege of competing for scholarships and of receiving scholarship-holders. But supposing there should still be found a Vidyasagar or two who would contemptuously spurn these bribes and prefer to keep his manhood? For that also this provident circular has provided. The school can be refused recognition, a refusal which will mean exclusion of its students from a college education. For this purpose the local Government will report to the University "which alone is legally competent to inflict the requisite penalty". But if this sole legal authority should decline to act on the report of the local Government? Then, it appears, there is another sole authority which is legally or illegally competent, the Government itself. The report is to be understood not as a report but as an order, and if it is disobeyed, the University "would fail to carry out the educational trust with which the law has invested it, and it would be the duty of the Government to intervene".

The next class is composed of university students. In their case the Government is not prepared to punish them, as a general rule, for merely attending political meetings. We take it that, in special cases, e.g., if it were a meeting addressed by Srijut Bepin Chandra Pal or Syed Haldar Reza or Mr. Tilak, they will not be punished. But if they take an active part in the meeting, then the need for discipline will begin. Any action which will bring undesirable notoriety upon their college, will be sufficient ground for Government interference. Picketing is of course forbidden to the student and so is open violence — such for instance as the defence of his father's house, person and property from Mahomedan Goondas or of the chastity of his wife, sister or mother from violation by political hooligans.

The schoolmaster is mercifully treated. He is graciously conceded the right of having his own opinions and even of expressing them within limits set by the alien bureaucracy. "If, therefore, the public utterances of a schoolmaster are of such a character as to endanger the orderly development of the boys under his charge by introducing into their immature minds doctrines subversive of their respect for authority and calculated to impair their usefulness as citizens and to hinder their advancement in after life, his proceedings must be held to constitute a dereliction of duty, and may properly be visited with disciplinary action." In plain unofficial English the schoolmaster will be allowed to teach loyalty and subservience, but if he teaches patriotism, he must be suspended, degraded or dismissed. If he takes his pupils or encourages them to go to political meetings, — barring celebrations of the Empire Day, — he will, of course, be dismissed at once. Finally, the College Professors, men like Srijut Surendranath Banerji, Aswini Kumar Dutt, Krishna Kumar Mitra, are not to be altogether gagged, but their hands are to be bound. "If he diverts his students' minds to political agitation", as Srijut Surendranath has done for decades; "if he encourages them to attend political meetings or personally" conducts them to such meetings, — this is obviously aimed at Srijut Krishna Kumar Mitra and the Anti-Circular

Society — "or if he adopts a line of action which disturbs and disorganises the life and work of the College at which he is employed", — whatever this portentous phrase may mean, — the College is to be disaffiliated or the offender expelled.

This ukase out-Russias Russia. Not even in Russia have such systematically drastic measures been taken to discourage political life and patriotic activity among the young. Not even the omnipotent Tsar has dared to issue an ukase so arbitrary, oppressive and inquisitorial. It means that no self-respecting patriot will in future enter or remain in the Government educational service in any position of responsibility; or if he remains, he will not be allowed to remain long. It means that the position of private schools and colleges will become unbearable and they will be compelled to break off connection with the Government University. It means, if there is a grain of self-respect left in the country, that the Government University will perish and a National University be developed. And for this reason we welcome the circular and hope that its provisions will be stringently enforced.

Bande Mataram, May 8, 1907

BY THE WAY

The Anglo-Indian Defence Association exists, we believe, in order to take up the cause of Anglo-Indians individually and generally, whether that cause be just or unjust, whether the individual be a good citizen or a criminal pursued by the law. It is not surprising that such a body should also be found championing the Mahomedan hooligans who, for the present, are the good friends, allies and brothers-in-arms of Anglo-India in its fight against Swadeshi. A certain Mr. Garth, said to be a son of the late Sir Richard Garth, Chief Justice and one of the cheap and numerous tribe of "Friends of India", was the oratorical hero of the occasion. This gentleman was delivered in Mangoe Lane on Monday of a speech which runs to more than a column of insults and misrepresentations against Swadeshi Bengalis. He informed a wondering world that things in East Bengal were quite the opposite of what the Bengali press reported. We do not exactly understand this phrase. Does Mr. Garth mean that it is the Mahomedans who are being plundered, their men wounded and injured, their women outraged, while the officials give their assailants a free hand and are busy repressing any attempt at self-defence? That would be the opposite of what the Bengali papers represent.

But Mr. Garth then assures the world — which ought by this time to be quite dumb with awe — that he, Mr. Garth, is quite satisfied of the absolute falsity of the charges against the local officials. He does not pretend — this easily-satisfied Mr. Garth — that there is a single fact or the smallest fragment of evidence to disprove these charges which the officials impugned have not tried and the Anglo-Indian journals have not been able to disprove. No, the inner consciousness, the subliminal self of Mr. Garth has assured the outer barrister in him of the innocence of Messrs. Clarke, Loghman & Co., and they are acquitted. Mr. Garth is equally cocksure that the Mahomedans did not begin any of the recent riots so — it was the Hindus who went and compelled them to riot and plunder and worse — so anxious were the people of Jamalpur and Dewangunj to bring on themselves the worst outrages and insults. With such brilliant powers of insight and reasoning Mr. Garth ought to have come much more to the front as a barrister than he has succeeded in doing.

The case for the Mahomedans as presented by this brilliant special pleader is that they were goaded to madness. In order to prove his point, he makes no bones about falsifying history. The Hindus, he says, tried their hardest to get the Mahomedans to join with them but absolutely failed. When we remember the unanimity of Hindus and Mahomedans at the time of the Partition Agitation, we cannot but admire such fearless lying. Well, the Hindus failed and then they tried intimidation on the poor sellers of Bideshi articles who are all, if you please, — yes, one and all Mahomedans in Mr. Garth's pleasant romance. But still Mahomedans would not lose their angelic patience, still they would not listen to the pipings of Hare Street. But at last the Hindus began to form bodies of volunteers and learn stick-play and sword-play. This was the last insult which drove the

Mahomedans to madness. That Hindus should learn sword-play and stick-play is enough, in Mr. Garth's opinion, to justify outrage, plunder, murder, mutilation, and the violation of women. After this, he says, no wonder the Mahomedans began to ask their leaders, "What is this?" All this tumult and violence, all these Armenian and Bulgarian horrors under British rule, are only the inoffensive, patient, loyal Mahomedan's gentle way of asking his leaders, "what is this?"

We have written the above in the very bitterness of our heart. It is clearer than ever that the unspeakable outrages inflicted on the Hindu community had the full moral support of the English in India. Officials allow them, Anglo-Indian papers sympathise with them, Anglo-Indian speakers defend them, and the speeches and writings in which they are defended, are full of intolerable insults to the whole Hindu population of Bengal. Yet we do not cease to buy the *Englishman* and *Empire*, we do not cease to give briefs to Mr. Garth and men of his kidney. We even hear that a prominent Swadeshi leader gave a brief to Mr. Garth the very next day after his speech, presumably as a reward for calling the whole Bengali Bar and Press a pack of liars. If it is so, we deserve every humiliation that can be inflicted upon us.

Bande Mataram, May 9, 1907

The Crisis

THE last action of the Minto-Morley Government has torn every veil from the situation and the policy of the British rulers. Whatever else may be the result of this vigorous attempt to crush Nationalism in the Punjab, it has the merit of clearing the air. We have no farther excuse for mistaking our position or blundering into ineffective policies. The bureaucracy has declared with savage emphasis that it will tolerate a meekly carping loyalism, it will tolerate an ineffective agitation of prayer, protest and petition, but it will not tolerate the New Spirit. If the Indian harbours aspirations towards freedom, towards independence, towards self-government in his mind, let him crush them back and keep them close-locked in his heart; for from English Secretary or Anglo-Indian pro-consul, from Conservative or from Liberal they can expect neither concession nor toleration. Indian aspirations and bureaucratic autocracy cannot stall together; one of them must go. The growth of the New Spirit had been so long tolerated in Bengal because the rulers, though alarmed at the new portent, could not at once make up their mind whether it was a painted monster or a living and formidable force. Even when its real nature and drift had become manifest, they waited to see whether it was likely to take hold of the people. They were not prepared for the enormous rapidity with which like a sudden conflagration in the American prairies, the New Spirit began to rush over the whole of India. By the time they had realised it, it was too late to crush it in Bengal by prosecuting a few papers or striking at a few tall heads. For the New Spirit in Bengal does not depend on the presence of a few leaders or the inspiration from one or two great orators. It has embraced the whole educated class with one unquenchable flame. If Srijut Bepin Chandra Pal were deported, and the *Bande Mataram*, *Sandhya* and other Nationalist journals suppressed, the fire would only become silent, pervading, irresistible. A hundred hands would catch the banner of Nationalism as it fell from the hands of the standard-bearer and a hundred fiery spirits rush to fill the place of the fallen leader. In Bengal, therefore, other measures have been adopted. But the moment the bureaucrats were sure that the fire had caught in the Punjab, they hastened to strike, hoping by the suppression of a few persons to suppress the whole movement. The first blow at the *Punjabee* was a disastrous failure. The second has been delivered with extraordinary precautions to ensure its success. The whole might of the British Empire has been summoned to drive it home. The pomp and prestige of its irresistible might, the tramp of its armies and the terror of its guns, the slow mercilessness of its penal law and the swift fury of its arbitrary statutes have all been gathered round two small cities, not to put down a formidable rebellion or affect the capture of dangerous military leaders, but to arrest a few respectable and unwarlike pleaders and barristers. Enveloped with a surge of cavalry under the mouths of British siege-guns, these fortunate individuals, most of whose names were till then hardly known outside their own province, — have been hurried to British jails and one eminent pleader whirled out of India with a panic haste. All this pomp and apparatus can evidently have no object but to terrify the New Spirit throughout India into quiescence by a display of the irresistible power of Britain. It is an emphatic warning from Mr. Morley and Lord Minto that they will not suffer the Indian to aspire to freedom or to work by peaceful self-help and passive resistance for national autonomy.

In this grave crisis of our destinies let not our people lose their fortitude or suffer stupefaction and depression to seize upon and unnerve their souls. The fight in which we are engaged is not like the wars of old in which when the King or leader fell, the army fled. The King whom we follow to the wars today, is our own Motherland, the sacred and imperishable; the leader of our onward march is the Almighty Himself, that element within and without us whom sword cannot slay, nor water drown, nor fire burn, nor exile divide from us, nor a prison confine. Lajpat Rai is nothing, Tilak is nothing, Bepin Pal is nothing: these are but instruments in the mighty Hand that is shaping our destinies and if these go, do you think that God cannot find others to do

His will? Lala Lajpat Rai has gone from us, but doubt not that men stronger and greater than he will take his place. For when a living and rising cause is persecuted, this is the sure result that in the place of those whom persecution strikes down, there arise, like the giants from the blood of Raktabij, men who to their own strength add the strength, doubled and quadrupled by death or persecution, of the martyrs for the cause. It was the exiled of Italy, it was the men who languished in Austrian and Bourbon dungeons, it was Poerio and Silvio Pellico and their fellow-sufferers whose collected strength reincarnated in Mazzini and Garibaldi and Cavour to free their country.

Let there be no fainting of heart and no depression, and also let there be no unforeseeing fury, no blindly-striking madness. We are at the beginning of a time of terrible trial. The passage is not to be easy, the crown is not to be cheaply earned. India is going down into the valley of the shadow of death, into a great horror of darkness and suffering. Let us realise that what we are now suffering, is a small part of what we shall have to suffer, and work in that knowledge, with resolution, without hysteria. A fierce and angry spirit is spreading among the people which cries out for violent action and calls upon us to embrace death. We say, let us be prepared for death but work for life, — the life not of our perishable bodies but of our cause and country. Whatever we do, let it be with knowledge and foresight. Let our first and last object be to help on the cause, not to gratify blindly our angry passions. The first need at the present moment is courage, a courage which knows not how to flinch or shrink. The second is self-possession. God is helping us with persecution; we must accept it with joy and use that help calmly, fearlessly, wisely. On the manner and spirit in which we shall resist and repel outrage and face repression, while not for a moment playing into the hands of the adversary, will depend the immediate success or failure of our mission.

Bande Mataram, May 11, 1907

In Praise of the Government

We cannot sufficiently admire the vigorous and unselfish efforts of the British Government to turn all India into a nation of Extremists. We had thought that it would take us long and weary years to convert all our countrymen to the Nationalist creed. Nothing of the kind. The Government of India is determined that our efforts shall not fail or take too long a time to reach fruition. It will not suffer us to preach nationalism to the people, but in its noble haste and zeal is resolved to preserve the monopoly of the Nationalist propaganda to itself. "Alone I will do it," they have evidently said to themselves, even as Louis XVI said to his people when he resolved to take the work of reform out of the hands of the States General into his own. The Government of India also has resolved to take the work of inculcating nationalism into its own hands. There is no further need of the inspiring oratory or compelling logic of a Bepin Chandra, the fine and vigorous lucidity and competent organisation of a Tilak, the attractive charm, self-sacrifice, moral force and steady, quiet work of a Lajpat Rai. The Government will brush them aside and take their place. We cannot deny that the methods of the Government far excel our poor efforts. Our methods are long, wordy, weary and when all is said and done, only half-effective; those of the Government are magnificent, brief, laconic, decisive, triumphantly effective. By its policy of leaving the Mymensingh Mahomedans for weeks together to inflict the utmost horrors of rapine and brigandage on a Hindu population sedulously disarmed and terrorised by official severity, they have convinced the country that the Pax Britannica is an illusion and no peace worth having which is not maintained by our own strength and manhood. By the deportation of Lala Lajpat Rai, they have destroyed the belief in British justice. By their Resolution for the prohibition of meetings they have convinced everyone that we possess the right of free speech, not as a right, not as a possession, but as a temporary and conditional favour depending for its continuance on despotic caprice. We await with confidence fresh developments of this admirable Nationalist propaganda.

Bande Mataram, May 13, 1907

How to Meet the Ordinance

WHEN we come to look at it closely, the new policy of the British Government in India is a real blessing to the country. We find ourselves in unexpected agreement with the Anglo-Indian Press in this matter. The Anglo-Indian Press is full of joy at these departures from pre-established policy and assevers in one chorus though in many keys, *ekam bahudhā*, that it is the very best thing the bureaucracy could have done in the interests of its own continued supremacy. We will not question their authority in a matter in which they alone are interested but we can certainly add that it is the very best thing the bureaucracy could have done in the interests of the country. Lord Minto ought therefore to be a very happy man, for it is not everyone whose actions are so blessed by Fate as to command equal approbation from the *Englishman* and the *Bande Mataram*.

Our reasons for this approval are obvious on the face of it. The great strength of British despotism previous to Lord Curzon's regime was its indirectness. By a singularly happy policy it was able to produce on the subject nations the worst moral and material results of serfdom, while at the same time it never allowed them to realise that they were serfs, but rather fostered in them the delusion that they were admirably governed on the whole by an enlightened and philanthropic people. We pointed out the other day that the relics of this superstition still lingered even in the minds of many thoroughgoing Nationalists of the new school. We did not indeed believe that the bureaucratic Government was a good government or the British people guided in their politics by enlightenment and philanthropy, but many of us believed that there were certain excesses of despotism of which they were not capable and that the worst British administration would not easily betray overt signs of moral kinship with its Russian cousin. We ourselves, although we were prepared for the worst and always took care to warn the people that the worst might soon come, thought sometimes that there was a fair balance of probabilities for and against frank downward Russianism. For such last relics of the old superstitions, for such overcharitable speculation, there is no longer any room. The whole country owes a debt of gratitude to Sirdar Ajit Singh and the Bharat Mata section of the Punjab Nationalists for forcing the hands of the bureaucracy and compelling them to change, definitely, indirect for direct methods of despotism. It has cleared the air, it has dispelled delusions; it has forced us to look without blinking into the face of an iron Necessity.

The question may then be asked, what farther room is there for passive resistance? A Punjab politician is said to have observed, after the arrests of Lala Hansraj and his friends and the first development of violent insanity in the Punjab authorities, "I do not see why the people should go on any longer with open agitation." But, in our opinion, there is still room for passive resistance, if for nothing else than to force the bureaucracy to lay all its cards face upward on the table; the oppression must either be broken or increased so that the iron may enter deeper into the soul of the nation. There is still work and work enough for the martyr, before the hero appears on the scene. Take for instance the Coercion Ukase, the new ordinance to restrict the right of public meeting at the sweet will of the executive. It is obvious that the matter cannot be allowed to rest where it is. We would suggest to the leaders that the right policy to begin with is to ignore the existence of the Ordinance. So far as we understand, the Lieutenant-Governor of Shillong has been empowered to proclaim any area in his jurisdiction, but as yet no area has been proclaimed. This is therefore the proper time for the leaders to go to East Bengal and hold meetings in every District; and those who go, should not be any lesser men, but the leaders of the two parties in Bengal themselves. We are inclined to think it was a mistake to recall Srijut Bepin Chandra Pal from Madras at this juncture; but since he has been recalled, it should be for a joint action in East Bengal against the policy of repression. If the bureaucracy lie low, well and good; it will be a moral victory for the people. But the moment any particular area is proclaimed, the leaders should immediately go there and hold the prohibited meetings as a challenge to the validity of the ukase, refusing to disperse except on the application of force by the police or the military. The bureaucracy will then have the choice either of allowing the Ordinance to remain a dead letter or of imprisoning or deporting men the prosecution of whom will so inflame the people all over India as to make administration impossible or of breaking up meetings by force. If they adopt the third alternative, the leaders should then go from place to place and house to house, like political Shankaracharyas, gathering the people together in groups in private houses and compounds and speaking to them in their gates, advising them, organising them. In this way the fire of Nationalism will enter into every nook and cranny of the country and a strength be created far greater than any which monster meetings can engender. How will the bureaucracy meet such a method of propagandism? Will they forbid us to congregate in our own compounds? Will their police enter our houses and force us to shut our gates to the guest and the visitor? Whatever they do, the country will gain. Every fresh object-lesson in bureaucratic methods will be a fresh impulse to the determination to achieve Swaraj and get rid of the curse of subjection. All that is needed to meet the situation, all that we demand of our leaders is a quiet, self-possessed, unflinching courage which neither the fear of imprisonment, nor the menace of deportation, nor the ulterior possibility of worse than deportation, can for a moment disturb.

The Latest Phase of Morleyism

That Mr. Morley should completely throw off the mask and unceremoniously declare his real attitude towards Nationalist aspirations is more than what was expected by most people. It is not customary with politicians to be so rudely and unnecessarily frank. Besides, such frankness is calculated to shake that faith in their benevolent professions which is the chief security of British domination in India. We have always been deceived by words. The effect of a series of repressive measures on the feelings of the people is at once counteracted by one kind word from a Viceroy or Secretary of State. Mere flattering promises have hitherto been sufficient to win and retain our allegiance. Why our bureaucrats have broken away from their policy of keeping their real intention veiled behind a number of cant phrases and now make no secret of their determination to put down Nationalism with a high hand can be easily understood by those who have been watching the progress of events during the last two years. The appearance of a Nationalist Party and the home truths they preach have been causing real anxiety to the bureaucracy. If this party gets the ear of the people whose patriotic impulses are never checked by considerations of expediency or immediate self-interest, then such a popular re-awakening is bound to strike at the very root of foreign overlordship. It has therefore become essentially necessary to intercept all communications between the people and their real leaders and well-wishers. It is for this reason that these openly despotic methods are being tried in order to demoralise the Nationalists. The other game is to tempt the Moderates to betray the country by ever dangling before their eyes the bait of administrative reform. This is in every way a great crisis for the country and by his conduct at this moment every man shall be judged. Persecution and temptation are God's methods for separating the showy dross from the true gold.

An Old Parrot Cry Repeated

The *Hindu Patriot* claims to have grown wise with age, and tries to argue us into serfdom. Happily oblivious of its younger days when it had not yet been prompted by senile prudence to sell itself to the alien lords, it comes forward to justify its backsliding and aim a few ineffective blows at the Swarajists. This is how it analyses the present situation:—

We want food for our nourishment; we want education; we want new outlets for the employment of our sons. But they give us none of these. They would make us swallow the bitter pill of autonomy even at the point of the bayonet and preach the Gospel of "Swaraj". It is to be our food, our raiment and the panacea for all our evils. Everything else they would throw overboard.

It would scarcely have called for notice had not this view been shared even now by a small section of the so-called educated community. The *Patriot* tries to establish what has been disproved by our experience during the last quarter of a century. We had been trying patch-works and half-measures — with what effect the *Patriot* knows as well as ourselves. It was only when we discovered that we had begun at the wrong end, that the ever-increasing drain on the country with its necessary accompaniments — plague and famine — could not be stopped so long as the people were left to the tender mercy of the foreign overlord, that the cry of Swaraj went forth, and people began to take politics more seriously than before. It is exactly because we cannot get food for nourishment, nor proper education nor even "employment for our sons", so long as we have to depend for these things on our unwelcome guests, that we have begun to think of managing our household, and surely it can serve no useful purpose to ignore our own experience and repeat the political farce over again. Are Englishmen here to give us food and education and provide fat berths for our own children? The whole political situation has been misunderstood, and where the very premises are wrong, the arguments can but lead astray.

Bande Mataram, May 15, 1907

Mr. Morley's Pronouncement

THE attitude assumed by Mr. John Morley in answer to the questions in Parliament about the latest act of mediaeval tyranny, cannot surprise those who have something more than surface knowledge of English politics and English politicians. Those who have been behind the scenes in English political life, know perfectly well that there sincerity is an element which does not exist. Professions, principles, ideals are the tinsel and trappings of the stage; each politician is an actor who has a part to play and plays it, certain set sentiments to mouth and mouths them. But the only reality behind is a mass of interests, personal interests, class interests, party interests, and the ruling principle of action is to "catch votes" and avoid the loss of votes. We have all noticed how persistently the Anglo-Indian Press out here talk of every movement as being artificial and the work of "professional agitators", and how persistently they refuse to credit the popular leaders, even when they are men of high moral worth like Lala Lajpat Rai, with sincerity. We generally put this down to the perverseness and wilful misrepresentation of a reptile press; the real truth is that they are judging us from their knowledge of their own country. They are perfectly well aware that in England politics is a huge piece of humbug; it professes to be a conflict of principles and is really a conflict of more or less sordid interests. They know that in England, a sincere politician is a contradiction in terms. They are therefore unable to believe in the existence in India of a sincerity and reality for which their own country offers no precedent. The only exceptions to the general rule of insincerity are the novices in politics — the maiden innocence of whose souls is soon rubbed off by a few Parliamentary sessions, — and a handful of independent-minded eccentrics who have no chance whatever of rising to influence, much less to office. Occasionally a man of absolute sincerity like Mr.

Bradlaugh breaks the record, but that is only once in half a century.

When Mr. John Morley entered politics, he entered as a literary man and austere philosopher and brought the spirit of philosophy into politics. His unbending fidelity to his principles earned him the name of Honest John, and this soubriquet, with the reputation for uprightness of which it was the badge, has survived long after the uprightness itself had perished in the poisoned air of office. No one can be long a Cabinet Minister in England and yet remain a man of unswerving principle. As Indian Secretary, Mr. Morley could not be expected to carry his philosophic principles into the India Office. On the contrary, there were several reasons why he should be even more reactionary than ordinary Secretaries of State. The Secretary of State does not represent India or stand for her interests; he represents England and his first duty is to preserve British supremacy; but Mr. Morley is also one of the foremost exponents of the most arrogant and exclusive type of enlightenment in nineteenth-century Europe, the scientific, rationalist, agnostic, superior type. As such he was the last man to think well of or understand Asiatics or to regard them as anything but semi-barbarous anachronisms. Moreover, as the *Bengalee*'s London correspondent pointed out this week, he is evidently showing signs of senile decay which is shown partly in his growing ill-temper and intolerance of contradiction, but most in the mental languor which prevents him from questioning or scrutinising the opinions and information served up to him by the India Office. The verbatim fidelity with which he reproduces whatever Anglo-India tutors him to say, is strikingly evidenced by his answers to Messrs. Rutherford and O'Grady. His remarks on the situation in East Bengal might have been taken for an extract from the *Englishman*'s editorials or from the imaginative reports of the special correspondent of the *Empire*.

Mr. Morley makes no attempt to justify the arbitrary action he has sanctioned except on the plea of necessity, the tyrant's plea, which no one in former days would have held up more eloquently to condemnation and ridicule than Mr. Morley himself.

He does not tell us why Lala Lajpat Rai was deported or what were the charges against him; probably he does not himself know, but simply accepted the assurance of the able and experienced Denzil and the level-headed Minto that the step was necessary. For they are the men on the spot, and Mr. Morley's conception of his position in the India Office is that he is there to act as a buffer between the men on the spot and adverse criticism. We need not discuss his utterances; they are merely faithful echoes of Anglo-Indian special pleading, in which there is nothing that is new and very little that is true. But the threat which he held out to the Moderate Party is worth noting. For some time Mr. Morley and Lord Minto, with whom the Secretary of State rather superfluously assures us that he has an excellent understanding, have been talking big of some wonderful reform that they have up their sleeves and feverishly assuring the world that these fine things are all their very own idea and by no means forced on them by Indian agitation. And now we are told or rather the Moderate leaders are told that they will lose these pretty toys if they do not help the bureaucracy to put down "disorder", or, in other words, to put down Nationalism. Mr. Morley offers them a certain administrative reform if they can give up for themselves or can induce their countrymen to give up the aspiration towards freedom. The Anglo-Indian journals all take up the cry and the absolute insincerity of it is sufficiently shown by the fact that even so venomous, reactionary and anti-Indian a print as the *Englishman* proses solemnly on the theme! The object of these threats is manifest. The sudden succession of coercive measures may for a moment have stunned the people, it may for a few days dismay the more timid, but it has certainly created a deep and settled exasperation throughout the country. The dismay is temporary, the exasperation will be permanent. Mr. Morley and Anglo-India hope to take advantage of the moment of dismay in order to half-bribe, half-intimidate the Moderate Party into detaching themselves from any opposition to these coercive measures. This is a vain hope. For even to the meanest political intelligence two considerations will at once occur. The first is that there is such a thing as buying a pig in a poke. Even the simplest buyer will want to see the animal before he puts down its price, and even the most confiding Moderate will want to know what is this wonderful reform of Mr. Morley's before he sells the country's future and risks his influence with the people for its sake. But on this point Mr. Morley preserves as studious a silence as on the charges against Lajpat Rai. Again, Mr. Morley and Lord Minto have hinted that their measure is an instalment of self-government, yet Mr. Morley emphatically declares that he will never strip the bureaucracy of any means of repression they possess, however barbarous and antiquated. It is evident therefore that whatever "self-government" may be in store for us, it is a "self-government" in which executive despotism will remain absolutely undiminished and unmodified. We have heard of a despotism tempered by epigrams and a despotism tempered by assassination, but this is the first time we hear of a self-government tempered by deportation. We do not think any section of Indian opinion is likely to rise to this lure. The *Bengalee* has already rejected the one-sided bargain with scorn and even the *Indian Mirror* has received it without enthusiasm. Coerce, if you will — we welcome coercion, but be sure that it will rank the whole of India against you without distinction of parties.

What does Mr. Hare Mean?

Writes the *Indian Mirror*: — "For one full week we have it constantly dinned into our ears, that Mr. Hare intends to visit the scenes of disturbance. Yet he has not left Shillong as yet, and disturbances are as rife as ever. What does Mr. Hare mean?"

Even Homer nods; and even Mahatmas are at times slow to understand the significance of events. Our contemporary declines to accept the Jamalpur affair as a link in a chain that has been forged by the people interested in the suppression not so much of Swadeshi and Boycott as of the spirit of nationalism. The Harrison Road case might have been a blow aimed at boycott, for at that time the new spirit had not made itself prominently manifest in Bengal and other parts of India. But the Barisal barbarities left no room for doubt. Then came the Comilla excesses.

Are we to believe that the Moslem population of East Bengal has really been deluded into the idea that East Bengal belongs to Salimullah? Are we, again, to believe that the British Government which now sees wraiths even in wreaths of smoke, contemplates with a sense of security, if not satisfaction also, the growth of this idea in the truculent population of the province and the consequent growth of the influence and power of an ordinary Zemindar? Are we then to believe that the British Government is too weak to check the spread of rowdyism in East Bengal and the distribution of the "red pamphlet"? Then comes the deportation of the Punjab leader by the Government in a manner which reminds one of the conduct of "Cunning old Fury" in *Alice in Wonderland*, who wanted to play the parts of judge and jury to convict the defendant in a case in which he himself was the plaintiff. The crowning act comes from Mr. Morley, once extolled by the Friend of India as the *beau idéal* of a man and a politician, who expresses his determination "not to strip the Government of India of any weapon or law for the suppression of native disorders".

The Jamalpur affairs are only a link in the chain. Accept this view and the whole situation, as well as the attitude of the local officers will be clear. We need no longer fight shy of the real significance of things. Let us take things as they are and face the situation boldly irrespective of consequences to individuals in the discharge of their duties.

Bande Mataram, May 16, 1907

The "Statesman" Unmasks

WE DO not know why the paper which calls itself the Friend of India and usually puts on a sanctimonious mask of liberalism, should have suddenly allowed its real feelings to betray themselves last Wednesday. Its attitude for sometime past has been extremely ambiguous. During the height of the disturbances in East Bengal this Friend of India maintained a rigid silence on Indian affairs and discoursed solemnly day after day on large questions of European policy. Like the Levite it turned its face away from the traveller wounded by thieves and passed by. Since the deportation of Lajpat Rai, it has cared less and less to preserve its tone of affected sympathy until on the 15th it appeared as the apologist of despotism and the mouthpiece not of an idea or of a policy, but of the individual grievances of a self-seeking politician whose influence has waned to nothing because he could not satisfy the new demand for courageous and disinterested patriotism. Professing to be a Liberal paper, the *Statesman* has defended the despotic regulation under which Lala Lajpat Rai was deported, — a regulation opposed to all the fundamental principles of Liberalism; it has defended the Coercion Ordinance as a proof of the leniency and liberalism of bureaucratic rule in India. Calling itself a friend of India, it has not scrupled to dissociate itself from its brother friends of India, the British Committee of the Congress, and sneer at them as ill-informed nobodies. After throwing the Congress, its principles and its friends overboard in this extraordinary manner, it has still the assurance to pose as the guide, philosopher and friend of the Moderate Party and lecture them on the necessity of supporting the Government in its action with regard to Lala Lajpat Rai.

The arguments with which the *Statesman* defends the deportation as a supreme act of Liberalism are of a remarkable kind. First, deportation "is not really so bad as it sounds", because "the lot of the so-called political exile is considerably happier than that of the criminal in the common jail". Prodigious! A man is arrested without any charge being formulated against him, without trial, without any chance of defending himself, separated suddenly from his family and friends, his country, his work for religion, society and motherland, and relegated to solitary imprisonment in a distant fortress; yet because he is not treated as Mr. Tilak was treated, as a common criminal with the daily harassment and degradation which is part of the criminal's punishment, this remarkable Liberal organ goes into ecstasies over the leniency of the British bureaucracy. Injustice and arbitrary oppression, in its opinion, is an admirable thing so long as it is not accompanied with vindictive personal cruelty. We remember a correspondent of an Anglo-Indian print at the time of Mr. Tilak's sentence, calling on the Marathas to admire the leniency of the British Government, because it treated him as an ordinary felon instead of impaling him or sawing him to pieces. The *Statesman* writes in the same spirit.

The second plea in defence of deportation is that no act of State is involved in the arrest, it is only a summary dealing under Municipal law. We do not know what to make of this rigmarole or what the *Statesman* understands by Municipal law, or by an act of State. Municipal law may mean the laws and rules which govern municipalities, but we presume it is not the Lahore Municipality which deported Lajpat Rai; or it may mean the ordinary laws and regulations by which local authorities arrange for local administration and the preservation of the peace. But here is an extraordinary action, above the ordinary laws, which needs the sanction of the Government of India and the sanction of the Secretary of State in which a political leader is arrested for mysterious political reasons and deported without trial. Yet this is Municipal law, not an act of State! and since it is Municipal law, no one need protest against it! Apparently an act of State in the *Statesman*'s opinion is an *illegal* act which there is no statute to cover. Any action however tyrannical, if covered by a statute, ought to be borne without complaint by Indians as an act of great leniency and liberalism. Mark again the friendship of this friend of India and the liberalism of this Liberal.

A third plea is that "the action of the authorities in India, if contrasted with that of the average European Government, is leniency itself." So then, tyranny is quite justifiable if it can site an example of another tyranny worse than itself. Let us remind the *Statesman* that the French and German bureaucracies are governments supported by the will of the people and that in the measures of stringency they adopt, they have the consent of the people behind them. And what have the police arrangements of Paris and Berlin to do with the punishment of a man without trial, a relic of medieval despotism of which no modern and civilised Government offers an example?

The real cause of all this special pleading for despotism is revealed in the latter part of the article. "Moderate men are apt to be pushed aside and their services forgotten by new men who seek to force the pace." "A long apprenticeship to journalism, a weary plodding in the musty by-paths of the law, are the chief or only means by which power and influence can be gained." This is where the shoe pinches. Who is this apprentice to journalism who is being pushed aside by young and extreme journals? Obviously the *Statesman* itself. Who is this weary plodder in the musty by-paths of the law, who claims that only lawyers or, say, only solicitors, have any right to be political leaders and whose "fame", if not his "fortune", has been affected by the new movement? It is plain enough now that the motive which so long actuated the *Statesman* was not liberal sentiment or high principles, but its own interest and influence. Since that interest was touched and that influence threatened by the increasing spirit of Swadeshism and self-reliance, the temper of this Friend of ours has been growing worse and worse until he has finally renounced his liberal principles and become a champion of bureaucracy.

The article closes with a curious attack which seems to be directed at Srijut Surendranath Banerji. "Violent speeches, inflammatory writings, a prosecution, a brilliantly unsuccessful defence, paragraphs in all the newspapers, *questions by ill-informed nobodies in the House of Commons*, the jail, the exit, fame and fortune, notoriety, may be a seat in Parliament — here we have not altogether a fancy picture of the modern Political Rake's progress." This is, we are told, not altogether a fancy picture; in other words, with the exception of the last touch about the possible seat in Parliament, it is taken from the life; and to whom can it be applied but Srijut Surendranath? For, obviously, no leader of the new school is meant, since no leader of the new school would aspire to a seat in Parliament. Yet after this ill-natured attack the *Statesman* yesterday had again the face to figure as the patron and councillor of Srijut Surendranath and advise him to sacrifice his feelings of personal friendship and respect for Lala Lajpat Rai, his principles, his patriotism, his reputation as a political leader and his influence with the people in order to get the approbation of Mr. John Morley and the *Statesman.*

A more complete unmasking could not be imagined. The *Statesman* not only attacks the new school, — that would be nothing new, — but turns round and rends his own associates, Srijut Surendranath, the British Committee, the friends of India in Parliament, renounces all liberal ideas and principles, throws off every disguise and stands forth naked and unashamed. We recommend this example of "friendship" to all Bengali customers of the *Statesman*'s heavy goods, and would advise them either to cease patronising a dealer of such doubtful candour or to insist that the goods they get shall be of the pattern they have paid for.

Sui Generis

The *Morning Leader* in casting about for reasons, — let us call them reasons, not excuses, — for defending Mr. Morley's Russian policy, has discovered the fact that the case of India is *sui generis*, a thing apart which stands on its merits and to which ordinary principles cannot be applied. The *Morning Leader* need not have taken refuge in Latin in order to hide its embarrassment. All India, Moderate and Extremist alike, have begun to realise that the principles of Liberalism which are so loudly mouthed about in Westminster and on the hustings, are not meant to be applied to India. They may be applied to England and the colonies but they are undoubtedly unsuitable to as subject a nation where the despotic supremacy of the white man has to be maintained, as it was gained, at the cost of all principles and all morality. Ireland also was *sui generis* once, until by moonlighting, Fenianism, dynamite and Passive Resistance, she managed to break down the barrier and place herself on the same level with other nations. Yes, India is a case apart. In England, politics is a question of parties. In India politics is a conflict of principles and of mutually destructive forces, the principle of bureaucracy against the principle of democracy, the alien force of Imperialism against the indigenous force of Nationalism. Our relations with our rulers are not those of protector and protected, but of eater and of eaten. As man and the tiger cannot live together in the same circle of habitation, so Indian Nationalism and bureaucratic despotism cannot divide India between them or dwell together in peace. One of them must go.

Bande Mataram, May 17, 1907

The "Statesman" on Mr. Mudholkar

NOTHING can be more instructive than the way in which recent events have arrayed all Anglo-Indians, "liberal" or reactionary, on one side and on the other hand brought all Indian politicians, moderate or "extremist", nearer to each other. It shows that the profound division of interests creates an unbridgeable gulf between the aliens in possession and the people of the country in their different degrees of aspiration.

Apparent alliances between Anglo-India and any section of the people can only be temporary adjustments of self-interest or of policy. When the crucial moment comes, each must return to his own camp and stand in sharply-defined opposition to his recent ally. We have had occasion to comment strongly on the recent unmasking of the *Statesman*. It was emphasised yesterday by the bitter and unscrupulous attack of that paper on Mr. Mudholkar. Mr. Mudholkar is the leading Moderate politician of the Berars, a man almost timid in his caution and one of the chief opponents of the new Nationalism. One would have thought therefore that the *Statesman* would have the decency at least to treat him with some affectation of respect. But Mr. Mudholkar is handled as roughly and hectored and lectured as insolently as if he had been a Tilak or a Bepin Pal. The attack is not only insolent; it is unscrupulous. The *Statesman* does not hesitate to misrepresent Mr. Mudholkar in order to serve its own ends. This is how it distorts Mr. Mudholkar's letter in one instance: "We read at the outset the theory of provocation is ridiculous and absurd; but in the succeeding sentence Mr. Mudholkar impliedly admits that it was the conduct of a few indiscreet young men that furnished the immediate occasion of the riot. *This, we believe, has now been definitely established.*" Anyone who takes the trouble to read Mr. Mudholkar's letter will see at once that he does not admit either impliedly or directly that there was provocation. He says, "Assuming, *what has yet to be proved*, that the impassioned advocacy of Swadeshi goods by the National Volunteers was distasteful to the Mahomedans, how could it possibly serve as a provocation?" And proceeding with this assumption, he asks in the next sentence how this alleged indiscretion of a few young men at the Mela could produce so fearful a riot? We cannot credit the *Statesman* with sufficient dullness or ignorance of the English language as to suppose that its distortion of Mr. Mudholkar's argument is not deliberate.

And when, may we ask, was it "definitely established" that the indiscretion of a few Volunteers was the cause of the riot? We know that it is so stated by the correspondents of Anglo-Indian papers whose evidence, being mere hearsay, has no value whatever, and we presume that this is what they have been told by the police officials who are accused of complicity in leading the Hindus into a carefully-prepared trap. But the statements of the Hindus, who were attacked, stand as yet uncontroverted by independent evidence and unrefuted by any reliable enquiry. The *Statesman*, feeling the weakness of its case, tries to justify the action of the Mahomedan rowdies by saying that there has been a rise of prices round about Jamalpur as the result of the Swadeshi agitation. This is, in the *Statesman*'s view, sufficiently grave provocation! Well, possibly so. There has been, we know, an immense rise of prices all over India owing to the British occupation, to which the present rise of prices is absolutely nothing. Would that, in the *Statesman*'s view, be sufficiently grave provocation for the whole of India to rise in riot of rebellion?

The *Statesman* has no real answer to Mr. Mudholkar's arguments. Its answer to him consists merely of a prolonged charge of exaggerated language. Mr. Mudholkar described the state of things in East Bengal by the words "anarchy, rapine, desecration, bloodshed". These words the *Statesman* stigmatises as "ludicrously inappropriate to the facts". Indeed? The facts are that for the space of several weeks village after village was plundered and property to the value of many lakhs looted; yet this is a state of things which we are not to be allowed to term rapine. During the same time images were destroyed, temples attacked and desecrated, a religious celebration forbidden by armed rowdies; yet all this did not amount to desecration! Life and person were unsafe, numbers of men were hurt, some so seriously as to be sent to the hospital, two or three were brutally murdered, yet the *Statesman* thinks there was no bloodshed. For this space of time life and property and the honour of women were unsafe over a large area, the Hindus had to flee from Jamalpur and in all neighbouring places to organise their own defence, panic and riot and outrage reigned supreme while the constituted authorities busied themselves repressing the community attacked and threatened, leaving a free hand to the rioters; but this is not to be called anarchy! No, all this, says this miraculous Friend of India, were mere ordinary local disturbances *which would scarcely have attracted notice* but for the profoundness of the Pax Britannica. Mark the opinions of your friend, people of India. The desecration of your temples, the violation of your women, the wholesale plunder of your property are to him things that scarcely deserve to attract notice.

The *Statesman* again rebukes Mr. Mudholkar for exaggerating the riot at Rawalpindi which it holds to be a very ordinary affair, and thinks that because Mr. Mudholkar has exaggerated this and other matters, therefore Indians are unfit to be entrusted with the administration of their own affairs. Yet in the same article the *Statesman* justifies the deportation of Lala Lajpat Rai, *even if he were innocent*, because the occurrences in the Punjab were considered by the Government so serious that his removal was a necessity. Here is a consistent Friend of India! But if Mr. Mudholkar's exaggerated ideas of the Rawalpindi disturbances unfit his countrymen for self-government, still more do Sir Denzil Ibbetson's and the *C. M. Gazette*'s yet more exaggerated ideas of the same occurrences show that Englishmen are unfit to rule India.

The only point that the *Statesman* successfully makes against Mr. Mudholkar is when it disproves his belief that such arbitrary and tyrannical proceedings are subversive of the principles of British law. This delusion of the Moderates ought now to be renounced. They have always laboured under the delusion that because the British Government, as apart from its local instruments, acts within the law, it is therefore incapable of oppression. On the contrary, as the *Statesman* points out, the British laws give ample room and provide adequate weapons for methods of despotic repression which are often indistinguishable in kind, though less direct and brutal than Russian methods.

None, says the *Statesman* sanctimoniously, has laboured more devotedly than ourselves in the case of India's political emancipation. We have heard legends that have come down to us from the times of our fathers of occasional active help given by the *Statesman* to their constitutional agitation, but we do not know what it has done recently beyond promising reforms which never come and thriving on the support of the Indian public. Certainly this is not enough to entitle it to lecture one of the leaders of public opinion and revile him as a "ranter". We hope that Mr. Mudholkar will learn his lesson, cease to appeal to English rulers and English journals and address himself in future to his own countrymen. Let him join hands with us in training them into a strength which will be a far greater security against "anarchy, rapine, desecration and bloodshed" than the protecting arm of the bureaucracy or the friendship of the *Statesman*.

Bande Mataram, May 20, 1907

Silent Leaders

We have been waiting day after day in the hope that the men who profess to be the leaders of the people would give out no uncertain instructions to the country as to how it could best meet the violent frontal attack which the bureaucracy has made upon the Nationalist agitation. We can quite understand that nothing hasty or impatient should be done and that a few days should have been taken for careful consideration before any lead was given to the nation at a peculiarly critical juncture. But it seems that the only thing our leaders can think of to do is — nothing. The struggle we are engaged in is of the nature of a battle and in a battle a quick eye and a prompt decision are of the first importance. It is not a big judicial case or a Bill in the Legislative Council in which slow decision or none is called for. We fear our leaders have been demoralised and the harsh and terrible reality, with which they are suddenly brought face to face, has frightened all the energy and volition out of them. If so, they are not the leaders for us. Men without courage, men who cannot hurl themselves upon the confronting danger when they see the crown of success beyond, or men whose eyes are blinded by selfish terror to the vision of the crown, these are not the men for times of revolution such as the present. We will look no longer to them for leading but take our own line and let those who have the courage go with us, and let them who have not, crouch in the temporary safety purchased by inglorious cowardice until the storm breaks upon fighter and trembler alike and sweeps away those first who thought to save themselves from its violence. Once more and for the last time we call upon these leaders of ours to give us the word for the battle. Where are they, these men who claimed to be our great men and our captains? Why are they hiding their heads in the hour of danger? Already murmurs are spreading among the rank and file and those who were once spoken of with honour are being called vile and shameful names. They must speak at once if they would save their reputation and influence.

Bande Mataram, May 21, 1907

The Government Plan of Campaign

THE bureaucracy is developing its campaign against Swadeshism with a great rapidity and a really admirable energy and decision. Barisal was naturally the first district to be declared, and now we learn that Dacca, Mymensingh, Faridpur, Pabna, Rungpur and Tippera, the Habiganj sub-division of the district of Sylhet and the Sudharam Thana in the district of Noakhali have also been proclaimed. Others, no doubt, will follow. All these districts have been selected for the prominence they have taken in the Swadeshi movement. It is significant also that in Backergunge the proclamation has been attended by a Magisterial order which forbids the carrying of lathis and sword-sticks between sunrise and sunset and the gathering of men in strength after nightfall. This can have no other effect than to prevent the Swadeshists offering an effective resistance in case of an attack being organised at night under orders from Dacca; for it is not likely that a lawless mob bent upon mischief would pay any heed to the Magisterial ukase. Meanwhile we have seen at Tangail a foreshadowing of the first line of attack on the Students under cover of the Risley Circular. The objective of the authorities is clear enough. It is to prevent the promulgation and organisation of the Swadeshi and Swaraj sentiment in Punjab and Bengal. In the promulgation of Swadeshism we have used three great instruments, the Press, the Platform and the students. The Press by itself can only popularise ideas, it cannot impart that motive impulse of deep emotion and enthusiasm which is given by the direct appeal, the personal magnetism of a born speaker. But the work of the Platform in its turn is not sufficient in itself. The motive impulse created by the orator is apt to be evanescent, unless it is confirmed by daily insistence on the note sounded, and the inspiring sight of the idea being actually carried into practice by devout and enthusiastic missionaries of the creed. In the Swadeshi agitation this part, the most important and necessary of the three, has been played by the students. It is they who have been the active missionaries of Swadeshism, carrying it into practice with the divine ardour and eagerness of youth, without the reserves of caution, temporising, doubt, half-belief with which colder age would have killed it in its birth; wherever they went, they have created a permanent Swadeshi *atmosphere* in which the tender plant of Nationalism could grow, could put forth leaf and bud, could flower into the religion of patriotism.

The English have a long exprience in the art of political agitation and it could not take them long to discover where the strength of the agitation lay. But they were for a long time at a loss how to deal with it without losing their prestige and reputation as a strong and benign Government. They tried experiments and would not carry them out to the end. They took up a policy of direct and violent coercion in a limited area and then, alarmed at the noise and opposition created, dropped it like a hot coal. Next they tried the effect of a general attitude of "sympathy" and calm toleration covering with its specious and ample cloak a great deal of petty local persecution and secret undermining of Swadeshism. Meanwhile they were preparing the ground for an anti-Hindu campaign through the instrumentality of the Mahomedans which was only to be brought into use if the policy of "sympathy" failed. The policy of sympathy did fail and the local authorities were allowed to let loose the Mahomedan mob on the Hindus. Here again there was a failure or a very partial success. The first attempt at Comilla miscarried owing to the high spirit and good organisation of Comilla Swadeshism. The second blow at Jamalpur fell with tremendous effect, but the additional outbreak on the 27th upset the official apple-cart. It went much farther, probably, than was originally intended; for, possibly, the original intention was simply to teach the Swadeshi Hindus a lesson and perhaps to give an excuse for exceptional measures. But the second outbreak went too far. It drove the Hindus out of Jamalpur, it identified the officials publicly and unmistakably with the hooligans, it lit a fire that spread all over Bengal and created a commotion throughout India; it gave a stupendous impulse to the self-defence movement all over the province; it found a few scattered Akharas and left the whole Hindu population feverishly drilling and standing on guard. Finally, it threatened to imperil Anglo-Indian trade by prolonging the disturbances into the critical part of the jute season. Moreover, the attempt of the officials to isolate Swarajism in East Bengal had failed. Swarajism had set fire to the Punjab, it had begun to permeate the United Provinces, it was spreading with great rapidity in Madras. Another year and the whole of India would have been submerged.

It was these circumstances, apparently, which led the Government to the resolution of grappling with the Frankenstein monster Lord Curzon had raised and of deploying all the powers and instruments of despotism for its suppression. The panic created by the Rawalpindi disturbance has only led it to unmask its batteries sooner and concentrate all its fire on Swadeshism with greater energy and rapidity than might otherwise have been the case. No direct attempt has yet been made to silence the Press, but we have no doubt it will be done, if the Government find that the deportation of Lala Lajpat Rai does not produce a permanent change in its tone. On the other hand, very effective measures have been taken against the platform. The wholesale arrests in Rawalpindi, the monstrous charges brought against Lala Hansraj and others for no worse offence than being present at a public meeting which happened to be followed in point of time by a riot, the deportation of Lala Lajpat Rai are all measures of intimidation against the platform. Lest these should prove insufficient, the bureaucracy has armed itself with powers which, if carefully used, will put an end to Swadeshi propaganda from the platform and can in any case crush it by violent and persistent coercion. It is applied, on the familiar principle of localising opposition and crushing it in detail, to East Bengal and Punjab only, but can easily be extended, should occasion arise. Finally, by the Risley Circular it is sought to strike out of the hands of Nationalism its chief strength, the young and rising generation whose political activity in their student days means the creation of a new race of men whom it will be impossible to rule by despotic methods. If we submit, therefore, to these bureaucratic measures it means that the three potent instruments of our movement will be rendered useless for our purposes and Swadeshism is at an end. The bureaucracy will necessarily wait to see how we take its attack. If we submit, they will not incur unnecessary odium by pressing the measures too hard but will hold them *in terrorem* over us and apply them lightly wherever necessary. If we try to carry on the movement, they will carry on the campaign of Russianism to the bitter end, regardless of ulterior consequences, unless the developments are such as to convince them that the Russian method is useless or worse. Meanwhile, as is shown by the deputation of Mr. Beatson Bell to Mymensingh, efforts will be made to get the Mahomedan outbreak under control again, if for nothing else than in the interests of jute. The Anglo-Indian cry of "jute in danger" is one which cannot be ignored. Until the gathering in of the jute, there will probably be no farther Mahomedan turbulence except in sporadic instances. What will happen afterwards will depend much on the course of events between. We may also expect other attempts besides the mere application of the Risley Circular to take the sting out of the volunteer movement.

Such is the prospect before us. It is high time that we should decide how we are to meet it. Our leaders have evidently abandoned the helm and are merely sitting tight watching the stormy waters roll. So poor is our organisation that even a meeting of mofussil and Calcutta delegates to consider the crisis has not been arranged. There is a talk, we learn from the Friend of India, of an extraordinary All-India Congress at which Mr. Gokhale and some other delegates will meet in Bombay under the aegis of Sir Pherozshah Mehta to protest against these new settled facts. All this will not help us and we must find out our own salvation. We shall devote the next few days to expressing our own opinion of the possibilities before us and we earnestly invite the attention and opinion of our readers upon them, — if they agree with us that there is still room for the open agitation for which we have always stood and which we still advocate.

Bande Mataram, May 22, 1907

And Still It Moves

WHAT is the precise difference which the recent Government measures have made in the conditions of the Swadeshi movement? The first to be considered, because the most `dramatic and striking of these measures, is the deportation of Lala Lajpat Rai. Has this deportation brought any really new element into the problem? When we began the movement we were prepared, or at least we professed to be prepared, for the utmost use by the Government of all the weapons the existing law puts in its hands. We were prepared for press-prosecutions, we were prepared to go to jail on false charges, we refused to be appalled by regulation lathis, broken heads and Gurkha charges. Whatever use the Bengal Government might make of the repressive laws which stand on its statute books, to whatever advantage the local magistracy might turn their powers of government by ukase, we were prepared for everything, we started with the fixed determination to allow nothing to daunt us. Deportation was also a pre-existing weapon of repression available to the bureaucracy under the existing laws. The difference its use has made is to bring in, in the place of provincial repression by the local government, imperial repression by the Government of India with the approval of the Secretary of State. It has also replaced the long and uncertain process of trial ending in a punishment of fixed duration by the swift and sudden process of kidnapping and a punishment — no, we apologise to the Friend of India, we should rather say, a leniency of uncertain, perhaps life-long duration. One other element it has introduced which patriots have had to face in all other countries, but which falls on our heads for the first time, — the punishment of exile. To speak the truth, this is the one and only terror of deportation to Indian patriots. The Indian mind with its passionate attachment to the very soil of the mother-country, its deep reverent feeling that mother and motherland are more to be cherished than paradise itself, must feel the deprivation with a force which no European race, except perhaps the passionate and emotional Italian, could understand. In jail the floor we tread is at least made of Indian soil, when we exercise in the prison yard the air that visits our cheeks is Indian air; the pulsation of Indian aspiration, Indian emotion, Indian life, Indian joys and sorrows beats around our prison walls and floods our hearts with the magnetic pervasiveness of which the air of India is more full than that of any other country. The bureaucracy blundered upon an ingenious way of striking us in a very vulnerable point when it hurried Lajpat Rai away to a remote corner of the world among alien men and cut him off from all sight of Indian faces and communion with Indian hearts. But what then? It is but one suffering the more and the deeper the suffering the greater the glory, the more celestial the reward. We cannot suffer more than Poeris in his Neapolitan dungeon or Silvio Pellico in his Austrian fortress or Mazzini in his lifelong exile. It is with the life-blood of a nation's best and the unshed tears that well up from the hearts of its strong men that the tree of liberty is watered. The greater the sacrifice, the earlier is its fruit enjoyed.

Yet it cannot be denied that the deportation came as a shock on the Moderates and as a surprise to the Extremists. It was a shock to the Moderates because of the source from which it came. They had never been able to shake off the idea that in the end Mr. John Morley, if not the sympathetic Lord Minto, would come to their help. To renounce that hope would be to reject the very keystone of the Moderate policy and turn their backs for ever on the illusions of thirty years. Even up to the moment almost of the deportation the *Bengalee* was clamouring for the recall of Mr. Hare and confidently expecting that his criminal inactivity in the East Bengal disturbances would be punished by a just and benign Secretary of State. On such high expectations the deportation came as a blow straight in the face and struck the Moderate Party dumb and senseless for a moment. The heaviness of the blow it had received can be judged by the sudden violence of the *Indu Prakash* which exceeded in the fierce anger of its utterances any Extremist organ. There is no disguising the fact that the Moderate's occupation is gone. British rule has so unmistakably, finally, irrevocably declared itself as despotism naked and unashamed, a despotism moreover which is firmly resolved to remain despotic, — the fiction of a constitution has been so relentlessly exposed as a sheer mockery and constitutional agitation has thereby been rendered such a patent elaborate and heartless farce that, although it will continue just as the snake continues to wriggle even after it has been cut into two, it has lost all life and all chance of carrying weight in the country. The temper of the Madras meeting, which a serious and influential paper like the *Madras Standard* asserts to have been composed mainly not of students but of adults, shows what the temper of the nation is likely to be. The deportation therefore has introduced a new element for the Moderate politician. His gods have failed him; the benign hand from which he expected favours has treated him instead to a whip of scorpions; the face of flowers he worshipped has had its veil torn away and stands revealed as a grinning death's head. Moderation lies wounded to death. It can no longer exist except as a pretence, an attitude. To the Nationalist the deportation came as a surprise because of the occasion for which it was employed. We knew that the benignant bureaucracy had this weapon in their armoury, that they had used it once and might well use it again; but we thought it had more respect for its prestige and more common sense than to waste it on an insufficient occasion. The Natus were deported because it was suspected that they were behind the Poona assassinations and that the assassinations themselves were part of an elaborate Maratha conspiracy. In the Punjab there was nothing but a riot; for the persistent wild rumours of the disarming of regiments and murder of Europeans have received no confirmation of any kind. Deportation, as directed against the Nationalist movement, was like the magic weapon of Karna which could be used only once with effect; it should therefore have been reserved for a supreme occasion when it might have averted, for the time at least, an incipient mutiny or formidable rebellion. It was used instead in a moment of panic to meet a *fancied* mutiny; it was used not against the formidable and indispensable leader of a great approaching rebellion; but against a boy-orator and a pleader of considerable influence who at the worst was no more than one of the many prophets of revolution. Meant for Arjuna, it has been hurled against Ghatothkach. This misuse deprives it of its utility; for as the *Empire* shrewdly pointed out the other day, the trick of deportation cannot be successfully played twice; the second time it will be a direct help to the strong revolutionary forces which are growing in the country. To the Nationalists therefore the menace of deportation does not bring in any new element into the situation, except in so far as it hastens their work or brings the leaders as well as the rank and file to the touchstone of peril where their value will be tested.

The new element of deportation, therefore, so far as it is a new element, merely facilitates the work of Nationalism. There is no reason why it should modify our action in any essential feature. We may be told of course that we cannot afford to imperil the leaders on whom the progress of the movement depends. We answer that the safety of the leaders can only be assured by sacrificing the vitality and force of the movement, a price too heavy to pay; secondly, where the will of a higher Power is active in a great upheaval, no individual is indispensable. The movement will not stop in the Punjab because Lajpat Rai is gone or Ajit Singh is hiding. *Eppur si muove*, "and still it moves", to its predestined end.

Bande Mataram, May 23, 1907

The Thunderer's Challenge

THE *London Times* has thrown out to us a far more comprehensive and significant challenge than the deportation of Lajpat and all the series of repressions accomplished or contemplated. This Thunderer has all this time been watching the growth of national sentiments in the East with increasing mortification and has at last called out to the surging waves: "Thus far and no further."

The British sword, which like King Arthur's Excalibur should have been thrown into these waves because its work in India, if it had any, is fulfilled and done with, is on the contrary being flourished vigorously as if its mere glitter would frighten the ocean back within its limits. Agitators are menaced and the whole East warned against her discontent with the overlordship of the West. The *Times* has done well to see the ongoings in the East in their proper perspective and not to belittle them as temporary and sporadic disturbances. It would have done better still if it had not talked of putting back a world-movement by the suppression of agitation or the waving of a sword in Fleet Street. The success of the "agitators" in bringing such a movement to a head should have convinced the *Times* that they are being aided by a higher power than any that Lala Lajpat or Ajit Singh can wield. The *Times* has got a superabundance of faith in its sword. But if it really thinks this much-flourished weapon a security against Indian progress, it should keep it waiting in the scabbard till the time for use. Familiarity breeds contempt and it is scarcely dignified for a power filling so important a place in the eyes of the world to indulge in puerile vauntings of its own strength in season and out of season. Let it strike at the right moment, if that will help, but unseasonable flourishings and proddings only give strength and speed to a movement which it is the Englishman's interest to weaken.

But England's folly is India's advantage. Imprudence and wrong-headedness on the part of the one nation are the sure provocatives to courage and manliness on the part of the other. It is in these challenges that the hope of our speedy salvation lies. National regeneration would have been quite an uphill work for us if the alien bureaucracy had continued unmoved in their profession and begun the actual practice of sympathy. But their increasingly militant attitude is helping the attainment of that solidarity which we could hardly have achieved but for this pressure from without. Nationalism which is a creed of faith, love and knowledge has no longer to creep in the petty pace of argument and persuasion, but is making rapid strides towards recognition by the whole people in the overwhelming reaction for which the present bullying by journals like the *Times* and hasty acts of repression like those in the Punjab are responsible. The whole of India is turning Nationalist by one swift revolution of feeling. When the Partition agitation of Bengal has created a universal unrest throughout India, when the cry of resistance that emanated from the small district town of Dinajpur in Bengal has been adopted by the whole country, united India can no longer be called an impossibility. The scepticism about our fitness, the superstition of philanthropy in politics, are fast disappearing before a dawning race-consciousness. The insolence of the ruling race and their constant talk of our inability have touched into life even our atrophied *amour-propre*. The covert and open resistance to the Swadeshi-boycott movement has revealed to us the true nature of foreign sympathy. The events of the last two years have completed our political education.

We used to be much exercised how to bring on that struggle which alone can call forth the energies of body and soul in a subject people. For circumstanced as we are, we cannot act on the offensive, but if others goad us by attack, then only can this degenerate race be saved. Misguided bureaucrats and virulent publicists have created our opportunity. We have only to make the right use of the challenges which are coming in quick succession, and we shall be able to effect in a few years a work which would otherwise take centuries.

An Irish Example

The refusal of the Irish Parliamentary Party under Mr. Redmond's leadership to have anything to do with the sham the Liberal Government has offered them in the place of Home Rule, is a step on which we may congratulate the Irish people. Had they been deluded into swallowing the bait which was devised for them with such unscrupulous skill by Mr. Birrell, they would have committed a false step of the worst kind and seriously compromised the Home Rule Movement. It is much better that Ireland should have to wait longer for any measure of self-government, than that she should commit political suicide by accepting Mr. Birrell's Bill. We call it Mr. Birrell's Bill but in reality it is Sir Antony Macdonnell's and has the stamp of "Liberal" Anglo-Indian upon it. Its object is obviously to kill the Home Rule Movement by kindness, to break up Irish unity and take the sting out of Irish Nationalism by a sham concession skilfully calculated to corrupt the natural leaders of the people. The measure proposed was a sort of bastard cross between a Colonial Parliament and an Indian-Legislative Council. Its acceptance would have committed Irish politicians to the abandonment of the policy of Parnell and to cooperation in future with the British Government. The Irish people were openly told that the concession of further self-government would depend on the way in which they used this precious opportunity, in other words, on their abandoning passive resistance and their principle of aloofness from Government and its favours and co-operating with it in a mutilated and ineffectual scheme of self-government. What would have been the result, if the Irish people had closed with this very bad bargain? They would not have got Home Rule which England is determined never to give them unless she has no other choice. The local self-government offered to Ireland would have been extended to Scotland and Wales and when Ireland demanded Home Rule, she would have been told to be satisfied with a measure of self-government which had satisfied the other parts of the United Kingdom. The British Government would by that time have broken the solid phalanx of Irish Nationalism and by the bribe of office, position and influence, succeeded in detaching from the cause a great number of the natural leaders of the people, men of intelligence, ability and ambition, whose talents would be used by England in keeping the people contented and combating true Nationalism. In this way the great ideal of an Irish Nation for which Emmett died, for which O'Connell and Parnell planned and schemed and which the Sinn Fein movement is making more and more practicable, would either have been entirely frustrated or postponed for another century. Instead of a separate nationality with its own culture, language, government, the Irish would have ended by becoming a big English county governed by a magnified and glorified Parish Council. The same kind of bait was offered to the Boers, but that shrewd people resolutely refused to associate themselves with any form of self-government short of absolute colonial Self-Government. The same kind of bait is promised to the Moderates in India by Honest John and the honest *Statesman*, if they will only consent to dissociate themselves from the New Spirit and all its works and betray their country. The *Statesman* says that Mr. Redmond has been forced to the refusal by the necessity of deferring to the Sinn Fein Party in Ireland, and hopes that the Indian Moderates will not commit the same mistake. Our sapient contemporary opines that the Nationalists in India are not really so strong as they seem, and that the Moderate leaders, if they desire to betray the country, can do so with impunity, without losing their influence and position. Well, we shall see.

Bande Mataram, May 24, 1907

The East Bengal Disturbances

WE HAVE said that the deportation of Lala Lajpat Rai brings no new element into the situation beyond hastening the processes of Nationalism and bringing us from a less to a more acute stage of our progress to independence. The second disturbing element has been the culmination of the alliance between Salimullah of Dacca and the bureaucracy in the anarchy and the outrages in the Mymensingh district. These disturbances are now almost over for the time being, though we must take full advantage of the lull allowed to us, so as to put our house in order against a possible recrudescence after the jute season. We should now seriously consider how far these disturbances have altered the situation and what we should do in order to meet these new conditions. We must first notice that neither the disturbances themselves nor their cause are in their nature a new element in the situation. The Salimullahi campaign, the use of Mahomedan Badmashes to terrorise Swadeshi Hindus, the official inactivity and sympathy with the lawbreakers, these have all been with us even before. The conclusions we arrived at at the time, the warnings and exhortations we addressed to the people have been proved to the hilt, justified beyond dispute, enforced in red letters of rapine, bloodshed and outrage. Our reading of the situation then was that no serious apprehension of trouble between Hindus and Mahomedans need be entertained except within that tract of country immediately under the influence of Nawab Salimullah, — Mymensingh, Dacca, Tipperah and possibly parts of Pabna. This is precisely what has happened. In Comilla the trouble was stopped before it could do real mischief, by the resolute spirit of the Hindus; in Dacca, in spite of small skirmishes, individual harassment and a minor outbreak or two, it never gathered to a head, because the great strength and early preparations of the Hindus overawed the prime movers and their instruments; Mymensingh alone felt the full force of the storm, while Pabna still hovers on the brink of it. It is not that the Nawab's campaign was not vigorously pursued in other parts. The Red Pamphlet has been ubiquitous throughout Eastern and Northern Bengal; the preachings of the Nawab's Mullahs have been as persistent, as malignant in Barisal, in Calcutta, in every strong centre of Swadeshism. But though there have been alarms and excursions even as far west as Allahabad and Benares, the campaign has for the present signally failed outside the limits of Nawab Salimullah's kingdom. This is a fact to be noted. We do not say that Salimullahism carries no dangers with it of general disruption and disunion between the two communities; an unscrupulous agitation of this kind, aided by official backing is always dangerous. But in the rest of the country the blind faith in the Nawab and his Mullahs is absent and other conditions and forces exist which, if properly used by the Nationalists, will permanently counteract the promoters of disunion. Even of themselves, they have been sufficient to prevent the Mahomedans from siding with the self-elected leader against the Swadeshists.

But however limited the area of the disturbances might be, we warned the country that Comilla was not the first and would not be the last of such outbreaks and we called upon it to be ready in time to follow the example of the Comilla Hindus. Moderate politicians, blind leaders of the blind, were rejoicing over the end of the disturbances brought about, they said, by their mysterious efforts — and crying peace, peace where there was no peace. We pointed out that the Comilla affair was not an isolated outbreak, but part of a policy and we knew the men we had to deal with too well to suppose that they would be put off their machinations by a single defeat. Beaten at Comilla, they were certain to try their luck again in Mymensingh. We warned the country also that when the disturbances came, it would be idle to look for protection to the officials and the police. By announcing Swaraj as our ideal we had declared war against the existence of the bureaucracy and we could not expect the bureaucracy to help us by making our efforts to put it out of existence safe and easy. On the contrary, the Nawab and his hooligans were practically, if not avowedly, the allies of the bureaucracy in their war against Swadeshism and must therefore command sympathy and helpful inactivity if not actual assistance from their friends. In all these respects our reading of the situation has been proved correct beyond cavil or dispute. The extent to which the Nawab has succeeded in turning the baser passions of the mob to his uses, the extent to which the Anti-Swadeshi army has gone in its outrages, not scrupling even to desecrate temples and violate women, the extent to which the officials carried their connivance with the excesses, an European police official actually leading the mob and the looting being carried on under the eyes of the police: these things were new, but the Salimullahi campaign itself, the use of the hooligans (our Indian Black Hundred), and the sympathy of the officials are elements which are old, of which the country had been warned and against which the leaders of the movement should have provided.

Even the extent to which these things were carried was due entirely to a feature of the Mymensingh occurrences which we had already warned the country to avoid — the non-resistance of the Hindus of Jamalpur. There are some who say that the recent events in India are a proof of the impracticability of the Nationalist programme. We do not follow the reasoning of these logicians. The Jamalpur incidents and their sequel are a terrible proof of the soundness of the Nationalist ideas and the utter unsoundness of the Moderate theories of our relations with the bureaucracy and the best way of enforcing the Swadeshi propaganda. The people of Comilla followed the Nationalist programme with brilliantly successful results. They boycotted the courts, schools and every other element of the bureaucratic scheme of things and announced their intention of continuing the boycott so long as the Nawab of Dacca was allowed to remain in Comilla — and the Nawab was packed off without ceremony. They met force with force and the hooligan army of Anti-Swadeshism underwent a crushing defeat. On the other hand, the people of Jamalpur did everything which the Nationalist programme excludes; they trusted to the promises of the alien, they chose to go to the Mela unarmed, like defenceless sheep, relying not on their own strong arm but on the protection of the British shepherd. At the order of the alien they laid down the lathis they carried for self-defence, at the order of the alien they trooped to the Mela, from which they had resolved to absent themselves, to be thrashed by Mahomedan cudgels. Then, when their sheepish trustfulness had had its reward, that one lesson was not enough; again they trusted to British protection and sent away the volunteers who stood between them and further outrage. And when the second storm came, they could think of nothing better than wholesale flight from the field of battle. Throughout we see the working of the old political superstitions, the old unworkable compromise which tried to oppose the bureaucracy and yet co-operate with it, to combine vigorous opposition with meek submission, to build up a nation under the most adverse circumstances and against the strongest opponents and yet be, first and foremost, docile, peaceful and law-abiding. These superstitions exploded in the explosions at Jamalpur and the conflagration that followed meant the collapse of a policy.

The hooligan disturbances in East Bengal bring therefore no new elements into the situation, but like the deportation of Lala Lajpat Rai, merely make it more acute and hasten the processes of Nationalism. They create no new conditions, but they have caused certain truths to be newly appreciated. The first is that the Pax Britannica is Maya and, if we mean to be Swadeshists and Swarajists, we must rely in future not on British protection but on self-protection. The second is that, as we have long insisted, our present means of self-defence are inadequate and better means and organisation are a pressing need. The third is the seriousness and true nature of the Mahomedan problem which our older politicians have always tried to belittle or ignore. Any one who wishes to deal successfully with the crisis in the country, must recognise these three lessons of experience and shape his methods accordingly.

Newmania

Yesterday the Special Correspondent of the *Englishman* finished his shilling shocker in many chapters, *The Dreadful Boy Despe-*

radoes of Dacca or *The Violent Volunteers of Barisal.* We have had many new things recently, the new Hinduism, the new School, the new Politics, the new Province, the new John Morley and now we have Newmania in the *Englishman.* The peculiarly delirious character of this disease can be easily understood from the Khulna telegram of the Secretary, People's Association. Mr. Newman had published from Barisal a peculiarly blood and thunder incident of the villainous drowning and stabbing of British goods by whiskerless young desperadoes of Khulna. The Magistrate of Khulna seems to have been so far taken in by the life-like vividness of Mr. Newman's style as to take this bit of heroic romancing quite seriously. He actually enquired into the alleged murder and sudden death and naturally found that nothing of the kind had happened. It is clear that we need a special liturgy for India. "From Denzil Ibbetson and deportation, from the stick of the Constable and the gun of the Goorkha, from sunstroke and the *Civil and Military Gazette*, from Pax Britannica and the Nawab of Dacca, from Sir Henry Cotton and Mr. Rees, from Fuller, Morley and Shillong Hare, Good Lord deliver us! From lesser plague and pestilence, from cholera and motor-cars, from measles and moderation, Good Lord deliver us! But most of all from the friendship of the *Statesman* and the ravings of Newmania, Good Lord deliver us!"

Mr. Gokhale on Deportation

We are glad to see that the *Statesman* does not happen to be the custodian of at least one prominent Moderate's conscience. Mr. Gokhale has written to the *Times of India* that "Lala Lajpat Rai has been sacrificed to a nervous apprehension that suddenly seized the Government." The menace held out to the prospects of administrative reform had no effect on him and like a patriot who on no account can be persuaded to throw overboard his fellow-worker in the field, he has concluded his letter to the *Times* with the characteristic observation: —

"Reforms which the Viceroy and the Secretary of State are contemplating will lose their meaning for us if they cannot be had without deportation out of India of such earnest and high-minded workers in the country's cause as Lala Lajpat Rai." It was an insult offered to the patriotism of our Moderate countrymen to seek to bay their support for measures like the deportation of Lajpat by dangling before them the bait of administrative reform. In the eye of the law both the giver and the taker of a bribe are equally criminal. It is no doubt gratifying that our moderate countrymen do not lay themselves open to the charge of criminality, not to speak of self-betrayal. As for Mr. Morley's offering the bribe his reputation is too philosophic and literary to suffer shipwreck by such a single stroke of diplomatic unscrupulousness. Besides, the ordinary standard of morality has never been observed in the case of black races. To touch politics is to touch tar, said Cardinal Newman, and in dealing with dark people there is an additional inducement for using this black commodity. Mr. Gokhale's white-washing of his high-minded friend will be of no use to the colour-darkened vision of Mr. Morley — it will be love's labour lost. All the same he has come out of the ordeal unscathed.

Bande Mataram, May 25, 1907

The Gilded Sham Again

The *Statesman* on Sunday came out with the startling fact that Mr. Morley has "finally formulated a workable scheme giving prominent natives a larger representation on the various bodies having effective control of Indian affairs". This is, we presume, the last and most authoritative of the special cablegrams with which the *Statesman* has been regaling us, for want of more substantial fare, ever since Mr. John Morley became Chief Bureaucrat for India. For, we are told, Mr. Morley will make an important announcement when introducing the Indian budget. We would call the attention of our readers to the wording of this portentous cablegram. There is going to be a larger representation on the bodies having effective control of Indian affairs, viz., the Legislative Councils and, perhaps, the Executive in which "natives" are at present unrepresented. Indians are not to be allowed any control over Indian affairs, they are only to be more largely represented on the bodies which have that control. They are to have a larger voice, but there is to be no guarantee that the voice will be at all effective. The share of Indians in the government has up to now been *vox et praeterea nihil*, a voice and nothing more, and in the future also it is to be a voice and nothing more. We notice, moreover, that it is not the country, not the people of India which is to be represented, but only "prominent natives". We shall have a few more Gokhales, a few more Bhupendranath Boses, a few more Nawabs of Dacca on the Councils — and there an end. There will be a little manipulation of light and shade, an increase in the number of dark faces, and Mr. Morley and the *Statesman* will triumphantly invite us to rejoice at the "important advance that has been made in the direction of self-government". A hint has been given from another source that there will actually be a non-official majority of elected and nominated members. In other words, Mr. Apcar, Mr. Gokhale and the Nawab of Dacca multiplied several times over will form a non-official majority in the Council. Is this the reform for which we are invited to give up Swadeshi, Nationalism and our future? Mr. Morley and the *Statesman* are grievously mistaken if they think that the newly-awakened spirit of Indian Nationalism can any longer be put off with a gilded sham.

National Volunteers

Our Barisal Correspondent seems, like the Khulna Magistrate, to have taken the *Englishman*'s Special Correspondent much too seriously. The fictions of Mr. Newman are too evidently fictions to deserve serious criticism. Whether they are the distortions of a panic-stricken imagination or actual inventions, we need not too closely enquire. They have a certain journalistic effectiveness, and they serve the political ends of this paper whose efforts are wholly directed towards urging on the Government to a policy of thoroughgoing repression. Everybody in Bengal knows that previous to the disturbances in East Bengal, there was no movement of the kind which has sent Mr. Newman into carefully calculated hysterics. There was a movement for physical training and the institution of Akharas, which was by no means so widespread or successful as it should have been. There was also a custom which had first grown up in the Congress and naturally extended to Conferences and then to public meetings, of employing the services of young men in making the arrangements and keeping order. It is those only who bore the name of volunteers and they were never a standing organisation, but merely organised themselves for the occasion and broke up when it was over, nor had they any connection with the Akharas. Finally, there was in the earlier days of the Swadeshi movement great activity among the young men in picketing and other means of moral suasion to enforce the boycott, but except in one or two places this has long fallen into desuetude except for occasional spasmodic attempts. Neither were the picketers ever formed into an organisation or termed volunteers. After the outbursts of anti-Swadeshi violence at Comilla and Jamalpur, the young men spontaneously united to present a firm defence against hooligan outrages and this is the terrible phenomenon which has made Mr. Newman delirious. In his ravings he has mixed up all these loose threads and woven out of them a web fearful and wonderful. As a matter of fact hundreds of youths who are taking part in the defence of hearth and home, never entered an Akhara or handled a lathi before, and are now first realising what they ought to have realised long ago, the necessity of physical exercise and training to self-defence.

With extraordinary ingenuity this imaginative Sherlock Holmes of Anglo-India has discovered that the Anti-Circular Society, the Bande Mataram Sampraday and the Brati-Samity — harmless and peaceful relics of the first Swadeshi enthusiasm, — are separately and unitedly the organising centre of these terrible Volunteers! We only wish our countrymen had shown themselves capable of forming such an organisation, deliberate, well-knit and pervasive. But we have still some way to travel before this becomes possible.

Bande Mataram, May 27, 1907

The True Meaning of the Risley Circular

WE HAVE seen that the effect of Lala Lajpat Rai's deportation is solely to bring the struggle between the bureaucracy and the people to a head and the leaders as well as the rank and file into the range of fire. We have also come to the conclusion that the disturbances in Mymensingh create no new problem but rather compel us to face as urgencies certain primary necessities we have too much neglected, — the necessity of no longer relying blindly on the purely hypnotic and illusory protection of the Pax Britannica which may at any moment fail us or be suspended; the necessity of an universal training in the practice of self-defence and a better orgnisation for mutual assistance; the necessity of recognising and practically grappling with the Mahomedan difficulty. But neither of these occurrences has really made impossible, or even altered the conditions of, our programme of defensive resistance.

The third fresh departure of the Government of India is the Risley Circular. This circular is only a more comprehensive and carefully studied edition of the Carlyle Circular. It brings therefore no unfamiliar element into the problem; but there is this very important difference, that while the Carlyle Circular was a local experiment hastily adopted to meet an urgent difficulty and dropped as soon as it was found difficult to work, the Risley Circular is a deliberate policy adopted by the Supreme Government, with full knowledge of the circumstances and of its possible effects, in the hope of striking at the very root of the Swadeshi movement. Everyone will remember the convulsion created by the Carlyle Circular. Its natural effect would have been to bring about an universal students' strike, and for a few days it seemed as if such a strike would actually take place. Unfortunately the movement immediately affected certain vested interests and the representatives of those interests happened also to be the political leaders to whom the country and the students especially were accustomed to look for guidance. The leading spirits among the young men in Calcutta were still immature and wanting in grit and tenacity; the influence on their minds of their old leaders was very powerful; the new men were comparatively unknown and influenced the course of events rather by the concrete directness of their views, the ardour of their feelings and the fiery energy of their speech and activity than by the weight of their personalities. The older leaders were, therefore, able by a strenuous and united effort of their authority to turn back the impetuous tide and dissipate the enormous motive-power which had been generated. They were too selfish to sacrifice their immediate interests, too blind and wanting in foresight to understand that the immediate loss and difficulty would be repaid tenfold by the inevitable effects of the movement. An universal educational strike at that moment, before the Government had become accustomed to the situation, would infallibly have unnerved the hand of power and brought about an almost immediate reconsideration of the partition. Whatever Government may say or do, it cannot afford to lose control of the education of the country; it cannot afford to hand over this immense mass of material, the India of the future, into the hands of the political leaders without the subtle control and check which membership of a Government University exercises, without the opportunity of unstringing the nerves of character and soul which the present system of education provides. The Government must keep its hold on the mind of the young or lose India. The magnitude of their blunder was dimly perceived afterwards by some of the leaders and one or two admitted it in private. We only recall that disastrous episode in order to lay stress on the fact that if again repeated the blunder will be worse than a blunder, it will be an offense against our posterity and a betrayal of the nation's future.

What is the position now? The Risley Circular is a desperate attempt of the bureaucracy not only to recover and confirm its hold on the student population and through them on the future, but to make that hold far more stringent, rigid, ineffugable than it ever was in the past. They do not care very much if certain academical ideas of liberalism or nationalism are imparted to the young by their teachers, but they desire to stop the active habit of patriotism in the young; for they know well that a mere intellectual habit untranslated into action is of no value in after life. The Japanese when they teach Bushido to their boys do not rest content with lectures or a moral catechism; they make them practise Bushido and govern every thought and action of their life by the Bushido ideal. This is the only way of inculcating a quality into a nation, by instilling it practically into the minds of its youth at school and college until it becomes an ingrained, inherent, inherited national quality. This is what we have to do with the modern ideal of patriotism in India. We have to fill the minds of our boys from childhood with the idea of the country, and present them with that idea at every turn and make their whole young life a lesson in the practice of the virtues which afterwards go to make the patriot and the citizen. If we do not attempt this, we may as well give up our desire to create an Indian nation altogether; for without such a discipline nationalism, patriotism, regeneration are mere words and ideas which can never become a part of the very soul of the nation and never therefore a great realised fact. Mere academical teaching of patriotism is of no avail. The professor may lecture every day on Mazzini and Garibaldi and Washington and the student may write themes about Japan and Italy and America without bringing us any nearer to our supreme need, — the entry of the habit of patriotism into our very bone and blood. The Roman Satirist tells us that in the worst times of imperial despotism in Rome the favourite theme of teachers and boys in the schools was liberty and tyrannicide; — but neither liberty nor tyrannicide was practised by the boys when they became men; rather they grew up into submissive slaves of the single world-despot. It is for this reason that the men of the new party have welcomed the active association of our students with political meetings, with the propagation and actual practice of Swadeshi, with the volunteer movement in its various forms, — not, as has been malevolently suggested, out of a turbulent desire to make use of unripe young minds to create anarchy and disorder, but because they see in this political activity in the young the promise of a new generation of Indians who will take patriotism earnestly as a thing to live and die for, not as the pastime of leisure hours. Nobody who believes that such patriotism is the first need of this country can consistently oppose the participation of students in politics. When Indian nationality is a thing realised and the present unnatural conditions have been remedied, then indeed this active participation may be brought under restriction and regulation; for then the inherited habit of patriotism, the atmosphere of a free country and the practice and teaching of the Bushido virtues within the limits of home and school life will be sufficient. But before them to submit to restrictions is to commit national suicide.

If our educated men do not understand this — as, indeed, with our want of direct political experience it is difficult for them to understand it, — our English rulers at least have grasped the situation. Study their circular and you will see what it means. School students are not even to attend political meetings nor school teachers to teach them patriotism. Why? Because at that age the mind is soft and impressionable and what is seen and heard, sinks deep and tends to crystallise not merely into fixed ideas, but into *character*. A teacher may by his personal influence and teachings so surround the minds of his students with the idea of the country, of work for the country, of living and dying for the country that this will become the dominant idea of their minds and, if associated with any kind of patriotic discipline or teaching in action, the dominant note in their character. The attendance of schoolboys as volunteers at political meetings, their work in the reception and service of men honoured by the country for patriotic service, their active participation in semi-political, semi-religious Utsavas are all part of such a patriotic discipline. It is this against which the efforts of the buraucracy are being directed, by the Risley Circular, by the prohibition of the Shivaji Utsava outside the Deccan, by the attack on our Melas and other public occasions where such training is possible. For the same reason the *active* participation of College students in political meetings is forbidden. At the age of College students ideas may be modified, the intellect may be powerfully influenced by what they hear and see, but character can only be influenced and modified by action. And it is of *character* in action that the bureaucracy is afraid, not so much of mere ideas, mere speeches, mere writings. Let the College students attend political meetings and Utsavas — that by itself will not hurt the bureaucracy; but let them not organise or take part in them, for that means the character affected, the habit of political action formed, the first elementary beginnings of service to the country commenced. Picketing and active participation in Swadeshi work is of course still more objectionable from the bureaucratic standpoint. For the same reason, again, College Professors are forbidden to influence their students or lead them to political meetings: for that brings in the powerful impetus of leading and example and threatens the bureaucracy with the beginnings of organisation.

The Risley Circular, with its sanctimonious professions of anxiety for the best interests of students and guardians, is in reality a powerful attack on the growing spirit of Nationalism at its most vital point. As such we must understand it and as such resist it.

Bande Mataram, May 28, 1907

The Effect of Petitionary Politics

We are glad to notice a ring of boldness and sincerity in all the writings of the *Indu Prakash* relating to the deportation of Lajpat Rai. We hope this tone will be an enduring change for the better. Mr. Gokhale's resort to the Anglo-Indian Press in preference to the Indian, on which its observations are very pertinent, is an example of the very common, almost inevitable effect of petitionary politics on patriotism. That a prominent leader of the Congress Party should show such an unreasonable partiality for the Anglo-Indian Press, whose recent campaign of misrepresentation and vituperation has been unpardonable in the eyes of every self-respecting Indian, is surprising at the first glance. But, in reality, it is the natural demoralizing effect of the association *cum* opposition politics. The very basis of constitutional agitation is reliance on the foreigner and the habit of appealing to him, which is the reverse side of a distrust and certain contempt for their own people. That this feeling should be, however unconsciously, betrayed by a man of Mr. Gokhale's position and character, is deplorable but inevitable. It is the logical outcome of that moderation and spirit of dependence which our contemporary has been so long preaching without perceiving, apparently, where its own dogmas led.

Bande Mataram, May 29, 1907

The Ordinance and After

WE HAVE pointed out in previous articles what we considered to be the individual effect of three of the measures of repression adopted by the bureaucracy in their fight with the Swadeshi movement. The review has led us to the conclusion that there is so far no new element in the situation beyond, on the one hand, the clear and universal conviction that has been carried home to the people of the nature and extent of the resistance which we may expect from the bureaucracy and, on the other, the more urgent necessity of adopting certain measures for national defence and resistance which ought to have been taken before. The conditions of the problem have not been materially changed, but its acuteness has been enhanced. The persecution of Swadeshi leaders and workers is nothing new, but it has increased in scale and in the atrocity of the punishments — and it is being carried out not by local officials but by the Government of India. The attempt to break the back of the movement by restricting the action of students and teachers is nothing new, but it is now being taken up deliberately, systematically, not by a local administration, but by the Government of India. The utilisation by the bureaucracy of Nawab Salimullah and by the Nawab Salimullah of hooligans to harass and, if possible, break the Boycott is nothing new, but the extent to which this sinister opposition has been carried and the wide space of country over which it has been attempted is a new phenomenon. But there is one measure of the Government which is in itself a new phenomenon and seriously affects, if it does not entirely alter, the whole situation. This is the Coercion Ordinance directed against public meetings. It would not be true to say that the ordinance was absolutely unforeseen. We at least had always held it extremely probable if not quite certain that this and even more violent and crushing methods of coercion would eventually be adopted by the bureaucracy in its struggle for self-preservation. But we did not anticipate so rapid a development of coercive measures, or that they would reach their height, as they threaten to do under a professedly Radical and Democratic Government. Not that we ever believed there was any essential difference between Liberals and Conservatives with regard to India, but there was a difference in their professions and we imagined that what the Conservatives would do immediately and without compunction, the Liberals would also do, but with hesitation and some show of reluctance. There has, however, been no slightest sign of reluctance. With alacrity and a light heart they have refused to India that right of free speech and free meeting which their political creed declares to be a common and fundamental right and to deny which is an act of tyranny. Nevertheless, though not expected so soon, the Coercion Ordinance was not a contingency which had altogether been left out of view.

What then is the new condition which it creates? One of immense importance. Up till now our whole programme with unimportant exceptions has fallen well within the law. We have worked against bureaucratic government, we have not worked against the law nor exceeded its restrictions to any of our methods. So careful have we been in this respect that the bureaucracy have been at a loss where to get a hold on the Swadeshi movement without losing their prestige and reputation, and in the end they have been obliged to throw their reputation overboard and allow the agents of their ally, the Nawab of Dacca, to create disorder so as to prepare the way for proclaiming the Swadeshi areas. This desire to keep within the law was not, as some of our disappointed adversaries suggested, born of fear or unwillingness to bear sacrifices for the country — for even without breaking the law many Swadeshi workers had to go to jail or undergo police and Goorkha violence, but part of a well-reasoned policy. To be able to keep within the law gives an immense advantage to a young movement opposed by a strong adversary in possession of all the machinery of legal repression and oppression; for it allows it to grow into adult strength before giving the enemy a sufficient grasp to strangle it while it is yet immature. Moreover, a nation which can show a respect for law even in the first throes of a revolution has a better chance of enjoying a stable and successful Government of its own when its chance comes. Nevertheless legality can never be the first consideration in a sturggle of the kind we have entered upon, and if new laws are passed which offend against political ethics,which make our service and duty to our country impossible and to obey which would therefore be an unpatriotic act, they cannot possibly command obedience. Still more is this the case when the measure in question is not a law, but an executive ukase which may be prevented from passing into law. This can best be done by a widespread and quiet but determined passive resistance which will make the ukase inoperative without a resort to measures of the most extreme and shameless Russianism. We have not concealed our opinion that this is the course the country ought to adopt in the present juncture, if for no other reason, then because it is our duty as men, as citizens, as patriots.

We recognise, however, that much is yet to be said on the opposite side. The strongest argument against the course we have suggested, is that the bureaucracy evidently desire an immediate struggle. The course of events at Barisal, the recent outrageous insult to a prominent Swadeshi worker and the insolent harassment of the townspeople by the local officials and their underlings, are extremely significant. The attempt to provoke a struggle between the Hindus and the Mahomedans culminating in the singular affair of the Barisal night panic which still calls for explanation, has been a failure. It seems that the police are now attempting to force on some demonstration which will give them an excuse for turning Barisal into a second Rawalpindi. The unprovoked blow given by a Goorkha to Srijut Satish Chandra Chatterjee was obviously a prearranged affair, leaving the victim the choice between swallowing the insult and an act of retaliation which might have led to an *émeute*. We think that Srijut Satish Chandra on the whole did well to subordinate his feelings to the good of his country, but the odds were the other way, and the police must have known it. That in case of resistance even of the most passive kind, the police or military would not "hesitate to shoot", is extremely probable from the action of the Punjab authorities and the known attitude of the local officials in East Bengal. Would it then be wise for us, it is argued, to expose ourselves passively to the arrest and deportation of our leaders, the dragooning of our towns and villages, the utmost outrages on men and women and all the violent ills of despotic repression, without any certain gain to the country to set in the opposite balance? The question really turns on the precise strength of the movement at its present stage of growth. If it is already strong enough to bear extreme Russian repressions without becoming unnerved and demoralised, the course we have suggested is the best, because it is the boldest. If not, it would be sounder policy perhaps to leave the bureaucracy to its Pyrrhic victory for a while and immediately turn all our energies to giving the movement the necessary strength, — in other words, the necessary organisation of men, money and means which it needs in order to cope with the bureaucracy on equal terms. The choice lies between these alternatives.

Common Sense in an Unexpected Quarter

It has given us quite a turn to find the following criticism of Mr. Morley's approaching "reforms" in the columns of India. "Tinkering with the Indian administrative machine will no longer avail. A thorough overhauling of its component parts has become imperative and unless the leaders of opinion in India are encouraged to play a part in the work of Government in a manner which is altogether denied to them today, the last state of India will be deplorably and ominously worse than the first." Of course *India* is much behind the times in imagining that "encouragement" to the leaders of public opinion will meet the situation. The least that India now demands is the admission of the people of the country to the management of its own affairs. But it is at once surprising and gratifying to find that the organ of Palace Chambers has at last realised the necessity of a complete and revolutionary change in the whole system of administration. It quotes against Mr. Morley an admirable passage of his own writings in which this pregnant observation occurs. "A small and temporary improvement may really be the worst enemy of a great and permanent improvement unless the first is made on the line and in the direction of the second." Precisely so. This is the main reason, even apart from their insufficiency, that any mere administrative reforms are looked on with suspicion by the Nationalist Party. The great and permanent improvement India demands is an entire change of the principles of Government in India, and a small and temporary improvement in details, leaving the principles untouched, would not be "on the line and in the direction" of the great improvement called for; it would be its worst enemy. Merely to temper absolute bureaucratic power by providing means for consulting the "leaders of public opinion" is a reform which would be the worst enemy of Indian self-government. We recommend this dictum of Mr. Morley, the philosopher, to Mr. Gokhale and other Moderates.

Drifting Away

Bombay is nearer London than Calcutta; and while Mr. Gokhale during his visit to Calcutta tried to organise a special session of the Congress at Bombay, the people of Bombay are contemplating the holding of the next session of the Congress in London. The *Guzerati* writes:—

"The idea of holding the next session of the Indian National Congress in London is a good idea. Years ago a similar proposal was put forward. But it was not taken up by Congressmen in right earnest. The extremists who are sure to quote Mr. Morley's reply to the anti-Partition memorialists in justification of their opposition to sending any petitions, will be probably also opposed to holding any session of the Congress in London. Excluding this class of Indians, the more thoughtful, sober-minded and responsible section of Congressmen who form the majority, will be in favour of the idea, provided financial difficulties could be overcome and the most representative Congressmen induced to visit England."

And it asserts that "a successful Congress session in London would be more fruitful especially at a juncture like the present than five sessions held in India". Fruitful in what respect? If our contemporary means fruitful in expenditure, humiliation and loss of self-respect, then we must agree with him. Why should the *National* Congress hold its session in London? The nation does not live in London and the root-idea of a *national* movement is opposed to this continual theatrical supplication to the very people who are interested in preventing us from becoming a nation. While our contemporary confidently asserts that a successful session in London would be more "fruitful" than five sessions held in India, we, belonging as we do to that section which Mr. Romesh Dutt during his two hours' presidentship of the Congress saw routed by the Moderates, may be permitted to suggest that one such session will do more injury to the country and the cause than five years without a session of the Congress. The attitude of British statesmen, moreover, is not encouraging even to the Moderates who still think of getting rights marked "Made in Great Britain" in the same consignment with Liverpool salt or Manchester piecegoods. The hand on the dial will be put back if we leave the nation and check the growing spirit of self-help and self-exertion to go and beg for "rights" in England and spend on this fruitless act sums which we badly require for the long-neglected task of national organisation. "The time," says our contemporary, "has come when Congressmen in a body should face the British public." Possibly; but not to "plead the cause of India and her inhabitants in the very metropolis of the Empire". This idea about the British public is a pure superstition. The British public will never interfere with the action of its representatives and kinsmen in India and in the India Office, unless and until it finds itself in danger of losing its Empire in the East. The quarrel has to be fought out between the people of India and the Anglo-Indian bureaucracy, and it must be fought out on the soil. To attempt to transfer the field of battle to London will be impracticable and harmful.

Bande Mataram, May 30, 1907

The Question of the Hour

THE writer of "A Word of Warning" which we publish today has voiced an opinion which we find to be held by several Nationalists who have the success of the movement sincerely at heart. Our correspondent, however, lays himself open to some misinterpretation when he speaks of "the suicidal folly of an unarmed and disorganised nation trying to measure its strength with that of the best-organised power in the land." The kind of resistance which seems to be suggested here is something in the nature of rebellion and it goes without saying that such resistance for "an unarmed and disorganised nation" would be not merely foolish but physically impossible; an armed revolt without arms is an absurdity. But to measure our strength, in a very different way, with the bureaucracy, however well-organised the latter may be, is the whole purpose and principle of the Nationalist movement. Our position has always been that the potential strength of the people is far greater than the actual strength of the close oligarchy which governs them without regard to their wishes or interests and that this potential strength can only be educated, organised and welded into compactness and coherence by a direct struggle against the antiquated and semi-mediaeval system with which the country is still cursed in this twentieth century, when all other nations "from China to Peru" are busy modernising and humanising their governments and institutions. In the actual course of the struggle questions will always arise as between rigid applications of principle and concessions to policy and between the contending claims of sheer courage and courage tempered by calculation. We must remember that throughout the movement the immense advance we have made is due to the enthusiasm for a great principle and the boldness, — in the opinion of many an almost foolhardy boldness, — with which we have met every fresh crisis. When the whole of Bengal flung itself into a passionate struggle with the bureaucracy, it was not from any consciousness of strength, for neither the people nor the rulers had any idea of the latent possibilities of political strength in the country. It was in a moment of uncalculating anger that Bengal took up the policy a few daring spirits suggested and was amazed to find that in doing so it had discovered itself and begun a new era of Indian history. The real point at issue now is whether it will or will not be wise to make a frontal in preference to a flank attack on the coercion ukase. We have defied an ukase before, but it was then the ukase of local officialdom and of doubtful legality. The present ukase is the deliberate act of the Government of India and the Secretary of State, and its legality is as undoubted as its political immorality. The question therefore is whether we shall persist in carrying on our movement rigidly within the pale of the law, however oppressive the law may be, or follow the example of the Irish and the English Nonconformists by passive resistance to the law itself with a view to bringing about its repeal. The answer really hangs upon the possible next move of the bureaucracy and our preparedness to meet it. If the bureaucrats try to break our resistance as at Rawalpindi by wholesale arrest, deportation and police and military violence, as well as the still more questionable methods we have seen in operation in East Bengal, shall we still be able to persist, and, if not, what will be our next course? This is the question which has given pause for a moment to the active prosecution of the Nationalist campaign, since it involves a serious issue of policy which must be settled before concerted action can take place. For if the ukase is to be passively resisted, the opposition must be offered in concert and ubiquitously. A sporadic resistance will be ineffectual and give the advantage to our adversaries.

We again repeat that in our opinion the boldest course is the best. If we thought, as the Anglo-Indian papers affect to think, that the movement was the result of our own efforts, a mere human creation, we might be of a different opinion. But throughout we have been conscious that our own efforts and the impulse given or the work done by leading men, whether Moderates or Extremists, have been so small, petty and inefficient that they are absolutely insufficient to explain the extraordinary results. The machinery has been absurdly inadequate, the organisation nil, the means at our disposal pitiably small, the real workers few and mostly obscure, and yet the Indian world has stood amazed and the Anglo-Indian aghast at the vast and incommensurate results of an apparatus so inefficient. We believe, therefore, that Divine Power is behind the movement, that the *Zeitgeist*, the Time-Spirit, is at work to bring about a mighty movement of which the world at the present juncture has need, that that movement is the resurgence of Asia and that the resurgence of India is not only a necessary part of the larger movement but its central need, that India is the keystone of the arch, the chief inheritress of the common Asiatic destiny. The Mongolian world, preserving the old strong and reposeful civilisation of early Asia, flanks her on the right and has already arisen. The Mahomedan world, preserving the aggressive and militant civilisation of Islam, flanks her on the left and in Egypt, in Arabia, in Persia, is struggling to arise. In India the two civilisations meet, she is the link between them and must find the note of harmony which will reconcile them and recreate a common Asiatic civilisation. Viewing the movement in this larger light we believe that as its progress and development has been in the past, so it will be in the future above ordinary human calculations, with only one thing certain about it, that no external force can frustrate it and no internal intrigue divert. Neither John Morley nor Denzil Ibbetson nor Nawab Salimullah, neither false friend nor open enemy, nor even our own mistakes and weakness can come in its way, but rather they are unconsciously helping it on and working for it. In this belief we are willing to take any risk and meet any expense of our blood and our labour for the great end. To husband our men or our resources and try to buy liberty in the cheapest market, would be a false and foolish economy. Lajpat Rai has been swallowed up in the maelstrom and hundreds more will follow him, but their disappearance will make no difference either to the strength of the movement or its velocity. Still it will move.

But, subject to this confidence and readiness to throw our all into the gulf, we recognise the necessity of relying on our human judgment to guide us in perplexity, leaving it to the Power behind to make our mistakes as useful, perhaps more useful to the final success than our wiser judgments. On one thing only we must lay fast hold, on the triple unity of Swadeshi, Boycott and Swaraj. These must be pursued with unremitting energy, and so long as we hold fast to them, we cannot go far wrong.

Bande Mataram, June 1, 1907

Regulated Independence

NEVER before were the utter helplessness and the deplorable demoralisation of the Native Princes of India more clearly demonstrated than at the present moment, when our political ideas and ideals are undergoing such a change. Writes the *Daily News*: "It is gratifying to learn that some of the Native States are following in the wake of the Government of India for the suppression of sedition, if not political agitation altogether. News comes from Srinagar that His Highness the Maharaja of Kashmir is about to issue a proclamation warning his subjects against the pitfalls of the so-called nationalist agitation. We do not doubt that his brother rulers in the Punjab will emulate so good an example." Some of us were at a loss to understand the cause of the *Daily News*'s jubilation. Section 124-A of the Indian Penal Code runs as follows: "Whoever by words either spoken or written, or by signs, or by visible representation, or otherwise brings or attempts to bring into hatred or contempt, or excites or attempts to excite disaffection towards His Majesty or the Government established by law in British India, shall be punished with transportation for life." So sedition in Kashmir is not sedition in British India; and by the attempts of the Kashmir Darbar to suppress sedition one naturally understood attempts to suppress the endeavours of Kashmir subjects to bring into hatred and contempt or excite or attempt to excite disaffection towards the Kashmir Darbar. But the Proclamation removed our doubt. We are asked to believe that the Maharaja of Kashmir, with a wonderful tact for self-effacement, was anxious only to protect the Government established by law in British India. The Maharaja's tender solicitude for the safety of the Power which had sold Kashmir to his ancestor and had, only the other day, condemned him unheard, was amazing indeed. But the matter did not end here. Following close upon the issuing of the Proclamation a Darbar was held in Kashmir. Sir Francis

Younghusband made a speech and the thanks of the British Government were conveyed to the Maharaja. The Maharaja, we are told, was so greatly affected that he could hardly find words to express his feelings, which is hardly wonderful considering the circumstances. He was able only to say that the tradition of his house was one of loyalty to the British Government. "This," says the *Hindu Patriot*, "is as it should be."

We cannot understand the logic of the "oldest native paper in India". Why should it be so? Did not the founder of the Kashmir house pay a very heavy price for Kashmir? True to a disgraceful understanding with the British Government, of which both parties ought to have been ashamed, Golab Singh — to quote Sir Thomas Holdich — "deserted his Sikh masters and paid for Kashmir with money looted from the Lahore treasury". So it was only "give and take".

But these pathetic and miraculous happenings appear more intelligible — and less pathetic — when we realise that though the voice is the voice of Jacob, the hands are the hands of Esau. And this fact becomes patent when we find that Kashmir does not present an isolated instance of such zeal on the part of Native Chiefs to safeguard the interests of the bureaucracy. If Kashmir can be made useful to suppress sedition, the Maharaja of Coochbehar can at least help in putting down the boycott. On the occasion of the distribution of prizes to the students of the Jenkins School the Maharaja of Coochbehar said that "schoolboys were ciphers in politics", and warned them against the danger of rushing into the whirlpool of politics, or joining in any political movement. Boys must read and play and ought never to concern themselves with matters beyond their grasp, and about which, on account of their age and inexperience, they have not the capacity to form sound, mature and correct opinions. With Swadeshism His Highness declared his full sympathy but he "was totally, entirely and absolutely against boycott". If anything approaching the boycott movement was seen in his territory His Highness gave in clear, emphatic and unequivocal language to understand that he would adopt very stringent measures to put it down. It is a pity that it should have been made necessary for the Maharaja to be so clear, emphatic and unequivocal and we can only extend to him our heart-felt sympathy.

But we cannot hold these Indian princes responsible for all they do or say. Their so-called independence is nothing more than a mere name. Though Lord Curzon called them his "colleagues and partners in the task of Indian administration", the truth was better expressed by Lord Dufferin who characterised the independence enjoyed by them as a "regulated independence", regulated by whom and to what extent it is superfluous to say. The incubus of the British Resident is always there. And the results of his intervention — often disastrous to the Chiefs — were thus summed up by the Gaekwar of Baroda in the *Nineteenth Century* in 1901: "Uncertainty and want of confidence in the indigenous Government is promoted. The influence of the Raja, which is indispensable for the individuality of the State, is thereby impaired. The ruler, being discouraged, slackens his interest in the continuity of his own policy." Then, of course, there are the annual visitations to relieve the States of their superfluous wealth and prove to the people that their Chief is no better than a pigmy before the viceregent of the King of England.

The attitude now taken by these Chiefs towards the spirit of Nationalism that is re-creating India, shows merely the degree to which the bureaucracy is determined directly and indirectly to stamp out the spirit. They have greater advantages in the States than in their own territory, for they can make the measures more thoroughgoing and rigorous than in British India and they can at the same time, through the Anglo-Indian Press, point to this rigour as a proof of the superior liberalism of British bureaucracy as compared with a native rule. This is indeed killing two birds with one stone.

A Consistent "Patriot"

Even Homer nods, and even the *Hindu Patriot* makes slips at times. Referring to the endeavours of the Kashmir Darbar to suppress "sedition" the *Patriot* wrote on the 22nd May: —

"The Maharaja of Kashmir's demonstration of fidelity is worthy of note. After upsetting the old law of the State against European settlements and earning thanks from the Masonic brotherhood for the great concession made to them, His Highness is extirpating from his dominions all sorts of 'undesirables' in a right autocratic spirit. But his brother chiefs do not seem ready to follow his noble example, and excepting the 'enlightened' Maharaja of Mysore, they may not care to do so. The Maharaja of Kashmir, however, is in right earnest. He has prohibited public and even private meetings of a revolutionary character and is the pet of the bureaucracy for playing this sort of masterly activity."

But this attempt to imbibe the spirit of the age, perhaps, got a rude shaking from some quarter, and the *Patriot* seized the first opportunity to rectify its "mistake". On the 30th it again referred to the subject and remarked: —

"The Maharaja of Kashmir's loyalty and anti-sedition measures have elicited from the Viceroy a tribute of warm appreciation. A grand Darbar was held at Srinagar to proclaim the Viceroy's message of thanks. Sir Francis Younghusband, late of the Tibet Mission, delivered a sombre sermon bristling with references to the efforts of the Maharaja to keep down sedition, and overflowing with advice and good words which no doubt went straight and deep into His Highness' heart and found a comfortable lodgment there. The Maharaja was so greatly affected that he could barely find words to give vent to his feelings. He was able only to say that the tradition of his house was loyalty to the British Government. This is as it should be."

This indeed is as it should be. And it reminds us of the *Hindu Patriot*'s sudden change of opinion in the matter of the site for the proposed Victoria Memorial Hall and other instances of the remarkable versatility and impressionability of this great organ of private opinion.

Bande Mataram, June 4, 1907

Wanted, a Policy

A SILENCE has fallen on the country since the inauguration of a new repressive policy by the bureaucracy, a silence broken only by Cocanada riots on one side and talk of a special Congress session on the other. Srijut Surendranath Banerji has gone to Simultala to think over the situation and other leaders are thinking over it wherever they happen to find themselves. The only gentleman in authority who has come forward publicly with a policy is Srijut Bhupendranath Bose and we are grieved to find that the country has received this honourable and legislative gentleman's proposals with the supreme contempt of neglect. It is natural that our adversaries should exult over this silence and point to it as an evidence of complete demoralisation, and it is natural that those of us who are not in constant touch with the mofussil should also feel the silence burdensome and talk of demoralisation. We do not believe that the country is demoralised. On the contrary we believe that circumstances have taken an extremely favourable turn. There is, to begin with, an immense revolution of opinion all over Bengal which has brought all but the inveterate loyalists to understand the situation and face realities. Secondly, if our information from the mofussil is correct, the people, the rank and file, are by no means cowed down, but rather from every part we hear news of men girding themselves for real work, now that the outer expression of our feelings is hampered and our hopes and aspirations driven in upon themselves. We are especially glad to find in West Bengal, so long apathetic, new stirrings of life and resolution. Nevertheless, in a certain small section there is undoubtedly bewilderment, hesitation and something like panic and we would be glad to believe that these feelings are not shared by any of our leaders or at least by those who have hitherto arrogated to themselves leadership and the credit for all the work that has been done. One cannot help thinking that they are, some of them, in the predicament of the Homeric heroes: — "They feared to take the challenge, to refuse it they were ashamed."

If they are not demoralised, if their hearts and hopes are as high as ever, they should take some trouble to show it. On the other hand, if they are demoralised, if they are suffering from sinkings and searchings of the heart, they ought to take some trouble to hide it. The words of the *Mahabharata* apply with particular force:

"Never should a prince and leader bow his haughty head to fear,
Let his fortune be however desperate, death however near.
If his soul grow faint, let him imprison weakness in his heart,
Keep a bold and open countenance and play on a hero's part.
If the leader fear and faint, then all behind him faint and fear.
So a king of men should keep a dauntless look and forehead clear."

What the country wants is a pronouncement of policy — it need not be a detailed or indiscreet pronouncement, but at least a lead is wanted. The bureaucracy has altered its front and changed its plan of campaign. Will it be enough to modify our old policy to meet a new but surely not unexpected situation or will it be necessary for us also to change our plan of campaign? One thing at least is certain, we in Bengal have no intention of giving up Swaraj, no intention of giving up Swadeshi, no intention of giving up Boycott; to this the Bhupendranaths and the others must make up their minds. If any leader tries to lower this triple banner of the cause, he forfeits his reputation and his position from that date. The country has no intention of withdrawing from a single essential position that has once been occupied.

Although we can make no claims to leadership, we have, as a responsible organ of public opinion, the duty of laying our views before the people and we have not failed to do so to the best of our ability. The policy we advocate now is the policy we have always advocated, the policy of the organisation of Swaraj and passive resistance. To push forward Swadeshi, to push forward National Education, to take up Arbitration in earnest and for the effective working of this positive side to create what we have not up till now created except in certain districts, — a compact, well-managed, earnest organisation; on the other hand, to follow a rational, effective and steady system of Boycott, and passively to oppose Government repression at every turn, to disregard the Risley Circular, to disregard the bureaucratic intimidation of the Press, to disregard or circumvent if we cannot disregard the Coercion Ordinance, to meet with silent contempt the danger of deportation and the threat of imprisonment; this is the policy we would favour if there are men in Bengal bold enough and steadfast enough to carry it out. Doubtless there are other dangers more serious than any that have yet threatened us, but if we lower the tone of the movement on account of anticipated calamities which may never happen, we may stand charged before posterity with the crime of sacrificing the future to vain and timid imaginations. Here again the wisdom of Vidula has a word in season for us: "Make not great thy foeman by thy terrors, panic eyes behind." The bureaucracy will use every method to kill the movement, guile as well as terrorism, they will try to bribe us with remedial measures as well as to bludgeon us with ordinances; they will wave the sword at us whenever we make the slightest movement and use it on occasion. Our future depends on our surmounting both inducement and intimidation. Let us take possible dangers into consideration, by all means, and provide against them, never run our heads against them wantonly and without occasion; but to be turned from our path by possible dangers is neither true manhood nor true prudence. The path to Swaraj can never be safe. Over sharp rocks and through thick brambles lies the way to that towering and glorious summit where dwells the Goddess of our worship, our goddess Liberty. Shall we dare to aspire to reach her and yet hope to accomplish that journey perilous with unhurt bodies and untorn feet? Mark the way; as you go it is red and caked with the blood of those who have climbed before us to the summit. And if that sight appals you, look up and forget it in the glory of the face that smiles upon us from the peak.

Preparing the Explosion

The Simla Government has again opened wide its mouth of thunder and another Resolution has issued from its capacious jaws. This time, as we had expected, it is aimed at the Press. The Resolution is full of sound and fury signifying little. It has been decided to institute, if necessary, a campaign against the liberty of the Press and throttle it as effectually as the Liberty of speech has been throttled by the Coercion Ordinance. But the Simla Government seems to be ashamed of having to do all this repressive work with its own viceregal hands and therefore it gradually retires behind the curtain and asks the local governments to take the stage. That is all. At the same time, the Press is a necessity to the foreign rulers and the Platform is not; they are therefore unwillingly, we take it, to apply the same absolute gag to the Press as they have applied to the Platform. They are trying first the effectiveness of the threat of prosecution. "Look, there is the policeman Andrew, (or the policeman Denzil, as the case may be). Mind you behave yourself. He has orders to run you in if you don't." This is a fair translation into vernacular English of Sir Herbert Risley's latest literary effort. We hardly think it will have much effect on the tone of the Press, unless our publicists are cursed with a much greater timidity than we give them credit for. A crop of Press prosecutions may therefore be confidently expected. If that is not sufficient, other measures will be used. And when they have silenced the Press and the Platform, Anglo-India will no doubt exult over its victory and avow wonderingly how easy it was to quell this absurd agitation. There is not enough statesmanship among these heaven-born rulers to perceive that they are playing into the hands of the most revolutionary section of opinion in India. Ajit Singh in his exile may rejoice, for his work is being done for him far more effectually than he could have done it himself. National feeling is like certain explosives which need resistance in order to be effective; unresisted they explode harmlessly and mildly into the air, but resisted, repressed and confined, they become devastating forces and annihilate the substance that resists and confines them.

Bande Mataram, June 5, 1907

A Statement

Mr. John Morley has committed himself in the House of Commons to a trenchant and unqualified statement that the whole blame for the disturbances in East Bengal lies upon the Hindus who, by a violent and obstreperous boycott attended with coercion and physical force, have irritated the Mahomedans into revolt. Whether Mr. Morley made this statement out of a sweet trustfulness in the man on the spot or relying upon his philosophical judgment and innate powers of reasoning does not concern us at all. Everyone knows that the statement is untrue. The boycott was no doubt the final cause of the hooliganism in the East just as the Russian revolutionary movement was the final cause of the excesses of the Black Hundred, but it was in no way the immediate and efficient cause. It was the final cause in this sense that its first success compelled Sir Bampfylde Fuller to look about for a counteracting influence and he found it in the Nawab of Dacca and the use that could be made of the Nawab's position to help on a breach between the Mahomedans and Hindus. That is the whole and sole connection of boycott with the Mymensingh disturbances. The rest followed by a natural course of evolution. Sir Bampfylde favoured the Mahomedans and depressed the Hindus, the Nawab excited his co-religionists against their fellow-countrymen. There was no concealment about this policy, no pretences. Sir Bampfylde Fuller openly declared that of his two wives the Mahomedan was his favourite and his favouritism was gross, open, palpable. He flourished it in the face of the public instead of concealing it. The Nawab of Dacca has also openly preached to his co-religionists about the wrongs they have suffered at the hands of the Hindus and called upon them to separate themselves from that evil and injurious connexion. There has been no concealment whatever about his anti-Hindu campaign. After the disappearance of Sir Bampfylde from the scene of his exploits, the philo-Mahomedanism of the

Shillong Government was no longer openly flourished in the face of the public but it was steadily continued in practice. The alliance of Anglo-India with the Nawab was from the beginning made the most of by the *Englishman* which for some time carried on a very active philo-Mahomedan and anti-Hindu crusade in its columns and did its best to stir up enmity between the two communities. So there came the first Mymensingh disturbances, the Comilla riots and finally the supreme conflagration that started from Jamalpur. That conflagration was brought about by Maulavis preaching outrage and plunder in the name of the Nawab of Dacca and the Government, an imputation which the Nawab of Dacca has made no attempt to repudiate, though, it is said, he has been challenged to do so in answer to his hollow professions of a desire to bring about amity between the two communities, while the Shillong Government has repudiated it only tardily and indirectly if at all, and only after the full mischief had been done. In all the incitements urged by the Maulavis and by the authors of the notorious Red Pamphlet, there has been no mention of a violent enforcement of the boycott on the Mahomedans, neither has any such connexion been established by any of the judicial proceedings which have hitherto been concluded. The theory of Mr. John Morley is therefore a dead thing and of no farther interest to any human being.

Of course the bureaucracy will go on playing with the bones of this dead scarecrow; it will wage war on Swadeshism on the plea that it leads to disorder; but that is only because, like all bureaucracies, it is sublimely indifferent to reason and fact and public opinion. It has served its turn by the fiction which it foisted through the mouth of Honest John on a loudly applauding though somewhat befogged House of Commons and it does not care even if the fiction is disproved a thousand times over. It will go on acting as if the fiction were a fact. We do not see therefore the utility of the statement which a majority of the Bengal leaders have published and which we hear is to be telegraphed or has been telegraphed to England. If the object is to set ourselves right in the opinion of the world, well, that is an innocent amusement. If it is to convince Mr. John Morley, it is a futility. It is absurd to suppose that Mr. John Morley at his age is going to allow himself to be convinced. He is far too old and wise to admit inconvenient facts. The statement contains a number of facts which all Bengal knows, which all India is sure to believe and all officialdom sure to deny. Beyond that the statement, a very able one in its way, merely encourages the consumption of stationery, patronises a printing-press, startles the Empire and enriches the Telegraph Office. Was it worth while?

Bande Mataram, June 6, 1907

Defying the Circular

IT WILL not be long now before the Colleges open and the students begin to return to Calcutta; the moment they come the struggle for the possession of the youth of the country must begin. The bureaucracy has thrown out the challenge and there is every sign that it will be taken up. Men of all parties, except the party of Mr. N. N. Ghose which, as it consists of only one man, need not concern us, are agreed that to acquiesce in the Circular is out of the question. If there is any difference of opinion, it is as to the best method of defying it, and that is not a matter of primary importance. For our own part, we have expressed ourselves in favour of an educational strike, because that is the most straightforward, the most masculine and the most aggressive form of passive resistance of which the occasion allows. We hold that in order to rise the nation must get into the habit of offering challenges rather than receiving them and when it is behind, it must take the swiftest and most direct form of demonstration open to it. Passive resistance can be carried on in an inert and passive spirit of mechanical reaction against pressure from above, or it may be carried on in an active and creative spirit, it may take the initiative instead of being driven; it may assail the citadels of the enemy instead of merely defending its own. What India needs especially at this moment is the aggressive virtues, the spirit of soaring idealism, bold creation, fearless resistance, courageous attack; of the passive tamasic spirit of inertia we have already too much. We need to cultivate another training and temperament, another habit of mind. We would apply to the present situation the vigorous motto of Danton, that what we need, what we should learn above all things is to dare and again to dare and still to dare.

Nevertheless we recognise that to leap at once from an overpoweringly tamasic condition of mind into the rajasic, the active, restless, bold and creative, is not easy for a nation and if we cannot have the best method, we will accept the second best, so long as the principle of resistance is maintained. A general defiance of the Circular will obviously make it unworkable, unless the Government is prepared to disaffiliate schools and colleges freely and give up its control of education. It is possible, of course, that they may do so in the hope of bringing the country to its knees by drawing home the conviction that it cannot take in hand its own education. But this will be a dangerous game to play; for the only thing that is needed to make the institution of a widespread and comprehensive system of national education possible and indeed eminently practicable, is the generation of an enthusiasm such as was beginning to gather force after the Carlyle Circular. A stern and bitter struggle between the people and the bureaucracy is the one thing that is likely to generate such an enthusiasm. National education is by no means impracticable or even difficult, it needs nothing but a resolute enthusiasm in the country and the courage to take a leap into the unknown. This courage is common in individuals but not in nations, least of all in subject nations; and yet when the fire is lit, it is perhaps subject nations more than any other which are found ready to take the leap.

We do not believe the bureaucracy will be willing to drive matters to such a crisis. It is more likely that they will use the Circular to harass the opposition and overcome our resistance by instituting measures of petty persecution wherever they can do it without upheaving the whole foundation of the educational system in Bengal. All that is demanded from us is therefore a persistent resolution to make the Circular unworkable regardless of loss and sacrifice. We must take every opportunity of challenging the Circular and testing the resolution of the bureaucracy and the campaign must be carried on simultaneously all over Bengal, if not in other parts of India as well. But it is Calcutta which must give the signal. Indeed, Calcutta has already given the signal. Meetings have been held in which teachers and students have attended and taken an active part; more meetings of the kind will be held and when the Colleges reopen, there must be a general defiance of the ukase. Once Calcutta leads the way, East Bengal will respond and West

Bengal follow the general example. The Risley Circular must go the way of its predecessors.

BY THE WAY

When shall We Three Meet Again?

The *Statesman*, which seems now to be the mouthpiece of the bureaucracy, published a semi-official communiqué to the effect that prosecutions are being launched against three of the journals in Bengal which have been the most violent in their recent utterances. This pleasant news opens the way to a most interesting line of speculation and we would suggest that one of our contemporaries, say, the *Sandhya*, might start a plebiscite or a prize competition for the correct list of the unfortunate victims. The prize would of course be given to the competitor who got the right names in the right order. It would be interesting to know whether the impressions of the people and of the Bengal Government tallied on this knotty question. If we ourselves are to be one of the recipients of this Government distinction, we must petition the authorities beforehand — even at the sacrifice of our principles — that the three editors may be allowed to share the same cell and assist each other at the same oakum picking or other exhilarating occupation in store for us, so that we may support each other "under the burden of an honour into which we were not born". Always provided that the editor of the *Indian Nation* is not one of the three.

*

The *Empire* is very much hurt that the Indian papers have not taken any notice of the Viceroy's magnanimous though somewhat belated refusal to sanction the Punjab Colonisation Bill. Our contemporary thinks that we kept silent out of pure cussedness. This is unkind. Could not our dear white brother — or, our dear green brother, we should say — realise that there were other reasons, honourable or natural — for this unanimous hush. It might have been out of sheer awe, it might have been out of a choked emotion. Some scruples of delicacy, some feelings of the "sorrow rather than anger" sort, perhaps even excessive loyalty may have stopped the flow of utterance. For instance, supposing in the rush of our gratitude one were to let slip unpleasant hints about the relations between the Rawalpindi row and the Viceroy's sudden and stupendous magnanimity! Who would like to hurt our sympathetic Viceroy's feelings by such ungracious truths! Or again, supposing the Bengal papers were contrasting silently events in the Punjab and Bengal? They do present a remarkable contrast. In Bengal we have agitated for two years; — first with repeated petitions, with countless protest meetings, with innumerable wails and entreaties from press and platform; but that could not help us, insult and ridicule were our only gain. Then we tried every lawful means of concrete protest, every kind of passive resistance within the law to show that we were in earnest. Result, — nil. But in Punjab they petitioned and protested only for a few weeks and then — went for Europeans, their persons, their property and everything connected with them. Result — the water tax postponed, the Colonisation Bill cancelled. Of course, as loyal subjects such as the *Empire* wants to be we must regard the contrast with sorrow rather than with anger. But if we were publicly to mention these matters, might not our feelings and even our motives be misunderstood? Might it not even happen that Police-Constable Andrew would run us in, under his new-old powers for sedition? And how could a loyal Press expose itself to such misunderstanding? The *Empire* will surely agree with us, on reflection, that silence was best.

*

It is a new and gratifying feature of present day politics to find the *Englishman* reporting Bengali meetings in the Calcutta squares with a full appreciation of their importance. The meeting in College Square at which Srijut Krishna Kumar Mitra presided has been favoured as well as Srijut Bepin Chandra Pal's meeting at Beadon Square. As to the accuracy of the reports we have our doubts, for the Bengali gentleman who reports for our contemporary is afflicted with the idea that he is very humorous, and there is nothing so fatal to accuracy as a sense of humour. We would not object to this amiable delusion, or the particular style of the reporter's wit, if it did not so persistently recall to us the imperial citizen of the British metropolis out on a spree who thinks it is a huge joke to tickle his fellow citizens with a peacock's feather or to comment on their possession of hair or the origin of their headgear with other light and cutting sarcasms. However, we note with satisfaction that teachers and students attended the meeting, that a teacher presided, another spoke and a student seconded a resolution. We too await with interest the action of the authorities in the matter.

*

Our venerable friend the *Indian Mirror* has solemnly assured us that it should be understood that no Government, Conservative or Liberal, will countenance violent methods, such as the Extremists have hitherto employed. For this surprising information, drawn no doubt from occult sources, much thanks. But still we cannot help inquiring, who the devil ever asked them to? No one in his senses, or out of them, either, ever dreamed of calling upon any Englishman to support the Extremist policy. We note with interest that the *Mirror* considers Boycott, Passive Resistance, National Education, Arbitration and Physical Training to be "violent" methods. On the other hand we find Srijut Narendra Nath Sen's signature affixed to the recently-issued statement in which the use of violent methods in Bengal is denied. Hail, holy light, divine re-effective *Mirror*!

*

The breathless speed with which the *Statesman* is legislating and administering the affairs of the nation, makes one's head whirl. One day the Simla Government, no doubt laying heads together with Mr. John Morley, issues a notice handing the Press over to the tender mercies of the local administrations, but with a rider that this is in the nature of a warning to the Press to behave itself and the effect will be watched before action is taken. After watching the effect for the space of twenty four hours the *Statesman* issues an order from Darjeeling to prosecute any three papers out of the long list of English and vernacular publications in Bengal, the selection to be made on the principle of the loudest first. Before the Press has recovered from this shock, while everybody from the *Englishman* down to the *Mihir Sudhakar* is brooding over his past sins and preparing for the arrival of the police with handcuffs, while even the *Mirror* and the *Nation* are trying to banish uncomfortable memories of an indiscreet article or two on the Jamalpur outrages, lo and behold, the *Statesman* in its Viceregal Council at Simla is forging a new Act which shall provide for the gagging of the Press without the trouble of a prosecution. We know that these are the days of the electric tram and the motor car, and telepathy and wireless telegraphy, but really this is overdoing it. A little slower, please.

Bande Mataram, June 7, 1907

The Strength of the Idea

THE mistake which despots, benevolent or malevolent, have been making ever since organised states came into existence and which, it seems, they will go on making to the end of the chapter, is that they overestimate their coercive power, which is physical and material and therefore palpable, and underestimate the power and vitality of ideas and sentiments. A feeling or a thought, Nationalism, Democracy, the aspiration towards liberty, cannot be estimated in the terms of concrete power, in so many fighting men, so many armed police, so many guns, so many prisons, such and such laws, ukases, and executive powers. But such feelings and thoughts are more powerful than fighting men and guns and prisons and laws and ukases. Their beginnings are feeble, their end is mighty. But of despotic repression the beginnings are mighty, the end is feeble. Thought is always greater than armies, more lasting than the most powerful and best-organised despotisms. It was a thought that overthrew the despotism of centuries in France and revolutionised Europe. It was a mere sentiment against which the irresistible might of the Spanish armies and the organised cruelty of Spanish repression were shattered in the Netherlands, which brought to nought the administrative genius, the military power, the stubborn will of Aurangzebe, which loosened the iron grip of Austria on Italy. In all such instances the physical power and organisation behind the insurgent idea are ridiculously small, the repressive force so overwhelmingly, impossibly strong that all reasonable, prudent, moderate minds see the utter folly of resistance and stigmatise the attempt of the idea to rise as an act of almost criminal insanity. But the man with the idea is not reasonable, not prudent, not moderate. He is an extremist, a fanatic. He knows that his idea is bound to conquer, he knows that the man possessed with it is more formidable, even with his naked hands, than the prison and the gibbet, the armed men and the murderous cannon. He knows that in the fight with brute force the spirit, the idea is bound to conquer. The Roman Empire is no more, but the Christianity which it thought to crush, possesses half the globe, covering "regions Caesar never knew". The Jew, whom the whole world persecuted, survived by the strength of an idea and now sits in the high places of the world, playing with nations as a chess-player with his pieces. He knows too that his own life and the lives of others are of no value, that they are mere dust in the balance compared with the life of his idea. The idea or sentiment is at first confined to a few men whom their neighbours and countrymen ridicule as lunatics or hare-brained enthusiasts. But it spreads and gathers adherents who catch the fire of the first missionaries and creates its own preachers and then its workers who try to carry out its teachings in circumstances of almost paralysing difficulty. The attempt to work brings them into conflict with the established power which the idea threatens and there is persecution. The idea creates its martyrs. And in martyrdom there is an incalculable spiritual magnetism which works miracles. A whole nation, a whole world catches the fire which burned in a few hearts; the soil which has drunk the blood of the martyr imbibes with it a sort of divine madness which it breathes into the heart of all its children, until there is but one overmastering idea, one imperishable resolution in the minds of all beside which all other hopes and interests fade into insignificance and until it is fulfilled, there can be no peace or rest for the land or its rulers. It is at this moment that the idea begins to create its heroes and fighters, whose numbers and courage defeat only multiplies and confirms until the idea militant has become the idea triumphant. Such is the history of the idea, so invariable in its broad lines that it is evidently the working of a natural law.

But the despot will not recognise this superiority, the teachings of history have no meaning for him. He is dazzled by the pomp and splendour of his own power, infatuated with the sense of his own irresistible strength. Naturally, for the signs and proofs of his own power are visible, palpable, in his camps and armaments, in the crores and millions which his tax-gatherers wring out of the helpless masses, in the tremendous array of cannon and implements of war which fill his numerous arsenals, in the compact and swiftly-working organisation of his administration, in the prisons into which he hurls his opponents, in the fortresses and places of exile to which he can hurry the men of the idea. He is deceived also by the temporary triumph of his repressive measures. He strikes out with his mailed hand and surging multitudes are scattered like chaff with a single blow; he hurls his thunderbolts from the citadels of his strength and ease and the clamour of a continent sinks into a deathlike hush; or he swings the rebels by rows from his gibbets or mows them down by the hundred with his mitrailleuse and then stands alone erect amidst the ruin he has made and thinks, "The trouble is over, there is nothing more to fear. My rule will endure for ever; God will not remember what I have done or take account of the blood that I have spilled." And he does not know that the fiat has gone out against him, "Thou fool! this night shall thy soul be required of thee." For to the Power that rules the world one day is the same as fifty years. The time lies in His choice, but now or afterwards the triumph of the idea is assured, for it is He who has sent it into men's minds that His purposes may be fulfilled.

The story is so old, so often repeated that it is a wonder the delusion should still persist and repeat itself. Each despotic rule after the other thinks, "Oh, the circumstances in my case are quite different, I am a different thing from any yet recorded in history, stronger, more virtuous and moral, better organised. I am God's favourite and can never come to harm." And so the old drama is staged again and acted till it reaches the old catastrophe. The historic madness has now overtaken the British nation in the height of its world-wide power and material greatness. In Egypt, in India, in Ireland the most Radical Government of modern times is bracing itself to a policy of repression. It thinks England has only to stamp her foot and all the trouble will be over. Yet only consider how many ideas are arising which find in British despotism their chief antagonist. The idea of a free and self-centred Ireland has been reborn and the souls of Fitzgerald and Emmett are reincarnating. The idea of a free Egypt and the Pan Islamic idea have joined hands in the land of the Pharaohs. The idea of a free and united India has been born and arrived at full stature in the land of the Rishis, and the spiritual force of a great civilisation of which the world has need is gathering at its back. Will England crush these ideas with ukases and coercion laws? Will she even kill them with maxims and siege-guns? But the eyes of the wise men have been sealed so that they should not see and their minds bewildered so that they should not understand. Destiny will take its appointed course until the fated end.

Comic Opera Reforms

Mr. Morley has made his pronouncement and a long-expectant world may now go about its ordinary business with the satisfactory conviction that the conditions of political life in India will be precisely the same as before. We know now what are the much talked of reforms which are to pave the way for self-government under an absolute and personal rule and to quiet Indian discontent. Let us take them one by one, these precious and inestimable boons. They are three in number, a trinity of marvels: an advisory Council of Notables, enlarged Legislative and Provincial Councils, admission of one or two Indians to the India Council.

An advisory Council of Notables — we can see it in our mind's eye. The Nawab of Dacca and the Maharaja of Darbhanga, the Maharajas of Coochbehar and Cashmere, the Raja of Nabha, Sir Harnam Singh, a few other Rajas and Maharajas (*not* including the Maharaja of Baroda), Dr. Rash Behari Ghose, Mr. Justice Mukherji, a goodly number of non-official Europeans, the knight of the umbrella from Bombay, etc. etc. with Mr. Gokhale bringing up the tail as the least dangerous of those whom Mr. Morley felt that he must reluctantly call "our enemies". And what will the business of the illustrious assembly be? It will find out what the opinion of the country is (on which the members will be better authorities no doubt than a highly inconvenient Press) and inform the Government; they will also find out the meaning of the Government (if that is humanly possible) and inform the country. We suppose it would be seditious to laugh at a Secretary of State, for is he not part of the Government established by law? So we will merely say that the right place for this truly comic Council of Notables with its yet more comic functions is an opera by Gilbert and Sullivan and not an India seething with discontent and convulsed by the throes of an incipient revolution.

As to the "enlarged" Legislative Councils we can say little. Mr. Morley does not enlighten us as to their composition but he has explicitly said that the official majority will be maintained — a piece of information, by the way, which the *Bengalee*'s "Own Correspondents" forget to cable out to Colootola. That is enough for it means that the Legislative Councils are to be precisely what they were before, only bigger. The people are not to be given any effective control of check on the management of their own affairs. We had gilted shams before; they will be bigger shams, with more gilt on them, but still shams and nothing but shams.

Finally, Mr. Morley says that the time has come when it will be really quite safe to have an Indian or even two (what reckless daring!) on the India Council. Really? A year or two ago, we suppose, it would have been very dangerous, — indeed, brought the Empire down with a sudden crash. So Mr. Romesh Dutt and Justice Amir Ali's expectations may at last be satisfied and we shall have two Indian tongues in the Council of India. We wish them luck; but for all the use they will be to India, they might just as well be in Timbuctoo, or the Andamans. Indeed they would probably be of much more use in the Andamans.

We find it impossible to discuss Mr. Morley's reforms seriously, they are so impossibly burlesque and farcical. Yet they have their serious aspect. They show that the British despotism, like all despotisms in the same predicament, is making the time-honoured, ineffectual effort to evade a settlement of the real question by throwing belated and now unacceptable sops to Demogorgon. We shall return to this aspect of the subject hereafter.

Paradoxical Advice

Mr. G. C. Bose, principal and proprietor of the Bangabasi College, has published a short signed article in the *Bangabasi* in which he sets forth very emphatically what he considers to be the duty of the students and their guardians in this critical moment. Mr. Bose is an educationist pure and simple who has never mixed himself up in politics, unlike another well-known principal whose weekly incursions into politics are more remarkable for their manner than for their matter. If therefore Mr. Bose had confined himself to the educational aspect of the question and the extent to which students may permissibly interest themselves in politics, we should have had nothing to say. Unfortunately Mr. Bose has allowed himself to be tempted by the prevailing political atmosphere outside his true province. He refrains from discussing the merits of the Risley Circular and merely advises the public to leave no stone unturned to get the circular withdrawn but to refrain scrupulously from defying it while it is in force. This is very much like telling us to leave no stone un-turned to get our dinner cooked, but at the same time refrain scrupulously from lighting a fire. Everyone, — even the veriest political tyro can see that if we submit to the circular it will remain with us in perpetuity, no amount of representations, such as it is now proposed to send to the Government, will get the circular recalled. Our only chance of getting rid of it is to make it a dead letter by a general refusal to abide by it. Mr. Bose represents a vested interest which will be seriously inconvenienced by an educational strike or a general refusal to abide by the circular and we fear the natural anxiety to avoid this inconvenience has blinded him to this very simple political fact. But will the student class listen to Mr. Bose's dulcet pipings? The wave of Nationalism in the land is surely not so spent, but will rise the higher for the obstacles thrown in the way of its advance.

Bande Mataram, June 8, 1907

An Out of Date Reformer

TIME was and that time was not more than two years ago, and indeed even less, when the reforms which Mr. Morley has announced would have been received in India by many with enthusiasm, by others with considerable satisfaction as an important concession to public feeling and a move, however small, in the right direction. Today they have been received by some with scorn and ridicule, by others with bitterness and dissatisfaction, even by the most loyal with a cold and qualified recognition. Never has an important pronouncement of policy by a famous and once honoured statesman of whom much had been expected, delivered moreover under the most dramatic circumstances possible and as a solution of a trying and critical problem, fallen so utterly flat on the audience which it was intended to impress. The outside world amazed at a change so sudden and radical may well ask what are its causes. The true cause is, of course, the revolution which has been worked in Indian opinion and Indian feeling in these two years. British Liberalism stands where it was and refuses to move forward. Indian opinion has advanced with enormous strides to a position far in front. The British Liberal has perhaps, from his standpoint, some reason for complaint. He had formed a sort of agreement with the section of Indian opinion which then dominated Indian politics. On our side we were to assure him of the permanence of British control, to acknowledge our present unfitness for self-Government and to accept perpetual subordination and dependence as an arrangement of Providence. On his side he has engaged to give us progressive alleviations of our subject condition, gradually increasing compensations for the renunciation of our national future; these he was prepared to concede to us by slow degrees according to his own convenience and ability. Nor was the prospect denied to India of becoming after the lapse of many centuries a trusted servant of England, or even something very like an adopted son.

The bargain was one-sided, but the political leaders had an overpowering sense of their own weakness, of the superior excellence of British civilisation, and of the unshakable might of Britain. They had too a profound trust in the justice of England and the genuineness of English Liberalism. They believed that the Liberal offers of small rights and privileges were made not as a bargain or out of a shrewd calculation of advantages and disadvantages, but from the sense of justice and from a true sympathy with liberal aspirations all over the world. They were therefore ready to take gratefully and contentedly whatever small mercies were conceded to them. Now the spirit of the people has changed. From a timid and easily satisfied dependence on the alien they have passed at once to a passionate and determined assertion of their separate national existence and a demand for an immediate recognition of their right to control their own affairs. It is not surprising that the old Friends of India should be alarmed and indignant at the change or that they should call upon the older leaders whom they know and think they can influence, to drive the Extremists out of their councils, return to their old allegiance and observe the terms of the contract. "We are where we were, we still offer you the same terms," they cry, "you shall have your reforms, but on the old conditions, the permanence of British control, the repression of all turbulent aspirations, dissociation from the forces of disorder and revolution." So they cry to the Moderate leaders to turn back and retrace their steps, and by main force to bring India back with them to the standpoint of twenty years ago. It is a vain cry. If the Moderate leaders wished to go back, they would have to go back alone as men without a following, lost leaders, prophets whose power had passed out of them. The force which has swept the country forward is a force no man has created and which no man can control. As well ask a man who has become adult to return to the age of childhood as India to go back to the standpoint it has left irrecoverably behind.

The British Government is like Tarquin with the Sybil; the terms it has refused will no longer be offered to it. It might have purchased contentment, a new lease of Indian confidence and a long spell of ease at a very small price only three or four years ago. Now at a price ten times as high it will be able to purchase at the most a short truce in a war which must be fought to the end. Mr. Morley recognised this fact when with an indiscreet frankness he referred to the educated class in India as "our enemies". A long era of repression and reaction culminating in Curzonism has opened the eyes of the Indian people. They have learnt that not only were the reforms of Liberal Viceroys and Governments small and ineffective in themselves, but that they were held on a precarious tenure. Mr. Morley or another might give "rights" and "privileges" of a dubious character, but the power of Liberalism in modern England is apt to be brief and succeeded by long periods of pure Imperialism in which those rights and privileges will surely be taken away or nullified. They have discovered also that the support they might expect from Liberalism is of a very limited and meagre nature and that, when in office, Liberal and Conservative are for India synonymous terms. The struggle which began with the Partition has generated a new ideal and a newborn Nationalism has sprung in a few days almost to its full stature. There was no chance therefore that any reform would be acceptable which did not ensure popular control, make reactionary legislation by despotic Viceroys impossible and open the way to Swaraj. And even if Mr. Morley's reforms had had any chance of being acceptable, it was ruined by the series of repressive measures which preceded them. Reforms simultaneous and compatible with the deportation of leaders, the prosecution of popular journals, the persecution of students and teachers and the prohibition of public meetings were of so patent a hollowness that the most moderate and loyal were compelled to receive them with a bitter scepticism. And as if to drive the moral home, the speech in which the reforming statesman introduced his measures was couched in the sour and autocratic spirit of a reactionary bureaucrat contemtuously doling out sops to the rabble to an accompaniment of hardly-veiled menace and insult. Mr. Morley has been unanimously complimented by the Liberal Press in England on his courage in coupling repression with reforms, kicks with breadcrumbs. For ourselves we are struck by his singular want of sagacity and of even an elementary knowledge of human nature and the feelings which govern great masses of men. As well might we call the policy of a Louis XVI or a Czar Nicholas courageous. The courage may or may not be there, but there can be no doubt of the unwisdom.

Bande Mataram, June 12, 1907

The Sphinx

Sir Henry Cotton has developed a sudden love for Lala Lajpat Rai. Though he has, like all Anglo-Indians — official, or ex-official, — condemned and condemned unheard Ajit Singh his love for Lajpat Rai knows no abating. He asked Mr. Morley to confirm his statement of the 6th June that Lajpat Rai's speeches had greatly dominated sedition in India and had been published broadcast, even on the floor of the House. The statement shows that Mr. Morley thinks he knows more about Indian affairs than we Indians do; and his reference, obviously, was to Members of the Parliament like Sir Henry Cotton who tease the Secretary of State for India with inconvenient questions about Indian subjects. With characteristic conceit, Mr. Morley replied that he should be very unlikely to make a statement without providing himself with fair and reasonable confirmation. It was surely such "fair and reasonable confirmation" that enabled him, the other day, to make an assertion about the proposed Victoria Memorial Hall which even the perverse ingenuity of the Anglo-Indian Press could not support. And it was surely such fair and reasonable confirmation that made him beat a retreat on the present occasion with the sage remark, that nothing would be more injudicious than to lay the facts on the table. Only deeds of darkness need be afraid of light. And people may be pardoned if they dare suspect that the fair and reasonable confirmation was as real as Mr. Morley's reforms so often advertised by himself as well as by the *Statesman*. Next, when Mr. Mackarness asked whether it was intended to formulate a definite legal charge against Lajpat Rai and Ajit Singh and also what the length of their banishment and confinement would be, Mr. Morley said that he was unable at present to state the intentions of the Government of India. It seems that as far as questions on matters Indian are concerned, the British House of Commons is as good as the Indian Legislative Councils. The reason is not far to seek. The British public have absolute faith in the infallibility of the "man on the spot" in India to maintain India for their benefit and they are ready and willing to give them a free hand in their dealings with the people of the country. Had it been otherwise — had the British taxpayers been guided by considerations other than those of advantage to Great Britain to take an intelligent interest in Indian affairs, the Sphinx would have found himself bound to speak. Yet to these people our deluded Moderate friends must go and spend the money of poverty-stricken India in the vain attempt to "educate" them — with a view to get political rights and privileges! What shadows we are, and what shadows we pursue!

Bande Mataram, June 14, 1907

Slow but Sure

Commenting on Mr. Morley's Budget Speech, the *Statesman* remarks — "It is to be hoped that the new concessions will be received in no carping spirit, and that there will be a resolute determination to make the best of them. Under English rule wherever it is found, reforms are almost invariably slow and gradual. England abhors a revolution, or even the logical working out of a principle — unless it be very gradually. It proceeds by compromises and half-measures. But this cautious policy has been justified by results. The advance, if slow, is sure, and a persistent well-reasoned agitation seldom fails to achieve its end. An example of the success which rewards perseverance is to be found in Mr. Morley's announcement that a Committee has been appointed to examine the distribution of the costs of the Indian Army as between the War Office and the Indian taxpayer."

So the Indian is asked to accept the so-called concessions in no carping spirit, nor to demand more like Oliver Twist, but to remember that beggars must not be choosers. But why should Englishmen interested in India be so anxious to confer concessions on Indians who in their present self-respecting mood are not likely to appreciate the generosity of the donors? New India — the India that has showed itself prepared to suffer sacrifices and brave dangers for political rights — has rejected as obsolete the methods of mendicant agitation and it is too late in the day to try to delude it with gilded toys and useless tinsel. Why waste your energy in granting "concessions" when none is wanted? After imparting this sage advice the *Statesman* proceeds to present a prose rendering of Tennyson's well-known description of England as the land "Where freedom slowly broadens down/ From precedent to precedent". In the case of countries conquered by England "reforms" slowly broaden down from Circulars to Ordinances. The bond is tightened and the lingering sparks of the spirit of self-help sought to be extinguished. It is useless to argue, for John Bull is — as our Friend admits — never logical. Yet we are advised to wait and suffer in silence till the millennium arrives and in the meantime to feel grateful for chance droppings from the basket of the bureaucracy. Let no Indian ask the inconvenient question — How long are we to wait? For that will be sheer impudence not to be brooked.

Bande Mataram, June 17, 1907

The Rawalpindi Sufferers

THE bureaucracy which has decided upon coercion as the most effective means of crushing the growing national spirit in India must necessarily turn the machinery of judicial administration also to its advantage. We have observed on previous occasions that a certain portion of the positive laws enacted by the British Government has been designed not so much to secure the rights and interests of the people as to repress their free manhood. There is a popular saying that almost every action of a man can be construed as an offence according to the Penal Code. This attempt to penalise many natural human activities in a conquered country, should have long ago convinced us of the true spirit of official-made British law but we instead have lived in a Fool's Paradise and run for safety to the institutions and professions of the foreigner, obstinately blind to the manner in which they illustrate the British genius for "ruling" subject races. Where the ordinary law does not cover all the conceivable offences against the interests of the foreigner, ordinances and ukases can easily be invented to put a stop to undesirable activities as we have lately seen. Thus the bureaucratic machinery grinds slow or grinds fast, but grinding is its object. In the ordinary course of things we do not become immediately conscious of its baneful consequence; but when the bureaucracy is face to face with an adverse force or interest it at once sets itself to the work of repression with all its demoralising consequences. Viewed in this light what is being described as unprecedented and "humanity-staggering" police violence and police licence in the alleged Rawalpindi riot case, is no more than natural and expected. The tales of police oppression while inducing the most whole-hearted sympathy with the noble sufferers have not the least feature of novelty in them. The *Patrika* is very much affected by the severe distress of the alleged rioters now on their trial; and moved by softer feelings, it has appealed to Lord Minto who according to our contemporary is "goodness personified" to come to their rescue. The *Patrika* is no doubt actuated by the very best of motives but our contemporary should remember that such nervousness while doing no good to the sufferers is demoralising to our firmness and high spirit. So far as the accused are concerned the die is cast. Suffer they must; their only care now must be so to suffer that their martyrdom may be a strength and inspiration to their countrymen. If their heroic and manful conduct during the trial and their readiness to face the grim sequel of a conviction puts courage into other hearts, then only will it be said that they have not suffered in vain. Otherwise there is not much on the credit side of the account. The duty of the publicist at such a time is to seek to brace the nerves of the martyrs and not to take away from the merit of their service to the country by any advocacy humiliating in form or abject in spirit. The public attitude at such a time reacts on that of the sufferer and if we give way to weakness at the report of their sufferings, we set them a bad example. We also have been moved, and not merely by feelings of grief and pity, at the dim, but only too sinister and significant hints of what is going on behind the decent show of a fair and public trial.

But this is not a time when we should give vent to feminine emotions. To try to rouse pity in the rulers is as unprofitable as it is unworthy of our manhood and of our cause and in these rough and still only superficially civilised descendants of the old sea-robbers it can only excite a deep contempt towards us and increase their arrogance. If we must show our grief and pity, let it be in substantial help to the victims or their relatives. If we must pray, let it be not to the goodness personified of any "sympathetic" repressor, but to the goodness unpersonified of the Power that makes and breaks kings and viceroys, empires and dominations. Let us pray to Him to give our brothers in Rawalpindi a stout and cheerful heart and a steadfast courage so that in the hour of their trial they may nothing common do or mean upon that memorable scene, and that we too, if our turn comes to suffer such things or worse for our country, may so bear ourselves that our country may profit by our sufferings. This is the only prayer that befits us in this hour of the new birth of our nation. For all that the country suffers now or will suffer hereafter are but the natural birth-pangs of a free and regenerated India.

Bande Mataram, June 18, 1907

The Main Feeder of Patriotism

THERE are many people who admit the superiority of Eastern civilisation, who recognise its humanitarian and socialistic aspect, who are not blind to its predominating feature of spirituality, who admire the absence of a militant Materialism in it, who praise the way in which it has balanced the interests of the different classes in the society, who are conscious how much attention it gives to the higher needs of humanity. But still patriotism is not a living and moving impulse with them. Apart from the natural attachment which every man has to his country, its literature, its traditions, its customs and usages, patriotism has an additional stimulus in the acknowledged excellence of a national civilisation. If Britons love England with all her faults, why should we fail to love India whose faults were whittled down to an irreducible minimum till foreign conquests threw the whole society out of gear? But instead of being dominated by the natural ambition of carrying the banner of such a civilisation all over the world, we are unable to maintain its integrity in its own native home. This is betraying a trust. This is unworthiness of the worst type. We have not been able to add anything to this precious bequest; on the contrary we have been keeping ourselves and generations yet unborn from a full enjoyment of their lawful heritage. For Eastern civilisation though it is not dead, though it is a living force, is yet a submerged force, and that not because it has no intrinsic merit but because it has been transmitted to a class of people devoid of a love for things their own. It seems as if they have no past to guide, instruct or inspire them. They are beginning, as it were, with a clean slate and what is worse, a foreign poetaster is calling upon his countrymen to take charge of them as "half devil, half child". Is not the humiliation sufficient to disturb our self-complacency?

We make no appeal in the name of any material benefit. No desire for earthly gain can nerve a people to such superhuman activity as the eager hope of maintaining their greatness and glory. We must first realise that we are great and glorious, that we are proud and noble, and it is through voluntary prostration that we are being stamped into the dust. No material ideal of riches and prosperity has ever made a nation. But when the sense of honour has been touched, when the consciousness of greatness has been re-awakened, then and then only have the scattered units of a fallen nation clustered round one mighty moral force.

What is now considered by political thinkers to be the chief incentive to conquest? What is the meaning of the imperial sentiment which is "now dominating every English breast"? "If we ask ourselves," says one writer, "seriously the question why we glory in the magnitude of our empire, it may be answered: partly because we think it adds to our riches, partly because we enjoy the sense of power and dominion, partly because we cling to old traditions and remember the great deeds of history; but beyond and above all these elements of satisfaction we feel that throughout the whole British empire we enforce those ideas of justice, personal freedom and religious toleration which are the results of the constitutional struggles of centuries." We are not concerned here with the discussion whether the Britisher's boast is well or ill-founded; but rightly or wrongly this sentiment has taken possession of him and he is invincible under its influence. For we find the same explanation in Mill. Sidgwick also in his *Elements of Politics* harps on the same strain. "Besides the material advantages," he says, "there are legitimate sentimental satisfactions derived from justifiable conquest which must be taken into account. Such are the justifiable pride which the cultivated members of a civilised community feel in the beneficent exercise of dominion and in the performance by their nation of the noble task of spreading the highest kind of civilisation, and a more intense though less elevated satisfaction — inseparable from patriotic sentiment — in the spread of the special type of civilisation distinctive of their nation, communicated through its language and literature, and through the tendency to catch its tastes and imitate its customs which its prolonged rule, specially if, on the whole, beneficent, is likely to cause in a continually increasing degree."

Thus, according to Sidgwick, physical expansion proceeds

from a desire for spiritual expansion and history also supports the assertion. But why should not India then be the first power in the world? Who else has the undisputed right to extend spiritual sway over the world? This was Swami Vivekananda's plan of campaign. India can once more be made conscious of her greatness by an overmastering sense of the greatness of her spirituality. This sense of greatness is the main feeder of all patriotism. This only can put an end to all self-depreciation and generate a burning desire to recover the lost ground.

Bande Mataram, June 19, 1907

Concerted Action

We publish in another column a letter from a correspondent signing himself "Organised Cooperation", in which a very elaborate plan is sketched out for ascertaining the opinion of the nation and following out in unison the programme arrived at. The scheme is, we fear, more elaborate than practicable. If the suggestion originally put forward by the Nationalists of the creation of Congress electorates had been adopted, such a plebiscite might have been possible; as it is, the necessary machinery does not exist. Moreover, such an all-India plebiscite covering the whole field of politics, even if it were possible, would neither be useful nor necessary. The national programme has already been fixed by the Calcutta Congress and there is no need of a further plebiscite to decide it; in Bengal at least it has been universally accepted, with additions and reaffirmed by the District Conferences and District Committees appointed to carry it out. Our correspondent seems to have misapprehended the nature and object of a plebiscite. A plebiscite can only be on a single definite and supreme issue, the decision of which is so important that the ordinary representative assembles cannot undertake the responsibility of a final decision. A plebiscite on a whole programme is an impossibility. Neither would it be binding. Bengal, for instance, is practically unanimous for Boycott. If the majority of votes went against Boycott, would Bengal accept the decision and tamely submit to repression?

Or if the majority were for Boycott, would Bombay City agree to carry out the decision? We sympathise with the hankering for united action, but united action is only possible in so much of the programme as all are agreed upon; it is not possible in those matters on which opinion is still widely divided.

The Bengal Government's Letter

The *Statesman* has recently become a confirmed sensation-monger and treats the public continually to its thick-coming opium visions. It has recently brought out a sensational statement about Government proceedings against the Nationalist Press in which a Bengal Government letter to three Calcutta journals received almost a fortnight ago, the recent Police raid on the Keshab Press, the *Bande Mataram*'s posters and some luxuriant imaginings of the *Statesman*'s own riotous fancy have been mingled together in wild confusion. We were one of the recipients of the Bengal Government's letter, and if we have not written on the subject, it is simply because the letter was marked confidential. Now, however, that the matter has got abroad, we may as well correct certain inaccuracies which have appeared not only in the *Statesman*'s bit of romancing, but in the *Amrita Bazar Patrika*'s correction. It is entirely untrue that on Monday afternoon or any other afternoon, evening or morning "a notice was served upon the proprietors, editor, manager and printer of this paper to the effect that proceedings would be adopted against them under section 124A and the other sections dealing with seditious publications, unless they moderated their tone". On Saturday before last, if our memory serves us, we received a communication from the Bengal Government addressed to the Editor, *Bande Mataram* in which we were informed that the Lieutenant-Governor had had under consideration certain articles (not specified) recently published in our paper "the language of which was a direct incitement to violence and breach of the peace". This sort of language the Bengal Government was determined to put a stop to, but before taking action they were gracious enough to give us a warning to mend our ways. That is all.

It is not true either that a conference was held with the directors or that the managers interviewed the legal advisers of the Company in connection with the notice. No such conference or interview was held for the simple reason that none was necessary. The Editorial Department is solely responsible for the policy of the paper and they have no need to consult lawyers about their duty to the public. The *Amrita Bazar Patrika* is therefore wrongly informed when it says that legal opinion has been taken and given in the matter. It is true that legal opinion is being taken by the Company, but it is on a point of law which arose previous to the receipt of the Bengal Government's letter and is entirely unconnected with it. The *Statesman* has also absurdly distorted the "proceedings against the *Yugantar* and *Nabasakti*". No proceedings have been instituted. The police while searching the Keshab Press for manuscripts in connection with the pamphlet *Sonar Bangla* — which has, by the way, no connection with Hare Street mare's nest — stumbled on the forms of the *Yugantar* then being printed. The Keshab Press is being proceeded against, but it is doubtful whether anything will be done to the *Yugantar*, as the printing of a paper in part or whole at another press in emergency is so common an occurrence that, even if it be a technical offence, which is not certain, to prosecute it would be purely vindictive. In any case the *Yugantar* business is not, as the *Statesman* represents, the first step in a campaign against the Nationalist Press. Our own position is very simple. The articles to which the Bengal Government refers are, we presume, those in which we called upon the Hindus to defend their temples and their women from insult and outrage. Every Hindu paper at the time did the same, even the *Indian Mirror* and the *Indian Nation*, and we do not think we did anything more than our plain duty to our countrymen. The Lieutenant-Governor, however, takes exception not to the purport of our articles but to their language — which was less violent than what English papers would have used if a similar campaign of outrage on European women had been in progress. Be that as it may, the occasion has passed and until it is repeated, the question of complying or not complying with the warning does not arise. We merely note it and pass on.

Bande Mataram, June 20, 1907

British Justice

THERE has been much to edify and instruct in the recent antics of the bureaucracy and, in the light of the object lessons they present, the people of India have been revising old ideas and out-worn superstitions with a healthy rapidity. The belief in British liberalism, in the freedom of the Press, in the freedom of the platform, in the Pax Britannica, in the political honesty of Mr. John Morley and many other cherished shibboleths have departed into the limbo of forgotten follies. But the greatest fall of all has been the fall of the belief in the imperturbable impartiality of British justice. There are two kinds of strain which no empire, however firmly bound in triple and quadruple bands of steel, can long bear; the strain of a burden of taxation which the people no longer find bearable and the strain of a series of perversions of justice which destroy all faith in the motives of the governing authorities. Justice and protection between man and man, between community and community, between rulers and ruled is the main object for which States exist, for which men submit to the restrictions of the law and to an equitable assessment of the expenses of the machinery which provides for protection and justice. But if the assessment of the expenses is grossly unjust, if the expenses themselves are exorbitantly high, if the revenue is spent on ways of which the taxpayers do not approve, then protection and justice are bought at a price which is not worth paying. And if in addition the protection is denied and the justice withheld, then the very object of the existence of a State ceases to be satisfied and from that moment the governing power, unless it can retrace its steps, is doomed by the inevitable operation of nature.

The bureaucrats who misgovern us at the present moment have totally forgotten these simple truths. Otherwise we would not have witnessed such scandalous scenes as are now being enacted at Rawalpindi or the gross infringements of equity and justice which are of frequent occurrence in Bengal. The amazing incidents of the Rawalpindi riot case are such as have hardly been paralleled in British India. The refusal of bail, which was the first scandal, has evidently become a part of bureaucratic policy. It is a sound principle of procedure that bail should not be refused except under exceptional conditions, such as the probability of the accused absconding; otherwise in a protracted case an innocent man may suffer seriously for the sole offence of being accused. In the Rawalpindi case there was not the least possibility of men like Lala Hansraj, Gurdas Ram or Janaki Nath absconding from justice and the apprehension of further riots in a city commanded by siege-guns and crowded with military was a contemptible and hollow pretence. Yet without hearing the case, on the mere statement of the prosecuting officials, the Chief Court of the Punjab, supposed to be the highest repository of impartial British Justice, prejudged the accused, declared them guilty and refused bail. This is British law and British justice! Again in the course of the present trial, although it was proved beyond dispute that the prisoners were suffering terribly in health as the result of a detention in which they are being deliberately subjected to unnecessary discomfort and privation, although, if there was ever any shadow of justification for the refusal of bail, even that shadow had by this time utterly vanished; yet on the strength of the airy persiflage of a Civil Surgeon, the relief to which they were entitled was refused. This gentleman held the view that the sufferings of the accused were not due to their detention and seems to be of the opinion that men of means and gentle nurture are rather in the habit of shedding several pounds of flesh off and on without apparent cause. And so the unfortunate martyrs, for the crime of being patriots, are punished with a long term of imprisonment before any offence has been proved against them. This too is British law and British justice. From the point of view of the executive it may no doubt be said that since the accused have to be punished whether they are guilty or innocent, it does not much matter whether their punishment begins before or after their conviction. That is good reasoning from the point of view of a bureaucratic executive, but not from that of a judicial authority. The refusal of bail to the Rawalpindi pleaders is one of the most deadly of the many wounds which the bureaucracy have been recently dealing to their own moral prestige and reputation for justice. The same spirit has been shown in the refusal of bail to Pindi Das, editor of *India*, and to Lala Dinanath of the *Hindustan*. In the latter case there is absolutely no excuse whatever for the refusal, except the vindictive fury of bureaucratic persecution which will omit no means however petty and base to make its opponents suffer.

But the most glaringly, paradoxically unsound case of all has occurred in our own midst. Srijut Girindranath Sen received at the hands of British justice a sentence of monstrous severity for a trifling offence. This same British justice, being moved to set aside the conviction and sentence, was graciously pleased to give the accused a chance of disproving the offence, but at the same time, in the plenitude of its justice and wisdom, refused to give him bail. In other words it admitted that the accused might be innocent, but at the same time decided that he must undergo a monstrously disproportionate punishment for a trifling offence of which it was admittedly doubtful whether he ever committed it! And then when the punishment had been served out, British justice lent a gracious and leisurely ear and admitted that this Swadeshi Volunteer Captain was very probably innocent, but as he had suffered punishment for his innocence, it was not necessary to go any further into the matter. This too is British law and British justice. If all this does not convince the Indian people that the British sense of justice is most marvellous and unique and *sui generis* and without any peer or parallel in the world, it must indeed be hard-hearted and dull of soul. For our part we are ready to acclaim British justice with hymns of adoration and praise. Hail, thou ineffable, incomprehensible, indescribable, unspeakable British Justice! Hail, thou transcendent mystery, *tubhyam bhūyiṣṭhām nama uktim vidhema.*

The Moral of the Coconada Strike

That the weapon of passive resistance is sometimes a match even for sword and bayonet, not to speak of milder instruments of repression, is being evidenced in the strike of the shipping coolies at Coconada. We may have to resort to this means of protest for some time to come until the Britishers so far forget themselves as to begin firing on strikers and boycotters — a contingency for which the country should now learn to be prepared. If the despot still entertains some doubt as to the working of the time-spirit, it should be set to rest by the instinctive resort of the Coconada coolies to a wholesale strike as an effective protest against the arrest of some of their own people for alleged participation in a riot. The drafting of the military and the punitive police to the locality has perhaps strengthened their firmness. The *Englishman* while alarmed at this unexpected combination among the lower class, hopes that the strike is not political in its character. This comfortable deduction has provoked a sort of subdued laughter from the Madras *Hindu.* Events alone make men wise. The opinion that is today punished and ridiculed as mere heresy, has its ratification tomorrow in experience. Our moderate contemporary now sees eye to eye with the Nationalists when it says: "If once the lower classes of the people begin to know and feel their real strength and power, it will be difficult to predict the results that would follow. No prudent administrator would, in our opinion, tempt the bringing into play of the capacity for combination which the lower strata of people have. They cannot be cowed down into submission with half the ease and celerity with which the educated classes can be brought down by the display of military strength." The whole plan of Nationalist campaign rests on the basis of this potential strength of the people which does not require for its re-awakening years of mass education as is contended by the Moderates, but only tangible instances of bureaucratic high-handedness. Education in the ordinarily accepted sense is not a very effective means of national regeneration, as the *Hindu* itself admits. The responsiveness of untampered and unsophisticated nature, its want of calculation and its speedy decision have to be turned to advantage.

Thus the Coconada strike comes handy with its moral to dispel another of our superstitions.

The "Statesman" on Shooting

While Mr. John Morley was being cross-examined by the Nationalist and Labour members in Parliament and was answering in his usual style of Demigod *plus* Aristides the just *plus* Louis XIV of France *plus* the Archangel Gabriel, the tiger qualities of an imperial race suddenly awoke in the breast of Sir Howard Vincent and roared out "Why not shoot Lajpat Rai?" In that single trenchant sentence the war-like Knight gave a sudden illuminating expression to the heart's desire of all Anglo-India and two-thirds of England. It was not decorous, it was not politic, but it was frank and sincere. Yesterday the Friend of India noticed the incident with great sympathy for Sir Howard Vincent's feelings, but it could not altogether approve of applying his panacea just at present. The *Friend*, however, looks forward to a day when the shooting will begin; it invites the attention of the Indian reactionaries — whoever they may be — to this blood-curdling Howard Vincent war-whoop and warns them that this is the prospect before them if a Tory Government comes into power while the present unrest continues. By its Indian reactionaries the *Friend* probably means not Nawab Salimullah and the *Mihir Sudhakar*, but the Democratic Nationalist Party in India; for the Friendly language must be usually interpreted by contraries, and it is quite natural for one who calls the *Statesman* a friend of India to call democracy and nationalism reactionary. Let us assure the *Friend* however that the Nationalist Party have from the beginning envisaged the possibility of the shooting being started; they did not need a Howard Vincent to open their eyes to it. The defenders of the established order of things have attempted almost every form of Russian repression except the taking of life. Deportation, condemnation without trial, punishment before conviction, flogging, the gagging of press and platform, police hooliganism, the employment of a Black Hundred, brutal personal persecution in jail and Hajat, have all been attempted though not as yet on the Russian scale. When all these methods have been found ineffective, it is quite possible that the order, "do not hesitate to shoot" may go out; already in the Punjab the threat has been used to prevent public meetings. The Friend of India is greatly mistaken if he thinks that his menaces will have any better effect than his abuse and cajolings; it is a wild dream for him to hope that any power can make Indian Nationalism fall down and kiss the feet of Archangel John.

Bande Mataram, June 21, 1907

Mr. A. Chowdhury's Policy

Mr. Ashutosh Chowdhury has used the opportunity given to him by his selection for the chair of the Pabna Conference to make a personal pronouncement of policy. This is the second time that Mr. Chowdhury has had an opportunity of this kind, the first being the Provincial conference at Burdwan. On that occasion he made a pronouncement which indicated a new departure in politics and created some flutter in the Congress dovecote. It would not be accurate to say that the Burdwan pronunciamento influenced the course of affairs; the propounder of the new policy, if such it could be called, had not sufficient weight of personality to become the leader of a New Party, nor was his policy either definite enough or sound enough to attract a following. But it had a certain importance. It was the immature self-expression of ideas and forces which had been gathering head in the country and groping about for means of entry into the ordinary channels of political action and expression. It was rather the prophecy of a new turn in Indian politics than itself a policy already understood and matured. The prophet himself was perhaps the one who least understood his own prophecy. The confusion of his ideas was shown soon afterwards by his identifying himself with the old current of Congress politics and thus turning his back on the two main positions in his Burdwan speech, the repudiation of mendicant politics and the dictum that a subject nation has no politics. He left it to others to develop the political ideas he had dimly and imperfectly outlined and give them a definite shape embodied in a clear political programme. Still more forcibly is this lack of comprehension evidenced by Mr. Chowdhury's attempt to revert, with modifications, to his Burdwan ideas even after the momentous changes of the last three years. He has once more reverted to his dictum that a subject nation has no politics; he once more proposes that we should give up our political agitation; once more he puts forward self-help as a substitute. When he spoke at Burdwan, industrial expansion was the idea of the day and Mr. Chowdhury offered it to us as a substitute for political mendicancy. Today Swadeshi, Boycott and National Education are the ideas of the day and Mr. Chowdhury offers them as a substitute for the struggle for Swaraj.

We do not wish to overrate the importance of Mr. Chowdhury's pronouncements. Mr. Chowdhury is not a political leader with a distinct following in the country who are likely to carry out his ideas. He is a sort of Rosebery of Bengal politics, a brilliant, cultured amateur who catches up certain thoughts or tendencies that are in the air and gives them a more or less striking expression, but he has not the qualities of a politician — robustness, backbone, the ability to will a certain course of action and the courage to carry it out. He has intellectual sensitiveness, but not intellectual consistency. Suave, affable, pliable, essentially an amiable and cultured gentleman, he is unfit for the rough and tumble of political life, especially in a revolutionary period; no man who shrinks from struggle or is appalled by the thought of aggression can hope to seize and lead the wild forces that are rising to the surface in twentieth-century India. But this very knack of catching up however partially the moods of the moment gives a certain interest to Mr. Chowdhury's pronouncements which make them worth examining.

When Mr. Chowdhury at Burdwan pronounced against the mendicant policy he was voicing two distinct and various currents of political tendency. The opprobrious term of mendicancy was applied to the old Congress School of politics not because remonstrance and protest are in themselves wrong and degrading, but because in the circumstances of modern India a policy of prayer, petition and protest without the sanction of a great irresistible national force at its back was bound to pauperise the energy of the nation and to accustom it to a degrading dependence. It was not only a waste of energy but a sapping of energy, and it was ruinous to manhood and self-respect. But the recognition of this fact only led to another problem. If we did not sue to others for help, we must help ourselves; if we did not depend on the alien's mercies, we must depend on our own strength. But how was that strength to be educated? Again, when we had decided that a subject nation has no politics, what then? Were we to renounce the birthrights inherent in our manhood and leave the field to the bureaucratic despotism or were we to resolve to cease to be a subject nation so that we might recover the right and possibility of political life and activity? There were two currents of political thought growing up in the country. One, thoughtful, philosophic, idealistic, dreamed of ignoring the terrible burden that was crushing us to death, of turning away from politics and educating our strength in the village and township, developing our resources, our social, economic, religious life regardless of the intrusive alien; it thought of inaugurating a new revolution such as the world had never yet seen, a moral, peaceful revolution, actively developing ourselves but only passively resisting the adversary. But there was another current submerged as yet, but actively working underneath, which tended in another direction, — a sprinkling of men in whom one fiery conviction replaced the cultured broodings of philosophy and one grim resolve took the place of political reasoning. The conviction was that subjection was the one curse which withered and blighted all our national activities, that so long as that curse was not removed it was a vain dream to expect our national activities to develop themselves successfully and that only by struggle could our strength be educated to action and victory. The resolve was to rise and fight and fall and again rise and fight and fall waging the battle for ever until this once great and free nation should again be great and free. It was this last current which boiled up to the surface in the first vehemence of the anti-Partition agitation, flung out the challenge of boycott and plunged the Bengali nation into a struggle with the bureaucracy which must now be fought out till the end.

All were carried away in the tide of that great upheaval; but it is needless to say that this was not what the advocates of self-help pure and simple had contemplated, Mr. Chowdhury least of all. He very early identified himself with the small knot of older leaders who from time to time struggled with the tide and tried to turn it back; but until now the tide was too strong for them. For a moment, however, the rush has been checked by superhuman efforts of repression on the part of the panic-stricken bureaucracy and it is natural that those who were not with their whole heart and conviction for the struggle for Swaraj, should begin to revert to their old ideas, to long to give up the struggle, to retreat into the fancied security of their fortress of unpolitical Swadeshism and a policy of self-help which seeks to ignore the unignorable. The tendency is to cry, "The old policy is a failure, the Briton has revealed his true nature; the new policy is a failure, we have not strength to meet the giant power of the bureaucracy; let us have the field, let us quietly pursue our own salvation in the peaceful Ashrams of Swadeshism and self-help." Mr. Ashutosh Chowdhury with his keen intellectual sensitiveness has felt this tendency in the air and given it expression. It is a beautiful and pathetic dream. We will develop our manufacture, boycott foreign goods, of course in a quite friendly and non-political spirit, and England will look quietly on while its tradc is being ruined! We will ignore the Government and build up our own centres of strength in spite of it, a Government the whole principle and condition of whose existence is that there shall be no centre of strength in the country except itself! Mr. Chowdhury's policy would be an excellent one if he could only remove two factors from the political problem; first, Indian Nationalism, secondly, the British Government. And how does he propose to remove them? By shutting his eyes to their existence. Ignore the Government, dissociate yourselves from the men of violence, — and the thing is done. Such is the political wisdom of Mr. Ashutosh Chowdhury.

A Current Dodge

Referring to the transfer to other places of Mr. Barneville and Maulavi Faizuddin Hossein who tried cases of looting in Jamalpur and recorded as their opinions that the riots were not provoked by Hindu boycotters and National volunteers, even the *Hindu Patriot* which has never been friendly to the Nationalist movement writes:—

"Transferring judges and magistrates whose decisions differ from the settled policy or preconceived views of the Executive officials, is a current dodge whereby the ends of justice are sought to be subordinated to political or other considerations. And this is but another very forcible illustration of the evils of the combination of Judicial and Executive functions, and it also explains the reason why there is so much opposition to the separation of the duties. All the same, however, we may frankly observe here that any attempt to destroy the integrity of the law courts will deepen the anxiety which is being manifested on all sides. It is the proverbial impartiality of British justice which is prized more than anything else."

But this current dodge is played not by the local executive officials but by the higher bureaucracy and need not be an argument in favour of the separation of Judicial and Executive functions. Our contemporary's attempt to smother facts in a profusion of side-issues cannot deceive those who can read between the lines. We must congratulate him all the same on his sudden flash of intelligent outspokenness. But our contemporary need not feel anxious about "the proverbial impartiality of British justice". The proverb is badly in need of a change. And as we said yesterday when referring to many cherished shibboleths of the people departing into the limbo of forgotten follies, the greatest fall has been the fall of the belief in the imperturbable impartiality of British justice. The transfer of Mr. Barneville and the Maulavi is only another count in the indictment.

Bande Mataram, June 22, 1907

More about British Justice

We commented the other day on the policy of refusing bail which has recently been adopted by the bureaucracy in a spirit of petty vindictiveness and the scandalous manner in which men accused of political offences are being punished before conviction. Of course it is all under the law, but that only proves the contention we have always advanced that the criminal law in this country on which our rulers pride themselves is barbarous, oppressive and semi-mediaeval in its spirit and that its provisions are governed far more by the principle of repressing the spirit of the people than by the principle of protecting the citizen. Moreover, in all judicial administration there are two elements, the letter of the law on one side, a humane and equitable practice on the other. To suspend the latter in favour of the former shows an oppressive and tyrannical spirit. The letter of the law enables the Government to appeal against any and every acquittal in a criminal case; equitable practice forbids it to take advantage of this barbarous provision except in important cases where it is convinced there has been a serious miscarriage of justice. But the first principle of bureaucratic rule in India is repression, to crush the spirit of the people and keep them down with the strong hand. Every acquittal is therefore considered by the executive a defeat to Government prestige and resented. Unless therefore there is a strong and independent High Court, the habit of appealing against acquittals is bound to become a standing feature of British justice. But the idea of a strong and independent High Court is becoming more and more a legend of the past. Future generations will be as sceptical of the possibility of its ever having existed as the modern world is of the existence of gnomes and fairies.

There is another equitable practice which has been violated with the most cynical openness in the Rawalpindi trial. It is a sound principle of legal procedure that the accused should not be hampered in his defence but on the contrary should receive every legitimate facility. The unjust judge who denies proper facilities of defence to a man whose life or liberty, honour or reputation is imperilled by an accusation which may be false or mistaken, the hanging judge whose diseased brain and morbid temperament are consumed with the desire to have the accused convicted, are survivals of mediaeval barbarity. Such men are the lineal descendants of Jeffreys and Torquemada. In England such men are rareties upon the Bench; in India especially among Civilian Magistrates and Judges, they are not uncommon. In England the prosecuting Counsel will seldom throw unnecessary difficulties in the way of the defence, in India it is too common for the prosecuting Counsel to regard the defence as an enemy to be beaten down and out-manoeuvred by any means which the technicalities of the law leave open to him. For the atmosphere is different. The spirit of bureaucracy in all countries tends to be narrow, hard and domineering, but in a country where a small alien element subsists in a huge native mass partly by the maintenance of a hypnotic illusion, partly by a cold legal repressive severity, ubiquitous and watchful to crush down every least unit of strength in the indigenous population, this temper is immensely heightened and exaggerated. Everybody knows that in the local administration of the law in this country conviction not impartial justice is the object. A Subordinate Magistrate is rated not by the soundness of his judgments but by the percentage of convictions to the total number of cases he has tried, and it is by this test that he is promoted. In that single fact we find the true and fundamental tendency of British justice in India.

When such is the spirit even in the ordinary administration of the law, it can easily be imagined to what lengths this spirit of semi-mediaeval barbarity is likely to be carried when political considerations are imported. To get justice in a Swadeshi case is nowadays almost impossible; even in the High Court only one or two judges have managed to keep a judicial frame of mind in relation to political cases. This is of course natural and inevitable. A struggle is going on between the ruling bureaucracy and the people of the country, and every judge or magistrate is a servant of the bureaucracy, generally a member of it and very often himself one of the caste and race whose monopoly of power is threatened. In his eyes the accused in a political case is not an ordinary accused but a rebel prisoner of war; he may not be guilty of the offence with which he is charged, but he is guilty of Swadeshism, he is guilty of being an opponent of the Government established by law. His punishment is therefore desirable in the interests of the ruling class and in the judge's own interests as a servant and member of that class. The judge is really a party to the case. It is not to be expected that in such circumstances any facilities will be allowed to the defence beyond what the letter of the law and bare decency require. A few magistrates may rise superior to these considerations, but the majority cannot be reasonably asked to do so. They are after all human beings — and Englishmen.

Still there is a limit, there is something due to decency and at Rawalpindi it seems to us that the limit has been overpassed and the dues have been denied. We have nothing to say as to the guilt or the innocence of the men under trial. We will assume that they are guilty, we will assume that their conviction is a thing settled. But still until the trial is over, they are in law regarded as men who are possibly innocent and should be allowed ordinary facilities to prove their innocence. One of the principal safeguards of accused innocence in India is the necessity of identification under stringent rules which prevent collusion between the police and the witnesses. In the Rawalpindi trial it has been repeatedly stated that the identification has been a scandalous farce; the prisoners have been under police custody all the time and have been repeatedly shown to the witnesses in the jail, and as if this were not enough, the police in Court are allowed to make signs to the witnesses so that they may be sure to identify the right persons. These statements have not been denied. They may be true or they may be false; but when such statements are advanced by the defence, it is the duty of an impartial judge to inquire into them and take every precaution against the barest possibility of such practices. Piteous complaints have been made by several of the accused of police violence and cruelty in Hajat. Into this also no inquiry has been made and the only answer the unfortunate men have received is a rough and uncivil command to keep silence.

If this were all, it would be scandalous enough, but the recent developments have been still more staggering. A hooligan crusade has been started against the pleaders for the defence so shamelessly persistent and open as to drive them to throw up their briefs. Sirdar Beant Singh's house has been invaded, himself and his brother brutally assaulted, his ladies' apartments entered and an ornament snatched from the person of his wife. While these brutal outrages were being committed, the police remained quiet in their Thana which is in the same compound as the Sirdar's house and made no attempt to give assistance, nor do we hear of any attempt to trace and punish the miscreants. The houses of other defence pleaders have been exposed to a campaign of theft and pilfering and none of them is safe against a repetition of the kind of intimidation which has been used against Beant Singh. All India has drawn its own conclusions from these singular occurrences, for indeed, the conclusions are not difficult to draw.

But the crowning scandal of all was the treatment of the witness Abdullah. It is possible that seditious speeches were delivered by the accused, but it is certain that the amazing literal unanimity of the witnesses has created, rightly or wrongly, an impression that their evidence was given according to police dictation. When, therefore, a Mahomedan witness actually declared in the witness box that his first evidence has been given under fear of the police, it was obvious that the whole foundation of the prosecution case was threatened; for the example of recantation might easily be followed. Then ensued a scene which we hope for the credit of humanity at large, has never had a parallel in recent judicial history. Immediately the prosecuting counsel leaps up and demands that this inconvenient witness be at once prosecuted for perjury and handed over to the tender mercies of the police against whom he has given evidence; immediately the judge complies with this amazing demand; immediately the unfortunate witness is hustled out of court into the grip of the police. It is not surprising that the miserable Abdullah should recant his recantation and balance his charge against the police by a charge against the leading pleader for the defence. And this too is British law and British justice. Nay, it is the climax, the apex, the acme, the culminating point which British justice has reached in this too fortunate country. After all, the British Empire must be saved at any cost.

Bande Mataram, June 24, 1907

Morleyism Analysed

THE fuller reports of Mr. Morley's speech to hand by mail do not in any essential point alter the impression that was produced by *Reuter*'s summary. The whole of the speech turns upon a single sentence as its pivot — the statement that British rule will continue, ought to continue and must continue. Mr. Morley does not say forever, but that is understood. It follows that if the continuance of British rule on any terms is the fundamental necessity, any and every means used for its preservation is legitimate. Compared with that supreme necessity justice does not matter, humanity does not matter, truth does not matter, morality may be trampled on, the laws of God may be defied. The principles of Liberalism, though they may have been professed a thousand times over, must be discarded by the English rulers of India as inapplicable to a country of "300 millions of people, composite, heterogeneous, of different races with different histories and different faiths". All these things weigh as dust in the balance against the one supreme necessity. If the continuance of British rule seems to be threatened by any popular activity, however legitimate, resort must be had to any weapon, no matter of what nature, in order to put down that activity. Reasons of State, "the tyrant's plea, necessity", must be held to be of supreme authority and to override all other considerations. Mr. Morley admits that the plea is a dangerous one, but sedition is still more dangerous. The danger of the reason of State is that it can cover and will inevitably be stretched to cover the repetition of "dangers, mischiefs and iniquities in our olden history and, perhaps, in our present history", in other words Mr. Morley's reasoning in favour of the present "iniquities" in India, can equally well be used to justify every utmost atrocity, cruelty, vileness with which tyrants ancient or modern have attempted to put down opposition to their sovereign will. Wholesale deportation, arbitrary imprisonment, massacre, outrage, police anarchy, torture of prisoners, every familiar feature of Russian repression, can be brought under the head of weapons necessary to combat sedition and can be justified by the plea of State necessity. This is the danger of reason of State, a danger that recent events in India and especially current events in the Punjab show to be by no means so remote as we might have some months ago imagined. But the danger of sedition is the cessation of British rule. And in the opinion of Mr. Morley, supported by an almost unanimous concensus of British opinion, the re-enactment by a British government of the iniquities and atrocities of ancient and modern tyranny are preferable to the cessation of British rule; it is better to take the risk of these than to take the risk of losing the absolute control of Britain over India. This is Mr. Morley's argument, approved by Conservative and Radical alike.... No, we are not distorting or exaggerating. There it is, plump and plain, in the speech of the great British Radical, the Liberal philosopher, the panegyrist of Burke and Gladstone. It is the last word of England to India on the great issue of Indian self-government.

What does Mr. Morley mean by British rule? Not the British connexion, not the continuance of India as a self-governing unit in a federation of free peoples which shall be called the British Empire. No, Mr. Morley is quite as hostile to the Moderate ideal of self-government on colonial lines, modified Swaraj, as to the Nationalist ideal of Swaraj, pure and simple. The educated minority in India have the presumption to think themselves capable of working the government of the country as smoothly as the heaven-born Briton himself, but Mr. Morley is persuaded that they would not work it for a week. This is final. If after a hundred years of English education and no inconsiderable training in the subordinate conduct of the bureaucratic machinery of government, the educated class are not fit to be entrusted even by gradual stages with the supreme government of Indian affairs, then they will never be fit. And we must remember that the policy of the rulers henceforth will be to control and restrict and not to encourage or promote the spread of education of the higher sort. From our own point of view, we may put it more strongly and say that if a hundred years of dependence and foreign control have so immensely impaired that governing capacity of the Indian races which they showed with such splendid results for the last three thousand years, then another century will absolutely and for ever destroy it. Mr. Morley is therefore logically justified in reiterating his conviction that personal and absolute foreign control must be the leading feature of Indian administration to the very end of time. This is what Mr. Morley means by the continuance of British rule, he means the continuance of a personal and absolute British control pervading the administration of affairs in every department, in other words, a bureaucratic despotism strongly flavoured by the independent personal omnipotence of local governors and local officials. The problem which former British statesmen professed to have before them was the problem of gradually training and associating the Indians in an European system of government until they were fit to take over absolute control of affairs and allow their patrons and protectors to withdraw. This problem does not any longer trouble the peace of British statesmen; on the contrary, it is definitely and forever disclaimed and put aside as a chimera — or a pretence. British rule in India will continue, ought to continue and must continue. What then is the problem which is troubling Mr. Morley? The problem is "the difficulty of combining personal government in our dependency with the rights of free speech and free meeting". Personal government, absolute government, despotism, that is the supreme necessity which must be continued for ever even at the sacrifice of morality, justice and every other consideration. Subject to that necessity Mr. Morley proposes to allow a certain amount of free speech if that be possible. Free speech was harmless as long as the Indian people had not set their heart on self-government; but now that they have resolved to have nothing short of self-government, free speech means seditious speech, and sedition is not consistent with the continuance of the absolute and personal British control. How then can free speech and British despotism be combined? How can fire and water occupy the same space? That is the problem, which Mr. Morley refuses to believe insoluble, and he solves it by proclaiming the areas where free speech has been chiefly employed, — and by establishing an Advisory Council of Notables.

It may be asked, if the continuance of absolute government

is the whole policy of British statesmanship, why does Mr. Morley trouble himself about free speech at all or propose any reforms? That question can be easily answered by a consideration of the suggested reforms. The first of these reforms is a Council of Notables. Mr. Morley has told us what is the object of this body; it is to be a sort of medium of communication between the government and the people. Of course Mr. Morley is quite mistaken in supposing that such a body can really serve the object he has in view, but we are concerned for the present not with the sufficiency of the means he is devising for his object, but with the object itself. The second reform is an expansion of the Legislative Councils and greater facilities to the elected members for the expression of their views; in other words the object of the expanded Legislative Councils is to keep the Government in India in touch with the views of the educated class. The third reform is the admission of Indian members to the India Council, and it is obvious that here again the object is that these Indian members should keep the Government in England in touch with the opinions of educated India, just as the elected members of the Legislative Council are to keep the Government in India in touch with the same opinion. The fourth reform is the decentralisation of the administration so that each local official may become an independent local despot. The object is clearly defined; first, to give him greater opportunities of being in touch with the people, secondly, to give him a greater power of personal despotic control within his own jurisdiction unhampered by the interference of higher authorities. All the reforms have one single object, one governing idea, — an absolute personal despotic British control *in touch with the people*. That is Mr. Morley's policy.

The object of keeping in touch with the people and knowing their opinions is not to redress their grievances, still less to allow their opinions any control over the administration. The object is quite different. A despotism out of touch with the people is a despotism continually in danger, ignorant of the currents of opinion, ignorant of the half-visible activities among its subjects, ignorant of the perils gathering in the vast obscurity, it must one day be suddenly surprised and perhaps overthrown by the unforeseen outburst of activities and dangers it had not anticipated. It is in order to avoid these dangers that Mr. Morley wishes to employ various means of keeping in touch with public opinion and its manifestations. He talks in his speech of the necessity of the rulers putting themselves in the skins of the ruled, in other words, of thoroughly understanding their thoughts, feelings and point of view. This does not mean that they shall rule India according to the sentiments, views and wishes of the Indian people. The whole conduct of Mr. Morley and the whole trend of his utterances shows that he means the opinions of the Government to prevail without regard to Indian opinions and sentiments. The rulers are to understand the ruled so that they may know how their measures are likely to affect the minds of the latter, how opposition can best be persuaded or Samjaoed into quiescence and how, if persuasion is useless, it can most swiftly and successfully be crushed. Through the Council of Notables, the Legislative Councils and the Indian members of the India Council, the Government will come to know the ideas, views, and feelings of the people; through the two former bodies they will try to present unpopular measures in such a way as to coax, cajole, delude or intimidate public opinion into a quiet acceptance. If they cannot do this, then through the decentralised local officers they can keep in touch with the popular temper, learn its manifestations and activities and successfully and promptly put down opposition by local measures, if possible, otherwise by imperial rescripts, laws and ordinances and every possible weapon of despotic repression.

We have analysed Mr. Morley's speech at length, because people in India have not the habit of following the turns of British parliamentary eloquence or reading between the lines of the speech of a Cabinet Minister. They are therefore likely to miss its true bearings and fail to understand the policy it enunciates. Read by an eye accustomed to the reservations and implications by which a British Minister makes himself intelligible without committing himself unnecessarily, Mr. Morley's speech is an admirably clear, connected, logical and, let us add, unusually and amazingly frank expression of a very straightforward and coherent policy. To maintain in India an absolute rule as rigid as any Czar's, to keep that rule in close touch with the currents of Indian sentiment, opinion and activity and to crush any active opposition by an immediate resort to the ordinary weapons of despotism, ordinances, deportations, prosecutions and a swift and ruthless terrorism, this is Morleyism as explained by its author.

Political or Non-political

We are glad to see that both at Jessore and Pabna the foolish idea of excluding politics from a political conference has been entirely abandoned. The attempt to parcel off our national progress into water-tight compartments, the attempts especially to put off political activity and political development to a far-distant area is, when not dictated by weakness or cowardice, a narrow, one-sided and short-sighted attempt. In one sense everything that concerns the welfare of the *polis*, the state or community is political. Education, social reconstruction, sanitation, industrial expansion, all these are a necessary part of politics; but the most important part of all is that to which the term politics is especially applied, the organisation of the state and its independence; for on these all the others depend. Just as an organism must first live and then attend to other wants and must therefore give the highest importance to the preservation of life, so also a state or nation must first win or maintain an organised independence, otherwise it will find itself baffled in all its attempts to satisfy its other wants. Swadeshi, Boycott, Arbitration, National Education are all doomed to failure if pursued separately and for their own sake; but as part of a single co-ordinated attempt to attain an organised independence, they are the necessity of the present time. They are merely component parts of Swaraj, which is made of all of them put together and harmonised into a single whole. It is mere ostrich politics to pretend to give up Swaraj, and confine oneself to its parts for their own sake. By such an attempt we may succeed in deceiving ourselves, we shall certainly not deceive anybody else.

Bande Mataram, June 25, 1907

The "Statesman" on Mr. Chowdhuri

The *Statesman* is naturally delighted with Mr. A. Chowdhuri's declaration in favour of leaving politics out of our programme. Here at least, cries the Friend of India, is a leader after our own heart. No doubt it would be extremely convenient for the Friend of India and its countrymen if Indians did give up their political aspirations and leave Anglo-India in undisputed possession of the field, but we do not think the friendly yearnings of the *Statesman* are likely to be gratified. Mr. Chowdhuri's message fell flat even in his own Pabna. At the same time our contemporary seems hardly to have taken the trouble to understand the speech of his new protégé. He fastens on the powerful indictment of the present system of education which is the most striking portion of Mr. Chowdhuri's address, and warmly approves of it. But he mildly rebukes the speaker for pinning his hopes on the new system of National Education which is gradually spreading throughout Bengal and advises him to transfer his affections to the old University. National Education will be a failure, says the Chowringhee prophet; Indians are too selfish and unpatriotic to make it a success. What then is to be done? Why, give up agitating for political reform since our agitation is so obviously a failure and begin agitating for educational reform. It is a luminous idea. After having wasted a century begging the British government to reform their administration, we are to waste another century begging them to reform their educational system, — with equal futility. The Government cannot give us a reformed and modern system of education for obvious reasons. It would mean the growth of highly-trained specialists who would immediately demand to be employed in preference to aliens, and either the bread of so many Europeans would be taken out of their mouths or there would be a fresh cause of discontent. It would equip Indians to oust the white man from his lucrative monopoly of commerce and trade and kill British trade in India by the development of indigenous industries. It would mean the transformation of our people into a highly-trained and well-equipped nation who would certainly not submit to Mr. Morley's personal and absolute

British control. Anything short of this would not meet Mr. Chowdhuri's ideal; but anything like this the bureaucracy could not give us without committing suicide. The *Statesman* has not, as we said, cared to understand Mr. Chowdhuri. He is for dropping politics, but he is also for self-help and denounces mendicancy. We fear the *Statesman* will have to look farther for its ideal Bengali leader. Why not try Sankharitola?

Bande Mataram, June 26, 1907

"Legitimate Patriotism"

LORD Minto has given us the historic expression "honest Swadeshi", and it was reserved for an Anglo-Indian publicist to startle the English-knowing world by an equally significant expression, "legitimate patriotism". Honesty, legitimacy and other kindred words of the English vocabulary are being newly interpreted by the Anglo-Indian bureaucrats and publicists. The natural sentiments and aspirations of men are to be regulated according to their convenience and notions.

If you give preference to the indigenous products of the country and ask your friends, relatives and countrymen to do the same, you are dishonest. This is stretching the meaning of honesty to suit the moral sense of our alien and benevolent despots. Today we hear from another Anglo-Indian Sir Oracle, the *Daily News* of Calcutta, that there is such a thing as legitimate patriotism. We have looked up the dictionaries to profit by the enlightenment so kindly vouchsafed to us, but we have failed in our efforts. According to Webster, patriotism covers all activities to zealously guard the *authority* and interest of one's country and we are at a loss to understand how what the Indians have hitherto done or proposed to do to ensure the authority and interest of their country can be stigmatised as illegitimate. We on the contrary believe, and that according to the best authority, that the patriotism which has hitherto wrested from Mr. Morley only an expanded Council with an official majority and a comic advisory Board of Notables, falls far short of the standard of lexicographers. Patriotism will never rest satisfied till it has recovered the authority of the country, however much the Anglo-Indians try to twist its meaning and implications.

If it is patriotic for an Englishman to say, as their greatest poet has said, that this England never did nor shall lie at the proud feet of a conqueror, why should it be unpatriotic and seditious for an Indian to give expression to a similar sentiment? If it is highly patriotic for a Roman "to die in defence of his father's ashes and the temples of his gods", why should it be madness and senseless folly for an Indian to be stirred by a similar impulse? If "self-defence is the bulwark of all rights", as Lord Byron has said, why should an Indian journalist be charged with an attempt to incite to violence when he asks his countrymen of East Bengal to defend the honour of their women at any cost? If Campbell is right in saying that virtue is the spouse of liberty, why should an Indian be exposed to the menace of siege-guns when entering on a legitimate and lawful struggle for the recovery of his lost freedom? If each noble aim repressed by long control expires at last or feebly mans the soul, why should not our countrymen benefit by the advice of Goldsmith and begin to chafe at the attempt to prolong this alien control? If Tennyson is justified in taking a pride in his country which freemen till, which sober-suited Freedom chose, where girt with friends or foes, a man may speak the thing he will, where freedom slowly broadens down from precedent to precedent, why should it be criminal on the part of an Indian to imagine a similar future for the land of his birth? It will not do to fling in our face the mockery of glittering generalities or blazing ubiquities of natural right with which they ridiculed the Declaration of Independence by the American colonists in 1776. Man cannot escape the influence of these glittering generalities and blazing ubiquities; the literatures of peoples who struggled for independence in former ages have always abounded with them and the awakened East must also talk in the same language. When some mighty sentiments dominate the human breast, they give rise to language which runs the risk of being scouted as mere platitude, they give rise to activities and demonstrations which are in danger of being traced to illegitimate sources. The students of Rajahmundry wore "Bande Mataram" badges, shouted "Bande Mataram" in the streets, gave a grand reception to a Nationalist speaker, formed themselves into a Balabharat Samiti, and the *Daily News* thinks all these to be the outcome of a patriotism hardly legitimate. What is then legitimate patriotism, pray? Our contemporary has given us no light on the point. We suppose it means a blind loyalty to the alien government, a helpless acquiescence in its most despotic measures, bowing our knee to every Anglo-

Indian, especially to the dicta of the Editor of the *Indian Daily News* and the *Englishman*. If we do not accept the ethics of the British and Anglo-Indian Press which calls the present patriotic movement immoral and ascribes it to the want of moral training in our schools and colleges, we may be guilty according to Anglo-Indian jurisprudence but the higher tribunal to whom alone all oppressed peoples look up, knows their hearts and shapes their destinies accordingly.

Bande Mataram, June 27, 1907

Personal Rule and Freedom of Speech and Writing

MR. John Morley is reported to have delivered himself of the following fatuity: "One of the most difficult experiments ever tried in human history was whether we could carry on personal government along with free speech and free right of public meeting," and he was cheered by the House. He might as well have said, "We are carrying on in India the most difficult experiment of hunting with the hounds and running with the hare," and no doubt he would have been applauded with the same enthusiasm. The average member of Parliament is gifted with no remarkable powers of understanding and such intelligence as they possess is never drawn upon in elucidation of matters Indian; and as there is a well-understood agreement between the two front benches that no real measure of liberty is to be given to India, the Secretary of State has a most enviable opportunity of saying anything he may please within the strict limits of such agreement about freedom of speech and similar topics, without the least fear of provoking any serious hostile criticism, and Mr. Morley has certainly taken his occasion by both hands.

Any power or privilege in order to deserve the title "free" must be based on the authority of an independent people possessing the supreme and ultimate power of control over its own government. It is this fundamental fact of self-government that must be their origin and sanction, and it is only in this sense that terms like "freedom of conscience" or "freedom of speech" are understood in the countries that actually enjoy them. Their 'freedoms' are the concrete expression, the sacred symbols, of the popular will that has realised its sovereignty and constitute the inviolable limitations under which the executive must work. They stand inaccessibly superior to the needs or wishes of those who actually carry on the government of the country; whose tenure of power primarily rests on their unquestioned submission to the sovereign will and freedom of the people as whose servants they administer. Take the situation in England during the late Boer War as an instance. Throughout that war the Pro-Boers carried on their propaganda all over the country without the least let or hindrance from the Cabinet or the administrative authorities, however much they might have desired to coerce them into silence. John Morley himself was the most outspoken exponent of those who sympathised with the Boers and denounced the war, but no ukase could reach him nor any Emergency Act hurry him out of England.

But when the right of spontaneous articulation comes as a gift from a foreign despotism with no limits on the power of its Executive, instead of proceeding from the consent and conviction of the people governed, it becomes then a mere licence strictly similar in kind to any other of the species, for example, a licence issued by the Excise Department. It is held during pleasure, the giving and the taking of it having not the least reference to the people's wishes. In fact the word "right" has no meaning in a subject country. A right can only be where the people are "free", and signifies some inalienable incident of citizenship the recognition of which is an absolute obligation on the Government. The things that masquerade in a country like India under the name of rights, are only concessions of might qualified by prudence and what is conceded in the prudential exercise of despotic power will be withdrawn out of the same consideration, the people remaining equally helpless before and after. The proclamation that is now brooding in a death-like hush over the Punjab and East Bengal is the amplest confirmation of the foregoing lines and disposes finally of the sickening cant of John Morley about the coexistence of free speech and personal rule. The freedom of a subject race is only the freedom to starve and die, all the rest of its existence being on sufferance from those who govern.

The pseudo sophies of the Radical philosopher who now rules our destinies, bear however some ugly results. They give in the first place a splendid opportunity to unblushing journals like the *Times* for insolent dissertations on the enlightened and democratic character of the Government that England has founded in the Orient and for illusory comparisons between the Indian Government and any other Government that might have possibly been established in this country if England had not come to bless her with her beneficent rule, the result of which is to place India in an entirely false light before the civilised world. They also fill the Briton, endowed by Nature with more than the ordinary mortal's share of pride, with an intoxicating sense of exultation as he thinks of the noble work his countrymen are carrying on in India. But far worse than all this is the poison they instil into the minds of those immoderate lovers of England in general, and John Morley in particular, who are known as Moderates amongst us hereby constantly borrowing from the language of English constitutionalism in order to designate the gewgaws given them by the Government. They have gradually deluded themselves into the belief that Indians possess like Englishmen the real incidents of citizenship and such belief hardens into a dogma when Mr. Morley lends it his sanction. The Queen's Proclamation becomes in the borrowed phraseology of the Moderate the Magna Charta of India; the indulgence granted to a subject people to ventilate their grievances is transmuted by the same jugglery of language into freedom of speech and writing, his membership of a helpless Dependency he must persist in describing as the citizenship of the Empire. No matter that the whole world laughs at him in utter contempt, and calls him a fool. There are two things that his English education and his reading of Morley have not given him — the sense of history and the sense of humour. And when a proclamation descends like thunder and shatters all his pretentious nonsense to slivers, he clings nevertheless to his illusion and blames the Extremist for having brought on the catastrophe by his foolhardiness. He weeps and wails because he has lost his primary right of citizenship without a moment's thought on the fact that he has neither rights nor citizenship, and that such things cannot be taken away by a Government. He has read in the history of free countries, but read in vain, that right and citizenship have behind them a sacred tradition of sacrifice, even to the shedding of blood, on a loyal adequate recognition of which their Government is founded. The Moderate does not see that what has been withdrawn from him by the proclamation is no such right as he pretends to have had, but the mere opportunity conceded by the master to the helot to pour forth his unavailing complaint. He confuses sufferance with freedom, the favour of a foreign despotism with the right of citizenship, and his ambition is to win liberty by a whimper. Unless he relearns History and undeceives himself, he will always remain unfit for freedom, a hindrance to his country, a mere dupe of Morleyism, the subject of utter scorn for the nations that are free. What he adores as liberty is a sorry sordid, delusive mask, not the high-throned, stern, exacting Goddess whose one incessant, unambiguous demand resounds through History and ever pierces across the night of time to the heart of the Indian who would worship her — "*Main bhukha hun, main bhukha hun.*"

Bande Mataram, June 28, 1907

The Acclamation of the House

A GREAT deal is being made in the Anglo-Indian press of the unanimous appreciation with which the House of Commons received Mr. Morley's speech on the Budget. The discovery that superior culture has not destroyed the primitive savage in the Anglo-Saxon has been welcomed with fierce gratification. One English paper writes: — "It was a healthy sign to which the attention of native sedition-mongers may be usefully directed that the House of Commons which gave an appreciative reception to the speech of the Secretary of State showed impatience at the captious and mischievous vapourings of Mr. C. J. O'Donnell." Well, but why draw attention to it? We have been arguing the same thing from the very beginning of our propaganda. We were among the first to point out to a too credulous nation that the friends of India in Parliament represented nobody but themselves. It was one of the principal items on the destructive side of the Nationalist programme, to prove the delusiveness of the prevalent faith in the ultimate sense of justice of the British people. If the House of Commons saves us the trouble of farther argument and itself conclusively proves the soundness of our reasoning, we accept its assistance with gratitude but without surprise. We may draw the attention of our monitor in return to an equally healthy sign in India. Nobody now, at least in Bengal, ventures in public to advocate an appeal to the bureaucracy or to the people in England for the redress of our grievances. There may not be agreement as to the best means of gathering strength by self-help but the hope of gaining rights and privileges by what is known as constitutional agitation has been given up by one and all. It is a faded superstition which has no longer any hold on the Indian mind. To warn us that the highly illiberal speech of Mr. Morley struck a responsive chord in every bosom in the House is therefore labour wasted. As nobody now looks with wistful eyes to that quarter, it is immaterial what they think or do. They may go into ecstasies over the speech of Morley, or they may gnash their teeth at the vapourings of O'Donnell; we in India are no longer affected by their frown or by their smile. The sympathy of people beyond the seas is no longer our guiding star and what happens at Westminster is no concern of ours. We have to improvise our own means of meeting the Regulation lathi and other bureaucratic means of repression and we neither hope for nor desire its mitigation.

If it were possible for anyone to re-evoke that dead phantom of a phantom, British sympathy, we should not be grateful to him for constraining our unbound spirit into bonds again. The legend of British sympathy misled us for a century and now that the phantasm has of itself ceased to haunt us, let no one try to juggle and deceive us again with the Mantras of that modern black art. Both Mr. Morley's speech and its effect on the British people are, we repeat, matters of supreme indifference to us, and the British and Anglo-Indian journals who want to frighten us into our old mendicant attitude by trumpeting the "sensible and resolute speech" of Mr. Morley and the appreciation it received in the House, merely show that they have no true conception of the Nationalist movement. The mind of our people has at last attained a certain amount of freedom. Faith in unrealities no longer clogs its progress. The Budget speech admirably exposed the true relation between England and India and betrayed the hollowness of the so-called liberal professions which have so long exerted their poisonous influence on the unsophisticated Indian mind, displaced as it was from its own orbit by an unnational education. Mr. Morley's outspokenness was welcome to the House? Well, it was tenfold more welcome to his "enemies" in India. Mr. Lalmohan Ghose in one of his more recent speeches, has said: "Dazzled by the meretricious glitter of a tawdry imperialism, conspicuous members of Parliament are now trying to sponge from their slate the teachings of men like Gladstone and Bright." It was reserved for Mr. Morley to tell all India what some of us had perceived long ago, that those teachings were never meant to be carried out in practice.

Whoever is a scourge of India must naturally be a demigod to the British people. The political instinct of a free people long accustomed to the international struggle for life, shrewd, commercial, practical, is not likely to be misled by humanitarian generalities as the politically inexperienced middle class in India have been misled; they have always felt that the man who trod down India under a mailed heel and crushed Indian manhood and aspiration was serving their own interests.

The sequel to the trial of Warren Hastings is an excellent example of this dominant instinct. Twenty-seven years after the impeachment, sixteen years after the death of Burke had left his orations as a classic to English literature, — a scene was enacted in the House of Commons similar in spirit to the unanimous acclamation of Mr. Morley's speech. Warren Hastings — an old man of eighty — appeared at the bar to give evidence in connection with the renewal of the East India Charter. He was received with acclamations, a chair was ordered for him, and when he retired the members rose and uncovered. The political instinct of the people perceived that this man, ruthless and monstrous tyrant though he had been, had consolidated for them a political Empire and basis of commercial supremacy, and the means by which this great work had been accomplished, were sanctified by the result. The scourge of India, a recital of whose misdeeds had 27 years before made some of Burke's listeners swoon with horror, was honoured as a hero and god, and biographies and histories have been written by the score to justify his action and exalt him to the skies. When therefore Mr. Morley declared his intention of preserving the Empire Hastings had consolidated, by any means however unjust or tyrannical, is it any wonder that an English House of Commons should recognise in him a worthy successor of Hastings and accord to him an unanimous applause?

Bande Mataram, July 2, 1907

Europe and Asia

THE London correspondent of a contemporary quotes, with the apposite change of a word, some verses from a poem by Wilfrid Blunt which so admirably express the basic motive of the Nationalist movement in India that we reproduce it here. It is often represented by our opponents that the cry for Swaraj is a mere senseless cry for freedom without any recognition of the responsibilities of freedom. This is not so. Those who have followed the exposition of the Nationalist ideal in *Bande Mataram* know well that we advocate the struggle for Swaraj, first, because Liberty is in itself a necessity of national life and therefore worth striving for for its own sake; secondly, because Liberty is the first indispensable condition of national development intellectual, moral, industrial, political (we do not say it is the only condition) — and therefore worth striving for for India's sake; thirdly, because in the next great stage of human progress it is not a material but a spiritual, moral and psychical advance that has to be made and for this a free Asia and in Asia a free India must take the lead, and Liberty is therefore worth striving for for the world's sake. India must have Swaraj in order to live; she must have Swaraj in order to live well and happily; she must have Swaraj in order to live for the world, not as a slave for the material and political benefit of a single purse-proud and selfish nation, but as a free people for the spiritual and intellectual benefit of the human race.

The verses quoted are from a poem called *The Wind and the Whirlwind* addressed to England. England, by her oppression of the Asiatic peoples under her sway, by her selfish and ruthless exploitation of their wealth, by her refusal to allow them the chance of national life and free development, is sowing the wind, and she will reap the whirlwind in the loss of her Empire, perhaps in national decay and death.

"Truth yet shall triumph in a world of justice;
This is of faith. I swear it. East and West
The law of Man's progression shall accomplish
Even this last great marvel with the rest.

Thou wouldst not further it. Thou canst not hinder.
If thou shalt learn in time, thou yet shalt live.
But God shall ease thy hand of thy dominion
And give to these the rights thou wouldst not give.

The nations of the East have left their childhood.
Thou art grown old. Their manhood is to come;
And they shall carry on Earth's high tradition
Through the long ages when thy lips are dumb,

Till all shall be wrought out. O lands of weeping,
Lands watered by the rivers of old Time,
Ganges and Indus and the streams of Eden,
Yours is the future of the world's sublime.

Yours was the fount of man's first inspiration,
The well of wisdom whence he earliest drew.
And yours shall be the floodtime of his reason,
The means of strength which shall his strength renew.

The wisdom of the West is but a madness,
The fret of shallow waters in their bed.
Yours is the flow, the fullness of man's patience,
The ocean of God's rest inherited.

And thou, too, India, mourner of the nations,
Though thou hast died today in all men's sight,
And though upon thy cross with thieves thou hangest,
Yet shall thy wrong be justified in right."

The view of the East as just emerging from its childhood and the West as old and senile, is contrary to received ideas, but there is a deep truth underlying it. The East is more ancient by many thousands of years than the West, but a greater length of years does not necessarily imply a more advanced age. The years which would mean only childhood to a long-lived species would bring old age and death to more ephemeral stocks. Asia is long-lived, Europe brief, ephemeral. Asia is in everything hugely mapped, immense and grandiose in its motions, and its life-periods are measured accordingly. Europe lives by centuries, Asia by millenniums. Europe is parcelled out in nations, Asia in civilisations. The whole of Europe forms only one civilisation with a common, derived and largely second-hand culture; Asia supports three civilisations, each of them original and of the soil. Everything in Europe is small, rapid and short-lived; she has not the secret of immortality. Greece, the chief source of her civilisation, matured in two or three centuries, flourished for another two, and two more were sufficient for her decline and death. How few in years are the modern European nations, yet Spain is already dead, Austria death-stricken and suffering from gangrene and disintegration, France overtaken by a mortal and incurable malady, England already affected by the initial processes of decay. Germany and America alone show any signs of a healthy and developing manhood. In the place which is left vacant by the decline of the European nations Asia young, strong, and vigorous, dowered with the gift of immortality and the secret of self-transmutation, is preparing to step forward and possess the future. She alone can teach the world the secret of immortality which she possesses and in order that she may do so, she must reign.

Asia has been described by the Europeans as decrepit; they will find to their amazement and dismay that she is rather emerging into her age of robust and perfect manhood. It is true that she reached ages ago heights of science, philosophy, civilisation which Europe is now toilfully trying to reach and that afterwards there was a slackening down, loss and disturbance from which she is only now recovering, but there was no decay or decline. It was rather the disturbance, the temporary arrest, disorganisation and derangement which marks the transition from boyhood to manhood. Her mighty civilisations, her great philosophies, her acute scientific observations and intuitions were the toys and games of her yet immature and imperfect powers, the light and easy play of a child-giant, and form merely a slight index of the far greater things she will accomplish in the coming days of her ripe strength and maturity. What she did, she did by the activity of intention and imagination, the first free penetrating sympathy of a mind fresh from the divine source of life. She will now learn the scientific method of the adult and senescent West and apply it with a far greater force and ability to lines of development in which Europe is a bungler and novice,

The wisdom of the West is but a madness,
The fret of shallow waters in their bed.

This shallowness proceeds from the fact that the West has developed materially and on the surface, but has not sought for strength and permanence in the deeper roots of life of which our outer activity is only a partial manifestation. The fundamental difference between East and West has been exemplified more than once in recent times. What European nation could have changed its whole political, social and economic machinery in a few years like Japan, with so little trouble, with such thoroughness and science, with the minimum of disturbance to its national economy? The phenomenon is so alien to European nature and European experience that even to this day Western observers have been unable to understand it. Japan is a "weird" nation, that is all the conclusion they can come to on the subject. What European nation again would deal so swiftly, directly and earnestly with its own national vices as the Chinese are dealing with the opium vice in China? The very idea that China really meant it was incredible to English observers. And well it might be, for one can imagine what would be the fate of any such attempt to deal with the national vice of drunkenness in England. If India is unable to show such signal triumphs, it is because she has been disorganised by the merciless pressure of the alien rule and all her centres of strength and action destroyed or disabled. Yet even so, she has shown and is still showing signs of a prolonged and unconquerable vitality such as no nation subject for an equally long time has evinced since history began. It is this moral strength, this ability to go to the roots, this gift of diving down into the depths of self and drawing out the miraculous powers of the Will, this command over one's own soul which is the secret of Asia. And he who is in possession of his soul, the Scripture assures us, shall become the master of the world.

Bande Mataram, July 3, 1907

English Obduracy and Its Reason

WE seriously invite our Moderate friends to ask themselves for a reason as to why Englishmen should invariably meet all their demands for political reforms with the one unalterable answer that they are not fit to receive them. Why should John Morley whose writings and sayings are so instinct with an ardent love of liberty, so lightly flout their prayer for some concessions of a democratic nature? He not only denies the Indians the least measure of liberty, but shuts the door of any possible hope abruptly in their face by telling them that as long as his imagination can travel into futurity so long must India remain under personal rule. In his last Budget speech also he took the opportunity to reiterate his faith in the efficacy of personal rule for India and even went a step further and indulged in the paternal prophecy that if the English left India today, she would plunge back into rapine, bloodshed and chaos within a week. Naturally a Secretary of State who entertains such a low opinion of the Indian character would consider it the maximum of human folly to give Indians any control over the government of their country. And the opinion of Mr. Morley only too truly represents that of the general body of the Europeans who have ever come into contact with India or thought about the problem she presents before humanity. The question is why should they all have arrived at this poor estimate of the Indian's political capability? The answer, however, is not far to seek; we have only ourselves to thank for this cosmopolitan contempt into which we have brought our country. The European remains today essentially as he was in the time of Aristotle, "a political animal". His nature has retained throughout history its ingrained and inalienable political bent; polity has played the greatest part in the moulding of his life and destiny; the ideas that have irresistibly moved him to heroic strivings, passionate hopes or death-defying sufferings have been mainly those of independence, freedom, liberty; the greatest names in his history are those of political heroes or governors; the one call that has ever sung truly in his ears and commanded his unquestioning obedience is the call to the service of his country; the courting of death for the fulfilment or the upholding of the above ideas has been as natural to him as breathing; the history of his country is the history of the increasing consummation of those ideas, in which faith and intellect have filled a subsidiary place. Such is the European by constitution. To him India is an insoluble riddle. How a country of three hundred million men can consent to be governed by a handful of foreigners he simply cannot understand. He thinks of the Indian as the member of a sub-human race, outside the pale of his privileges, his code of morality, his civilisation. And that new-fangled specimen of the Indian race, the educated Indian, only intensifies his contempt. That a man who has been nurtured in the literature of England, and has read the history of Europe, can still have failed to be touched by the European ideal, to be visited by an insatiable longing for liberty, and can continue, on the other hand, in a life of contented acquiescence in foreign rule, and feel happy and proud merely to serve under it and ensure its continuation, strikes the native of Europe as a most monstrous mockery, as some unimaginable and unaccountable perversion of human nature. He gradually gets to believe that whatever may be the excellence of his domestic life or the greatness of his philosophy, the Indian is by birth fit only to be a slave, and education succeeds in perfecting him only in the art of slavery. And as slavery means to the European the permanent extinction of all the nobler possibilities that lie before man, servile India ceases altogether to engage his least consideration or enlist his sympathy; let her alone with her slave's philosophy and art, thinks he, she can be of no service to the future of the human race.

And the politics and politicians of India heighten further his convictions about the lowering nature and effect of slavery, and the impossibility of India ever lifting herself to the level of civilised humanity. Her politics are the slave's politics whose method is prayer and petition and whose resentment or disapproval can find expression only in weeping and sobbing. And rebuff merely urges the Indian politician to greater efforts of supplication and to higher feats of wailing. And by such persistent mendicancy alone he aspires to win his country's liberty — liberty to which Europe has wilfully waded her way through a welter of blood after her struggles of centuries. No, cries the irritated European, India can never be fit to govern herself. This is the secret of John Morley's point-blank refusal to satisfy Moderate aspirations; he has thrown to them a plaything or two, for they deserve nothing better. And because Mr. Morley loves and prizes liberty more highly than the average man, therefore has he been the more intolerant of the Moderate's pretensions, the more merciless in felling to the ground all his cherished delusions based on his inverted conception of liberty. The Partition of Bengal Mr. Morley admits to be a wrong, but he will not undo it because it is a settled fact; in other words, in dealing with dependent India he refuses to observe the rules of political morality which he has himself so clearly enunciated; in enunciating them, he would say, he had in contemplation only the rights and obligations that arise between one free people and another, and not the relationship between a ruling race and their abjectly servile subjects. All his other pronouncements point to the same moral. And have we not heard of the common English labourer who on being harangued eloquently by a Moderate Missionary about Indian grievances asked him bluntly if he was really relating the true state of affairs, and on being answered in the affirmative told the Missionary without much ceremony that a people who could submit to such wrongs and could think of nothing better than the sending of representatives to England to plead for their removal, fully deserved to be ruled by an arbitrary despotism? Unknowingly perhaps he was summarising the verdict of the civilised world on Indian politics. The money-making middle class in England say the same thing, and further strengthen their argument with the interesting inquiry, "What is to become of our boys if we leave the management of India in your hands?" The man from the Continent or America asks plainly, "How can the whole three hundred million of you be kept under by 70,000 tommies?"

Ought not all this to give our Moderate friends furiously

to think? We can appreciate the humanity of their desire to emancipate the country without dragging her through the red horror of a revolution. But let them reconsider how best to achieve this end. Surely their failure to obtain anything worth having after thirty years of patient supplication culminating in the supreme tragedy of the refusal of John Morley, the one man of whom they had expected more than of any other — even to listen to their prayers with any seriousness, ought to impel them to some introspective inquiry regarding the soundness of their political faith. We also invite their thoughts to the changing attitude of England and of the whole world towards India since the declaration of the Boycott and the rise of the New Party. We conjure the Moderate to spend his best and sincerest thoughts on these two most vital topics; and once he has begun to *think*, we know the days of his creed are numbered, and there can be but one party in India, the Nationalists.

Bande Mataram, July 11, 1907

Work and Speech

We often hear that the time for speeches has gone by and action, silent, strenuous, sacrificing action is all that is necessary at the present moment. Denunciation of speeches has almost passed into a fashion and to rescue at least a certain class of speeches from undeserved contempt is a duty we owe to the speakers and the country they are serving no less by their speech than by other kinds of activity.

Those who happen to be in any kind of touch with the people will agree with us when we say that there is no consensus of opinion even amongst the educated section as to the wisdom of pursuing a great and bold ideal or our capacity of making the least possible progress towards its realisation. The indifference towards all patriotic activities still too common is not infrequently the result of a total lack of grasp of the situation and of the lines of activity which the situation demands. Most people are so immersed in their own affairs, so much oppressed by the anxieties and cares of the average life that they cannot study for themselves the actual condition of the country, the causes that have brought about its miseries and the true way of escape from them. Much help can be obtained from them if they are once convinced that many of our ills are the necessary results of subjection and everyone who desires to leave his country better than he found it, should either by thought or action, help the assertion of a separate national existence and an administration which can maintain and perfect such an existence. We have until now resigned ourselves to the absolute sway of a small alien body and by passive obedience had almost rid ourselves of the capacity for political animation. Real self-examination, real study of our political condition and the endeavour to discover a practical line of work which will build up a free nation, have only begun. If therefore the need for action is great, the need for speech is not yet over. Speech in itself is an instrument for good and not a mere waste of energy. But what we need is that the speeches shall be by men who can think, see and feel and not by mere mouthers of political commonplaces and unrealities. Patriotic propagandists who understand the situation themselves and have formed a tolerably good idea as to how work should begin can always make converts who will help them in promoting the cause. But mere declaimers who have no light to give, but rather give out mere darkness and confuse practical issues, have brought and will continue to bring the gift of speech into discredit and alienate public sympathy from propagandist work. But after all propagandist work has only begun. In Bengal, Barisal is the best-organised district; by a successful organisation of propaganda and moral pressure the Boycott has been almost a complete success. Yet we have been informed that the masses have not been reached and the opposition offered by a section of them must be put down to this deficiency of missionary work. It is therefore clear that there is still much to be done in this direction of bringing home to our people the necessity of the Boycott and kindred activities. And for this purpose we want men whose ideas are clear and who can act as an inspiring force by pouring into their speech the strength of a convicted intellect and a powerfully moved heart and will. They must radiate the light from a highly reflective surface. A fine illustration is the Shivaji address of Mr. Tilak recently delivered at Poona. The force and effectiveness of the address has been acknowledged in the editorial columns of journals like the *Indian Patriot* of Madras. Mr. Tilak took the occasion of the Shivaji celebration to make it clear that we are all being moved by a mighty impulse, by a natural aspiration and to desist from its forceful expression for fear of consequences is not only unmanly but prejudicial to the best interests of the country. Now such a pronouncement can only come from one with whom the aspiration is a guiding reality of his life and who is so much possessed by the certainty of its realisation as to be careless of the persecutions and sufferings its pursuit must involve. The Maratha leader does not conceal truth in the hope of conciliating the bureaucracy nor resort to such diplomacy on the platform as may obscure the purity of the ideal or demoralise the ardour of its pursuit in his followers. His admirable judgment saves him from utterances which may imperil the cause either by excess or by unseasonable reservations. A courageous and clear-sighted utterance which inspires and gives nerve and strength to the hearer, it observes the limitations which our own environments impose on our speech and actions. Powerfully directing the mind to the goal in view, emphasising the necessity of a perfect sacrifice, there is no touch in it of irresponsibility, no froth and foam of mere unmeaning rhetoric. The extreme course is not concealed; the sacrifice is not excused; but nothing is demanded of us which our present capacities and surroundings do not warrant.

Nothing, for instance, can be better than the exposition of the use and meaning of the national festivals which have now become a part of our public life. Helpful to the cultivation of courage — such courage as the appreciation of heroes securing their salvation against odds can give, they are not held for raising the standard of revolt; not because revolt is in itself a thing accursed, — no such loyalist cant is to be expected from a true Nationalist leader, — but because it is not under present circumstances either possible or necessary; for neither have we the means to revolt nor have we yet exhausted all possibilities of action within the law. Speeches of such an admirable temper shedding a dry light, as the *Indian Patriot* well says, fearless, cogent, outspoken and statesmanlike — who shall say that they are no longer needed, or that action can long endure in our present stage of preparation if we deliberately deny ourselves the stimulus of such utterances? The cry for work, the cry against mere noise we can sympathise with, but the cry against public propaganda has no meaning. No great movement has ever been able to do without it.

Bande Mataram, July 12, 1907

From Phantom to Reality

THE action of the omnipotent and irresponsible executive in obstructing District Conferences alike in the proclaimed and unproclaimed areas of Bengal ought to carry home to every mind, however persistent in self-deception, the absurdity of vaunting the rights and privileges of a subject people. There is a taunt writ large over these ukases and it is this: "Fools and self-deceivers who think that rights can be held as the gift of a superior! Nothing is a right till it has been purchased by sacrifices as great as the aspiration is high. You were allowed to speak and pass resolutions so long as speeches and resolutions were all; but now that you are breaking the tacit contract by turning your movement into a serious thing, we order you to be silent and disperse." *Māyā* dies hard. Illusion is the chief obstacle to salvation, man clings to illusions by a natural impulse; but to rid oneself of them is the beginning of wisdom. Illusions have long stood in the way of our political salvation and the lingering faith of our prominent men in persistent constitutional agitation, even when the alien bureaucracy stands completely unmasked before our eyes, is an illustration of the obstinate cherishing of illusions. The Magistrate prohibits the holding of the District Conference at Khulna. The High Court is moved and the illegal ukase is precipitately withdrawn: but the withdrawal was merely a change of tactics. A bureaucracy never lacks pretexts to harass the undesirables. The promoters of the Conference are now on their trial for making seditious speeches in the Conference.

At Faridpur a local leader, whose faith in the ultimate good sense of the autocratic rulers has outlived even the recent violent strain, arranged for a District Conference on a grand scale notwithstanding the protests of a section of the public against holding meetings with permission from the Police. As the recent District Conferences, though compromising our self-respect to a certain extent, have at last been justified by their results, we have preferred not to press the point of honour. We have submitted to the Ordinance by not holding meetings; Faridpur and Pabna carry their weakness a little further, that is all. And on the whole it was well that the attempt to hold the Conference was made. For the Faridpur leaders adopted to a certain extent the Nationalist programme and have, as a consequence, come in conflict with the bureaucracy. The prohibitory ukase of the Magistrate of Faridpur leaves no doubt as to the attitude of the bureaucracy towards opposition in any form. They demand a tame acquiescence in their arbitrary regulations and are determined to put down any expression of adverse opinion under the pretext of preventing the spread of disaffection and the disturbance of public tranquillity. Is further explicitness wanted? Cultivate the art of "wooing", hold meetings to issue loyalist manifestos or celebrate the Empire Day, but if you are audacious enough to express your discontent, the British truncheon is ready for you. This is the whole meaning of these ukases; this is the moral repeatedly inculcated through the various prohibitory circulars. As the old superstitions have still their hold on some minds, we welcome the repetition of such browbeating. But in the meantime we must not fail to turn them to account. If we are not capable of offering any active opposition to the encroachment on our natural rights, the intensified sense of wrong should at least give a healthy direction to the patriotic efforts of all. From such continued rebuffs we should draw the energy and inspiration to work out our national well-being on independent lines. Every fresh blow should impart a greater impetus to the Boycott, to National Education, to the organisation of discontent, with a view to leaving the aliens severely alone. But hitherto our Moderate friends have rather been anxious to ram their heads more vigorously against the stone wall of bureaucracy than to learn by their failure the necessity of taking our own road. They still persist in trying to resurrect the dead phantom of British sympathy and good will. Henceforth they should seek rather the resurrection of our own national strength and greatness. When Lord Curzon aimed his first blow at self-government by giving his seal of approval to the Calcutta Municipal Bill, the *Pratibasi* published a cartoon exposing the unsubstantial nature of our rights and privileges. The Calcutta Municipality was represented as a shrouded corpse surrounded by weeping relatives to whom a *padre* with the physiognomy of Sir John Woodburn soothingly remarked, "The Lord hath given, the Lord hath taken away; blessed be the name of the Lord." It drew forth from the *Pioneer* the following retort: "The quaint conceit might have been rounded off by some hope of future resurrection." This false hope which the bureaucracy till now sedulously fostered, has been a curse to the country. Privileges granted as favours have no true life in them; they are mere illusions and what is the use of striving for the fitful return, of ghosts who are again bound to disappear? Let *māyā* pass out of us, let the illusions die; let us turn with clear eyes and sane minds from these pale and alien phantoms to the true reality of our Mother as she rises from the living death of a century, and in her seek our only strength and our sufficient inspiration.

Swadeshi in Education

There is an interesting article in the *Modern Review* on Swadeshi in Education, interesting not only because of the subject and its importance, or of the undoubted thought and ability which has been devoted to the subject, but also and still more because of the limitations of the present education to which it bears striking evidence. The mind trained by the present system of education, even when it is somewhat above the average, is almost invariably deficient in practicality and the robustness to shake off cherished superstitions and face and recognise facts. The attempt at Swadeshi Education under the official Universities has been made both in Calcutta and under particularly favourable circumstances at Poona. At Poona an immense amount of self-sacrifice went to the making of the New English School and the Ferguson College, and some of the best intellects and noblest hearts in the Deccan devoted themselves to the work. Yet the end was failure. The Ferguson College is in no way superior to any other institution in the Bombay University, although also in no way inferior. Its education is the same vicious and defective education — utterly unsuited to modern needs — academic, scrappy, unscientific, unpractical, unideal. It takes aid from the officials, submits to their dictation and excludes politics at their bidding. Yet the proposal of the *Modern Review* writer is merely to concentrate the best intellects of the country in the Poona Institution in order to make it "an Indian College superior to any existing College", and as summarily, dismisses the idea of a National University merely on the score of expense. We fail to see how this will meet the problem or how such an institution can really deserve the name of Swadeshi in Education. Swadeshi in Education does not mean teaching by Indian professors only or even management by Indians only. It means an education suited to the temperament and needs of the people fitted to build up a nation equipped for life under modern conditions and absolutely controlled by Indians. The proposed Model College might avail itself of the services of Drs. Bose and Ray and Ziauddin, but they would after all have to teach on the lines and up to the standard of the Bombay University and submit entirely to the rules and orders of the Bombay Government, as conveyed through an officialised Senate and Syndicate. We should still be confined within the vicious circle of which the writer complains. We should be no nearer "taking the higher education of this country into our own hands and ceasing to look to Englishmen for help" than we were thirty years ago. Independence is the first condition and any scheme which disregards it is doomed to failure.

Bande Mataram, July 13, 1907

Boycott and After

THE twentieth century dawned on a rising flood of renascent humanity surging over Asia's easternmost borders. The first report of it reached the astonished world in the victorious thunder of Japan. And it spread onward, this resurgent wave of human spirit, swiftly, irresistibly, overflooding in a sweeping embrace China, India, Persia and the farther West. India received the ablution of the holy waters singing her sacred hymn *Bande Mataram* that filled the spaces of heaven with joyous echoes heard of the Gods as of old — and the nations of the earth listened to the song of unfree India and knew what it was — a voice in the chorus of Asiatic liberty. The unpremeditated and spontaneous declaration of the Boycott was the declaration of the country's recovery to life from its death-swoon of centuries, of her determination to live her own life — not for a master, but for herself and for the world. All was changed. Patriotism, the half-understood catchword of platform oratory, passed out of its confinement into the heart of the people, — the priest and the prince and the peasant alike — giving to each that power of sacrifice which has now translated itself according to the confessions of the *Times* into the concrete fact of 42 million yards less of English cotton goods. And the demonstrations of the sixteenth of October joined in by the Hindu and the Mahomedan, the Buddhist, the Jain and the Sikh, the police and the people, through the mystic compulsion of an instinctive fraternity, was the enchanting prevision of the India to be. Such a vision is vouchsafed only to the man or the nation that stands on the threshold of emancipation; it came to the Rishi filling him with the immortal longing to be one with the Divine, to the medieval monk penetrating him with the life-long love of Christ, and it has ever come at the mature moment to the down-trodden peoples of the earth revealing to them in a flash the mission and the destination of their life. It remains but a moment, but those that have seen it can never forget or rest; they pursue the glory, even while it seems to recede into the distance, over the even and uneven walks of life, past the smiles of the tempter, through the prison-gate and exit, on through the jaws of death. Its effect on the individual is immediate, on a whole nation necessarily spread over a longer time during which the seer of it bears its message to him who has not seen. But the progress of the pursuit none can arrest till the vision is reached, realised and reinstalled in all the beauty of its first appearance. Ever since the Partition day, India has pressed on this path; the boycott of foreign goods, the return of the weaver to his loom, the dissociation of the people from the government, the strikes, the deluge of meetings all over the land, the insulting of the National leaders, the breaking up of the Barisal Conference, the dismissal of Fuller, the appointment of Hare, the persecution of boys, the dismissal of the school masters, who loved liberty more than money, the foundation of the National Council of Education, of National schools, the institution of technical education, the insolvency of dealers in Bideshi goods, the social ex-communication of anti-boycotters, the unbidden repetitions of the Rakhi-day first, the passing of the Swadeshi resolution by the Congress, the prosecution of the Punjabees, the Rawalpindi riot, the Mahomedan rowdyism in East Bengal, the loan to Salimullah, Newmania, the changed and respectful attiude of Anglo-Indians towards Indians, the deportation of Lajpat and Ajit Singh, the proclamation, the unmasking of English liberalism, the awakening of Madras, the prosecutions at Rajahmundry and Coconada, the continuing prosecution in the Punjab and Bengal, the admission by the *Times* of the success of the Boycott, the throwing of 150,000 English labourers out of employment, and the necessity of easing overstocked markets, are some of the landmarks of the country's progress. Before her now lies the valley of the shadow of death full of trials and unknown perils and temptations, but the light that leads her cannot fail; the inspiration of the Power that gives her strength is irresistible, superior to death; she will go on till the fulfilment of the vision of the 16th of October. There is a Divinity that has been shaping her ends — no mere might of man, for nothing but the renovating touch of Divinity can account for the difference between now and then, between the days before and after the Boycott.

Bande Mataram, July 15, 1907

The Khulna Comedy

THE result of a political case is always a foregone conclusion in this country in the present era of Anti-Swadeshi repression, for the object of the proceedings is not to detect and punish crime but to put down Swadeshi under the forms of law; whether the accused is innocent or guilty of the particular charge it has been thought convenient to formulate against him, is a matter of very trifling importance. Neither the people nor the bureaucracy really accept a conviction as proof of any offence against the law. Indeed it is more or less a matter of caprice or convenience whether one offence or another is selected. When the crime is not chosen with a view to the punishment it is desired to inflict, or the greater ease of securing evidence, or the necessity of convicting when there is no evidence, the problem is probably determined by the sense of humour of the prosecuting Magistrate or by an aesthetic perception of the fitness of things. Generally the Swadeshi worker is charged with sedition or assault or breach of the peace or wishing to break the peace, or thinking of doing something which somebody in authority pretends to believe likely to break the peace; but he might just as well be charged with burglary or abduction or with contempt of the Magistrate's Khansamah or with the Bengal stare or the Coconada grimace. The main object is to send him to prison or bind him over not to do any work for Swadeshi for six months or a year, and the pretext is a mere bagatelle. The real point is not whether the accused is innocent or guilty of the particular offence but whether he is innocent or guilty of Swadeshi, whether he is innocent or guilty of patriotism, whether he is innocent or guilty of Nationalism. For this reason no disgrace attaches to conviction, rather it is the passport to fame, honour and public esteem. The prosecution is a farce, the defence is a farce, and the judgment is the most exquisite farce of all. The bureaucracy go through the farce because they cling to the shadow of moral prestige even when the substance of it is gone; they like to adopt Russian methods, but they do not like them to be called Russian and still hug the delusion that by going through the legal forms of which Justice makes use they can cover the nakedness of their tyranny with the rags of law. The accused go through the farce with the sole object of so managing the defence as to dispel even the last shadow of the old moral prestige and to expose the nakedness of bureaucratic oppression more and more. It is a political fight with the law courts for its scene.

In no recent political case except Rawalpindi has the veil of law been so ridiculously thin as in the Khulna case. Partly, no doubt, this is due to the personal gifts of the prosecuting Magistrate who decided the case. Mr. Asanuddin Ahmed is a very distinguished man. The greatest and most successful achievement of his life was to be a fellow-collegian of Lord Curzon. But he has other sufficiently respectable if less gorgeous claims to distinction. Arithmetic, logic, English and Law are his chief fortes. His mastery over figures is so great that arithmetic is his slave and not his master; it is even said that he can assess a man at Rs. 90 one day and bring him down 200 per cent in estimation the other. It is whispered that it was not only for a masterly general incompetence but also for this special gift that he was transferred to Khulna. His triumphant dealings with logic were admirably exampled by the original syllogism which he presented to the startled organisers of the District Conference. "I, Asanuddin, am the District Magistrate; the District Magistrate is the representative of the District; ergo, I, Asanuddin, am the one and only representative of the district. Now only a representative of the district has a right to hold a District Conference or to do anything in the name of the district, or to use any expression in which the word district occurs; I, Asanuddin, am the sole and only representative of the district; ergo, I, Asanuddin, have the sole and only right to call a District Conference." Mr. Ahmed's English is the delight of the judges of the High Court, who are believed to spend sleepless nights in trying to make out the meaning of his judgments. In one case at least, it is said, a distinguished judge had to confess with sorrow and humiliation that he could make nothing of the English of the learned Magistrate and after reading the judgment in the present case, we can well believe the story. As for his knowledge of law, the best praise we can give it is that it is on a level with his knowledge of, say, English. Such was the brilliant creature who appointed himself prosecutor, jury and judge in the Khulna sedition case.

Under such auspices the conduct of the case was sure to be distinguished by a peculiarly effulgent brilliancy. In order to prove that Venibhushan Rai talked sedition it was thought necessary to prove how many volunteers were present at the Conference. This is a fair example of the kind of evidence on which the case was decided and which the great Asanuddin declared to be particularly relevant. Beyond evidence of this stamp there was no proof against the accused except the evidence of police officers unsupported by any verbatim report, while on the other side were the statements of the respectable pleaders, the verbatim copy of the speech and a whole mass of unshaken testimony. But our one and only Asanuddin declared that the evidence of respectable men was not to be believed because they *were* respectable and graduates of the Calcutta University and partakers in the Conference; the police apparently were the only disinterested and truthful people in Khulna. But the most remarkable dictum of this remarkable man was that when one is charged with sedition it is not necessary to prove the use of any particular seditious utterances; it is quite enough for the Magistrate to come to the conclusion that something untoward might, could or should have happened as the result of the accused having made a speech. In fact, it is hardly necessary under the section as interpreted by Daniels of this kind, to prove anything against the accused; the only thing necessary is that the Magistrate should think it better for convenience official or unofficial that he should be bound over. The section answers the same purpose in minor cases which the Regulation of 1818 answers in the case of more powerful opponents of irresponsible despotism.

The Khulna case has been from the point of view of Justice an undress rehearsal of the usual bureaucratic comedy; from the point of view of Mr. Asanuddin Ahmed it has been a brilliant exhibition of his superhuman power of acting folly and talking nonsense; from the point of view of Srijut Venibhushan Rai it has been a triumph greater than any legal victory, a public certificate of patriotism, courage and sincerity, an accolade of knighthood and nobility in the service of the Motherland.

Bande Mataram, July 20, 1907

The Korean Crisis

The chorus of jubilation with which the English Press receives news of any danger to the last shred of independence of any ancient people is characteristic. The Koreans cannot see their way to acquiesce in Japanese rule, ergo, they are arch-intriguers. Europe in her present temper seems to be the most uncompromising enemy of the liberty of all peoples except her own. The disturbances that have followed the deputation to the Hague, the meeting of the Korean troops and the active participation of the populace in the same, seem to have filled Europe with a grim gratification at the prospect of Korea being placed permanently under the heel of Japan. Europe is a worshipper of success, and we need not wonder if she is glad to see an Eastern power taking a leaf out of her book, in threatening the liberty of Nations.

Bande Mataram, July 22, 1907

One More for the Altar

Srijut Bhupendranath Dutt has been sentenced to one year's rigorous imprisonment for telling the truth with too much emphasis. As to that we have nothing to say, for it is a necessary part of the struggle between Anglo-Indian bureaucracy and Indian democracy. The bureaucracy has all the material power in its hands and it must necessarily struggle to preserve its unjust and immoral monopoly of power by the means which material strength places in its hands, by the infliction of suffering on the bodies of its opponents and on their minds, so far as they allow the suffering of the body to affect the mind, by forcible interference with the outward expression of their feelings, by intimidation and a show of brute power and force. But if the bureaucracy has all the material power in its hands, the democracy has all the spiritual power, the power and force of martyrdom, of unflinching courage, of self-immolation for an idea. Spiritual power in the present creates material power in the future and for this reason we always find that if it is material force which dominates the present, it is spiritual which moulds and takes possession of the future. The despot in all ages can lay bonds and stripes and death on our body; his power is only limited by his will, for law is an instrument forged by himself and which he can turn to his own uses and morality is a thing which he regards not at all, or if he affects to regard it, he is cunning enough to throw a veil of words over his actions and mislead the distant and ill-informed opinion which is all he cares for. But if the despot can lay on the body the utmost ills of the scourge and the rack and the sword, if he can directly or indirectly plunder the goods of those who resist him and seek to crush them by wounding them in their dearest point of honour, the enthusiast for liberty can also turn suffering into strength, bonds into a glorious emancipation and death into the seed of a splendid and beneficent life. He can refuse to allow the tortures of the body to affect the calm and illumined strength of his soul where it sits, a Divine Being in the white radiance of its own self-existent bliss, rejoicing in all the glorious manifestations of its Will, rejoicing in its pleasures, rejoicing in its anguish, rejoicing in victory, rejoicing in defeat, rejoicing in life, rejoicing in death. For we in India who are enthusiasts for liberty, fight for no selfish lure, for no mere material freedom, for no mere economic predominance, but for our national right to that large freedom and noble life without which no spiritual emancipation is possible; for it is not among an enslaved, degraded and perishing people that the Rishis and great spirits can long continue to be born. And since the spiritual life of India is the first necessity of the world's future, we fight not only for our own political and spiritual freedom but for the spiritual emancipation of the human race. With such a glorious cause to battle for, there ought to be no craven weakness among us, no flinching, no coward evasion of the consequences of our action.

It is a mistake to whine when we are smitten, as if we had hoped to achieve liberty without suffering. To meet persecution with indifference, to take punishment quietly as a matter of course, with erect head and undimmed eyes, this is the spirit in which we must conquer.

Bande Mataram, July 25, 1907

The Issue

THE bureaucracy as usual has over-reached itself in instituting a case under the sedition clause against the editor of the *Yugantar*. The Punjabee prosecution did untold harm to their prestige and helped to shatter the not over-abundant remnants of their moral ascendancy; its work was negative and destructive. But the *Yugantar* prosecution has been a positive gain to the national cause; it has begun the positive work of building up the moral ascendancy of the people which is to replace that of the alien and nullify his mere material superiority. This momentous result the editor of the *Yugantar* has brought about by his masterly inactivity. His refusal to plead has been worth many sensational trials. It has produced an enormous effect on the public mind all over India, not only as an individual instance of moral courage and readiness to suffer quietly and simply, without ostentation and self-advertisement, as a matter of course and one's plain duty to the country, but as the first practical application in the face of persecution of the sheer uncompromising spirit of Swarajism. For the first time a man has been found who can say to the power of alien Imperialism, "With all thy pomp of empire and splendour and dominion, with all thy boast of invincibility and mastery irresistible, with all thy wealth of men and money and guns and cannon, with all thy strength of the law and strength of the sword, with all thy power to confine, to torture or to slay the body, yet for me, for the spirit, the real man in me, thou art not, thou art only a phase, a phenomenon, a passing illusion, and the only lasting realities are my Mother and my freedom."

It is well that we should understand the real issue which is not primarily one of law or of political forms and institutions, but a spiritual issue on which all others depend and from which they arise. The question is not whether one Bhupendranath Dutt published matter which he knew to be likely to bring the Government established by law, to wit certain mediocrities in Belvedere,

Darjeeling, Shillong or Simla who collectively call themselves the Government of Bengal or of India, into contempt or hatred or to encourage a desire to resist or subvert their lawful authority. If that were all, we might argue the question whether what he did was wise or what he wrote was true or mistaken, legal or illegal. As it is, these things do not matter even to the value of a broken cowrie. The real issue for us Nationalists is something quite different and infinitely more vital. It is this, "Is India free?" — not even "Shall India be free?" but, is India free and am I as an Indian free or a slave bound to the service, the behest or forced guidance of something outside and alien to myself and mine, something which is *anātman*, not myself? Am I, are my people part of humanity, the select and chosen temple of the Brahman, and entitled therefore to grow straight in the strength of our own spirit, free and with head erect before mankind, or are we a herd of cattle to live and work for others? Are we to live our own life or only a life prescribed and circumscribed for us by something outside ourselves? Are we to guide our own destinies or are we to have no destiny at all except nullity, except death? For it is nonsense to talk of other people guiding our destinies, that is only an euphemism for killing our destinies altogether; it is nonsense to talk of others giving us enlightenment, civilisation, political training, for the enlightenment that is given and not acquired brings not light but confusion, the civilisation that is imposed from outside kills a nation instead of invigorating it, and the training which is not acquired by our own experience and effort incapacitates and does not make efficient. The issue of freedom is therefore the only issue. All other issues are merely delusion and Maya, all other talk is the talk of men that sleep or are in intellectual and moral bondage.

We Nationalists declare that man is for ever and inalienably free and that we too are, both individually as Indian men and collectively as an Indian nation, for ever and inalienably free. As freemen we will speak the thing that seems right to us without caring what others may do to our bodies to punish us for being freemen, as freemen we will do what we think good for our country, as freemen we will educate ourselves in our own schools, settle our differences by our own arbitrators, sell and buy our own goods, build up our own character, our own civilisation, our own national destinies. Your schools, your administration, your Law Courts, your manufactured articles, your Legislative Councils, your Ordinances and sedition laws are to us things alien and unreal, and we eschew them as Maya, as *anātman.* If men and nations are for ever and inalienably free, then bondage is an illusion, the rule of one nation over another is against natural law and therefore a falsehood, and falsehood can only endure so long as the Truth refuses to recognise itself. The princes of Bengal at the time of Plassey did not realise that we could save ourselves. We were not enslaved by Clive, for not even a thousand Clives could have had strength enough to enslave us, we were enslaved by our own delusions, by the false conviction of weakness. And the moment we get the full conviction of our strength, the conviction that we are for ever and inalienably free, and that nobody but ourselves can either take or keep from us that inalienable and priceless possession, from that moment freedom is assured. So long as we go on crying "We are unfit, we are unfit", or even doubt our fitness, so long we shall make and keep ourselves unfit. It is only the conviction of fitness for freedom and the practice of freedom that makes and keeps men fit for freedom. To create that conviction, to encourage and make habitual that practice is the whole aim of the new movement. Nationalism is the gospel of inalienable freedom. Boycott is the practice of freedom. To break the Boycott and to stop the preaching of Nationalism is the whole object of the bureaucracy. The *Times* saw this when it singled out the writings of *Bande Mataram* and *Yugantar*, the speeches of Bepin Chandra Pal and his like and above all, the Boycott as the root of all evil. Behind all technicalities this is the true and only issue in these sedition cases. The Nationalists declare that Indians are for ever and inalienably freemen and vindicate their right to preach this gospel; Mr. Morley and the bureaucrats tell us we are for ever and inalienably the property of England and would pursue our preaching as a crime. Who or what shall reconcile this fundamental and irreconcilable opposition?

Bande Matatam, July 29, 1907

The 7th of August

THE approaching celebration of the 7th of August has a double importance this year, for it has not only its general and permanent importance as the commemoration of our declaration of independence, but an occasional though none the less urgent importance as an opportunity of reaffirming our separate national existence against the arbitrary and futile attempt of the bureaucracy to reaffirm and perpetuate a vanishing despotism. The 7th of August will be recognised in the future as a far more important date to the building up of the nation than the 16th October. On the 16th October the threatened unity of Bengal was asserted against the disingenuous and dangerous attack engineered by Lord Curzon; and since it is on the solidarity of its regional and race units that the greater Pan-Indian unity can alone be firmly founded, the 16th October must always be a holy day in the Indian Calendar. But on the 7th of August Bengal discovered for India the idea of Indian independence as a living reality and not a distant Utopia, on the 7th of August she consecrated herself to the realisation of that supreme ideal by the declaration of the Boycott. The time has not come yet when the full meaning of that declaration can be understood; even the whole of Bengal has not yet understood, much less the whole of India. But the light is coming; partly by the efforts of the preachers of the light, still more by the efforts of the enemies of the light, it is coming: and in the dim wide glimmer of the mighty dawn we can see the vast slow surge of Indian life quickening under the breath of a stupendous wind, we can discern the angry fringes of the tide casting themselves far beyond the old low level, we can almost hear the roar of the surf hurling itself on the flimsy barriers it had once accepted as an iron and eternal boundary. The waters are at last alive with the breath of God, the flood which is to overwhelm the world has begun.

The 7th of August was India's Independence Day. A big

word, it may be said, far too grandiose for the little that was accomplished. To those who judge only by the gross material event it may seem so, but to those who look beneath and watch the course of events as they shape themselves in the soul of a nation, the phrase will not seem one whit too excessive. It is the soul within us that decides, that makes our history, that determines Fate, and the material nature, material events only shape themselves under the limitations of Space and Time to give an outward body and realisation to the decisions of the soul. The day of a nation's independence is not the day when the administrative changes are made which complete the outward realisation of its independence but the day when it realises in its soul that it is free and must be free. For it is the self-sufficing separateness of a nation that is its independence, and when that separateness is realised and recorded as a determined thing in ourselves, the outward realisation is only a question of time. The seventh of August was the birthday of Indian Nationalism, and Indian Nationalism, as we pointed out the other day, means two things, the self-consecration to the gospel of national freedom and the practice of independence. Boycott is the practice of independence. When therefore we declared the Boycott on the seventh of August, it was no mere economical revolt we were instituting, but the practice of national independence; for the attempt to be separate and self-sufficient economically must bring with it the attempt to be free in every other function of a nation's life; for these functions are all mutually interdependent. August 7th is therefore the day when Indian Nationalism was born, when India discovered to her soul her own freedom, when we set our feet irrevocably on the only path to unity, the only path to self-realisation. On that day the foundation-stone of the new Indian nationality was laid.

Let us then celebrate the day in a spirit and after a fashion suitable to its great and glorious meaning. Let it be a reconsecration of the whole of Bengal to the new spirit and the new life, a purification of heart and mind to make it the undivided possession and the consecrated temple and habitation of the Mother. And, secondly, let it be a calm, brave and masculine reaffirmation of our independent existence. The bureaucracy has flung itself with savage fury on the new activities of our national life; it has attempted to trample on and break to pieces under its armed heel our economical boycott; it has made the service of the motherland penal in her young men; it has visited with the prison and deportation the preaching of Nationalism by the elder men. The 7th of August must be an emphatic answer to these persecutions and prohibitions. The Boycott must be reaffirmed and this time in its purity and simplicity as the national policy to which all are committed. The Risley Circular must be definitely and unmistakably challenged and negatived in action. Let there be a procession of students led by those venerable leaders of Bengal who are also professors of the Government University. And let us see afterwards what the bureaucracy can do and what it dare do to the men who refuse to give up their lifelong and sacred occupation at an alien bidding and to the youths who refuse to abstain from initiation in the same sacred service out of sordid hopes and fears.

But most of all the day should be a day of rejoicing and a day of consecration. The whole Indian part of the town should be illumined in honour of the divine birth which saw the light two years ago. And along with the outer illumination it should be a day of the illumination of hearts. It is the sacrament of our religion that can alone give the perfect and effective blessing to our movement, and the celebration of this great day will not be complete until every Indian makes it a sacred observance, worshipping God in his own way, the Hindu in his temple, the Brahmo in his Mandir, the Mahomedan in his mosque, to consecrate himself anew on that day to the service of that single and omnipresent Deity through the task He has set to the whole nation, the upbuilding of Indian nationality by self-sacrifice for the Motherland.

The "Indian Patriot" on Ourselves

We gave in full yesterday the article of the *Indian Patriot* in which our contemporary criticised the action of the Bengal Government in searching the *Bande Mataram* office as a preliminary, it is presumed, to a prosecution under the sedition clause. We thank our contemporary for his sympathy, but we are bound to say that he does not seem to have entirely grasped the political gospel preached by *Bande Mataram*. The *Patriot* seems to be under the impression that it is a gospel of violent despair. Because England has refused to hear our prayers and melt at our tears, therefore we advocate an appeal to force. But this is not and has never been our attitude. Those who are at present responsible for the policy of this paper were never believers in the old gospel of mendicancy and at no time in their lives were associated with Congress politics, they publicly opposed the Congress propaganda as futile and doomed to failure at a time when the country at large was full of a touching but ignorant faith in prayers and resolutions and British justice. Despair and disappointment therefore could not possibly be the root of their policy. It is rather a settled, reasoned and calm conviction we have always held, but for which the country was not ripe until it had gone through a wholesome experience of disillusionment. Neither is our teaching a mere gospel of brute force. We preach on the contrary a great idea in the strength of which we are confident of victory. All that we contend is that we must reach the realisation of that idea in the same way as other nations by utter self-devotion, by self-immolation, by bitter struggle and terrible sacrifices, and that we cannot hope and ought not to wish to have liberty given to us at less than its eternal and inevitable price.

Bande Mataram, August 6, 1907

To Organise

Srijut Surendranath Banerji in his remarkable speech in College Square, the other day, observed that what the country now needed was not oratory but statesmanship, for the only effective answer to bureaucratic repression is the organisation of the whole strength of the country to carry out its natural ideal in spite of all repression. We think the veteran leader has gauged the situation very accurately, but we confess we do not see at present where the statesmanship is to come from which is to carry out the difficult, arduous and delicate task before us. What we have done hitherto we have done without leadership, almost without clear purpose, under an inspiring and impelling force which we must necessarily think divine. Where that force has visibly guided us, we have done astonishing things: but at the same time there has been much confusion, one-sidedness and incoherence in our work. And now that a powerful and organised Government has set itself in grim earnest to destroy our movement it is imperative that we too should organise and make our whole potential strength effective for self-defence. The divine guidance will only be continued to us if we show ourselves in our strength and wisdom worthy of it. But it cannot be denied that the first effect of the repression has been to disorganise our work. Since it began, there has been no concerted and coherent action, every man has done what seemed good in his own eyes or else remained inactive. The result has been much weakness, supineness and ineffectiveness. Barisal fights for its own hand to maintain the boycott. The *Yugantar* attacked carries on a heroic struggle with the bureaucracy with what stray assistance, individual generosity or patriotism may offer it. But organised resistance, organised persistence even there is none.

This unsatisfactory condition of things is traceable to one main cause. All Bengal is heartily agreed in Swadeshi and professedly all are agreed on the necessity of industrial Boycott. But a majority of the older leaders, trained in another school of politics cannot adapt themselves to the new state of things, they cannot even throw themselves heartily into the only measures which can make the individual boycott crushingly effective, and they are out of sympathy with the wider developments of boycott which are becoming indispensable if we are to meet the bureaucratic attack with full success. They object personally to the new men and decline to work in co-operation with them. The new men, on the other hand, who have immensely increased their following and influence in the country are not in possession of the machinery of Congress and Conference, are, in fact, zealously excluded from it by the present possessors and have but small following among the richer men who might provide the sinews of war. They are moreover prevented, by a natural unwillingness to hopelessly divide the nation, from organising a machinery of their own. Yet to talk of organising the nation while excluding the new men is absurd. If the older party have the greater solidity and resources, the younger men have the lion's share of the energy and driving force, they divide the great middle class and are no longer there in a hopeless minority, but are gathering adherents all over the country (even in Madras they commanded one third of the votes at the last Conference) and they exercise an overwhelming empire over the minds of the rising generation. To organise the nation means to make all its elements of strength efficient for a single clear and well-understood work under the leadership of a recognised central force. To exclude such important forces as these we have described, simply means to leave the nation unorganised.

The country is in need of a statesman, yes; but what kind of statesman? He must be a man thoroughly steeped in the gospel of Nationalism, with a clear and fearless recognition of the goal to which we are moving, with a dauntless courage to aim consciously, steadily, indomitably towards it, with a consummate skill to mask his movements and aims when necessary and to move boldly and openly when necessary and, last but not least, with an overmastering magnetic power and tact to lead and use and combine men of all kinds and opinions. Such a leader might organise the nation to some purpose, but those who shrink from following where their hearts and intellects lead them or who form party feelings or personal dislike or jealously try to exclude powerful forces from the common national work cannot claim the name of statesman. It is an encouraging sign of the times that Surendranath is coming more and more into sympathy with thoroughgoing Nationalism but will he have the courage and magnanimity to hold out his hand to the new men and if he does will he be able to retain the loyalty of his principal followers? If not, he will never be able to carry out the task he has declared to be the one and supreme need of the nation.

Bande Mataram, August 8, 1907

A Compliment and Some Misconceptions

We extract in another column the opinions and interpretations of the London *Times* anent the *Bande Mataram*. It is gratifying to find the Thunderer so deeply impressed with the ability with which this journal is written and edited, even though the object of this generous appreciation be to point us out as the tallest oak of all on which the lightning may most fitly descend. But we feel bound to correct certain misapprehensions into which the *Times* has too readily fallen. It suits the *Times* to pretend that the Nationalist movement in India is a pure outcome of racial hatred and that the creation and fomentation of that hatred is the sole method of Indian agitators and the one object of their speeches and writings. But Nationalism is no more a mere ebullition of race hatred in India than it was in Italy in the last century. Our motives and our objects are at least as lofty and noble as those of Mazzini or of that Garibaldi whose centenary the *Times* was hymning with such fervour a few days ago. The restoration of our country to her separate existence as a nation among the nations, her exaltation to a greatness, splendour, strength, magnificence equalling and surpassing her ancient glories is the goal of our endeavours: and we have undertaken this arduous task in which we as individuals risk everything, ease, wealth, liberty, life itself it may be, not out of hatred and hostility to other nations but in the firm conviction that we are working as much in the interests of all humanity including England herself as in those of our own posterity and nation. That the struggle to realise our ideal must bring with it temporary strife, misunderstanding, hostility, disturbance, — that in short, it is bound to be a struggle and not the billing and cooing of political doves, we have never attempted to deny. We believe that the rule of three hundred millions of Indians by an alien bureaucracy not responsible to the nation is a system unnatural, intrinsically bad and inevitably oppressive, and we do not pretend that we can convince our people of its undesirability without irritating the bureaucracy on one side and generating a strong dislike of the existing system on the other. But our object is constructive and not destructive, to build up our own nation and not to destroy another. If England chooses to feel aggrieved by our nation-building, and obstruct it by unjust, violent or despotic means, it is she who is the aggressor and guilty of exciting hatred and ill-feeling. Her action may be natural, may be inevitable, but the responsibility rests on her, not on Indian Nationalism.

Pal on the Brain

We have commented on one misconception of the *Times* about ourselves which it perhaps could not help, so necessary was the error to justify its own position, but it has perpetrated another which seems wilful, — unless it is the result of monomania. The Thunderer seems to have Srijut Bepin Chandra on the brain; it sees him gigantically reflected in every manifestation of Nationalism and is rapidly constructing him into a sinister Antichrist of British rule. So it insists on identifying him with the *Bande Mataram* and will take no denial. Somebody has been pointing out to it that Bepin Babu severed his connection with the paper nine months ago, and this is how the *Times* disposes of the attempt to dissipate its cherished delusions: "Mr. Bepin Chandra Pal has nominally ceased to edit the paper, but there can be no question that he is the dominating force behind its policy and comments, which are stated with a literary ability rare in the Anglo-native Press." The *Times* is evidently not going to be deceived. The literary ability with which the *Bande Mataram* states its views is rare in the "Anglo-native" Press but it is known that Bepin Pal has a rare literary ability, therefore it is unquestionably Bepin Pal and no other, who really edits and writes in the *Bande Mataram.* There seems to be a flaw somewhere in the Thunderer's logic, and we do not think the Bengal Government in its recent affectionate enquiries has come to the same conclusion. Bepin Babu has his own sufficient portion of anti-bureaucratic original sin without being burdened with ours. The *Times* should realise that almost the whole literary ability of Young Bengal is behind the movement of which we are the daily expression, so that the ability and literary excellence of our paper is not to be wondered at.

Bande Mataram, August, 12, 1907

To Organise Boycott

That Boycott is the central question of Indian politics is now a generally recognised fact, recognised openly or tacitly by its supporters and its opponents alike. The Anglo-Indian papers are busy trying to make out that it is a chimera, and a failure; the executive are straining every nerve to crush it by magisterial interference, by police Zulum, by prosecution of newspapers and all the familiar machinery of repressive despotism; the friends of the alien among ourselves are reiterating that the movement is a foolish affair and that no nation ever was made by Boycott. If Boycott had really been an impossibility or a failure, it is obvious that all this elaborate machinery would not have been brought into play to crush it. On the contrary it has become a very substantial reality, a very palpable success, and now stands out, as we have said, the central and all-important question of Indian politics. Those who say that no nation was ever made by boycott, do not know what they are talking about, do not understand what boycott is, do not know the teachings of history. Boycott is much more than a mere economical device, it is a rediscovery of national self-respect, a declaration of national separateness; it is the first practical assertion of independence and has therefore in most of the national uprisings of modern times been the forerunner of the struggle for independence. The American struggle with England began in an enthusiastic and determined boycott of British goods enforced by much the same methods as the Indian boycott but with a much more stringent and effective organisation. The Italian uprising of 1848 was heralded by the boycott of Austrian cigarettes and the tobacco riots of Milan. The boycott was the indispensable weapon of the Parnell movement in Ireland, and boycott and Swadeshi are the leading cries of Sinn Fein. The first practical effect of the resurgence of

China was the Boycott of American goods as an assertion of China's long down-trodden self-respect against the brutal and insolent dealings of the Americans towards Chinese immigrants. In India also Boycott began as an assertion of national self-respect, and continued as a declared and practical enforcement of national separateness, liberty, independence and self-dependence. "We will no longer tamely bear injury and insult, we will no longer traffic and huckster with others for broken fragments of rights and privileges; we are free, we are separate, we are sufficient to ourselves for our own salvation," that was what boycott meant and what its enemies have understood it to mean: its economical aspect is only an aspect.

The economical boycott has been on the whole an immense success, — not indeed in every respect, for the crusade against foreign sugar has not diminished the import, though it may have checked to some extent the natural increase of the import, and the Tarpur sugar factory is, we understand in danger of failing because people will not buy the dearer Swadeshi sugar, — an example of the futility of "honest" Swadeshi unsupported by a self-sacrificing boycott: but enormous reductions have been made in the import not only of cotton goods but of all kinds of wearing apparel, and salt has been appreciably affected. But now the whole weight of bureaucratic power is being brought to bear in order to shatter the boycott, and if we intend to save it we must oppose the organised force of the bureaucracy by the organised will of the people. What the unorganised will of the people could do, it has done; it has indeed effected miracles. But no statesman will rely on the perpetual continuation of a miracle, he will seek to counteract weaknesses, to take full advantage of every element of strength and to bring into action new elements of strength; he will in short utilise every available means towards the one great national end. Srijut Surendranath has said well that we must answer the campaign of repression by organising the country. And the readiest way to organise the country is to organise boycott.

The chief weakness of the movement has been the want of co-ordinated action. We have left everything to personal and local enthusiasm. The consequence is that while in East Bengal the Boycott is a fact, in West Bengal it is an idea. There is some Swadeshi in West Bengal, there is no Boycott. Moreover Bengal has not brought its united influence to bear upon the other provinces in order to make the Boycott universal. The whole force of this vast country is a force which no Government could permanently resist. But this force has not been brought to bear on the struggle, Bengal and Punjab have been left to fight out their battles unaided, without the active sympathy of the rest of India. This must be altered, the rest of India must be converted and we must not rest till we have secured a mandate from the Congress for an universal boycott of British goods. Meanwhile we must bring West Bengal into a line with East Bengal, and for that purpose we must have a stringent and effective organisation. We need not go far for the system which will be most effective. We have only to apply or adapt to the circumstances of the country the methods used by the American boycotters against England. How this can be done we propose to discuss in another article.

The Bloomfield Murder

The *Bengalee* seems to be much surprised and rather hurt at the unkind conduct of the *Statesman* in adversely criticising Justices Mitter and Fletcher for their judgment in the Bloomfield Murder Case. Our contemporary's invincible faith in the *Statesman* is really pathetic. One would have thought that the attitude of the Chowringhee paper with regard to Lala Lajpat Rai and its support of the policy of repression would have opened the eyes of the blindest. What does the *Bengalee* expect? The *Statesman* is a Liberal Imperialist organ wedded to the eternal continuance of the British control and all that it implies, but willing to concede unsubstantial privileges and a carefully modified liberty because that will make the task of the British ruler easier. It cannot be expected to sympathise with Swadeshi and Nationalism. No patriotic Englishman, Sir Roper Lethbridge has said, can support Swadeshi: no patriotic Indian can help supporting Swadeshi. The opposition of interests is complete and irreconcilable. When therefore the *Bengalee* and other Moderates took up Swadeshi, they forfeited all claim to the support of the *Statesman*. No patriotic Englishman again can support anything which can possibly injure the prestige, supremacy and exceptional position of the white community in India; no patriotic Indian but must desire to see that prestige lowered and that supremacy and exceptional position replaced by the equality of all communities before the law, as well as socially and politically. Cases like this Bloomfield murder raise, therefore, a crucial point. When the whole basis of a political system is the despotic rule of a small alien handful over the immense indigenous numbers, it is an essential condition of its continuance that the persons of the foreigners should be held sacred, that those who lay hands on them, no matter under what provocation, should be overtaken by the most terrible retribution the other conditions of the rule may permit. While therefore there may be two opinions among Anglo-Indians as to the advisability of allowing European murderers of Indians to go free, there can be no two opinions on the necessity of avenging every loss of a European life by the execution of as many Indians as the police can lay their hands upon. No matter whether the revenge be unjust or inhuman, no matter whether it be even monstrous. The principle it is sought to uphold is itself unjust and monstrous, and squeamishness about means is out of place. Terrorism is indispensable, whether it be the naked, illegal and unashamed terrorism of Denshawi or terrorism in the fair disguise of legal forms and manipulating for its own purposes the Criminal Procedure Code and the Evidence Act. It is not the fault of the Anglo-Indians but of their position, and it is that position which must be altered if such massacres as that which the calm judicial temper of Justices Mitter and Fletcher prevented in the Bloomfield Case, are to be rendered an impossibility.

Bande Mataram, August 14, 1907

The Foundations of Nationality

MR. N. N. Ghose of the *Indian Nation* has some name in this country as an educated and even a learned man. He himself does not conceal his opinion that he is almost if not quite the only well-educated man in India and is perpetually asking the acknowledged exponents of public opinion on the Nationalist side what educational qualifications they possess which would justify them in advising or instructing their countrymen in politics. At one time it is the conductors of *Bande Mataram* who are put to the question; at another it is so able a political thinker and orator as Srijut Bepin Chandra Pal whose speeches and writings have extorted the reluctant admiration of our bitterest opponents in England; at another it is the editor of *Yugantar* who is apostrophied as an ill-educated adolescent — a paper every single issue of which evidences more knowledge, reading and power of thought and expression than the whole year's output of the *Indian Nation*. In the latest issue of his weekly Mr. Ghose has penned an article on the prospects of Nationality in India — which he thinks to be very bad indeed — and in trying to support his thesis by examples from history he has perpetrated such astonishing blunders, of so gross and elementary a character, that one wonders what ill-educated adolescent usurped the editorial chair usually occupied by the Principal of the Metropolitan College. We will give only a few samples of Mr. Ghose's historical knowledge. The unification of the Italian republics into a nation, he says, was not so much the effect as the cause of Italian independence. We leave for the moment the truth of the statement which is contrary to the facts of history; but we should like to know what on earth our universal critic means by his Italian republics? There were republics in mediaeval Italy, but we did not know that Naples and Sicily were republics under King Bomba, or Rome under the Popes, or Tuscany under the Grand Duke, or Lombardy under the Austrians, or Sardinia and Piedmont under the descendants of Victor Amadeus. Then again Mr. Ghose has "observed" that the different States of Greece developed a National unity as soon as they had a common enemy in the Persian. Really? We had always thought that the one outstanding fact of Greek history was the utter inability of these states to develop national unity at all, the sentiment of Panhellenism never having a look-in against the separatist spirit of the city-states. And then he tells us that the provinces and states of ancient Italy (whatever that may mean) also readily united into a great national state in the presence of a foreign enemy. Yet those foolish historians tell us that Italy was united not at all willingly by the Roman sword and the Carthaginian invasion simply tested the solidity of the Roman structure; it certainly did not create it. But it would be a wearisome task to hunt down all the errors with which the article is packed. We think that after this Mr. N. N. Ghose had better stop questioning other people about their qualifications for instructing the people and examine his own.

But in spite of his historical blunders he has succeeded in giving expression to a very common error which troubles many patriotic people and unnerves their faith and weakens the quality of their patriotism. "Let it be distinctly remembered and never forgotten that the essential conditions of a nationality are unity of language, unity of religion and life, unity of race." And because there is diversity of race, religion and language in India he thinks that there is no possibility of creating a nationality in this country. This is a very common stumbling-block, but is there any reality in it? Rather we find that every nationality has been formed not because of, but in spite of, diversity of race or religion or language, and not unoften in spite of the co-existence of all these diversities. The *Indian Nation* has itself admitted that the English nation has been built out of various races, but he has not stated the full complexity of the British nation. He has not observed that to this day the races which came later into the British nationality keep their distinct individuality even now and that one of them clings to its language tenaciously. He has carefully omitted the striking example of Switzerland where distinct racial strains speaking three different languages and, later, professing different religions, coalesced into and persisted as one nation without sacrificing a single one of these diversities. In France three different languages are spoken; in America the candidates for White House address the nation in fourteen languages, Austria is a congeries of races and languages, the divisions in Russia are hardly less acute. That unity in race, religion or language is essential to nationality is an idea which will not bear examination. Such elements of unity are very helpful to the growth of a nationality, but they are not essential and will not even of themselves assure its growth. The Roman Empire though it created a common language, a common religion and life, and did its best to crush out racial diversities under the heavy weight of its uniform system failed to make one great nation.

If these are not essential elements of nationality, what, it may be asked, are the essential elements? We answer that there are certain essential conditions, geographical unity, a common past, a powerful common interest impelling towards unity and certain favourable political conditions which enable the impulse to realise itself in an organised government expressing the nationality and perpetuating its single and united existence. This may be provided by a part of the nation, a race or community, uniting the others under its leadership or domination, or by an united resistance to a common pressure from outside or within. A common enthusiasm coalescing with a common interest is the most powerful fosterer of nationality. We believe that the necessary elements are present in India, we believe that the time has come and that by a common resistance to a common pressure in the shape of the boycott, inspired by a common enthusiasm and ideal, that united nationality for which the whole history of India has been a preparation, will be speedily and mightily accomplished.

Bande Mataram, August 17, 1907

Barbarities at Rawalpindi

THE process of terrorism that is going on at Rawalpindi in the name of administering justice is too open and transparent to require any unravelling. Of course, every one who takes politics seriously thought that the British law and administration would at once reveal their true nature if the people were to enter on a real struggle for self-improvement and the repression that is being resorted to in the Punjab under the pretext of trial has caused no surprise to those with whom the work for the nation's future is a duty demanding enormous self-sacrifice. But the series of episodes connected with the Rawalpindi trial in which humanity has been outraged and decency defied should nevertheless be taken to heart by the people. They demand an adequate response of stern and resolute work as an atonement and recompense for the sufferings of these martyrs. No patriot would shrink even from the agonies to which the accused are being subjected during the course of their trial at Rawalpindi if he could at least faintly hope from the attitude of his countrymen that they would carry on the patriotic work undaunted and with a greater amount of determination and energy. The man of faith no doubt is never depressed. His faith is always his stay and support. But the martyrdom becomes easier if there is the prospect of some immediate benefit to the country resulting from his sufferings.

From the very beginning of the Rawalpindi trial, the bureaucratic law seems to have been whetted against the alleged offenders. The refusal of bail to the accused amongst whom there are men of unquestioned respectability and integrity testifies to the petty vindictiveness of the judiciary which ostensibly exists to diminish crimes and not to exasperate people into their perpetration. The ill-treatment of the accused can without the least exaggeration be characterised as wanton cruelty. The accused after their experience of the British law courts will find it difficult to distinguish a judge from a mediaeval executioner. The Judge could not be moved to the most elementary feeling of humanity when the accused were overwhelmed by the most painful domestic calamities. One man was not allowed to see his dying son till he actually expired and was past all help or need of help. This ferocity on the part of a tribunal, whose special study should be to abstain from writing the least punishment on a man till his guilt has been fairly established is a violation of the first principle of justice and turns a court of law into a torture chamber. A judge should not lack firmness in repressing crime but to pursue an alleged offender with implacable wrath from the moment of his arrest is an exhibition of vindictiveness and not of due judicial austerity. The trial has now extended over nearly two months and the sickening details of inhumanity practised upon the accused continue to be as distressing as ever.

Lala Hansraj and two or three others of his position have been detained in the prison without any justification. They are not the men who can even think of shirking the consequences of their patriotic actions under an alien rule. But why anti-date their punishment from the very time of their arrest. They are not men accustomed to privations and they have all been showing signs of failing health during this pretty long period of police custody. They have already served out a term of punishment disproportionate to the nature of their alleged offence. It is a brand new feature of British justice to go on with the trial of men stretched on their sick-bed in the court room. Our latest telegram from Rawalpindi says that on the 16th Lala Hansraj was shaking with fever and ague on a string cot borrowed from a constable. The internal pain was so intense that tears ran down his cheeks though he tried to be firm and cheerful and pretended that something had fallen into his eyes.

We need not multiply the details of the prisoner's sufferings. We have already sampled the treatment which the Pindi martyrs are receiving at the hands of the judiciary. We expect no mitigation of their sufferings. The alleged offence of rousing people to a spirit of active resistance perhaps justifies these barbarities in the eyes of the ruling class. They are innocent of all compunction and are calmly watching the effect on the people. The *Englishman* once opined that even the suspected offence of inciting to a riot excuses the most monstrous treatment of the offenders. But we believe their lesson will not be lost on our own countrymen. The heavy price that these men are paying for inducing the spirit of self-assertion in us should nerve others to greater and greater sacrifices in the service of the Motherland.

The High Court Miracles

The situation in Bengal is one of a very peculiar kind and of extraordinary interest. There is a deep and widespread unrest in the country; a movement has commenced which the bureaucracy holds to be fraught with serious danger certainly to the British monopoly of commercial exploitation, possibly to the supremacy of British officialdom. In order to save these threatened citadels the bureaucrats in the Punjab and Eastern Bengal have embarked on a policy of thoroughgoing repression in which the practically unlimited and arbitrary power of an autocratic executive is backed up and confirmed by a zealous judiciary. The union of these two forces is essential to the success of the bureaucratic plan of campaign; for the strength of the bureaucratic position lies in the fact that all the powers of legislation and administration are centred unreservedly and without limitation in its hands. It controls the men by whom the law and the executive administration are carried out, for it not only exercises all the patronage of both services, but wields immense disciplinary powers. It can appoint and favour such men as are likely to do its will and it can punish with substantial marks of its displeasure those who disregard its interests or do not act according to its expectations. In an hour of crisis like the present when there is a powerful movement undisguisedly directed against the continued supremacy of the present ruling community in all its aspects, this concentration of all powers against the insurgence of the subject peoples is of the most vital importance. The executive must have a free hand to deal with the opposition of the demos without being hampered by inconvenient and trammelling considerations of legal procedure and the narrow limits of legality. But in a fight with an acute and intelligent people, a nation of born lawyers, this is only possible on condition that the judiciary are willing to support and confirm the actions of the executive unhesitatingly and without a qualm. These conditions have been secured in East Bengal and still more completely in the Punjab. But there is one weak point, the Achilles' heel in the otherwise invulnerable constitution of the bureaucracy, and that is the High Court of Bengal. The oldest and most venerable institution of British rule with the most honourable traditions of integrity and independence maintained by a series of judges learned in the law, trained to the love of justice and equity and a calm judicial habit of mind, the High Court had become a thing cherished and valued, a refuge to the oppressed, a guarantee of eventual relief against executive vagaries. It had therefore attracted an almost superstitious reference and was the chief moral asset of British rule. But the inevitable tendency of bureaucratic rule when threatened by the increasing self-assertion of the people, began eventually to affect the High Court. It is true that the High Court is independent of the executive authorities, but it is under the control of the Chief Justice, and by the simple device of securing a Chief Justice of weak personality and multiplying civilian judges of the right kind the institution can easily be converted into a source of strength to the bureaucracy instead of a source of weakness. Since the beginning of the reactionary policy which followed the Viceroyalty of Lord Ripon, this has been the increasing tendency of the High Court and the trust and reverence of the people has decreased proportionately, and the hold of British rule on their imaginations has decreased with it. We have always held that British justice as between Indians and Europeans or in cases in which the bureaucracy was judge, jury and accuser, must obviously and inevitably be a farce unless and until human nature ceases to have any resemblance to its present self. Neither had we any of that enthusiastic admiration for British law and its administration which was not so very long ago the fashion among Indians of the educated class. On the contrary we were compelled to regard its procedure as costly, dilatory and often calculated to defeat justice, its penal system repressive and its punishments savage and barbarous with the cold civilised brutality of a half-baked incomplete civilisation. Our respect for the High Court was tempered by a perception of the ease with which it could be captured by the bureaucracy for its own ends. We have therefore always decried the old moribund belief in the excellence of the British courts and the tendency to run to them for protection in all cases of oppression and injustice. Have the recent transactions in the High Court proved us wrong? They have certainly proved that there are still Judges Indian and English who can rise above the depressing atmosphere and lowered traditions of this once venerated institution and equal the distinguished record of these strong fearless Judges who have now become a memory, almost a legend of the past. There has been nothing like the series of important decisions given in a few days by Justices Mitter and Fletcher since the 7 Bishops were acquitted. The bold opposition of the sense of justice and respect for law to the interests of an irritated and determined government in a time of great political unrest and disturbance, is an episode which history will love to record. But is it more than an episode? We apprehend it is the last flaring up of the old fire previous to extinction. The executive will surely take care not to repeat the error by which a fearless, just and religious Hindu lawyer has been placed on the Criminal Bench side by side with a young barrister Judge fresh from England and still full of the uncorrupted moral temper natural in a free country. The bureaucracy has blundered in its management of the High Court, but the power to utilise it is still on its hands and will no doubt be better handled in the near future than in the past. Let us not be unduly elated by the victory in the High Court; great as it has been its causes are transient and its tenure insecure.

Justice Mitter and Swaraj

Justice Mitter's conduct in connection with the cases which were more or less of a political nature, has been a surprise to many of his own countrymen. He has risen high above the servile impulses which our education, surroundings and life raise in us, and is giving his country the full benefit of the advantageous position he holds under an alien bureaucracy. His native independence and uncommon intellectuality seem to have been specially invigorated by the spiritual re-awakening of which the whole country is giving some indication, and in all the cases he has lately tried he has done his utmost to annihilate the vast distance between absolute and bureaucratic justice. He has shewn the service-holding section of his countrymen an example which they will do well to imitate in the interests of their country and humanity. The moral of his conduct is that our duty as men and Indians should always get the precedence of our duty as servants. If we be true to ourselves, we cannot be false to anyone. Self-reverence cannot fail to extort respect even from our enemies. But this is by the way.

Justice Mitter's explanation of Swaraj is now the subject of talk amongst the thinking portion of our people. It has almost thrown into comparative oblivion his luminous and unexceptionable judgment in the now famous Comilla Case. And we propose to offer our opinion on his interpretation of Swaraj. His explanation of Swaraj as Home Rule under British control no doubt echoes the sentiment of Mr. Dadabhai Naoroji who is considered the prophet of this new message. But Saroda Charan is not only a Justice but a scholar too. Without seeking to justify the ideal of Swaraj under the somewhat narrow meaning which Mr. Naoroji has given to it, Justice Mitter might have taken an excursion into our Vedic literature, traced the word to its very source, and pointed out that it represents an ideal which, having regard to its inspired scriptural origin and high moral and spiritual significance can never lack the sanction of law and justice, if law and justice are of divine origin and concern themselves with promoting the real welfare of mankind. The Vedas say that if we pursue real happiness we must seek the great, the universal. Our aspiration can be satisfied with nothing short of the Omnipresent. In littleness there is no bliss. So we must not run after petty ideals. The Universal alone should be the one object of our knowledge and pursuit. Then the Vedas explain the nature of the Universal. It is independent, self-protecting, and stands by its greatness, and in its greatness — stands *sva-mahimni*, as we have it in the text. This *sva-mahimni* is synonymous with Swaraj as everyone who understands Sanskrit can very well see. According to the Vedanta which is only the philosophical exposition of the Vedas, every individual self is nothing but divinity itself and should stand by and in its own greatness. To be impressed with the dignity of one's own self, to realise its identity with the Universal is the goal of our aspiration, the end of our being. If this is the object of an individual life, the nation also should set its heart on the same ideal. The nation also should try to know itself, to work out its potentialities, to realise its mightiness and identity with the Universal. Such an ideal does not at all brook the notion of dependence. The very radical meaning of the term Swaraj excludes it. Swaraj emphasises the idea of self-sufficiency and insists on it. It mitigates against the idea of there being any limit to our expansion. We must be full, we must be perfect, we are the divinity in embryo and when fully developed we shall be coextensive with God Himself. This is what Swaraj unmistakably means. It at once embodies the ideals of independence, unity, liberty. It can never compromise itself with anything having a limit. It is the ideal of infinite possibility and Justice Mitter has not fully used the opportunity to point out to his countrymen the ideal which alone should engage their attention if they really mean self-improvement as a nation. But what he has done is so much, in his position, that the admiration and respect of the whole country for his fearless sense of Justice is no more than his right.

Bande Mataram, August, 19-20, 1907

Advice to National College Students*

I HAVE been told that you wish me to speak a few words of advice to you. But in these days I feel that young men can very often give better advice than we older people can give. Nor must you ask me to express the feelings which your actions, the way in which you have shown your affection towards me, have given rise to in my breast. It is impossible to express them. You all know that I have resigned my post. In the meeting you held yesterday I see that you expressed sympathy with me in what you call my present troubles. I don't know whether I should call them troubles at all, for the experience that I am going to undergo was long foreseen as inevitable in the discharge of the mission that I have taken up from my childhood, and I am approaching it without regret. What I want to be assured of is not so much that you feel sympathy for me in my troubles but that you have sympathy for the cause, in serving which I have to undergo what you call my troubles. If I know that the rising generation has taken up this cause, that wherever I go, I go leaving behind others to carry on my work, I shall go without the least regret. I take it that whatever respect you have shown to me today was shown not to me, not merely even to the Principal, but to your country, to the Mother in me, because what little I have done has been done for her, and the slight suffering that I am going to endure will be endured for her sake. Taking your sympathy in that light I can feel that if I am incapacitated from carrying on my work, there will be so many others left behind me. One other cause of rejoicing for me is to find that practically all my countrymen have the same fellow-feeling for me and for the same reason as yourselves. The unanimity with which all classes have expressed their sympathy for me and even offered help at the moment of

* Sri Aurobindo delivered the above address on the 23rd August, 1907, before the students and teachers of the Bengal National College, in a meeting assembled to record their deep regret at his resignation of the high office of Principalship of the College.

my trial, is a cause for rejoicing, and for the same reason. For I am nothing, what I have done is nothing. I have earned this fellow-feeling because of serving the cause which all my countrymen have at heart.

The only piece of advice that I can give you now is — carry on the work, the mission, for which this college was created. I have no doubt that all of you have realised by this time what this mission means. When we established this college and left other occupations, other chances of life, to devote our lives to this institution, we did so because we hoped to see in it the foundation, the nucleus of a nation, of the new India which is to begin its career after this night of sorrow and trouble, on that day of glory and greatness when India will work for the world. What we want here is not merely to give you a little information, not merely to open to you careers for earning a livelihood, but to build up sons for the Motherland to work and to suffer for her. That is why we started this college and that is the work to which I want you to devote yourselves in future. What has been insufficiently and imperfectly begun by us, it is for you to complete and lead to perfection. When I come back I wish to see some of you becoming rich, rich not for yourselves but that you may enrich the Mother with your riches. I wish to see some of you becoming great, great not for your own sakes, not that you may satisfy your own vanity, but great for her, to make India great, to enable her to stand up with head erect among the nations of the earth, as she did in days of yore when the world looked up to her for light. Even those who will remain poor and obscure, I want to see their very poverty and obscurity devoted to the Motherland. There are times in a nation's history when Providence places before it one work, one aim, to which everything else, however high and noble in itself, has to be sacrificed. Such a time has now arrived for our Motherland when nothing is dearer than her service, when everything else is to be directed to that end. If you will study, study for her sake; train yourselves body and mind and soul for her service. You will earn your living that you may live for her sake. You will go abroad to foreign lands that you may bring back knowledge with which you may do service to her. Work that she may prosper. Suffer that she may rejoice. All is contained in that one single advice. My last word to you is that if you have sympathy for me, I hope to see it not merely as a personal feeling, but as a sympathy with what I am working for. I want to see this sympathy translated into work so that when in future I shall look upon your career of glorious activity, I may have the pride of remembering that I did something to prepare and begin it.

Bande Mataram, August 23, 1907

Sankharitola's Apologia

THE omniscient editor of the *Indian Nation* exposed himself last week to a well-deserved castigation at our hands by trespassing into history, of which he evidently knows less than a fifth form schoolboy in an English public school. We gave him his deserts, but were careful to couch our criticism, however deservedly severe, in perfectly courteous language. We find, however, that the courtesy was thrown away on the most hysterically foul-mouthed publicist in the whole Indian Press. The late Sambhunath Mukherji ironically described Mr. N. N. Ghose as a thundering cataract of law: he might more aptly have described him as a thundering cataract of billingsgate. He has attempted to answer our criticism in this week's *Indian Nation*, but the answer is so much befouled with an almost maniacal virulence of abuse that most of our friends have advised us to ignore his frenzies and never again give him the notoriety he desires by noticing him in our columns. It is true that the *Indian Nation* addresses itself to a microscopic audience and expresses the personal vanities, selfishness, jealousies of a single man, but so long as it enjoys a false reputation for learning and wisdom even with a limited circle or trades on that reputation to attack and discredit the National movement, it is our duty to expose its pretensions, and we shall not be deterred by any abuse, however foul.

Mr. N. N. Ghose's reply falls into three parts, of which one consists merely of rancorous vituperation, another of a feeble attempt to wriggle out of the uncomfortable position he has got into by his failure to consult a few historical primers before writing, and the third is a restatement of his opinions about nationality formulated this time in the shape of general ideas without any basis either of historical fact or of Metropolitan College fiction. As to the abuse we can only say that it might have been more skilfully done. At least it might have been more coherent. The aggrieved sage of Sankharitola picks out from all the *Bande*

Mataram writers Srijut Aurobindo Ghose for the object of his wrath and among other elegant terms of abuse calls him a prig and a *Graeculus esuriens.* To those who may not be such accomplished Latin scholars as the Principal of the Metropolitan College, we may explain that the last expression means a starving and greedy scholar who is prepared to commit any vileness for the sake of earning a livelihood. We will not stop to ask whether this description applies to Srijut Aurobindo Ghose or to a Principal who daily exhorts his students to subordinate honour, high feeling and patriotism to the supreme consideration of bread and himself practises the lofty philosophy he preaches. We will only ask Mr. Ghose whether a man can be at once a prig and an *esurient Greekling.* Srijut Aurobindo Ghose may be one or the other or neither, but he can hardly be both. Either Mr. N. N. Ghose's knowledge of Latin is as distinguished and correct as his knowledge of history, or else he is so ignorant of English as to be even ignorant what the word prig means. We can understand his being in a rage at the merciless exposure of his pretended scholarship, but that does not excuse his incoherence: nor is it a sufficient reason for what was once a fair counterfeit of a gentleman and a scholar turning himself into the image of a spitting and swearing tom-cat. And with that we leave Mr. N. N. Ghose the fishwife and pass on to Mr. N. N. Ghose the historian.

He does not try to justify his blunders, — that would be hopeless — but he does try to excuse them. He practically admits that his Italian republics are a blunder and that he was thinking of the Middle Ages when he was writing of the nineteenth century. But he pleads that Burke uses the word commonwealth in the sense of state and therefore Mr. N. N. Ghose can use the word republic in the same sense. This is Metropolitan College logic and Metropolitan College knowledge of English. Does Mr. Ghose really think that republic and commonwealth mean the same thing precisely or that Burke would have talked of the Russian republic when he meant the Russian monarchy? But, says Mr. Ghose, it does not matter, as I was not talking about forms of government. But if Mr. Ghose in his class was to talk about adjectives when he meant nouns, would it be an excuse to say that he was not talking about the difference between various parts of speech? His defence of his other blunders is still more amusing.

Says the Oracle: "To combat our proposition about ancient Greece an academic commonplace is trotted out, namely, that the people of Greece never developed a panhellenic sentiment." Really this is enough to take one's breath away. Mr. Ghose told us last week that the Greeks became an united nation under the pressure of the Persian invasion; this week he coolly tells us that it is an academic commonplace that the Greeks never even developed a panhellenic sentiment. We certainly never said anything of the sort. The Greeks, as any tyro in history knows, did develop a panhellenic sentiment but it was never strong enough — and that was all we said — to unite them into a nation. But Mr. Ghose flounders still deeper into the mire in the next sentences. "What does it signify whether they did or not? The whole question is, could the Greek states have been set against one another? Athens and Sparta, for instance, against each other? And if not, why not?" Really, Mr. Ghose, really now! Is it possible you do not know that soon after the Persian invasion which you say made Greece an united nation, Athens and Sparta were at each other's throats and the whole of the Greek world by land and sea turned into one vast battlefield on which the Hellenic cities engaged in a murderous internecine strife? What would we think of a "scholar" who pretended to know Indian history and yet asserted that the Hindus became an united nation under the pressure of the Mahomedan invasion and that it was impossible to set the Hindu states against each other, Mewar and Amber for instance? Yet this is precisely the blunder Mr. Ghose has committed with respect to Greek history. But he pleads bitterly that his facts are no doubt all wrong, but the conclusions he bases on them are right. What do facts matter? It is only Mr. N. N Ghose's opinions which matter.

Mr. Ghose accuses us of incapacity to understand the substance of his article. We quite admit that it is difficult to understand the mystic wisdom of a sage who asserts that the soundness of his premises has nothing to do with the soundness of his conclusions. Mr. Ghose stated certain facts as supporting a conclusion otherwise unsupported. We have proved that his facts are all childish blunders. He must therefore accept one of the two horns of a dilemma: either his facts had nothing to do with his "truism" or his "truism" itself is an error. But we had another object in view in exposing the pretentious sciolism of this arrogant publicist. Our business with him is not so much to disprove his opinions as to convince the few who still believe in him of the hollowness of his pretensions. It was for this reason that we dwelt on his blunders last week and have done the same this week, — in order to show that this gentleman who claims a monopoly of culture and wisdom in India, is a half educated shallow man whose boasted mastery of the English language even is imperfect and who in other subjects, such as history and politics, is an ignoramus pretending to knowledge.

Bande Mataram, August 24, 1907

Our False Friends

The *Englishman* has been warning us against our false friends. We have been asked to avert our eyes from those Indian delegates who have asked the socialistic Conference at Stuttgart to liberate one-fifth of the human race from serfdom. The *Englishman* unblushingly calls these Indian delegates our enemies and perhaps points to himself as our only friend, guide and philosopher. With the *Englishman* for our friend, and the *Civil and Military Gazette* for our ally and the rest of the Anglo-Indian Press for our well-wishers it is no doubt sinful to long for a change for the paradise of universal brotherhood. India is the freest of lands, retorts the Hare Street Journal to the misrepresentation of our false friends in the above socialistic Conference. Here under British rule the people enjoy religious freedom, they are allowed to stick to their absurd social customs, they are not denied food, clothing and luxuries. What is there wanting to their freedom the *Englishman* is at a loss to discover. Does our contemporary seriously desire enlightenment on the point? Or is he indulging in a bit of Hare Street humour at our expense? Is it owing to this freedom of which we are the enviable possessors that he himself as well as his prototype in Lahore enjoy the monopoly of pouring daily vile abuses on us with perfect safety and immunity? Is it due to this freedom that we are threatened with imprisonment for republishing the articles of the *Yugantar* and they are supported and patronised for the very same offence? Is it for this enviable freedom that some innocent men of Comilla were very near being hanged and transported without a shred of evidence against them? Is it in consequence of this freedom that a highly respectable accused at Rawalpindi is taking his trial on a sick bed? Is it in the exercise of their rights as free citizens of the British Empire that Lala Lajpat Rai and Ajit Singh have been deported without even the mention of the charge against them? This freedom is perhaps responsible for the banishment of an Arya Samajist from his country though the trying magistrate has declared him quite innocent of the charge brought against him. Is it a tangible demonstration of our freedom that we cannot keep our food grains for our own use even when there is a terrible famine in the land? Is it because we are free to think and act that the Partition of Bengal has been carried out in the teeth of an unanimous and protracted opposition? The disarming of a whole people is another incontrovertible evidence of their freedom. They are not allowed the use of arms because they are free. Their manhood is repressed because they are free. They are converted into so many harmless cattle because their Mothercountry is the freest of all countries! If we had even a jot of freedom the *Englishman* could not have flung in our face such a mocking statement. The world has come to know of India's true condition, and these interested and shameless perversions of truth can deceive nobody.

Bande Mataram, August 26, 1907

Repression and Unity

One of the most encouraging signs of the present times is the effect of repression in bringing together men of all views who have the future welfare and greatness of their country at heart. At this time last year the great fight between the old and new parties was just beginning to pass from the stage of loose occasional skirmishes into a close and prolonged struggle. The emergence of Nationalism as a self-conscious force determined to take shape and fight for the domination of the national mind was indicated by the appearance of the *Bande Mataram* as the first out and out Nationalist daily in the English tongue published in India. For the first time a gospel of undiluted Nationalism without any mitigating admixture of prudent concealment or diplomatic reservation was poured daily into the ears of the educated class in India. At first the *Bande Mataram* and the cause it came to champion had to make a hard fight for existence and for a voice in the country, and in the struggle which culminated in the last session of the Congress, many hard words were used on both sides, strong animosities aroused and what seemed incurable misunderstandings engendered. Those times are now fading into a half-remembered past. The second year of the paper's existence has begun with a prosecution for sedition, but circumstances have so changed that in its hour of trial it has the sympathy of the whole of Bengal at its back. We note with satisfaction and gratitude that all classes of men, rich and poor, all shades of opinion, moderate or extremist, the purveyors of ready made loyalty alone excepted, have given us a sympathy and support which is not merely emotional. This growing unity is mainly due to the action of the bureaucracy in attempting to put down by force a movement which has now taken possession of the nation's heart beyond the possibility of dislodgment. This is the last and crowning blessing of British rule.

Bande Mataram, August 27, 1907

The Three Unities of Sankharitola

MR. N. N. Ghose has again attempted to answer us in his issue of the 26th August. As usual the bulk of his answer is composed of irrelevant abuse, but we are glad to note that except towards the end where his passion of spite and wounded vanity has broken out in a furious yell of hatred, he has tried to curb his natural inclination to couch the logic of Billingsgate in the language of the gutter. We pointed out that Mr. N. N. Ghose's "historical facts" — which he had brought forward to prove his theory that Nationality was possible everywhere except in India, were all blunders of which a schoolboy would have been ashamed, and we drew the inevitable conclusion that the sage of Sankharitola was an ignoramus in history. That was exceedingly plain language, no doubt, but it was relevant to the issue. A man who knows nothing about history, has no business to argue from history and foist on the public conclusions drawn from his own imagination or from others and distorted in the borrowing under the disingenuous pretence that they are the "laws of national growth" as ascertained from an accurate study of the world's past experience. And what is Mr. N. N. Ghose's answer? His answer is that Srijut Aurobindo Ghose is a coward and had not courage to ride a horse and that he would never have been a patriot if he had not failed in the Indian Civil Service. Even if that be true, — and we can hardly blame the Principal of the Metropolitan College for judging others by his own standard of courage and patriotism, — we do not see how it helps his case or goes to prove that his bad premises do not vitiate his conclusions or that Nationality is impossible in India. The question is not whether Srijut Aurobindo Ghose is a coward and a self-seeker but whether Mr. N. N. Ghose is wrong in his facts and in his conclusions. With regard to the facts he has practically admitted defeat. He admits that he is an ignoramus, he admits that the depths of his ignorance have been proved to be unfathomable. We can therefore leave him alone in the future and confine ourselves to his opinions. An ignoramus who pretends to a monopoly of knowledge and wisdom, and is always questioning other people about their educational qualifications, makes himself offensive and deserves to be exposed but an ignoramus who confesses that he is an ignoramus is harmless and even an object of kindly pity.

Mr. Ghose argues that though his facts were wrong, that does not prove that his conclusions were not right. Perhaps not, but it at least creates a presumption in that direction. We shall however leave his self-justification on this point for future treatment and deal with the more substantial issues he has raised in his defence.

Mr. N. N. Ghose's position — and we notice it only because it is the position of better men than he — is contained in the following luminous sentence: "The bookish politician is not able to cite a single instance where a nation was made by boycott or under any conditions other than the unities we have more than once referred to." Here there are two propositions, one, that boycott never made a nation, the other that in every case of the building up of a nationality there have been present as indispensable conditions and the only causes of the growth of nationality Mr. Ghose's three precious unities, — viz., a single language, a single race, a single religion. A more shallow, ignorant and unfounded brace of assertions it would be difficult to imagine. We pointed out in the first article in which we condescended to notice Mr. Ghose's flounderings, several instances of nations which have been welded into unity and maintained their unity without possessing a single one of these indispensable "unities". As for unity of race there is not a single one of the European nations which is not a compound of several races, except, possibly, the Scandinavian peoples. In England up to the present day the Celtic races preserve their separateness and distinct individuality: in Austria there are a superfluity of different races and languages: Russia is a congeries of peoples: Italy was built up out of various races and even after the accomplishment of national unity the Gallo-Lombard of the North and the Latins, Oscans, Umbrians, Tuscans of the Centre find it difficult to understand and live with the Graeco-Italians of the South: in Germany the Prussian, the Slav, the Pole, and the South German are of different race-types and temperaments: in Spain the Iberian, the Goth and the Moor have mingled their blood: in France there are the Breton, still a distinct race, the Provençal and the Frank as well as the Celts of the Centre and the Aquitanian, each with noticeable marks of their separate origin: in Switzerland there are three races speaking three different languages. Does Mr. N. N. Ghose want any more instances? We can give him plenty if he does. If he had even the most insignificant knowledge of common facts, he would not have needed our assistance to enlighten him on the subject. Every one knows, except the Shankaritola sage, that race and nationality are two totally different things which have no necessary relation to each other, since one depends upon common descent while the other is a geographical and political unity. One might just as well say that different chemical elements cannot combine into a single substance as that different races cannot combine into a single nation. There is no such irreconcilable divergence between the races in India as to make their union an impossibility. If we turn to unity of language we find a respectable number of nations which do not speak a single language. Three languages are spoken in Switzerland, the same number in France, while Welsh holds its own in Great Britain. Unity of language, therefore, is not necessary to nationality, only the recognition of one prevalent language as the State language is required. If America, needing to be addressed in fourteen languages by her would-be Presidents is a nation, if the Swiss speaking three different languages on equal terms are a nation, what reason is there that the people of India should not federate into a single political unity? As for the religious difficulty, it is an old bogey. We do not deny the difficulty created by the divisions between the Mahomedans and Hindus, but it is idle to say that the difficulty is insuperable. If the spirit of nationalism conquered the much fiercer intolerance of the religious struggles in Europe after the reformation, it is not irrational to hope as much for India in the twentieth century. We have not seen in Mr. N. N. Ghose's polemics a single argument or favourable instance for his pretentious theory of the three unities of nationalism. We do not deny that it would be a great help to us if we had a single language or professed a single religion. But we do deny that these "unities" still less the unity of race, are indispensable. There is no warrant for such a view in history or in reason.

Bande Mataram, August 31(?), 1907

Eastern Renascence

When the mailed fist of young Japan was striking blows after blows at the huge Russian bear our benevolent rulers who were secretly dismayed and astonished tried to put on a smiling face as best they could and persuade us into the belief that Japan was only an exception which proved the rule of Eastern worthlessness. Somehow or other, however, inconvenient facts cropped up to challenge their favourite theory and Persia, and even Afghanistan began to raise their heads. Even China threw away her phial of laudanum and opened her eyes to the rays of the rising sun. Our honest Anglo-Indian Press tried to ignore this ugly fact as long as it could; but now with a deep sigh it has to confess that the Eastern nations have secured a fresh lease of life and have begun in right earnest to set their houses in order. Here is an extract published by the *Pioneer* from a circular issued by the Chinese authorities:

"Those who are able to promote agricultural enterprises, mechanical arts and handicrafts, trade and mines or any other kind of business, or aid merchants to subscribe capital for industrial enterprises, and succeed in them — such officials or gentry who have worked to such an end, will be rewarded by the Throne to an extraordinary degree. Should any one be able to show that he has succeeded in starting a manufactory or industrial work with a capital of over ten million taels, where the workmen number several thousand, such persons will be even more greatly rewarded — even to the extent of being raised to the peerage."

Japan joined in the race of commercial enterprise later than

India and outstripped her in no time and now China, where there are no "honest Swadeshi" officials to let loose mercenary Goorkha bands to crush all spirit of enterprise, may very well be expected to do the same. Here in India we lag behind and lose the race not because the other Eastern nations are naturally more gifted than we are but because there is that benevolent despotism which like a leaden extinguisher puts out all the fire of our genius. There is scarcely a word of encouragement, and in fact there cannot be; but of repression and Swadeshi cases there is plenty.

But the Time-Spirit is abroad, and out of the extinguishers leap forth the tongues of fire that will at no distant date set all obstacles ablaze. The nations of the East will rear up their heads and India will be herself again. Repression will only enhance the glory of her victory and help in putting her in the vanguard of nations.

Bande Mataram, September 3, 1907

The Martyrdom of Bepin Chandra

WE HAVE felt considerable delicacy hitherto in writing on the prosecution of Srijut Bepin Chandra Pal for refusing to take the oath in the *Bande Mataram* Case, as that prosecution has arisen directly out of our own. In fact, all the more important events of recent occurrence in Calcutta have been so closely connected, directly or indirectly, with this case that we have been practically compelled to keep our lips closed on current public affairs. The imprisonment of the Nationalist orator and propagandist, the most prominent public figure of the New Party in Bengal, is nevertheless a matter of capital importance on which we cannot remain silent. Without touching on the relations of this affair with the *Bande Mataram* Case we shall say what we have to say on the political aspect of the vindictive sentence passed by the third Presidency Magistrate, an obscure servant of the bureaucracy, on the man with a great and historic mission whom the strange incongruous humour of Fate brought before his petty judgment-seat.

Srijut Bepin Chandra Pal has been condemned to six months' simple imprisonment, the maximum penalty permitted by the law for the crime of possessing a conscience, Mr. Hume asked for a conviction on the ground that Bepin Babu had baulked the prosecution in the *Bande Mataram* Case. Apart from the large assumption involved in the assertion that his evidence would have materially assisted the prosecution, this appears to us a singular plea for a lawyer to put forward. It has not yet been made a crime punishable under the Penal Code to baulk a Government prosecution and if it was the intention to draw the Magistrate's attention to the political bearings of the case, it was at least maladroit to allow the suggestion to be palpable. We will take it, however, that the Magistrate sentenced Bepin Babu for a breach of the law which the defendant did not deny, not for an action of which there was no evidence and which is not an offence under the law. What then was Bepin Babu's offence? Certainly it was not that he carried the policy of Boycott beyond the limits of legality and preferred adhesion to his own political programme before the dictates of the alien's law. That would have been an action which, however pardonable or praiseworthy in the eyes of patriots engaged in a life and death struggle with the bureaucracy, must necessarily figure as a serious offence in the eyes of the bureaucracy itself and we could hardly quarrel with its servant for trying to serve the interests of his employers by the infliction of a severe punishment. But it was distinctly declared by Bepin Babu that it was not as a boycotter, not with the political intention of making the working of the bureaucratic law courts impossible, that he declined to give evidence or take the oath. The boycott in Bengal has not yet been extended in practice to the law courts, and even in theory it is proposed to extend it only to voluntary resort to the protection of the alien authorities and not to cases in which one is compelled to them by a warrant or a summons. A few men like Bhupendranath Dutt who have realised freedom in their souls and refuse to be bound by any limitations of an alien making, may decline to have anything to do with the law which the nation had no hand in framing and the courts over which the nation has no control, but this has not yet become the accepted policy of the New Party and there was no moral compulsion on its leader to make any such refusal. If it had been an ordinary case of crime, he would not have refused to give evidence. It was, in fact, as an individual case of conscience that he regarded the question. In his first statement Bepin Babu declared that it was the duty of a citizen to refuse to take any part in such cases which are manifestly unjust and injurious to society and the peace of the country. In his later statement the expression about the duty of the citizen was, wisely we think, dropped: for we in India are not citizens and having no rights of citizenship cannot be saddled with any duties of citizenship. The members of a subject nation absolutely destitute of any inalienable rights cannot have any moral obligations as citizens: they can only have moral obligations as patriots and subject to their patriotic obligations, as members of a social order. If therefore we recognise any obligation to respect and obey the law, it is not as citizens but as members of the social order who are interested in its maintenance and in the maintenance of peace and order so long as, and no longer than, that order and peace do not militate against the well-being of the society instead of promoting it. The moment obedience to the law involves a wound to society, the individual is brought face to face with a difficult case of conscience.

It was in such a difficult situation that Bepin Babu found himself. He was called on to associate himself as a prosecution witness with a political policy carried on under the forms of law, a policy which he considered fatal to the well-being and peace of the nation, but which he had no means of challenging except by the passive protest of refusing to perform the function required of him. He had to obey either the dictates of his conscience or the requirements of the law and he held the imperative command of his conscience a more sacred and binding law than the Penal Code. The law had a right to assert itself by inflicting on him a nominal or slight penalty, it had no right to punish a man vindictively for obeying his conscience. The Magistrate thought perhaps that he was serving the interests of the present system and ensuring its stability by putting Bepin Pal in prison for six months, but what has he really done? Merely made people believe that the bureaucracy is so savage in its repression, so enamoured of power, that for its sake it will not even allow a man to possess a conscience, that an honest and reluctant protest on the part of a distinguished and honourable man against a misuse of the law will be punished by it with eager severity if it happens to conflict with its own interests or its repressive policy.

The country will not suffer by the incarceration of this great orator and writer, this spokesman and prophet of Nationalism, nor will Bepin Chandra himself suffer by it. He has risen ten times as high as he was before in the estimation of his countrymen: if there are any among them who disliked or distrusted him, they have been silenced, for good we hope, by his manly, straightforward and conscientious stand for the right as he understood it. He will come out of prison with his power and influence doubled, and Nationalism has already become the stronger for his self-immolation. Posterity will judge between him and the petty tribunal which has treated his honourable scruples as a crime.

Bande Mataram, September 12, 1907

The Unhindu Spirit of Caste Rigidity

THE *Bengalee* reports Srijut Bal Gangadhar Tilak to have made a definite pronouncement on the caste system. The prevailing idea of social inequality is working immense evil, says the Nationalist leader of the Deccan. This pronouncement is only natural from an earnest Hindu and a sincere nationalist like Srijut Tilak. The baser ideas underlying the degenerate perversions of the original caste system, the mental attitude which bases them on a false foundation of caste, pride and arrogance, of a divinely ordained superiority depending on the accident of birth, of a fixed and intolerant inequality, are inconsistent with the supreme teaching, the basic spirit of Hinduism which sees the one invariable and indivisible divinity in every individual being. Nationalism is simply the passionate aspiration for the realisation of that Divine Unity in the nation, a unity in which all the component individuals, however various and apparently unequal their functions as political, social or economic factors, are yet really and fundamentally one and equal. In the ideal of Nationalism which India will set before the world, there will be an essential equality between man and man, between caste and caste, between class and class, all being as Mr. Tilak has pointed out different but equal and united parts of the Virat Purusha as realised in the nation. The insistent preaching of our religion and the work of the Indian Nationalist is to bring home to everyone of his countrymen this ideal of their country's religion and philosophy. We are intolerant of autocracy because it is the denial in politics of this essential equality, we object to the modern distortion of the caste system because it is the denial in society of the same essential equality. While we insist on reorganising the nation into a democratic unity politically, we recognise that the same principle of reorganisation ought to and inevitably will assert itself socially; even if, as our opponents choose to imagine, we are desirous of confining its working to politics, our attempts will be fruitless, for the principle once realised in politics must inevitably assert itself in society. No monopoly, racial or hereditary, can form part of the Nationalist's scheme of the future, his dream of the day for the advent of which he is striving and struggling.

The caste system was once productive of good, and as a fact has been a necessary phase of human progress through which all the civilisations of the world have had to pass. The autocratic form of Government has similarly had its use in the development of the world's polity, for there was certainly a time when it was the only kind of political organisation that made the preservation of society possible. The Nationalist does not quarrel with the past, but he insists on its transformation, the transformation of individual or class autocracy into the autocracy, self-rule or Swaraj, of the nation and of the fixed, hereditary, anti-democratic caste-organisation into the pliable self-adapting, democratic distribution of function at which socialism aims. In the present absolutism in politics and the present narrow caste-organisation in society he finds a negation of that equality which his religion enjoins. Both must be transformed. The historic problem that the present attitude of Indian Nationalism at once brings to the mind, as to how a caste-governed society could co-exist with a democratic religion and philosophy, we do not propose to consider here today. We only point out that Indian Nationalism must by its inherent tendencies move towards the removal of unreasoning and arbitrary distinctions and inequalities. Ah! he will say, this is exactly what we Englishmen have been telling you all these years. You must get rid of your caste before you can have democracy. There is just a little flaw in this advice of the Anglo-Indian monitors, it puts the cart before the horse, and that is the reason why we have always refused to act upon it.

It does not require much expenditure of thought to find out that the only way to rid the human mind of abuses and superstitions is through a transformation of spirit and not merely of machinery. We must educate every Indian, man, woman and child, in the ideals of our religion and philosophy before we can rationally expect our society to reshape itself in the full and perfect spirit of the Vedantic gospel of equality. We dwell on this common sense idea here at the risk of being guilty of repetition.

Education on a national scale is an indispensable precondition of our social amelioration. And because such education is impossible except through the aid of state-finance, therefore, even if there were no other reason, the Nationalist must emphasise the immediate need of political freedom without which Indians cannot obtain the necessary control over their money. So long as we are under an alien bureaucracy, we cannot have the funds needed for the purpose of an adequate national education, and what little education we are given falls far short of the nationalist ideal, being mainly concerned with the fostering of a spirit of sordid contentment with things that be. Apart from the question of the cultivation of those virtues which only come in the wake of liberty, apart from the question of reorganisation of the country, if we were to look into the problem in its purely social aspect, even then we are confronted with the primary need of political emancipation as the condition precedent of further fruitful activity.

The Nationalist has been putting the main stress on the necessity of political freedom almost to the exclusion of the other needs of the nation, not because he is not alive to the vital importance of those needs of economic renovation, of education, of social transformation, but because he knows that in order that his ideal of equality may be brought to its fullest fruition, he must first bring about the political freedom and federation of his country.

Bande Mataram, September 20, 1907

Caste and Democracy

WE FEAR our correspondent who has criticised on another page the consistency of our views on caste, has hardly taken any trouble to understand the real drift of our articles. His attitude seems to be that we must be either entirely for caste as it at present exists or entirely against the institution and condemn it root and branch in the style of the ordinary unthinking social reformer. Because on the one hand we protested against the ignorant abuse of the institution often indulged in simply because it is different in form and spirit from European institutions, and on the other hand emphasised the perversions of its form and spirit and the necessity of its transformation in the pure spirit of Hinduism, our correspondent imagines that we are inconsistent and guilty of adopting successively two different and incompatible attitudes. Our position is perfectly clear and straightforward. Caste was originally an arrangement for the distribution of functions in society, just as much as class in Europe, but the principle on which the distribution was based in India was peculiar to this country. The civilisation of Europe has always been preponderatingly material and the division of classes was material in its principles and material in its objects, but our civilisation has always been preponderatingly spiritual and moral, and caste division in India had a spiritual object and a spiritual and moral basis. The division of classes in Europe had its root in a distribution of powers and rights and developed and still develops through a struggle of conflicting interests; its aim was merely the organisation of society for its own sake and mainly indeed for its economic convenience. The division of castes in India was conceived as a distribution of duties. A man's caste depended on his *dharma*, his spiritual, moral and practical duties, and his *dharma* depended on his *svabhāva*, his temperament and inborn nature. A Brahmin was a Brahmin not by mere birth, but because he discharged the duty of preserving the spiritual and intellectual elevation of the race, and he had to cultivate the spiritual temperament and acquire the spiritual training which could alone qualify him for the task. The Kshatriya was a Kshatriya not merely because he was the son of warriors and princes, but because he discharged the duty of protecting the country and preserving the high courage and manhood of the nation, and he had to cultivate the princely temperament and acquire the strong and lofty Samurai training which alone fitted him for his duties. So it was with the Vaishya whose function was to amass wealth for the race and the Sudra who discharged the humbler duties of service without which the other castes could not perform their share of labour for the common good. This was what we meant when we said that caste was a socialistic institution. No doubt there was a gradation of social respect which placed the function of the Brahmin at the summit and the function of the Sudra at the base, but this inequality was accidental, external, *vyavahārika*. Essentially there was, between the devout Brahmin and the devout Sudra, no inequality in the single *virāṭ puruṣa* of which each was a necessary part. Chokha Mela, the Maratha Pariah, became the Guru of Brahmins proud of their caste purity; the Chandala taught Shankaracharya: for the Brahman was revealed in the body of the Pariah and in the Chandala there was the utter presence of Shiva the Almighty. Heredity entered into caste divisions, and in the light of the conclusions of modern knowledge who shall say erroneously? But it entered into it as a subordinate element. For Hindu civilisation being spiritual based its institutions on spiritual and moral foundations and subordinated the material elements and material considerations. Caste therefore was not only an institution which ought to be immune from the cheap second-hand denunciations so long in fashion, but a supreme necessity without which Hindu civilisation could not have developed its distinctive character or worked out its unique mission.

But to recognise this is not to debar ourselves from pointing out its later perversions and desiring its transformation. It is the nature of human institutions to degenerate, to lose their vitality, and decay, and the first sign of decay is the loss of flexibility and oblivion of the essential spirit in which they were conceived. The spirit is permanent, the body changes; and a body which refuses to change must die. The spirit expresses itself in many ways while itself remaining essentially the same, but the body must change to suit its changing environments if it wishes to live. There is no doubt that the institution of caste degenerated. It ceased to be determined by spiritual qualifications which, once essential, have now come to be subordinate and even immaterial and is determined by the purely material tests of occupation and birth. By this change it has set itself against the fundamental tendency of Hinduism which is to insist on the spiritual and subordinate the material and thus lost most of its meaning. The spirit of caste arrogance, exclusiveness and superiority came to dominate it instead of the spirit of duty, and the change weakened the nation and helped to reduce us to our present condition. It is these perversions which we wish to see set right. The institution must transform itself so as to fulfil its essential and permanent object under the changed conditions of modern times. If it refuses to change, it will become a mere social survival and crumble to pieces. If it transforms itself, it will yet play a great part in the fulfilment of civilisation.

Our correspondent accuses us of attempting to corrupt society with the intrusion of the European idea of Socialism. Socialism is not an European idea, it is essentially Asiatic and especially Indian. What is called Socialism in Europe is the old Asiatic attempt to effect a permanent solution of the economic problem of society which will give man leisure and peace to develop undisturbed his higher self. Without Socialism democracy would remain a tendency that never reached its fulfilment, a rule of the masses by a small aristocratic or monied class with the consent and votes of the masses, or a tyranny of the artisan classes over the rest. Socialistic democracy is the only true democracy, for without it we cannot get the equalised and harmonised distribution of functions, each part of the community existing for the good of all and not struggling for its own separate interests, which will give humanity as a whole the necessary conditions in which it can turn its best energies to its higher development. To realise those conditions is also the aim of Hindu civilisation and the original intention of caste. The fulfilment of Hinduism is the fulfilment of the highest tendencies of human civilisation and it must include in its sweep the most vital impulses of modern life. It will include democracy and Socialism also, purifying them, raising them above the excessive stress on the economic adjustments which are the means, and teaching them to fix their eyes more constantly and clearly on the moral, intellectual and spiritual perfection of mankind which is the end.

Bande Mataram, September 22, 1907

Impartial Hospitality

The *Englishman* is ever predicting new horrors for the agitators. The agitator in the Press has been taken in hand, the present law is being tried to intimidate him into silence and as its inadequacy in this respect is being increasingly felt the coming winter will be taken advantage of to convert its present elasticity into a cast-iron rigidity. It will then crush the agitators at a single blow and the bureaucracy will have a merry time of it. In the meantime political considerations are expected to do the duty of the amended law. The present deficiency in quality is to be made up by an extensive enforcement of the law against all the miscreants. Prosecutions have already been instituted against all the seditious newspapers, and this ill-tongued messenger of the bureaucracy has brought us the latest news that seditious speakers will shortly meet with their deserts. The College Square and the Beadon Square must not be allowed to blow the pestilential seditious winds and the mild bracing air of the Pax Britannica should again form their healthy atmosphere. The prisoners' dock in the Police Court is now, we hear, to be occupied by guests from those quarters. The speakers are justly envious of the hospitality which is being lavished on the writers and as the *Englishman* now assures us of an impartial treatment, let no one complain of any partiality of British justice.

Bande Mataram, September 23, 1907

Free Speech

The *Nation* to hand has some pertinent observations as to the true meaning of free speech. Its interpretation of free speech clearly shows that we are content with mere shadows and that we exhaust our energies in clamouring for so-called rights and privileges which when analysed prove to be mere shams that cannot at all satisfy people who are in the least serious about them. Unless politics were a mere pastime or a means of making name and fame with us we would have never deluded ourselves with the belief that we possess any political rights and privileges under an alien bureaucracy. The bureaucracy never makes any secret of the fact that its policy will always be to safeguard its own supremacy. Popular rights and such a supremacy go ill together. Right means a power which has some sort of sanction behind it and as a power it can never be tolerated by another power always over-anxious for its existence and supremacy. The power of the state is never afraid of the power of the citizen in free democratic countries because there the objects pursued by both are identical. But this cannot be the case in a subject country where the so-called state interferes for its own benefit or the pretended benefit of the people under its assumed tutelage. But no people with any pretension to self-respect and intelligence can consent to be dictated to by a small governing body whether foreign or of the country as to what conduces to their real interests. This is where the necessity of free speech comes as an essential requisite for promoting and guarding the true well-being of the people. Free speech should therefore be not only an unfettered expression of the ideas of the people as to what alone will do them good but should also be recognised as a force by the executive body. The *Nation* explains the true meaning of free speech in the following words: —

"Free speech in any liberal and statesmanlike sense of the term means something more than the right of a subject people to perorate in vain in a free Press, to hold public meetings, and to record its hopeless aspirations at unrecognised congresses.

It means, if we are sincere, the provision of facilities for the focusing and expression of public opinion."

Judged by this standard our crying in the wilderness with the full risk of being run in whenever the bureaucracy chooses is only aimless and dangerous prattle.

Bande Mataram, September 24, 1907

"Bande Mataram" Prosecution

THE prosecution of the *Bande Mataram*, the most important of the numerous Press prosecutions recently instituted by the bureaucracy, commenced with a flourish of trumpets, eagerly watched by a hopeful Anglo-India Press, has ended in the most complete and dismal fiasco such as no Indian Government has ever had to experience before in a sedition case. The failure has not been the result of any lukewarmness or half-heartedness in the conduct of the prosecution or any unwillingness to convict on the part of the trying Magistrate. The Police left no stone unturned to get a particular man convicted, the Standing Counsel did not hesitate to press every possible point and make the most of every stray scrap or faint shadow of evidence against the accused, the Magistrate was a Civilian Magistrate whose leanings have never been concealed, the same who gave two years to the *Yugantar* Printer, who sent Bepin Pal before a subservient Bengali Magistrate with a plain hint to give him a heavy punishment, who sentenced Sushil Kumar to fifteen stripes, who brushed aside the evidence of barristers in favour of Police testimony, and every paragraph of whose judgment in the present case shows that he would readily have dealt out a handsome term of hard labour if the evidence had afforded him the slightest justification for a conviction. All the winning cards in the game are in the hands of the bureaucracy in such a trial. They can command the best legal knowledge in the country, they have a detective and secret service system which for political purposes is popularly supposed to be second only in its elaborateness to the Russian, they have their own servants sitting on the bench to try a case in which they are deeply interested, there is no trouble about juries who might be unwilling to convict, the Police have unlimited powers of search and can even turn the Post Office into a branch of the detective department; their methods of discovering witnesses are various and effective; yet with all this they were unable to bring forward a single scrap of convincing evidence to prove that the particular man they were bent on running down was the Editor. The Magistrate in his judgment and the affectionate Friend of India in Chowringhee in his comments have drawn from this failure the lesson that the laws against the freedom of the Press should be made more stringent. An ordinary unilluminated intelligence would have come rather to the conclusion that the executive authorities would do well to reform their method of instituting proceedings in a political trial.

The one important lesson of the *Bande Mataram* Case is the light which it throws on the spirit in which the bureaucracy have been instituting the political prosecutions and persecutions which have latterly seemed to be their only reason of existence. This spirit has been exposed in a lurid and sensational manner in the Comilla case, when an innocent man with difficulty escaped the gallows to which a political prosecution had condemned him. But in the *Bande Mataram* Case also there has been a less sensational though sufficient exposure of the same sinister spirit. What has been the whole meaning and aim of this prosecution? Certainly not an honest impartial desire to vindicate outraged law and check without personal animus or any purely political aim a wanton tendency to disturb the public tranquillity, which would be the only excuse for a sedition prosecution. It has been an obvious attempt to crush a particular paper and a particular individual. The bureaucracy has sought to cripple or silence the *Bande Mataram* because it has been preaching with extraordinary success a political creed which was dangerous to the continuance of bureaucratic absolutism and was threatening to become a centre of strength round which many Nationalistic forces might gather. It has sought to single out and silence a particular individual because it chose to think that he was, as the Friend of India expresses it, the master mind behind the policy of the paper. If we are challenged to justify this assertion, it will be sufficient to point to the conduct of this case from its very inception. The *Bande Mataram* has been for over a year attacking without fear and without disguise the present system of Government and advocating a radical and revolutionary change. It has advocated that change on grounds of historical experience, the first principles of politics and the necessity of national self-preservation. It has not minced matters or sought to conceal revolutionary aspirations under the veil of moderate professions or ambiguous phraseology. It has not concealed its opinion that the bureaucracy cannot be expected to transform itself, that the people of India and not the people of England must save India, and that we cannot hope for any boons but must wrest what we desire by strong national combination from unwilling hands. Hundreds of articles have appeared in the paper in this vein and the bureaucrats had only to pick and choose. But they have not attacked one of these articles, nor did their counsel venture to cite even a single one of them to prove seditious intention. The fact is that, however dangerous such a propaganda may be to an absolutist handful desiring to perpetuate their irresponsible rule, no government pretending to call itself civilised can prosecute it as seditious without forfeiting all claim to the last vestige of the world's respect. But though the paper could not be characterised as seditious, it was highly inconvenient, and there was a growing clamour which extended even to the cloudy home of the Thunderer in London, for its prosecution and, if possible, suppression. And so watch is kept to find the paper tripping over some trifle, for which it can be hauled up and got into trouble on a side issue. What is the matter for which the *Bande Mataram* was prosecuted? A reprint of the official translations of certain articles from a vernacular paper, translations issued as part of a case in the law courts and reproduced as such, — that is one count; and an insignificant correspondence which does not even profess to give voice to the policy of the paper, — that is the second and third; and there is no other. The *Yugantar* was prosecuted on articles expressing its essential policy; the *Sandhya* has been proceeded against on articles expressing its views on important matters; but it was sought to crush the *Bande Mataram* partly for a technical offence and partly on a side issue. So eagerly, so carelessly is the casual chance given snatched at that the executive do not even trouble to know what is the article on which action is being taken; they give sanction to prosecute on an advertisement in the righthand corner of the paper, and but for the compassionate correction vouchsafed by an officer of the company the mistake would have had to be rectified in the course of the trial itself. Sanction is given to prosecute a nameless Editor and the Police at once proceed to ask for a warrant against Aurobindo Ghose. It is in evidence that they had nothing better to go on than hearsay. But they had no hesitation in immediately pouncing on one particular writer of the *Bande Mataram* without possessing the least scrap of evidence against him. Obviously they cannot have done this without instructions. It was popularly believed that Srijut Aurobindo Ghose was all in all on the *Bande Mataram* staff, that all the best articles were written by him, that he gave the tone of the paper and that it could not last without him. Why did the Police take a body-warrant against Aurobindo Ghose to the office and why, having taken it, did they not arrest him? Obviously they took it because they thought that they would find plenty of evidence against him in the search, and they did not execute it because they found that not a scrap of proof rewarded their efforts. After that there was a pause till Anukul Mukherjee's testimony was secured, and on that flimsy evidence the trial was started. Had it been honestly intended to deal only with the Editor, whoever he might turn out to be, the proceedings against Aurobindo Ghose would have been given up, but the Police made no secret of the fact that it was this one man who was wanted and that no other, whatever the evidence against him, would be thought worth capture. Even when the case for the prosecution was complete without any evidence fit to raise more than a flimsy presumption, the Standing Counsel would not give up, but in an outrageous address in which he rode roughshod over the higher traditions of his office, pressed weak points and wrested ambiguous evidence to get the charge framed. And after Anukul had broken down in cross-examination and made admissions fatal to their case, still the prosecution struggled for a verdict. And with what result? Even a Civilian Magistrate willing to support the prestige of the Government had more sense of law and justice than the bureaucracy and its advisers and was able to see that a man could not be sent to two years' rigorous imprisonment without any shadow of evidence. Their prey escaped them; the Manager who seems to have been arrested on spec and tried without even any pretence that there was any evidence against him was acquitted, and only an unfortunate Printer who knew no English and had no notion what all the pother was about, was sent to prison for a few months to vindicate the much-damaged majesty of the almighty bureaurcacy.

Bande Mataram, September 25, 1907

The Chowringhee Pecksniff and Ourselves

THE collapse of the *Bande Mataram* Prosecution and acquittal of Srijut Aurobindo Ghose, which have been welcomed with relief and joy by our countrymen all over India, are naturally gall and wormwood to the opponents of Indian Nationalism; but to none has the fiasco caused bitterer disappointment than to the Friend of India in Chowringhee. Sharing the common but mistaken impression that our paper depends on the writings of one man for its continued existence, the *Statesman* had evidently hoped that with the incarceration of Srijut Aurobindo Ghose the one paper in Bengal which it fears and which has ruthlessly exposed the falsehood and duplicity of its sanctimonious Liberalism, would be removed out of its path. It cannot conceal its chagrin and mortification at the disappointment of its cherished hopes, and as a *pis aller* it tries to discredit the *Bande Mataram* and informs our subscribers that they ought not to support us any longer because it has been proved that we are either guilty of having put forward a false defence or of the unpardonable immorality of having an editorial staff instead of a single Editor. The tone and method of this attack are worthy of this unctuous and mealy-mouthed Pecksniff of Anglo-Indian journalism. It unscrupulously supports its malicious insinuations by calling the witnesses summoned by the prosecution "defence witnesses" as if the accused had put men into the witness-box to tell a false story: and it shelters itself from the charge of libel by the use of 'ifs' and 'ors'. Yet it has the impudence to claim a superior sense of honour for English pamphleteers and editors! "The great English political writers," it says, "have never been afraid to own their handiwork and we cannot recall a single instance in which an English pamphleteer or editor has endeavoured to evade the law by raising technical difficulties as to his share of responsibility." There are three separate insinuations in this carefully written sentence; first, it is hinted that Srijut Aurobindo Ghose was the real writer of the correspondence, "Politics for Indians", but falsely denied his handiwork; secondly, that he was the responsible Editor of the paper and his denial of responsibility was "technical" and untrue; thirdly, that any writer for the paper was morally bound to accept responsibility for anything that might appear in the paper as a part of the political propaganda in which he was engaged and Aurobindo Ghose, knowing himself to be so bound, evaded his responsibility out of fear. Certainly the writer of this article need not disown his handiwork or evade his responsibility, for he has brought the art of safe slander to its utmost possible perfection.

We have no hesitation in saying that if we had invented a system of divided responsibility with the object of baffling a possible bureaucratic prosecution, we should have been entirely within our rights. In England a publicist or propagandist has always had the advantage of being tried by a jury of his own peers and in all but rare cases enjoyed every reasonable chance of a fair trial, but the reverse is the case in countries circumstanced as India is circumstanced today. Where the whole armoury of an absolute power is arrayed against him, the Judge a servant of his prosecutor, the law an instrument specially designed for his suppression, the wealth and power of a despotic executive and the activity of a not over-scrupulous police his pursuers, and his only supporters are his own patriotism and the sympathy of his people, the Nationalist is entitled to use any means for his own self-defence which will not be inconsistent with his mission nor injure his claim to national sympathy and support. He owes no moral obligation of quixotic candour to antagonists who themselves recognise no moral obligation in their struggle with him. Whatever he owes is to his people and the mission he has to discharge. If he will serve his country best by leaping into the fire, that is his duty; if self-defence is more to the interests of the country and the cause, no other consideration ought to weigh with him. The primary object of the Nationalist organs must be to keep up their propaganda until it is rendered physically impossible by the growing severity of bureaucratic enactments. Bhupendranath and Basanta deliberately exposed themselves to the worst effects of bureaucratic wrath in order to give an example to the country of heroic self-sacrifice and a living demonstration of the spirit of Swarajism; but they did it in the full confidence that the *Yugantar* would continue undaunted and unchanged in the course it conceived to be its duty to the nation. Had they exposed themselves with the knowledge that their disappearance would have meant the death of the paper, their action would have been heroic but foolish, an outburst of patriotic sentiment but not an act of patriotic wisdom. To allow the voice of Nationalism to be silenced would be to play into the hands of the adversary to whom we owe no duty. The gospel of Nationalism has to be preached with unflinching candour, but Nationalist organs will be perfectly within their rights if they prctect their writers so long as it is humanly possible to protect them and so prolong their own career of propagandist usefulness.

No such arrangement was made in the case of the *Bande Mataram.* Had we intended to protect ourselves, we would have done it by the simple and convenient Japanese device of a jail editor. The device imputed to us would be neither illegal nor immoral, but it would be cumbrous and unsafe. It is perfectly true that it throws great difficulties in the way of the prosecution, but it is equally obvious that it leaves the bureaucracy free to single out any one they choose for harassment, and does not protect him at all, since the police have only to be clever enough in their choice of witnesses and the arrangement of the evidence, and the accused, whether really responsible or not, is doomed. Everybody can feel that if Anukul Mukherjee had had more backbone and lied more cleverly in the cross-examination, Srijut Aurobindo Ghose would now be a convict in the Central Jail. Had we thought of putting forward a false defence, we could have done it very effectively by producing an Editor on the spot. There were at least three men on the staff who were anxious to immolate themselves in this manner, and it was only prevented by the refusal of the accused to accept any such sacrifice and by the singular conduct of the prosecution in calling the officers of the Company as their witnesses. The moment Srijut Sailendranath Ghose entered the witness box, there was no course left open to the defence but to take their stand on the facts as elicited by the prosecution. For a member of the staff to come forward and by a splendid falsehood take upon himself the responsibility of the matter complained of, if not of the whole editorial function, would have been morally permissible; but it was obviously impossible for the Secretary of the Company to perjure himself by fixing a non-existent responsibility on any particular individual. The one defect in the conduct of the defence was that the circumstances which brought about the state of things described by the Secretary, were not elicited in cross-examination. When we come to deal with the facts of the case in detail, we shall mend that deficiency and our readers will see that the evolution of that arrangement was natural and even inevitable.

In the diatribe of the Chowringhee Pecksniff against us there is one bit of Pecksniffian logic which we fail to appreciate. He seems to think that a paper cannot be respectable unless it has a single autocratic Editor and that the readers of a paper not so blessed must be disreputable. Why, pray? We had always thought that what one man could do in the way of management could be done as well by a board or committee of men acting in unison and with one clearly understood policy; we used even to think that such conjoint management was in politics the characteristic of democratic times. But Chowringhee liberalism evidently thinks no arrangement respectable which does not involve absolute control by a single master-mind. It argues that the *Bande Mataram* policy being the joint product of several minds must be the result of distracted counsels, since only an autocrat can think clearly. After that we can hardly be surprised at the affection of the Friend of India for absolutism and absolutist methods or the support it has given to the new Grand Mogul who now governs India on mediaeval principles from Westminster.

Bande Mataram, September 26, 1907

The "Statesman" in Retreat

THE strong censures which the *Statesman*'s article on the *Bande Mataram* Case has called forth from the Bengali Press in Calcutta, have forced that journal to enter into some explanation of its conduct. While professing to stand by every word it had written, it manages under cover of the plea that it has been misunderstood, to unsay much that it had said. The article was on the face of it a malignant attack on the *Bande Mataram*, an attempt to create the impression that this paper was either a journal managed on a dishonest, disreputable and impossible principle or else that its staff were a gang of liars and cowards with an Editor who made a false or practically false defence in order to avoid the responsibility for his political propaganda. We were told that from this dilemma there was no possible escape. The *Statesman* has now considerably altered its tone. In order that we may not be accused of wilfully misinterpreting our very Liberal contemporary, we will give his explanation of his own meaning in his own words and answer him point by point. "We maintained," he says, "that there had been in essence a miscarriage of justice in the *Bande Mataram* Case, since the trial had resulted in the conviction of the Printer, whereas the real offender — the author of the article or articles complained of — was not brought to book. We pointed out in the next place, that in England the person really responsible for the articles could readily have been found, for no attempt would have been made to evade the issue on the divided liability principle adopted in the *Bande Mataram* office, still less to make a scapegoat of an ignorant workman. We maintained, lastly, that unless every public journal had a responsible head of some sort, the liberty of the Press would degenerate into a licence under which no institution of organised society, no man's reputation would be safe." We do not for a moment deny that there was a very serious miscarriage of justice in the *Bande Mataram* Case, but we are certainly astonished at the malignity of the *Statesman* in trying to fasten the responsibility for the Printer's conviction on the *Bande Mataram* or on the other accused. It writes as if it were we who took out a warrant against the Printer, knowing him to be nothing but an ignorant workman, or who sentenced him to three months' rigorous imprisonment in spite of the evidence that he knew nothing of the matter and could not have had any criminal knowledge or intention, or as if we had asked the Printer to take any responsibility upon himself for the articles. Does the Friend of India find anywhere in the records of the case or out of them either that any of the accused tried to shield himself by putting the responsibility on the Printer? The blame for the miscarriage of justice must rest on the unjust British law which makes an ignorant workman responsible, on the bureaucrats who sanctioned his prosecution and on the Magistrate who sentenced him, and the attempt to fasten it on our shoulders is as grotesque as it is malicious. The *Statesman* is, farther, much exercised because the real author of the offending article has escaped punishment, but this is not a calamity over which we can affect to be greatly grieved. After all, miscarriages of justice, whether in the shape of the conviction of innocent Indians or the immunity from punishment of European criminals, are not so rare in this country that society will be shattered to pieces because the writer of a chance letter disagreeable to the sacred feelings of the bureaucracy, has not been sent to turn the oil-mill for a couple of years. "In England the person really responsible for the article could readily have been found." If the real writer is meant, we deny this altogether. In England it would be absolutely impossible to discover the true writer of an unsigned article, for it is not considered binding on him to come forward even if another suffers for his offence or his indiscretion; and when the *Statesman* claims a chivalrous sense of honour for English writers, political or other, and asserts that they always come forward to claim their handiwork, it is trading on the ignorance of English life which is prevalent in this country. If, on the other hand, the Editor is meant, we would advise our contemporary to study the history of the English Press more minutely. He will find that English editors have not always been so enamoured of legal penalties as to forego any opportunity of evading responsibility which the law allowed them. We will admit that ordinarily in England there is a single responsible head of some kind, though he is not always the writer of the articles, but this is not the case in every country nor with every newspaper, and we cannot admit that any such arrangement is necessary in the interests of society. When the *Statesman* says that no man's reputation is safe unless every paper has its one responsible head, it is talking and knows that it is talking pure nonsense. A man who thinks himself libelled has always his remedy in civil law and it cannot matter to him whether he gets his damages from the actual writer of the libellous matter or from the proprietor or from a company or syndicate owning the paper. Was Mr. Lever's reputation unsafe because his damages were paid by the Harmsworth Trust and not by the actual libeller? If the proprietor happens to be a corporate body, the aggrieved person is no doubt deprived of the vindictive pleasure of sending his critic to prison, but we hardly think it can be said that society is mortally wounded by his loss. But of course what the *Statesman* is really troubled about is the safety of the bureaucratic groups who administer the country at present and whom it dignifies and disguises by describing as "institutions of organised society". This anxiety of the *Statesman*'s is rather humorous. The bureaucracy has armed itself with such liberal powers of repression that a journalist attacking it is like a man with no better weapon than a pebble assailing a Goliath panoplied from head to foot, armed with a repeating rifle and supported by howitzers and maxim guns. For a backer of the giant to complain because the unarmed assailant throws his pebble from behind a bush or wall is, to say the least of it, a trifle incongruous.

The gravamen of the *Statesman*'s charge, however, lies in the question it triumphantly posits at the end of its rejoinder as a final settler for its critics. The impugned "articles in the *Bande Mataram* must have been written by someone; is it courageous and honourable conduct on the part of their unknown author, this precious 'patriot', that he should elect to remain in hiding and let a poor unfortunate Printer go to jail in place of himself?" And our contemporary asks its critics either to affirm that it is right for a journalist to allow an innocent man to suffer in his place, — or else be silent. We admit our contemporary's luminous suggestion that someone must have written the article "Politics for Indians" and the better to clear up the confusion of his ideas we will add that the someone must have been either a member of the staff or an outside correspondent. The evidence showed that he must have been the latter, and, if so, his conduct in not coming forward was in accordance with those traditions of English journalism by which the *Statesman* sets such store. It may not have been ethically the most heroic or exalted conduct possible, but it does not lie in the mouth of an Englishman to question it. And we presume that the *Statesman* will not seriously suggest that it was our duty, even if we had recorded the name, to peach against a correspondent in order to save our own man, or that such a betrayal would have been either courageous or honourable. If, on the other hand, the real writer were a journalist on the staff, he must have been someone other than Aurobindo Ghose to whom no one in his senses would attribute such a half-baked effusion. He would then be one who was not accused and could only take the responsibility by giving evidence against himself as a witness for the defence. No Englishman in a similar situation would have done it unless actually put in the witness box, but for an Indian patriot, we admit, it would have been the natural course if the Printer could have been saved by his self-devotion, but it is perfectly obvious that the Printer would still have been liable under the statute and got his three months. The imputation made by the *Statesman* is not true in fact, as it was an outside contributor who wrote the article, but even were it otherwise, it is absurd in theory. It was the bureaucracy and the Magistrate who made a scapegoat of the Printer and not the *Bande Mataram* or any one on its staff. The *Statesman* is intelligent enough to understand this without having it pointed out and malice alone prompted its dishonest attempt to discredit us.

Bande Mataram, September 28, 1907

True Swadeshi

The *Times of India* like other Anglo-Indian journals of its class loses no opportunity for discrediting the Nationalist movement in Bengal. In the issue to hand it has an appreciative leader on the New Iron Industry initiated by the late Mr. J. N. Tata and now placed on a sound business footing as a Joint Stock concern with a handsome capital subscribed by the people of India. The *Times* has been constrained to admit that Indian capital is no longer shy and the spirit of enterprise too is much in evidence. The *Times* would not be itself if it omitted to mention that the Government has been doing its best to help the new industry thus giving a proof of its substantial sympathy with the true Swadeshi. But the sting is in the tail. While praising the public spirit and enterprise of Bombay, it concludes with the customary fling at Bengal where agitators are absorbed in mouthing sedition in the Beadon Square. The *Times* should remember that but for the dissemination of so-called sedition in the Beadon Square the recent striking industrial activity of Bombay as evidenced in the erection of new mills and the addition of new looms would hardly have been possible. The impartial observer must also admit that Bengal is also waking up to her industrial needs. The "true" Swadeshi of the *Times* draws its vitality from the larger Swadeshi which Bengal has made its own.

Bande Mataram, October 4, 1907

Novel Ways to Peace

We learn from the *Empire* that on Wednesday evening the Paharawallas got completely out of hand and that a number of them afterwards traversed the streets indulging in looting, destruction of property and assault. We are farther told by our contemporary that the moment the peace was broken, the Budmash element asserted itself. And the *Empire* winds up with a genial and smiling prophecy to the effect that the atmosphere will be more or less disturbed for a month (that is till the Puja is over and the European merchants have been able to get their consignments through) and there will be considerable bloodletting over the business; at the end of that period, we are told, the relations between the Government and the people, especially the Extremists, will be substantially improved, because the latter will have fully realised by then what Calcutta would be like if the British Government were actually "overthrown". We rather fancy the *Empire* has carefully forgotten to include two very important and indeed essential considerations in its amiable prosings on the orgy of hooliganism and police outrage to which the unarmed Bengalis have been subjected in the interests of foreign trade. The first is that if the present bureaucratic government were to be, let us not say "overthrown" but to be driven to retire in a dungeon from the scene, the Arms Act would deal with them and the people would very soon have the means as well as the will to defend themselves. The second is that the police in a free India would be compelled to protect the citizens instead of supplementing the deficiencies of the hooligans. It is easy to wrench all means of self-defence out of the hands of people, savagely repress all attempts at mutual protection, leave them to the mercy of the turbulent classes, allowing even the police whom we pay to protect the peace to "get completely out of hand" and loot unpunished, and then taunt the victims with their inability to defend themselves and the necessity of an alien and irresponsible third party for keeping the peace. The argument has worn thin and can no longer serve its purpose. The *Empire* errs grievously in thinking that police violence and hooliganism are the royal road to peace and conciliation. East Bengal and the Chitpur outrages will not pacify and conciliate Calcutta. The only result will be to more fiercely embitter the struggle. One other result there may indeed be — to eventually dethrone the nationalist leaders and destroy their control over the van of the movement as the control of the Moderates has already been destroyed; for as the exasperation increases their attempts to regulate the movement will be resented and themselves condemned as cowards and moderates at heart. But who will fill the vacant place? Police Commissioner Halliday or Mr. Blair, does the *Empire* think? Or prophets of desperation beside whom Bepin Chandra Pal will shine like an angel of loyalty in the eyes of Anglo-India? Yes, the bureaucrats and their underlings are doing much to break down the creed of passive resistance which we have promulgated and to prove our policy impossible. But will passive resistance be replaced by quiescence? If so, we have much misread history. The immediate future looks dark and gloomy, a chaos the end of which no man can foresee. But whatever God does is good and still our cry to our Mother is the same, "Though thou slay us, yet will we trust in thee."

"Armenian Horrors"

It has been pointed out to us that the tone of our reporter's account of Thursday's doings was hardly in consonance with the creed and the spirit of which the *Bande Mataram* is the exponent. The facts reported are not materially different from those attested by other Indian dailies, but there is too much hysterical and lachrymose exaggeration of phrase in describing them. As it is no part of our policy to conceal our own lapses, we will at once admit that there is truth in the complaint. To talk of Armenian horrors in such a connection is the rhetoric of an excited Moderate disappointed in his reliance on European humanity and "superior" civilisation, not of a sturdy Nationalist organ which has always foreseen the possibility of this and worse things as the price we shall have to pay for liberty. We withdraw therefore this and all similar expressions. Calcutta has as yet suffered nothing like what East Bengal has suffered, to say nothing of Armenia and Bulgaria. We are as yet only at the beginning of our journey and have not gone down into the valley of death through which our way lies to the promised land. It will not do to whine or shriek over some shops looted and men robbed and beaten or even over a few corpses of our countrymen floating in the Ganges, if the report be true, — this and far worse than this we shall have to meet with a calm brow and a brave heart. Not merely in goods and money but with the blood from our hearts we shall have to pay for the sins of our forefathers.

Bande Mataram, October 5, 1907

The Vanity of Reaction

THE devices of reactionary absolutism have a curious family resemblance all the world over. Reaction is never intelligent and never imaginative. Limited to the narrow horizon of its own selfish interests, committed to the preservation of the impossible and the resuscitation of corrupt systems and dead forms it has neither the vision to understand and measure the forces that have been new born to replace it, nor the wisdom to treat and compromise with the strength of Demogorgon while yet unripe so as to prolong its hour of rule for a little, — the only grace that Heaven allows to doomed institutions and forfeited powers. Like Kamsa of old, it seeks to confirm its failing grip on the world by murderous guile and violence or like the Jupiter of Prometheus Unbound gropes for safety through vain diplomacies and the martyrdom of the champions of suffering humanity. Poor in invention except in the cunning variation of savage tortures or petty brutalities, it reiterates the old wornout spells, the once-potent lies which had been powerful to prolong the death-sleep of the peoples and sees not that the mumbling of its incantations only awakes the scorn and rage of strong men indignant that such deceptive bonds should so long have availed to bind their strength. Barren of resources, it blindly persists in the old stupid violences that can hurt and enrage but cannot kill, the old menaces and outbursts of barbarous rage that have lost their power to intimidate an incensed and stubborn people, and will not realise that every blow evokes a mightier reaction, that every missile of death it hurls is returning with fearful rapidity upon the thrower, that the chains with which it binds the limbs of the nation's martyrs are so much iron which the nation will forge into weapons against its oppressors, that the blood it sheds is so much water of life to foster the young plant of liberty, that, when sentence has been passed upon men or class or institution, every device invented for safety becomes an instrument for destruction and the fiercer the attempts to escape, the swifter the motion straight towards doom. Through the clanking of the chains of its prisoners, through the cries of its victims, through the red mist of blood and torture and suffering which it seeks to set between itself and God and blind His vengeance and baffle His decrees, still there rings the ancient sentence of Fate. "In Gokul He groweth still from day to day. Who thee shall slay." The genius, the wisdom, the strength of the servants of Reaction turns naturally to their opposites, and posterity wonders that such wise men should have been so blind, that such giants should have been slain by the throwing of a pebble, that so much energy of strong action and cunning speech should have been of no more avail than the staggerings and babblings of a drunkard in his cups. For they have set their strength and wit against God's will, and it is His ironic decree that their wisdom shall be baffled by children and the weak hand of a woman shall be enough to shatter their might.

Men had once deemed of England that she was not as other peoples and that the lessons of history would be reversed by the unselfish glories of her rule, and the weakness of human nature would be belied by the splendour of her generosity and the candour of her enthusiasm. For the English are a great and wonderful people. It is true that her statesmen and soldiers slew and murdered and ravished in Ireland so that the Celt might remain quiet under her iron heel, — but they planned and fought for the freedom of nations subject to other domination than her own. It is true that they have taken the bread out of the Indian's mouth that her own children might be filled and seek to turn her dark-skinned subjects everywhere into helots of her commerce and trade, — but they paid down hard cash that her West Indian Negro might be free. It is true that her politicians deny the institutions of liberty to her own subjects, but she has been the examplar of a bourgeois liberty and a limited democracy to the whole world. Other nations turned, it was thought, but one side of themselves to the gaze, the side of national self-seeking and grasping land-hunger. England had two sides, and the one which dazzled men was very bright. And now all the world is watching what England will do now that the same problem is once more set for her which every nation has failed to solve, whether she will tread the same path of futile bloodshed, violence and defiance of irresistible decrees which other nations have trod before her or be wise in her generation as she was wise when her own children rose against her in Canada, as she has once more been wise after her hour of bloodthirst and madness in the Transvaal. The selfish fury of Anglo-India is answering for her, the greed of her merchants and capitalists is pushing her on into the abyss. Still her rulers have qualms, hesitations, fears, still they dare not utterly set their own law and the law of God at defiance. At the last moment a palsy overtakes their hands, a relenting works in their souls. After their long torture the Rawalpindi prisoners are free; Nibaran has hardly escaped from the gallows by a strange mercy of Fate; here and there the monotonous roll of repression is brightened by occasional acquittals, by stray glimpses of justice if not of forbearance. But the Anglo-Indian bureaucrats have set out on the slippery path where futile ferocity and vain blood guiltiness hurry down the car of empire to sink in the sea of shame and blood below. Seldom and by a miracle can the wheels that have once gone some way down by that slope be retarded and stopped.

What is it that you seek, rulers who are eager to confuse the interests of a handful of white administrators with the welfare of humanity, or what is it that you dream, traders who think that God made this India of ours only as a market for your merchandise? This great and ancient nation was once the fountain of human light, the apex of human civilisation, the examplar of courage and humanity, the perfection of good Government and settled society, the mother of all religions, the teacher of all wisdom and philosophy. It has suffered much at the hands of inferior civilisations and more savage peoples; it has gone down into the shadow of night and tasted often of the bitterness of death. Its pride has been trampled into the dust and its glory has departed. Hunger and misery and despair have become the masters of this fair soil, these noble hills, these ancient rivers, these cities whose life story goes back into prehistoric night. But do you think that therefore God has utterly abandoned us and given us up for ever to be a mere convenience for the West, the helots of its commerce, and the feeders of its luxury and pride? We are still God's chosen people and all our calamities have been but a discipline of suffering, because for the great mission before us prosperity was not sufficient, adversity had also its training; to taste the glory of power and beneficence and joy was not sufficient, the knowledge of weakness and torture and humiliation was also needed; it was not enough that we should be able to fill the role of the merciful sage and the beneficent king, we had also to experience in our own persons the feelings of the outcaste and the slave. But now that lesson is learned, and the time for our resurgence is come. And no power shall stay that uprising and no opposing interest shall deny us the right to live, to be ourselves, to set our seal once more upon the world. Every race and people that oppressed us even in our evening and our midnight has been broken into pieces and their glory turned into a legend of the past. Yet you venture to hope that in the hour of our morning you will be able to draw back the veil of night once more over our land as if to read you a lesson. God has lighted the fire in a quarter where you least feared it and it is beginning to eat up your commerce and threaten your ease. He has raised up the people you despised as weaklings and cowards, a people of clerks and babblers and slaves and set you to break their insurgent spirit and trample them into the dust if you can. And you cannot. You have tried every means except absolute massacre and you have failed. And now what will you do? Will you learn the lesson before it is too late or will you sink your Empire in the mire of shame where other nations have gone who had not the excuse of the knowledge of liberty and the teachings of the past? For us, for you, today everything is trembling in the balance, and it is not for us who have but reacted passively to your action, it is for you to decide.

The Price of a Friend

Recent events are daily putting a greater and greater strain on the sweet and cordial relation of the Friend of India with her people. It is no doubt hard to part when friends are dear, perhaps it will cost a sigh, a tear. Under the circumstances the poet's advice is to steal away and choose one's own time. But the Friend of India is giving us warning after warning that it will cease to be our friend unless we consent to do its bidding. When the people do not much mind the sundering of this tie the Friend should be prepared for the inevitable and devise some means for avoiding the heart-wrench which the sudden severance of such a long-standing connection must necessarily cause. The Friend so fondly hoped that the Moderates compared with whom the Extremists are "a mere drop in the ocean" would ever remain docile and teachable, sit at its feet for all time and hang on its lips with the attention and reverence they show to their spiritual preceptors. But this sudden change in their attitude has come to our friend as a surprise. The Moderates are now most indecently and openly hobnobbing with the Extremists. When a prominent Extremist goes to jail the Moderates stand by him, nay shed tears over his unjust incarceration. When an Extremist newspaper is prosecuted and the bureaucracy fails to spot the real offender on account of its having been conducted under an arrangement which whatever its merit, lacks the fairness and candour of delivering the management at once into the hands of the enemy whenever so required, the Moderates do not realise the enormity of the latter's offence and what is more, resent the Friend of India's pious demand that the conductors of the paper should have thrust their neck, down the wolf's throat. This ill-advised obstinacy the friend can hardly excuse and we quite understand its righteous indignation. There is time yet for the Moderates to come round, go on their knees before their justly offended friend and sign a pledge to go back to his guidance. This the friend demands and hopes that the Moderates will accede to it. The friend also reaffirms his claim to their allegiance and that is his persistent support of their "just aspirations". It is by their unjust aspirations that they have forfeited the sympathy of this precious friend. There cannot be a greater iniquity than the attempt at self-realisation; justice and equity demand that one nation should for ever be in the leading strings of another. Whoever wants to alter this most reasonable and fair arrangement must be shunned and expelled from the Congress and all other institutions which desire the countenance of the *Statesman*. The friend also contends that though the constitutional method has not hitherto paid, that does not mean that it will never pay. Even if it does not pay at all, the Moderates have no business to rub the shoulders with the Extremists; for in that case they stand to lose the most valuable thing they possess, the friendship of the Friend of India.

A New Literary Departure

We have received from the publisher Srijut Abinash Chandra Bhattacharya, a small volume in Bengali, entitled *Bartaman Rananiti* or the Modern Science of War. The book is a small manual which seeks to describe for the benefit of those who, like the people of Bengal under the beneficent Pax Britannica, are entirely unacquainted with the subject, the nature and use of modern weapons, the meaning of military terms, the uses and distribution of the various limbs of a modern army, the broad principles of strategy and tactics, and the nature and principles of guerilla warfare. These are freely illustrated by detailed references to the latest modern wars, the Boer and the Russo-Japanese, in the first of which many new developments were brought to light or tested and in the second corrected by the experience of a greater field of wafare and more normal conditions. The book is a new departure in Bengali literature and one which shows the new trend of the national mind. In the old days of a narrow life and confined aspirations, we were satisfied with the production of romantic poetry and novels varied by occasional excursions into academic philosophy and criticism. Nowadays the heart of the nation is rising to higher things; history, the patriotic drama, political writings, songs of national aspiration, draughts from the fountain of our ancient living religion and thought are almost the sole literature which command a hearing. There are signs also that books recording the results of modern science and the organisation of modern life in war and peace will ensure a ready sale if there are writers who can give the public exactly what they want. The new born nation is eagerly seeking after its development and organisation and anything which will help it and widen its sphere of useful knowledge, will deserve and gain its attention. Two years ago this small volume would have fallen still-born from the Press, today we have no doubt it will be eagerly sought after. It is perfectly true that no practical use can be made of its contents at the moment; but the will and desire of thousands creates its own field and when the spirit of a nation demands any sphere of activity material events are shaped by that demand in ways that at the time seem to be the wild dreams of an unbridled imagination. Our business is to prepare ourselves by all kinds of knowledge and action for the life of a nation, by knowledge and action when both are immediately permitted us, by knowledge alone for action which, though not permitted now, is a necessary part of the future nation's perfect development. When the earnest soul prepares itself by what Sadhana is possible to it, however imperfect, God in his own good time prepares the field and the opportunity for perfect Sadhana and complete attainment.

Bande Mataram, October 7, 1907

Mr. Keir Hardie and India

The visit of Mr. Keir Hardie to Bengal, so much feared by the English papers, has come and gone and the reactionist Press have taken care that it should create the right sort of sensation in England, so that whatever he may tell of the carefully-hidden truth about the "unrest" in India may be discredited beforehand. We have been watching these manoeuvres with some amusement, mingled with a kind of admiration for the sheer bare-faced impudence of the lies which these amiable gentry are administering so liberally to a willing British public. Anything is good enough for British consumption, and accordingly Anglo-India sets itself no limits in the grossness and incredibility of the inventions it circulates. Mr. Hardie's presence is responsible for the riots, for the Union Jute Mills strike, for every development of the political struggle which has occurred since the formidable Labourite set foot on Indian soil. We shall hardly be surprised if we see it next asserted in the *Englishman* and then telegraphed by the *Englishman*'s faithful Reuter that the boldness of Brahmobandhab Upadhyay's statement in the dock was caused by the expectation of Keir Hardie's visit or that some dim prophetic anticipation of it moved Basanta Bhattacharjee when he faced the terrors of British law. We are ready to give Anglo-India credit for very great lengths of denseness, ignorance and folly, but it is hard to believe that they cannot realise the change which has come over Indian political life and still think that the words or presence of an Englishman can ever again influence the minds of the people even in an ordinary way much less in the fabulous fashions which Newmania concocts. Anglo-India feared that if the truth travelled to England, the campaign of repression might be stopped and measures of conciliation adopted. For ourselves we never entertained any such fear. It is not ignorance of the truth, but their own self-interest as a nation which determines the attitude of all English parties, not excluding the Labourites. The interest of the monied classes is bound up with the continuance of arbitrary British domination, and for that domination Liberal as well as Tory will fight tooth and nail. As for the Labour Party, it will support that domination if they think it is to the interest of the working classes, otherwise they will oppose it. We have met and talked with Mr. Keir Hardie and we found him a strong, shrewd-witted man possessed of a great deal of clear common sense. He is a Labourite and a Socialist. As a Labourite he will do whatever he thinks best in the interests of Labour; as a Socialist, the interests of whose creed are bound up with the progress of internationalism, he may take Indian questions with a greater sincerity than the Cottons and Wedderburns. But as we said before in our article on Mr. Keir Hardie, to suppose that he can do anything for us is a delusion. India like other countries, must work out her salvation for herself, and the less she trusts to foreign help, the swifter will be her deliverance.

Bande Mataram, October 8, 1907

The Nagpur Affair and True Unity

THE Nagpur Nationalists are now being run down in every quarter for having failed to work in unison with the Moderates. The cause of rupture as disclosed by the *Indian Social Reformer*, a hostile critic of the Nationalist Party, will convince every right-thinking man that the Nationalists had ample provocation for what is being denounced as a highly reprehensible conduct on their part. They had a Nationalist majority in the Executive Committee and the Moderates were arranging for a fresh meeting of the Reception Committee to alter this state of things. This unconstitutional step led to the subsequent unpleasant development. It is very difficult to disentangle the truth from the apparently exaggerated reports of "Nationalist rowdyism" of which so much has been heard of late. But we have a suspicion that it is the wonted game of the Moderates to have it all their own way and then to try to discredit the opponents by making them responsible to the country for the disunion and dissension in the camp. Why do they not adopt a straightforward course from the very beginning? It is they who stand in the way of a united India by denying a fair representation to those who hold advanced political views. They always want the Nationalists to compromise their principle by an appeal in the name of unity. But their selfishness and autocracy never allow them to reflect on the true way of achieving unity.

There is a cant phrase which is always on our lips in season and out of season, and it is the cry for unity. We call it a cant phrase because those who use it, have not the slightest conception of what they mean when they use it, but simply employ it as an effective formula to discourage independence in thought and progressiveness in action. It is not the reality of united thought and action which they desire, it is merely the appearance of unity. "Do not let the Englishman think we are not entirely at one on any and every question," that is the bottom idea underlying this formula. It is a habit of mind born of the spirit of dependence and weakness. It is a fosterer of falsehood and encourages cowardice and insincerity. "Be your views what they may, suppress them, for they will spoil our unity; swallow your principles, they will spoil our unity; do not battle for what you think to be the right, it will spoil our unity; leave necessary things undone, for the attempt to do them will spoil our unity;" this is the cry. The prevalence of a dead and lifeless unity is the true index of national degradation, quite as much as the prevalence of a living unity is the index of national greatness. So long as India was asleep and only talking in its dreams, a show of unity was possible but the moment it awoke and began to live, this show was bound to be broken. So long as mendicancy was our method and ideal, the show was necessary, for a family of beggars must not vary in its statements or in the nature of its request to the prospective patron; they must cringe and whine in a single key. Under other circumstances, the maintenance of the show becomes of less paramount importance.

There is another idea underlying the cry for unity and it is the utterly erroneous impression that nations have never been able to liberate themselves and do great deeds unless they were entirely and flawlessly united within. History supplies no justification for this specious theory. On the contrary when a nation is living at high pressure and feelings are at white heat, opinions and actions are bound to diverge far more strongly than at other times. In the strenuous times before the American War of Independence, the colony was divided into a powerful minority who were wholly for England, a great hesitating majority who were eager for internal autonomy but unwilling to use extreme methods, and a small but vigorous minority of extremists with men like John Adams at their head who pushed the country into revolt and created a nation. The history of the Italian revolution tells the same story. We are fond of quoting the instance of Japan, pointing to its magnificient unity and crying shame on ourselves for falling below that glorious standard; but those of us who talk most of Japan often betray a sovereign ignorance of its history. Nowhere was there a more keen, determined and murderous struggle between parties than in Japan in the days of its preparation, and the struggle was not over the ultimate ideal or object

— the freedom and greatness of Japan, on which all parties were agreed, but on questions of method and internal organisation. Until that question as between the moderate Shogun Party and the extremist Mikado Party had been settled, it was felt by all that the approach to the ultimate ideal of all could not be seriously attempted.

True national unity is the unity of self-dedication to the country when the liberty and greatness of our motherland is the paramount consideration to which all others must be subordinated. In India at the present hour there are three conflicting ideals; one party set the maintenance of British supremacy above all other considerations; another would maintain that supremacy in a modified form; a third aspires to make India a free and autonomous nation, connected with England, if it may be, but not dependent on her. Until one of these conflicting ideals is accepted by the majority of the nation, it is idle to make a show of unity. That was possible formerly because the ideal of a modified British supremacy was the prevailing ideal, but now that new hopes and resolves are entering the national consciousness, these must either be crushed or prevail, before true unity of a regenerated nation can replace the false unity of acquiescence in servitude.

Bande Mataram, October 23, 1907

The Nagpur Imbroglio

It is difficult to get authentic and undisputed news of the Nagpur imbroglio, but if report is to be believed, there is a better chance than before of a satisfactory working compromise. It is in every way desirable that the present difficulties should be smoothed over if that can be done without any sacrifice to essential principle, and for any such compromise it is essential for both sides to recognise that while they may and should fight stubbornly for their principles both outside and inside the Congress, yet the National Assembly itself is not the monopoly of either. A great deal of clamour has been raised by the Moderates of Nagpur and Bombay over the outbursts of excited popular feeling in which a few Loyalists were roughly handled, and use has been freely made of them to obscure the real issue. It is well therefore that this incident, which we must all regret, should be understood in its true light. The Moderate majority on the Nagpur Reception Committee happens to be a factitious majority and most of the members take no sustained interest in the Committee work, while the Nationalist minority are alert and active. At the meeting which elected the Executive Committee the Moderates did not attend except in small numbers and a strong Nationalist majority was elected. The inconveniences of this tactical defeat were very soon felt by the Moderate Party and after a fashion to which they are unfortunately too much addicted, they tried to remedy their original error by riding roughshod over procedure and the unwritten law that guides the conduct of all public bodies. Mr. Chitnavis, one of the Secretaries, called on his own initiative a fresh meeting to elect a new Executive in which the Moderates should predominate. Dr. Munje, also a Secretary, was perfectly within his rights in opposing the bare-faced illegality of this unconstitutional procedure and refusing to allow the meeting to be held. Meanwhile, great popular excitement had been created and there was a strong feeling of indignation among the students and people in general against the Moderate aristocrats of Nagpur and when they issued from the abortive meeting, they were angrily received by the crowd waiting outside and handled in a very rough and unseemly manner. This was certainly regrettable, but it is absurd to make the Nationalist leaders in Nagpur responsible for the outburst. All that they did was to baffle a very discreditable attempt to defy all constitutional procedure and public decorum in the interests of party trickery, and in doing so they were entirely right.

A persistent attempt has also been made to prejudice the Nagpur Nationalists in the eyes of the country and obscure the real question by grossly misrepresenting their action with regard to the issue about the Presidentship. By the rule formulated at last year's Congress — a rule we have always considered foolish and unworkable — the local Reception Committee has to elect the President for the year by a three-fourths majority, and, if they cannot do so, the decision rests with the All-India Congress Committee. This arrangement is admirably conceived for swelling the Congress funds on the one hand and for defeating public opinion on the other. The Reception Committee is not an elected or representative body but is constituted on a money basis, as any one who can pay twenty-five rupees or get another to pay it for him can have his name enrolled as a member. Whichever side has the longer purse can secure the election of the President of its choice. Such an election is no more likely to represent public opinion than Mr. Morley's Council of Notables is likely to represent it. Like the Council of Notables, it will represent the opinion of the moneyed aristocracy, the men of position and purse, the men "with a stake in the country". Nevertheless, the rule is there and so long as it stands, it must be observed. The position in Nagpur as in the Deccan is this, that the Loyalist Moderate Party is composed of the wealthy, successful and high-placed men, the retired officials, the Rai Sahebs and Rai Bahadurs, the comfortable professional men and those who pride themselves on their English education and Western enlightenment and look down with contempt on the ignorant masses. On the other hand, the young men and the poorer middle class form the bulk of the Nationalist Party, although it contains a minority of the wealthier men. The lines of divergence are therefore somewhat different from those in Bengal and the gulf between the two parties wider both in opinion and in spirit. In Bombay or Nagpur it would be perfectly impossible for a man like Srijut Surendranath Banerji to be a leader of the Moderates; he would be looked on with suspicion, continually checked, snubbed, thrust into the shadow and eventually forced out of the camp.

The struggle over the Presidentship in Nagpur followed lines necessitated by the character of the two parties. The Moderates relied on the length of their purse, the Nationalists appealed to the people. A few Moderates of wealth advanced money and filled the Reception Committee with men of their persuasion, who were therefore in a sense paid to vote for any President proposed by their wealthy patrons. The Nationalists, on the other hand, created a Nationalist organisation or Rashtriya Mandali and invited all who were willing to become members of the Reception Committee *on condition that Mr. Tilak became President* to send in the requisite sum, not to the Reception Committee but to the Rashtriya Mandali. Eventually it was found that though the total sum raised by the Nationalists was much larger than that contributed by the Moderate magnates, yet the votes it represented fell short of three-fourths. It was decided, therefore, after paying in the sums sent in unconditionally to the Congress funds, to devote the rest to some Nationalist purpose, preferably the creation of a National School in Nagpur. This decision has been deliberately misrepresented as a perversion of Congress funds and a refusal on the part of the Nationalist Party to contribute their share of the Congress expenses. The money was expressly sent in on the condition and with the proviso that the contributors would become members of the Reception Committee *only* if there was a certainty of Mr. Tilak's being elected, and for this reason it was sent in to the Rashtriya Mandali and not to the Congress Committee, as the latter could not accept conditional contributions. In the disposal of these monies, therefore, Mr. Tilak not having been elected, the Congress has no concern whatever and the Moderate Party less than none; it is a matter entirely between the Nationalist organisation and its contributors. Yet it is on these and similarly flimsy pretexts that the Moderate magnates have withdrawn from the Reception Committee.

A compromise can now be arrived at only on condition that the present constitution of the Executive Committee is not interfered with and that the Congress session will be duly held at Nagpur. To transfer the Congress to Madras or any other centre for the convenience of the Moderate Party while there are men willing to hold it in Nagpur, would mean a definite and final split in the Congress camp, which would turn the Congress into a Rump of Loyalists and Moderates possibly with a Nationalist Assembly standing in opposition to it. The All-India Committee is not likely to force on such an undesirable consummation. Whoever may or may not retire himself from the Reception Committee, the body itself remains and is the only one constitutionally capable of holding the session this year. On the other hand, the rule of the three-fourths majority remains and if Mr. Tilak's followers cannot secure this for their nominee, the Nationalists cannot lower themselves by attempting to secure his election by any unfair or unconstitutional means. They may also meet the Moderates halfway by raising further funds as their share of the Congress expenditure. If Mr. Tilak is not elected, it does not matter to us, in the absence of Lala Lajpat Rai, whether Dr. Rash Behari Ghose or any other figurehead graces the Presidential seat, and this need not be a cause of further quarrel. On the basis of Dr. Ghose's election and the *status quo* in other respects a compromise ought not to be impossible, and at the present juncture it is undoubtedly desirable. We hope that good sense and not party feeling will prevail.

Bande Mataram, October 29, 1907

English Democracy Shown Up

SCRATCH an Englishman and you will find an Anglo-Indian, — this is what we said in these columns sometime ago. The Anglophilous Indian enthusiast who goes to England saturated with the old Congress poison of a morbid faith in the native generosity of English character, in the innate amenability of Englishmen to reason and persuasion regarding matters Indian, is doomed to a very rude awakening. He has not to stay long in the country before he finds every Englishman he may come across turning a deaf ear to his story of grievance and injustice. He is no doubt loudly applauded and called a "true Briton" when he declaims against the tyranny in Russia, but is invariably called "ungrateful" if he happens to tell home truths about England's dominion in Hindusthan. He meets with the same callous disapprobation from all Englishmen alike, from the Liberal whose motto is "Government with consent" just as much as from the Tory whose principle avowedly is "let things be". On the Indian question the Englishman will tell you his position is that of a "patriot", not of a "partisan". Imperialism is far above party; every Englishman therefore is an Imperialist when he is thinking of the Indian question, he has then ceased to be either a Liberal or a Conservative. To this rule there are some exceptions, a few old ladies here and there (who however hardly count in politics yet), and some truly noble men who hold humanity far higher than Imperialism. These men certainly frankly admit that England's arbitrary and tyrannous tenure of power in India is a standing libel on herself, a gross violation of those political principles which she proclaims from the housetops to the whole of Europe. The voice of such men however is hardly heard in the Councils of the Empire, and if ever heard, contemptuously ignored.

The hasty, hideous, indecent, savage yell that has been raised by the whole of the English Press against Mr. Keir Hardie because he has dared to tell the truth about the present situation in this country is a striking confirmation of what we have said above, and what we stated before in the *Bande Mataram.* We must not commit the mistake of supposing that the English Press is indignant because it doubts the truth of Mr. Hardie's statements against the Indian Government; not that at all; they know very well, one and all of that yelling throng, that every word of what he has said is true, and that Reuter has wired a grossly mendacious version of his statements; but they are full of wrath because the leader of the Independent Labour Party has told the unvarnished truth respecting the character of the rule that England has established here. They are bursting with rage because their long and unscrupulously kept-up fiction of a just and benevolent Indian rule has been exposed in all its ugliness at last by one who happens to be an *Englishman*, (Oh the sting of it!) and an Englishman of power and prestige too, who easily has the ear of the civilised world. He is a traitor, shout the impious fraternity of the British Press, because he has the nobleness of mind, the honesty of conviction, to be able to tell the truth against his own country when he finds it attempting without a blush to perpetuate an outrage upon humanity. He is no longer a statesman because he could not deliberately suppress a truth in consideration of the reasons of state, which in the present instance means, in the interest of the sickening British lie — repeated *ad nauseam* before Europe and America — that England governs India for the benefit of the Indians. The paper which so often contains articles from the pen of Sir Henry Cotton joins in this infamous chorus of denunciation no less than the *Daily News* which always so overflows with the pure milk of undiluted Liberalism, that is to say British Liberalism.

Let us hope this at least will serve to open wide the eyes of those of our countrymen who are still troubled now and then with the visitings of their old faith in England. England *will not* give us anything unless we can force her to her knees, this is the only moral to which the present outrageous clamour of the English Press points. We may present our case with as much eloquence, logic and precision as we please; they in England will always brush our representations insolently aside as mere "Babu rodomontade". If an Englishman with a disengaged mind has the courage to take up our cause, and tell the world the most elementary facts about the wrong England is doing us, his voice is drowned in the roar of the ruling nation whose one aim is mercilessly to exploit India and let the rest of the world know as little about their real Indian policy as possible, and even to deceive it whenever opportunity offers. How humane it sounded, how extremely Christian, when Lord Lansdowne declared in the House of Lords with that supreme unction of which Englishmen alone are capable, that one of *the* motives of the war with the Boers was the righting of the grievous wrongs to which "our *Indian fellow-subjects* were forced to submit in the Transvaal". That grandiose declaration was not without its effect in the international world, though we know only too well that the Transvaal Indians live under infinitely more humiliating conditions now than they ever did under the government of Paul Kruger. And one need not feel surprised if one hears an Englishman, even at the present day, repeating the pronouncement of Lord Lansdowne in all solemnity in order to prove England's constant anxiety and watchfulness on behalf of her Indian subjects.

There can hardly be any doubt that the Press has been shamelessly encouraged in its campaign of foul misrepresentation against Mr. Keir Hardie by Mr. Morley's speech at Arbroath. The philosopher-Secretary betrayed not a little ruffling of his philosophic calm in his undisguisedly hostile and somewhat petulant references to Mr. Keir Hardie's opinion that India should be given the same autonomy that is enjoyed by Canada. The wonderful allegory of the fur-coat though hardly giving us an encouraging indication of any power of imagination or perception, of any historical insight, of any sense of humour or relevancy on the part of its author, certainly furnishes abundant proof of his ill-natured impatience of the generous ideal that the labour leader cherishes for the people of this country.

But, after all, we perhaps do the Indian Secretary an injustice in charging him with lack of historical insight; in one sense, it may be said, he shows an abundance of it. For we learn from Reuter, that "he paid a tribute to the courage, patience and fidelity of the House of Commons, from which he augured that the democracies were going to show their capacity to tackle difficult and complicated problems." The one remarkable feature of European democracies from the days of Athens to those of England, has throughout been that whilst they always most jealously keep vigil over the integrity of their own republican constitution, they revel at the same time in the despotic sway of unlimited power over the peoples they conquer. This is strictly true of the Pagan republics of Hellas and Rome as well as of the Christian Communes and Country-states of Mediaeval and Modern Europe. The ideal that has shaped the polity of Europe is always consciously or unconsciously Hellenic and not Hebraic; the Christian ideal of human brotherhood the European is apt to regard as part of the privilege of his citizenship, it is not to be extended to a conquered people. This is strictly true, the Christian missions and missionaries of Europe notwithstanding. In other words, Christian Europe flings her Christianity aside in her treatment of those who have had the misfortune to come under her rule; these she looks upon as Athens and Rome did on their subject peoples. Mr. Morley whilst congratulating the English democracy on the determination they have shown to keep their Indian Empire their own, might very well have been feeling the secret glow of an historic enthusiasm in insensibly thinking of similar figures in ancient and modern European history extolling their countrymen on similar occasions.

What we meant by taxing him with want of historic perception was that he has betrayed a sad ignorance of Asiatic history. Asia has never embraced an ideal without universalising it. To profess the Christian faith and persist in confining the Christian ideal of human brotherhood to one's own nation strikes the Asiatic as a monstrous hypocrisy. Nor, as we have had occasion to remark before, has an ideal had to win its way to the heart of the Orient through a welter of its martyr's blood, as has been the case with all kinds of ideals in Europe. This is the secret of the willingness and readiness with which the monarchies of Asia are democratising the constitutions of their country. The period of English History dating from 1066 and ending with 1832, the Shah of Persia has had the magnanimity to summarise into a few years of Persian History. It is therefore that the average Indian who has studied England's history and literature feels so extremely perplexed, and is just now beginning to feel indignant at her strenuous and persistent refusal to give India that liberty which she has so prized all through her history.

England, on the other hand, and quite consistently enough thinks she is rightly acting in withholding from the Indian the citizenship of the British Empire, for in so doing she is strictly in the wake of European tradition, and has the full justification of history as she has known and understood it. And consequently John Morley hastens to remind Indians of the "weary steps" necessary before they can attain liberty, the weary steps that the countries of Europe have had to traverse before they secured it.

We fully understand the import of the latest speech of the Indian Secretary, and of the latest outburst of the British Democracy — India will only have liberty when she has the strength, physical and moral, to wrench it from the selfish grasp of the ruling country.

Bande Mataram, October 31, 1907

How to Meet the Inevitable Repression

THE Swadeshi that you have started in Bengal is a move in the right direction, said some highly placed members of the Indian Civil Service to an Indian on their way back to this country from England; but they continued, we shall try to break the back of it in every possible way, we shall put the staying power of the Bengalee people to the severest test, before we allow them to develop their new nationalism. Thus spoke they, and what has happened since has certainly been singularly confirmatory of their frank avowal. The Declaration of the 7th of August, 1905, came as a surprise upon the English people; to their discerning ear trained hereditarily to true and false political notes, the resolution of the people of Bengal to live of their own and not to repose any longer on an unmanly faith in England's charity and benevolence, sounded like the very death-knell of the Anglo-Indian autocracy. The consciousness of potential strength that lay at the bottom of the people's determination to boycott English goods would, as it developed, inevitably render England's arbitrary tenure of power in India progressively difficult to maintain. The oversea overlords therefore made up their mind at the very outset to crush this ominous phenomenon in Bengal. But the Briton is by nature an optimist, a born believer in his own immense power and in the insignificance of others. And thus, though visited by a secret dread of ultimate possibilities, he at first nursed the fond illusion that the discontent in Bengal was only a mere surface-simmer, the Declaration of the 7th a mere petulant outcry, that the boycott was an impossibility in Bengal because it required for its success a higher patriotism than was to be expected of the Bengalee character. And many English people in England as well as in this country kept speaking in this strain for sometime, always finishing up with the confident and pleasant prediction that the Boycott movement in Bengal was doomed to a speedy and complete failure. It is this condition of the British mind that accounts for the somewhat mental attitude of the Government during the first phase of the movement in Bengal. But as soon as the success of the boycotters was patently manifest in the substantial and steady diminution of the imports from England, the self-assurance of the English people and their scepticism of the Bengalee character vanished into thin air, and they definitely launched upon their policy of "breaking the back of the movement".

The country must fully realise the seriousness of the struggle on which it has entered with the Bureaucracy; it must be strong enough to withstand and triumph over the most merciless act of hostility from an immensely powerful opponent. To extinguish the boycott at any cost is clearly now the one policy of the Anglo-Indian autocrats. The weapons in their hands are many, some possessed of such subtle potency as easily to elude the comprehension of those who are not always on their guard. The policy of breaking up the dawning sense of Indian nationality into a congeries of conflicting forces that have been initiated under the guise of reform by the Secretary of State who happens, by the way, to be a commentator of the Prince of Machiavelli, shows the consummate cunning of the foe with whom we have joined action on behalf of our country. The treatment meted out to Liakat Hossain, Saroda Charan Sen and the Printer of the *Sandhya* gives us a glimpse of the relentlessness that we must be prepared as a nation to face; the protected hooliganism that fell like a scourge on the city but a few days ago, is a luminous indication of what is to come with increasing intensity (does it not remind one of very similar happenings at Naples in the days of Austrian tyranny?) The Seditious Meetings Bill that has been ushered into birth with such a blare of the legislative trumpet shows the boldness with which the Bureaucracy can fling defiance in the face of those who have dared to dream of Indian unity. And behind it all can you hear the roar — like that which the Christian martyrs heard when the gentler methods of persuasion had failed to shake their Christianity?

Providence has however simplified our task. Nowhere in the world has an absolutism been so helplessly dependent on the loyalty and cooperation of those over whom it is set. The day that cooperation comes to a stop the English cease to be the rulers of this country. And it is this that sets a strict limit to the extent to which the Indian Government can carry on its repressive policy. There are acts from which even the Indian police will recoil with horror; there are policies against which even the loyal Subordinate Civil Service will revolt; and such acts and policies therefore are beyond the range of practical politics in this country — acts and policies of which we consantly read in connexion with the Russian and Turkish tyrannies. No one could accuse us of the intention to minimise to the country the immensity of the sacrifice it must nerve itself to face in the struggle with the powers that be; but at the same time we do not agree with those who turn away from the thought of liberty because it must necessarily involve the country, they think, in all those bloodcurdling inhumanities which they have read of, say, in the memoirs of Prince Kuropatkin. The position of the Indian Government, it must be borne in mind, is much less secure than that of any other Government in the world. Many Englishmen, not unpossessed of some culture and learning, were grossly scandalised to see Bepin Chandra Pal going about freely after he had refused to give evidence in the case against the *Bande Mataram*; he would have been hurried into Newgate the very next moment after his refusal to help the prosecution, had he been in England, they said, or he would have been immediately led off to Siberia had he been guilty of a similar defiance of the Government in Russia. The obvious answer to these plaintive hypotheses was that the Indian Government possesses none of that strength that is enjoyed by the Government either in England or Russia. In our national preparation against arbitrary rule we must not be wanting in a correct appreciation of our own strength and of the points of weakness of our opponents. The problem of the Bureaucracy, to state it finally, is to push its policy of repression against the Indian Nationalists as far as it can without alienating the moral sympathy of those on whose collaboration their tenure of power rests.

Our duty is thus obviously to train up the moral consciousness of our people to that level of development at which it will refuse as a whole to tolerate for any space of time at all the rule of the few over the many. And in doing this work we must press up all the avenues that lead to the common goal. The missionary work of preaching the ideal of self-rule in every part of the country, as the essential precondition of our National realisation, is of course of superlative importance, and the bold and unflinching facing of persecution in the faithful discharge of this sacred task is of equal service. But apart from this work we must also endeavour to foster the growth of those conditions that favour the easy and rapid germination of the love of liberty. Even a cursory glance at Indian life would convince everybody that it is only in the independent professions in our country that the ideal of Indian liberty struck its first root and is now most widely prevalent. The vast majority of our educated countrymen are absorbed in Governmental or quasi-Governmental services where the growth of the liberty ideal is naturally inhibited and where at best it acquires but a stunted development, being condemned from birth to deafness and dumbness. It would be difficult to think of anything more ruinously unfortunate for a country than that the greater majority of its educated men should be debarred throughout the most fruitful period of their life from participation in patriotic work, should be robbed of their only chance of livelihood if they ever happened to give explicit utterance to their love for the land that gave them birth. One can easily realise how unspeakably demoralising the influences of such a service must be, and yet the overwhelming proportion of our educated countrymen are constantly subject to them. The only way to remove this gross anomaly is to create rival sources of employment which will provide Indians an independent living. The existing professions are too few for this purpose, and are, further, filled already to choking. The only adequate means to this end is therefore the industrial development of the country which will open to our present and coming generations a much more attractive and promising avenue of employment than the services, the strictly subordinate services, let us not forget, of the alien Bureaucracy. The uprise of a numerous industrial class will thus spell a great and invaluable accession of strength to the political interest of the country. It is this that lends to the question of India's industrial development its main fascination and interest, and serves to remind us forcibly of the vital interaction that exists between the different branches of human activity. The stir and activity in the various industries of the country that have already been caused by the Swadeshi boycott movement is full of happy augury. We must strain every nerve to fill the whole country with trained industrial ability, we must send our young men in hundreds and thousands all over the world to learn the scientific methods of production so that India may in a very few years be covered with a network of industrial centres that will supply work to hundreds of thousands of our educated men, and rescue them from the inanition of a living death in Government service. The work already begun in this direction by the Association for the Advancement of Scientific and Industrial Training of Indians cannot be too much praised and deserves the most liberal encouragement. How very many more Basantas we may very reasonably expect to see rising up in an industrial India, ready to court suffering in the name of the Motherland.

And besides, the successful working of the handful of trades union in Bengal mostly composed as yet of illiterate men, certainly give us a most promising insight into the latent possibilities that lie in the direction of a general policy of passive resistance that may be adopted by the country. If the people of India are one day to signify their intolerance of arbitrary rule, it will very probably be, as Seely and Meredith Townsend foretell, by a general declaration of passive resistance. And before we can expect our countrymen in the services seriously to entertain the thought of refusing to serve the Bureaucracy, we must see that the country has other means of obtaining their subsistence to offer them.

Bande Mataram, November 2, 1907

Difficulties at Nagpur

THE difficulties experienced at Nagpur in bringing about the compromise which at one time seemed on the point of being effected, do not strike a mind outside the whirlpool of local excitement and controversy as either obvious or insurmountable; yet it is evident that so much importance is being attached to them as to seriously imperil the chance of a Congress session being held at all this year. It is imperative that some decision should be arrived at in the course of the next few days either one way or the other. Both sides lay the blame of the failure to arrive at an agreement on its opponents. The Nationalists say that the Moderate Party will not accept any reasonable terms and the Moderates charge the Nationalists with backing out of the compromise on the question of the money subscribed to the Rashtriya Mandali. It appears that the Nationalists are willing to co-operate if Srijut Surendranath Banerji be nominated as President in lieu of Mr. Tilak. The reasons for this proposal and its rejection are not far to seek. Sj. Surendranath is recognised all over India as the acknowledged leader of one of the two great parties in Bengal, a man with a great name and a great following in the country and, what is more important from the Nationalist standpoint, one who, whatever vagaries his ideas or policy may lead him into, is believed to be a thoroughgoing Boycotter and Swadeshist and in no sense a Government man. Dr. Rash Behari Ghose, on the other hand, is a dark horse in politics. All that the rest of India knows of him is that he is a distinguished jurist, the Chairman of last year's Reception Committee and — a Legislative Councillor. None of these titles to distinction is sufficient to justify his being suddenly put forward as President of the National Congress; for the time has passed away, not to return, when appointment to the Legislative Councils, provincial or imperial, was sufficient to raise a successful man of intellectual distinction or social influence, not before politically notable, to the position of a leader or at least a sort of Congress grandee entitled to the respect of the common herd. A seat on the Legislative Council is nowadays an obstacle and not a help to leadership, a cause of distrust and not of trust: the man to whom the bureaucracy lends ear is not one whom the people can trust and follow, and one who consents to sit in a Council where he is not listened to and can command no influence, has not the self-respect and backbone which are necessary to a popular leader — in days of stress and struggle. To us Nationalists a seat on the Council is not merely an obstacle but an absolute bar to popular leadership, for it means that the man has one foot in the enemy's camp and one in the people's. It is easy to understand therefore why the Nagpur Nationalists are opposed to the idea of Dr. Ghose's Presidentship, specially as his political views are not understood nor has he, like Mr. Gokhale, a record of past services and self-sacrifice to set against the disqualification of a seat on the Legislative Council. Nor is it difficult to understand why the Moderates of Nagpur have shied at the idea of Srijut Surendranath's Presidentship. The Moderatism of Western India is much more Loyalist than Moderate, unlike that of Bengal, where except in the case of a small minority Moderatism wears loyalty more or less loosely as a sort of cloak or garment of respectability than as an essential part of its politics. This tendency is exaggerated in places like the Central Provinces where before the Nationalist upheaval the pulse of political life beat dull and slow. For a Moderate of the Nagpur Rai Bahadur type to be asked to take Surendranath as a substitute for Tilak, is as if they were asked to exchange Satan for Beelzebub; both are to them, as to the *Englishman*, devils of Extremism, one only less objectionable than the other.

But the rights of this question are so simple that there is no excuse for allowing the Congress to break up over it. If the Moderates want Dr. Rash Behari Ghose or any other Loyalist or Legislative Councillor as President, they must be satisfied with their three-fourths majority on the Reception Committee and pay the bulk of the expenses of the session. If they desire a larger co-operation on the part of the Nationalists, they should meet them halfway by accepting the nomination of Surendranath or any other President acceptable to both parties as a compromise. And if they will take neither course, they should leave it to the Nationalists to arrange for the holding of the Congress with Mr. Tilak as President. But for them to insist on the Rashtriya Mandal funds, raised on the clear understanding that they should only be devoted to Congress purposes if Mr. Tilak were nominated President, being given into their hands to hold a Congress with a Loyalist President in the chair is a preposterously childish and unreasoning obstinacy. We cannot understand how the Rashtriya Mandali could take this step even if they wished, since it would be a distinct contravention of the condition on which the money was given and a misuse of public money. Yet it is because the Rashtriya Mandali will not comply with this unreasonable demand that the Moderates of Nagpur seem to have given the *coup de grâce* to the Nagpur session. The plea of the fear of schoolboy rowdyism is plainly disingenuous, for these gentlemen were willing to face that terrible danger provided the Nationalists paid in their funds to the Reception Committee and accepted their nominee as President; these therefore are the real points on which the Moderate Party is unwilling to compromise and the plea of rowdyism is only a convenient if undignified excuse to cover an untenable position. For our part, we do not think the question of the Presidentship need be made a cause of final cleavage. Dr. Rash Behari Ghose is pledged, like most public men in Bengal, to Swadeshi and Boycott and this is still the most important issue before the Congress. If therefore the Loyalists can still be got to listen to reason in the matter of the Rashtriya Mandal funds, we think the Nationalists might give way on this point to avoid a national scandal. If, on the other hand, the Rai Sahebs and Rai Bahadurs are obdurate, it is time for Nationalists all over the country to consult together as to the course they will follow in the two possible contingencies of no session being held or of the Moderate Party deciding to hold the Congress in another province. The situation in the country is a critical one and it is our action with regard both to the bureaucracy and the Congress at this juncture that will chiefly determine the course of the future.

Bande Mataram, November 4, 1907

Mr. Tilak and the Presidentship

WHILE writing of the Nagpur imbroglio we have touched very lightly on the question of Mr. Tilak's Presidentship, the dispute over which was the beginning and real cause of the discord at Nagpur. We regard this issue as one of immense importance and shall today try to make clear our position in the matter and the reasons why we attach such a supreme importance to it. The Bombay Moderates with their usual skill in the use of their one strong weapon, misrepresentation, have been writing and speaking as if the question of Mr. Tilak's election to the President's chair were a personal issue; they blame Mr. Tilak for not withdrawing from the field, talk of us as Tilakites and assume throughout that we are fighting for a man and not for a principle. If it were a personal matter, Mr. Tilak who has always been an unselfish and unassuming patriot, always averse to pushing himself or to figuring personally more than was necessary for his work, always a strong fighter for the success of his ideas and methods but never for his own hand, would be the first to obviate all discord by withdrawing. But it is not a personal matter and Mr. Tilak has not himself come forward as a candidate for the Presidentship. His name was put forward last year by the Bengal Nationalists without consulting him and was again put forward this year as the embodiment of a principle. This being so, Mr. Tilak has no voice in the matter except as an individual member of the Nationalist Party, and is not entitled to withdraw his name except with the consent of his party. In fact, his personal right of accepting or refusing the Presidentship can only arise when and if it is offered him by the local Reception Committee or the All-India Committee. That the Moderates should not be able to understand this is natural; their conception of a leader and the Nationalist conception of a leader are as the poles asunder. Mr. Tilak by his past career, his unequalled abilities and capacity for leadership, his splendid courage and self-sacrifice, his services to the cause and the disinterestedness and devotion with which he used his influence, is naturally the most prominent of the Nationalist leaders, and our party looks up to his experience, skill, cool acuteness and moral strength for guidance on great occasions like the Congress session when it has to act as a single body. But our idea of a leader is not and will never be one whom we have to follow as an individual for his own sake, whether he is right or wrong; we follow him only so long as he is faithful to the principles of Nationalism and is ready to fight its battles in accordance with the collective will of the party.

The question was first raised last year in Bengal when at a meeting of the Nationalists in Calcutta it was decided to suggest to the country the name of Mr. Tilak as President of the Calcutta Congress and in accordance with this decision Srijut Bepin Chandra Pal, who was then touring in the Mofussil, was communicated with and asked to bring the question forward and take the sense of the public upon it in Eastern Bengal. We have never concealed the fact that this was deliberately done in order to throw down the gauntlet publicly to Loyalism, Anti-Swadeshism, Moderatism and every other *ism* which seeks to bring in foreign considerations and alloy or weaken the pure and uncompromising Nationalist creed. The nomination of Mr. Tilak was a crucial point as between the two parties, for three separate reasons. At that time the country was divided between the Swadeshists on principle and the Anti-Swadeshists — or, let us say, "honest" Swadeshists of the Mehta-Wacha type and still more sharply between Boycotters and those who trembled at the very name of Boycott. From this point of view, the attempt to secure Mr. Tilak's nomination was an attempt on our part to have the Swadeshi-Boycott propaganda recognised on the Congress platform. Secondly, there was and still is a small ring of Congress officials who treat the Congress as their own private property, decide in secret conclave what it shall do or not do, and hand round the Presidentship among themselves and the occasional newcomers admitted to their ranks from the Legislative Councils, except when a live M.P. can be secured from England or a Mahomedan had to be nominated to demonstrate Hindu-Musulman unity. The second object of the attempt to get Mr. Tilak nominated was to break through this oligarchic ring and establish the true nature of the Congress as no mere machinery to be engineered by a few wealthy or successful proprietors, but a popular assembly in which the will of the people must prevail. Thirdly, the opposition to Mr. Tilak and the attempt to force him always into the background arose largely from the feeling that Mr. Tilak's views and personality are objectionable to the bureaucracy and that the nomination of a public man once convicted of sedition would deprive the Congress and, what was more important to Loyalists, leading men of the Congress, of all chance of Government favour. But these very reasons which made the name of Mr. Tilak an offence and a stumbling-block to the Loyalists, imposed upon the Nationalist Party the duty of bringing forward Mr. Tilak's name year after year until he is elected. Leadership in the Congress must no longer be regarded as a convenient and profitable road to appointments on the Bench and in the Government Councils but as a post of danger and a position of service to the people and it must depend on service done and suffering endured for the cause and not in the slightest degree on bureaucratic approval, and the national movement must be recognised as a sacred cause which exists in its own right and cannot consent to be regulated by the smiles and frowns of the bureaucracy which it is its first object to displace. These are the principles for which our party are contending when they insist on Mr. Tilak's nomination and they are principles which are essential to the Nationalist position and are as living today as they were last year. The question of Mr. Tilak's Presidentship will be always with us until it is finally set at rest by his election, for until then we shall pass it year after year.

But so far as the Nagpur session is concerned, the question no longer exists. The attempt to make this question wholly responsible for the difficulty is disingenuous and the demand that Mr. Tilak should throw over his own party by a gratuitous refusal to be President if ever he is asked, so as to reassure irreconcilable Loyalists in their fears, is absolutely preposterous. The Nagpur Nationalists have put his name forward and they alone are competent to withdraw it. But such withdrawal is not necessary. They have failed to secure the necessary three-fourths majority and they can therefore no longer insist on his name unless they are asked to hold the Congress with their own funds. They are willing to withdraw in a body from the Reception Committee if the Moderates so desire; they are willing to co-operate on lines both definite and reasonable; and they are willing, if called upon, to hold the Congress with any Moderate President in the chair if the funds in Mr. Dixit's hands are paid in. But they are not willing to misappropriate public money for the Congress funds and they are not willing to walk into the Loyalist trap by an admission of any personal responsibility for the disturbances that have taken place, in the shape of a guarantee that no disturbance of any kind shall take place at the time of the Congress. Such a guarantee can only be given by those who were responsible for the rowdyism or instigated it, and this unwarrantable charge has already been emphatically denied by the leading Nationalists; to ask them to give a guarantee is to ask them to admit what they have already denied. If therefore the Moderates insist on these preposterous conditions, the public will know whom they have to blame.

Bande Mataram, November 5, 1907

Nagpur and Loyalist Methods

THE decision of the All-India Congress Committee, holding its session appropriately enough not in any place of meeting suitable to its character as a public body but in "Sir Pherozshah Mehta's bungalow", has put the crown on one of the most discreditable intrigues of which even Bombay Loyalism is capable. We held our peace about the real meaning of the Nagpur affair so long as there was the remotest possibility of the sense of shame and decency reawakening among even a section of the Nagpur Loyalists, lest a too trenchant exposure of the whole intrigue might imperil that slender chance. Now that the die is cast, it is time for us to speak our minds. From the whole course of the Loyalist manoeuvres in Nagpur since the strength of the Nationalist Party in the Central Provinces became apparent, it was quite evident that from the first the Loyalists had made up their minds under inspiration from Bombay to prevent the holding of the Congress at Nagpur. To effect this object they were prepared to bring about a public scandal of the most shameful kind and bring discredit on the Congress if only their party might win a tactical advantage and, as the chief Moderate organ in Bombay frankly put it, keep the Congress out of the hands of the Extremists. It was in order to keep the Congress out of the hands of the Extremists that the session was originally arranged to be held at Nagpur and the prior claims of the Punjab ignored. For Nagpur was then supposed to be a sleepy hollow of politics, a happy hunting-ground of Rai Bahadurs and Government pets and tame patriots with the official collar round their necks, where there was no fear of Mr. Tilak's nomination becoming even a remote possibility and Sir Pherozshah Mehta might safely hope to retrieve the crushing blow his dictatorship had received at Calcutta. The Congress cabal had, unfortunately for themselves, reckoned without the fiery energy and indomitable self-confidence which have always been the characteristics of Nationalism in every country and every age of its emergence. The Nationalists of the Berar and Central Provinces took the work of proselytisation in hand and as the result of several tours undertaken by leading members of the party from town to town and village to village the sleepy hollow awoke to life, a great revolution of opinion was effected and Nationalism became in a few months a power to be reckoned with. It soon appeared that in Nagpur there was on one side the small body of wealthy, respectable and successful elders with their dependents, hangers-on and satellites and on the other side, behind a growing body of true patriots among the men of name and standing, the great bulk of the young men and the poorer middle class. When a trial of strength came over the question of Mr. Tilak's nomination the Loyalists could muster a large body of votes on the Reception Committee only by the wealthy men paying for the admission of their dependents and hangers-on, while even so against the Rs. 21,000 they could muster, the Rashtriya Mandal was able to show a total of more than Rs. 30,000 representing what would have been a substantial majority of votes if the rule of a three-fourths majority had not been in force. It thus became apparent that the Nationalist Party might easily command a majority of the local delegates and, since the place of session was within easy reach of Bengal and a strong body of Nationalist votes from the North, from Madras and from the Deccan might be expected, Loyalism was evidently in danger of a serious reverse compared with which its experiences at Calcutta might sink into insignificance. Nor was the outlook made rosier by the fact that there was on the Nagpur Executive Committee an active Nationalist majority led by a strong and fearless stalwart. It had become imperative, if the primary object of loyalist politics, "to keep the Congress out of the hands of the Extremists" and so avoid a rupture with the bureaucracy, was not to be hopelessly frustrated, either to drive the Extremists out of the Executive Committee and turn it into a convenient instrument for Sir Pherozshah Mehta's masterly manoeuvres or to transfer the Congress to a less central and thoroughly Loyalist locality where the Dictator's will could reign supreme.

From this point onward the hand of the great wire-puller behind the scenes can be observed in all the developments on the

Nagpur stage. Left to themselves there is little doubt that the two local parties would have come to some understanding; nor can it be for a moment supposed that the audacious and high-handed attempt at a shamelessly unconstitutional *coup d'état* on the 22nd September was conceived in the brain of so harmless and insignificant a personality as Mr. Chitnavis. The attempt to expel Dr. Munje and his Nationalist colleagues from the Executive Committee was a failure because leonine tactics require a leonine personality to carry them through and Mr. Chitnavis was trying to wear the giant's robe without possessing the bulk and sinews of the giant. But their failure and the disturbance that followed it served the alternative plan of the Loyalists. That disturbance was obviously not engineered by the Nationalist leaders since, their point having been gained, it could serve no purpose whatever and on the contrary might do them harm, as it was bound to give and did give the Loyalists a handle for discrediting the Nationalists and stood them in good stead as a convenient and always serviceable pretext for breaking the Nagpur session if every other trumped-up excuse should fail. The same guiding hand is seen in the skill with which the very success of the Rashtriya Mandal, was turned to the uses of the intrigue by the preposterous and cynical demand that the condition under which money had been paid in to it should be disregarded and a breach of faith with the public committed. Neither can we regard seriously the much advertised visits of Moderate leaders to Nagpur to effect a reconciliation, followed as they were by ostentatiously sorrowful and misleading telegrams to the effect that both sides refused to accept any compromise while the simple truth was that the Nationalists in their eagerness to have the session at Nagpur were making every time larger and larger concessions and it was the Loyalists who throughout showed themselves intractable. It is not to be believed that if such influential peacemakers had been in earnest, the Nagpur Loyalists would have showed this spirit of inflexibility; it was obviously not a local product but made in Bombay, and all these attempts at conciliation were simply meant to prepare the public mind for the transfer to Surat which had already been decided on by the master mind in Bombay. Meanwhile the wires were pulled at Surat and Madras and the Surat respectables and Mr. Krishna Swami Aiyer and his Mahajan Sabha danced to the skilful manipulation. We do not believe the Madras offer was anything but a feint, for Madras is much too near to Bengal and there is already a strong Nationalist Party in the northern parts of that province; but to have only the single offer from Surat would have been to leave the whole intrigue too bare to the public eye. Our belief is confirmed by the Bombay correspondent of the *Bengalee*, who openly says that Madras was not chosen because there were men in Madras pledged to Extremist views. Finally, the last act of the farce supplies the key to all that has gone before. An informal and unofficial representation from a minority of the Reception Committee is precipitately seized upon by the All-India Congress Committee, a meeting is announced not at Nagpur where the members might have gone into the matter on the spot and arranged a working compromise, but in Bombay and at Sir Pherozshah Mehta's bungalow, as if the Committee and the Congress itself were Sir Pherozshah's personal movable property; and instead of calling for a report of the Reception Committee or taking cognisance of the fact that there were citizens of Nagpur willing and able to reconstitute the Committee and hold the session as arranged at Calcutta, the Moderate majority records a predetermined decision to transfer Sir Pherozshah's movable property to Surat at a safe distance from Bengal where the Loyalist position is as yet unbreached and there is no time for the Nationalists to instruct public opinion before the holding of the session.

The intrigue is now complete, to the huge delight of the *Englishman*, and officialdom is full of hope that Sir Pherozshah will this year save the British Empire. For the Nationalists it should be a spur to redoubled efforts to spread their creed into every corner of the country so that Loyalism may nowhere find a secure resting place for its footsoles. As to the Surat Pherozshah Congress it would be the logical course for us regarding the decision of the All-India Committee meeting as a misuse of the powers of that body, to abstain and allow the Loyalists to hold a purely Moderate Congress of their own. The other alternative is to arrange forthwith the organisation of Nationalist propaganda in Gujerat and make full use of the opportunity such as it is which the session will provide. In either case, a conference of our party is necessary, for, in view of the bureaucratic campaign on one side and the danger of a retrograde step on the part of the Congress on the other, the times are critical and concerted action imperative.

Bande Mataram, November 16, 1907

The Life of Nationalism

FOR all great movements, for all ideas that have a destiny before them, there are four seasons of life-development. There is first a season of secret or quasi-secret growth when the world knows nothing of this momentous birth which time has engendered, when the peoples of the earth persist in the old order of things with the settled conviction that that order has yet many centuries of life before it, when Krishna is growing from infancy to youth in Gokul among the obscure and the despised and the weak ones of the earth and Kamsa knows not his enemy and, however he may be troubled by vague apprehensions and old prophecies and new presentiments, yet on the whole comforts himself with the thought of his great and invincible power and his mighty allies, and by long impunity has almost come to think himself immortal. Then there comes the leaping of the great name to light, the sudden coming from Gokul to Mathura, the amazement, alarm and fury of the doomed powers and greatnesses, the delight of the oppressed who waited for a deliverer, the guile and violence of the tyrant and his frantic attempts to reverse the decrees of fate and slay the young deity, — as if that godhead could pass from the world with its work undone. This is the second period of emergence, of the struggle of the idea to live, of furious persecution, of miraculous persistence and survival, when the old world looks with alarm and horror on this new and portentous force, and in the midst of wild worship and enthusiasm, of fierce hatred and frantic persecution, of bitter denunciation and angry disparagement, assisted by its friends, still better assisted by its foes, the new idea, fed with the blood of its children, thriving on torture, magnified by martyrdom, aggrandised by defeat, increases and lifts its head higher and higher into the heavens and spreads its arms wider and wider to embrace the earth until the world is full of its indomitable presence and loud with the clamour of its million voices and powers and dominations are crushed between its fingers, or hasten to make peace and compromise with it that they may be allowed to live. That is its third period, the season of triumph when the tyrant meets face to face the man of his own blood and sprung from the seed of his own fostering who is to destroy him, and in the moment when he thinks to slay his enemy feels the grasp of the avenger on his hair and the sword of doom in his heart. Last is the season of rule and fulfilment, the life of Krishna at Dwaraka, when the victorious idea lives out its potent and unhindered existence, works its will with a world which has become in its hands as clay in the hands of the potter, creates what it has to create, teaches what it has to teach, until its own time comes and with the arrow of Age, the hunter, in its heel, it gives up its body and returns to the great source of all power and energy from which it came.

But in its second period, the season of ordeal and persecution, only the children of grace for whom the gospel is preached are able to see that vision of its glory. The world admires and hates and doubts, but will not believe. The enemies of the idea have sworn to give it short shrift. They promulgate an ordinance to the effect that it shall not dare to live, and pass a law that it shall be dumb on pain of imprisonment and death, and add a bye-law that whoever has power and authority in any part of the land shall seek out the first-born and the young children of the idea and put them to the sword. As in the early days of the Christian Church, so always zealous persecutors carry on an inquisition in house and school and market to know who favour the new doctrine; they "breathe out threatenings and slaughters against the disciples of the Lord" and "make havoc of the Church entering into every house and, haling men and women, commit them to prison". The instruments of death are furbished up, the rack and thumb-screw and old engines of torture which had been rusting in the lumber-room of the past are brought out, and the gallows is made ready and the scaffold raised. Even of the nation to which the gospel is preached, the rich men and the high-priests and Pundits and people of weight and authority receive its doctrine with anger, fear and contempt; — anger, because it threatens their position of comfortable authority amongst men; fear, because they see it grow with an inexplicable portentious rapidity and know that its advent means a time of upheaval, turmoil and bloodshed very disturbing to the digestions, property and peace of mind of the wealthy and "enlightened few"; contempt, because its enthusiasms are unintelligible to their worldly wisdom, its gigantic promises incredible to their cautious scepticism and its inspired teachings an offence and a scandal to their narrow systems of expediency and pedantic wisdom of the schools. They condemn it, therefore, as a violent and pernicious madness, belittle it as a troublesome but insignificant sect, get their learned men to argue it or their jesters to ridicule it out of existence, or even accuse its apostles before the tribunal of alien rulers, Pontius Pilate, a Felix or a Festus, as "pestilent fellows and movers of sedition throughout the nation". But in spite of all and largely because of all the persecution, denunciation and disparagement, the idea gathers strength and increases; there are strange and great conversions, baptisms of whole multitudes and eager embracings of martyrdom, and the reasonings of the wise and learned are no more heeded and the prisons of the ruler overflow to no purpose and the gallows bears its ghastly burden fruitlessly and the sword of the powerful drips blood in vain. For the idea is God's deputy, and life and death, victory and defeat, joy and suffering have become its servants and cannot help ministering to its divine purpose.

The idea of Indian Nationalism is in the second season of its life history. The Moderate legend of its origin is that it was the child of Lord Curzon begotten upon despair and brought safely to birth by the skilful midwifery of Sir Bampfylde. Nationalism was never a gospel of despair nor did it owe its birth to oppression. It is no true account of it to say that because Lord Curzon favoured reaction, a section of the Congress Party lost faith in England and turned Extremist, and it is vain political trickery to tell the bureaucrats in their councils that it was their frown which created Extremism and the renewal of their smiles will kill it. The fixed illusion of these moderate gospellers is that the national life of India is merely a fluid mirror reflecting the moods of the bureaucracy, sunny and serene when they are in a good humour and stormy and troubled when they are out of temper, that it can have no independent existence, no self-determined character of its own which the favour of the bureaucracy cannot influence and its anger cannot disturb. But Nationalism was not born of persecution and cannot be killed by the cessation of persecution. Long before the advent of Curzonism and Fuller-ism, while the Congress was beslavering the present absolutist bureaucracy with fulsome praise as a good and beneficent government marred by a few serious defects, while it was singing hymns of loyalty and descanting on the blessings of British rule, Nationalism was already born and a slowly-growing force. It was not born and did not grow in the Congress Pandal, nor in the Bombay Presidency Association, nor in the councils of the wise economists and learned reformers, nor in the brains of the Mehtas and Gokhales, nor in the tongues of the Surendranaths and Lalmohuns, nor under the hat and coat of the denationalised ape of English speech and manners. It was born like Krishna in the prison-house, in the hearts of men to whom India under the good and beneficent government of absolutism seemed an intolerable dungeon, to whom the blessings of an alien despotic rule were hardly more acceptable than the plagues of Egypt, who regarded the comfort, safety and ease of the Pax Britannica, — an ease and safety not earned by our own efforts and vigilance but purchased by the slow loss of every element of manhood and every field of independent activity among us, — as more fatal to the life of the people than the *poosta* of the Moguls, with whom a few seats in the Council or on the Bench and right of entry into the Civil Service and a free Press and platform could not weigh against the starvation of the rack-rented millions, the drain of our life-blood, the atrophy of our energies and the disintegration of our national character and ideals; who looked beyond the temporary ease and opportunities of a few merchants, clerks and successful professional men to the lasting pauperism and degradation of a great and ancient people. And Nationalism grew as Krishna grew who ripened to strength and knowledge, not in the courts of princes and the schools of the Brahmins but in the obscure and despised homes of the poor and ignorant. In the cave of the Sannyasin, under the garb of the Fakir, in the hearts of young men and boys many of whom could not speak a word of English but all could work and dare and sacrifice for the

Mother, in the life of men of education and parts who had received the *mantra* and put from them the desire of wealth and honours to teach and labour so that the good religion might spread, there Nationalism grew slowly to its strength, unheeded and unnoticed, until in its good time it came to Bengal, the destined place of its self-manifestation and for three years, unheeded and unnoticed, spread over the country, gathering in every place the few who were capable of the vision and waiting for the time that would surely come when oppression would begin in earnest and the people look round them for some way of deliverance.

For, that an absolute rule will one day begin to coerce and trample on the subject population is an inevitable law of nature which none can escape. The master with full power of life and death over his servant can only be gracious so long as he is either afraid of his slave or else sure that the slave will continue willing, obedient and humble in his servitude and not transgress the limits of the freedom allowed him by his master. But if the serf begins to assert himself, to insist on the indulgence conceded to him as on a right, to rebel against occasional harshnesses, to wag his tongue with too insolent a licence and disobey imperative orders, then it is not in human nature for the master to refrain from calling for the scourge and the fetters. And if the slave resists the application of the scourge and the imposition of the fetters, it becomes a matter of life and death for the master to enforce his orders and put down the mutiny. Oppression was therefore inevitable, and oppression was necessary that the people as a whole might be disposed to accept Nationalism, but Nationalism was not born of oppression. The oppressions and slaughters committed by Kamsa upon the Yadavas did not give birth to Krishna but they were needed that the people of Mathura might look for the deliverer and accept him when he came. To hope that conciliation will kill Nationalism is to mistake entirely the birth, nature and workings of the new force, nor will either the debating skill of Mr. Gokhale nor all Dr. Ghose's army of literary quotations and allusions convince Englishmen that any such hope can be admitted for a moment. For Englishmen are political animals with centuries of political experience in their blood, and though they possess little logic and less wisdom, yet in such matters they have an instinct which is often surer than reason or logic. They know that what is belittled as Extremism is really Nationalism and Nationalism has never been killed by conciliation; concessions it will only take as new weapons in its fight for complete victory and unabridged dominion. We desire our countrymen on their side to cultivate a corresponding instinct and cherish an invincible faith. There are some who fear that conciliation or policy may unstring the new movement and others who fear that persecution may crush it. Let them have a robuster faith in the destinies of their race. As neither the milk of Putana nor the hoofs of the demon could destroy the infant Krishna, so neither Riponism nor Poona prosecutions could check the growth of Nationalism while yet it was an indistinct force; and as neither Kamsa's wiles nor his *viṣakanyās* nor his mad elephants nor his wrestlers could kill Krishna revealed in Mathura, so neither a revival of Riponism nor the poison of discord sown by bureaucratic allurements, nor Fullerism plus hooliganism, nor prosecution under cover of legal statutes can slay Nationalism now that it has entered the arena. Nationalism is an *avatāra* and cannot be slain. Nationalism is a divinely appointed *śakti* of the Eternal and must do its God-given work before it returns to the bosom of the Universal Energy from which it came.

Bande Mataram, November 16, 1907

BY THE WAY

In Praise of Honest John

Mr. John Morley is a very great man, a very remarkable and exceptional man. I have been reading his Arbroath speech again and my admiration for him has risen to such a boiling point that I am at last obliged to let it bubble over into the columns of the *Bande Mataram*. Mr. Morley rises above the ordinary ruck of mortals in three very important respects; first, he is a literary man; secondly, he is a philosopher; thirdly, he is a politician. This would not matter much if he kept his literature, politics and philosophy apart in fairly watertight compartments; but he doesn't. He has not only doubled his parts, he has trebled them; he is not merely a literary philosopher and philosophic littérateur, he is a literary philosopher-politician. Now this is a superlative combination; God cannot better it and the devil does not want to. For if an ordinary man steals, he steals and there are no more bones made about it; he gets caught and is sent to prison, or he is not caught and goes on his way rejoicing. In either case the matter is a simple one without any artistic possibilities. But if a literary philosopher steals, he steals on the basis of the great and eternal verities and in the choicest English.

*

And so all along the line. An ordinary man may be illogical and silly and everybody realises that he is illogical and silly; but the literary man when he goes about the same business will be brilliantly foolish and convincingly illogical, while the philosopher will be logically illogical and talk nonsense according to the strictest rules of philosophical reasoning. An ordinary man may turn his back on his principles and he will be called a turncoat or he may break all the commandments and he will be punished by the law and society, — unless of course he is an American millionaire or a member of the ruling race in India; — but the literary philosopher will reconcile his principles with his conduct by an appeal to a fur-coat or a syllogism from a pair of jackboots; he will abrogate all the commandments on the strength of a Solar Topee. A politician again will lie and people will take it as a matter of course, especially if he is in office, but a literary philosopher-politician will easily prove to you that when he is most a liar, then he is most truthful and when he is juggling most cynically with truth and principle, then he most deserves the name of Honest John; and he will do it in such well-turned periods that one must indeed have a very bad ear for the rhythm of a sentence before one can quarrel with its logic. Oh yes, a literary philosopher-politician is the choicest work of God, — when he is not the most effective instrument in the hands of the Prince of Darkness. For the Prince of Darkness is not only a gentleman as Shakespeare discovered, but a gentleman of artistic perceptions who knows a fine and carefully-worked tool when he sees it and loves to handle it with the best dexterity and grace of which he is capable.

*

Of course it is not his speeches alone for which I admire John Morley. I admire him for what he has done almost as much as for the way in which he has done it. He is not so great a man as his master Gladstone who was the biggest opportunist and most adroit political gambler democracy has yet engendered and yet persuaded himself and the world that he was an enthusiast and a man of high religious principle. But Gladstone was a genius and his old henchman is only a man of talent. Still Mr. Morley has done the best of which he is capable and that is not a poor best. He has served the devil in the name of God with signal success on two occasions. The first was when he championed the cause of the financiers in Egypt, the men who gamble with the destinies of nations, who make money out of the groans of the people and coin into gold the blood of patriots and the tears of widows and orphans, — when abusing his influence as a journalist, he lied to the British public about Arabi and urged on Gladstone to crush the movement of democratic and humanitarian Nationalism in Egypt, the movement in which all that is noble, humane and gracious in Islam sought fulfilment and a small field on earth for the fine flowering of a new Mahomedan civilisation. The second is now when he is trying in the sordid interests of British capital to crush the resurgent life of India and baffle the attempt of the children of Vedanta to recover their own country for the development of a revivified Indian civilisation. The two foulest crimes against the future of humanity of which any statesman in recent times could possibly have been guilty, have been engineered under the name and by the advocacy of honest John Morley. Truly, Satan knows his own and sees to it that they do not do their great work negligently.

*

Mr. Morley is a great bookman, a great democrat, a great

exponent of principles. No man better fitted than he to prove that when the noblest human movements are being suppressed by imprisonment and the sword, it is done in the interests of humanity; that when a people struggling to live is trampled down by repression, pushed back by the use of the Goorkha and the hooligan, the prison walls and the whipping-post into the hell of misery, famine and starvation, the black pit of insult, ignominy and bonds from which it had dared to hope for an escape, the motive of the oppressor finds its root in a very agony of conscientiousness and it is with a sobbing and bleeding heart that he presses his heel on the people's throat for their own good; that the ruthless exploitation and starvation of a country by foreign leeches is one of the best services that can be done to mankind, the international crimes of the great captains of finance a supreme work of civilisation and the brutal and selfish immolation of nations to Mammon an acceptable offering on the altar of the indwelling God in humanity. But these things have been done and said before; they are the usual blasphemous cant of nineteenth century devil-worship formulated when Commerce began to take the place once nominally allowed to Christ and the Ledger became Europe's Bible. Mr. Morley does it with more authority than others, but his own particular and original faculty lies in the direction I indicated when drawing the distinction between the ordinary man and the extraordinary Morley. What he has done has been after all on the initiative of others; what he has said about it is his own, and nothing more his own than the admirably brilliant and inconsequential phrases in which he has justified wickedness to an admiring nation.

*

Man has been defined sometimes as a political animal and sometimes as a reasoning animal, but he has become still more pre-eminently a literary animal. He is a political animal who has always made a triumphant mess of politics, a reasoning animal whose continual occupation it is to make a system out of his blunders, a literary animal who is always the slave of a phrase and not the least so when the phrase means nothing. The power of the phrase on humanity has never been sufficiently considered. The phrase is in the nostrils of the vast unruly mass of mankind like the ring in the nose of a camel. It can be led by the phrase-maker wherever he wishes to lead it. And the only distinction between the sage and the sophist is that the phrases of the sage mean something while the phrases of the sophist only seem to mean something. Now Mr. Morley is an adept in the making of phrases which seem to mean something.

*

Take for instance his phrase "The anchor holds." Mr. Morley complains that he who has served Liberalism so long and so well, is not allowed to be illiberal when he likes, that when he amuses himself with a little reaction he is charged with deserting his principles! "It is true, gentlemen," says Mr. Morley, "that I am doing things which are neither liberal nor democratic; but, then, my anchor holds. Yes, gentlemen, I dare to believe that my anchor holds." So might a clergyman detected in immorality explain himself to his parishioners, "It is true I have preached all my life continence and chastity, yet been found in very awkward circumstances; but what then? My anchor holds. Yes, dear brethren in Christ, I dare to believe that my anchor holds." So might Robespierre have justified himself for the Reign of Terror, "It is true, Frenchmen, that I have always condemned capital punishment as itself a crime, yet am judicially massacring my countrymen without pause or pity; but my anchor holds. Yes, citizens, I dare to believe that my anchor holds." So argues Mr. Morley and all England applauds in a thousand newspapers and acquits him of political sin.

But of course Mr. Morley's crowning mercy is the phrase about the fur-coat. It is true that the simile about the coat is not new in the English language; for a man who abandons his principles has always been said to turn his coat; but never has that profitable manoeuvre been justified in so excellently literary and philosophical a fashion before. Mr. Morley has given us the philosophy of the turn-coat. "Principles," he has said in effect, "are not a light by which you can guide your steps in all circumstances, but a coat which is worn for comfort and convenience. In Canada, which is cold, you have to wear a fur-coat, there is no help for it; in Egypt, which is hot, you can change it for thin alpaca; in India, where it is very hot indeed, you need not wear a coat at all; the natives of the country did not before we came and we should not encourage them to go in for such an uncomfortable luxury. It is just so with principles, democratic and other." The reasoning is excellent and of a very wide application. For instance, it may be wrong in England to convict a political opponent for political reasons of an offence of which you know him to be innocent and on evidence you know to be false, or to sentence a man to be hanged for a murder which you are quite aware somebody else committed, or to disregard the plainest evidence and allow a bestial ravisher to go free because he happens to be a dog with a white skin, but it is absurd to suppose that such principles can keep in the heat of the Indian sun. It is difficult to know what inequity reasoning of this sort would not cover. "I thoroughly believe in the Ten Commandments," Caesar Borgia might have said in his full career of political poisonings and strangulations, "but they may do very well in one country and age without applying at all to another. They suited Palestine, but mediaeval Italy is not Palestine. Principles are a matter of chronology and climate, and it would be highly unphilosophical and unpractical of me to be guided by them as if I were Christ or Moses. So I shall go on poisoning and strangling for the good of myself and Italy and leave 'impatient idealists' to their irresponsible chatter. Still I am a Christian and the nephew of a Pope, so my anchor holds, yes, my anchor holds."

*

Mr. Morley's fur-coat is one of the most comprehensive garments ever discovered. All the tribe of high-aiming tyrants and patriotic pirates and able political scoundrels and intelligent turncoats that the world has produced, he gathers together and covers up their sins and keeps them snug and comforted against the cold blasts of censure blowing from a too logical and narrow-minded world, all in the shelter of a single fur-coat. And the British conscience too, that wondrous production of a humorous Creator, seeking justification of the career of cynical violence its representatives have entered on in India, rejoices in Mr. Morley's fur-coat and snuggles with a contented chuckle into its ample folds. Am I wrong in saying that Honest John is a wonder-worker of the mightiest and that Aaron's magic rod was a Brummagem fraud compared with Mr. Morley's phrases? *Vivat* John Morley!

Bande Mataram, November 18, 1907

Bureaucratic Policy

THE policy of the bureaucracy at the present moment would be a curious study to any dispassionate observer of politics. It is not an unmixed and fearless policy of repression, yet the repression, wherever entered on, is as thoroughgoing, ruthless and without scruple as the most virulent advocate of the strong hand could desire. It is not a policy of frank and wise concession, though concessions of a kind are fitfully made with no very apparent rhyme or reason. A Coercion Act is put upon the Statute-book of the most thoroughly Russian severity; it is supposed to be passed in hot haste to meet a crisis of an exceptional kind and to be urgently and imperatively demanded by the Chief Bureaucrats of three provinces who decline to be responsible otherwise for the preservation of peace and the British rule within their respective jurisdictions; yet when it has been passed, it is only applied to a single district in the whole of India. The protests of Moderate politicians against the deportations and their urgent pleas for the release of the prisoners in Mandalay are brushed aside with contempt, yet the very next news is that Lajpat Rai and Ajit Singh are released and on their way homeward. Simla, vowing it will ne'er consent, has consented. On the other hand Liakat Hossain is pursued with relentless severity, a politically-minded High Court Bench discharges with a contemptuous impatience the appeals brought before it in political cases, and the wholesale persecutions of young men in the mofussil centres and the campaign against the Nationalist Press does not relax. The official explanation given by the *Englishman* is that the Extremists have collapsed, Sir Pherozshah Mehta is once more master of the situation, the Moderate Party has come suddenly by its own and the Government recognising its own victory and the victory of its friends, is willing and can afford to be generous. With all respect to Hare Street we will offer another explanation which we think will be found nearer to the mark.

The policy of the Anglo-Indian bureaucrats has always been

checked by their strong sense of the weakness of their position in India. They know perfectly well that if the whole population of India gets to be infected by the enthusiastic beliefs and insurgent spirit of Nationalism, their present absolute sway over the country will at once become an impossibility. They know that the almost universal conversion of the educated class to Nationalism is a contingency of the near future and that Nationalism having once taken possession of the educated class must immediately proceed to invade the masses; such a consummation is sure to be immensely hastened by a policy of unflinching repression which will alienate the whole educated community. The bureaucracy have indeed no love for the educated class, and the policy dearest to their hearts would be to create in the masses a counterpoise to the intellectuals, such as another bureaucracy once hoped to create in Russia. It is not likely that they will fix any permanent hope, still less their main hope, on the policy of setting Hindu and Mahomedan by the ears by an unstinted pampering of the latter community, however thoroughly they may have resorted to that expedient in the terror of the moment; for by doing so they will not only help to weld the Hindu population into a homogeneous whole, but they will be creating a new and dangerous power in the country in a Mahomedan community excited by new hopes and eager to recover their old ascendency. On the other hand, the masses under present circumstances are not easily accessible to a foreign and unsympathetic handful of aliens chiefly known to them through a corrupt, brutal and cruelly oppressive police, while the work of educating them into loyalty will take a long time and may be no less a failure in the end than the old plan of creating a permanently loyal middle class as a support to foreign rule against the regrets of the aristocracy and the possible fanaticism of the masses. Awaiting therefore the launching and success of their experiment with the masses the bureaucrats would like to keep the more pliable portion of the educated classes as long as possible in their own hands and set them against Nationalism. But they are not prepared to purchase this support at the sacrifice of any least fragment of their absolute authority and irresponsible power; they are only willing to appease the rising unrest by sham concessions or any temporary and isolated step which will not affect their prestige or their authority. The difficulty is that with the exception of the Loyalist section of the Moderate Party led by men like Sir Pherozshah Mehta, no one would be satisfied with apparent concessions sufficient only to meet the claims of the wealthier upper ten of the educated community to titles, honour and position; the more advanced section which places patriotism before loyalty demand in addition such a substantial concession as would in their opinion pave the way for complete self-government in the future; but this the bureaucracy are not prepared to concede. Yet the Loyalists are precisely those whose support is least worth having. Really strong in commercial centres like Bombay and Surat, wearing an appearance only of strength, in other parts where Nationalism has not yet put forth a strength, it is a waning force constitutionally prone to inertia and incapable of exciting enthusiasm.

Such is the position which the bureaucrats have to face, and once we realise it their policy becomes quite coherent and intelligible. They have to be prepared against the possibility of the flood of Nationalism submerging the whole country in spite of all the dams they may erect, and for this reason they are arming themselves with extraordinary powers which will enable them to check its future expansion and crush it where it has already established itself. At the present moment they hope to get it under without persisting in a general repression which would drive the whole educated community into the Nationalist camp. They have got Bepin Pal and Liakat under lock and key, Brahmabandhab is dead, Aswin Dutta may be paralysed by a rigorous enforcement of the new Act in Backergunge, and of all the more powerful Nationalist speakers and writers one or two only have so far escaped the attack made upon them. The bureaucracy may well hope that the back of the movement is broken and relax their legal thumbscrew, at least until they have seen what Sir Pherozshah can do at Surat. Any fresh development of Nationalism they are prepared to meet by ruthless repression. Wherever they see it spreading itself by open propaganda, they will forthwith apply the Gagging Act; wherever it spreads by its own force without the aid of the platform they will attack it through the young men as at Rangpur, Dinajpur, Dacca and Midnapur, and whatever leader or active propagandist comes forward, they will find some pretext to thrust into prison. Meanwhile they will pursue their policy of isolating the movement, locally by crushing it where it is bold and vehement while they will play with and indulge it for a time where it is milder and more cautious, politically by setting all other forces in the country against it.

This is their second line of defence, to find for themselves as many points of support as possible against Indian Nationalism amongst the Indians themselves. Their first hope is in the Mahomedans whom they will encourage enough to buy their hostility to the Hindus, but not enough to make them really powerful or give an impetus to a Mahomedan revival. Their second hope is in the landed aristocracy whom they broke and ground into the dust with the aid of the newly created middle class and would now call in in their turn to help in crushing that very middle class grown too powerful for its creator. Their third hope is in the masses whom they expect to dominate partly by a carefully-conceived primary education, partly by decentralising their administration sufficiently to give the District Officer direct touch with and autocratic control over the peasantry and partly by creating in officially-controlled Panchayets instruments of check and supervision among the masses themselves. Their fourth point of support is in the Loyalist-cum-Moderate Party in the Congress. It is to keep the way open for a reconciliation with that party that Lajpat Rai has been released, the Gagging Act kept in abeyance outside Backergunge and overtures made in the demi-official Press, notably in such foul-mouthed revilers of all educated India as the *C. M. Gazette* and the *Englishman* to the more sensible and sober elements in the Congress. The word has gone round to rally the Moderates to the Government and that party is notified by act and word that if they will accept the olive branch, be even temporarily satisfied with Mr. Morley's reforms and dissociate themselves from Boycott, Swaraj and Extremism, the bureaucracy will not confound them in one common ruin with the Extremists, but on the contrary give them its paternal blessing and a fair number of new playthings.

Such is the complete Minto-Morley policy as it now stands developed, and nobody will deny that, subject to the incurable defects of the bureaucratic position in India and the overruling decrees of Providence, it is a well-planned and skilful policy. The question is "what chance has it of success? and what should be the line taken by the Nationalist Party to frustrate this curious mixture of force and guile?" That is the chief problem to which we have now to turn our attention.

Bande Mataram, November 19, 1907

The New Faith

THE political struggle in India is entering on a new phase; and now that the Nationalists have been given a foretaste of its persecuting ability, the bureaucracy is making an awkward attempt to patch up a reconciliation with the Moderate leaders. The olive branch has been already held out; Lala Lajpat Rai and Sirdar Ajit Singh have been released, and vague rumours of other conciliatory measures are in the air. Press prosecutions, deportations and police hooliganism have done their work. It is now fondly believed that Nationalism is crushed and what remains is but to exchange a complimentary smile with Moderate politicians and swear eternal peace and good will. The bureaucracy has acted its part well; and in fact we expected from it no less, no more. But what the country is eagerly waiting to see is, whether those who profess to guide public opinion will forfeit their leadership and swallow the bait. They may hail with delight the relaxation of stringent measures and offer loud assurances of good will but they will have lost the authority of doing it in the name of the people.

The centre of authority has been shifted during the recent popular upheaval. The nation has become self-conscious and knows its mission, and individuals, however gifted and influential, will not be allowed to pass off their own opinions for those of the people. The real issue at stake has been revealed. All compromise is now out of the question, and Freedom's battle once begun must be carried on to the bitter end. The tortures undergone by the people have been for them an initiation in the worship of liberty, and if their sufferings have been great, the energy of their rising will be equally so. They have now learnt a truth with every tear and every month of their suffering has been for them a preparation for complete redemption. Will they now tolerate men who have no faith in popular strength and who have never understood the genius of the country to trifle with their sorrows and act as their spokesmen before the alien bureaucracy? These leaders have never had sufficient insight to perceive that it is not strength but the consciousness of strength that we lacked in the past; and now that the struggle with opposing forces has evoked the national consciousness, it is too late to talk of a compromise. Compromise here cannot be from the very nature of the case, for it is not a question of removing particular grievances and setting the machinery of government in order, but of changing our political status as a nation. Decentralisation Commissions and Advisory councils can help us no longer. Even in the midst of the din and bustle of the struggle, the people have caught a glimpse of the glorious future and they will not be easily accessible to discouragement.

The bureaucracy will not have to reckon this time with a few self-styled leaders who are only too eager to fall down and worship the idol of the hour, but with a newly-awakened people to whom the political freedom of the country has been elevated to the height of a religious faith. The mist that clouded their intellect for ages has at least partially cleared away; and they have begun to feel that if only they will, they can and therefore ought to make themselves in their own country what other nations are in theirs. The political strife has assumed a religious character, and the question now before the people is whether India — the India of the holy Rishis, the India that gave birth to a Rama, a Krishna and a Buddha, the India of Sivaji and Guru Gobinda — is destined for ever to lie prostrate at the proud feet of a conqueror. Are we going to sacrifice our national destiny to the whims and interest of the foreigner or are we again to take ourselves seriously and struggle for the right to live that we may fulfil in this world our Heaven-appointed mission? It is well to state clearly the real nature of the issue, for no nation has been regenerated by a lie. Those who want liberty must buy it for themselves, and it is poor statesmanship to try to hide the real nature of the struggle by a falsehood which, after all, deceives nobody and least of all our alien lords. Plain speaking may be unpalatable and persecutions may follow, but persecutions have never yet killed a religious faith, and a self-conscious India is too mighty a power to be put down by a despot's rod. Persecutions do not crush but only fortify conviction and no power on earth can exterminate the seed of liberty when it has once germinated in the blood of earnest and sincere men.

The days of timid dabblers in politics are over and men who have no faith in enthusiasm and who cannot believe in anything beyond the cold calculations of diplomacy by which they have been a thousand times bought and sold and who cannot believe in the possibility of uniting the people in a single aim and purpose have no more business to loiter in the political field. They have no right to assume the direction of an enterprise they are incapable of grasping or conceiving in its entirety. Those hugely credulous worthies who have still the heart to lend their ears to the siren voice of a Morley, have never understood the true way to salvation, and dismayed by the greatness of the undertaking, have contented themselves by scoffing at an enthusiasm they extinguished by their timidity and hesitation.

But every error they have committed has served as a stepping-stone to truth. The effect of their accumulated errors has been to dispel the illusion, and new circumstances today have called forth new men, men untrammelled by old habits and systems, men in whom the great Idea is incarnate, who have realised that the true secret of power is faith, who know that true virtue is sacrifice and that the true policy is to prove one's self strong.

To them belongs the future. The line of work is to mix with the masses and to organise and reduce to a system the ideas and aspirations now scattered and disseminated. They will put their trust in the nation and they will make all compromise impossible till the Indian soil is free.

Bande Mataram, November 30, 1907

About Unity

OUR esteemed contemporary, the *Bengalee*, has recently been reading us eloquent sermons on the uses and advantages of unity. We confess we cannot follow our contemporary's argument. We gave utterance to the very obvious and we thought, undeniable sentiment that Unity is a means and not an end in itself. But the *Bengalee* asserts, and it has now got the strong authority of Mr. Myron Phelps to back it, that unity is an end in itself and not a means, but it seems to us that neither our contemporary nor his authority have anything but their *ipse dixit* to prove their assertion. We have great respect for Mr. Myron Phelps who is evidently a sincere well-wisher of our nation, but it does seem to us that he is forgetting the history of his own country when he asserts that unity is an end in itself. The end his countrymen aimed at during their quarrel with England was certainly not unity but independence, and to the attainment of that end there was a strong loyalist minority opposed and unfriendly. Even among the American Liberals the democratic Extremists were a minority while the greater number would have been glad to combine submission to the English crown with American liberty. It was the fiery vehemence and energy of the Extremists aided by the intensity of popular indignation which hurried the Moderate majority into the Boycott and the same force which plunged them half against their will into war with the suzerain and into ultimate democracy. The same thing has happened in India, for there is not the slightest doubt that the Moderates have been carried at the fiery chariot-wheels of Extremism into the perpetuation of the Boycott and the angry struggle between people and bureaucracy from which they would have gladly withdrawn and more than once made motions to withdraw, if left to themselves. We insist that the end of national action is the acquisition and maintenance of national independence and greatness, and unity is only a means to that end. Moreover, political unity which is an essential condition of independence differs from unity of ideas and methods which are not essential. Political unity can be prepared by men of all parts of the country joining in a common struggle for the creation of a single national government, but the other unity is only possible if the whole nation is inspired by one spirit and one idea. The *Bengalee* thinks there is substantially such a unity between, say, Sir Pherozshah Mehta, Srijut Surendranath Banerji and Srijut Bepin Chandra Pal; but we have our doubts. Surendranath wants Colonial Self-government, Pherozshah would be hugely pleased with something infinitely less; Bepin Chandra wants absolute autonomy. Where is the unity? If Colonial Self-government for India, that political monstrosity, means anything, it means a hampered and provincial autonomy; the Nationalists strive for a complete and international autonomy, and if our contemporary thinks that is a small or merely academic difference, we cannot compliment him on his knowledge either of history or politics. We will admit however for the sake of argument that our aim is identical, though in one case frankly expressed and in the other hidden under a veil, but that our methods are different. How then can there be that unity of action for which the *Bengalee* so sonorously but hazily pleads? Unity of action along with and unaffected by difference of methods is a kind of unity which we do not understand, and we rather suspect it is a chimera from the land of confused ideas very much on a par with the "Colonial Self-government for India" of our friends or Mr. Morley's wonderful reconciliation of a free Press and Platform with an autocratic government. If one party has petitioning for its method and another rejects it for passive resistance, how can there be unity of action? Or if one party insists on association with and opposition to the bureaucracy (another twynatured and self-contradictory figment from dreamland) and the other repudiates the association, how can there be united action? If united action is at all possible in Bengal, it is because the Moderate Party in Bengal has ceased to be wagged by its loyalist tail and is now following the lead of its small but advanced head which is in sympathy with many of the Nationalist ideas though it is not prepared to carry them to their complete and logical end with the thoroughness and audacity which true Nationalism requires.

The Moderates have given up for the present the policy of mendicancy, they have given in their adherence to the programme of passive resistance though only in part. So far therefore as the methods of the two parties agree, united action is possible, though difference of fundamental ideas and difference of spirit make it impossible for that concord to be real and whole-hearted, even if personal misunderstandings and dislikes did not stand in the way. But it is only in Bengal that even so much unity is possible, though there is a tendency in that direction in Madras. In the rest of India Moderatism is in its public professions and actions frankly loyalist and is quite prepared to eject the Nationalists from the Congress so far as it can be done with safety to itself. The Nagpur affair and the action of the All-India Congress Committee prove that beyond doubt. Where then is the basis of unity? For that matter, the Bengal Moderates while they sing dulcetly to us the praises of Unity, have invariably joined heartily in Loyalist attempts to suppress the voice of Nationalism in the Congress. They were, we are convinced, consenting parties to the unconstitutional political trickery by which Sir Pherozshah transferred the meeting place of the Congress to one of his own pocket boroughs. Again we ask, on what ground can we meet for heartily united action? We have our work to do and cannot wait for ever on sweet words and professions used as a veil for secret — well, shall we say, diplomacy? We are ourselves anxious to carry the support of our Moderate countrymen with us in our struggles, but their friendship must first become less of the "I love you and kick you downstairs" kind than it is at present. Sincerity has great healing properties and without it professions are a poor salve for old sores.

Bande Mataram, December 2, 1907

Personality or Principle

Our contemporary, the *Punjabee*, has in its last issue a balanced and carefully impartial comment on the Congress trouble and the action of the All-India Congress Committee, or rather of Sir Pherozshah Mehta in the exercise of his role of Congress Lion and Dictator. There is one remark of our contemporary's, however, which seems to us unfair to the Nationalist Party and with which therefore we feel bound to join issue. He censures the Nagpur Nationalists for forcing on a division in the camp over a personal question like the election of Mr. Tilak as President. The question of the Presidentship is, in his opinion, not only a purely personal issue but also extremely trivial, as the President has no function of importance and a democratic body like the Congress ought not to make a vital issue out of a nomination to a purely honorific post. We have already given our reasons for originally raising and still persisting in this question and we again assert that we are not swayed in the slightest degree by personal questions. It will not raise Mr. Tilak in our eyes if he becomes President, it will not lower him in our eyes if he is never nominated. To a certain extent the Presidentship is a position of honour, and so far as it is so, a man of ability and reputation, an acknowledged leader and moulder of opinion, who has suffered courageously for the country is entitled to that honour. But that is not the position we take. The Presidentship is in our view much more a position of responsibility and service. We cannot agree that it is of no importance who is chosen to fill the chair, even if the Congress be a democratic body, which, as at present constituted and conducted, it is not. In no democratic assembly is the choice of the President, whether he be a virtual ruler, as in America, or only a Moderator, as in France, a question of no importance. Our Congress is not as yet either a deliberative or a legislative body, but even so the Presidentship is a function of considerable importance. The President is the embodiment to all observers of the dignity and personality of that year's session and as such his address, though it may not be binding on the whole body, is an utterance of great weight and is or ought to be largely indicative of the national temper and policy. The Congress shows the importance it attaches to his address by devoting the first day to it, an arrangement which, if the address has no weight or value as a manifesto of Congress views and policy, is an absurd and reprehensible waste of time. Besides, the President is a moderator of debate in the Subjects Committee, and of rule and decorum in the public sitting. When divided views are before the national gathering it depends on him whether all sides shall get a fair hearing and a chance of impressing their views on the Congress. We raised the question of Mr. Tilak's Presidentship at a time when Swadeshi was the question before the country partly in order that the most powerful Swadeshi worker in the country might pronounce for Swadeshi from the President's chair, and the Congress by electing him might show its sympathy with the movement. We made no secret of our object at the time and it was certainly not of a personal nature. But there was a second point at issue which was in the minds of all though it was never formulated, and this too was a point of principle, viz. that the Congress should not in any of its actions be influenced by the desire of bureaucratic favour or the fear of bureaucratic displeasure, that it should declare its complete independence as a body which looked to the people alone and not to the bureaucracy. This could not be better done than by the election of a great man and leader who was not a *persona grata* with the bureaucrats and had undergone sentence of imprisonment for the crime of patriotism. That is the real difficulty in the way of the Moderates' accepting Mr. Tilak and it is equally the reason why the Nationalists refuse to give up their point. An apparently personal question often conceals one of essential principle, even when the person is not as in this case a great patriot and leader. It was not for profligate John Wilkes that the people of Middlesex fought in the eighteenth century but for the liberty of the Press which was attacked in his person. We too fight not for honour to be done to a man however great and noble, but for the liberty of the Congress from all shadow of bureaucratic influence and its new creation as an independent, popular and democratic assembly.

Persian Democracy

The progress of democracy in the East will, if signs can be trusted, receive a powerful impetus from the creation of the Persian Parliament. In Persia the people are proving themselves too powerful for both the Crown and the Church and rapidly taking all power into their hands. When the second of Asia's Parliaments came into being, the European critics wrote, patronisingly or scornfully as the mood took them, about this new departure of these funny Asiatics who will not understand that it is only Europeans who are capable of self-government or fit for democracy and that God made Asia only to be civilised, exploited and ruled by white men, and they were liberal of prophecies that the Shah would re-establish absolutism by the sword before the world was many months older, or that Persia would be mis-governed by fanatical Mullahs. The prophets were evidently very much out of it, for the reverse has happened. The Shah is evidently being overwhelmed in the tide of democracy and the clergy who took the first step towards revolution find themselves, like the French noblesse after a similar step, already in the position of reactionaries threatened by the flood they set going. Democracy is not only the natural bent of Mahomedanism, but it is obviously the only hope of Persia where there is no wise and powerful aristocracy to lead and organise the people as in Japan. Only the fire of the democratic idea and the resurgence of the whole people, can save Persia from the European menace. Democracy is not merely the dream of "the young and ignorant" in Bengal, it is a rising force throughout Asia. Sir Harvey Adamson will have it that democracy is neither conceivable nor desired in India. Well, well, the proof of the pudding is in the eating and we will see by practical experiment whether you are right or we.

Bande Mataram, December 3, 1907

More about Unity

THE *Bengalee* has again returned to the charge about unity. The line of argument adopted by our contemporary savours strongly of the peculiar style of political thinking which underlay all our movements in the last century. The old school of politics was chiefly remarkable for a blithe indifference to facts and an extraordinary predilection for vague abstractions which could not possibly apply to the conditions with which our political action had to deal. The nineteenth century Indian politician never cared to study history, but used a ready-made and high-sounding philosophy of politics based chiefly on the circumstances and conditions of modern English politics which had no validity at all for India. The result of this divorce from real life was a tendency to use words without caring to consider their real practical meaning. We find the *Bengalee* in its article learnedly repeating these old mistakes. It builds wordy arguments from the terms of modern Science without grasping the true facts and hard realities of life without a knowledge of which the terms cannot be correctly applied. It argues from evolution that progress is an ever-increasing unity of ever-developing parts, that therefore progress is nothing but unity, ergo unity is not a means but an end, not an important or necessary help to arriving at progress, freedom and greatness but itself at once progress, freedom and greatness. This is merely playing with words. The question is, what is this unity which the *Bengalee* makes so much of and which it asks us to prefer to our principles and in its name to join in action which we believe to be harmful to the country? If our contemporary means political unity, the formation of all the communities and races in the country into a single political organism with a common centre of life, that is certainly, as we have already admitted, a necessary condition of independence and greatness; but it is a thing of the future which is impossible so long as the centre of life in the country is alien and external, and all we can do towards it is to unite people of all communities and races in one common struggle to replace the alien and external centre of political life by an indigenous and internal centre in the national organism itself. Very good, but the question still remains, by what method can that result be attained? We believe the methods proposed by the Loyalists to be futile and injurious, we understand their aim to be not the independence of the national organism, but an impossible scheme of two centres of political life controlling the country at the same time of which the alien shall be the supreme and yet the indigenous shall be free! What the *Bengalee* asks of us is to disregard this vital difference of opinion and aim and be united — in what? In aiming at an object which we believe to be absurd, by means which we believe to be futile. It does not matter, says the *Bengalee*, in what we are united, so long as we are united; for unity is progress, unity is freedom and greatness. So that if we are united in petitioning we are by the very fact of that unity free and great! The error of the *Bengalee*'s argument is that it confuses political unity, which is a necessary condition of independence, with unity of opinion and action which is an immense help, if the opinion and the action are in the right direction, but certainly not indispensable. It is not true that unity, even political unity, is identical with freedom, for a nation may be united in bondage or united in submission to a foreign and absolutist rule. Still less is it true that unity in following the wrong road is the true means to the goal, much less the goal itself. We tried to prove from history that nations had been made free not by a scrupulous pursuit of unanimity or of unity in action but by faith, energy and courage in a number of its more energetic sons carrying away the bulk of the nation into a strenuous effort to reach a great ideal. For the sake of brevity we gave one instance where we might have given a dozen. The *Bengalee*, however, like all Moderate politicians will have nothing to do with history or at least with the facts of history. History, it says in effect, is a record of human error, and the methods of which it tells us, involve great waste. So we in India are to invent something brand new, an ingenious and carefully calculated method of revolution which will bring us freedom and greatness without any waste, without any risk, by a minimum expenditure of trouble, disturbance and sacrifice. We fear it has left out of consideration the fact that waste also is one of Nature's methods, indeed, what we call waste is one of the most subtle parts of her economy. No man or nation that refused to venture hugely like a gambler for huge ends ever arrived at freedom, none who has not been prodigal of his best has ever risen to greatness, and what has been in the past will be in the future; for human nature and the laws of human action remain the same, and cannot be new-shaped in Colootola. Politics is for the Kshatriya and in the Kshatriya spirit alone can freedom and greatness be attained, not by the spirit of the Baniya trying to buy freedom in the cheapest market and beat down the demands of Fate to a miser's niggard price. That which other nations have paid for freedom we also must pay, the path they have followed we also must follow. And if you will not learn from history, you will have to be taught by a harsher teacher the same lesson — and taught perhaps at a much more tremendous price than that which you stigmatise as waste. We Nationalists have no desire to break the Congress or to part company with our less forward countrymen, but we have our path to follow and our work to do, and if you will not allow us a place in the assembly you call National, we will make one for ourselves out of it and around it, until one day you will find us knocking at your doors with the nation at our back and in the name of an authority even you will not dare to deny.

Bande Mataram, December 4, 1907

BY THE WAY

The Scots *wha hae* not with Wallace bled but emigrated from the land of Bruce and his spider to exploit and "administer" spider fashion the land of Shivaji and Pratap, met again this year for their great national feed. The menu began with relishes and proceeded through the wedded delights of ice-pudding and liqueurs to a regale of confidences and confessions by Sir Harvey Adamson which was perhaps the most enjoyable dish of the evening. The inventive Briton has discovered the great truth that out of the fullness of the stomach the heart speaketh and the result is that great British institution, the after-dinner speech. So the clans gathered and Sir Harvey of the clan of the sons of Adam spoke from "beneath the spreading antlers of a Monarch of the Glen", (so at least the *Englishman* dropping into poetry in its fervour assured us in sonorous blank verse) and behold! even as was the state of his stomach, so was the speech of Sir Harvey full-stomached and packed with choice titbits, comfortable, placid and well-pleased.

*

Of course Sir Harvey talked of the unrest, but his speech was eminently restful; it had all the large benevolence, sweet reasonableness and placid self-satisfaction of a man who had legislated as he had dined, wisely and well. It reeked of the olives and turtle soup and bannocks o' barley meal, it had the generous flavour of the liqueurs and the champagne. He first assured the assembled clans that the unrest was not purely a seditious movement nor an anti-partition movement, — Sir Harvey has found out that, and we congratulate him on his statesmanlike perspicuity. But he has found out other things too. He has not only found out what the unrest is not, he has also found out what it is. It is simply this, that the educated classes are learning to realise their own position and to aspire to "a larger share" in the government of their own country. Now at last we see this luminous reading of the situation has shed a flood of light on Mr. Morley's policy. The educated classes want their present share in the government enlarged. Most natural, most laudable! A benevolent Minto, a Radical Morley are not the men to stand in the way of such admirable aspirations. The present share of the people in the government of their own country is nothing; they want more of it; very good, we will give them a larger share of nothing. The Legislative Council is a nothing; go to, we will enlarge that nothing; we will add fresh nothings in the shape of an Advisory Council of not-ables to assist the educated class in doing nothing; and lest the burden of such an arduous task should be too heavy for their educated shoulders, we will give them upon the Councils plenty of capable helpers some of whom have been doing nothing all their lives and ought by now to be experts. If after that the educated class does not feel satisfied in its aspirations, if it does not feel as full-fed and happy as Sir Harvey after his haggis, well, they are ungrateful brutes and there is an end of it.

*

Unkind people have said that the intention of the Government was not to satisfy the aspirations of the educated class but to exclude them from the Councils under the cover of a misnamed "reforms". Sir Harvey is naturally shocked at so gross an imputation against his benevolent Government. All that the Government desires is to make the representation of the lawyers and educated men a "fair" representation. It does not want to exclude educated men, but only to swamp them with Zemindars, Mahomedans and Europeans; and it does not want to "suppress the middle class" but only to reduce them to a nullity. And this because they will not have "what is scornfully known in the East as a vakil-ridden country". It was evidently the generosity of the champagne that made Sir Harvey expand all India into the East. We are not aware that the vakil class as it exists in India is to be found anywhere except in India. It is the happy result of British rule in this favoured land that the nation now consists of a huge mass of starving peasants, a small body of dumb Government servants, and sweated office clerks, a landed aristocracy habitually overawed, fleeced and for the most part well advanced on the road to ruin, a sprinkling of prosperous middlemen, and as the only independent class, a handful of lawyers, journalists and schoolmasters. That is what Sir Harvey calls a vakil-ridden country. We have heard the expression Vakil-Raj, but we have not heard it used "scornfully" except by Anglo-Indians. But no doubt when he talks of the East, Sir Harvey means himself and his brother Scots out to make money in the East, just as by Indian trade is always meant Anglo-Indian trade and by Indian prosperity the prosperity of Anglo-India. This is a sort of official slang which has become a recognised idiom of the English language.

Anglo-India is equal to India, India is equal to the East, therefore Anglo-India is the East. The Anglo-Indian has mastered the practice of the Vedanta, for, he sees himself as the whole world and the whole world in himself; why should he then make any bones about attributing his own sentiments to a whole continent?

The government, we are gratified to learn, have no intention of stemming the flowing tide. It wants instead to cut a new channel for the tide and divert it into a lake of not-ables, where it will cease from its flowing and be at rest. As for the old channel of Swadeshi and Swaraj, it will be carefully stopped up with a strong compositive of sedition laws, Goorkhas and regulation lathis. But meanwhile what does the tide itself think about this neat little plan? Well, says Sir Harvey, Moderate politicians are delighted, but the native press dissatisfied. We had to look twice at this remarkable assertion to make sure that the champagne (or was it good old Scotch) which Sir Harvey had drunk to the health of the unrest, had not missed its way and wandered into our eyes instead of Sir Harvey's legislative cranium. All the native papers then are Extremist organs! What, all, Sir Harvey? The *Bengalee* no less than the *Bande Mataram*, the *Indu Prakash* in the same boat with the *Kesari*? All Extremists, for have not all expressed dissatisfaction with reform, which would have been received two years ago with an unanimous shriek of infantine delight? Who then can be Moderates? Sir Harvey was right after all. It is the virus of extremism which has entered secretly into the unsophisticated Congress mind and taught it to ask for something more than its long-cherished baubles. But in that case who are the Moderate politicians who are satisfied with the new playthings? Why, of course, Mr. Malabari and the Maharaja of Burdwan and Nawab of Dacca. For at this rate even Sir Pherozshah is suspected of extremism.

*

Sir Harvey has much to say about sedition and what he says is very interesting. He explains what sedition is and the explanation is of course authoritative, since it comes from the Law

Member. First, the preaching of active rebellion against the British Government. To that of course there can be no objection. Whoever preaches an armed rebellion, does it with the gaol and gallows before his eyes, and is not likely to complain if he is punished. Secondly, efforts to reduce the native army from its allegiance, and then we get a remarkable sentence. "The Government has been publicly charged with instigation of dacoity and sacrilege," etc. As we all know, a charge was made by the whole press, Moderate, Extremist, and Loyalist, against local officials, of having given a free hand to Mahomedan hooliganism, and the charge was never refuted and now Sir Harvey identifies the Government with these officials and lays down the law that whoever brings a charge against any official is guilty of sedition! "I and my Father in Simla are one," the local official may now say, "and he who blasphemeth against me blasphemeth against him." Secondly the Government has been charged with "propagating famine and plague". We note therefore that it is sedition to say that the economic conditions created and perpetuated by the present system of government are responsible for famine and poverty and the diseases which thrive on poverty! Thirdly, the Government is seditiously charged with draining the resources of India for the benefit of England. So it is sedition too to talk of the drain or refer to Lord Curzon and his luminous remarks about administration and exploitation! These are, it seems, "turgid accusations which are made to sell and do not influence sober-minded men". So Mr. R. C. Dutt is not a sober-minded man, nor Mr. Dadabhai Naoroji, nor Mr. Gokhale, nor even the knighted Bombay Lion. They are all turgid seditionists whose utterances are "made to sell". One wonders who and where the devil are these sober-minded men of Sir Harvey's whom he warrants immune from turgidity, and again one has to fall back on Mr. B. M. Malabari, the Maharaja of Burdwan and the Nawab of Dacca. O blest and sainted trio.

*

Of course Sir Harvey is strong on the seditious press, in other words, the organs of anti-bureaucratic Nationalism. Our newspapers are "of a low class", their editors have "discovered that sedition is a commercial success", and so write, it is suggested, what they do not believe because it sells. Fudge, Sir Harvey! If you could be transformed from a perorating official Scot into the manager of a Nationalist newspaper for the first year or two of its existence, you would "discover" at what tremendous pecuniary and personal sacrifice these papers have been established and maintained. If Sir Harvey knew anything about the conditions of life in the land he is helping to misgovern, he would know that an Indian newspaper, unless it is long established, and sometimes even then, can command immense influence and yet be commercially no more than able to pay its way, especially when on principle it debars itself from taking all but Swadeshi advertisements. Fudge, Sir Harvey! The Nationalists are not shopkeepers trading in the misery of the millions; they are men like Upadhyay and Bepin Chandra Pal and numbers more who have put from them all the ordinary chances of life to devote themselves to a cause, and in the few instances in which a Nationalist journal has been run at a profit, the income has gone to Swadeshi work and the maintenance of workers and not into the pockets of the proprietors, while in almost every case men of education and ability have foregone their salary or half-starved on a pittance in order to relieve the burden of the struggling journal. These are your editors of low newspapers, traders in sedition, "interested agitators", men without sense of responsibility or "matured understanding". You say the thing which is not and know it, a licensed slanderer of men a corner of whose brains has a richer content than your whole Scotch skull and whose shoes you are unworthy to touch.

*

It is refreshing to learn that Sir Harvey thinks he has got under one chief means of sedition, the platform, by his gagging ordinance turned into law. He has stiffened it he says into a tap which can be turned on wherever his vigilant eye sees a travelling spark of sedition, so on that side the British Empire and the profits of the clans are safe. But against the press he has not been able to find an equally effective extinguisher. The Government were apparently equal to the manufacture, but they want to try those tools they have before forging others that we know not of. The British public also might turn nasty if there were too rapid a succession of such stiffenings and Morley might find the fur-coat an insufficient protection against the cold biting blasts of his friends' ingratitude. So Sir Harvey means to try a few more prosecutions first. But if Kingsford's pills prove ineffective, well, then Sir Harvey, in spite of the British public and Mr. Morley's sufferings, will be the first to recommend the smothering of the patient who refuses to be cured. After that the orator passed off into complaints about his bearer and praises of whiskey and soda and other subjects too sacred to touch. And so on the note of "whiskey in moderation" Sir Harvey closed his historic speech. And the British Empire knew itself safe.

Bande Mataram, December 5, 1907

Caste and Representation

THE policy of the Bureaucracy in the face of the national movement, so far as it is anything more than crude repression, is a policy of makeshifts and dodges, and, though skilful in a way, it shows throughout an extraordinary ignorance of the country they rule. The latest brilliant device is an attempt to reshuffle the constituent elements of Indian politics and sort them out afresh on the basis not only of creed, but of caste. The *Pioneer* has come out with an article in its best style of business-like gravity, in which it settles the basis on which representation should be given to India. For two years of unrest have brought us so far that Anglo-India is awakened to the necessity of giving some kind of representation to the Indians, and petty details of administrative reform, the demand for which was then considered as much a crying for the moon as the cry for Swaraj nowadays, are fast coming into the range of "practical politics". Great are the virtues of unrest! Of course it is only representation and not representative government which Anglo-India is bending itself to think within the range of possibility; for government means control and control is the last thing which they will consent to yield to us. When Viceroys and Law Members talk of giving us a larger share in the government of our country, they mean of course not control but what they call a voice, and they will take good care that this voice shall be *vox et praeterea nihil*, a voice and nothing more. But even a voice may be a serious inconvenience to an absolute government and pains are therefore to be taken to substitute an echo for a voice, an echo of bureaucratic whisperings for the living utterance of a nation. In the representative institutions which the bureaucracy are likely to give us, it is the drone of many notables and the mechanical squeaking of officially manipulated puppets that we shall hear, and this, the world will be told, is the voice of the Indian people.

But Anglo-Indian statesmanship will not rest satisfied with

tuning the ineffective voice with which they desire to delude our aspirations, to the character of a flat and foolish echo; they will farther make every arrangement to turn it into a source of fresh weakness to the growing nationality instead of a source of strength. They began of course long ago, the attempt to make capital of the religious diversities of Indian society and recently the policy of setting the Mahomedans as a counterpoise to the Hindus has been openly adopted. In the new Legislative Councils the Mahomedans are to have representation not as children of the soil, an integral portion of one Indian people, but as a politically distinct and hostile interest which will, it is hoped, outweigh or at least nullify the Hindus. The bureaucratic Machiavels have not realised that the conditions of the new struggle which has begun, are of so different a kind from any yet known in British India that the Mahomedans cannot be turned into an effective tool in the hands of the bureaucracy without becoming at the same time a danger to the artisan of discord who uses them. For the field of the struggle is not nowadays in Simla or on the floor of the House of Commons or on any lists where outside opinion can have a decisive or even a material influence. It is not a voice which they have to set against a voice or a show which they have to outface with a better show, but a force which they will have to call into being to oppose a force. The Hindus have become self-conscious, they have heard a voice that cries to them, "Arise from the dead, live and follow me," and they are irresistibly growing into a living and powerful political force. Unless the Mahomedans can be built up also into a self-conscious, living and powerful political force, their assistance to the rulers will be a mere handful of dust in the balance. But the moment they become a living and self-conscious power the doom of bureaucracy will be sealed. For no self-conscious community aware of its strength and separate life will consent to go on pulling chestnuts out of the fire for Anglo-Indian Machiavel. Even if they do not coalesce with the Hindus, they will certainly demand a share of the power which they maintain. Not in that direction lies any permanent hope of salvation for the absolute power of the bureaucracy. Perhaps the more thinking part of Anglo-India perceives this truth, hence the desire to find additional points of support and other principles of discord by which Indian Nationality can be hopelessly divided and cut to pieces in the making.

Of course the *Pioneer* does not avow the real object of this scheme for creating and perpetuating as political entities divisions which every healthful political organism progresses by subordinating and discharging of all political significance; but it is obvious enough. If it were possible for the bureaucracy to turn the social divisions of the community into political divisions, there could be no more fatal instrument of political disorganisation, and just as a natural indigenous rule finds its safety in better political organisation, so an unnatural alien rule finds its safety in disorganisation of what it preys upon. If it can, it destroys all centres of political organisation except itself; otherwise it tries to create unnatural centres whose action will hamper and distract the organic growth. Caste with the proper safeguards is an admirable means of social organisation and conservation, but it has not and should not be allowed to have any political meaning. In India with the exception of Maharashtra it has had no political meaning at all. In the old times it was different. All the executive power and functions of war and politics were in the hands of the Kshatriyas for the good reasons that the whole work of war and protection of the country from internal and external disorder was assigned by Society to them, and classes which did not give of their blood to preserve the peace and freedom of their country could not claim a direct control of administration. The Brahmin legislated, but legislation was then a religious function which implied no political power or position, and the people at large exercised only an indirect control by the pressure of a public opinion which no ruler could afford to neglect. Afterwards when Chandragupta and Asoka had created the tradition of a powerful absolutism with a strong bureaucratic organisation to support it, things changed, but not in the direction of a polity based on caste. On the contrary all classes, Brahmin, Kshatriya, Vaishya, Sudra could and did rise to any position of political power, even the throne itself, and except in Rajasthan where the Kshatriya ideals and institutions were preserved, caste came to count less rather than more in politics as time went on. All the great nation-builders have ignored caste as a political factor and it was only when the national spirit of the Marathas declined after Panipat that a cleavage on the lines of caste took place which is still a slight danger to Nationalism in the South. It is curious to find the British rulers who have done their best to undermine caste as a social institution now dreaming of perpetuating and using it as a political instrument. We do not think they will make much by this move. The centripetal impulse in Hindu society is already too strong and with most of us political division by castes is too foreign to our habits of thought to take root. The very idea of making a constituency of Bengal Kayasthas or Bengal Brahmins is absurd. Only where certain classes are much depressed and submerged a temporary strife may be created, but the onward sweep of the national movement, profoundly democratic as it is, will lift these classes to a nobler function in society and give them prizes which a Government post or title cannot hope to rival. If we listened to our Loyalists and continued to depend on alien favours and look on them as the crown of our political life, then indeed discord might be sown and castes learn to view themselves as distinct and hostile political interests, but against the force of the National movement such devices will array themselves in vain; its democratic and unifying spirit will make light of all such feeble attempts to divide.

Bande Mataram, December 6, 1907

About Unmistakable Terms

WE answered yesterday in general terms the claim advanced in the columns of the *Bengalee* to implicit and blind obedience from all Bengalis to the Calcutta Moderate leaders and to any local representatives of loyalty and moderation whom they may be pleased to erect to the gaze of an adoring public. But the *Bengalee*'s article contained also certain passages which demand more direct and plain-spoken answers and this today we will give. The *Bengalee*, not contented with its arrogant demand for submission, goes on to declare that the Nationalists, because they refuse this claim, are traitors to their country, that the men who opposed Mr. Chitnavis' autocracy at Nagpur or Sir Pherozshah's at Calcutta or Mr. K. B. Dutt's at Midnapur are rowdies and the Nationalist leaders, Mr. Tilak and Mr. Khaparde in the West of Srijuts Bepin Pal, Aurobindo Ghose or Brahmabandhab Upadhyay in Calcutta have been abettors of rowdies, and it calls on the whole country to speak out in unmistakable terms against us. Unmistakable terms? Well, then, let us have an understanding about terms, to begin with. What is the definition of a traitor to his country? Are men traitors who have exposed themselves to persecution, imprisonment and harassment for the sake of their country? Are those traitors who have made large sacrifices and devoted themselves to the cause of the Motherland? Or are those young men traitors who have stood in the forefront of the battle of boycott, braving the full fury of the bureaucrats and their police, and but for whom the boycott agitation would have flagged and perished after the first six months of excitement? The *Bengalee* says they are: for they may have done all these things, and yet if they oppose Mr. K. B. Dutt or Srijut Surendranath, they are traitors to their country. On the other hand, have not those rather the complexion of traitors who are ready to call in police assistance against their countrymen in a Swadeshi conference although there has been no riot or violence, who boast that the police are in their hands and they can get all arrested who oppose them, who are ready to forget all the oppression from Barisal till now and call in Magistrates and police superintendents to the place of honour in national meetings, who are ready to take the lathis out of the hands of volunteers to please a District official? Or those, to take other examples, who wrote with brilliant success to Anglo-Indian papers to get Mr. Tilak prosecuted at the time of the Poona murders? Or those who pointed out Lala Lajpat Rai to the bureaucracy as the man to strike at when the Punjab was in a ferment over the Colonisation Bill? But, by the *Bengalee*'s reasoning, men may be the moral descendants of Mir Jafar and Jagat Seth and yet be excellent patriots so long as they obey Moderate leaders and respect age and authority.

The second term we want to see so defined as to be unmistakable, is the term "leaders". The *Bengalee* calls for discipline and submission to leadership, but who are the leaders to whom we are to yield this unquestioning military obedience? What is the qualification in Mr. K. B. Dutt of Midnapur, for instance, by virtue of which we are called upon to sacrifice for his sake our national self-respect, our convictions, and our natural right to a free exercise of our individual reason and conscience? The *Bengalee* talks of age, but it is preposterous to set up age by itself as the claim to leadership in politics; nor did the Moderate leaders themselves show an overwhelming deference to age when they were themselves younger and more ardent. Respect for age as a part of social discipline we can understand, but leadership by seniority is a new doctrine. Then again the *Bengalee* talks of authority. What authority? The authority of social position, wealth, professional success? Are we to obey Mr. K. B. Dutt because he is the leader of the Midnapur bar just as the East Bengal Mahomedans obey Salimullah because he is the Nawab of Dacca? We decline to accept any such law of obedience. Authority is always a delegated power which does not rest in the individual but proceeds to him from a definite source and returns to that source. Official authority proceeds from an organised government executing the law which can both delegate its power to individuals and take them away again as it pleases. In popular movements the people are the only source from which authority can proceed. The people follow a leader because he best interprets their ideas, aims and feelings or because he shows himself the best fitted to organise and lead the popular forces to the realisation of popular aspirations and ideals, and the moment their confidence is shaken, the moment they begin to think he does not represent their best ideas and aspirations or that his methods of leadership are mistaken, the authority begins to depart out of him. There can be no other kind of authority in democratic politics, nor can popular leadership be self-constituted. Those who demand military obedience to self-constituted leaders are not preparing self-government but killing it, striking at its very roots. If what the Moderate leaders want is to replace bureaucracy not by popular self-government but by the government of particular persons or classes, if they want the movement to be not democratic but oligarchic, or plutocratic, let them say so clearly, in God's name and let us have done with this juggling with words, and henceforward on both sides "speak in unmistakable terms".

Finally, while we are about defining terms, let us know when a man becomes President of a Conference or Congress session. The *Bengalee* says, "The attempt that was made to heckle the President and to bring into contempt his position as the head of the Conference was unique in the history of our Conferences and Congresses. We never witnessed in the whole course of our public life a proceeding...so derogatory to the authority of the President." The "heckling" took place before Mr. K. B. Dutt was elected, when the President's chair was vacant. Are we then to suppose that a man becomes President before he is elected? It is curious that Mr. K. B. Dutt himself made this unwarrantable claim when the trouble first began. By custom the Reception Committee designates a President but the decision of the Committee has no binding force on the delegates of the Conference who have always the power to elect any one else whom they may prefer and not till a public confirmation by the votes of the delegates, has the President designated by the Reception Committee any authority or tenure of office. Until then he is merely a public man nominated for a particular function and the public have every right to "heckle" him so as to be sure that he will properly represent them before they give him their votes. Because till now this right has not been enforced, it does not follow that the public has forfeited its right, nor are we bound by "traditions" which mean simply the absence of lively popular interest and have no sanction in any reasonable principle of procedure.

The *Bengalee* sets up discipline as the one requisite of a popular movement and to back up its proposition it is so ill-advised as to quote the example of Parnell and his solid Irish phalanx. The choice of this example shows a singular ignorance of English politics. Before Parnell's advent, the Irish Party in Parliament was a moderate party of Irish Liberals of very much the same nature as the old Congress Party before the Boycott. It was balanced in Ireland by a revolutionary organisation using the most violent means employed by secret societies. When Parnell first appeared on the scene, his first action was to revolt against the leader of the Irish Party and make a party of his own. Consisting at first of a mere handful it soon captured the whole of Ireland and created the solid phalanx. But what was the secret of Parnell's success? Parnell, unlike our Moderate leaders, did not dwarf the ideal of a national movement but always held the absolute independence of his country as the goal: he made it a fixed principle to accept no half-way house between independence and subjection short of an Irish Parliament with independent powers; he suffered no man to enter his party who did not pledge himself to refuse all office, honour or emolument from the alien government and he showed his people a better way of agitation than mere dependence on England on one side and secret outrage on the other — the way of passive resistance, obstruction in Parliament and refusal of rent in the country. Only so could Parnell succeed in creating the solid phalanx, and when it was broken, it was by the folly of his adherents who receded from his principles and sacrificed their leader at the bidding of an English statesman. If Srijut Surendranath wishes to have the country solid behind him, he must be a Parnell first and not shrink from a Parnellite policy and ideals. Only clear principles and unambiguous conduct can secure implicit obedience.

Bande Mataram, December 12, 1907

The Surat Congress

WHEN the All-India Congress Committee first betrayed its charge and degraded itself from the position of a high arbiter and guide in all national affairs to that of a party machine subservient to a single political tactician, we said that there were but two courses open to us, either to refuse to accept a party trick engineered in defiance of justice, decency and all the common rules of public procedure and to hold our own Congress at Nagpur, or to go in force to Surat and, if we could not swamp the Congress, at least to show that into whatever farthest nook or corner of India Sir Pherozshah Mehta might fly for refuge, he could not get rid of the presence of Nationalism, to fling ourselves at once on Gujerat and organise Nationalism there, so that the Loyalist's chosen haven of refuge might become another place of shipwreck. In any case, we said, we must have a Conference of Nationalists this year and organise Nationalism all over the country. We have not concealed our opinion that the session at Nagpur would be the preferable course, as being both the most logical and the manliest and involving the least waste of energy now and in future. But such a course was out of the question unless all could agree upon it, and this was not found possible. Especially when Mr. Tilak and Lala Lajpat Rai, fresh from his exile, were in favour of attending the Surat session, there could be no further question of our course. It has been decided, then, to attend the Surat Congress in what force we can muster at this short notice and do our best to hold the ground we have gained, as well as to see that certain questions which were held over last year are not held over again. A Nationalist Conference has also been arranged by the efforts of the Nationalists at Surat and arrangements will be made for Nationalist delegates, a ticket of one rupee being issued to each delegate for the recovery of expenses.

We call upon Nationalists in Calcutta and the Mofussil, who are at all desirous of the spread of Nationalist principles and

Nationalist practice all over India, to make ready at whatever inconvenience and, if they find it humanly possible, go to Surat to support the Nationalist cause. We are aware of the tremendous difficulties in our way. Surat is far-distant, the expenses of such a journey are almost prohibitive, for only a small percentage of our party are men of means, and the time for preparation is almost nil. And yet we must go. What is a Nationalist good for if he cannot make up by his enthusiasm and energy for his other deficiencies, if he cannot make nothing of difficulties and turn the impossible into the possible? It is to sweep away difficulties and to strike the word impossible out of the Indian's dictionary that our party has arisen. The leaders of the Deccan call us; Lala Lajpat Rai, a name now made sacred to us all, is waiting to see the first fruit of his sufferings in the increase of patriots wedded to the principles for professing and practising which he has suffered, and the people of Gujerat are waiting eagerly for our advent. If Bengal goes there in force it will, we believe, set flowing such a tide of Nationalism as neither bureaucrats nor Bombay Loyalists are prepared to believe possible. The Christmas concessions given by the Railway companies reduce the expense to a minimum and for those who travel by the intermediate, Rs. 75 at the outside should be enough. For we are going not as holiday sight-seers making a national occasion an excuse for a Christmas jaunt and we do not demand comfort on the way or luxuries when we arrive. We must go as poor men whose wealth is our love for our Motherland, as missionaries taking nothing with them but the barest expenses of the way, as pilgrims travelling to our Mother's temple. We have a great work to do and cannot afford to be negligent and half-hearted. Be sure that this year 1907 is a turning-point of our destinies, and do not imagine that the session of the Surat Congress will be as the sessions of other years. Let us fear to miss by absenting ourselves the chance of helping to put in one of the keystones of the house we are building for our Mother's dwelling in the future, the house of her salvation, the house of Swaraj.

Bande Mataram, December 13, 1907

Reasons of Secession

WE HAVE now placed all the facts of the Midnapur Conference before the public and the reasons which made a Nationalist secession inevitable are sufficiently obvious. The Loyalist legend that the Nationalists came prepared to break up the Conference by force, but were either baffled, say some authorities, by the "mingled tact and firmness" of Mr. K. B. Dutt, or overawed, say others, by the presence of the President's bureaucratic friends and allies, and in their rage and disappointment seceded and held a separate meeting, is too contemptible a lie to be treated seriously. "Why should they secede? What was the necessity of a second Conference?" ask our opponents with a holy simplicity, "Did we not pass the same resolutions? Was not a translation of the President's marvellous address offered to the audience? What does it matter if the President broke his word? As for the interpretation of Swaraj as colonial self-government, it is an unimportant matter, a prejudged matter, no Conference pretending to be a branch of the Congress organisation has any right to pass a resolution for Swaraj pure and simple and no responsible politician can support such a resolution. The Police Superintendent? Well, he was there only to see that the train wrecking outrage was not repeated by the Nationalists in the Conference Pandal!"

Let us clear the matter of this jungle of irrelevancies. It was not over the resolutions passed by the Moderate Subjects Committee and Conference that the secession took place. When the Moderates saw that they had succeeded in disgusting and tiring out their opponents and had the field themselves they quietly adjourned to the Bailey Hall and held their own Committee and passed their own resolutions — this is a favourite trick with this party which they perform in the full confidence that their opponents will in the end acquiesce in the accomplished fact for the sake of "unity". We are informed that two resolutions were seriously modified in Committee at the command of the President, but whether these modifications stood, or repentance came with the morning, does not matter: for the resolutions were not the cause of the secession. The question of the language in which the President's speech should be delivered was a detail on which the Mofussil delegates felt strongly and it is obvious that if these Conferences are to serve the purpose for which they are created, the vernacular must be the medium employed. It is absurd to have the President's speech in English and then to patch up matters by offering a translation, when the audience is already wearied out by listening to a long address in a foreign tongue which they do not understand. If Mr. K. B. Dutt had to address all India, though no one asked him to, he could have delivered a lecture in the British Indian Association or published a pamphlet or written an article in the *Bengalee*; the Conference Pandal was not the place for his dissertation. But in any case the question of language was not a determining cause of the secession. Again we do not think it a light thing that a gentleman who fills the important and dignified position of the President of a District Conference, should, after he has been nominated without opposition on the strength of a clear promise, go back upon his word and yet cling to his post. Honour is not a light thing, a public undertaking is not a light thing, and that the President did promise, has been testified to by honest Moderates as well as Nationalists who were present on the occasion. But the seceders did not take this ground for secession, for they had consented, on the strength of Srijut Surendranath's qualified assurance, to the election which, once made, could not be unmade. As to Swaraj, we do not think it an unimportant matter, nor can we see that a District or Provincial Conference is debarred from passing a resolution in its favour; for by this rule several District Conferences, including the Bhola Conference, presided over by Srijut Ambica Charan Mazumdar, have forfeited their right to be considered branches of the Congress organisation. But we will let that too go, for it was not to pass a resolution on unqualified Swaraj that a second Conference was held. The secession took place because of the arbitrary conduct of the President supported by his party in evading the right of the whole body of delegates to express its opinion effectively on disputed matters and because of the use made by him of his alliance with the Police to support his arbitrary authority.

The emergence of two distinct parties in Indian politics has altered the whole nature of our political problems and our political activity and it is absolutely necessary that the constitution, methods and procedure of the Congress and the subordinate bodies should be constructed accordingly. Formerly it mattered nothing how the Congress was conducted, because there was no overt difference of opinion and whatever the Congress chiefs did or thought good was accepted without question or murmur. If there were dissentients they were easily silenced. But now there are two distinct parties with different ideals, different methods of work, a different spirit and standpoint, each struggling to get the ear of the country and the control of our public activities. It is clear that if these two parties are to live together in the Congress, there must be some procedure which both can recognise as just, some means of determining their relative strength and giving each a means of influencing the course of Congress work in proportion to its strength. This can be done by constituting the Subjects Committee so that each party shall be represented according to the strength it can muster or by allowing each section of the delegates to choose by vote its own representatives; the representatives of both sides can come to an agreement in Committee on disputed points and where agreement is impossible, the majority of votes will decide the matter, subject always to an inalienable right of appeal by amendment to the whole body of delegates. With such rules of procedure there would be no reason why two parties should not exist side by side and the deliberations of the Congress and Conferences be conducted with decorum, order and dignity. But if one side refuses to acknowledge the existence of the other, if it tries, when it cannot ignore it, to put it down by bullying or by the personal authority of its own leaders, and when even that is not possible by what it calls a combination of tact and firmness but the other side calls a mixture of trickery and arbitrariness, when it keeps procedure vague and disregards the rules common to all public assemblies, then to live together seems almost impossible. This is the reason why the fight over the nomination of the President is so unnecessarily bitter. One side feels that it cannot allow the election of a Nationalist President because that would mean official recognition of the right of the other to share in influencing and guiding the Congress work. The other side feels that a Moderate President will simply be an instrument for Moderate tactics, not an impartial speaker of the House. He will rule Nationalist proposals and amendments out of order, refuse to take the sense of the House when called upon and by other arbitrary exercise of his authority serve his party. The rowdiness of which the Moderates complain is simply the clamorous persistence which is the sole means left to the other party to compel justice and a hearing. All this the Nationalists have again and again endured in the hope that by sheer persistence they might get their existence recognised and such rules formulated as would permit of differences being automatically settled. But when the Moderate goes so far as to call in a third party to weigh down the balance in his favour, and that third party the common enemy, the bureaucrat and his police, the limit of sufferance is over-passed and nothing is left but to separate before difference of opinion degenerates into civil war. This was the stage which by the grace of Mr. K. B. Dutt was reached at Midnapur. We bring no charge against the Calcutta leaders except that of supporting a man instead of considering the interests of the country; we prefer to believe that they had nothing to do with the underhand methods of their local lieutenant; but the support they rendered him made him impervious to reason and left the Nationalists no resource but secession. The Nationalist Conference, the Nationalist organisation is now an accomplished fact. If the local Moderates come to their senses, a *modus vivendi* may in future be found, but in any case our Conference and Association will remain and work. Midnapur has taken the initiative in giving Nationalism an organised shape and form.

Bande Mataram, December 14, 1907

The Awakening of Gujerat

WHEN the word of the Eternal has gone abroad, when the spirit moves over the waters and the waters stir and life begins to form, then it is a law that all energies are forced to direct themselves, consciously or unconsciously, willingly or against their will, to the one supreme work of the time, the formation of the new manifest and organised life which is in process of creation. So now when the waters of a people's life are stirred and the formation of a great organic Indian state and nation has begun, the same law holds. All that the adversaries of the movement have done whether they have tried to repress or tried to conciliate, has helped what they sought to destroy and swelled the volume and strength or purified as by fire the forces of Nationalism. So also the efforts of those among ourselves who are afraid of the new movement or distrustful of it to check the pace and bring back the nation's energies into the old grooves, have only helped to increase the vehemence of the National desire to move forward. When Sir Pherozshah Mehta juggled the Congress into Surat, he thought he was preparing a death-blow for Nationalism: he was only preparing the way for a Nationalist awakening in Gujerat. Nationalism depends for its success on the awakening and organising of the whole strength of the nation; it is therefore vitally important for Nationalism that the politically backward classes should be awakened and brought into the current of political life; the great mass of orthodox Hinduism which was hardly even touched by the old Congress movement, the great slumbering mass of Islam which has remained politically inert throughout the last century, the shopkeepers, the artisan class, the immense body of illiterate and ignorant peasantry, the submerged classes, even the wild tribes and races still outside the pale of Hindu civilisation, Nationalism can afford to neglect and omit none. It rejoices to see any sign of life where there was no life before, even if the first manifestations should seem to be ill-regulated or misguided. It is not afraid of

Pan-Islamism or any signs of the growth of a separate Mahomedan self-consciousness but rather welcomes them. It is not startled by the spectacle of a submerged class like the Namasudras demanding things which are, under existing circumstances, impracticable from Hindu society. When a community sues for separate rights from the bureaucracy, that is a sign not of life but of stagnant dependence which is death, but when it seeks a larger place in the national existence and it tries to feel its own existence and its own strength, it is a true sign of life, and what Nationalism asks is for life first and above all things; life, and still more life, is its cry. Let us by every means get rid of the pall of death which stifled us, let us dispel first the passivity, quiescence, the unspeakable oppression of inertia which has so long been our curse; that is the first and imperative need. As with backward communities, so with backward provinces. It is vitally important to Nationalism that these should awake. Behar, Orissa, the Central Provinces, Gujerat, Sindh must take their place in the advancing surge of Indian political life, must prepare themselves for a high rank in the future federated strength of India. We welcome any signs that the awakening has begun. It is for instance a cause of gratification that Orissa is beginning to feel its separate consciousness, and to attempt to grow into an organised life under a capable and high-spirited leader, although we consider his political attitude mistaken and believe that he is laying up for himself bitter disappointment and disillusionment in the future. But when the inevitable disappointment and disillusionment come, then will the new political consciousness, the new organised life of Orissa become an immense addition of strength to the forces of Nationalism. Yet it remains true that the only way these provinces can make up for lost time and bring themselves up swiftly to the level of the more advanced races, is by throwing themselves whole-heartedly into the full tide of Nationalism, and we do not know that we ought not to thank Sir Pherozshah for giving us a unique chance to light the fire in Gujerat.

The Gujeratis have only recently been touched by the tide of political life. Largely split up into Native States, large and small, and only partially under the direct rule of the bureaucracy, immersed in commerce and fairly prosperous until the last great famine swept over the once smiling and fertile province destroying life, human and animal, by the million they had slumbered politically while the rest of India was accustoming itself to some kind of political activity. It was at the Ahmedabad Congress that Gujerat was for the first time moved to a political enthusiasm, an awakening perhaps helped on by the association of a thoroughly Swadeshi Exhibition with the session of the Congress and the inclusion, however timid and half-hearted, of industrial revival in our political programme. Then came the outburst of the Swadeshi by which Gujerat, unlike some of the other politically backward provinces, was profoundly affected. The ground has been prepared and Nationalist sentiment has already spread among the educated Gujeratis. The Surat Congress provides an opportunity to give a fresh and victorious impulse which will make Gujerat Nationalism a powerful working and organised force. The importance of winning Gujerat to the Nationalist cause is great. The Gujeratis labour as the Bengalis did, until the present awakening, under a reproach of timidity and excessive love of peace and safety. The truth probably is that so far as the reproach has any foundation either in Bengal or Gujerat the defect was due not so much to any constitutional cowardice as to indolence born of climate and a too fertile soil and to the prevalence of the peaceful and emotional religion of Chaitanya and Vallabhacharya. Be that as it may, Bengal under the awakening touch of Nationalism has wiped out that reproach for ever and there is no reason why Gujerat, stirred by the same influences, awakened to the same energy, should not emulate her example and take like her a foremost place in the battle of Swaraj. We must not forget that she also has great traditions of old, traditions of learning, traditions of religion, traditions of courage and heroism. Gujerat was once part of the Rajput circle and her princes fought on equal terms with Mahmud of Ghazni. Her people form valuable and indispensable material for the building of the Indian nation. The *savoir-faire*, the keen-witted ability and political instinct of her Brahmins, the thrift and industry of her merchants, the robust vigour and common sense of her Patidars, the physique and soldierly qualities of her

Kathis and Rajputs, the strong raw human material of her northern and southern hills, are so many elements of strength which Nationalism must seize and weld into a great national force. Even if Sir Pherozshah Mehta overwhelms us with numbers at Surat, even if we cannot carry a single proposition in the Congress Pandal, yet if we can give this great impulse to Gujerat and organise our scattered forces for a great march forward, all the energy, all the expenditure we can devote to this session at Surat will be amply rewarded. It is not merely or chiefly by victories in the Congress but by victories in the country that we must record the progress of Nationalism.

Bande Mataram, December 17, 1907

"Capturing the Congress"

WE HAVE asked the Nationalists all over India to muster strong at Surat during the Congress session. It is believed in some quarters that we intend to march upon the Congress and re-enact a Pride's Purge. Another insinuation is that we form a band of vain, petulant upstarts who delight in wrecking and breaking for its own sake. The *Bengalee* calls upon the people to repudiate these traitors, and the *Tribune* of Lahore, the *Indu Prakash* and *Social Reformer* of Bombay, the *Indian People* of Allahabad have by this time swelled that cry. The principle that underlay our attempt to get Lajpat elected to the Presidential chair has not been appreciated by the *Punjabee*, the *Hindu* and even Lala Lajpat Rai himself. Capital is being made of this fact and unworthy motives attributed to the Nationalists. Our enemies have got a splendid opportunity to discredit the Nationalist movement by saying that even those who are avowedly sympathetic towards the propaganda cannot support all its senseless manifestation. The emergence of a new school of thought, their vigorous and menacing activity and enthusiasm have always made the votaries of established order uneasy and vindictive. In the frenzied anxiety to retain all power, in a paralysing fear of change they raise a terrible clamour and try to play upon the timidity and the spirit of routine of the unthinking people. They cry for the blood of the new messengers without even patiently listening to their message. Even master minds succumb to this weakness. When Dr. Price delivered his eloquent sermon on the great impetus given to national freedom by the revolutionary propaganda in France, Burke became quite unnerved and was so much carried away by an unreasonable fear as to wreck his own reputation as a sedate and practical statesman by setting to work to write that hysterical diatribe against the French Revolution, which even his admirers could not help regretting.

It is no wonder therefore that the Nationalists should be

assailed with the most unjustifiable vehemence in their attempt to awaken and organise the people and to shift the centre of power and authority to them. But while the Nationalists should pursue their line of action with unabated zeal, they are also to consider, in view of the fierce and vindictive opposition which they have provoked not only from the bureaucracy but also a section of their own countrymen, whether they should not work in their own way without coming into collusion with those whose ideals and methods of work render any concerted action hardly possible. We invite the Nationalists to Surat not so much to capture the Congress by violence, as our enemies maliciously put it, but to see that the Nationalist sentiment and Nationalist programme find their place in the deliberations and finally prevail. Many of us think that the Nationalists cannot pull on with the Moderates and Loyalists who are determined to baffle their patriotic activities to democratise the Congress by a cobweb of malicious misrepresentation and vilification. The Nationalists indulge in no vague charges against the Moderates. They expose their high-handedness with an unequivocal statement of facts. But these people do not meet us on the charges brought against them, but try to evade the real issue by irrelevant and senseless denunciations. Under the circumstances, some of us thought it wiser and easier for the Nationalists to have an organ of their own, without giving the Moderates and Loyalists a chance of misrepresenting and vilifying them. The experience of the Midnapur Conference shows that the delegates, young and old, all smart under the autocracy of the old workers, which is leading many to think a separatist movement preferable to a perpetual friction. But for the present we must put all such thoughts from us. It has been decided to continue the attempt to fight out the battle of Nationalism in the Congress Pandal until at last a majority of the delegates declare for our views. To that end we must now devote all our energies.

Lala Lajpat Rai's Refusal

The refusal of Lala Lajpat Rai to accept nomination to the Presidentship of the Congress as against Dr. Rash Behari Ghose has given great cause for rejoicing to the Moderates and to Anglo-Indian journals like the *Empire*. The refusal is natural enough, for when a man who has not been nominated is under such circumstances pressed for a reply to the question whether he will accept nomination or not, he is put into a delicate position in which he must either appear to be wanting in modesty or give away his supporters. This was the dilemma in which the Loyalists have placed Lala Lajpat Rai. Evidently, he has been persuaded to think that he was being asked to stand against Dr. Rash Behari Ghose and that the proposal of the Nationalists was intended as a personal honour to himself. Needless to say, the Nationalists have not asked Lajpat Rai to stand as a candidate. The step they have taken is simply to ask from Dr. Rash Behari Ghose the magnanimity to withdraw and leave the field clear so that a great principle might be vindicated in the most striking way of which the circumstances admitted. Had Dr. Ghose shown that magnanimity there would have been no necessity for Lajpat Rai to be asked to stand as a candidate; the unanimous will of the country would have called him to the Presidential chair. Our proposal was not meant as an invitation to do honour to a particular individual, nor, great as is our personal regard for Lajpat Rai, was it dictated by personal affection. We look upon him as the embodiment of an ideal and his nomination as the nation's answer to the repressions of the bureaucracy. Lala Lajpat Rai, out of feelings which we respect, has declined to give us that opportunity. We are sorry to have lost it, but glad at least that of the two men put forward, one should have shown the magnanimity to which the other has not been able to rise.

The Delegates' Fund

Many who are desirous of contributing to the Delegates' Fund, have addressed enquiries to us about the manner in which it is to be disposed of. The object of the fund is to send to Surat a number of delegates with uncompromising views and of an uncompromising spirit who will see to it, so far as lies in their power, that the Congress at Surat shall make no backward step but, if possible, move a step further towards associating itself with the new life of the country. We hope that no attempt will be made to take any backward step, but we know that there is a reactionary element in the Congress which would be only too glad to recede, and if by negligence we give them their opportunity, the responsibility for any backsliding will be ours. We hope also that Bengal will present a solid front against any reaction, but we have no right to be sure of it, and only if there is the strong moral backing of a number of delegates, who will not compromise with their principles or allow respect of persons or utter persuasion or browbeating to sway them from their firm position, can we expect the Bengal leaders to stand fast against the pressure that may be brought to bear on them. The delegates who will be assisted out of the fund must therefore pledge themselves to stand firm for Boycott as a general principle, for the Swadeshi resolution as it was framed last year, for National Education and Arbitration as prominent planks in the Congress platform and to do their best to see that the Congress takes up the cause of the Transvaal Indians, rejects Mr. Morley's reforms or any other sham and simulacrum of self-government and takes a sensible step forward in the direction of national organisation. The precise proposals which will be pressed upon the Subjects Committee will be formulated after due discussion in the Nationalist Conference which meets on the 24th at Surat, but these are the broad lines on which we propose to frame them. We may mention finally that all we propose to give out of the fund is assistance; no single delegate will be given all his expenses to and from or at Surat. If it should be decided to propose constitutional changes in the direction of democratising the Congress, our delegates will support such proposals. Those, therefore, who contribute to the Fund should understand that they are contributing to send delegates who will support progress and to save the National Assembly from the danger of a disastrous and ignominious relapse into the past methods and ideas which the nation is fast outgrowing and which Bengal has altogether renounced.

Bande Mataram, December 18, 1907

The Present Situation*

My Fellow-Countrymen, Mr. Ranade has said that there is no President here, but that God himself is our President. I accept that remark in the most reverent spirit, and before addressing you, I ask Him first to inspire me. I have been asked to speak on the "Needs of the Present Situation". What is the present situation? What is the situation of this country today? Just as I was coming in, this paper (*showing the copy of the 'Bande Mataram' newspaper*) was put into my hands, and looking at the first page of it, I saw two items of news, "The *Yugantar* Trial, Judgment delivered, the Printer convicted and sentenced to two years' rigorous imprisonment." The other is "Another Newspaper Prosecution, The *Nabasakti* Office sacked and searched, Printer let out on a bail of Rs. 10,000." This is the situation of the country today. Do you realise what I mean? There is a creed in India today which calls itself Nationalism, a creed which has come to you from Bengal. This is a creed which many of you have accepted when you called yourselves Nationalists. Have you realised, have you yet realised what that means? Have you realised what it is that you have taken in hand? Or is it that you have merely accepted it in the pride of a superior intellectual conviction? You call yourselves Nationalists. What is Nationalism? Nationalism is not a mere political programme; Nationalism is a religion that has come from God; Nationalism is a creed which you shall have to live. Let no man dare to call himself a Nationalist if he does so merely with a sort of intellectual pride, thinking that he is more patriotic, thinking that he is something higher than those who do not call themselves by that name. If you are going to be a Nationalist, if you are going to assent to this religion of Nationalism, you must do it in the religious spirit. You must remember that you are

* A lecture delivered under the auspices of the Bombay National Union by Sri Aurobindo to a large gathering at Mahajan Wadi, Bombay, on Sunday, the 19th January, 1908.

the instruments of God. What is this that has happened in Bengal? You call yourselves Nationalists, but when this happens to you, what will you do? This thing is happening daily in Bengal, because, in Bengal, Nationalism has come to the people as a religion, and it has been accepted as a religion. But certain forces which are against that religion are trying to crush its rising strength. It always happens when a new religion is preached, when God is going to be born in the people, that such forces rise with all their weapons in their hands to crush the religion. In Bengal too a new religion, a religion divine and sattwic has been preached and this religion they are trying with all the weapons at their command to crush. By what strength are we in Bengal able to survive? Nationalism has not been crushed. Nationalism is not going to be crushed. Nationalism survives in the strength of God and it is not possible to crush it, whatever weapons are brought against it. Nationalism is immortal; Nationalism cannot die; because it is no human thing, it is God who is working in Bengal. God cannot be killed, God cannot be sent to jail. When these things happen among you, I say to you solemnly, what will you do? Will you do as they do in Bengal? (*Cries of 'Yes'*) Don't lightly say "yes". It is a solemn thing; and suppose that God puts you this question, how will you answer it? Have you got a real faith? Or is it merely a political aspiration? Is it merely a larger kind of selfishness? Or is it merely that you wish to be free to oppress others, as you are being oppressed? Do you hold your political creed from a higher source? Is it God that is born in you? Have you realised that you are merely the instruments of God, that your bodies are not your own? You are merely instruments of God for the work of the Almighty. Have you realised that? If you have realised that, then you are truly Nationalists; then alone will you be able to restore this great nation. In Bengal it has been realised clearly by some, more clearly by others, but it has been realised and you on this side of the country must also realise it. Then there will be a blessing on our work, and this great nation will rise again and become once more what it was in the days of its spiritual greatness. You are the instruments of God to save the Light, to save the spirit of India from lasting obscuration and abasement. Let me tell you what it is that has happened in Bengal. You all know what Bengal used to be; you all know that "Bengali" used to be a term of reproach among the nations; when people spoke of Bengal, with what feelings did they speak of it? Was it with feelings of respect? Was it with feelings of admiration? You know very well what people of other countries used to say of the Bengali. You know well what you yourselves used to say of the Bengali. Do you think that now? If anybody had told you that Bengal would come forward as the saviour of India, how many of you would have believed it? You would have said, "No. The saviour of India cannot be Bengal; it may be Maharashtra; it may be the Punjab; but it will not be Bengal; the idea is absurd." What has happened then? What has caused this change? What has made the Bengali so different from his old self? One thing has happened in Bengal, and it is this that Bengal is learning to believe. Bengal was once drunk with the wine of European civilisation and with the purely intellectual teaching that it received from the West. It began to see all things, to judge all things through the imperfect instrumentality of the intellect. When it was so, Bengal became atheistic, it became a land of doubters and cynics. But still in Bengal there was an element of strength. Whatever the Bengali believed, if he believed at all — many do not believe — but if he believed at all, there was one thing about the Bengali, that he lived what he believed. If he was a Brahmo, or if he was a social reformer, no matter whether what he believed was true or not, but if he believed, he lived that belief. If he believed that one thing was necessary for the salvation of the country, if he believed that a thing was true and that it should be done, he did not stop to think about it. He would not stop to consider from all intellectual standpoints whether the truth in it was merely an ideal and to balance whether he would do honestly what he believed or whether he could hold the belief intellectually without living it, but without regard to consequences to himself, he went and did what he believed. And if he was not a Brahmo, if he was an orthodox Hindu, still if he really believed what the Hindu Shastras taught, he never hesitated to drive even his dearest away, rather than aid by his weakness in corrupting society. He never hesitated to enforce what he believed to the uttermost without thinking of the consequences to himself. Well, that was the one saving element in the Bengali nature. The Bengali has the faculty of belief. Belief is not a merely intellectual process, belief is not a mere persuasion of the mind, belief is something that is in our heart, and what you believe, you must do, because belief is from God. It is to the heart that God speaks, it is in the heart that God resides. This saved the Bengali. Because of this capacity of belief, we were chosen as the people who were to save India, the people who were to stand foremost, the people who must suffer for their belief, the people who must meet everything in the faith that God was with them and that God is in them. Such a people need not be politically strong, it need not be a people sound in physique, it need not be a people of the highest intellectual standing. It must be a people who can believe. In Bengal there came a flood of religious truth. Certain men were born, men whom the educated world would not have recognised if that belief, if that God within them had not been there to open their eyes, men whose lives were very different from what our education, our Western education, taught us to admire. One of them, the man who had the greatest influence and has done the most to regenerate Bengal, could not read and write a single word. He was a man who had been what they call absolutely useless to the world. But he had this one divine faculty in him, that he had more than faith and had realised God. He was a man who lived what many would call the life of a madman, a man without intellectual training, a man without any outward sign of culture or civilisation, a man who lived on the alms of others, such a man as the English-educated Indian would ordinarily talk of as one useless to society. He will say, "This man is ignorant. What does he know? What can he teach me who have received from the West all that it can teach?" But God knew what he was doing. He sent that man to Bengal and set him in the temple of Dakshineshwar in Calcutta, and from North and South and East and West, the educated men, men who were the pride of the university, who had studied all that Europe can teach, came to fall at the feet of this ascetic. The work of salvation, the work of raising India was begun. Consider the men who are really leading the present movement.

One thing I will ask you to observe and that is that there are very few who have not been influenced by the touch of a Sadhu. If you ask who influenced Babu Bepin Chandra Pal, it was a Sadhu. Among other men who lead in Bengal is the man who started this paper which is being prosecuted. You may not know his name here, but he is well known throughout Bengal, and he had done much to forward this movement; he is a man who has lived the life of a Sadhu, and taken his inspiration and strength from that only source from which inspiration and strength can come. I spoke to you the other day about National Education and I spoke of a man who had given his life to that work, the man who really organised the National College in Calcutta, and that man also is a disciple of a Sannyasin, that man also, though he lives in the world, lives like a Sannyasin, and if you take the young workers in Bengal, men that have come forward to do the work of God, what will you find? What is their strength? What is the strength which enables them to bear all the obstacles that come in their way and to resist all the oppression that threatens them? Let me speak a word to you about that. There is a certain section of thought in India which regards Nationalism as "madness". The men who think like that are men of great intellectual ability, men who have studied deeply, who have studied economics, who have studied history, men who are entitled to respect, men from whom you would naturally accept leading and guidance, and they say that Nationalism will ruin the country. What is it that makes them talk like this? Many of them are patriots, many of them are thoroughly sincere and honest, many of them desire the good of the country. What is it that is wanting in them? This is wanting. They are men who have lived in the pure intellect only and they look at things purely from the intellectual standpoint. What does the intellect think? What must it tell you if you consult the intellect merely? Here is a work that you have undertaken, a work so gigantic, so stupendous, the means for which are so poor, the resistance to which will be so strong, so organised, so disciplined, so well-equipped with all the weapons that science can supply, with all the strength that human power and authority can give, and what means have you with which to carry out this tremendous work of yours? If you look at it intellectually, and these men look at it from the intellectual standpoint, it is hopeless. Here are these men who are being prosecuted. How are they going to resist? They cannot resist. They have to go straight to jail. Well, these gentlemen argue and they are arguing straight from the intellect; they ask, "How long will you be able to resist like that? How long will this passive resistance work? All your leaders, all your strong men will be sent to jail, you will be crushed and not only will you be crushed, the nation will be completely crushed." If you argue from the intellect, this seems to be true. I cannot tell you of any material weapon with which you will meet those who are commissioned to resist your creed of Nationalism when you try to live it. If you ask what material weapons we have got, I must tell you that material weapons may help you no doubt but if you rely wholly upon material weapons then what they say is perfectly true, that Nationalism is a madness. Of course, there is another side to it. If you say that Nationalism cannot avail, then again I ask the intellect of these people, what will avail? Intellectually speaking, speaking from the Moderate's standpoint, what will avail? What do they rely upon? They rely upon a foreign force in the country. If you do not rely upon God, if you do not rely upon something mightier than material strength, then you will have to depend solely upon what others can give. There are men who think that what God cannot give for the salvation of India, the British Government will give. What you cannot expect from God you are going to expect from the British Government. Your expectation is vain. Their interests are not yours, their interests are very different from yours, and they will do what their interests tell them. You cannot expect anything else. What then does this intellectual process lead you to? This intellectual process, if it is used honestly, if it is followed to the very end, leads you to despair. It leads you to death. You have nothing which can help you, because you have no material strength at present which the adversary cannot crush and the adversary will certainly not be so foolish as to help you, or to allow you to develop the necessary strength unmolested. What then is the conclusion? The only conclusion is that there is nothing to be done. The only conclusion is that this country is doomed. That is the conclusion to which this intellectual process will lead you. I was speaking at Poona on this subject, and I told them of my experience in Bengal. When I went to Bengal three or four years before the Swadeshi movement was born, to see what was the hope of revival, what was the political condition of the people, and whether there was the possibility of a real movement, what I found there was that the prevailing mood was apathy and despair. People had believed that regeneration could only come from outside, that another nation would take us by the hand and lift us up and that we have nothing to do for ourselves. Now that belief has been thoroughly broken. They had come to realise that help cannot come from this source, and that they had nothing to rely upon. Their intellect could not tell them of any other source from which help could come, and the result was that apathy and despair spread everywhere and most of the workers who were really honest with themselves were saying that there was no help for this nation and that we were doomed. Well, this state of despair was the best thing that could have happened for Bengal, for it meant that the intellect had done its best, that the intellect had done all that was possible for it and that the work of the unaided intellect in Bengal was finished. The intellect having nothing to offer but despair became quiescent, and when the intellect ceased to work, the heart of Bengal was open and ready to receive the voice of God whenever He should speak. When the message came at last, Bengal was ready to receive it and she received it in a single moment, and in a single moment the whole nation rose, the whole nation lifted itself out of delusions and out of despair, and it was by this sudden rising, by this sudden awakening from dream that Bengal found the way of salvation and declared to all India that eternal life, immortality and not lasting degradation was her fate. Bengal lived in that faith. She felt a mightier truth than any that earth can give, because she held that faith from God and was able to live in that faith. Then that happened which always happens when God brings other forces to fight against the strength which he himself has inspired, because it is always necessary for the divinely appointed strength to grow by suffering; without suffering, without the lesson of selflessness, without the moral force of self-sacrifice, God within us cannot grow. Sri Krishna cannot grow to manhood unless he is called upon to work for others, unless the Asuric forces of the world are about him and work against him and make him feel his strength. Therefore in Bengal there came a time, after the first outbreak of triumphant hope, when all the material forces that can be brought to bear against Nationalism were gradually brought into play, and the question was asked of Bengal, "Can you suffer? Can you survive?" The young men of Bengal who had rushed forward in the frenzy of the moment, in the inspiration of the new gospel they had received, rushed forward rejoicing in the new-found strength and expecting to bear down all obstacles that came in their way, were now called upon to suffer. They were called upon to bear the crown, not of victory, but of martyrdom. They had to learn the real nature of their new strength. It was not their own strength, but it was the force which was working through them, and they had to learn to be the instruments of that force. What is it that we have learned then? What is the need of the situation of which I am to tell you today? It is not a political programme. I have spoken to you about many things. I have written about many things, about Swadeshi, Boycott, National Education, Arbitration and other subjects. But there was one truth that I have always tried, and those who have worked with me have also tried, to lay down as the foundation-stone of all that we preached. It is not by any mere political programme, not by National Education alone, not by Swadeshi alone, not by Boycott alone, that this country can be saved. Swadeshi by itself may merely lead to a little more material prosperity, and when it does, you might lose sight of the real thing you sought to do in the glamour of wealth, in the attraction of wealth and in the desire to keep it safe. In other subject countries also, there was material development; under the Roman Empire there was material development, there was industrial progress, but industrial progress and material development did not bring life to the Nation. When the hour of trial came, it was found that these nations which had been developing industrially, which had been developing materially, were not alive. No, they were dead and at a touch from outside they crumbled to pieces. So, do not think that it is any particular programme or any particular method which is the need of the situation. These are merely ways of working; they are merely particular concrete lines upon which the spirit of God is working in a Nation, but they are not in themselves the one thing needful. What is the one thing needful? What is it that has helped the older men who have gone to prison? What is it that has been their strength, that has enabled them to stand against all temptations and against all dangers and obstacles? They have had one and all of them consciously or unconsciously one over-mastering idea, one idea which nothing can shake, and this was the idea that there is a great Power at work to help India, and that we are doing what it bids us. Often they do not understand what they are doing. They do not always realise who guides or where he will guide them; but they have this conviction within, not in the intellect but in the heart, that the Power that is guiding them is invincible, that it is Almighty, that it is immortal and irresistible and that it will do its work. They have nothing to do. They have simply to obey that Power. They have simply to go where it leads them. They have only to speak the words that it tells them to speak, and to do the thing that it tells them to do. If the finger points them to prison, to the prison they go. Whatever it bids them to endure, they gladly endure. They do not know how that enduring will help, and the worldy-wise people may tell them that it is impolitic, that by doing this they will be wasting the strength of the country, they will be throwing the best workers away, they are not saving up the forces of the country. But we know that the forces of the country are other than outside forces. There is only one force, and for that force, I am not necessary, you are not necessary, he is not necessary. Neither myself nor another, nor Bepin Chandra Pal, nor all these workers who have gone to prison. None of them is necessary. Let them be thrown as so much waste substance, the country will not suffer. God is doing everything. We are not doing anything. When he bids us suffer, we suffer because the suffering is necessary to give others strength. When he throws us away, he does so because we are no longer required. If things become worse, we shall have not only to go to jail, but give up our lives, and if those who seem to stand in front or to be absolutely indispensable are called upon to throw their bodies away, we shall then know that that also is wanted, that this is a work God has asked us to do, and that in the place of those who are thrown away, God will bring many more. He himself is behind us. He himself is the worker and the work. He is immortal in the hearts of his people. Faith then is what we have in Bengal. Some of us may not have it consciously; some may not call it by that particular name. As I said, we have developed intellectuality, we have developed it notably and we are still much dominated by it. Many have come to this greater belief through the longing to live for their countrymen, to suffer for their countrymen, because God is not only here in me, he is within all of you, it is God whom I love, it is God for whom I wish to suffer. In that way many have come to do what God bade them do and he knows which way to lead a man. When it is his will he will lead him aright.

Another thing which is only another name for faith is selflessness. This movement in Bengal, this movement of Nationalism is not guided by any self-interest, not at the heart of it. Whatever there may be in some minds, it is not, at the heart of it, a political self-interest that we are pursuing. It is a religion which we are trying to live. It is a religion by which we are trying to realise God in the nation, in our fellow-countrymen. We are trying to realise him in the three hundred millions of our people. We are trying, some of us consciously, some of us unconsciously, we are trying to live not for our own interests, but to work and to die for others. When a young worker in Bengal has to go to jail, when he is asked to suffer, he does not feel any pang in that suffering, he does not fear suffering. He goes forward with joy. He says, "The hour of my consecration has come, and I have to thank God now that the time for laying myself on his altar has arrived and that I have been chosen to suffer for the good of my countrymen. This is the hour of my greatest joy and the fulfilment of my life." This is the second aspect of our religion, and is the absolute denial of the idea of one's separate self, and the finding of one's higher eternal Self in the three hundred millions of people in whom God himself lives.

The third thing which is again another name for faith and selflessness is courage. When you believe in God, when you believe that God is guiding you, believe that God is doing all and that you are doing nothing, — what is there to fear? How can you fear when it is your creed, when it is your religion to throw yourself away, to throw your money, your body, your life and all that you have, away for others? What is it that you have to fear? There is nothing to fear. Even when you are called before the tribunals of this world, you can face them with courage. Because your very religion means that you have courage. Because it is not you, it is something within you. What can all these tribunals, what can all the powers of the world do to that which is within you, that Immortal, that Unborn and Undying One, whom the sword cannot pierce, whom the fire cannot burn, and whom the water cannot drown? Him the jail cannot confine and the gallows cannot end. What is there that you can fear when you are conscious of him who is within you? Courage is then a necessity, courage is natural and courage is inevitable. If you rely upon other forces, supposing that you are a Nationalist in the European sense, meaning in a purely materialistic sense, that is to say, if you want to replace the dominion of the foreigner by the dominion of somebody else, it is a purely material change; it is not a religion, it is not that you feel for the three hundred millions of your countrymen, that you want to raise them up, that you want to make them all free and happy. It is not that, but you have got some idea that your nation is different from another nation and that these people are outsiders and that you ought to be ruling in their place. What you want is not freedom for your countrymen, but you want to replace the rule of others by yours. If you go in that spirit, what will happen when a time of trial comes? Will you have courage? Will you face it? You see that is merely an intellectual conviction that you have, that is merely a reason which your outer mind suggests to you. Well, when it comes to be put to the test, what will your mind say to you? What will your intellect say to you? It will tell you, "It is all very well to work for the country, but, in the meanwhile, I am going to die, or at least to be given a great deal of trouble, and when the fruit is reaped, I shall not be there to enjoy it. How can I bear all this suffering for a dream?" You have this house of yours, you have this property, you have so many things which will be attacked, and so you say, "That is not the way for me." If you have not the divine strength of faith and unselfishness, you will not be able to escape from other attachments, you will not like to bear affliction simply for the sake of a change by which you will not profit. How can courage come from such a source? But when you have a higher idea, when you have realised that you have nothing, that you are nothing and that the three hundred millions of people of this country are God in the Nation, something which cannot be measured by so much land, or by so much money, or by so many lives, you will then realise that it is something immortal, that the idea for which you are working is something immortal and that it is an immortal Power which is working in you. All other attachments are nothing. Every other consideration disappears from your mind, and, as I said, there is no need to cultivate courage. You are led on by that Power. You are protected through life and death by One who survives in the very hour of death, you feel your immortality in the hour of your worst sufferings, you feel you are invincible.

Now I have told you that these three things are the need of the present situation, because, as I said, the situation is this: you have undertaken a work, you have committed yourselves to something which seems to be materially impossible. You have undertaken a work which will rouse against you the mightiest enemies whom the earth can bring forward. As in the ancient times, when the Avatars came, there were also born the mightiest Daityas and Asuras to face the Avatars, so it always is. You may be sure that if you embrace this religion of Nationalism, you will have to meet such tremendous forces as no mere material power can resist. The hour of trial is not distant, the hour of trial is already upon you. What will be the use of your intellectual conviction? What will be the use of your outward enthusiasm? What will be the use of your shouting "Bande Mataram"? What will be the use of all the mere outward show when the hour of trial comes? Put yourselves in the place of those people who are suffering in Bengal, and think whether they have the strength and whether if it comes to you, you have the strength to meet it. With what strength will you meet it? How can you work invincibly? How can you meet it and survive? Can you answer that question? I have tried to show you that not by your material strength can you meet it. Have you the other strength in you? Have you realised what Nationalism is? Have you realised that it is a religion that you are embracing? If you have, then call yourselves Nationalists; and when you have called yourselves Nationalists, then try to live your Nationalism. Try to realise the strength within you, try to bring it forward, so that everything you do may be not your own doing, but the doing of that Truth within you. Try so that every hour that you live shall be enlightened by that presence, that every thought of yours shall be inspired from that one fountain of inspiration, that every faculty and quality in you may be placed at the service of that immortal Power within you. Then you will not say, as I have heard so many of you say, that people are so slow to take up this idea, that people are so slow to work, that you have no fit leaders and that all your great men tell you a different thing and that none of them is ready to come forward to guide you in the path that is pointed out. You will have no complaints to make against others, because then you will not need any leader. The leader is within yourselves. If you can only find him and listen to his voice, then you will not find that people will not listen to you, because there will be a voice within the people which will make itself heard. That voice and that strength is within you. If you feel it within yourselves, if you live in its presence, if it has become yourselves, then you will find that one word from you will awake an answering voice in others, that the creed which you preach will spread and will be received by all and that it will not be very long — in Bengal it has not been very long, it has not taken a century or fifty years, it has only taken three years to change the whole nation, to give it a new spirit and heart and to put it in front of all the Indian races. From Bengal has come the example of Nationalism. Bengal which was the least respected and the most looked-down on of all the Indian races for its weakness has within these three years changed so much simply because the men there who were called to receive God within themselves were able to receive him, were able to bear, to suffer and live in that Power, and by living in that Power they were able to give it out. And so in three years the whole race of Bengal has been changed, and you are obliged to ask in wonder, "What is going on in Bengal?" You see a movement which no obstacle can stop, you see a great development which no power can resist, you see the birth of the Avatar in the Nation, and if you have received God within you, if you have received that power within you, you will see that God will change the rest of India in even a much shorter time, because the Power has already gone forth, and is declaring itself, and when once declared, it will continue its work with ever greater and greater rapidity. It will continue its work with the matured force of Divinity until the whole world sees and until the whole world understands him, until Sri Krishna, who has now hid himself in Gokul, who is now among the poor and despised of the earth, who is now among the cowherds of Brindaban, will declare the Godhead, and the whole nation will rise, the whole people of this great country will rise, filled with divine power, filled with the inspiration of the Almighty, and no power on earth shall resist it, and no danger or difficulty shall stop it in its onward course. Because God is there, and it is his Mission, and he has something for us to do. He has a work for this great and ancient nation. Therefore he has been born again to do it, therefore he is revealing himself in you not that you may be like other nations, not that you may rise merely by human strength to trample underfoot the weaker peoples, but because something must come out from you which is to save the whole world. That something is what the ancient Rishis knew and revealed, and that is to be known and revealed again today, it has to be revealed to the whole world and in order that he may reveal himself, you must first realise him in yourselves, you must shape your lives, you must shape the life of this great nation so that it may be fit to reveal him and then your task will be done, and you will realise that what you are doing today is no mere political uprising, no mere political change, but that you have been called upon to do God's work.

Bande Mataram, January 19, 1908

Bande Mataram*

Sj. Aurobindo said that he was exceedingly pleased to know that the song had become so popular in all parts of India and that it was being so repeatedly sung. He said that he would make this national anthem the subject of his speech. The song, he said, was not only a national anthem to be looked on as the European nations look upon their own, but one replete with mighty power, being a sacred *mantra*, revealed to us by the author of *Ananda Math*, who might be called an inspired Rishi. He described the manner in which the *mantra* had been revealed to Bankim Chandra, probably by a Sannyasi under whose teaching he was. He said that the *mantra* was not an invention, but a revivification of the old *mantra* which had become extinct, so to speak, by the treachery of one Navakishan. The *mantra* of Bankim Chandra was not appreciated in his own day, and he predicted that there would come a time when the whole of India would resound with the singing of the song, and the word of the prophet was miraculously fulfilled. The meaning of the song was not understood then because there was no patriotism except such as consisted in making India the shadow of England and other countries which dazzled the sight of the sons of this our Motherland with their glory and opulence. The so-called patriots of that time might have been the well-wishers of India but not men who loved her. One who loved his mother never looked to her defects, never disregarded her as an ignorant, superstitious, degraded and decrepit woman. The speaker then unfolded the meaning of the song. As with the individual, so with the nation, there were three bodies or *koṣas*, the *sthūla*, *sūkṣma* and *kāraṇa śarīras*. In this way the speaker went on clearing up the hidden meaning of the song. The manner in which he treated of love and devotion was exceedingly touching and the audience sat before him like dumb statues, not knowing where they were or whether they were listening to a prophet revealing to them the higher mysteries of

* This is the summary of a lecture delivered by Sri Aurobindo in the Grand Square of the National School, Amraoti, Berar, on Wednesday the 29th January, 1908. The meeting commenced with the singing of Bande Mataram.

life. He then concluded with a most pathetic appeal to true patriotism and exhorted the audience to love the Motherland and sacrifice everything to bring about her salvation.

Bande Mataram, January 29, 1908

Revolutions and Leadership

AMONG many of those who are our leaders, there is a feeling of resentment against Nationalists because there is so little recognition of their past services, so strong a disposition to find fault with their actions and question their authority. It is asked of us whether we are going to upset all authority, disregard discipline and overthrow the natural pre-eminence of men who have long worked for their country. This question is the expression of an inevitable feeling of personal pique forced from them by the sense of exasperation which the loss of prestige and power cannot fail to create. If we answer this question at all, it is because it takes its stand on points of general importance instead of appearing in its native character of personal feeling. The authority of a political leader depends on his capacity to feel and express the sentiments of the people who follow him; it does not reside in himself. He holds his position because he is a representative man, not because he is such and such an individual. To take the position that because he has led in the past therefore his word must be law so long as he lives is to ignore the root principles of political life. This past service can only give him the claim to be regarded as leader in preference to others so long as he voices the sentiments of the people and keeps pace with the tendencies of the time. The moment he tries to misuse his position in order to impose his own will upon the people, instead of making their will his own, he forfeits all claim to respect. If he has fallen behind the times, his only course is to stand aside; but to demand that because he is there and wishes to remain, the march of the world shall wait upon his fears and hesitations is to make a claim against which the reason and conscience of humanity rebels.

What the Moderate leaders ask is that the immense revolution which has begun in India, shall ask for their permission before it chooses its course or rolls forward to its great goal. Like so many Canutes they set their chairs, Presidential or other, on the margin of the tide of Nationalism and looking over the stormy waters command them to respect their thrones and stay the upsurging wrath of their billows so that their robes may not be drenched by the spray. It is a vain and fantastic demand. This tide was not created by any human power, nor can any man impose on it a limit or a bourne. As well ask the thunderbolt to respect the tallest oaks or the avalanche to regulate the line of its descent so that ourselves may go safe, as ask this tremendous revolution to obey the will of the insignificant individuals whom chance has lifted to a momentary eminence. Nationalism is itself no creation of individuals and can have no respect for persons. It is a force which God has created, and from Him it has received only one command, to advance and advance and ever advance until He bids it stop, because its appointed mission is done. It advances, inexorably, blindly, unknowing how it advances, in obedience to a Power which it cannot gainsay, and every thing which stands in its way, man or institution, will be swept away, or ground into powder beneath its weight. Ancient sanctity, supreme authority, bygone popularity, nothing will serve as a plea.

It is not the fault of the avalanche if it sweeps away human life by its irresistible and unwilled advance; nor can it be imputed as moral obliquity to the thunderbolt that the oak of a thousand years stood precisely where its burning hand was laid. Not only the old leaders but any of the new men whom the tide has tossed up for a moment on the crest of its surges, must pay the penalty of imagining that he can control the ocean and impose on it his personal likes and desires. These are times of revolution when tomorrow casts aside the fame, popularity and pomp of today. The man whose carriage is today dragged through great cities by shouting thousands amid cries of "Bande Mataram" and showers of garlands, will tomorrow be disregarded, perhaps hissed and forbidden to speak. So it has always been and none can prevent it. How can such and such a barrister, editor, professor whom his personal talents have brought forward for a time, say to Revolution, "Thou shalt be my servant" or to Chaos, "I will use thee as the materials of my personal aggrandisement"? As the pace of the movement is accelerated, the number of those who are left behind will increase. Men who are now acclaimed as Extremists, leaders of the forward movement, preachers of Nationalism, and embodiments of the popular feeling will tomorrow find themselves left behind, cast aside, a living monument of the vanity of personal ambition. The old leaders claim eternal leadership because they have rendered services — some few eloquent speeches or well-written petitions to wit; but before we are much older, those who are serving their country by personal suffering and self-sacrifice will find that they too must not presume on their services. Only the self-abnegation which effaces the idea of self altogether and follows the course of the revolution with a childlike belief that God is the leader and what He does is for the best, will be able to continue working for the country. Such men are not led by personal ambition and cannot therefore be deterred from following the will of God by personal loss of any kind.

Revolutions are incalculable in their goings and absolutely uncontrollable. The sea flows and who shall tell it how it is to flow? The wind blows and what human wisdom can regulate its motions? The will of Divine Wisdom is the sole law of revolutions and we have no right to consider ourselves as anything but mere agents chosen by that Wisdom. When our work is done, we should realise it and feel glad that we have been permitted to do so much. Is it not enough reward for the greatest services that we can do, if our names are recorded in History among those who helped by their work or their speech or better, by the mute service of their sufferings to prepare the great and free India that will be? Nay, is it not enough if unnamed and unrecorded except in the Books of God, we go down to the grave with the consciousness that our finger too was laid on the great Car and may have helped, however imperceptibly, to push it forward? This talk of services is a poor thing after all. Do we serve the Mother for a reward or do God's work for hire? The patriot lives for his country because he must; he dies for her because she demands it. That is all.

Bande Mataram, February 6, 1908

THE SLAYING OF CONGRESS

A Tragedy in Three Acts

Act One

SCENE I

Calcutta.

Dadabhai, Mehta, Gokhale, Surendra, Tilak and others; Democracy, Congress.

DADABHAI

Much have I laboured, toiled for many years
To see this glorious day. Our Lady Congress
Grown to a fair and perfect womanhood,
Who at Benares came of age, is now
With pomp and noble ceremony arrived
In this Calcutta to assume the charge
Of her own life into her proper hands.
Mehta and Gokhale, Tilak, Suren, all,
Our anxious years of guardianship are ended.
Only is left to tell our lovely ward
The name, dimensions and exact extent
Of her estate which now in alien hands
She must recover — Swaraj is the name
And the dimensions wide as all this Hind.

CONGRESS

I thank you all, and swear to win Swaraj
Back from the hands that keep me from my own.

MEHTA

I like this not. If once this girl escapes
From my supreme control, I fear that she
Will run quite wild. Look with what covert eyes
She gazes at this young Democracy,
This roistering, robustious young Democracy.
A crew of plotters seek to push us out
From our established seats, Lal, Pal and Tilak,

Extremists babbling frantic heresies,
Boycott, Swadeshi, National Control.
This scatter-brained, unripe Democracy
Goes shouting at their heels and they intend
To wed young Congress to Democracy.
But I am here to baulk their fell designs
With all Bombay behind: Gokhale, be firm;
Aiyer and Malaviya, be ready, friends,
When I shall give the word, at once to speak
Lest mischief brewing with a perilous haste
Prevent us.

DADABHAI

Now much dispute there is of late
About the means, whether to take a course
Stout and bold and by heroic war
Win Swaraj from the usurper's mighty hands
Or yet once more to his great throne repair
And sue for Swaraj. Yet I do believe
That in her heart of hearts Britain is just
And will allow our plaint. Once more then try
The ancient way. And if it fail, let then
Defiance be declared and war begin.

PAL

Defiance need not wait on your beliefs:
Bengal already with a trumpet voice
Declares defiance and her youthful sons
Banding to win Swaraj prepare their souls
To bear imprisonment, blows, stripes and bonds
Rather than bow again at the tribunal
Of British justice.

TILAK

Let this dispute be settled
By a just compromise, and while you bow
Before the throne we in Bengal, Punjab
And Maharashtra will at our own risk

Declare the boycott. Only we desire
Permission and the gracious word should fall
From Lady Congress here that bids us war
For her just rights withheld. Swadeshi, Boycott
And Education under National Control,
Swaraj, these four allow, the rest we yield.

MEHTA

These four shall not be given.

MALAVIYA

Not one, not one.

AIYAR

Who dare give these, Madras refusing?

GOKHALE

Something
May be allowed, but not the whole demand.

DEMOCRACY

My voice is for the four, and when my voice
Declares my will, there's not a man in Hind
Whose will outweighs my voice.

MEHTA

I quite forbid it.

DEMOCRACY

Who art thou to forbid?

MEHTA

Pherozshah I.

DEMOCRACY

Pherozshah, no Pherozshahs. I stand here
And claim the sovereignty which is my right.

MEHTA

Mehta I am who rule with absolute sway
The Corporation.

DEMOCRACY

There then give commands.
This is Calcutta where I am arisen
And let no man dispute my will.

AIYAR

I speak
For all Madras.

CRIES

No, no!

MALAVIYA

I for the North.

CRIES

We quite deny it.

MEHTA

This is a public place,
Let us withdraw.

DEMOCRACY

My rights are not for thee
To settle; let Tilak, Gokhale and the rest
Confer together; and their just award
Shall bind this Congress.

CONGRESS

I agree.

SCENE II

The same.

Mehta, Gokhale, Aiyar and others.

MEHTA

So it is settled? Gokhale, thou art weak.

GOKHALE

How else can this dispute be brought to end?

AIYAR

By vote.

GOKHALE

That would be shameful in the view
Of all the world.

MEHTA

What care I for the world?
Mehta is Mehta whose unquestioned will
Must be supreme.

AIYAR

And Aiyar says the same.

MEHTA

Now for the future. To amend our fault
We will take the Congress to some far retreat
Impregnable where we can do our will,
Binding her hand and foot, and close immure
From clamorous Democracy; what else
Must be resolved, in Bombay let it be.

GOKHALE

There is the great Committee which will be
A tool to do our will.

MEHTA

See that it meets
Not in a public place but in our house.
Let it be secret so that we may plot,
Not rudely censored by the public voice,
In calm security.

AIYAR

Then at Madras
Let Congress have her seat.

GOKHALE

No, at Nagpore
Where all is quiet, and Democracy
Can find no entrance, we shall sit at ease
Nor anyone shall question what we do.

MEHTA

It shall be Nagpore.

ALL

Nagpore let it be.

SCENE III

Bombay.

Gokhale solus.

GOKHALE

What shall I do? Mehta's inexorable
And bent on blood. If I dispute his will
What footing will I have in all Hind? Tilak
Calls me, but him I too completely hate
To take his hand. Distrust between us stands,
No friendship possible; Mehta's support

I hold quite indispensable, so must
Obey him wholly. If I take my course
Who will support me in my journeys hence
To plead at Britain's throne for India's good?
And if I do not plead at Britain's throne,
How shall poor India fare? But my heart bleeds
For Congress. Must I slay her whom I love?
No, no, there's yet some chance of saving her
From her own predilection for the love
Of wild Democracy. I will invent
A constitution forged with deftest skill
Which so shall bind her that she cannot stir
One inch from her accustomed chair of ease.

Enter Mehta.

MEHTA

Well, Gokhale, have you thought the project over?

GOKHALE

I have. But let not our accustomed hands
Be stained with innocent blood. Although Nagpore
Is now the home of wild Democracy,
Are there not other places in the land
Where we are safe? Surat is thine, and we
Shall carry Congress there and bind her fast,
Not interfered with. Make a constitution
Most cunningly devised to fasten down
Congress to her accustomed chair of ease.
Democracy shall be shut out from her.
Moti, Pal, Tilak, Lajpat, Aswini
May plague their heads but find no remedy.

MEHTA

But if you fail?

GOKHALE

I shall not fail.

MEHTA

Well, then,
Do what you can.

GOKHALE

I haste to see it done.

Exit.

MEHTA

You are too foolish, hesitating, weak,
I will persist but will not let you know
What I intend. Surat is full of men
Bound to my will and they shall do the deed.
What then can Gokhale do? He must submit.
Suren, I can win over or deceive.
But when I have slain Congress, I will choose
Some other ward to take her place who will
Be subject to me. I will set her up
In Congress' place and give her the estate.
For Britain's might will stand behind me then
Unwitnessed. Let me then be quick, prepare
Murder and make the dagger sharp. Congress,
I reared thee up but thou, ungrateful fool,
Rebelst and choosest vain Democracy
To be thy lord. Rather than let thee wed
The protégé of Tilak, Lal and Pal,
I will put an end to thee. Mehta endures
No rival near his throne nor will he bow
This haughty head to vile Democracy.

SCENE IV

Bombay.

Mehta, Gokhale, Tilak, Aiyar, Nagpore and others.

MEHTA

Once more we meet. What else but to decide
Whether we choose Nagpore for the abode
Of Congress or to change her mighty seat
To Surat or Madras.

TILAK

Nagpore, I say.

GOKHALE

Nagpore has forfeited her right.

AIYAR

Madras
Shall take the place left vacant by Nagpore.

MEHTA

Surat is first to make the offer.

AIYAR

No,
Madras. I claim priority.

GOKHALE

Aiyar,
Art thou so sure that thou art quite supreme?

AIYAR

Some few dispute it.

GOKHALE

Surat's quite sure. She is
Impenetrable.

MEHTA

Surat then let it be.

NAGPORE

My lords, I know not by what dire offence
I lose my right, but this permit me say, —
"Whatever sin committed bars my right
I will atone. Let not my name be stained."

MEHTA

Who gave thee right of entrance? Out! out! out!

TILAK

I called her.

MEHTA

When Congress weds thy ward, be king.
But I am now supreme; go from this place!

NAGPORE

But hear me.

MEHTA

No.

NAGPORE

Let me beseech thee, hear me.

MEHTA

Get out, get out. Ho! Servants. Watch, Gokhale,
Turn out this wench.

NAGPORE

Mehta, I will not here brawl
With thee.

Exit.

TILAK

This was not well nor wisely done.

MEHTA

I need not thy advice. Let us decide.
Surat is here.

TILAK

Where Nagpore is excluded
What right has Surat to be heard?

MEHTA

My will.
Surat, come in.

Enter Surat.

TILAK

Sirs, we protest.

GOKHALE

Well, then,
Let Surat speak.

SURAT

I am prepared, my lords,
To bear the expenses of the three days' sojourn
Of Congress all unhelped. Let me have hearing.

GOKHALE

Mehta will judge.

TILAK

Surat, hast thou consent
Of all thy people?

MEHTA

Who gave thee our ward?
I am the lord of Congress and decree
Surat shall be her seat.

TILAK

We still protest.

MEHTA

Protest, but Surat is decided on.—
It is settled. Let us go.

Exeunt.

Act Two

SCENE I

Poona.

Tilak, A Friend.

TILAK

My friends are full of wrath and mean revolt,
But in my view this would be utter madness:
For if we hope to wed our Lady Congress
To bold Democracy, what better plan
Than to bear all with firm but patient love
And let proud Mehta make himself obnoxious
To every honourable man? Therefore
Let Nagpore now submit. But if he purpose
Betrayal, we shall raise so wild a storm
Of opposition that his friends shall fear
And leave him to himself. Go, friend, and speak
To Moti of these things, request his aid
To keep Bengal united. If Bengal
Make common cause then shall proud Mehta find
Congress too strongly hedged with friendly spears
For his vile plots to injure her.

SCENE II

Bombay.

Mehta, Gokhale.

GOKHALE

Mehta, all's ready.

MEHTA

Make everything so sure,
That Tilak shall be utterly undone.
We must not suffer Boycott to be made
Part of our programme.

GOKHALE

To omit it quite
Is hardly possible. The fierce revolt
Of all Bengal will shake us from our seats
And give control into the hands of those
Who favour wild Democracy. I mean
To juggle skilfully with all the four:
Swadeshi, Boycott, Education National,
Swaraj. With Congress bound, we can explain
Whatever we have done in such a light
As to keep Britain pleased.

MEHTA

But when 'tis known
What you have done, what will the people say?

GOKHALE

What, Mehta fears the people? When we speak,
Will not the mob accept our princely word?

MEHTA

So be it. Well, Gokhale, thou art full of guile
Which makes thee useful; but thy courage, friend,
Too flimsy to support the smallest strain.
Who's there?

A SERVANT

What's it, my lord?

MEHTA

Call in the man
Who waits outside. My mind is full of spite,
Murderous and fell, it will not be at rest
Until I have revenged myself by blood.
What will the fate be of Democracy
When Congress falls? The bold uproarious youth
Is of his strength so proud he cannot feel
That 'tis my strength protects him from the wrath
Of Britain. When she's dead, all ties are snapped
And he, grown beggared of our help, is left
To the fierce persecution of the king.
Then I shall be avenged for the insolence
He showed me at Calcutta in his den.

Enter a Surat Moderate.

MEHTA

Well, are you resolute?

SURAT MODERATE

We are.

MEHTA

Is all
Made ready?

SURAT MODERATE

It is. We have secured the aid
Of many ruffians from the Tapti's banks
Who for a hire will slay their mothers, wives
Or sons.

MEHTA

Be sure of them.

SURAT MODERATE

They are stored with coin
For drink; for which they'd sell their souls to Satan
And do his fiendish will.

MEHTA

Then let us go. We shall perfect
The plot when we have seen what Tilak does.

SCENE III

Surat.

Tilak.

TILAK

The plot is perfect. To prepare the way
Congress is brought here where proud Mehta's lord.
When she will stand among her friends and his,
We shall be quite a handful, so he does
His will upon her; binds her in the chains
Of this strange constitution; so that she
Is utterly made helpless, bound and gagged.
Meanwhile the four great planks are sawn apart
Which we had introduced beneath her throne,
And when we are driven out, they will be broken
And Congress hurled into a dungeon deep
There to be starved to death, while in her place
Another wearing both her name and robes
Usurps her place. Oh vile conspiracy!
But let me see if we have not the strength
Of members. Nagpore and Amraoti stand
Behind me, all the Deccan's at my back,
Madras has sent a valiant band, Bengal
Some of her choicest sons, and there are some
Even from the North — six hundred stalwart men

To back me. But if the Committee's packed
These numbers will not help. This Gujerat,
Untouched till now by our great National Creed,
Sends half the numbers; her unaided voice
May overbear the will of the whole land.
What then? Let us then from the first oppose
And show the people that it is a voice
Local at best which seeks to bind our Lady
And drive from her Democracy. It may be
That if our opposition is too strong
From the beginning, we may force the friends
Mehta relies on to compel their chief
To meet us and give up this fatal plot.
When Suren comes, I'll meet him and appeal
To him to save their Congress from her fate.
There's Moti too, who'll do his best, Lajpat
And others. It may be some compromise
Is possible; we would not then oppose
From the beginning, but with friendly hearts
Agree how best to keep dear Congress safe.
Meanwhile 'tis best to be prepared for worst.
(*Calls*)
Go, friend, and tell our party to be ready
With all its chiefs. We must be bold but calm
And let young, rash Democracy be patient,
For Congress' life's in peril.

SCENE IV

Surat.

Suren, Moti, Tilak.

SUREN

I am quite one with you, and mean to insist
Upon the four. But you must also yield,

Nor let our Rash Behari be opposed.

TILAK

There is the rub. Our friends are full of wrath
And if you wish us to yield up our points,
Some pledge, some plain assurance we must have
That Congress' freedom and the four supports
Of her great throne are safe.

SUREN

For my own self
And for Bengal I give the pledge. Gokhale
May join us.

TILAK

So let it be. Or if another
In some authority can give the pledge
We shall be satisfied.

SUREN

That too I'll try
Or try yourself.

TILAK

Well, then, try Gokhale you.
Myself will seek some other out whose word
May satisfy my friends.

SUREN

That is agreed.

MOTI

When Congress takes her throne, be then prepared
To give the pledge.

SUREN

I am prepared.

TILAK

That is done.

I hope this day will be a peaceful day
Of friendly union, and the threatened storms
Disperse. Come, let us do our part.

SCENE V

Surat.

Gokhale, Mehta, Suren, Tilak, Congress, Democracy and others.

GOKHALE

I cannot give the pledge.

SUREN

Why can you not?

GOKHALE

Why, what am I? A humble single man
Whose voice is but a voice and nothing more.
I dare not be presumptuously bold
To speak for Congress, who alone can say
What she intends.

SUREN

There's something in your plea.

TILAK

Nothing but an unreal humbleness
Concealing fell designs. But if 'tis meant
Congress to bind, then let the storm begin.

SUREN

I am prepared.

TILAK

What is your single word?

SUREN

Bengal's.

TILAK

But not for Gujerat you speak.
And 'tis the voice of Gujerat will stand
For India's here.

SUREN

Well, I will do my part,
Whatever happens.

DEMOCRACY

We will not hear your voice.

SUREN

How now? What is this boldness on the part
Of pestilential bold Democracy?
Shall I not then be heard, Suren, who lead
Bengal?

DEMOCRACY

I lead Bengal and all the world.

SUREN

I know thee, upstart. When at Midnapore
I stood before the people, 'twas thy voice
Insulted me. Traitor and pestilence,
Be silent, let me speak.

(*Tumult*)

DEMOCRACY

'Twas thou, I think,
Traitor thyself, who broughtest the police
To sit beside thee there lest my bold hand

Should thrust thy friend from his unmerited
And misused eminence. Be silent.

SUREN

I.............

DEMOCRACY

Be silent.

(*Tumult*)

SURAT MODERATE

Who art thou to bid him hush?

DEMOCRACY

Democracy, whose voice must be supreme.

SURAT MODERATE

I am supreme.

DEMOCRACY

Silence. I will prorogue
This sitting.

SUREN

What, my voice will not be heard?
Who shall prevent me?

DEMOCRACY

I. Hold thy glib tongue.
(*Tumult*)
I here prorogue the session.

SUREN

This despite
Shall be repaid.

Act Three

SCENE I

Surat.

Gokhale, Mehta, Suren, Aiyar.

SUREN

Now I am with you. Mehta, do thy worst.
Whatever purpose brews within thy brain,
Though it be fell as darkest Erebus,
I will support.

GOKHALE

I sympathise with you,
Suren. This is the plotted spiteful deed
Of Tilak.

MEHTA

He has set Democracy
Against thee so that he alone may rule.

AIYAR

Abandon them and be our first and chief.

GOKHALE

It is decided then. Let Congress die,
Convention take her place.

AIYAR

And a good riddance.

GOKHALE

I do not this without a deep regret.
Congress was dear to me as my own child.

AIYAR

But children gone astray are best removed.

GOKHALE

Our enemies have played into our hands,
Have they not, Mehta? Suren is wholly ours.

SUREN

Now what remains?

GOKHALE

We must let people think
'Twas Tilak did the deed.

MEHTA

Trust me for that.

SUREN

Well, as you will. Though Tilak was my friend,
This wipes out every previous record. Come,
Let us prepare tomorrow's piteous deed,
So fell it is, almost I hesitate.
Democracy, Democracy, thou evil
Upstart and hooligan, 'tis thou, 'tis thou
That drivest me to this crime.

GOKHALE

Waver not now.
All's for the sake of Hind.

SUREN

And I am hers.

GOKHALE

So are we all. Who works for selfish ends?
Let Tilak do his worst, we are prepared.

MEHTA

Moderate of Surat, art thou ready?

SURAT MODERATE

I am,

The dagger's sharp, our men are armed with sticks
And at thy word the tumult will begin.

MEHTA

That's well.

SCENE II

The same.

Tilak, Moti, Democracy, Aswini.

TILAK

Whatever provocation pushed you on,
You were a fool to pick this quarrel; see,
Suren is lost.

DEMOCRACY

We are too strong to care
Who stays with us or who remains.

TILAK

Imprudent.
If Congress falls, the country will be wroth
Because 'twas we who first began the strife.
Well, well, to sorrow now is vain. Henceforth
Be patient, let not thy tumultuous heart
Break out in words.

DEMOCRACY

Why should I curb myself?

TILAK

For Congress' sake.

DEMOCRACY

I would do much for her,

But not renounce my freedom.

ASWINI

What a man!
Be patient now that henceforth thou mayst be
Sovereign and lord.

DEMOCRACY

I am already lord.

MOTI

You will spoil everything.

DEMOCRACY

So let it be.
I will not give my right of liberty
For any sovereignty Congress can give.

TILAK

If she should wed thee, then thou getst with ease
What otherwise must be with labour got
And fierce revolt.

DEMOCRACY

Why, is it not our creed
That nations are with labour and revolt
Set free?

TILAK

That is from foreign hands,
Not from our countrymen.

DEMOCRACY

You are too subtle,
I only understand my right and strength,
Not these distinctions. But this time I'll yield.

TILAK

That's good. Now, Moti, let us do our best.

It may be even now that they will hear us.

DEMOCRACY

It is not to be hoped.

TILAK

I am more sanguine.

MOTI

Well, try and if we fail the fault is theirs.

TILAK

Good, let us go about it.

Bande Mataram, February 16, 1908

Swaraj

NATIONALISM was filled at the Pabna conference with a new spirit unlike anything yet known to us. Whatever resolutions were passed or steps taken, were taken in a spirit of practical utility, which has been hitherto absent from our Congresses and Conferences. We have hitherto been engaged in dispute about ideals and methods. We are confident that the country, at least Bengal, has now reached a stage when this dispute is no longer necessary. Whatever we may say out of policy or fear, the whole nation is now at one. Swaraj is the only goal which the heart of Bengal recognises, Swaraj without any limitation or reservation. Even the President in his second and closing speech was so much moved by the spirit in the air that he forgot the feeling of caution which obliged him in his opening address to deprecate ambitious ideals, and out of the gladness of his heart there burst from him a flood of inspiring eloquence which made the whole audience astir with feelings of impassioned aspiration. Swaraj was the theme of his eloquence and to anyone listening carefully it was evident that 'Swaraj', unlimited and without reservation, was the ideal enthroned in the heart of the poet. Even Surendranath or those who voted for colonial Swaraj knew well in their heart of hearts that their ideal was not the ideal of the nation. Long habit and apprehension were the only obstacles in their way which prevented them from throwing themselves into the current. But the rest of the audience were visibly moved by the passionate eloquence which flowed from the lips of Rabindranath. What matters it what resolutions may be passed or rejected? Swaraj is no longer a mere word, no longer an ideal, distant and impossible, for the heart of Bengal has seized upon it, and the intellect of Bengal has acknowledged it. We hold no brief for anyone, but we believe that Srijut Manoranjan Guha was an inspired speaker when he told the Conference never to lose sight of God in the movement. Mighty aspirations are in the heart of the people and he is false to the inspiration within him who tries to dwarf them. Let us work practically at the smallest details, but let us never forget that the work is not for its own sake but for the sake of Swaraj. We shall be false to our inspiration if we forget the goal in the details; we shall condemn ourselves to the fate of the man who in the eagerness of picking up pebbles on the seashore threw away the alchemic stone, which God had for a moment given into his hands. Swaraj is the alchemic stone, the Parash-Pathar, and we have it in our hands. It will turn to gold everything we touch. Village Samitis are good, not for the sake of village Samitis but for the sake of Swaraj. Boycott is good, not for the sake of Boycott but for the sake of Swaraj. Swadeshi is good, not for the sake of Swadeshi but for the sake of Swaraj. Arbitration is good, not for the sake of arbitration but for the sake of Swaraj. If we forget Swaraj and win anything else we shall be like the seeker whose belt was turned indeed to gold but the stone of alchemy was lost to him for ever.

Never should we forget that but for the hope of Swaraj we should never have done what we have done during the last three years. No lesser hope, no ideal of inferior grandeur could have nerved us to the tremendous efforts, the great sacrifices, the indomitable persistence in the face of persecution which has made these three years ever memorable as the birth-time of a nation. Who could have borne what we have borne for the sake of some petty object? No good can result from denying what God has revealed to us. When Peter denied his master, half of his virtue went out of him. Let not our people have to repent as Peter had to repent, and shed tears of bitter sorrow because the divinity has been expelled by their own folly from their bosom. When a light has been revealed, folly alone will try to shut it out behind a screen. When a mighty power has entered into the heart, madness alone can wish to forfeit it. Swaraj is the direct revelation of God to this people, — not mere political freedom but a freedom vast and entire, freedom of the individual, freedom of the community, freedom of the nation, spiritual freedom, social freedom, political freedom. Spiritual freedom the ancient Rishis had already declared to us; social freedom was part of the message of Buddha, Chaitanya, Nanak and Kabir and the saints of Maharashtra; political freedom is the last word of the triune gospel. Without political freedom the soul of man is crippled. Only a few mighty spirits can rise above their surroundings, but the ordinary man is a slave of his surroundings and if those be mean, servile and degraded, he himself will be mean, servile and degraded. Social freedom can only be born where the soul of man is large, free and generous, not enslaved to petty aims and thoughts. Social freedom is not a result of social machinery but of the freedom of the human intellect and the nobility of the human soul. A man who follows petty ends cannot feel his brotherhood with his fellows, for he is always striving to raise himself above them and assert petty superiorities. If caste makes him superior or money makes him superior, he will hug to his bosom the distinctions of caste or the distinctions of wealth. If political freedom is absent, the community has no great ends to follow and the individual is confined within a narrow circuit in which the superiority of caste, wealth or class is the only ambition which he can cherish. If political freedom opens to him a wider horizon, he forgets the lesser ambitions. Moreover a slave can never be noble and broad-minded. He cannot forget himself in the service of his fellows; for he is already a slave and service is the badge of his degradation, not a willing self-devotion. When man is thus degraded, it is idle to think that society can be free.

So too spiritual freedom can never be the lot of many in a land of slaves. A few may follow the path of the Yogin and rise above their surroundings, but the mass of men cannot ever take the first step towards spiritual salvation. We do not believe that the path of salvation lies in selfishness. If the mass of men around us is miserable, fallen, degraded how can the seeker after God be indifferent to the condition of his brothers? Compassion to all creatures is the condition of sainthood, and the perfect Yogin is he who is *sarvabhūtahite rataḥ*, whose mind is full of the will to do good to all creatures. When a man shuts his heart to the cries of sufferings around him, when he is content that his fellow-men should be sorrowful, oppressed, sacrificed to the greed of others, he is making his own way to salvation full of difficulties and stumbling-blocks. He is forgetting that God is not only in himself but in all these millions. And for those who have not the strength, spiritual freedom in political servitude is a sheer impossibility. When India was free, thousands of men set their feet in the stairs of heaven, but as the night deepened and the sun of liberty withdrew its rays, the spiritual force inborn in every Indian heart became weaker and weaker until now it burns so faintly that aliens have taken upon themselves the role of spiritual teachers, and the people chosen by God have to sit at the feet of the men from whose ancestry the light was hidden. God has set apart India as the eternal fountain-head of holy spirituality, and He will never suffer that fountain to run dry. Therefore Swaraj has been revealed to us. By our political freedom we shall once more recover our spiritual freedom. Once more in the land of the saints and sages will burn up the fire of the ancient Yoga and the hearts of her people will be lifted up into the neighbourhood of the Eternal.

Bande Mataram, February 18, 1908

The Future of the Movement

When a great people rises from the dust, what *mantra* is the *sanjīvanī mantra* or what power is the resurrecting force of its resurgence? In India there are two great *mantras*, the *mantra* of "Bande Mataram" which is the public and universal cry of awakened love of Motherland, and there is another more secret and mystic which is not yet revealed. The *mantra* of "Bande Mataram" is a *mantra* once before given to the world by the Sannyasins of the Vindhya hills. It was lost by the treachery of our own countrymen because the nation was not then ripe for resurgence and a premature awakening would have brought about a speedy downfall. But when in the great earthquake of 1897 there was a voice heard by the Sannyasins, and they were conscious of the decree of God that India should rise again, the *mantra* was again revealed to the world. It was echoed in the hearts of the people, and when the cry had ripened in silence in a few great hearts, the whole nation became conscious of the revelation. Who imagined when the people of Bengal rose in 1905 against the Partition that that was the beginning of a great upheaval? It is a passing tempest, said the wise men of England, let it go over our heads and we will wait. But the tempest did not pass, nor the thunders cease. So there was a reconsideration of policy and the wise men said, — "The people of Bengal are easily cowed down, and we will try whether force cannot do what patience has failed to do". When Sir Bampfylde Fuller met Lord Curzon at Agra, this was the policy agreed on between them — to hammer the Bengalis into quietude. But Sir Bampfylde Fuller has gone and the movement remains. Hare too will go, and many will go, but the movement will remain. The regulation lathi, the Police truncheon, the threat of the Goorkha rifle are as straws in the wind before the Divine breath of God. Human power is mere weakness when measured with the will of the Eternal. So the movement will continue. It is now time to look deeper into it and know its fountain sources. So long we were content with the superficial aspects, but the time has come for God to reveal Himself, and the powers of the world to look on in amazement at His wonderful workings. When we left Pabna we knew that He was at work to unite the Bengali race. We hope yet to see that He is at work to unite the Indian people. When the Convention Committee meets at Allahabad, it will be seen whether it is His will to unite the parties into a single whole or to separate them from each other, so that the work of salvation may be hastened by the energy of the Nationalist Party being separated from the steadiness of the Moderates. Whatever may happen, it is His will. We look forward to the Easter meeting for light on what He intends. If the Moderate leaders of Bengal are wise, they will realise that Bengal at least is destined to become predominatingly Nationalist, that it is her mission to lead and force the rest of India to follow. Whoever tries to prevent her from fulfilling that mission, is setting himself against the decrees of God and will be blown away like stubble before the tempest.

Bande Mataram, February 19, 1908

Work and Ideal

We are being advised by many nowadays not to quarrel over ideals but to attend to the work lying nearest to our hands. We must not talk of faith and hope, or revel in Utopian visions but run to the nearest scene of work, be one of the drudging millions, try to improve their lot and set ourselves to the task of mitigating human sufferings. The old villages are so many pictures of desolation and distress, they are the hot-beds of malaria, the sepulchres of our greatness; so go to them and try to reinstate our tutelary angel in his ancient seat. Or we must erect mills, start small industries, educate the masses, do philanthropic work and not talk of free or united India until this is done. When the spade work has not yet begun, why talk of a fine superstructure and create difficulties in the way of solid and substantial work? You have not yet put the plough to your land, why quarrel over the prospective produce and sow seeds of dissension amongst yourselves before you have sown the seed that is to yield any good to the country? The buoyant Nationalism of the day is sought to be repressed by such timid truisms and guarded amenities with which our advisers justify their placid course of life. They want us to take note of our limitations, environment and not to tempt the country to the skies with wings so heavily weighed down. Common sense, it is said, should be our guide and not imagination.

All this is well, and we would be the last to deny the necessity of the work so much insisted upon. But the work is nothing without the ideal, and will be fruitless if divorced from its inspiring force. Which is common sense? To tread the right path or to avoid it because it promises to be thorny? Which is common sense? To mislead ourselves or to speak the truth and do the right? The uplifting of a nation cannot be accomplished by a few diplomatic politicians. The spirit to serve, the spirit to work, the spirit to suffer must be roused. Men in their ordinary utilitarian course of life do not feel called upon to serve any one except themselves.

The daily duties are engrossing enough for the average man. His own individual prospects in life generally become his sole concern. He is propelled by the inertia of his own individual needs, and if any other sort of work is expected of him a different and more intense force must be continuously applied to him to produce the necessary energy. Or, in other words, we must continuously appeal to his better nature, we must evoke the spiritual in him, we must call forth his moral enthusiasm.

These may not be human nature's daily food, they may not be necessary for our daily life, they may not have their use in the ordinary selfish pursuits, but they are essential for working a change in our social or political life. Buddha only preached and lived a holy life, Christ only preached and lived a holy life, Sankar only preached and lived a holy life, and they have each worked a mighty revolution in the history of the world. Inspiration is real work. Let the truly inspiring word be uttered and it will breathe life into dry bones. Let the inspiring life be lived and it will produce workers by thousands. England draws her inspiration from the names of Shakespeare and Milton, Mill and Bacon, Nelson and Wellington. They did not visit the sickroom, they did not do philanthropic work in the parishes, they did not work spinning jennies in Manchester, they did not produce cutlery in Sheffield, but theirs are the names which have made nationhood possible in England, which have supplied work and enterprise with its motive and sustaining force. England is commercially great because Adam Smith gave her the secret of free-trade. England is politically great because her national ideals have been bold and high, not because of her parish work and municipalities. He was no fool or Utopian who wished to be the maker of songs for his country rather than its law giver. Wolfe had Gray's elegy recited to him on his death-bed, and said he would rather be the author of these lines than the captor of Quebec. These are the utterances of great workers and heroes, they have given the greatest credit to the givers of ideas and ideals, because they have felt in their own life where the inspiration for work comes from. Work without ideals is a false gospel.

BY THE WAY

Notables

When we wrote of the days of ancient greatness, we did not think that we were about to witness the singular spectacle of a Hindu society professing to restore the purity of the old religion bowing down at the throne of Minto, who could recognise in the Lords of today the Rajas and Maharajas of modern India, the sons of the great Kshatriya blood? Minto and Morley are the representatives of Yavana and Saka of old. Did the princes of ancient India go out of their way to kneel before their throne? Was that the glory of Hinduism? Or are we witnessing a revival of the days when Asoka ruled over the Asiatic peoples? The Bharat Dharma Mahamandal aim at the revival of Hinduism but they are working for its final extinction.

Minto Worship

When we speak of the Notables bowing at the feet of Minto, we are aware that we shall lay ourselves open to the charge of disloyalty. Well, that is a charge we have never been anxious to avoid. When sedition is found in all we write then it is no advantage picking and choosing our expressions. But we have one thing to say. Who made Lord Minto ruler of India? Not the hand of any earthly power. But the decree of God, and if the Hindu people bow down before Minto, it is only as the Viceroy of God. Is that the logic of the Bharat Dharma Mahamandal? If so, it is a logic based on outward facts, not on the inner truths. God is today manifesting himself again, but where? Not in the glory of England — which is on the wane, but in the resurgence of Asia.

Minto-Morley

Minto is an archangel of peace, says Romesh Chandra Dutt;

Morley an archangel of benevolence. With so many archangels to look after us, we are unfortunate indeed if we cannot be happy. Poor India!

Within and Without

Romesh Chandra Dutt is a statesman according to his own idea of himself and statesmen are always looking out for their fellows. Romesh Chandra with his large-hearted appreciation of the ruling qualities of the British race, Surendranath with his unswerving loyalty, Narendranath with his gratitude are, one would imagine, so many pillars of British rule. What about Romesh Chandra's letters to Lord Curzon, Surendranath's boycott or Narendranath's secret hopes of Theosophical rule of Mahatmas? Whoever says one thing with his lips and another in his heart, can never hope to help his country.

Truth and Falsehood

When we are on the subject, let us be frank. Truth is the rock on which the world is built. *Satyena tiṣṭhate jagat*. Falsehood can never be the true source of strength. When falsehood is at the root of a movement, that movement is doomed to failure. Diplomacy can only help a movement if the movement proceeds upon truth. To make diplomacy the root-principle is to contravene the laws of existence.

Bande Mataram, February 20, 1908

The Latest Sedition Trial

WE DO not generally concern ourselves with the results of trials in bureaucratic law-courts. The law that is now recognised by the civilised world is the will of a people. The law that is really binding on a people is the mature deliberation of its own representatives as to the proper want and scope of individual activity in relation to the common weal. Law if it is to be beneficial to society cannot be divorced from the truths established by science, on the contrary derives its binding force from being based on them. That a bureaucratic law is not so much meant to ensure social well-being but designed for restricting even a legitimate freedom of action sanctioned by science has been amply illustrated in the judgment of the Police Magistrate of Calcutta in the *Nabasakti* case. The Magistrate was confronted with the difficulty that neither common sense nor jurisprudence can penalise the preaching of a political truth. The strange syllogism with which he has sought to bring the preaching of an ideal within the purview of the bureaucratic law is ridiculous to the extreme. The Magistrate in his judgment does not seem even to know his own mind. In the earlier part of his judgment he talks as if the preaching of independence as an ideal were in itself sedition. "To my mind," he says in powerful magisterial fashion, "the meaning and intention of this article admit of no doubt whatever. The writer is advocating independence and the article is seditious." Later on he has misgivings. Glimpses of a common sense buried deep away under long habits of reading political necessity into judicial interpretation seem to visit the official mind:

"The ideal of national independence is one which appeals to Englishmen with very strong force, and it is one which when reasonably and temperately expressed will always meet with a great deal of sympathy. There is undoubtedly at the present day, a growing belief amongst men of liberal and statesmanlike views that India will at a future date attain this national independence. Moreover it is an object with which the use of force need not be associated at all for it is an object attainable by constitutional means. I believe therefore that no Liberal Government would ever take serious exception to the temperate expression of the ideal."

The only fault to be found with this expression of a common sense view of things is that the Magistrate seems to lay down the proposition that it depends on the feelings and views of Englishmen whether the preaching of independence is seditious or not. That is so in practice, no doubt, but judicially it is a strange principle of interpretation. On this ground, clearly stated by the Magistrate, that the preaching of national independence is not in itself seditious and does not become seditious unless coupled with excitations to revolt or violence or with matter tending to bring the Government into hatred or contempt, — the Printer of the *Nabasakti* was entitled to an acquittal. But the Magistrate immediately afterwards falls back from light into a thick fog in which he flounders helplessly for some way of unsaying what he has said.

"An Indian writer, however, who holds up national independence as an immediate panacea for the wrongs of his countrymen, is a mere visionary, and it is most unfortunate that so much of the political writing in Bengali newspapers should be the crude product of ignorant and ill-trained minds." And he goes on to say that the accused had published articles of this description and coupled them with others inciting to violence. Therefore he is convicted of sedition. Are we then to understand that the Printer is found guilty of sedition not because he advocated independence but because he advocated independence in an ignorant and ill-trained manner and his article was a crude product? If an article is to be declared seditious merely because it does not please the literary taste of a Police Court Magistrate, a new terror will be added to the law of sedition. Or are we to understand that the article is not seditious, is quite innocent, since to preach independence is not seditious, but it is declared seditious because other articles in the paper which contain nothing about independence are violent in tone? So far as we can see from the judgment of this learned Magistrate, the article in question is not seditious, though it may or may not be "a crude product", the other articles are not seditious though they may come under some other Section of the penal Code than 124A, and in any case they are not the subject matter of the charge. But because one article preaches independence and another which has no connection with it is written in a violent tone, therefore the first non-seditious article is transmuted into sedition by some strange magisterial alchemy. We come out of the reading of this judgment with a bewildered brain and only one clearly grasped idea, *viz.*, that whether what we write is seditious or not, depends not on the law, but on the state of "public opinion" in England and Anglo-India, and on the intellectual vagaries of a Magistrate who cannot even misinterpret the law consistently. And after all that is "all we know or need to know" on the subject of the law of sedition.

Bande Mataram, February 21, 1908

The Soul and India's Mission

Wind and Water

WIND and water are always types of the human soul in our literature. Wind is so light a substance that we cannot grasp it, water so fluid that we cannot seize it. When the soul is in a state of lightness and fluidity, it is then that it is compared to wind and water. When it is hard and rigid, then it is a stone. Wind and water are the light and fluid soul, stone the hard and rigid. Soul is variable and not easily distinguished from the European description of mind. Such a description may seem fanciful but it is true. Whoever has practised *prāṇāyāma* knows that sometimes the breath is as light and fluid as wind or water, sometimes as hard and rigid as stone. This changefulness of the soul is the true reason for *māyā*. If the soul were not changeable, it would be too much akin to the *brahman* — but because it is changeable, it lays itself open to the influence of *māyā*.

Light

Light is an emanation from the sun, but the sun is itself an emanation from God. When it is full of Him, then it is full of light. So the ancient Rishis used to say that He was in the sun. *Yo'sau puruṣaḥ* etc. But this was only a manner of speaking. When the sun is full of God's presence, it is full of light and heat, when it is empty of Him, the light and heat are withdrawn. So too the human soul is like the sun: When it is full of light and heat, it is said to be alive, when the light and heat are withdrawn, it is said to die. But this too is only a manner of speaking. The soul is imperishable. When the body feels the presence of God within, it is conscious of life, but when the light and heat of His presence are withdrawn it ceases to become active and conscious. This is called death. There is no hard and fast line to be drawn between life and death. The one is only the positive, the other the negative of God's presence.

Body and Soul

Soul is a presence, body a piece of *māyā*. When the body is full of the presence of the soul it lives, but when the soul withdraws from it it dies. In other words, the soul while in the body feels a sense of imprisonment which ceases as soon as the body falls from it. This is the work of *māyā* who lives by creating the sense of restriction in the illimitable and free *brahman*. *Māyā* is the negative quality of *brahman* making for darkness, *vidyā*, the positive quality making for light. They subsist together in the soul, and sometimes one prevails, sometimes the other. When *māyā* prevails, the soul thinks itself bound, when *vidyā* prevails, it thinks itself free. But there is no bondage. So too when a people feels itself bound and subject it acquiesces in its bondage, but the moment a light from God is sent into it, and the prophet of God is commissioned from on high, the nation wonders at its blindness and wakes to the sense of its inalienable freedom.

Immortality

Death, we have said, is a mere phase. There is no death, only the change from bondage to freedom. Death of the body is the first release from physical bondage, death of the soul the last release from spiritual bondage. The soul does not really die, but merely shakes off the false sense of separateness from *brahman*. Who then will fear death? Death is no enemy, no King of Horrors, but a friend who opens the gates of Heaven to the aspiring soul. Heaven is a myth in the opinion of modern science, but if Heaven means eternal happiness then Heaven is no myth. It is the state of the soul released from *māyā*, rejoicing in the sense of its own illimitable being; and those attain it who are in this world able to rise above the self to the knowledge of the higher self either by *yoga* or by selfless action for the sake of others.

Heaven awaits the patriot who dies for his country, the saint who passes from this life with the thought of God in his heart, the soldier who flings his life away at the bidding of his nation, all who can put the thought of self away from them.

Rest

When the soul is at rest, peace unutterable becomes its possession. How is rest to be attained? By the thought of *brahman*. Whoever thinks of Him at the time of death, passes into Him. Not the mere act of intellectual cognition, but the thought which dwells in the heart. The heart is the meeting place of God and the Soul. When the two meet then all action ceases, and rest becomes the possession of the soul. Whoever wishes to realise this truth must try to seek God in his heart. If he can find Him there he will experience rest.

Final Cessation

Nirvana is the goal of the soul's progress. Nirvana is the cessation of all phenomenal activity. Saints and sages are agreed in all religions on this one common truth, that so long as the phenomenal world is present to the soul, there can be no communion with God. Whoever imagines that by communion with the phenomenal world he can reach God is committing error, for the two are incompatible. The West is full of interest in phenomena, and it is for this reason that no great religion has ever come out of the West. Asia on the other hand is full of interest in Brahman and she is therefore the cradle of every great religion. Christianity, Mahomedanism, Buddhism and the creeds of China and Japan are all offshoots of one great and eternal religion of which India has the keeping.

India's Mission

So with India rests the future of the world. Whenever she is aroused from her sleep, she gives forth some wonderful shining ray of light to the world which is enough to illuminate the nations. Others live for centuries on what is to her the thought of a moment. God gave to her the book of Ancient Wisdom and bade her keep it sealed in her heart, until the time should come for it to be opened. Sometimes a page or a chapter is revealed, sometimes only a single sentence. Such sentences have been the inspiration of ages and fed humanity for many hundreds of years. So too when India sleeps, materialism grows apace and the light is covered up in darkness. But when materialism thinks herself about to triumph, lo and behold! a light rushes out from the East and where is Materialism? Returned to her native night.

Bande Mataram, February 21, 1908

The Glory of God in Man

WHOEVER is still under the influence of intellectual pride, is shocked when people depreciate the reason as the supreme guide. He asks how is it posssible for a man of culture to depreciate the reason and exalt some extraneous influence like that which people call God? But these doubters are under the influence of European materialism which tries to confine man to his material portion and deny him the possibility of a divine origin and a divine destiny. When Europe left Christianity to the monk and the ascetic and forgot the teachings of the Galilean, she exposed herself to a terrible fate which will yet overtake her. God in man is the whole revelation and the whole of religion. What Christianity taught dimly, Hinduism made plain to the intellect in Vedanta. When India remembers the teaching she received from Shankaracharya, Ramanuja and Madhva, when she realises what Sri Ramakrishna came to reveal, then she will rise. Her very life is Vedanta.

If anyone thinks that we are merely intellectual beings, he is not a Hindu. Hinduism leaves the glorification of intellectuality to those who have never seen God. She is commissioned by Him to speak only of his greatness and majesty and she has so spoken for thousands of years. When we first received a European education, we allowed ourselves to be misled by the light of science. Science is a light within a limited room, not the sun which illumines the world. The *aparā vidyā* is the sum of science but there is a *higher vidyā*, a mightier knowledge. When we are under the influence of the lower knowledge, we imagine that we are doing everything and try to reason out the situation we find ourselves in, as if our intellect were sovereign and omnipotent. But this is an attitude of delusion and *māyā.* Whoever has once felt the glory of God within him can never again believe that the intellect is supreme. There is a higher voice, there is a more unfailing oracle. It is in the heart where God resides. He works through the brain, but the brain is only one of His instruments. Whatever the brain may plan, the heart knows first and whoever can go beyond the brain to the heart, will hear the voice of the Eternal. This is what Srijut Aurobindo Ghose said in his Bombay speech. But our contemporary, the *Indian Patriot*, has lamented his downfall from the high pedestal of culture he once occupied. Our contemporary has forgotten the teachings of Vivekananda which were once so powerful in Madras. What does he think was the cause of the great awakening in Bengal?

When Lord Curzon thought to rend Bengal asunder, he deprived her of all her old pride and reliance upon her intellectual superiority. She had thought to set her wits against British power; and believed that the intellect of her sons would be a match for the clumsy brains of the English statesmen. Lord Curzon showed her that Power is too direct and invincible to be outwitted. The brains of Bengal did their best to cope with him and they failed. No course remained open to Bengal which her intellect could suggest. But when she was utterly reduced to despair, the time came for her own power to awake and set itself against that of the foreigner. She flung aside the devices of the Greek and took on herself the majesty of Roman strength and valour. When she declared the Boycott, she did so without calculation, without reckoning chances, without planning how the Boycott could succeed. She simply declared it. Was the intellect at work when she declared it? Was it her leaders who planned it as a means of bringing the British to their knees?

Everybody knows that it was not so. It was Kishoregunj, it was Magura, the obscure villages and towns of East Bengal which first declared the Boycott. What brain planned it, what voice first uttered it, history will never be able to discover. None planned it, but it was in the heart of the nation and God revealed it. If human brains had thought over the matter, Boycott would never have been declared. Srijut Bepin Chandra Pal is the most powerful brain at present at work in Bengal, but Srijut Bepin Chandra has himself often related that he was opposed to the Boycott in its inception, because his intellect refused to assent to the economic possibility of Boycott. So with all the men who were then the recognised brains and voices of Bengal. Only the nation had Boycott in their hearts and the heart of Bengal refused to be silenced by its brain. So Boycott was declared. Had the *Indian Patriot* been the mouthpiece of Bengal it would have asked for a plan of operations. But what plan of operations could have been given? So we see from this one great example what Srijut Aurobindo Ghose meant when he said that it was God's work and not man's. If the *Indian Patriot* can show us who planned the Boycott, or how it has been guided to success by human intellect, we will accept his view of things. Meanwhile, we shall take leave to approve of the view expressed by Srijut Aurobindo Ghose. God is behind this movement and He does not need anyone to tell Him how to bring it to success. He will see to that Himself. Whatever plans we may make, we shall find quite useless when the time for action comes. Revolutions are always full of surprises, and whoever thinks he can play chess with a revolution will soon find how terrible is the grasp of God and how insignificant the human reason before the whirlwind of His breath. That man only is likely to dominate the chances of a Revolution, who makes no plans but preserves his heart pure for the will of God to declare itself. The great rule of life is to have no schemes but one unalterable purpose. If the will is fixed on the purpose it sets itself to accomplish, then circumstances will suggest the right course; but the schemer finds himself always tripped up by the unexpected.

Bande Mataram, February 22, 1908

A National University

THE idea of a National University is one of the ideas which have formulated themselves in the national consciousness and become part of the immediate destiny of a people. It is a seed which is sown and must come to its fruition, because the future demands it and the heart of the nation is in accord with the demand. The process of its increase may be rapid or it may be slow, and when the first beginnings are made, there may be many errors and false starts, but like a stream gathering volume as it flows, the movement will grow in force and certainty, the vision of those responsible for its execution will grow clearer, and their hands will be helped in unexpected ways until the purpose of God is worked out and the idea shapes itself into an accomplished reality. But it is necessary that those who are the custodians of the precious trust, should guard it with a jealous care and protect its purity and first high aim from being sullied or lowered.

There have been many attempts before the present movement to rescue education in India from subservience to foreign and petty ends, and to establish Colleges and Schools maintained and controlled by Indians which would give an education superior to the Government-controlled education. The City College, the Ferguson College and others started with this aim but they are now monuments of a frustrated idea. In every case they have fallen to the state of ordinary institutions, replicas of the Government model, without a separate mission or nobler reason for existence. And they have so fallen because their promoters could not understand or forgot that the first condition of success was independence — an independence jealously preserved and absolute. In other words there can be no national education without national control.

A certain measure of success has been secured by two institutions of a later birth, the Benares Hindu College and the Dayanand Anglo-Vedic College. These are successful institutions, but isolated. They have not developed into centres of a network of schools affiliated to them and forming one corporate body. They have not in themselves the makings of Universities. So far as they give religious teaching they are a wholesome departure from the barren official form of education, but that is only one part of education on national lines. National education cannot be defined briefly in one or two sentences, but we may describe it tentatively as the education which starting with the past and making full use of the present builds up a great nation. Whoever wishes to cut off the nation from its past is no friend of our national growth. Whoever fails to take advantage of the present is losing us the battle of life. We must therefore save for India all that she has stored up of knowledge, character and noble thought in her immemorial past. We must acquire for her the best knowledge that Europe can give her and assimilate it to her own peculiar type of national temperament. We must introduce the best methods of teaching humanity has developed, whether modern or ancient. And all these we must harmonise into a system which will be impregnated with the spirit of self-reliance so as to build up men and not machines — national men, able men, men fit to carve out a career for themselves by their own brain-power and resource, fit to meet the shocks of life and breast the waves of adventure. So shall the Indian people cease to sleep and become once more a people of heroes, patriots, originators, so shall it become a nation and no longer a disorganised mass of men.

National education must therefore be on national lines and under national control. This necessity is the very essence of its being. No one who has not grasped it can hope to build up a National University. Mrs. Besant has recently begun a campaign in favour of national education and in a recent speech has outlined her idea of a National University. We have every respect for this great orator and organiser, but we are bound to point out that an university organised by Mrs. Besant will not be a National University. In the first place the future University must be one built up by the brain and organising power of India's own sons. It shall never be said that the first National University in India was the creation of a foreigner and that the children of the Mother were content to follow and imitate but could not lead and originate. Such a charge would be fatal to the very object of the University. Secondly, Mrs. Besant has forgotten that the basis of a National University has already been laid. The National Council of Education in Bengal has already commenced the great work on lines which have only to be filled in, and their work has received the blessing of God and increases. But Mrs. Besant has omitted to make any mention of their work and speaks as if she intended to have the Benares College as the basis of the National University. But the Benares College has shown itself unfit for so huge a task. It has been obliged to rely on foreign funds and to court Government patronage. Even the Dayanand Anglo-Vedic College is a more robust growth, for it has been built up by the munificent self-sacrifice of the Arya Samaj. No institution which cannot rely on the people of India for its support and build itself up without official support or patronage, can be considered to have established its capacity of developing into a National University. Finally, Mrs. Besant shows by her scheme that she is not in possession of the true secret of the movement. She wants a Charter from England. We are aware that she talks of organising the University with the help of Indian talent and keeping it as a preserve for Indian control, but when she asks for a Charter it is evident that she has not realised what national control implies. No Government will give a Charter which excludes them from all control. There may be no provision for control in the Charter itself, but the power that gives the Charter can at any moment insist on seeing that the University merits the Charter. Once this constructive possibility of control is allowed to overshadow the infant institution, goodbye to its utility, its greatness, its future. It will follow the way of other schools and colleges and become a fruitless idea, a monument of wasted energy and frustrated hopes.

A Misconception

The *Englishman* is waiting with bated breath for the amendment of the Press Act. As soon as a sedition trial is concluded and savage sentence meted out to the supposed offender the *Englishman* feels the necessity of a stricter law providing for the extinction of the whole seditious lot, including the editor, contributors, printer, publisher and proprietor. The *Englishman* complains that in this respect the law in India is behind even that of China where all the different persons connected with the publication of a newspaper can be satisfactorily dealt with. The *Englishman*'s idea of progressiveness in these matters is no doubt peculiar and does not call for any serious notice. According to our contemporary the Press Law will perhaps be perfectly modernised if provision is made to shoot down everyone found to be in possession of any of the alleged seditious prints. However, we are not much concerned with the curious notions of the bureaucracy and its advisers about freedom of speech. We want to remove one misconception both from the minds of our Anglo-Indian and Indian critics in this connection. Whatever may be the literary ability of the printers and publishers of these prosecuted papers they thoroughly understand their mission and willingly offer themselves as sacrifices in spite of dissuasion, to keep alive this sort of patriotic literature in the country. They come forward out of a strong patriotic impulse and offer to shield ability behind their heroism to ensure the continuity of propagandist work according to their own ideas and ideals. Printers or publishers, theirs is the moral and legal responsibility for the dissemination of the ideas which are sought to be put down. These men are really the prophets and martyrs and those for whose blood the Anglo-Indian Press and the bureaucracy seem to be so thirsty are merely the dressers of their ideas. The new batch of printers and publishers who are rushing to jail one after another are not mere mercenary instruments but young men fired with divine enthusiasm and heroic devotion to the cause of their country. Those who talk lightly of the printers and publishers of these alleged seditious papers should take note of this fact, and then judge if any severity of the Press Act can at all put an end to this sort of literature.

Bande Mataram, February 24, 1908

Mustafa Kamil Pasha

WE published yesterday among our selections a full account of the life and death of Mustafa Kamil Pasha, the great Nationalist leader in Egypt, who has regenerated Nationalism in his motherland and will be remembered in history as the chief among the creators of modern Egypt. The early death of this extraordinary man will be a blow to the movement, but we must remember what we are apt to forget that the life-work of a great man often does not begin till he dies. While the body fetters the activities of the spirit within, his work is limited in its scope and imperfect in its intensity, but when the material shackles are struck off by the friendly hand of death, then the spirit ranges abroad in perfect freedom and the sudden and startling rapidity with which its work develops, forms a theme for the amazement and admiration of posterity. Whatever else Mustafa Kamil may have been, he was a sincere and enthusiastic patriot. When he left Egypt to help the cause of his country in foreign countries, he was welcomed even in England by those who had the generosity to appreciate patriotism; but the moment it appeared that his work was beginning to bear practical fruit in Egypt itself, a storm of misrepresentation began to beat about his devoted head which has not even yet ceased. He was denounced as an intriguer, a paid tool of the Khedive, a Turcophil emissary of the Sultan. But Egypt felt the heart of a patriot in his writings and his speeches and her people responded to his call. The steady growth of the Nationalist Party has been mainly the work of Mustafa Kamil. It attained its consummation in the meaning of the recognised Nationalist Party when he was on the brink of the grave and his last self-forgetful service to his country was the speech which he rose from his death-bed to deliver upon that memorable occasion.

The programme of the Nationalist Party in Egypt has some resemblances to that of the Indian Nationalists. Its object is the independence of Egypt, its method is the appeal to the self-consciousness of the nation, and its reliance is on the help which God always gives to the cause of righteousness when it is pursued in a lofty and disinterested spirit. In his earlier career Mustafa relied too much on foreign sympathy and he persisted till the end in clinging to the hope of some assistance, moral if not material, from the foreign Powers financially interested in Egypt. But his trust in this chance of outward help never extended to the folly of expecting British statesmen to co-operate of deliberate purpose in hastening the day of Egypt's liberation. He was a statesman as well as a prophet of Nationalism. If he relied too much on foreign sympathy, it was because the national sentiment in Egypt was as yet local and he trusted in the moral support of other countries to prevent England from putting it down with the strong hand before it had become sufficiently self-conscious to survive oppression. The Sultan stood between Egypt and complete annexation to England, and therefore he always persisted in laying stress on the suzerainty of the Sultan. The religious solidarity of Islam was a moral asset in his favour and he insisted on this solidarity but never suffered it for a moment to interfere with the distinct existence of Egyptian Nationality. The cause of Nationality was his first object; the rest merely helps and supports. Towards the end of his career as the sentiment of Nationality grew more and more self-conscious and self-reliant in his countrymen, he too came to perceive in its fullness the truth that Egypt must rely on herself first and not on others. Foreign help can only be safe and beneficial if the nation has already grown strong enough to rely mainly on itself for its own separate existence.

Mustafa Kamil was a man of the type of Mazzini in one respect, his intense idealism and lofty idea of cosmopolitan unity embracing national independence. It is this idealism which will keep Egypt alive and secure the immortality of the Nationalist movement. When a movement for independence begins with diplomacy and Machiavellianism, it is doomed to failure as the Carbonari movement failed in Italy. God is not with it. It does not rely on the eternal principles of truth and virtue, but on the finite strength of human intellect and human means and to that finite strength God leaves it. When that strength comes to its limits, there is nothing left, and failure is final. But when a movement takes its stand on truth and justice, then it appeals to God Himself and He will see to it that the trust reposed in Him is not falsified. Failures may come but they will be only fresh incentives to purer and nobler effort. An immortal power will stand behind the movement and death will be afraid to come near it. Its leaders may be snatched away by the hand of death, hurried into exile or imprisonment, given to the hand of the executioner, but fresh leaders will arise. Its means may change from time to time, it may pass through ever-new phases and sometimes men may fail to recognise it as the same old movement, but God is within it always as its eternal and undying Self and it lasts till it receives its consummation.

Bande Mataram, March 3, 1908

A Great Opportunity

THE release of Srijut Bepin Chandra Pal will take place in a few days and the bureaucracy is undoubtedly looking with anxiety to see what kind of reception the people give to this great leader and propagandist after his six months' incarceration for conscience' sake. They will do their best to prevent by a surreptitious release any expression of public feeling either at the jail doors or at the station, but it does not matter whether or not we welcome him at the precise moment and place of his release, so long as the heart of the people goes out unmistakably in some mighty demonstration of feeling. That Srijut Bepin Chandra Pal is one of our most powerful workers on the platform and the press, is a fact which even his opponents have acknowledged. That his services to the country have been of an incalculable value, few will care to gainsay. Among a large section of his countrymen he is recognised as the prophet of a great political creed. Whenever men of his type fall under the displeasure of the powers that be, they return to the field of work with greater vigour and a fresh vitality, for theirs is a mission which thrives upon oppression and gains by exile and imprisonment. Srijut Bepin Chandra also will come out of prison like a giant refreshed and renew his labour for his nation. But if his incarceration had been a source of strength to himself, has it or has it not been a source of strength to his country? This is the question which we must answer on the 9th of March. In what terms shall we answer it? Are we to confess that the cunning policy of mingled repression and occasional forbearance has had its effect? There are some among us who advise caution and look with fear on such demonstrations as likely to provoke fresh persecution, as if it were the outward ebullitions of sentiment and not the fact of national aspiration which it is sought to repress. Shall we by an imperfect welcome to this great tribune of the people show that these counsels of imprudent prudence have weight with us? Shall we not rather make the occasion one of universal rejoicing all over the country so that all may feel that the pulse of the movement is not slower, that the heart of this people beats as high as before the incarceration of their well-loved apostle and teacher?

How then are we to welcome Bepin Chandra Pal back to the scene of his labours? By illuminations, by processions, by rejoicing of every kind. We would have every town and village where the nation is awake write his welcome in letters of fire on balcony and roof of their dwellings not only in Bengal but in Madras, in Maharashtra, in the Punjab, wherever Nationalism is alive and the name of the Mother is honoured. We invite our countrymen all over India to become one with Bengal in the act of a rejoicing which is not for a man but for the cause he has served. Let us also arrange to lead him in procession from his house after his return to a place of public meeting with such pomp and ceremony as befits one who returns from a great victory to his native land; for the jail is a place of exile and the prisoner released is a soldier who has waged a great moral conflict for his country and returns triumphant carrying with him his unblemished patriotism and the unlowered flag of his courage as the trophies of the fight. And in the place of assembly let all parties unite to do him honour so that the return of this Nationalist leader may be the best answer to those who rejoice in our dissensions and seek in them the safety which they cannot hope for from the justice of their bureaucratic rule or the righteousness of their absolutist cause. And if in addition every considerable society of workers and patriots expresses separately its appreciation and respect, the welcome will be worthy of the occasion, and a great opportunity for fresh national inspiration and the upwelling of a living enthusiasm will have been nobly used. Whoever thinks that this is a time for nourishing old grudges or remembering past feuds, is wanting in patriotism and insight. The hour is one of growing national unity and there is in the heart of the people a desire to have done with barren dispute and set themselves to the sacred work to which this generation has been called. Whoever stops now to weigh and consider whether he is at one with Bepin Chandra in the views of which he is the chief exponent or can entirely appreciate the reasons of his refusal to give evidence, is allowing trifles to obscure the greatness of the thing which Bepin Chandra for the moment represents. It is not the man or the action which will be honoured by a public demonstration. The man is nothing but the cause is everything. The action is nothing, but the sacrament of suffering is everything. This sacrament of suffering has been in this instance the privilege not of the rank and file of the national army but of a great leader and captain, whose name is honoured in every part of India. Such an occasion is one of rare occurrence, for it is usually the private soldiers who are food for powder and the leaders stand out of range for the better safety of the work. Yet when one is struck down, it is a matter for national rejoicing, that so illustrious a name has been added to the roll of those who have been chosen to give proofs of the noblest patriotism and courage.

We therefore invite all to join in this demonstration. We do not wish this occasion to be marred by the memories of past dissension but to be ennobled by the growing hope of a great united movement forward in the future. In the person of Bepin Chandra let the present impulse towards a better understanding find a consummation which all the world cannot fail to understand. Let it be the seal of reconciliation which began at Pabna, and the beginning of united action for the better organisation of the work to which all Bengal without distinction of parties is now irrevocably pledged.

The Strike at Tuticorin

The struggle at present in progress at Tuticorin is one of absorbing interest. This is not the first instance in which Madras has shown how deeply it is imbued with the spirit of a strong and enthusiastic Nationalism. But on this occasion there is a note of firm serious strength in the attitude of the people which is proof of a great advance on former outbreaks of Nationalist feeling. Why the authorities should have chosen to apprehend a miniature rebellion in Tuticorin, they themselves alone know. The people are conducting themselves with a marvellous combination of firmness and dignity, with quiet self-control and have given absolutely no hold to the excited local bureaucrats. We can only suppose that as the self-assertion of Indian labour has evoked the enthusiastic support of the people, so the menace to the despotic control of the labour market by British capital has been taken by the bureaucrats as a blow aimed at British rule. The identity of the interests of administration and exploitation of which Lord Curzon was the prophet is, no doubt, at the root of this unseemly alliance between the Coral Mills and the British Government. The people seem to have found worthy leaders in Sjts. Chidambaram Pillai and Subramaniya Siva and have so far held their own in the struggle. We await further developments with interest and with confidence in their courage and discretion.

Bande Mataram, March 4, 1908

Swaraj and the Coming Anarchy

WHOEVER tries to read the signs of the time, will be no little perplexed at first by their complexity. The beginnings of a great revolution which is destined to change the whole political, social, and economic life of a great country, are always full of ebb and flow, perplexing by the multitude of details and their continual interaction. The struggle going on at Tuticorin exemplifies this remarkable diversity and intermingling of numerous tendencies each of which would, in ordinary times, be a separate movement. Society is full of anomalies which clash and jostle together in an inextricable chaos of progress and reaction; economic India is in the throes of a violent transition from the old mediaeval basis of life to the modern; politics is at a parting of the ways. All these various and independent activities of the Indian body politic unite into a huge and confused movement of which the main impulse is political and the others are largely inspired, if not motived, by the passions which are at the root of the political upheaval. Great issues of economics wear the guise of a political conflict; immense political aspirations become mixed up with a purely industrial struggle between indigenous labour and foreign capital. So also in society the old reform movement which was a separate and ineffectual attempt to transform our society according to European ideas, has given place to disquiet and aspiration in the society itself. So long the educated men of the upper castes debated among themselves about the better ordering of society, and outside Bengal and the Punjab it was no better than an academic dispute on the Social Conference platform or between the reforming and orthodox Press. Even in Bengal and the Punjab, the movement was sectional, a revolt of a small minority of the educated few, and did not touch the heart of the people. So far as society as a whole was affected, it was by the new environments of the nineteenth century bringing an irresistible pressure to bear on its outworks, and sometimes by the force of economical necessity born of the modern conditions of India under British rule. The change was from outside and therefore injurious rather than beneficial, for an organism is doomed which, incapable of changing from within, answers only to the pressure of environment. But this immobile state of Hindu society has now begun to pass away and we see the beginning of a profound and incalculable life in the heart of the great organism. Yesterday we hardly needed to reckon with the lower strata of society in our political life; today they are beginning to live, to move, to have a dim inarticulate hope and to grope for air and room. That is a sign of coming social revolution in which neither the conservative forces of society nor the liberal sympathies of the educated few will have much voice. The forces that are being unprisoned will upheave the whole of our society with a volcanic force and the shape it will take after the eruption is over does not depend on the wishes or the wisdom of men. These social stirrings also are mingling with the political unrest to increase the confusion. The question of the Namasudras in Bengal has become a political as well as a social problem and in other parts of the country also the line between politics and social questions is threatened with obliteration.

The future is not in our hands. When so huge a problem stares us in the face, we become conscious of the limits of human discernment and wisdom. We at once feel that the motions of humanity are determined by forces and not by individuals and that the intellect and experience of statesmen are merely instruments in the hands of the Power which manifests itself in those great incalculable forces. In ordinary times, we are apt to forget this and to account for all that happens as the result of this statesman's foresight or that genius' dynamic personality. But in times like the present we find it less easy to shut our eyes to the truth. We do not affect to believe, therefore, that we can discover any solution of these great problems or any sure line of policy by which the tangled issues of so immense a movement can be kept free from the possibility of inextricable anarchy in the near future. Anarchy will come. This peaceful and inert nation is going to be rudely awakened from a century of passivity and flung into a world-shaking turmoil out of which it will come transformed, strengthened and purified. There is a chaos which is the result of inertia and the prelude of death, and this was the state of India during the last century. The British peace of the last fifty years was like the quiet green grass and flowers covering the corruption of a sepulchre. There is another chaos which is the violent reassertion of life and it is this chaos into which India is being hurried today. We cannot repine at the change, but are rather ready to welcome the pangs which help the storm which purifies, the destruction which renovates.

One thing only we are sure of, and one thing we wear as a life-belt which will buoy us up on the waves of the chaos that is coming on the land. This is the fixed and unalterable faith in an over-ruling Purpose which is raising India once more from the dead, the fixed and unalterable intention to fight for the renovation of her ancient life and glory. Swaraj is the life-belt, Swaraj the pilot, Swaraj the star of guidance. If a great social revolution is necessary, it is because the ideal of Swaraj cannot be accomplished by a nation bound to forms which are no longer expressive of the ancient and immutable Self of India. She must change the rags of the past so that her beauty may be readorned. She must alter her bodily appearance so that her soul may be newly expressed. We need not fear that any change will turn her into a second-hand Europe. Her individuality is too mighty for such a degradation, her soul too calm and self-sufficient for such a surrender. If again an economical revolution is inevitable, it is because the fine but narrow edifice of her old industrial life will not allow of Swaraj in commerce and industry. The industrial energies of a free and perfect national life demand a mightier scope and wider channels. Neither need we fear that the economic revolution will land us in the same diseased and disordered state of society as now offends the nobler feelings of humanity in Europe. India can never so far forget the teaching which is her life and the secret of her immortality as to become a replica of the organised selfishness, cruelty and greed which is dignified in the West by the name of Industry. She will create her own conditions, find out the secret of order which Socialism in vain struggles to find and teach the peoples of the earth once more how to harmonise the world and the spirit.

If we realise this truth, if we perceive in all that is happening a great and momentous transformation necessary not only for us but for the whole world, we shall fling ourselves without fear or misgivings into the times which are upon us. India is the *guru* of the nations, the physician of the human soul in its profounder maladies; she is destined once more to new-mould the life of the world and restore the peace of the human spirit. But Swaraj is the necessary condition of her work and before she can do the work, she must fulfil the condition.

Bande Mataram, March 5, 1908

Back to the Land

THE life of a nation is always rooted in its villages but that of India is so deeply and persistently rooted there that no change or revolution can ever substitute for this source of sap and life the Western system which makes the city the centre and the village a mere feeder of the city. Immense changes have taken place, great empires have risen and fallen, but India is still a nation of villagers, not of townsmen. This has been perhaps an obstacle to national unity but it has also been an assurance of national persistence. It is an ascertained principle of national existence that only by keeping possession of the soil can a nation persist; the mastery of the reins of government or the control of the trade and wealth of a country, does not give permanence to the people in control. They reign for a while and then the virtue departs out of them and they wither or pass away and another takes their place; but the tillers of the soil, ground down, oppressed, rack-rented, miserable, remain, and have always the chance of one day overthrowing their oppressors and coming by their own. When a small foreign oligarchy does the trading and governing and a great indigenous democracy the tilling of the soil, it is safe to prophesy that before many generations have passed the oligarchy of aliens will be no more and the democracy of peasants will still be in possession.

When the poison of Western education was first poured into our veins, it had its immediate effect, and the Hindus, who were then the majority of the Bengali-speaking population, began to stream away from the village to the town. The bait of Government service and the professions drew away the brightest intellects and the most energetic characters by their promise of wealth, prestige and position. They won for their community the rewards which they had set out to win. The Hindu community has now a monopoly of Government service, of the professions, of prestige, wealth and position; but it has lost possession of the soil, and with the loss of the soil it has sacrificed the source of life and permanence. The *Amrita Bazar Patrika* has long been drawing attention to the dwindling of the higher castes, and Mr. A. Chowdhuri at the Pabna Conference pointed out what has been known to the few for some time but not the general public, that this decrease is not confined to the higher castes but is common to the Hindu population. We are a decadent race, he cried, and inconsistent as the cry may seem with the splendid and leading position which the Bengali Hindu occupies in the public and intellectual life of the country, it is perfectly true. Intellectual prominence often goes hand in hand with decadence, as the history of the Greeks and other great nations of antiquity has proved; only the race which does not sacrifice the soundness of its rural root of life to the urban brilliance of its foliage and flowering, is in a sound condition and certain of permanence. If the present state of things is allowed to continue, the Mahomedan will be the inheritor of the future and after a brief period of national strength and splendour the Bengali Hindu, like the Greek, will disappear from the list of nations and remain only as a great name in history. Fortunately, the national movement has come in time to save him if he consents to be saved. With the deepening of the movement, as it turns its eyes more and more inwards, it is earning wisdom and acquiring insight, and one of the more powerful tendencies of the moment is the reversion of interest to the village. Srijut Jogesh Chowdhuri has an instinct for the need of the moment and just as he threw himself into Swadeshi activity long before the leaders of the hour awoke to its importance, so now he has started his Palli Samaj propaganda while the rest of the political leaders are unable to extend their view beyond the fields of activity already conquered. Srijut Rabindranath Tagore at Pabna laid stress on the same necessity. "Back to the land," is a cry which must swell with time and, if the Bengali Hindu is wise, he will listen and obey. Swadeshi was the most pressing need of the nation till now, because we were threatened with a commercial depletion which would have rendered agricultural life impossible by turning famine into a chronic disease. The peasant must live if he is to keep possession of the soil, and a flourishing national commerce is the only sure preventive of famine. But now Swadeshi has become an integral part of our politics, the gradual growth of Indian industry is assured until this growth is complete, the struggle with famine will continue and this also is getting to be recognised as an essential part of our political activity. We must now turn to the one field of work in this direction which we have most neglected, the field of agriculture. The return to the land is as essential to our salvation as the development of Swadeshi or the fight against famine. If we train our young men to go back to the fields, we shall secure the perpetuation of the Hindu in Bengal which is now imperilled. They will be able to become mentors, leaders and examples to the village population and by introducing better methods of agriculture and habits of thrift and foresight and by organising the institution of Dharmagolas and securing more equal position for the peasant in his dealings with the merchant and the moneylender they will materially assist the Swadeshi manufacturer and the organiser of famine relief in the fight for survival. To settle more Hindu agriculturists on the land is the first necessity if the Hindu is to survive.

National Education has followed the trend of the political movement and its first energies have been devoted to literary and technical instruction. In the latter branch it has already, in spite of insufficient help from the public, achieved a signal success; if it has been able to make only a beginning, yet that beginning has been so sound, so admirably and intelligently done, that we can already perceive in this little seed the mighty tree of the future. We understand that the literary instruction is now being organised with a view to make the College in Calcutta a home of learning and fruitful research as well as a nursery of intelligence and character. But we look to the organisers of the College to make equal provision for agricultural training, so that a field may be created for its students on the soil whence all national life draws its sap of permanence. The establishment of the Pabna School is of good omen in this respect, but a single institution in East Bengal will not be sufficient, as the conditions of Pabna are not universal in Bengal, and model farms on drier soil such as we have in Comilla and West Bengal will also be needed. If the work is taken in hand from now, it will not be a moment too soon, for the problem is urgent in its call for a solution, and the mere organisation of village associations will be only partially effective if it is not backed up by a system of instruction which will bring the educated Hindu back to the soil as a farmer himself and a local leader of the peasantry of the race.

Bande Mataram, March 6, 1908

The Village and the Nation

We wrote yesterday of the necessity of going back to the land if the Bengali Hindu is to keep his place in the country and escape the fate of those who divorce themselves from the root of life, the soil. But there is another aspect of the question which is also of immense importance. The old organisation of the Indian village was self-sufficient, self-centred, autonomous and exclusive. These little units of life existed to themselves, each a miniature world of its own petty interests and activities; like a system of planets united to each other indeed by an unconscious force but each absorbed in its own life and careless of the other. It was a life beautifully simple, healthy, rounded and perfect, a delight to the poet and the lover of humanity. If perfect simplicity of life, freedom from economic evils, from moral degradation, from the strife, faction and fury of town populations, from revolution and turmoil, from vice and crime on a large scale are the objects of social organisation, then the village communities of India were ideal forms of social organisation. Many look back to them with regret and even British administrators who were instrumental in destroying them have wished that they could be revived. So valuable indeed were the elements of social welfare which they secured to the nation, that they have persisted through all changes and revolutions as they were thousands of years ago when the Aryans first occupied the land. Nor can it be denied that they have kept the nation alive. Whatever social evils or political diseases might corrupt the body politic, these little cells of national life supplied a constant source of soundness and purity which helped to prevent final disintegration. But if we owe national permanence to these village organisations, it cannot be denied that they have stood in the way of national unity.

Wherever a nation has been formed, in the modern sense, it has been at the expense of smaller units. The whole history of national growth is the record of a long struggle to establish a central unity by subduing the tendency of smaller units to live to themselves. The ancient polity of Greece was the self-realisation of the city as an unit sufficient to itself while the deme or village was obliged to sacrifice its separate existence to the greater unity of the city-state. Because the Greeks could not find it in their hearts to break the beautiful and perfect mould of their self-sufficient city life, they could never weld themselves into a nation. So again it was not till the Romans had subdued the tendency of the Italian cities to live to themselves, that the first European nation was created. In mediaeval times the city-state tried to reassert itself in the Municipalities of France and Germany and municipal freedom had to be blotted out by an absolute monarchy before national unity was realised. Whenever a smaller or different unity, whether it be that of the province, the church or feudal fief, tends to live for itself, it is an obstacle to national unity and has to be either broken up or subordinated if the nation is to fulfil its unity. Ancient India could not build itself into a single united nation, not because of caste or social differences as the European writers assert, — caste and class have existed in nations which achieved a faultless national unity, — but because the old polity of the Hindus allowed the village to live to itself, the clan to live to itself, the province or smaller race-unit to live to itself. The village, sufficient to itself, took no interest in the great wars and revolutions which affected only the ruling clans of the kingdom including it in its territorial jurisdiction. The Kshatriya clans fought and married and made peace among themselves, and were the only political units out of which a nation might have been built. But the clan too was so attached to its separate existence that it was not till the clans were destroyed on the battlefield of Kurukshetra that larger national units could be built out of their ruins. Small kingdoms took their place based on provincial or racial divisions and until the inrush of foreign peoples an attempt was in progress to build them into one nation by the superimposition of a single imperial authority. Many causes prevented the success of the attempt, and the provincial unit has always remained the highest expression of the nation-building tendencies in India. One cause perhaps more than any other contributed to the failure of the centripetal tendency to attain self-fulfilment, and that was the persistence of the village community which prevented the people, the real nation, from taking any part in the great struggles out of which a nation should have emerged. In other countries the people had to take part in the triumphs, disasters and failures of their rulers either as citizens or at least as soldiers, but in India they were left to their little isolated republics with no farther interest than the payment of a settled tax in return for protection by the supreme power. This was the true cause of the failure of India to achieve a distinct organised and self-conscious Nationality. It is worthy of notice that the Indian race in which the national idea attained its most conscious expression and most nearly attained realisation, was the Maratha people who drew their strength from the village democracies and brought them to interest themselves in the struggle for national independence. If the Marathas had been able to rise above the idea of provincial or racial separateness, they would have established a permanent empire and neither of the Wellesleys could have broken their power by diplomacy or in the field. The British, historians have told us, conquered India in a fit of absence of mind. In a fit of absence of mind also they destroyed the separate life of our village communities, and, by thus removing the greatest obstacle in the way of national development, prepared the irresistible movement towards national unity which now fills them with dismay. The provinces have been brought together, the village has been destroyed. It only remains for the people to fulfil their destiny. We are now turning our eyes again to the village under the stress of an instinct of self-preservation and part of our programme is to re-create village organisation. In doing so we must always remember that the village can be so organised as to prove a serious obstacle to national cohesion. One or two of our leading publicists have sometimes expressed themselves as if our salvation lay in the village and not in the larger organisation of the nation. Swaraj has been sometimes interpreted as a return to the old conditions of self-sufficient village life leaving the imperial authority to itself, to tax and pass laws as it pleased — ignored because it is too strong to be destroyed. Even those who see the futility of ignoring Government which seeks to destroy every centre of strength, however minute, except itself, sometimes insist on the village as the secret of our life and ask us to give up our ambitious strivings after national Swaraj and realise it first in the village. Such counsel is dangerous, even if it were possible to follow it. Nothing should be allowed to distract us from the mighty ideal of Swaraj, National and Pan-Indian. This is no alien or exotic ideal, it is merely the conscious attempt to fulfil the great centripetal tendency which has pervaded the grandiose millenniums of her history, to complete the work which Srikrishna began, which Chandragupta and Asoka and the Gupta Kings continued, which Akbar almost brought to realisation, for which Shivaji was born and Bajirao fought and planned. The organisation of our villages is an indispensable work to which we must immediately set our hands, but we must be careful so to organise them as to make them feel that they are imperfect parts of a single national unity, and dependent at every turn on the co-operation first of the district, secondly of the province, and finally of the nation. The day of the independent village or group of villages has gone and must not be revived; the nation demands its hour of fulfilment and seeks to gather the village life of its rural population into a mighty, single and compact democratic nationality. We must make the nation what the village community was of old, self-sufficient, self-centred, autonomous and exclusive — the ideal of national Swaraj.

Bande Mataram, March 8, 1908

Welcome to the Prophet of Nationalism

TODAY Srijut Bepin Chandra Pal is due in Calcutta, a free man once more until it shall please irresponsible Magistrates and easily-twisted laws to repeat his seclusion from the work which God has given him to do. A true leader of men today in India holds his liberty as a light thing to be lost at a moment's notice; when he chooses to defend himself, he does so with the knowledge that no skill of defence but the choice of his prosecutors is the arbiter of the trial, no soundness of the law in his favour, but the convenience of those who employ and pay his judge, determines whether he goes free or incurs the honourable pains of martyrdom — brief or long according to the caprice or policy of his political adversaries. To one who loves his country above all things, life in India today is as insecure as in the worst days of despotic caprice and arbitrariness from which British benevolence is fabled to have rescued us; he walks about under the constant sense of an insecurity which is the condition of his labours, not knowing whether the next day will not see him under arrest with the practical certainty of a sentence already fixed and awaiting only the idle formalities of a nominal trial for its confirmation. The price of safety, if he desires it, is the sacrifice of his soul, to be silent when God has bidden him to speak, to refrain from action which his duty and conscience call on him to perform. Bureaucracy sometimes promises him safety for the moment at an apparently lighter price, the loss of personal self-respect and honour. It does not, as it once did, call upon him to fall down and worship it, it does not demand affection from its opponents; but it is content to barter acquittal for an apology. Recantation was the alternative which the old persecutors of Christianity and the Christian persecutors of Jews and heretics offered to those whom they threatened with the cross and the arena, with the rack and the fire, and it was offered for the same reason that it is offered today to the political martyr. The force with which the old religious persecutors had to struggle was a moral force which fought tyranny not with material weapons but with the weapons of the spirit and it was by intimidating the spirit and breaking the moral force of the resistance that they hoped to destroy the movement which they feared.

Recantation meant a diminution of the moral force of the movements, so much to the credit of the tyrant, to the loss of the cause. Today also it is a great religious movement disguised for the moment in a political and Western garb with which the bureaucracy is faced and the weapons which it uses are the weapons of the spirit, the force which makes it formidable is a spiritual force. We have nothing to oppose to the immense material engines of the bureaucracy except the exalted faith, the unflinching courage, the unswerving devotion to principle which has been so strangely, suddenly born in the hearts of this generation of young men in Bengal. There lies the true strength of Nationalism and the enemies of Nationalism instinctively feel it. They are concerned therefore not so much to crush the inadequate and rudimentary material means which the movement has so far generated but to destroy the moral force which makes it a power. They are willing to forego the satisfaction of vindictiveness, if they can secure the solid advantage of an apology or recantation of some kind such as would fatally injure the moral force of at least one champion of Nationalism and by cumulative examples beat down the enthusiastic self-confidence of the nation. Once or twice they have succeeded, but these solitary instances of weakness have been a beacon-light of warning to the country and the stern resolution not to flinch has been strengthened by the perception of the incalculable harm a single instance of recantation can do to the whole cause. On the other hand, every one who can say to the bureaucratic tempter, "Get thee beind me, Satan", is scoring a victory for the cause of his country.

Yet, there are signs that the counsels of prudence and the wisdom of the diplomat are beginning to gain upon us, we are growing wise in our generation and calculate the harm that can be done to the success of the movement by rashness or the advantages to be gained by a little care and economy of life or suffering. The exaltation of the movement is in danger of being lowered by an accommodating spirit. We have referred before to this growing danger and we are led to dwell on it by a perception of the relaxation in popular enthusiasm and fire which is apparent in Bengal. Now that Bepin Chandra is coming out of prison, we look to his triumphant oratory, the Pythian inspiration of his matchless eloquence to reawaken the spirit of lofty idealism, of unflinching devotion to principle which it was his mission to confirm if not awaken, and which is now more evident in Madras where his influence is the chief inspiring force than in Bengal, the home of Nationalism. The voice of the prophet will once more be free to speak to our hearts, the voice through which God has more than once spoken. We shall remember once more that the movement is a spiritual movement for prophets, martyrs and heroes to inspire, help and lead, not for diplomats and pinchbeck Machiavels; we shall realise that the spirit of India reawakened is the life of the movement and not a borrowed Western patriotism; we shall shrink once more from accommodation and paltering with the high call of our conscience as a fatal concession to the adversary and feel again that only by perfect faith, perfect self-sacrifice, perfect courage can we generate that Brahmatej in the nation which will raise up the Kshatriya spirit to protect it. Without this Brahmatej, this spiritual force in our midst, all else will be vain; Swadeshi will cease, National Education fail, the great hopes and schemes now forming in our midst disappear like idle wreaths of smoke and the whole movement stain the pages of history as an abortive and premature impulse, a great chance of freedom lost because the body of the nation was not strong enough and the soul of the nation was not pure enough to sustain the tremendous inrush of spiritual force which had suddenly come upon it. Bepin Chandra stands before India as the exponent of the spiritual force of the movement, its pure 'Indianity', its high devotion to principle; this has been the kernel of his teaching, the secret of the almost miraculous force which often breathed from his eloquence. To give this message was the work particularly chosen for him. We need that message to be repeated in yet mightier language and with more convincing logic; the voice has been too long silent, the word of inspiration wanting. We welcome back today not Bepin Chandra Pal, but the speaker of a God-given message; not the man but the voice of the Gospel of Nationalism. He comes to us purified by an act of self-immolation, with a soul deepened by long hours of solitude and self-communion to repeat the word of hope and inspiration, to call us once more to the task of national self-realisation. Welcome to him and thrice welcome.

Bande Mataram, March 10, 1908

The Voice of the Martyrs

WE ARE now rejoicing over the release of Srijut Bepin Chandra Pal, but who among us is prepared to forget that so many have suffered for the country not less or more than he, and are still suffering? Yesterday when we welcomed the great orator, the man of high thoughts and inspired eloquence, the prophet of new ideas to his people, our thoughts went for a while to those who are now in British prisons, to Bhupen, to Basanta, to the Editor of the Barisal *Hitaishi* and the Rangpur *Vartabaha*, to the aged Moulavi spending the last years of his noble life in the severities of a criminal jail, to our fellow martyrs of East Bengal, to the few who are suffering in other provinces. For what are these men suffering? What was the hope that stirred them to face all rather than be unworthy of the light that had dawned in their hearts? No petty object fired their soul, no small or partial relief was the hope in which they were strong. It was the star of Swaraj that shone upon them from the darkness of the night into which they willingly departed, it is the light of Swaraj which creates a glory of effulgence in the squalid surroundings of the jail and makes each hour of enforced labour a sacrament and an offering on the most sacred of earthly altars. Today let us remember these brothers of ours even as yesterday was devoted to the joy of welcoming our beloved leader back into our midst. Today let us recall what it is that they expect from us; forgetting for a while our selfish preoccupations, our little fears, our petty ambitions, let us identify ourselves in heart with these nobler spirits whom it is our privilege to call fellow-countrymen, and ask ourselves whether we are really working to bring about the great ideal for which they have immolated themselves. Who is there who can really say that his work is worthy of these heroic martyrs? Prometheus chained to the rock and gnawed by the vulture's beak endured in the strong hope of man's final deliverance from the tyrant powers of the middle-heaven who sought to keep him from his divine destiny;

but the human race for whom he suffered forgot Prometheus, forgot the dazzling hope to which his life had pointed them and, involved in petty cares and mean ambitions, allowed their champion to suffer in vain and their destiny to call them to no purpose. We, like the woman whom Christ censured, the careful, prudent woman of the world, are busied with many things, but forget the one thing needful. We are waiting to see whether the Congress will be revived or not, or we are watching the progress of Swadeshi with self-satisfaction, or we are anxious for this or that National School, while the fight for Swaraj seems to have ceased or passed away from us into worthier hands. Madras has taken up the *herol* out of our hands, and today it is over Tuticorin that the gods of the Mahabharat hover in their aerial cars watching the chances of the fight which is to bring back the glorious days of old. Gallant Chidambaram, brave Padmanabha, intrepid Shiva defying the threats of exile and imprisonment; fighting for the masses, for the nation, for the preparation of Swaraj, these are now in the forefront, the men of the future, the bearers of the standard. The spirit of active heroism and self-immolation has travelled southward. In Bengal the spirit of passive endurance is all that seems to remain and the bold initiative, the fiery spirit that panted to advance is dead or sleeping. "Work, there is no need to aspire; labour for small things and the great will come in some future generation", is the spirit which seems to be in the ascendant. But the voices of the martyrs from their cells cry to us in a different key, "Work, but aspire, so that your work may be true to the call you have heard and which we have obeyed; labour for great things first and the small will come of themselves. Cherish the might of the spirit, the nobility of the ideal, the grandeur of the dream; the spirit will create the material it needs, the ideal will bring the real to its body and self-expression, the dream is the stuff out of which the waking world will be created. It was the strength of the spirit which stood with us before the alien tribunal, it was the force of the ideal which led us to the altar of sacrifice, it is the splendour of the dream which supports us through the dreary months and years of our martyrdom. For these are the truth and the divinity within the movement."

Constitution-making

Schemes for the constitution of the Congress are now being drawn up in various quarters but we fear that some important and indeed essential points are being lost sight of by the framers. A constitution may be drawn up with one of two motives, either to suit the convenience of a party or to assure the orderly and harmonious procedure of a representative assembly in which conflicting opinions are to be allowed free entrance. In the former case the country at large is not interested in the result, for a party organisation is free to make the arrangements most suitable to itself. But if the Congress is to be a Congress of all opinions and not of one section only, the Constitution must be so drafted as to remove the causes of quarrel which led up to the Surat fiasco. One of these was the conflict between authority and freedom in the proceedings of the session. The Moderates stand for official authority, the Nationalists for the freedom of debate and the rights of the delegate as a popular representative. The conflict between the Chairman of the Reception Committee and Mr. Tilak was on the issue whether the authority of the President or Chairman is absolute and autocratic or whether the individual delegate has a right to be heard according to the rules observed in all free assemblies and to appeal to the full assembly if his right is unjustly denied. The Moderates desire to establish a sort of official oligarchy in the Congress; the leaders officially recognised in previous years, must be implicitly obeyed; the voice of the President is to be absolute and final irrespective of the validity of his decision or the rights of free discussion. The Nationalists contend that the President is a servant of the Congress and not its master: — his function is to administer the rules of debate and not to make his own will and pleasure the law. There can be no doubt which attitude is in consonance with the practice of free peoples, the spirit of modern politics and the principles of democracy. Mr. Tilak has established his position by his articles in the *Kesari* and *Maratha* with the most crushing completeness and there is no possible answer to the array of authorities, precedents and sound argument which he has marshalled in those pieces of perfect political reasoning unrivalled in their force and clearness of exposition. Whoever wishes to draft a constitution for the Congress must take this great issue into consideration and lay down clearly, first the powers of the President and their limits, secondly the proper procedure with regard to the Subjects Committee, and thirdly, the rights of the delegates in full Congress as against the President and the Subjects Committee. We propose to take up this quesition of the constitution and deal with it at length, for it is a subject of immense importance and it is essential that those who handle it should try to grasp the principles involved. We wish to take the Congress seriously as a body which may and ought to form a seed out of which the future Indian Parliament must grow, and not a sham representative assembly meant for passing exigencies the constitution of which can be settled offhand.

What Committee?

There are signs that the compromise arrived at at Pabna will be ignored by the Moderates at Allahabad. We have received a communication from two leading gentlemen of Barisal enclosing a draft constitution for the Congress which seems to be a reply to another draft forwarded in the name of some Calcutta Committee. This is described in the forwarding letter as a committee of "our leaders". If it is the Calcutta Committee of the Surat Convention, it should have made its origin and nature clear while forwarding its views to the Mofussil. We are entirely unaware of any general Committee having been formed of the leaders in Calcutta which can speak authoritatively to Bengal, or of any draft constitution prepared by the common consent of Bengal's foremost men. The Convention Calcutta Committee met in secret and seem to have issued their draft in secret to a select few in the Mofussil. The Mofussil gentlemen who sent their draft appear to be under the impression that the leaders of the Nationalist Party are in the know. We must remind them that there are two Committees, one appointed by the Moderate Convention at Surat, the other by a meeting of the delegates pledged to the four Calcutta resolutions. No attempt to arrogate to the Convention Committee the sole inheritance of the Congress can succeed; and if the people of Bengal desire union on the lines of the Pabna resolution they must insist either on the All-India Congress Committee being entrusted with the work of reviving the Congress or on both the Surat Committees uniting to arrange the lines on which the Congress shall be reconstructed. A section has no right to lay down a law by which the whole will be bound and if they persist in the attempt they will be only inviting a permanent secession.

Bande Mataram, March 11, 1908

A Great Message

THE stupendous success of the reception to Srijut Bepin Chandra Pal, a success which outdid all previous occasions of the kind, was a convincing proof of the popular feeling and left no doubt in the minds of those who saw it that the nation is alive. We have always believed that God is at work in the hearts of the people to effect His mighty purpose. When Sj. Bepin Chandra spoke at College Square in answer to the welcome he received from the people of Calcutta, the same deep conviction breathed from his lips and expressed itself in words of an inspired fervour, "The man is nothing, the personality is nought, and it is a vain egoism to think that we are doing anything. There is One in whose hands we are instruments and puppets, One who directs all our motions." This is the conviction that the Prophet of Nationalism has brought with him from his deep self-communing in the solitude of the cell to which the enemies of Nationalism had consigned him. They sent him there in the hope of silencing for a while the mighty and inspiring voice which had stirred the heart of India and created a revolution in sentiment and opinion. But they were mere instruments in the hand of One who is ordering all things so that Asia may move steadily to its resurgence. He it was who secluded Bepin Chandra for a while from the stir and movement of the outside world so that his heart might be forced in on itself and lie open to the new thought which the nation must now learn, so that Nationalism may enter on a new chapter of its history. No farther progress, no new development is possible until the divine nature of the movement is thoroughly understood by those who have been selected to lead it. The one thing which can bring it to nought and drag this nation back into servitude is selfishness, weakness and egoism in those who are entrusted severally with different departments of the work which has to be done so that Swaraj may be fulfilled. It has therefore been made an indispensable condition of the success of the movement that those who lead it shall learn this lesson that it is God's movement and not theirs, that, as Bepin Chardra declared in his speech at College Square, the men are nothing, there is One who directs and controls all their movements. In the stir and clamour of the political struggle, in the clash of factions with their petty meannesses and paltry rancours, with the voice of thousands shouting accalmations to him as the creator of the movement, even so powerful a mind as Bepin Chandra's would have been led away and another might have been added to the mighty minds and strong personalities whom egoism has stopped short in their work for India and through India for the world. Therefore he was removed for a while from the busy scene which was so largely filled with his great personality and far-sounding eloquence, removed by a means which man would never have dreamed of, by a chain of petty circumstances which seemed mere fortuity so that for six months his soul might be alone with itself and he might take stock of his personal strength and weakness and realise that his strength was not his own but God's, his eloquence was not his own but God's, his fruitful, strong and subtle brain was not his own, but God's. When we heard him on Tuesday avow the struggle in his soul and its deep consequence, we felt once more convinced of the divine workings. All great teachers have to go through this hour of lonely self-communion and deep mental travail in order that they may learn the nature of their commission and whence it proceeds. It is only after this hour has come to them that their mission really begins, and all that went before was merely a preparation for that hour; for they must feel the power within them before they can realise who gave them the power. Bepin Chandra went to prison, — the leader of a section and the spokesman of a party; but if he lives in the revelation he has received in his sojourn in the desert, he will be in future something far greater, and become the prophet and inspirer of a nation consecrated to that mission by a power whose wisdom will lead him and whose strength will protect throughout the struggle that lies in front. Others, we hope, will realise the meaning of the words which fell from him in his first utterance after his return. There are many powerful spirits now in the ranks of Nationalism who have also their share of the work, some of whom are still under the influence of egoism and believe that by their own skill, courage and ability they will bring the movement to a success. Unless they learn the lesson which Bepin Chandra has learned, they will be in danger of misleading the people and themselves being withdrawn from the field as unfit instruments. To them as to all this country it was a great and necessary message that the foremost man among us has delivered as the word that God spoke to him in the silence of his prison.

Bande Mataram, March 12, 1908

The Tuticorin Victory

THE success of passive resistance at Tuticorin ought to be an encouragement to those who have begun to distrust the power of the new weapon which is so eminently suited to the Asiatic temperament. When the Boycott was declared in Bengal, the whole of the energy of the people was thrown into the attempt to get the Partition repealed and if that concentration of effort had been continued, the Partition would by this time have become an unsettled fact; but for two different reasons the attempt to unsettle the Partition was unstrung and the energy diverted to a different goal. In the first place, a great thought entered into the heart of the people and displaced the petty indignation against an administrative measure which was the immediate cause of the Boycott. Swaraj displaced the idea of a mere administrative unity and Swaraj is too mighty an object to be effected by a single and limited means. Secondly, the first magnificent unity of the movement was lost. The Mahomedans, lured by specious promises, broke away from the ranks and within the circle of the leaders themselves a division arose between those who believed in Swaraj pure and unadulterated and those whom policy or caution dissuaded from so mighty an aspiration. For passive resistance to succeed unity, perseverance and thoroughness are the first requisites. Because this unity, perseverance and thoroughness existed in Tuticorin, the great battle fought over the Coral Mill has ended in a great and indeed absolutely sweeping victory for the people. Every claim made by the strikers has been conceded and British capital has had to submit to the humiliation of an unconditional surrender. Nationalism may well take pride in the gallant leaders who have by their cool and unflinching courage brought about this splendid vindication of Nationalist teaching. When men like Chidambaram, Padmanabha and Shiva are ready to undergo exile or imprisonment so that a handful of mill coolies may get justice and easier conditions of livelihood, a bond has been created between the educated class and the masses, which is the first great step towards Swaraj.

There has been only one other instance of a victory as complete for passive resistance against the might of a great Government. We refer to the struggle in the Transvaal which was carried on with equal unity, perseverance and thoroughness to a success less absolutely unconditional but even more striking from the strength and stubbornness of the enemy it had to overcome. We publish in another column a letter from a brother in the Transvaal on the subject. The conditions of political struggle in the Transvaal are different, the objects less vast than those of the movement in India. The Transvaal Indians demand only the ordinary rights of human beings in modern civilised society, the right to live, the right to trade, to be treated like human beings and not like cattle. In India which is our own country, our aspirations have a larger sweep and our methods must be more varied and strenuous. Moreover, in the Transvaal the Asiatics form a small and distinct community in a foreign and hostile environment and can more easily rise above petty differences of creed and caste, opinion and interest; but in this vast continent with its huge population of thirty crores and its complex tangle of diversities the task is more difficult, even as the prize of success is more splendid. The unity will be longer in coming, the perseverance more difficult to maintain, the thoroughness less perfect; but the might of three hundred millions welded into a single force will be a potency so gigantic that the imagination fails to put a limit to the final results of the movement now in its infancy.

Meanwhile, the lesson of Tuticorin, the lesson of the Transvaal is one which needs to be learnt and put frequently into practice. We should lose no opportunity of letting our strength grow by practice. There have been many labour struggles in Bengal, but with the exception of the Printers' strike none has ended in a victory for Indian labour against British capital. Either the unity among the operatives was defective or the support of the public was absent or the perseverance and thoroughness of the strike was marred by hesitations, individual submissions, partial concessions. The Tuticorin strike is a perfect example of what an isolated labour revolt should be. The operatives must act with one will and speak with one voice, never letting the temptation of individual interest or individual relief get the better of the corporate aim in which lies the whole strength of a labour combination, and the educated community must give both moral and financial support with an ungrudging and untiring enthusiasm till the victory is won, realising that every victory for Indian labour is a victory for the nation and every defeat a defeat to the movement. The Tuticorin leaders must be given the whole credit for the unequalled skill and courage with which the fight was conducted and sill more for the complete realisation of the true inwardness of the Nationalist gospel which made them identify the interests of the whole Indian nation with the wrongs and grievances of the labourers in the Coral Mill.

Bande Mataram, March 13, 1908

Perpetuate the Split!

The Mehtaist Press in Western India seems to be unable to make up its mind for a compromise or against a compromise. It cannot conceal its repugnance to the idea of giving up its darling scheme of excluding the Nationalists from the Congress or the creed which Mr. Gokhale had so skilfully drawn up for that purpose. On the other hand, the Pabna Conference has filled it with dismay, for it perceives a force in Bengal which may prove strong enough to separate the Bengal Moderate leaders from the ranks of pure Moderatism in this crucial matter. It is curious that while trying to throw the whole blame of the Surat fiasco on the Nationalists, the Bombay Moderates have never concealed the fact that it was their intention to jockey the Nationalists out of the Congress. Their chief organ openly declared that it had been the Moderate plan to get rid of passive resistance and other Extremist heresies which had been read into the Calcutta resolution by the Extremists. The *Gujerati* is equally plain about the creed, its object is to get rid of the spectre of Swaraj by exorcism and the creed is the magic formula which is to drive Swaraj and Swarajists out of the National Assembly. Mr. R. C. Dutt has declared that the split was a consummation much to be desired and must be perpetuated and the *Gujerati* heartily endorses the sentiment. The Pabna Conference, it contends, was a got-up affair arranged by Mr. Tilak, and so its opinion has no value. The Mahomedans and Parsis will join the movement if the Nationalists are driven out and the British Public and British Government are, according to Babu Bhupendranath Bose, an excellent authority, deeply interested in seeing the creed preserved. For all these reasons let the creed be preserved. We wonder whether these cogent reasons will confirm the wavering allegiance of Srijut Surendranath Banerji and his followers and keep them in the Mehtaist fold! They ought at least to show unprejudiced people all over the country who were really desirous of the split and with what motives it was engineered.

Loyalty to Order

The action of the Bharat Dharma Mandal in presenting themselves before the Viceroy as representatives of Hindu Society and offering their loyalty and the post of defender of the Hindu faith has been so severely criticised by the vernacular Press in Calcutta that it would be unkindness to add a final stroke. We cannot refrain, however, from reminding the Mahamandal that the foundations of Hinduism are truth and manhood, *eṣa dharmaḥ sanātanaḥ*. Hinduism is no sect or dogmatic creed, no bundle of formulas, no set of social rules, but a mighty, eternal and universal truth. It has learned the secret of preparing man's soul for the divine consummation of identity with the infinite existence of God; rules of life and formulas of belief are only sacred and useful when they help that great preparation. And the first rule of life is that man must live the highest life of which he is capable, overcoming selfishness, overcoming fear, overcoming the temptation to palter with truth in order to earn earthly favours. The first formula of belief is *satyānnāsti paro dharmaḥ*, there is no higher law of conduct than truth. We leave it to the conscience of the Mahamandal to decide how much of truth and manhood there was in their demonstration of loyalty and their ridiculous appeal to a representative of Western materialism and practical atheism to defend Hinduism and its institutions.

Bande Mataram, March 14, 1908

Asiatic Democracy

ASIA is not Europe and never will be Europe. The political ideals of the West are not the mainspring of the political movements in the East, and those who do not realise this great truth, are mistaken; for they suppose that the history of Europe is a sure and certain guide to India in her political development. A great deal of the political history of Europe will be repeated in Asia, no doubt; Democracy has travelled from the East to the West in the shape of Christianity, and after a long struggle with the feudal instincts of the Germanic races has returned to Asia transformed and in a new body. But when Asia takes back democracy into herself she will first transmute it in her own temperament and make it once more Asiatic. Christianity was an assertion of human equality in the spirit, a great assertion of the unity of the divine spirit in man, which did not seek to overthrow the established systems of government and society but to inform them with the spirit of human brotherhood and unity. It was greatly hampered in this work by the fact that the European races were in a state of transition from the old Aryan civilisation of Greece and Rome to one less advanced and enlightened. The German nations were wedded to a military civilisation which was wholly inconsistent with the ideals of Christianity, and the new religion in their hands became a thing quite unrecognisable to the Asiatic mind which had engendered it. When Mahomedanism appeared, Christianity vanished out of Asia, because it had lost its meaning. Mahomed tried to re-establish the Asiatic gospel of human equality in the spirit. All men are equal in Islam, — whatever their social position or political power, — nor is any man debarred from the full development of his manhood by his birth or low original station in life. All men are brothers in Islam and the bond of religious unity overrides all other divisions and differences. But Islam also was limited and imperfect, because it confined the ideal of brotherhood and equality to the limits of a single creed, and was further deflected from its true path by the rude and undeveloped races which it drew into its embrace. Another revelation of the old truth is needed.

India from ancient times had received the gospel of Vedanta which sought to establish the divine unity of man in spirit; but in order to secure an ordered society in which she could develop her spiritual insight and perfect her civilisation, she had invented the system of caste which by corruptions and departures from caste ideals came to be an obstacle to the fulfilment in society of the Vedantic ideal. From the time of Buddha to that of the saints of Maharashtra every great religious awakening has sought to restore the ancient meaning of Hinduism and reduce caste to its original subordinate importance as a social convenience, to exorcise the spirit of caste-pride and restore that of brotherhood and the eternal principles of love and justice in society. But the feudal spirit had taken possession of India and the feudal spirit is wedded to inequality and the pride of caste.

When the feudal system was broken in Europe by the rise of the middle class, the ideals of Christianity began to emerge once more to light, but by this time the Christian Church had itself become feudalised, and the curious spectacle presents itself of Christian ideals struggling to establish themselves by the destruction of the very institution which had been created to preserve Christianity. When the ideals of liberty, equality and fraternity were declared at the time of the French Revolution and mankind demanded that society should recognise them as the foundation of its structure, they were associated with a fierce revolt against the relics of feudalism and against the travesty of the Christian religion which had become an integral part of that feudalism. This was the weakness of European democracy and the source of its failure. It took as its motive the rights of man and not the *dharma* of humanity; it appealed to the selfishness of the lower classes against the pride of the upper; it made hatred and internecine war the permanent allies of Christian ideals and wrought an inextricable confusion which is the modern malady of Europe. It was in vain that the genius of Mazzini rediscovered the heart of Christianity and sought to remodel European ideas; the French Revolution had become the starting-point of European democracy and coloured the European mind. Now that democracy has returned to Asia, its cradle and home, it will be purged of its foreign elements and restored to its original purity. The movements of the nineteenth century in India were European movements, they were coloured with the hues of the West. Instead of seeking for strength in the spirit, they adopted the machinery and motives of Europe, the appeal to the rights of humanity or the equality of social status and an impossible dead level which Nature has always refused to allow. Mingled with these false gospels was a strain of hatred and bitterness, which showed itself in the condemnation of Brahminical priestcraft, the hostility to Hinduism and the ignorant breaking away from the hallowed traditions of the past. What was true and eternal in that past was likened to what was false or transitory, and the nation was in danger of losing its soul by an insensate surrender to the aberrations of European materialism. Not in this spirit was India intended to receive the mighty opportunity which the impact of Europe gave to her. When the danger was greatest, a number of great spirits were sent to stem the tide flowing in from the West and recall her to her mission; for, if she had gone astray the world would have gone astray with her.

Her mission is to point back humanity to the true source of human liberty, human equality, human brotherhood. When man is free in spirit, all other freedom is at his command; for the Free is the Lord who cannot be bound. When he is liberated from delusion, he perceives the divine equality of the world which fulfils itself through love and justice, and this perception transfuses itself into the law of government and society. When he has perceived this divine equality, he is brother to the whole world, and in whatever position he is placed he serves all men as his brothers by the law of love, by the law of justice. When this perception becomes the basis of religion, of philosophy, of social speculation and political aspiration, then will liberty, equality and fraternity take their place in the structure of society and the *satya-yuga* return. This is the Asiatic reading of democracy which India must rediscover for herself before she can give it to the world. It is the *dharma* of every man to be free in soul, bound to service not by compulsion but by love; to be equal in spirit, apportioned his place in society by his capacity to serve society, not by the interested selfishness of others; to be in harmonious relations with his brother men, linked to them by mutual love and service, not by shackles of servitude, or the relations of the exploiter and the exploited, the eater and the eaten. It has been said that democracy is based on the rights of man; it has been replied that it should rather take its stand on the duties of man; but both rights and duties are European ideas. *Dharma* is the Indian conception in which rights and duties lose the artificial antagonism created by a view of the world which makes selfishness the root of action, and regain their deep and eternal unity. *Dharma* is the basis of democracy which Asia must recognise, for in this lies the distinction between the soul of Asia and the soul of Europe. Through *dharma* the Asiatic evolution fulfils itself; this is her secret.

Charter or no Charter

We have already said what we had to say on Mrs. Besant's idea of a National University. In her speech on Education delivered at the Corinthian Theatre, she referred again to the subject of the Charter and invited the National Council of Education to get a Royal Charter to confer degrees. She gave the instance of the English Universities which have got such a Charter from the King, but "it did not follow that those Universities were under Government control, the Charter being but a guarantee for the education which the University undertook to give". It is surprising that so acute an intellect as Mrs. Besant should not perceive the fallacy of appealing to English precedents. An arrangement which works in England for the benefit of the country, may easily be worked in India to its disadvantage, for the simple reason that in India the interests of the governing bureaucracy and the people are not identical, while in England the people and the Government are one. Socialistic State control may work well in England, in India it means the control of public business in the interests of a small and alien caste. So with the proposed Charter. Mrs. Besant gives away her case when she admits that the

Charter is a guarantee for the education given in the University. Certainly, the authority having the guarantee has the right to see that the guarantee is not abused and that the education is up to a standard consistent with the dignity of a Royal Charter. This means at least potential State control. In England the control is not exercised, because no public interest can be served by interfering with the work of the educational experts who conduct these Universities, but if the Universities were to fall very much behind in their educational standard, it is conceivable that the potential right of interference might be exercised. If the National Council of Education were to get a Royal Charter, this potential right of interference would be in the hands of the authority issuing the Charter, in other words, with the King, which means, for India, with the Secretary of State, which again means with the Anglo-Indian bureaucracy; and we know how that bureaucracy would be likely to use the power. At any moment the Council might have to face the alternative of either accepting practical control by officialdom or sacrificing the Charter; this would mean a crisis which might wreck the new education altogether. Quite apart, therefore, from the sacrifice of that principle of robust independence and faith in its own future which is its true strength, the Council would be guilty of an impolitic step, if it accepted, much more if it asked for a Charter. The latter idea is indeed inconceivable. The exclusion of the Council's students from the learned professions means only exclusion from the Government service and the Law, and it is more wholesome for the new institution to be removed from these temptations till it is strong enough to make these professions seek for its students instead of its students seeking for them. The hankering after a Charter is born of weakness and deficient faith; it will be no gain to National Education and may easily be fatal to it.

Bande Mataram, March 16, 1908

The Warning from Madras

The outbreak at Tinnevelly is significant as a warning both to the authorities and to the leaders of the popular party. For the bureaucracy, if they have eyes to see or ears to hear, it should be an index of the fierceness of the fire which is burning underneath a thin crust of patience and sufferance and may at any moment lead to a general conflagration. Whence does this fire come or what does it signify? It is a suddenly blazing fire of straw, say the bureaucrats, kindled by the hands of mischievous agitators; it means nothing except that the authors of the mischief must be vigorously repressed. Even if this were true, it is at least a subject which might well cause reflection in minds not blinded by selfish infatuation why it is so easily kindled, why it blazes out so fiercely and in so many places far apart from each other. Some years ago agitators might have spoken themselves hoarse and yet there would have been no such upsurging of the population of a whole city in reckless revolt against established authority. Still more significant is the defiant spirit of the people which neither the imprisonment of the leaders, nor the shots of the military could quell, but rather lashed into fiercer rage. This is no light fire of straw, but a jet of volcanic fire from the depths, and that has never in the world's history been conquered by repression. Cover it up, trample it down, it may seem to sink for a moment, but that is only because part of the imprisoned flame has escaped; every day of repression gives it a greater volume and prepares a mightier explosion. To the popular leaders it is a warning of the necessity to put their house in order, to provide a settled leading and so much organisation as is possible so that the movement may arrive at a consciousness of ordered strength. At Tuticorin it was the inspiring voices, the cheerful and confident faces, the strong and calm example of their leaders in which the people felt their strength, and enabled them also to act with a restrained enthusiasm and a settled courage. The removal of that inspiring, yet quieting force, led inevitably to the resort to violence which has startled the whole country by its devastating fierceness, — though at the same time it was mild enough compared with what an European mob would have done at a similar pitch of excitement. Throughout the country the same fire is burning or beginning to burn and where it has gathered force, it can only be calm and restrained so long as it feels either that it is well led or that it is developing an ordered strength. Any weakness, any failure of a serious kind on the part of the leaders will be the signal for storms before which the 'unrest', so alarming to English politicians, will prove a mere bagatelle. It is only conscious strength, it is only organised courage that can afford to be calm and patient. This is not the time to be inventing creeds and constitutions which a year or two will tear into shreds, but to recognise facts, to put ourselves in touch with the present and make ourselves strong to control the future.

Bande Mataram, March 17, 1908

The Need of the Moment

ALL that we do and attempt proceeds from faith, and if we are deficient in faith nothing can be accomplished. When we are deficient in faith our work begins to flag and failure is frequent; but if we have faith things are done for us. No great work has ever been done without this essential courage. Misled by egoism, we believe that we are working, that the results of what we do are our creation, and when anything has to be done we ask ourselves whether we have the strength, the means, the requisite qualities, but in reality all work is done by the will of God and when faith in Him is the mainspring of our actions, success is inevitable. Sometimes we wish a thing very intensely and our wish is accomplished. The wish was in fact a prayer, and all sincere prayer receives its answer. It need not be consciously addressed to God, because prayer is not a form of words but an aspiration. If we aspire, we pray. But the aspiration must be absolutely unselfish, not alloyed by the thought of petty advantages or lower aims if it is to succeed. When we mingle self with our aspirations, we weaken to that extent the strength of the prayer and the success is proportionately less.

Whoever believes in God, rises above his lower self; for God is the true Self of the Universe and of everything within the Universe. When we rely upon our lower self, we are left to that lower self, and succeed or fail according to our strength of body or intellect under the law of our past life and actions. There is one law for the lower self and another for the higher. The lower self is in bondage to its past; the higher is lord of the past, the present and the future. So the will of the lower self is born of *ahaṅkāra* and limited by *ahaṅkāra*, but the will of the higher self is beyond *ahaṅkāra* and cannot be limited by it. It is omnipotent. But so long as it works through the body, it works under the laws of time, space and causality and we have to wait for its fulfilment till the time is ready, the environment prepared, the immediate causes brought about. The will once at work infallibly brings about the necessary conditions; all we have to do is to allow it to work.

Apply this great psychological law to what is happening in India. The aspiration towards freedom has for some time been working in some hearts, but they relied on their own strength for the creation of the necessary conditions and they failed. Of those who worked, some gave up the work, others persisted, a few resorted to *tapasyā*, the effort to awake in themselves a higher Power to which they might call for help. The *tapasyā* of those last had its effect unknown to themselves, for they were pouring out a selfless aspiration into the world, and the necessary conditions began to be created. When these conditions were far advanced, the second class who worked on began to think that it was the result of their efforts, but the secret springs were hidden from them. They were merely the instruments through which the purer aspiration of their old friends fulfilled itself.

If the conditions of success are to be yet more rapidly brought about, it must be by yet more of the lovers of freedom withdrawing themselves from the effort to work through the lower self. The aspiration of these strong souls purified from self will create fresh workers in the field, infuse the great desire for freedom in the heart of the nation and hasten the growth of the necessary material strength.

What is needed now is a band of spiritual workers whose *tapasyā* will be devoted to the liberation of India for the service of humanity. The few associations already started have taken another turn and devoted themselves to special and fragmentary work. We need an institution in which under the guidance of highly spiritual men workers will be trained for every field, workers for self-defence, workers for arbitration, for sanitation, for famine relief, for every species of work which is needed to bring about the necessary conditions for the organisation of Swaraj. If the country is to be free, it must first organise itself so as to be able to maintain its freedom. The winning of freedom is an easy task, the keeping of it is less easy. The first needs only one tremendous effort in which all the energies of the country must be concentrated; the second requires a united, organised and settled strength. If these two conditions are satisfied, nothing more is needed, for all else is detail and will inevitably follow.

For the first condition the requisite is a mighty selfless faith and aspiration filling the hearts of men as in the day of Mazzini. For the second, India, which has no Piedmont to work out her salvation, requires to organise her scattered strengths into a single and irresistible whole.

For both these ends an institution of the kind we have named is essential. The force of a great stream of aspiration must be poured over the country, which will sweep away as in a flood the hesitations, the selfishnesses, the fears, the self-distrust, the want of fervour and the want of faith which stand in the way of the spread of the great national awakening of 1905. A mightier fountain of the spirit must be prepared from which this stream of aspiration can be poured to fertilise the heart of the nation. When this is done, the aspiration towards liberty will become universal and India be ready for the great effort.

The organisation of Swaraj can only be effected by a host of selfless workers who will make it their sole life-work. It cannot be done by men whose best energies and time are given up to the work of earning their daily bread and only the feeble remnant to their country. The work is enormous, the time is short, but the workers are few. One institution is required which will train and support men to help those who are now labouring under great disadvantages to organise education, to build up the life of the villages, to spread the habit of arbitration, to help the people in time of famine and sickness, to preach Swadeshi. These workers must be selfless, free from the desire to lead or shine, devoted to the work for the country's sake, absolutely obedient yet full of energy. They must breathe the strength of the spirit, of selfless faith and aspiration derived from the spiritual guides of the institution. The material is ready and even plentiful, but the factory which will make use of the material has yet to be set on foot. When the man comes, who is commissioned by God to do it, we must be ready to recognise him.

Bande Mataram, March 18, 1908

The Early Indian Polity

THE principle of popular rule is the possession of the reins of government by the mass of the people, but by the possession is not intended necessarily the actual exercise of administration. When the people are able to approve or to disapprove of any action of the Government with the certainty that such approval or disapproval will be absolutely effective, the spirit of democracy is present even if the body is not evolved. India in her ancient polity possessed this spirit of democracy. Like all Aryan nations she started with the three great divisions of the body politic, King, Lords and Commons, which have been the sources of the various forms of government evolved by the modern nations. In the period of the Mahabharata we find that the King is merely the head of the race, possessed of executive power but with no right to legislate and even in the exercise of his executive functions unable to transgress by a hair's breadth the laws which are the sum of the customs of the race. Even within this limited scope he cannot act in any important matter without consulting the chief men of the race who are usually the elders and warriors; often he is a cipher, a dignified President, an ornamental feature of the polity which is in the hands of the nobles. His position is that of first among equals, not that of an absolute prince or supreme ruler. We find this conception of kingship continued till the present day in the Rajput States; at Udaipur, for instance, no alienation of land can take place without the signature of all the nobles; although the Maharaja is the head of the State, the sacred descendant of the Sun, his power is a delegated authority. The rule of the King is hereditary, but only so long as he is approved of by the people. A tyrannical king can be resisted, an unfit heir can be put aside on the representation of the Commons. This idea of kingship is the old Aryan idea, it is limited monarchy and not the type of despotism which is called by the Western writers Oriental, though it existed for centuries in Europe and has never been universal in Asia.

The Council of Chiefs is a feature of Indian polity universal in the time of the Mahabharata. That great poem is full of accounts of the meetings of these Councils and some of the most memorable striking events of the story are there transacted. The *Udyoga Parva* especially gives detailed accounts of the transactions of these Council meetings with the speeches of the princely orators. The King sits as President, hears both sides and seems to decide partly on his own responsibility, partly according to the general sense of the assembly. The opinion of the Council was not decided by votes, an invention of the Greeks, but as in the older Aryan systems, was taken individually from each Councillor. The King was the final arbiter and responsible for the decision, except in nations like the Yadavas where he seems to have been little more than an ornamental head of an aristocratic polity.

Finally, the Commons in the Mahabharata are not represented by any assembly, because the times are evidently a period of war and revolution in which the military caste had gained an abnormal preponderance. The opinion of the people expresses itself in public demonstrations of spontaneous character, but does not seem to have weighed with the proud and self-confident nobles who ruled them. This feature of the Mahabharata is obviously peculiar to the times, for we find that the Buddhist records preserve to us the true form of ancient Indian polity. The nations among whom Buddha lived were free communities in which the people assembled as in Greek and Italian States to decide their own affairs. A still more striking instance of the political existence of the Commons is to be found in the Ramayana. We are told that on the occasion of the association of Rama as Yuvaraj in the government, Dasaratha summoned a sort of States General of the Realm to which delegates of the different provinces and various orders, religious, military and popular were summoned in order to give their sanction to the act of the King. A speech from the throne is delivered in which the King states the reasons for his act, solicits the approval of his people and in case of their refusal of sanction, asks them to meet the situation by a counter proposal of their own. The assembly then meets "separately and together", in other words, the various Orders of the Realm consult first among themselves and then together and decide to give their sanction to the King's proposal.

The growth of large States in India was fatal to the continuance of the democratic element in the constitution. The idea of representation had not yet been developed, and without the principle of representation democracy is impossible in a large State. The Greeks were obliged to part with their cherished liberty as soon as large States began to enter into the Hellenic world; the Romans were obliged to change their august and cherished institutions for the most absolute form of monarchy as soon as they had become a great Empire; and democracy disappeared from the world until the slow development of the principle of representation enabled the spirit of democracy to find a new body in which it could be reborn. The contact with Greek and Persian absolutism seems to have developed in India the idea of the divinity of Kinghood which had always been a part of the Aryan system; but while the Aryan King was divine because he was the incarnate life of the race, the new idea saw a divinity in the person of the King as an individual, — a conception which favoured the growth of absolutism. The monarchy of Chandragupta and Asoka seems to have been of the new type, copied perhaps from the Hellenistic empires, in which the nobles and the commons have disappeared and a single individual rules with absolute power through the instrumentality of officials. The Hindu King, however, never became a despot like the Caesars, he never grasped the power of legislation but remained the executor of laws over which he had no control nor could he ignore the opinion of the people. When most absolute, he has existed only to secure the order and welfare of society, and has never enjoyed immunity from resistance or the right to disregard the representations of his subjects. The pure absolutist type of monarchy entered India with the Mahomedans who had taken it from Europe and Persia, and it has never been accepted in its purity by the Hindu temperament.

***Bande Mataram*, March 20, 1908**

The Fund for Sj. Pal

THE question of a fund for Srijut Bepin Chandra Pal was raised at first in a private way and without the idea of a public appeal, but as soon as it was suggested to the leaders of the Nationalist Party, they rejected the idea of any action which would seem like an appeal to the private charity of the friends, admirers and sympathisers of Srijut Bepin Chandra. They resolved to ask the public for funds to present to Srijut Pal as a recognition of his services to the country well knowing that he would insist on the money being utilised for further service to his country instead of for his own personal benefit. Nevertheless certain friends and fellow-workers are under the impression that the purse will be a personal gift to the Nationalist leader to be used for his personal benefit, and they have questioned the suitability of the form which the appreciation of his services has taken. Among others Sj. Rabindranath Tagore while associating himself with the appeal wrote to us suggesting that the question of the advisability of introducing this European form of material recognition into the more spiritual atmosphere of India might be publicly discussed in our columns. The question is an important one and since it is likely to recur as our political life develops, it is as well to clear the air from the beginning.

The principle of rewarding distinguished public services by material forms of recognition as well as by honours and titles is common to East and West, not only so but rank and title were usually associated with the gift of an estate or Jagir to support the expenditure suitable to the rank and the dignity of the title. Sometimes gifts of land were given by the State without any fresh rank or title either as a reward or as a security for future service. In modern times the State has no land to give and the only material appreciation it can show of great merit or distinguished services is either a pension or annuity for the former or a vote of money for the latter. An annuity serves the purpose of securing a man of ability against want and enabling him to devote himself entirely to the work which has procured him the recognition and therefore serves the purpose of securing the future services to the community once guaranteed by the State gift of land. The vote of money on the other hand is usually given to a distinguished man who is above want and is a substitute for the Jagir of feudal times. No European soldier or statesman, however great his position, his rank or his wealth, would consider it a degradation to accept such a gift from the nation.

In India the State is not the people, and the servants of the people are likely to fall under the displeasure of the State to be persecuted and even ruined by official wrath rather than to enjoy honours, dignities and rewards at its hands. It is therefore the duty of the people to show its own appreciation of their services, not because they demand such recognition, but as a duty to itself and an assertion of its own dignity and claims. Many of those who suffer for its sake are ruined by the persecution of the bureaucrats and leave their families to want or even to destitution, and in such cases the people are bound to come to their assistance. Such funds as the Basanta Bhattacharya Fund belong to this category, and there can be no question about their fitness, nor can any blot come to the honour of the recipient by his acceptance. But public vote of money to a leader falls under a different head and introduces new questions of propriety. There can be no question either of the right of the public to offer such a substantial mark of recognition or of this right under certain circumstances becoming a duty; and until the new movement there would have been no question of the propriety of a public leader accepting such a gift; for in those days the standard was a Western standard and whatever was held right and honourable by the Western standard, was necessarily right and honourable in Indian politics. But the new movement has abolished the Western standard and returns to national ideals and principles. The first question is whether the public ought to be allowed to give a purse, the second whether the leader should accept it. To the first question the answer is that the purse takes the place of the feudal Jagir which either secures the services of ability by placing it above want or is meant as a substantial recognition of past services. The public is entitled to adopt this form because there is no other, except such titles and honours as have been given by common consent to men like Raja Subodh Chandra Mallik or the brilliant but passing honour of a public reception. But this right is limited by the obligation not to demoralise the people's servants, not to stain the purity of their motives or lower the high ideal of self-sacrifice and self-effacement which is growing up in our midst. The new servant of the people is a different type from the old political leader. He is as often as not a man who is poor, without resources, pursued by difficulties in his private life, yet is debarred from devoting himself to earning his private bread except by such occupations as are themselves an act of service to the people. This poverty, this indigence is the glory of the man and his great honour. Such an ideal, like that of the Brahmin, is a possession of great price which should not be lightly thrown away. If the presentation of a purse destroys it, then this form of recognition should be eschewed. But how then is the public to mark its sense of appreciation, to put something in the balance against the material injuries which the bureaucracy have it in their power to inflict just as they are able to outweigh the moral stigma of the jail or legal condemnation by marks of their love and admiration? The solution lies in such rare instances as that of Sj. Bepin Chandra in the public exercising its right and leaving it to the representative of the New Spirit to deal with their gift in the new spirit. We expect the people of India to show by the substantial nature of the purse their high appreciation of the services of the great Nationalist leader, of his noble self-immolation and of the oppressive nature of the monstrous sentence which was inflicted upon him. They may safely leave it to Sj. Bepin Chandra to make such a disposition of their gift as will effect the purpose for which it was given and yet preserve the ideal purity of the standards which he himself has done so much to bring into public favour and acceptance.

Bande Mataram, March 21, 1908

The Weapon of Secession

THERE has been much talk recently of drawing up a constitution for the Congress, but even if we are able to decide the question of the constitution, the next step before us will be to carry it out. To think that a paper constitution will help to bring about peace between the parties, is to ignore the fact that men are swayed by feelings and not by machinery. Paper constitutions have always failed to effect their object, except when they are in harmony with the feeling of the nation and express the actual situation in their arrangements. Whatever constitution we may draw up, must be one which will suit the conditions of the country and meet the difficulties of the present crisis. We propose to go into the question from time to time and deal with the chief points which in our opinion ought to be decided in order to form a real starting-point for the fresh life of the Congress. The first and initially essential question is the object of the Congress, the function which it proposes to discharge and the aim which it sets before itself. We agree with the Moderates that this is the first point on which a clear understanding is necessary, but we do not follow them in their contention that the decision of this question need imply the exclusion of all who differ from the precise terms in which it is decided. The Congress is an expression of the life of the nation, and the will and aspiration of the nation must decide the function and object of the Congress; but that will and aspiration are not immutable; they develop, change, progress, and it is always the function of the dissentient minority to stand for that potential development and progress without which life is impossible. The exclusion of the minority by a rigid shibboleth means the perpetuation in the Congress of a state of things which may correspond for the moment to the desire of the nation, but may cease so to correspond in a few years. It means the conversion of a national assembly into a party caucus.

The function of the Congress has hitherto been to pass inoperative resolutions, its aim to influence British opinion. Needless to say, the originators were men of ability and wide views, and they had an ulterior object in instituting this body and giving it the shape it took. The situation in India as they envisaged it, resembled that of the patricians and plebeians in Rome; for they accepted the permanence of British control almost as a law of Nature though they were anxious to alter its conditions. A caste of white patricians arrogated the control of the State in all its functions and effected an inborn social superiority accompanied not only by an intolerable arrogance and aloofness but often by actual brutality; yet it was the indigenous mass that supplied the sinews of war and did the substantial work which secured the peaceful and efficient conduct of the administration. The political and social grievances were farther accentuated by the economical sufferings of the proletariat, which were largely caused by the selfish policy of the ruling caste. Yet there was no legal or constitutional means of redress, the people had no votes, no means of checking directly or indirectly either executive or legislature, no power over the purse. The only force at their command was the vague strength of public opinion. The object of the Indian leaders, like that of the Roman plebeians, was to give a definite form to that public opinion, — focus it, as it is commonly expressed, and, secondly, to make that definitely formulated opinion effective. In each case a new body was formed within the State which served the purpose of formulating popular sentiment with a view to bring pressure on the ruling caste and bring about a change in political conditions. But while the Roman comitia became a new sovereign assembly in the State, existing side by side with the already recognised organs of Government, invested with full legislative powers, governing by means of plebiscites or resolutions of the people and appointing magistrates of its own who were empowered to exercise a check on every action, legislative, executive or fiscal of the Government, the Congress has remained from beginning to end a nullity. The difference lay partly in the conditions, partly in the means employed.

The originators of the Congress had undoubtedly before them an object very similar to that of their Roman prototypes.

The Congress has sometimes been described as His Majesty's permanent Opposition; but the aim of the originators was to make it something less futile than a mere meeting of powerless critics; they certainly hoped that the plebiscites or resolutions of the Congress would eventually come to have a sovereign force and translate themselves almost automatically into laws. But they took no sufficient notice of the immense difference in the conditions of a struggle for popular rights which is introduced by the foreign character of the ruling caste. There can always be an accommodation between the contending factions or classes within the same nationality, even though the accommodation may not come till after a severe and even violent struggle, but when the ruling caste is a caste of foreigners, it is unlikely to give up its powers, on any lesser compulsion than the alternative of extinction and will often prefer extinction to surrender. Even when the Congress leaders discovered that the bureaucracy were implacable and irreconcilable, they did not lay their hands on the right source of strength. The bureaucracy in India is in itself weak and powerless; it subsists greatly by the acquiescence and support of the people, partly by the existence behind it of the strength of the British Empire. The Congress leaders saw only the second source of its strength and sought to cut it off by depriving the bureaucracy of the moral support of the British public. Their initial miscalculation pursued them. They forgot that the British justice to which they appealed was foreign justice, the justice of alien to alien, of self-satisfied and arrogant masters to discontented dependents with whom they have no bonds of blood, culture, religion or social life. Justice might be on their side, but nature and self-interest were against them. Therefore they failed.

The real strength of their position lay in the other source of bureaucratic security, the acquiescence and support of the people. As at Rome, so in India the ruling caste cannot last for a moment except by this aid and acquiescence of the plebeian mass and when the plebeian leaders found their rulers deaf to the opinions and loudly-expressed feelings of the oppressed populace, they discovered an infallible weapon, a *brahmāstra* of peaceful political struggle, the weapon of secession. They gave the patricians notice that they would cease to give their aid and acquiescence to the patrician rule and would form a new city over against Rome. In India, by force of a similar situation, we rediscovered this weapon of secession. For boycott is nothing but this secession; we threaten to secede industrially, educationally, politically, to refuse our aid and acquiescence to the maintenance of British exploitation and British education and British administration in India, and build ourselves a new city, a State within the State, by creating our own industries, our own schools and colleges, our own instruments of justice and protection, our own network of public, executive and administrative bodies throughout the realm. Only while it was enough for the Romans to threaten, we have to carry out our threat before the weapon can be effective, because our ruling caste, being foreign, will certainly refuse to recognise the Congress as a sovereign body whether existing side by side with the present organs of Government or replacing them until it has such a position as an actual fact; they will recognise only the realised aspiration, not the distant possibility. The party of peaceful secession of thoroughgoing passive resistance does not forget that besides the support and acquiescence of the people the bureaucracy have another source of strength in the military force of the British Empire. They are often accused of forgetting it, but they realise it fully, only they also realise that this weapon of secession, of boycott and self-help, is the only chance which yet remained of a peaceful solution of the problem, — and they are willing to make full use of that chance.

The question of the function of the Congress hinges upon this acceptance or rejection of this weapon. Whatever be the aim of the Congress, whether it be Swaraj or Colonial Self-government or administrative reform, it cannot be brought about by inoperative resolutions, it can only be brought about by pressure; and the only means of pressure in our hands is the threat or the practice of boycott or secession. If the function of the Congress is merely to focus public opinion, it need do nothing but pass resolutions and a few slight changes of procedure will be sufficient. But if its function is to pass effective resolutions, if it is not only to focus public opinion but to collect and centralise national strength, it will have to use the weapon of secession to organise a State within the State, and for that purpose the body will have not only to be readjusted but gradually reconstructed.

Sleeping Sirkar and Waking People

In commenting on the helplessness of the frontier Hindus, the Afridi raids and the callous indifference of the British authorities, the *Punjabee* reports the conversation between the old Chowdhury of a raided village and a high officer of the district. "Were you awake or asleep when the raiders came in?" asked the belated Heaven-born. "Sir," was the old man's reply, "we were all asleep, for we thought our great Sirkar was wide awake. Had we known the Sirkar had gone to sleep, we would have, in that case, taken care to keep awake." The reply carried with it a lesson which lies at the very root of all stable government. The king is king because he tries to please his people; he rules not by right of strength and power which are given to him by God to help him in his duties, but by service, — because he gives protection, because he deals justice, because he helps his people in their wants and in their sorrows. That is the ideal on which kingship is based, and when the ruler wilfully falls short of the ideal, he is punished first by demoralisation, last, by loss of the strength and power which are not his but delegated. The British are in India because they had a certain mission to perform; but the condition of their tenure was justice, protection and sympathy, and if their rule has lasted for these hundred years, it was because some of them tried to satisfy the condition. Unfortunately for them, they allowed commercial greed to overcome their kingly instincts and the punishment of demoralisation has come upon them in full measure. Their sympathy exists only in Mr. John Morley's stock of liberal cant phrases, their justice is no longer believed in and their protection is now following the other virtues. Protection is vested in a corrupt and oppressive police of which the ruler of a great Province does not feel ashamed to be greeted as the friend and protector. Protection takes the form of making Afridi raids an excuse for military practice on the frontier and then quietly allowing the raids to continue. The other kingly qualities, provident wisdom, calm courage, the instinct for the right action and the right moment are already decayed. Only the power and the strength remain and that will disappear when the people are compelled to feel their own strength. The strength of God in the people has slumbered because they "thought that the great Sirkar was awake". But they find, like the old Punjabi that the Sirkar is asleep and it is time for them to awake. Self-protection, not the protection of military exercises in the frontier; self-protection, not the curse of a police enquiry — when this ideal wakes in the heart of the people, what will become of mere power and strength which has no office left but selfishness and self-aggrandisement? How long will it be before it is withdrawn as the strength of Arjuna was withdrawn when Krishna went from him; as the strength of Ravana was withdrawn when Rama beheld the Power of God protecting the Rakshasa in her arms, and prayed to the Mother?

Anti-Swadeshi in Madras

The *Madras Standard* has undoubtedly hit the right nail on the head when it derives the Tinnevelly disturbances from the establishment of the Swadeshi Steam Navigation Company and the attempt to throw difficulties in the way of its success. The struggle generated an acute feeling on both sides and when the commercial war extended itself and the people took sides with Indian labour against British capital in the affair of the Coral Mills, the patience of the English officials gave way and they rushed to the help of their mercantile caste-fellows, misusing the sacred seal of justice and the strong arm of power as instruments to maintain their trade supremacy. This unjust and unwarrantable action has been responsible for the riots and the corpses of dead men lying with their gaping wounds uncared for in Tinnevelly streets, — uncared for but not forgotten in the book of divine reckoning. Nations as well as individuals are subject to the law of *karma,* and in the present political and industrial revolt British rule in India is paying for the commercial rapacity which impelled it to prefer trade returns to justice and kingly duty and use its political power to turn India from a land of fabulous wealth into a nation of starving millions. The payment has only just begun — for these karmic debts are usually repaid with compound interest.

Bande Mataram, March 23, 1908

Exclusion or Unity?

WE DEALT yesterday with the question of the function of the Congress, whether it should be merely to focus public opinion and proceed no farther or to gather up the life of the nation and deploy its strength in a struggle for national self-assertion.

When this question is decided, the next which arises is that of the aim towards which the Congress is to work. If its function is merely to focus public opinion, its aim can only be to submit grievances to the Government for redress, to beg for privileges and to petition for favours. It will then admit the absolute authority of the bureaucracy and fulfil the purpose of collective petitioning instead of leaving each individual class or community to approach the omnipotent seat of power by itself. The absolute rule of the Moghuls admitted this right of petition; it recognised no status in the applicant; it offered no promise of justice, but decided according to the will of the sovereign. The position of the Congress in that case is no better than that of the suitor at the justice seat of Akbar or Aurangzebe. To ask without strength, to aspire without effort, to submit if refused by the sovereign power, will be the limit of its duties. The negation of national life which this attitude implies, is too reactionary to have a chance of acceptance. If the few who cling to these mediaeval notions, desire to keep the Congress to a role so beggarly, they must, when they enter the Congress Pandal, leave the nation outside. For a time by raising party cries and confusing issues they may get the bulk of the Moderate Party to follow them, but the moment they show their hand, there will be a second split and they will be left alone with a handful of well-to-do men on the Congress platform.

The function of the Congress must obviously be to gather the life of the nation together for the purpose of national self-assertion. The question which divides us is as to the nature and extent of that self-assertion. Whether we are to carry the self-assertion to its logical conclusion or to stop halfway, whether we are to separate ourselves from association with the Government or combine association with opposition, whether we are to use boycott as a local protest against a local grievance or a grand universal means of establishing a State within the State, these are the points at issue between the Moderate Party and the Nationalists. The Nationalists desire Swaraj, the Moderates desire Colonial Self-government. The Nationalists wish to exclude all petitionary resolutions, all, that is to say, which depend on the will of the bureaucracy for their execution and not on our own exertions; they would keep the deliberative side of the Congress for ascertaining the sense of the nation as to the work which should be done and the principles which should govern it, and would add a working or executive side to review the work already done, settle the future programme and supervise its execution. The Moderates wish to keep the petitionary side of the Congress as its chief function, but to admit a certain amount of self-help as a subordinate feature. Finally, the Nationalists proclaim the boycott as a movement of secession by which the nation can gradually withdraw itself from association with a control in which it has no voice or share and assert its own and separate life; the Moderates will not have a boycott *movement* at any price and are prepared only to admit a commercial boycott as temporary local action to bring about the redress of local grievances. The minor questions which divide the parties have no importance by themselves and would not give any trouble if there were no acute feeling engendered by these important differences of opinion or principle.

The importance of these differences cannot be denied and ought not to be belittled. We cannot agree with those who try to smooth over difficulties by saying that they do not exist or that there are no parties. This evasion of great political issues, this attempt to slink away from disagreeable facts and shirk the inevitable is likely to discourage the growth of a robust political sense in the people. People with a sound political instinct always take care to recognise and give their proper importance to great issues. They welcome keen discussion and even contention and eager struggle over them, but they do not allow these differences to override the sense of national unity or the struggle of parties to degenerate into a war of factions. This is the only sound way to deal with the difficulty, not by the principle of exclusion, not by breaking apart into sectional bodies and destroying the chance of a regular progression towards a single coherent and self-conscious political life, but by the principle of inclusion, by admitting differences of opinion, regulating procedure and accepting the result. The Nationalists are not in favour of Colonial Self-government as an ultimate ideal, but they accepted the resolution on Self-government as an expression of the immediate aim of the Congress at Calcutta, because they knew that the bulk of the nation was not yet prepared to accept Swaraj as an immediate purpose. They are in favour of boycott as an universal movement throughout India, but they accepted its restriction to Bengal because other provinces were not yet ready to declare in favour of boycott. They are always ready in principle to accept the decision of the Congress for the time being, reserving the right to get that decision altered in the future. The severity of the struggle at Surat was due to the attempt to use a local majority in order to effect a revolution in the Congress constitution, which would turn it into a Moderate Congress and exclude the Nationalist element altogether. They took strong exception to any use of this local majority for altering the mutual composition arrived at by common consent at Calcutta, and decided to record their protest by opposing on all contested points beginning from the election of the President, but they had no intention of seceding even if the Calcutta resolutions were dropped or modified; they would simply have strained every nerve to get the wrong redressed at the next session. This attitude which was clear from the speech and action of the Nationalist leaders throughout, has been obscured by the cry raised against them of wrecking the Congress and the falsehoods which not only attributed the whole blame of the second day's disturbance to them but represented it as preconceived by them and deliberately planned. The Nationalist Party recognises only one sufficient ground for secession, a resolution, constitution or procedure expressly or practically excluding them from the pale of the Congress. Temporary withdrawal as a protest not against the nature of the resolutions passed but against unconstitutional procedure, stands on a different footing and has been often practised, by the Punjab, for instance, when it abstained for several years from the Congress because of the arbitrary refusal to allow the question of the constitution to be dealt with or properly raised.

This we hold to be the only possible attitude if an organised political unity is to be achieved. Full right of discussion, free use of every legitimate means of protest, but not secession on account of opinions. The Moderate Party outside Bengal is, at present, keen for separation. It holds the view, loudly preached by the Bombay papers, that if certain resolutions are passed, if a certain colour is given to the proceedings of the body or to agitation carried on by any section of its members in the country, they are not only entitled but bound to withdraw if they are in the minority or to expel the Nationalists if they are in the majority. They seem to base this view on two grounds, first, that they cannot allow opinions not their own to be expressed in Congress resolutions, secondly, that such opinions or poitical association with those who hold them, will discredit Congress in the eyes of the Government. The first presupposes either a claim to hold the Congress as their personal property or an intolerance which is consistent with the essential conditions of a self-governing body; the second, either a dependence on bureaucratic in place of public opinion which is also incompatible with the spirit of self-government or an implied right of control by bureaucratic influence which no patriot will admit. We assert the right of the Congress to determine its own aims, functions, aspirations, constitution; we do not admit the right of any party sitting in convention to determine them for the Congress. If the Moderates desire to have the creed of the Congress fixed, they must get it done by the Congress, which is alone competent to decide the question, they must not couple it with a proviso of exclusion against those who cannot subscribe to every article of the creed. The ideal of the Congress may be complete Self-government or it may be partial, its methods may be petitionary or they may be self-assertive. That is a question not of constitution but of the balance of opinion. The only constitutional question to be decided in connection with the determination of the aim or ideal is whether those who pitch their ideal either higher or lower than the precise key settled at a particular session are to be excluded in future or admitted, whether the Congress is to be a stationary and sectional body or comprehensiveness is to be aimed at and progress and movement to be allowed.

Biparita Buddhi

The infatuation which drives men to destroy themselves seems to have taken full possession of the bureaucrats in this country. So long as they touched only the political or commercial interests of their subjects, the Lord of *karma* might delay his avenging hand; but the bounds are exceeded when the hand of power is turned against philanthropy and religion. The news published in our yesterday's issue that the bureaucratic police are interfering with the famine work of Lala Lajpat Rai and intimidating his agents, is a sign that the cup is growing full and will soon brim over. It is when the soul of India is attacked that Nemesis feels the call and turns her eyes on the transgressor. Power may do its worst against power but when it becomes the enemy of the saint, the helpless, the innocent, it is then that God is bound to interfere. The Lala's work of famine relief is a saintly work, spontaneous, unforced, not called for as a duty of position or power, taking its root in love and disinterested service, it is a work of *tapasyā* which generates *brahmatejas* in the doers, and when obstructed, the fire will turn upon the assailant and consume him. The jealousy and fears of the bureaucracy are hurrying them into all the excesses that prepare a disastrous recoil and bring about the fall of the proud and the destruction of the mighty.

***Bande Mataram*, March 24, 1908**

Oligarchy or Democracy?

APART from questions of aim and method, a fruitful source of discord between the two parties has been the divergence of views with regard to the spirit of the Congress, whether it is to be the Congress of the few or the Congress of the many. This divergence has been chiefly operative in bringing about struggles over the election of the President and his method of conducting the proceedings, over the selection of the Subjects Committee and the rights of the delegates to express their opinion and use every means to make it operative. One side demands implicit obedience to the authority of the President and a small circle of leaders, the other claims that the President is only a servant of the Congress with a delegated and limited power, that the Congress is supreme and no small circle of leaders has a right to dictate to it, and that the obscurest delegate is by his very position equal in rights and status to the most distinguished men in the country. One side tries to form a Subjects Committee of the leading men in each province, the other tries to enforce the right of the delegates to make their own unhampered choice. One side wishes the Congress to register obediently the resolutions framed for it by wiser heads, the other claims a sovereign dignity and activity for the whole body and the utmost latitude of debate on all important questions. This difference of spirit has been the cause of even more discord and bitterness than the difference of aims and methods, and the most difficult and debatable points in the Congress Constitution will be those into which this issue enters.

In the early days of the world political development was the result of the needs of the civic organism; in modern times it is powerfully swayed by ideas, and often the idea creates the need. English education has brought in the idea of democracy, of the sovereign right and power of the people, and a predilection for the forms of a democratic assembly. When, therefore, the Congress was instituted, the originators tried to cast it in the democratic mould, to clothe it in democratic forms. But the idea by itself cannot become operative, it must first create a corresponding need. The Congress, therefore, while democratic in theory, was in reality a close oligarchy of the most primitive type. Claiming to realise in obedience to the most developed modern ideas the course of modern democratic development, it really followed in obedience to the actual political conditions of the country a course of primitive development very like in its essential features to the primitive constitutions of early times when democracy was unconsciously evolving. There was no electorate which could make the principle of election operative, no political vitality or habit of political thought in the people to put life into the forms of a democratic assembly, no battle of opinions which could hammer out the complete mould of a great deliberative assembly from the rough and shapeless mass called the Congress.

Nominally, the Congress was a sort of imitation Parliament and its delegates were supposed to be elected by the people and representatives of the people; in reality, there was no electorate to represent and the forms of election degenerated into a farce; five people often meeting to elect a hundred out of whom those only attended the Congress session who had time and leisure. In effect, therefore, the Congress was not a modern Parliament but a popular assembly like the old Aryan assemblies in which the whole body of the citizens could attend and all did attend who had the inclination and the leisure. But while the old Aryan assembly was actually the mustering of the citizens, the Congress was rather like those early federal assemblies held in a central place in which as many as could attended from distant places and the bulk of the gathering was made up of local citizens. The peculiarity of the Congress has been the failure to provide against the preponderance of the local majority except by the habit of aiming at unanimity in its resolutions. This flaw in the foundation has been largely responsible for the final tumbling to pieces of the structure. Nominally, again, the resolutions of the Congress were passed by the vote of the assembled delegates, as in a democratic chamber; in reality, the delegates did not vote at all but, like the primitive assemblies, simply accepted by acclamation resolutions ready prepared for them by a few influential men sitting in secret council. Nominally, the President was elected by the Congress and presided over the proceedings according to recognised rules of debate, but in reality he was chosen out of and by the small oligarchical circle which ruled the Congress, effected their decisions and carried out their will. His authority over the proceedings was unfettered by any written rules; the custom and the precedents of the assembly were the sole guide and these were interpreted by him according to the convenience of the Congress oligarchs. Thus the pretence of a modern democratic assembly reduced itself in practice to the reality of an oligarchy. A small circle meeting in secret called the Congress, decided its place of meeting, fixed its policy, framed its resolutions, selected its officers, governed its proceedings and took the opinion of the assembly by acclamation. The assembly listened to the speakers selected by the oligarchs and passed by acclamation the resolutions they had framed. The President was simply a temporary chief of the oligarchs and not the real head of a democratic assembly. In all these respects the Congress reproduced with extraordinary fidelity the essential features of a primitive Greek ecclesia or the Roman comitia in the most oligarchical period.

The first attempt to democratise the Congress was the creation of the Subjects Committee, as a sort of temporary Senate or Council which should prepare the business of the Congress. It was an unconscious reproduction of the Greek boulē or preliminary Council which had similar functions; but it failed to democratise the Congress, it only widened the basis of the Congress oligarchy. It was supposed to be elected by the assembly but was really selected by the oligarchs whose nominations were accepted by the Congress. The Subjects Committee meetings were indeed the scene of frequent encounters between the oligarchs and the free lances who represented a growing strain of popular discontent; but there was no popular party which these men could set against the prestige of the old leaders, and they themselves were usually young and ambitious men who soon passed into the charmed circle and became its chief supports. Those of a robuster type, a Tilak or a Bepin Pal, were held at arm's length and, having no organised following, were unable to prevail.

Another direction in which the incipient democratic tendency sought to fulfil itself was in the demand for a fixed and written constitutution for the Congress. Unwritten law administered by a coterie, class or caste, has always been a strength to oligarchy, and we find in early times that the first demand of an infant democracy is for the codification of law and a fixed and written constitution. We have ourselves experienced in the last two years what a powerful weapon in the hands of the Congress oligarchy has been this absence of a written constitution, law and procedure for the Congress. The demand for a written constitution early manifested itself and led for some time to an actual secession of a whole Province from the Congress, but the privilege of administering the body without fixed or written restrictions was too highly valued by the official clique to be lightly parted with, and by procrastination and masterly inaction they succeeded in baffling the growing demand.

To democratise the Congress was, in fact, impossible without a popular awakening and widening of the political consciousness. Democracy is impossible without a demos, a people politically awake and active, and it was only in the upheaval of 1905 that the rudiments of such a demos began to form. The Nationalist Party which sprang out of that upheaval, showed its character by the democratic nature of its demands and the increasing tendency to democracy in its own composition. It demanded that the President should be elected according to popular sentiment and not by a coterie, that the Subjects Committee should be elected in due form and not nominated by a coterie, that the President and the Congress official circles should act constitutionally and not at their caprice or convenience, that the constitution should be reduced to writing, that the full assembly of delegates should be in fact as well as in theory the sovereign body and that the rights of discussion, amendment and rejection of resolutions should be allowed to be put in practice. In brief, they claimed that the theoretically democratic Congress should become democratic in effect and reality. The keenness of the struggle not only in the Congress but outside it has been largely if not principally due to this onslaught on the charmed oligarchical circle and the determination of the latter to preserve their position at any cost. At Midnapur, for instance, the struggle was over this issue, and not over any serious difference of opinion. And though the issue at Surat was much larger and complicated, it is significant that the battle was joined over a question of constitutional procedure, and it was on a claim of the official oligarchy to override the constitutional rights of a delegate that the Surat Congress broke up in admired disorder. Oligarchy or democracy, authority or freedom are the issue, and no settlement can work which does not decide the question whether the Congress is to remain a mute assembly swayed by a handful of men or a democratic body of as modern a development as the political conditions of the country will allow.

Bande Mataram, March 25, 1908

Freedom of Speech

THE questions in Parliament about the change of the existing law and Mr. Morley's answers seem to point to a coming repressive measure intended to suppress the small amount of free speech still existing in India. The rights of free speech and free meeting were once reckoned among the priceless blessings which British rule had brought to India. Nowadays one can with difficulty put oneself back into the frame of mind which made such a conception possible. The entire dependence on British protection, the childlike faith in the machinery of European civilisation, the inability to perceive facts or distinguish words from realities, the facile contentment with the liberties of the slave to which that conception testified, are happily growing obsolete. They persist in the survivors of the old generation and in those of the present generation who cannot open themselves to new ideas, but are dead in the minds of those who will be the future people of India. In the course of another fifty years men will look back to the times when such ideas were possible, in the same spirit that the nineteenth century looked back to the Middle Ages, as a period of absolute ignorance and darkness when the national mind and consciousness were in a state of total eclipse. The blessings of British rule have all been weighed in the balance and found wanting. The Pax Britannica is now seen to be the cause of our loss of manliness and power of self-defence, a peace of death and torpor, security to starve in, the ease of the grave. British law has been found to be a fruitful source of demoralisation, an engine to destroy ancient houses, beggar wealthy families and drain the poor of their little competence. British education has denationalised the educated community, laid waste the fertile soil of the Indian intellect, suppressed originality and invention, created a gulf between the classes and the masses and done its best to kill that spirituality which is the soul of India. The petty privileges which British statecraft has thrown to us as morsels from the rich repast of liberty, have pauperised us politically, preserved all that was low, weak and dependent in our political temperament and discouraged the old robust manhood of our forefathers. Every Municipal or District Board has been a nursery of dependence and pampered slavery, and the right of public meeting and freedom of the Press only served to complete this demoralisation, while at the same time cheating us into the belief that we were free.

The ancient Romans had a class of slaves born in the family and pampered in their childhood by their masters, who were called *vernae* and enjoyed a peculiar position of mingled licence and subjection. They were allowed to speak with the most unbounded licence, to abuse their masters, to play tricks sometimes of a most injurious character and were yet indulged — so long as the master was in a good humour; let the master's temper turn sour or break into passion and the lash was called into requisition. The freedom of speech enjoyed by us under the bureaucratic rule has been precisely of this kind. It depended on the will of a despotic administration, and at any moment it could be withdrawn or abridged, at any moment the lash of the law could be brought down on the back of the critic. This freedom of speech was worse than the Russian censorship; for in Russia the editor laboured under no delusion, he knew that freedom of speech was not his, and if he wrote against the administration, it was at his own risk; there was no pretence, no dissimulation on either side. But our freedom of speech has demoralised us, fostered an ignoble mixture of servility and licence, of cringing and impudence, which are the very temperament of the slave. We were extravagantly pleased with the slightest boons conceded to us and poured out our feelings with fulsome gratitude, or we grew furious at favours withheld and abused the withholders in the same key. Our public expressions were full of evasions, falsehoods, flatteries of British rule coupled with venomous and damaging attacks on that which in the same breath we lauded to the skies. A habit of cowardly insincerity became ingrained in us, which was fatal to the soundness of the heart, an insincerity which refused to be confined to our relations with the rulers and pursued us into our relations with our own countrymen. The same dry rot of insincerity vitiated all our public action and even our private lives, making a farce of our politics, a comedy of our social reform, and turning us from men into masks. The strenuous attempt to live what we believed, which was the result of the ancient Indian discipline, left the educated class altogether and a gulf was placed between our practice and our professions, so that the heart of India began to beat slower and slower and seemed likely to stop.

It was the proud privilege of the Nationalist Party to strike at the root of this terrible evil. From the first outburst of the Swadeshi movement, their speakers and writers decided to be no longer masks but men, to speak and write the truth that was in their minds, the feeling that was in their hearts without disguise, without equivocation, as freemen vindicating their freedom,— a freedom not bestowed but inborn. The poison passed out of the national system and the blood began to circulate freely in our veins. Once more we stood up as men and not as gibbering spectres of a vanished humanity. The attitude of the *Sandhya* and *Yugantar*, consistently maintained in the dock, stood for a revival of Indian sincerity, truthfulness, manliness, fearlessness; it was the resurgence of the Arya, the ideal of honour and quiet manhood which made our forefathers great. But when the prosecutions failed to crush the papers for which the martyrs offered themselves as a sacrifice, the cry was raised that they were being sacrificed by designing men who kept themselves in the background. The persistence of the same tone and the same writings showed that those who maintained the spirit of the paper were untouched, and it was obvious that only by putting them under lock and key, could the journal itself be snuffed out. So the threat of a change in the law which would hunt out the real culprits, has been persistently held before our eyes, and, if disregarded, may be carried out. The threat is an empty one, because no change of law can find out those whom the nation is determined to save, lest the light of truth be prematurely put under eclipse. Only by the abrogation of all law, by an arbitrary measure extinguishing the freedom of speech altogether can these journals be snuffed out of being by the hand of Power. Such a measure may at any moment be hurried through the Legislative

Council, and the fear of it troubles our Moderate friends and sometimes finds expression in objurgations against our past indiscretions or our policy of protecting our writers and contributors coupled with more or less bland invitations to commit suicide so that their journals may survive. But the existence of one paper which does not shrink from expression of the heart and mind of the nation is of a higher value than that of many journals which fill their columns with insincerities and platitudes. The freedom of speech which the Moderate Party are so anxious to save from extinction is a badge of slavery, a poison to the national health, a perpetuation of servitude, and it is better that it should be extinguished than that the recovered freedom of a nation's soul should cease. God will find out a way to spread the movement, even as it was found out in Russia, if the bureaucracy are so ill-advised as to gag the Press. This voice is abroad and what law shall prevail against it?

The Comedy of Repression

The campaign of repression proceeds merrily in Madras. Srijuts Chidambaram Pillai and Subramaniya Shiva are to be prosecuted for sedition, (we notice, by the way, that Srijut Pillai was not allowed to see his Vakils in jail, a typical piece of bureaucratic "justice") the Tuticorin lawyers are being bound down to keep the peace, and "it is reported that instructions have been issued to the Sub-Magistrate, Tinnevelly, to issue warrants for the arrest of persons shouting 'Bande Mataram' within the Municipal limits of Tinnevelly and Palancotta." The bureaucrats of Madras are profiting by lessons in Russianism both from East Bengal and from the Punjab. Meanwhile the people crowd round the jail gates and line the roads to get a glimpse of the faces of their imprisoned leaders, and Chidambaram Pillai, agent of the Swadeshi Steam Navigation Company, whose name yesterday was little known outside one corner of Madras, is now a popular hero; his name will be a household word; his photograph will hang on the walls of private houses as one of the family gods; and when he comes out from the term of imprisonment which is now a foregone conclusion, he will be a man of mighty influence and, where he swayed thousands before, will sway millions of men throughout his native Presidency. It is the old story, so old, so hackneyed, so certain in its dénouement that one wonders the despotisms of the world do not get tired of playing it.

Bande Mataram, March 26, 1908

Tomorrow's Meeting

THE great opportunity of Srijut Bepin Chandra Pal's return has been utilised for a demonstration such as Calcutta has not yet witnessed, but the occasion will not be perfect unless the public complete their homage to the soul of Nationalism by coming in their thousands to hear him at the Federation Hall Ground on Saturday when the congratulations of the country will be given to him on his return to the great work he has yet to accomplish. He has returned with a double strength, a position of impregnable security in the hearts of his countrymen and a new conception of his work which is precisely what is needed for its fulfilment. On Saturday we expect to hear his first deliberate utterance after his imprisonment. As a leader of the Nationalist Party, he has spoken before, but he will speak now as a voice of prophecy, a thinker whose thoughts do not proceed from himself but are guided from within.

Tomorrow the life of Nationalism will resume its mighty current. Since Bepin Chandra went to prison, it has been half deprived of its old impetuous flow, wandering amid shoals and quicksands, distracted by cross-currents, uncertain whither its course was bound. The constant inspiration of his thoughts was wanting, the impetus of his presence ceased to move the springs of Nationalist endeavour. Tomorrow he resumes his place at the post of honour, the standard-bearer of the cause, the great voice of its heart, the beacon-light of its enthusiasm. We were in a semi-darkness while that light was absent, uncertain and bewildered as to our course while that voice was silent and the standard was held by weaker hands, the post of honour filled by untried champions.

When the Federation Hall Ground is filled and overflowing tomorrow, we shall realise how great was the loss of his presence, how weak we were in the absence of the man with a mission; for each of the men who stand before the country today has a work set for him to do and which he alone can do aright. It is the mission of Bepin Chandra to lead the thought of the movement, to inspire it with his utterances, to keep the fire of its enthusiasm burning, while others carry out the detail work, education, propaganda, Swadeshi, arbitration, self-defence or whatever other things may be given to their hands to do. From Bengal the ideas of the new age must proceed, from Bengal must come the life of the movement, its high sense of principle, its fearless courage, its greatness, its broadness of view and keenness of vision. From Bengal the stream must flow, which will cleanse India of her impurities. If the work is to be well done, each man must recognise his proper work and do it. The clash of conflicting egoisms, the desire to monopolise, the pride of success must disappear from our midst, and be replaced by our intense self-effacement, an enthusiasm of sacrifice, an exalted conception of the high Power at work and the constant sense that we are only His instruments. It is for this reason that we have recently laid stress on this great truth; no advance can be made, no mighty success obtained unless we are able to perceive the divinity of the movement, realise the necessity of subordinating ourselves, overcome the tendency to break into cliques and cabals and apportion to each his allotted portion in the one united work. If anyone tries to outstep his sphere and appropriate the work of others, there will be confusion, disturbance of harmony and temporary failure. The only way to avoid it is for all to realise that the work is not theirs, that their right is only to a portion, that no man is indispensable and only so long as he acts within his own province and on the lines laid down for him by his capacities, his inspiration and his circumstances, is he even useful. This harmony is necessary for the rapid progress of the movement. If each man knows his place and keeps to it, the harmony is possible. All the discords, the quarrels, the failures which have marred our work have been due to the desire of leadership, the obstinacy of prepossessions, the arrogance of egoism which wishes to claim the ownership of God's work.

Bepin Chandra's place has been marked out for him by his powers of oratory, his knowledge of politics, his enthusiasm and unconquerable vitality of hope and confidence, his unequalled power to excite and inspire. The awakening of Madras is the sign-manual of the Almighty upon his mission. He has only to be true to himself and the cause to complete that stupendous beginning and send the same stream of life beating through the atrophied veins of all India, till one unanimous voice, one tremendous impulse works from the Himalayas to Cape Comorin, from Assam to Bombay and the whole country, molten into a burning mass of enthusiasm, is finally fused in one and ready to be hardened into steel of perfect temper, beaten into shape and fined to perfect sharpness by the workmanship divine, so that it may be a weapon in the hands of the Most High to slay ignorance and barbarism throughout the world.

Well Done, Chidambaram!

A true feeling of comradeship is the salt of political life; it binds men together and is the cement of all associated action. When a political leader is prepared to suffer for the sake of his followers, when a man, famous and adored by the public, is ready to remain in jail rather than leave his friends and fellow-workers behind, it is a sign that political life in India is becoming a reality. Srijut Chidambaram Pillai has shown throughout the Tuticorin affair a loftiness of character, a practical energy united with high moral idealism which show that he is a true Nationalist. His refusal to accept release on bail if his fellow-workers were left behind, is one more count in the reckoning. Nationalism is or ought to be not merely a political creed but a religious aspiration and a moral attitude. Its business is to build up Indian character by educating it to heroic self-sacrifice and magnificent ambitions, to restore the tone of nobility which it has lost and bring back the ideals of the ancient Aryan gentleman. The qualities of courage, frankness, love and justice are the stuff of which a Nationalist should be made. All honour to Chidambaram Pillai for having shown us the first complete example of an Aryan reborn, and all honour to Madras which has produced such a man.

The Anti-Swadeshi Campaign

The official campaign against the Swadeshi Steam Navigation Company is now drawing to a head. The enquiries made by Sub-Collector Ashe as to the list of shareholders are sufficiently ominous, while the case against the Tuticorin lawyers is an almost undisguised attempt to ruin the Company by making it practically illegal to farther its interests. All India is looking on with interest to see the end of this campaign. If it succeeds, we shall know that the peaceful development of Swadeshi is impossible under British rule. Whatever disguises the local bureaucracy may try to throw over the issue, there is no man in India who has not understood the issue.

Bande Mataram, March 27, 1908

Spirituality and Nationalism

MANKIND have a natural inclination to hero-worship and the great men who have done wonders for human civilisation will always be the inspiration of future ages. We are Hindus and naturally spiritual in our temperament, because the work which we have to do for humanity is a work which no other nation can accomplish, the spiritualisation of the race; so the men whom we worship are those who have helped the spiritual progress of mankind. Without being sceptical no spiritual progress is possible, for blind adoration is only the first stage in the spiritual development of the soul. We are wont to be spiritually sceptical, to hesitate to acknowledge to ourselves anything we have not actually experienced by the process of silent communion with God, so that the great sages of antiquity were as sceptical as any modern rationalist. They did away with all preconceived notions drawn from the religion of the Vedas, plunged into the void of absolute scepticism and tried to find there the Truth. They doubted everything, the evidence of the senses, the reality of the world, the reality of their own existence, and even the reality of God. This scepticism reached its culmination in the teachings of Buddha who would admit nothing, presuppose nothing, declare nothing dogmatically, and insisted only on self-discipline, self-communion, self-realisation as the only way to escape from the entanglement of the intellect and the senses. When scepticism had reached its height, the time had come for spirituality to assert itself and establish the reality of the world as a manifestation of the spirit, the secret of the confusion created by the senses, the magnificent possibilities of man and the ineffable beatitude of God. This is the work whose consummation Sri Ramakrishna came to begin and all the development of the previous two thousand years and more since Buddha appeared has been a preparation for the harmonisation of spiritual teaching and experience by the Avatar of Dakshineshwar.

The long ages of discipline which India underwent are now

drawing to an end. A great light is dawning in the East, a light whose first heralding glimpses are already seen on the horizon; a new day is about to break, so glorious that even the last of the *avatārs* cannot be sufficient to explain it, although without him it would not have come. The perfect expression of Hindu spirituality was the signal for the resurgence of the East. Mankind has long been experimenting with various kinds of thought, different principles of ethics, strange dreams of a perfection to be gained by material means, impossible millenniums and humanitarian hopes. Nowhere has it succeeded in realising the ultimate secret of life. Nowhere has it found satisfaction. No scheme of society or politics has helped it to escape from the necessity of sorrow, poverty, strife, dissatisfaction from which it strives for an outlet; for whoever is trying to find one by material means must inevitably fail. The East alone has some knowledge of the truth, the East alone can teach the West, the East alone can save mankind. Through all these ages Asia has been seeking for a light within, and whenever she has been blessed with a glimpse of what she seeks, a great religion has been born, Buddhism, Confucianism, Christianity, Mahomedanism with all their countless sects. But the grand workshop of spiritual experiment, the laboratory of the soul has been India, where thousands of great spirits have been born in every generation who were content to work quietly in their own souls, perfect their knowledge, hand down the results of their experiments to a few disciples and leave the rest to others to complete. They did not hasten to proselytise, were in no way eager to proclaim themselves, but merely added their quota of experience and returned to the source from which they had come. The immense reservoir of spiritual energy stored up by the self-repression was the condition of this birth of *avatāras*, of men so full of God that they could not be satisfied with silent bliss, but poured it out on the world, not with the idea of proselytising but because they wished to communicate their own ecstasy of realisation to others who were fit to receive it either by previous *tapasyā* or by the purity of their desires. Of all these souls Sri Ramakrishna was the last and greatest, for while others felt God in a single or limited aspect, he felt Him in His illimitable unity as the sum of an illimitable variety. In him the spiritual experiences of the millions of saints who had gone before were renewed and united. Sri Ramakrishna gave to India the final message of Hinduism to the world. A new era dates from his birth, an era in which the peoples of the earth will be lifted for a while into communion with God and spirituality become the dominant note of human life. What Christianity failed to do, what Mahomedanism strove to accomplish in times as yet unripe, what Buddhism half-accomplished for a brief period and among a limited number of men, Hinduism as summed up in the life of Sri Ramakrishna has to attempt for all the world. This is the reason of India's resurgence, this is why God has breathed life into her once more, why great souls are at work to bring about her salvation, why a sudden change is coming over the hearts of her sons. The movement of which the first outbreak was political, will end in a spiritual consummation.

***Bande Mataram*, March 28, 1908**

The Struggle in Madras

THE new spirit of spiritual and political regeneration which is today becoming the passion of the country, has arrived at a crisis of its destinies. All movements are exposed to persecution, because the powers that be are afraid of the consequences which may result from their sudden success and cannot shake off the delusion that they have the strength to suppress them. When Kamsa heard that Krishna was to be born to slay him, he tried to prevent the fulfilment of God's will by killing His instrument, as if the power which warned him of approaching doom had not the strength to enforce the doom. So too, when the vague prophecies of a Messiah reached the ears of Herod and he heard that Christ was born in Bethlehem, the fear of his earthly dominion passing into the hands of another drove him to massacre all the children of the Jews in order to avoid his fancied doom. These examples are a parable of the eternal blindness of men when face to face with movements divinely inspired which threaten or seem to threaten their temporal dominion. The bureaucracy are here to be replaced when their work is over, and if they had been able to put aside their selfish interests, and were really capable of governing India and India's interests as they have so long professed, they would have recognised in the upheaval of 1905 the signal of their approaching dismissal from their task, and made the way smooth for a peaceful transference of power to the people, thus securing a glorious euthanasia which would have been remembered in history as a unique example of self-denial and far-seeing statesmanship. But human nature is too feeble to arise to such heights of wisdom and self-abnegation, except in those rare instances when the divine breath enters into a nation and lifts it to a pitch of enthusiasm which ordinary human weakness cannot support.

The persecution of Swadeshism which is now reaching the most shameless lengths in Madras, is a sure sign that God has withdrawn Himself from the British bureaucracy and intends their rapid fall. Injustice is an invitation to death and prepares His advent. The moment the desire to do justice disappears from a ruling class, the moment it ceases even to respect the show of justice, from that moment its days are numbered. The cynical disregard of all decorum with which the shows of law are being used to crush the Swadeshi Steam Navigation Company in Tuticorin will exasperate the whole of the mercantile community in the country. It will convince those who still dream that industrial development is possible without political power, of their mistake. The Marwaris are already alienated, the whole Jain community seething with an indignation too deep-rooted for words. The Tuticorin reign of terror directed against the one Swadeshi enterprise which can prevent all the rest from being rendered futile by the refusal of British Steam services to help the carriage of Swadeshi goods has begun to shake the complaisant acquiescence of the commercial classes in bureaucratic absolutism. The collapse of the Swadeshi Steam Navigation Company will mean that from Cape Comorin to Budaricashram the cry will go forth of "Swadeshi in Danger" with the result that the whole nation will awaken to the necessity of uniting in one desperate struggle to force the bureaucracy to surrender its monopoly of power. Swadeshi is now the dream and hope of all India. Loyalist, Moderate, Nationalist, all are at one on this point, all are agreed, that without Swadeshi there is no hope for the people of India. When it becomes evident that the bureaucracy is bent on destroying the only means by which Swadeshi can be secure of its existence, the greatest supporter of the present Government will feel that his choice lies between loyalty to his country and the hope of her resurgence on the one hand and loyalty to the bureaucracy and the destruction of his people and his motherland on the other.

When Srijut Chidambaram Pillai set himself to the task of establishing a Swadeshi Steam Navigation Company between Tuticorin and Colombo, he was taking a step which meant the beginning of the end for the British commercial monopoly in India. There are three departments of Swadeshi which have to be developed in order to make India commercially independent, first, the creation of manufactures, secondly, the retail supply, thirdly, the security of carriage from the place of manufacture to the place of supply. Of all these the third is the most essential, because the others are bound to lead a precarious existence if all the means of carriage are in the hands of the enemies of Swadeshi. The difficulties experienced in East Bengal by those who tried to import Swadeshi goods from Calcutta in the face of the control of the railway and the steam services by hostile interests, are only a slight foretaste of the paralysing obstacles which will be thrown in our way the moment it is seen that Swadeshi has got the upper hand. The only remedy for this state of things is for the people of the country to organise steamer services both by sea and by river, so that all carriage by water at least may be in their hands. The carriage by land cannot come into our hands without a political revolution, but if we hold the waterways, we shall not only hold an important part of the system of communications but be able to use our possession of it as a weapon against British trade if the railway is utilised against us. The instinct of the country had seized on this truth and the organisation of Swadeshi steam services has been one of the first and most successful outcome of the new movement. The Chittagong Company and Tuticorin Company have both been a phenomenal success and, owing to the spirit of self-sacrificing patriotism which has awakened in the hearts of the people, they have been able to beat their British rivals without entering into a war of rates, for the British steamers charging extravagantly low rates have been unable to command as much custom as the dearer Swadeshi services. A network of Companies holding the water carriage from Rangoon to Karachi and the Persian Gulf would soon have come into existence and the waterways of East Bengal would have been covered with boats plying from town to town in the ownership of Swadeshi concerns. If the Swadeshi Steam Navigation Company is crushed, this fair prospect will be ruined and all hope of commercial independence disappear for ever. The bureaucracy well know the tremendous importance of the issue at stake and have sacrificed everything, honour, justice, decency, to the one all-important chance of success. We also must awaken to the necessity of saving Swadeshi in this hour of danger. The time is a critical one and it is as if Providence had determined to test the spirit of the people and see whether it was strong enough to deserve assistance. The Swadeshi Steam Navigation Company was on the point of crushing its British rival, if the bureaucracy had not interfered; it is now on the point of being crushed itself unless the people interfere. The people have the power to save it by blotting out its rival. If the merchants refuse in a body to ship by the alien service, if the people refuse to tread its decks, no amount of bureaucratic help, no amount of magisterial injustice and police tyranny can save it from the doom it deserves. We look to the Nationalists of Madras to see that this is done. The British jails are not large enough to hold the whole population of Tinnevelly district; let every man follow the noble example of Chidambaram Pillai and, for the rest, let God decide.

A Misunderstanding

We have noticed a paragraph in the last issue of *Basumati* which may lead to some misunderstanding in the public mind and needs therefore to be corrected. The *Basumati* practically charges the National Council with disregarding the claims of Srijut Aurobindo Ghose to reoccupy the post of Principal and Srijut Satish Chandra Mukherji who has done so much to organise the College, with clinging to the post to the exclusion of his colleague. We are able to state the real facts. Srijut Aurobindo Ghose left the College when he was implicated in the *Bande Mataram* sedition trial and a conviction seemed, from the temper of the authorities, to be a foregone conclusion. He expressed in his letter of resignation a readiness to rejoin his duties at some future date if the Council thought his services required. After his acquittal the Executive Committee at an early date passed a resolution appointing Srijut Aurobindo Ghose a Professor of History and Political Science in the College, but as the result of a special request from Srijut Aurobindo himself to the Secretary to excuse him from the onerous duties of a Principal which he had neither the time nor, as he himself thought, the necessary capacity to discharge, the post of Principal was not included in the reappointment. Srijut Satish Chandra Mukherji had no hand or voice in the matter; he had taken the post of Principal with reluctance and holds it now as a duty until it pleases the Executive Committee to relieve him. Many groundless rumours have been afloat from time to time about the National College, and it is a pity that they should be printed without previous verification. Srijut Aurobindo Ghose sent in his resignation spontaneously, and would certainly not have returned if, as it was at one time persistently rumoured, he had been compelled to retire; and his return as Professor and not as Principal was also due to his own unwillingness to accept the latter charge. Neither the National Council nor any one else can be held responsible in either case.

Bande Mataram, March 30, 1908

The Next Step

THE condition of the poorer classes in this country is a subject which has till now been too much neglected, but can be neglected no longer if the blessing of God is to remain with our movement. The increasing poverty of the masses has been the subject of innumerable pamphlets, speeches and newspaper articles, but we are apt to think our duty done when we have proved that the poverty problem is there; we leave the solution to the future and forget that by the time the solution comes, the masses will have sunk into a condition of decay from which it will take the nation many decades to recover. We have been accustomed to deal only with the economical side of this poverty, but there is a moral side which is even more important. The Indian peasantry have always been distinguished from the less civilised masses of Europe by their superior piety, gentleness, sobriety, purity, thrift and native intelligence. They are now being brutalised by unexampled oppression; attracted to the liquor shops which a benevolent Government liberally supplies, bestialised by the example of an increasingly immoral aristocracy and gradually driven to the same habits of looseness and brutality which disgrace the European proletariats. This degeneration is proceeding with an alarming rapidity. In some parts of the country it has gone so far that recovery seems impossible. We have heard of districts in which the peasantry are so far reduced to poverty by the exactions of Zemindars, planters and police that the sturdier classes among them are taking to highway robbery and dacoity as the only possible means of livelihood. We have heard of villages where the liquor shop and the prostitute, institutions unknown twenty-five years ago, have now the mastery of the poorest villagers. Many of the villages in West Bengal are now well supplied with these essentials of Western civilisation. The people ground down between the upper millstone of the indigo planter and the nether millstone of the

Zemindar, are growing full of despair and look to violence as their only remedy. These conditions of the worst districts tend to become general and unless something is done to stem the tide of evil, it will sweep away the soul of India in its turbid current and leave only a shapeless monstrosity of all that is worst in human nature.

We are convinced, of course, that India is destined to rise again, we await with confidence the coming of the Avatar of strength who will follow the Avatar of love, but in order that He may come, we must prepare the atmosphere, purify it by our own deeds of love, strength and humanitarian self-sacrifice. The educated classes are now the repositories of the hope of resurgence; it is in them that the spirit has entered, to them the masses look for guidance. Their duty is to be worthy of their mission, to bring hope, strength and light into the lives of their down-trodden countrymen. We have so far been occupied with Swadeshi as the economical means of saving the people: we must now set ourselves to the restoration of the moral tone of the nation by ourselves setting an example of mercy, justice, self-denial, helpfulness and patient work for the people. The work is one for the young. It was they who made the Swadeshi movement a success and ensured its permanence; they also must set themselves to the task which now calls us and go to the succour of their suffering countrymen, point their spirits to the help which is to come, support them in their present sufferings, relieve them so far as possible and bind the educated class and the masses together by the golden bond of love and service. This is the next step in the development of the present movement. Swadeshi is fairly begun and will now go on of its own impetus; but when the work of which we speak is taken in hand, Swadeshi will receive a fresh impetus which will make it so irresistible that all the tyranny of the officials, all the police oppression, every obstacle and hindrance which man can interpose will be swept away like so much chaff, and all Bengal become the fortress of Swadeshi, its temple and its domain. This is the work to which the finger of God has been pointing us from the beginning of the present year, by the success of the *Ardhodaya Yoga* organisation, by the call to the village which was the dominant note of the Pabna Conference, by signs and omens of many kinds which those who keep their eyes open will easily understand. We have now Samitis for spreading Swadeshi, Samitis for physical culture and self-defence, Samitis for the organisation of meetings, festivals and other great occasions. All these are good, but we want now Samitis for giving help and light to the masses. The Anusilan Samiti has given a right direction to its activities when it undertook Famine Relief, but Famine Relief is a temporary work, one which needs an immense fund to be really effective, and only a united body of the leading men of Bengal could successfully cope with it. What our Samitis can do is to take up the work which we have indicated as a permanent part of their duties, put themselves in touch with the people, lead them to hope, inspire them with the spirit of self-help, organise them and make them ready for the coming of the Avatar.

A Strange Expectation

The *Indian People* of Allahabad writes in a tone of mingled pathos and disgust at the supineness of the Government in allowing the Extremists to gain ground in the country by its obstinate refusal to dance to Moderate piping. It depends entirely on the Government, says our contemporary, which party is to prevail; if the Government will only take the Moderate Party as the keeper of its conscience, it will be saved from the Extremist peril. We do not know which is to be most pitied, the Moderate Party or the Government. The former is, according to its own confession, a helpless puppet depending for its very existence on the actions of an external power over which it has no influence or control, for its popularity on the favour of the bureaucracy and for its continuance on the self-sacrifice of an official class which it invites to commit suicide in order to keep an opponent in existence. Such is the grotesque position of the party which boasts for itself a monopoly of statesmanship and sober wisdom that it has to depend for its continued existence not on its statesmanship and wisdom, but on the will of its enemy! And as for the Government, the only choice offered to it is either to fall into the Extremist fire or singe in the Moderate frying-pan. We would remind our contemporary that the English people have sufficient political intelligence to see that once they begin giving "substantial gifts" instead of the present "toys and rattles" and "shadowy and ridiculous reforms", it is simply a question of time when they will have to part with the last vestige of their present absolute control. Whether the bureaucratic system dies a lingering death at the slow fire of Moderatism or is burned to ashes in the Nationalist conflagration, the choice is one to which the bureaucracy may be pardoned if it violently objects and even prefers to take the risk of the second alternative rather than the certainty of the first. The Nationalists do not expect substantial concessions from the bureaucracy not because they attribute to the present rulers a double dose of original sin, but because they believe them to have sufficient insight to see the danger of concessions but not the almost superhuman penetration which would show them the lofty magnanimity and real wisdom of a timely surrender.

A Prayer

Spirit of God that rulest, lord and king
Of all this universe, who from Thy throne
In heaven, besieged by prayers, lookst down on man,
Immeasurable Spirit, if any thought
Of human frailty in my mind should dwell,
While at Thy feet I lay myself, forgive.
Not for myself but for the land where Thou
Wert once a mighty warrior, lord and king,
For India, for her sons, I pray, who now
Fallen, abject, cringing to a foreign hand,
Forget Thee. Thou immeasurable Lord
Of all this universe, august, unborn,
By Thy unspeakable compassion urged
Enteredst a human body, of Thy huge

Empire a little province camest down
From foes within and foes without to save.
Again the land is full of Thee and full
Of hope; a stir is in the air, a cry
Is in men's hearts, the whole terrestrial globe
Thrills and vague rumours, huge presentiments
Move like the visions born of mist and dream
Across the places where Thou once wast born
Prophesying Thy advent. Wilt Thou come
Lord, in a form such as Thou worest once
When Mathura was free, when Kamsa fell,
And from Brindavan came the avenging sword
Till then concealed. So would we have Thee come.
The nations of the earth are full of sin;
Greed, lust, ambition are their gods, and keep
Revel with Science for their caterer
To give the food by which they live. All forms
Of mercy, gentleness and love are lost
While strength alone is worshipped, strength divorced
From justice, uninspired by noble aims.
The greatnesses of earth forget their source
And limit; they desire to break and build,
To fill their lust, to hold majestic rule
For ever, but forget the source of strength,
Forget the purpose for which strength is given.
Oppression fills the spaces of the world,
Hatred and pain reply with murder, One
Is needed who will break the strengths of earth
By His diviner strength; and till He comes
In vain we struggle and in vain aspire.
Come therefore, for Thou saidst that Thou wouldst come;
Whenever strong injustice lifts her head
To slay the good, — Thou saidst that Thou wouldst come
For rescue of the world. Today the globe
Waits for Thy coming, as it waited then
When Ravan was the master of the world
And Lanka, full of splendid strength and sin,

Possessed mankind. Now many Ravans rule
And many Lankas. Therefore come; the earth
Can bear no more the burden of their pride,
Hellward she sinks. Unless Thou come, the end
Approaches. Save Thy fair creation, Lord.

Bande Mataram, March 31, 1908

India and the Mongolian

WHEN Srijut Bepin Chandra Pal in his speech at the Federation Ground was speaking of the possibility of China and Japan overthrowing European civilisation, how many of the audience understood or appreciated the great issues of which he spoke? We have lost the faculty of great ideas, of large outlooks, of that instinct which divines the great motions of the world. This huge country, this mighty continent, once full of the clash of tremendous forces, stirring with high exploits and gigantic ambitions, loud with the voices of the outside world, has become a petty parish; the palace of the Aryan Emperors is now the hut of a crouching slave, small in his ideas, mean in his aspirations, his head sunk, his eyes downcast, so that he cannot see the heavens above him or the magnificent earth around. If one speaks to him of his mighty possibilities of great deeds that he yet shall do, or seeks to remind him that he is the descendant of kings, he takes the speaker for a madman talking vain things and a derisive smile of pity is his only reply. We hold it to be the greatest injury of all that England has done us, that she has thus degraded our soul and dwarfed our imagination. It is only by the grace of God that a reawakening has come, that we are once more becoming conscious of our divine inheritance and the grandiose possibilities of our future.

Of all the minds that have stirred to the breath of God among us, refreshed themselves from the fountain of strength and inspiration and risen to their full height and stature Srijut Bepin Chandra's is the most penetrating, the most alive to the thoughts that are filling the modern world, the first to divine the future and prophesy the movements of God in the nation. While others were the slaves of Western ideals, his mind first caught the meaning of the sudden arising of India, first proclaimed the spiritual character of the movement, first discovered that it was not only the body but the soul of India that was awaking from the sleep of the ages. On Saturday when he spoke of India as the saviour of Europe, he again gave expression to a prophetic thought, again looked with more than human insight into the future. The truth was not one which his hearers could grasp; many must have gone away scoffing, few could have appreciated the luminous penetration of insight which lay behind the thought of the speaker. The awakening of Asia is the fact of the twentieth century, and in that awakening the lead has been given to the Mongolian races of the Far East. In the genius, the patriotic spirit, the quick imitative faculty of Japan, — in the grand deliberation, the patient thoroughness, the irresistible organisation of China, Providence found the necessary material force which would meet the European with his own weapons and outdo him in that science, strength and ability which are his peculiar pride. The political instinct of the European races has enabled them to understand the purpose of the Almighty in the awakening of the Mongol. A terror is in their hearts, a palsy has come upon their strength, and with blanched lips they watch every movement of the two Eastern giants, each wondering when his turn will come to feel the sword of the Mikado or what will happen when China, the Titan of the world, shall have completed her quiet, steady, imperturbable preparation. The vision of a China organised, equipped, full of the clang of war and the tramp of armed men, preparing to surge forth westwards is the nightmare of their dreams. And another terror of economic invasion, of the Mongol swamping Europe with cheap labour and stifling the industries of Europe adds a fresh poignancy to the apprehensions which convulse the West. Hence the panic in America, in Australia, in Africa, the savage haste to expel the Asiatic at any cost before the military strength of China is sufficiently developed to demand entrance for her subjects with the sword emphasising her demand. This is the Yellow Peril, and every European knows in his heart of hearts that it is only a question of time necessary for his vision to translate itself into the waking world. But one thing the European has not yet perceived and that is that the Mongolian is no wild adventurer to go filibustering to Australia or bombard with his siege-guns San Francisco or New York before Asia is free. The first blow given by the Mongolian fell upon Russia because she stood across the Asiatic continent barring the westward surge of his destiny. The second blow will fall on England because she holds India.

The position of India makes her the key of Asia. She divides the Pagan Far East from the Mahomedan West, and is their meeting-place. From her alone can proceed a force of union, a starting-point of comprehension, a reconciliation of Mahomedanism and Paganism. Her freedom is necessary to the unity of Asia. Geographically, she occupies an impregnable position of strength commanding the East of Asia as well as the West, from which as from a secure fortress she can strike the nations of the Persian or the Chinese world. Such a position held by an European Power means a perpetual menace to the safety of Asia. It will therefore be the first great enterprise of a Chino-Japanese alliance to eject the English from India, and hold her in the interests of Asiatic freedom and Asiatic unity. This necessity of India's position is one which neither the English nor the Mongolian can escape. No treaties, no attempts to reconcile conflicting interests will stand against the secret and inexorable necessity which forces nations to follow not the dictates of prudence or diplomacy, but the fiat of their environment. When the inevitable happens and the Chinese armies knock at the Himalayan gates of India and Japanese fleets appear before Bombay harbour, by what strength will England oppose this gigantic combination? Her armies which took two years to overcome the opposition of forty thousand untrained farmers in the Transvaal? Her fleets which have never fought a battle with a trained foe since Trafalgar? They will be broken to pieces by the science and skill of the Mongolian. And the key of Asia will pass into Mongolian hands and the strength of India, the Sikh and the Rajput and the Maratha, the force of Mahomedan valour and the rising energy of new nations in Bengal and Madras will all be at the service and under the guidance of the Mongolian who will not fail to use them as England has failed, letting them run to waste, but will hammer them into a sword of strength for the fulfilment of his mission, the extrusion of the European from Asia, Africa, Australia, the smiting down of European pride, the humiliation of Western statecraft, power and civilisation and its subordination to the lead of the dominant Asiatic.

The doom is drawing very near and the awakening of Bengal has come just in time to give India a chance of recovering her freedom of action. If she strains every nerve to use the chance, if she is able to develop her self-consciousness, her unity, her warlike instincts, her industrial independence, she will be in a position to assert her own will, to offer herself as an ally and not an instrument, it may be even, as Bepin Babu suggested, to mediate between the civilisation of Europe and Asia, both of them so necessary to human development. Two great obstacles stand in her way. The blindness of the bureaucracy which is straining every nerve to crush the Indian renascence in the vain hope that it can continue to rule, is the least of the two. Far more formidable is the greater though more excusable blindness of the people themselves who still persist in connecting their future with the rule of England. Our Moderate politicians refuse to allow their minds to shake off the delusion that the British rule is a dispensation of Providence and meant to endure. All their thoughts of the future assume that the present is perpetual, that what is, will be. As one long in darkness cannot see the light when it enters suddenly his prison, so our people even when the dawn has come, cannot believe that it is really daybreak. They persist in assuming that the night will continue and are content with merely turning a little in bed instead of rising and swiftly accoutring themselves for the work of the day. The warning which Srijut Bepin Chandra addressed to the British people, is also a warning to the people of India. British rule can only continue in India, if India is willing that it should continue and strong enough to defend it against all comers. If a rejuvenated India decides to be free, it depends on the present action of the bureaucracy whether free India will be a friend of England and a mediator between Europe and the triumphant Mongol or an ally of the latter in the approaching Armageddon. Even if the movement in India is crushed, it will not be England that will reap the fruit of her crime in strangling an infant Nationality. She will before long be swept out of India by the Mongolian broom and the latent forces which she refused to utiiise will be used against her by a bolder and more skilful statesmanship. The people of India too will have to reap the fruits of their present Karma. On them far more than on the bureaucracy it depends whether they will meet the coming Mongolian as a destined slave and instrument, an ally or an equal whose voice shall override all others in determining the fate of the world.

Religion and the Bureaucracy

The measure of the panic into which the new movement has thrown the bureaucracy can be taken from its interference with the religious life of the people. Time was when the rulers shrank from any interference with religion lest it should arouse what they were pleased to call the fanaticism of the people. But one ghost drives out another, and the old fear of fanaticism has given place to the greater fear of the new Nationalism, just as the fear of the Mahomedans has given place to the more tangible terror of the resurgent Hindu community. The expulsion of a religious preacher from Travancore is significant of the direction in which the fears of the bureaucracy are tending. That this act of tyranny was not the work of the Maharaja goes without saying, since no Hindu prince would dream of interfering with the religion of his subjects. The dictation of the Resident is the only explanation of this political act. Whatever activity may help the growth of national spirit or foster self-respect in the people, is now suspect to the rulers and will be stopped wherever possible, impeded where direct prohibition cannot be exercised. The famine relief work of Lala Lajpat Rai is being interfered with as seditious, and the religious preaching of the Madras Brahman has been vetoed because it calls on the people to revive the spiritual glories of ancient India. The struggle will soon overpass the political limits; for the next stage in Swadeshi will be a return of the nation to its old spirituality and active habit of philanthropy with the revival of the nation as its motive. When the bureaucracy interferes with this development as it will be driven to interfere by the instinct of self-preservation, as it has already begun to interfere, the true struggle will begin, the Avatar will be ready to manifest himself and the end will come.

The Milk of Putana

A spirit of conciliation is evident in some of the recent acts of the bureaucracy, such as the separation of Judicial and Executive of which Sir Harvey Adamson has given the details in his speech in Council. The policy of Sir Sydenham Clarke in Bombay is of the same type, and from the Mofussil we hear of politician Magistrates who are busy re-establishing the use of foreign articles by skilful exhibitions of sympathy attended with intimidating of Swadeshists carried out through the instrumentality of Indian subordinates on whom the whole blame is thrown. This is the milk of Putana by which Kamsa hoped to poison the infant Krishna. The modern Kamsa comes of a shopkeeping breed and is careful only to let the infant have as much of the milk and no more as will do his business for him. The separation of Judicial and Executive functions, the pet scheme of the old mendicancy, will be carried out only in a district or two of Eastern Bengal as an experiment. The policy of Sir Sydenham Clarke has confined itself to sweet words and abstention from repression, and the milk of Mr. Morley's sympathy is limited to so much as can be bottled for use in a Council of Notables. So too the politician Magistrates take care to do nothing except occasionally rescind oppressive orders which they have already issued in the names of their Indian subordinates. Their policy is to throttle Swadeshi with one hand while stroking the District paternally on the head with the other. What shall we do with this milk of Putana? Sri Krishna drained the breasts of Putana and killed her, and if the bureaucracy begins giving real concessions, that will be its fate. But this watered milk of Morleyan sympathy is a different matter. To drink it is to weaken ourselves and help the adversary.

Bande Mataram, April 1, 1908

Oligarchy Rampant

The *Indu Prakash*, commenting on the Poona District Conference, again raises the note of dissension. It draws attention to the conflicting nature of the reports telegraphed respectively to the *Hindu* from Nationalist sources and to the *Tribune* from a Moderate correspondent. The Poona Conference had passed a resolution in favour of an united Congress, and the telegram in the *Hindu* represents this as a *fiat* to the Congress leaders, the telegram to the *Tribune* as a pious wish meant only to operate if the leaders chose to agree. The *Indu* resents the speech of the President and the Nationalist interpretation of the resolution as a threat to the leaders menacing them with the intervention of the nation if they refuse to compose their quarrels. Whatever may have been the circumstances under which the resolution was passed, the speech of the President was unmistakable; it asserted the sovereignty of the nation, the purely delegatory character of the power of the leaders and the right of the former to dictate to the latter. The Bombay organ of Moderatism resents the claim of the nation to dictate to the leaders; it holds that it is the leaders who ought to dictate to the nation. In our articles on the Congress Constitution we described the present constitution of the Congress as an oligarchy and we hear that some of our Moderate readers resented this description. We ask them whether this attitude of the *Indu* is not the very spirit of oligarchy? Can any more narrow and exclusive claim be set up for a small circle of men than this that the nation shall have no right to dictate to them their course in a crisis when the whole future of the country depends on their action? The *Indu* says that an united Congress shall only be held if the leaders were willing to hold it. Again pure oligarchy! It does not matter what the nation thinks, but because Mr. Gokhale and Mr. Tilak cannot get on together, or because Sir Pherozshah Mehta or Dr. Rash Behari Ghose are of a different opinion from Srijut Bepin Chandra Pal, the nation has to see the Congress broken asunder for ever. And such considerations are to rule the destiny of a great people!

***Bande Mataram*, April 2, 1908**

The Question of the President

THE union of the two parties in the Congress is now in sight. If the Convention Committee which is about to meet at Allahabad, will be guided by the country and not by the single will of one masterful and obstinate personality, the reconciliation of the parties is certain. When this desirable consummation is brought about, the next step will be the formation of a Constitution under which a harmonious working may be possible. We have already formulated what in our opinion should be the principles of the Constitution; the basis should be democratic and not oligarchic, the scope of the Congress should be widened so as to embrace actual work, the aim left indeterminate. It is the function of this body to gather around it the strength of the nation, and no creed should be promulgated which would have the result of excluding any section of the people.

Taking these principles as our starting-point, we shall proceed to discuss the chief questions which must be settled in order to ensure harmonious working between the two parties. The first issue which will present itself is the choice of a President. In his speech at the Federation Ground, Sj. Bepin Chandra Pal threw out a suggestion which he thought might obviate the difficulties which now attend the choice of a President. The present method of election is wholly unsatisfactory. A Reception Committee formed on the basis of wealth, not of democratic election is the primary authority; and the choice of the President is determined by a three-fourths majority which it is under present circumstances impossible to secure. Failing this impossibility, the All-India Congress Committee proceeds to nominate a President who may be the choice not of the country but of a party, and the nomination is confirmed by the consent of the Congress which the Moderates declare to be a mere formality of election not implying any right of the delegates to withhold their consent or reverse the decision of the Committee. This method of election is about the most irrational, undemocratic and perversely unconstitutional which can be imagined. The whole value of a democratic constitution lies in the relation of the parts of the commonwealth to each other on the basis of a definite delegation of power by the people to its officials, magistrates or governing bodies. The present system eliminates the sovereignty of the people altogether; it sets up an irresponsible body temporarily created for a different purpose as the primary authority and creates in the All-India Committee a power of final election which makes it independent of the people.

Srijut Bepin Chandra proposes to leave the election of the President to the Reception Committee, permitting the anomaly to continue for the sake of peace; but the voice of the people is not to be entirely silent, inoperative in the election, it finds its opportunity in the criticism of the President's address which is to be open to discussion and amendment like the King's Speech in Parliament. This right of criticism and amendment will act as a check on the party proclivities of the President and tend to bring his speech to the colourless nature of a pronouncement embracing what the whole nation is agreed upon and omitting the points of difference which still divide men's minds. It is possible that an obstinate President might face the disagreeable certainty of a division on his address, in which case the check would not work; but this would be too unlikely a possibility to be a serious drawback to Sj. Bepin Chandra's proposal. The defect in it as a complete solution lies elsewhere, it provides against the misuse of the Presidential chair to deliver a party pronouncement wounding to the susceptibilities of a part of the audience, but it does not provide against the misuse of the Presidential authority to prevent the passing of resolutions disagreeable to the party to which the President for the year happens to belong. This can be done, however, without altering Bepin Babu's suggestion.

There are two aspects of the Presidential position. In one he is the spokesman of the nation issuing a manifesto on its behalf with regard to the questions of the day. The Moderate Party usually tries to belittle this aspect by the contention that the President's speech binds no one but himself. If that is so, then he has no right to take up a whole day of the brief time available for work with utterances and opinions which are of no conceivable importance to the country or the world at large. Either the President's speech is a national manifesto and should be denuded of its party character, or it is a personal expression of opinion and should be either eliminated altogether or reduced to the brief proportions of an acknowledgement of the honour done to him in his election, so that the Congress may at once proceed to real business. In that case the President will become a Speaker of the House and nothing more, which he is at present, but only in his second and subordinate capacity. In this secondary capacity he is master of the deliberations of the Congress and can, if he so wishes, try to rule out of court or declare as lost without division any proposal or amendment which is displeasing to his party. Indeed, as everybody knows, it is this which has been at the root of all the bitterness that has gathered round the question and which led to the fracas at Surat. It will not therefore be enough to provide against the party character of the address, it is still more necessary to provide against the party use of the President's authority. In the House of Commons the Speaker is a non-party man whose sole business is to interpret impartially the rules of the House, and, if we are to avoid the repetition of such scenes as took place at Surat, the President of the Congress must be compelled to assume the same character. The difficulties in the way are two: first, the absence of any well-understood rules of procedure in the Congress; secondly, the absence of a strong public opinion which would unanimously resent the misuse of his authority whatever party might be benefitted. If the now unwritten procedure of the Congress is reduced to writing and provision made for the right of delegates to lay their views in due form before the Congress, the first difficulty may be got rid of, and a very necessary step taken in the democratisation of the Congress. But the interpretation of the rules is always liable to misuse, as all free countries have found, and the only safeguard against it is a strong sense of the supreme importance of free discussion which will override party feeling and discourage the temptation to acquiesce in anything which will bring about a party victory. To develop such a feeling will take time. In the meanwhile such checks should be devised as would both deter the President from misusing his authority and foster the growth of a public sentiment such as governs the proceedings of free assemblies in free countries; Mr. Tilak at the Surat Congress appealed to the Congress against the decision of the Chairman of the Reception Committee, disallowing his notice for the adjournment of the election of the President. This right which is inherent in every free assembly, ought to be specifically recognised. We cannot find a better means of checking any tendency to abuse authority than the knowledge that an appeal lies against one's decision to the whole assembly of the delegates, nor any stronger incentive to the growth of the public sentiment we desire to create than the knowledge that the final responsibility for dishonest party tactics will rest on the whole body of the delegates. If these precautions are added to the suggestion of Srijut Bepin Chandra the difficulties at present arising out of the anomalous election of the President will largely disappear. At the same time, the anomaly remains and if we overlook it for the present for the sake of peace, it should be clearly recognised that the present system can only be a temporary device pending the growth of a definite electorate in the country which can take over the function of electing the President.

The suggestions we put forward therefore are that the President should be elected by a bare majority of the Reception Committee or, failing a clear majority in favour of one name over all others combined, by the All-India Congress Committee; that the President take his seat the moment the Congress sits, before the Chairman of the Reception Committee begins his address of welcome; that the address of the President after delivery be open to formal discussion, in other words, that the Congress be asked to accept the address and that the right of amendment be permitted; that the President be governed by definite rules of procedure, and that his decision be subject to an appeal to the whole House.

Bande Mataram, April 3, 1908

Convention and Conference

WHEN the leaders of the Moderate Party meet at Allahabad, they will be on their trial before India and all the world. They have done much in the past for the country. Whatever we may think of the views they hold or the methods dear to them, they are the survivors of a generation which woke the nation from political apathy and helped to break the spell which British success had thrown upon the hearts of the people. They turned a critical eye on things which had been taken for granted, British peace, British justice, British freedom. Even while they lauded, they criticised, and the habit of fault-finding which they turned into a weapon of political warfare, helped to break the hypnotic power of the bureaucratic domination. This was no small or unimportant result for so abjectly prostrate a generation as the one into which they were born. If the nation is passing out of their hands, it is largely on account of the change in the popular mind which they brought about by their ceaseless attacks on the bureaucracy. But if they did so much to raise the nation, the political influence which they acquired by their services was an ample recompense. They are now losing that influence; the minds of the rising generation are widening to receive ideas which they have chosen to oppose, to envisage hopes which they are anxious to discourage, to attempt enterprises with which they are either unwilling or afraid to associate themselves. The Surat Congress failed because they desired to throw an insuperable barrier across the path of the onward march of the rising generation, because they hoped to confine the future to the formulas of the present and leave the mould of their ideas as the rigid form out of which the nation would not be permitted to grow. The Convention is an attempt to drag back the Congress out of the twentieth century into the nineteenth. It is as much a futile piece of reaction as Mr. Morley's Council of Notables. The same exclusive, oligarchical spirit of the past trying to dominate the future, of the few with wealth, position and fame for their title claiming the monopoly of political life, animates the idea of the Convention. Perhaps, if the Convention becomes a living fact, it may, who knows, be accepted by Mr. Morley as the basis for his Council of Notables? But if the Moderates of Bombay would welcome such a consummation, the Bengal leaders ought to know that the attempt to separate the Congress from the life of the people will be disastrous to the future of the movement for which Bengal stands. If they associate themselves with any such attempt to bring back the country to the footstool of the bureaucracy, they will have given the last blow to their influence and popularity. They may remain Notables, they will cease to be popular leaders. The resolution of the Pabna Conference which was accepted by them leaves them no ground to stand upon if they associate themselves with the Bombay attempt to turn back the wheels of time and put an end to the natural evolution of the Congress. The Convention was the creation of Sir Pherozshah Mehta who will leave no stone unturned to save his offspring when the Convention Committee meets at Allahabad; it will be seen whether the fear of Sir Pherozshah Mehta or the fear of the country is strongest in the hearts of the Moderate leaders. They are still, it seems, undecided as to their course, a dangerous condition of mind since the powerful will of Sir Pherozshah is likely to carry all before it, if it is not met by a settled determination to give effect to the plainly expressed wishes of the people.

Whatever happens at the Convention, the leaders of the Moderate Party will be held responsible for the result. If the Congress breaks asunder for good, the blame will rest on them and they will no longer be able to throw it upon the Nationalists who have since the break-up at Surat laid themselves open to the charge of weakness and cowardice rather than stand in the way of reconciliation. From the first meeting of the Nationalist Conference after the fracas on the second day of the session to the present moment the attitude of the party has been accommodating to a fault. They allowed the Moderates to score a seeming triumph at Pabna rather than allow a second split. At Poona in their stronghold they invited the co-operation of the Moderates at Dhulia, they even consented to the question of the Boycott being allowed to stand over, unless otherwise decided by the Provincial Conference, rather than forfeit Moderate co-operation. The public utterances of Nationalist papers and Nationalist speakers from the speech of Mr. Tilak after the fracas to the latest speeches at the Poona Conference have all been pervaded by the thought of reconciliation, the anxiety for union. The Nationalists make no stipulation except that no creed shall be imposed on the Congress from outside, no action be taken which implies that the Convention is the arbiter of the destinies of the Congress and that no constitution or change of policy shall be drawn up by anyone as binding on the Congress before the Congress itself decided on its future course. This is an attitude to which no one can take reasonable exception. The Nationalists also appointed a Committee after the fiasco, but the instructions issued to this Committee were merely to watch the results of the split, to see that a reconciliation be effected and only in the last resort to take up the work of the Congress where it had broken off, if no accommodation proved possible. The Committee has therefore taken no action beyond watching the course of events and exercising the influence of its authorised officials to bring about such resolutions as would help the reconciliation of the parties. It depends entirely on the result of the meeting at Allahabad whether the Committee is to assert its existence or quietly allow itself to cease when the main object for which it came into being has been accomplished. Convention and Conference are both mere party organisations and, if either of them affects to be the Congress, it will be guilty of a parricidal action leading to the death of the parent body.

BY THE WAY

The annual meeting of the European and Anglo-Indian Defence Association took place last Monday without the world being any the worse for the calamity. There were speeches and there was a report. Each of the orations was in the usual key of solemnity and the Association conducted itself with imperturbable seriousness — a feat of muscular self-control which should be put down to its credit. A sense of humour is an obstacle to success in life and the British nation has always avoided or controlled it, especially since the union with Scotland. It is, indeed, since the Scotchman became a member of the British nation that the great development of England as an Empire has taken place. Now the Anglo-Indian Defence Association hails largely from beyond the Tweed.

*

The first speaker who took the affairs of the Empire under his patronage, was a certain Mr. Lockhart Smith. He gave some firm but kindly advice to the leaders of Indian thought as to the best way of managing their business forgetting that his time would have been more usefully employed in minding his own. It appears that the unrest was a natural and healthy aspiration of the people, but all the same it created a natural and healthy alarm in the manly breasts of the Anglo-Indian Defence Association and it is a good thing that it has quieted down to some extent. Unfortunately the position is still far from clear or satisfactory to Mr. Lockhart Smith. This healthy unrest is still too healthily restless for Mr. Smith's nerves. He therefore calls upon the leaders of Indian thought to rise to the occasion and handle the situation with a statesmanlike reposefulness. They must learn to be quietly unquiet, restfully restless, humbly aspiring, meekly bold. If they are restless in their unrest, the Government will "put back the hands of the clock", to the great inconvenience of old Father Time. Perhaps Mr. Lockhart Smith is in the habit of putting back the hands of the clock in his office so as to give his clerks a longer spell of work; otherwise we cannot understand his sublime confidence in the effectiveness of this trick with the clock or his evident belief that it will stop the march of Time.

*

On the whole the advice of Mr. Smith may be summed up as an appeal to spare his nerves. The Viceroy will recognise the position "as clear and satisfactory" if the leaders are content to 'aspire' without being over-anxious to get their aspirations realised. We have no doubt he will.

*

After Mr. Lockhart Smith had locked up his heart from farther speech, there was a shower of sparks. Mr. H. W. S. Sparkes chose the unrest for the theme of his eloquence. Every sentence in the report of his speech is a scintillating piece of brilliance. He said "if the wishes of the people of India, the Extremists, who are thinking of driving the British out of India were granted, they would be the first to go down on their bended knees and ask the Government to stay back and dictate any terms they liked." That the people of India are all extremists, is the first proposition we gather from this remarkable prophecy, that they all want to drive the British out of India is the second. It appears that their wishes are going to be granted, but whether by God or John Morley the prophet does not inform us. At some psychological stage of the process of eviction — after the wishes have been granted and the British have been driven out of India, — the Government and Mr. Sparkes are to be intercepted on the Apollo Bunder by a deputation of Bepin Pal, Tilak and Khaparde on bended knees asking them to stay back on any terms rather than deprive India of their beatific presence. This is the first spark.

*

The second spark is of a somewhat fuliginous character. Mr. Sparkes hastened to disclaim this remarkable prophecy, it is his fosterchild and not his own and only begotten son. "These were not his own views, but of the Bengalis and men who never mixed in politics." They are the views, it seems, of two classes of men, first, of the Bengalis, then, of men who never mixed in politics; and the opinion of the latter on a political question is no doubt exceptionally valuable, but if this is the opinion of the Bengalis, who then are the people of India who are all Extremists and want to drive the British out in order to have the luxury of asking them back on their bended knees? There seems to be a confusion of Sparkes somewhere.

*

It appears that "the Indians are trying to be registered as a nation of the world, but they were fools if they thought that that time had come". Here is another brilliant classification, but we do not quite grasp the distinction between a nation of the world and a nation not of the world. It seems to savour of German metaphysics and is too deep for us. Anyway, we observe that Mr. Sparkes differs from the Transvaal authorities, he will not allow Indians to register themselves in the book of the world. What, not even their thumb impressions, Mr. Sparkes?

*

"The Partition wounded the people of Bengal to the quick but Mr. Morley had done well in refusing to reopen that question." This was the last fitting coruscation of Sparkes, and yet neither the Ganges nor the Maidan was ablaze. After this Mr. Summons with his blood-curdling references to the train-wrecking incident and the Allen affair fell quite flat. He discovered a distinct attempt made to shield the wrong-doers. This is a charge against the police to which we invite the prompt attention of Sir Andrew Fraser. Mr. Summons ought to be called upon either to substantiate his allegation against the Lieutenant-Governor's friends or withdraw it.

Such was the feast of fancy and the flow of soul which came off last Monday. The end of this once potent Association threatens to be as pitiful as that of the Roman way — which began in massive dignity and ended in a bog.

Bande Mataram, April 4, 1908

The Constitution of the Subjects Committee

WHEN we first wrote of the Constitution we pointed out the importance of the Subjects Committee as the first approach towards the democratisation of the Congress. The whole assembly of delegates is too large and too loose a body to discuss what resolutions shall be placed before it or what particular form of words should be used. This has necessarily to be done by a smaller body. But before the Subjects Committee came into existence these questions were decided irresponsibly by a small cabal of leaders in secret. When the first difference arose between the old leaders and younger men, the prospect of a difference of opinion on the platform of the Congress was sufficient to bring about the substitution of a Committee for the cabal. It was a step forward but a very small step. The Committee was nominated by the cabal, not elected by the Congress, with the result that only those who were likely to be subservient to the cabal, their satellites, their mofussil lieutenants or others who were too prominent to be ignored, became members of the Committee. The change widened the basis of the oligarchy, it did not introduce a democratic principle. The Committee met to consent to what the leaders proposed, the Congress met to consent to what the Committee suggested. Freedom of discussion was restricted in the Committee by the autocratic intervention of dominant members of the cabal, in the Congress it was tabooed as a violation of unity.

In any future constitution of the Congress the election of the Subjects Committee must be regulated by the principles of democratic representation, not of oligarchic nomination. The state of things during the last two years has been one of transition, the leaders attempting to dictate their choice to the delegates, the delegates attempting to force theirs on the leaders, and the formation of the Subjects Committee has been invariably the occasion of scenes of tumult, confusion and chaos which were painful to all lovers of orderly procedure. The only remedy is the frank acceptance of the principle of democratic representation. At Surat when the Bengali delegates were electing their representatives on the Subjects Committee, Srijut Surendranath Banerji let fall a remarkable expression of sentiment which explains the difficulty felt by the leaders in frankly accepting the principle of district or divisional election which can alone ensure that the Subjects Committee will represent the will of the country. "If the delegates are allowed to elect their representatives," he said, "the best men will not be chosen." The aristocratic nature of the objection was a surprise to many of the delegates, for it contains the very essence of the oligarchical spirit. The distrust of the people, the sense of aristocratic superiority, the confidence of superior wisdom which it conveyed are the stamp of this spirit in all ages. The best men are the men of position, rank, status, the men with a stake in the country, the men who have succeeded and are on the top of the ladder, and these have a right to lead by virtue of their position apart from the will of the people. The party of privilege in all ages have posed as the superior people, the monopolists of wisdom, the *optimates* or best men, the *boni* or good people. The party opposed to them are the ignorant, the pestilent demagogues, the crazy fanatics, the men without stake or substance who wish to create a revolution in order to benefit themselves. If democratic election is allowed, these men will be elected in increasing numbers and shoulder out their betters. This spirit of oligarchical exclusiveness is the secret of all the friction which has been evident and the scenes of anger, strife and disorder, the frequent outbreaks of popular indignation which have marked the Conferences and Congresses since the birth of the democratic spirit. The Congress oligarchs, unwilling to allow that spirit to assert itself, are yet unable to disavow openly the principles of democracy in the name of which they demand from the bureaucracy rights and privileges which they themselves refuse to the rank and file of their own followers. The conflict goes on behind the scenes and the outbreaks in the Conference or Congress are rare and the results of a growing impatience of the evasions, tricks, shufflings by which the leaders try to hold an untenable position. They can neither disown democracy nor frankly accept it. They are eager to keep up its forms, determined to exclude its spirit. We shall not dwell farther on this aspect of the question, for the democratic spirit cannot be permanently repressed or baffled by evasions. That the constitution must be based on democratic principles is one of the axioms with which we have started. The Subjects Committee is the brain of the Congress and must be democratised if the Congress itself is to be democratic. Otherwise we shall have a repetition of the scenes which we are all anxious to avoid. An oligarchical Subjects Committee preparing resolutions which have to be repeatedly challenged in the full house, is an unworkable arrangement. The delegates must be made to feel that the Committee is really representative of their wishes and opinions and the inclination to scan with suspicion the Subjects Committee's resolutions and amend them in full house, will then disappear.

The election of the members of the Committee is at present no election at all, but a scramble for the membership. It must be reduced to order and rule by a serious, settled and deliberate form of election. The representatives of each division in a province must be allowed to sit separately and vote their choice of representatives for their own division, the names must be written down by a temporary secretary and handed in to the Secretary for the Province who will read out the full list of names to the assembled delegates of the Province. These names should be sent in to the Secretaries of the Congress who will put in the full list as soon as the President's address is over. In this way the business of forming the Subjects Committee can be done quietly, timely and thoroughly. No objection should be allowed from one division against the choice of another division or from one Province against the choice of another Province.

But the method of election is not the only obstacle in the way of full correspondence between the will of the Subjects Committee and the will of the Congress. The method of discussion in the Committee is at present hampered by irregularities which often prevent the real sense of the Committee from being properly ascertained. It is only when a strong and conscientious President acquainted with the forms of discussion in a free country sits in the chair, that the proceedings of the Committee are worthy of itself. These irregularities arise partly from ignorance of the rules of debate, partly from over-eagerness to make points and score tactical successes. The only remedy is for the rules of discussion to be formalised, made known to each member and rigidly enforced by the President. When this is done, the habit of orderly discussion will gradually create a public sentiment against excess of party spirit. Finally, the secrecy of the sitting is a feature which ought not to be continued. It is undemocratic in its origin, fosters irresponsibility and helps to create misunderstanding and facilitate crooked methods. There is no reason why our discussions should not be carried out in the full light of day, since we have nothing to conceal; on the contrary, the knowledge of the discussion in the Subjects Committee will serve the same end as the publicity of Parliamentary discussions in free countries. It will keep up a living interest in the people, educate the public mind to deal with political questions in a graver and more responsible spirit, accustom the representatives of the people to feel that they are speaking and acting with the eye of all India upon them and train the country to prepare itself the habits of mind, speech and action which are necessary for the success of representative government. Secrecy is the enemy of good government, but it is still more fatal to self-government. Publicity is the very breath of life to democratic institutions.

These then are the changes which we would suggest for the democratisation of the Subjects Committee — the members to be elected by the divisions of each Province by a regular and orderly method, the discussions of the Committee to be regulated by fixed rules of procedure and the sitting to be thrown open to the Press and the public or at least to the delegates. When these changes have been effected, the foundations of representative government in India will have been laid, for it is only out of the Congress that representative institutions can arise in India. The Congress is the seed and only by the proper development of the seed can the life of the tree be ensured.

Bande Mataram, April 6, 1908

The New Ideal

THE need of a great ideal was never more keenly felt than it is in India at the present day. Nowhere have so many weaknesses combined to stand in the way of a nation in the whole range of history. Nowhere have the rulers reduced their subjects to so complete, pervading and abject a material helplessness. When the Mogul ruled, he ruled as a soldier and a conqueror, in the pride of his strength, in the confidence of his invincible greatness, as the lord of the peoples by natural right of his imperial character and warlike strength and skill. He stooped to no meanness, hedged himself in with no army of spies, entered into no relations with foreign powers, but, grandiose and triumphant, sat on the throne of a continent like Indra on his heavenly seat, master of his world because there was none strong enough to dispute it with him. He trusted his subjects, gave them positions of power and responsibility, used their brain and arm to preserve his conquests and by the royalty of that trust and noble pride in his own ability to stand by his innate strength, was able to hold India for over a century until Aurangzebe forgot the Kuladharma of his house and by distrust, tyranny and meanness lost for his descendants the splendid heritage of his forefathers. The present domination is a rule of shopkeepers who are at the same time bureaucrats, a combination of the worst possible qualities for imperial Government. The shopkeeper rules by deceit, the bureaucrat by the use of red tape. The shopkeeper by melancholy meanness alienates the subject population, the bureaucrat by soulless rigidity deprives the administration of life and human sympathy. The shopkeeper uses his position of authority to push his wares and fleece his subjects, the bureaucrat forgets his duty and loses his royal character in his mercantile greed. The shopkeeper becomes a pocket Machiavel, the bureaucrat a gigantic retail trader. By this confusion of *dharmas*, *varṇasaṅkara* is born in high places and the nation first and the rulers afterwards go to perdition.

This is what has happened in India under the present regime. The bureaucracy have ruled in the spirit of a mercantile power, holding its position by aid of mercenaries, afraid of its subjects, with no confidence in its destiny, with no trust even in the mercenaries who support it, piling up gold with one hand, with the other holding a borrowed sword over the head of a fallen people. It has sought its strength not in the mission with which God had entrusted it, nor in the greatness of England, her mastery of the ocean, her pride of unconquered prowess, her just and sympathetic principle of government, but in the weakness of the people. The strength of England has been held as a threat in the background, not as a source of quiet and unostentatious self-confidence which enable the rulers to be generous as well as just. The liberal principles of English rule have been chanted as a sort of magic *mantra* to hypnotise the nation into willing subjection, not used as a living principle of government. What have been the real sources of bureaucratic strength? An Arms act, a corrupt and oppressive police, an army of spies, a mercenary military force officered by Englishmen, a people emasculated, kept ignorant, out of the world's life, poor, intimidated, abjectly under the thumb of the police constable or the provincial prefect. Such a principle of rule cannot endure. It contradicts the law of God and offends the reason of man; it is as unprofitable as it is selfish and heartless.

The nation which has passed through a century of such a misgovernment must necessarily have degenerated. The bureaucracy has taken care to destroy every centre of strength not subservient to itself. A nation politically disorganised, a nation morally corrupted, intellectually pauperised, physically broken and stunted is the result of a hundred years of British rule, the account which England can give before God of the trust which He placed in her hands. The condition of the people is the one answer to all the songs of praise which the bureaucrats sing of their rule, which the people of England chorus with such a smug self-satisfaction and which even foreign peoples echo in the tune of admiration and praise. But for us the people who have suffered, the victims of the miserable misuse which bureaucrats have made of the noblest opportunity God ever gave to a nation, the song has no longer any charm, the *mantra* has lost its hypnotic force, the spell has ceased to work. While we could we deceived ourselves, but we can deceive ourselves no longer. Pain is a terrible disillusioner and the pangs which had come upon us were those of approaching dissolution. It was at the last moment, when further delay would have meant death, that a higher than earthly physician administered through a proud viceroy the potent poison of Partition and saved the life of India. The treatment of the disease has been drastic and will continue to be drastic. There are those who dream of mild remedies, whose beautiful souls will not bear to think of the fierceness of strife, hatred or agony which a revolution implies; but strong poisons are the only salvation in desperate diseases and we fear that without these poisons India will not easily or ever recover from the fatal and consuming disease which has overtaken her. What will support her under the stress of the agony she will have to undergo? What strength will help her to shake off the weaknesses which have crowded in on her? How will she raise herself from the dust whom a thousand shackles bind down? Only the strength of a superhuman ideal, only the gigantic force of a superhuman will, only the vehemence of an effort which transcends all that man has done and approaches divinity. Where will she find that strength, that force, that vehemence? In herself. We have seen Ramamurti, the modern Bhimasen, lie motionless, resistant, with a superhuman force of will-power acting through the muscles while two carts loaded with men are driven over his body. India must undergo an ordeal of passive endurance far more terrible without relaxing a single fibre of her frame. We have seen Ramamurti break over his chest a strong iron chain tightened round his whole body and break it by the sheer force of will working through the body. India must work a similar deliverance for herself by the same inner force. It is not by strength of body that Ramamurti accomplishes his feats, for he is not stronger than many athletes who could never do what he does daily, but by faith and will. India has in herself a faith of superhuman virtue to accomplish miracles, to deliver herself out of irrefragable bondage, to bring God down upon earth. She has a secret of will power which no other nation possesses. All she needs to rouse in her that faith, that will, is an ideal which will induce her to make the effort. That ideal is now being preached by Srijut Bepin Chandra Pal in every speech he delivers and never has it been delivered with such beauty of expression, such a passion of earnestness and pathos, such a sublimity of feeling as at Uttarpara on Sunday when he addressed a meeting of the people in the compound of the Uttarpara Library. The ideal is that of humanity in God, of God in humanity, the ancient ideal of the *sanātana dharma* but applied, as it has never been applied before, to the problem of politics and the work of national revival. To realise that ideal, to impart it to the world is the mission of India. She has evolved a religion which embraces all that the heart, the brain, the practical faculty of man can desire but she has not yet applied it to the problems of modern politics. This therefore is the work which she has still to do before she can help humanity; the necessity of the mission is the justification for her resurgence, the great incentive of saving herself to save mankind is the native power which will give her the force, the strength, the vehemence which can alone enable her to realise her destiny. No lesser ideal will help her through the stress of the terrible ordeal which she will in a few years be called to face. No hope less pure will save her from the demoralisation which follows revolutionary strife, the growth of passions, a violent selfishness, sanguinary hatred, insufferable licences, the disruption of moralities, the resurgence of the tiger in man which a great revolution is apt to foster. Srijut Bepin Chandra speaks under an inspiration which he himself is unable to resist. The public wish to hear him on Swaraj, Swadeshi, Boycott, National Education — the old subjects of his unparalleled eloquence, and he himself may desire to speak on them, but the voice of a prophet is not his own to speak the thing he will, but another's to speak the thing he must. India needed the gospel of Swaraj, Swadeshi, Boycott and National Education to nerve her to her first effort, but now that she is drawing nearer to the valley of the shadow of Death she needs a still mightier inspiration, a still more enthusiastic and all-conquering faith. The people have not yet understood, but the power to understand is in them, and if any voice can awake that power, it is Bepin Chandra's.

Bande Mataram, April 7, 1908

The "Indu" and the Dhulia Conference
Non-Party Lines

The Reception Committee of the Dhulia Conference has fallen under the ban of the *Indu Prakash* because it has dared to attempt a compromise in which the views of the "Extremists" have not been completely ignored. The only "compromise" which Moderates are prepared to accept is one in which Nationalism is ignored and the Nationalists make a complete surrender. It is strange to find these irreconcilable fanatics of separatism posing as men of sobriety and moderation, these ignorers of every principle of constitutional action posing as constitutionalists. The framing of two or three resolutions of self-help and the repetition of three of the Calcutta Congress resolutions is described by the organ of Sir Pherozshah as the capture of the Conference by Extremism. The Dhulia Reception Committee have framed fifteen resolutions of which the first three are the Congress resolutions on Self-Government, Swadeshi and National Education; the fourth is a resolution for an united Congress on the lines settled at the Calcutta Congress; the fifth is for village organisation and arbitration; the ninth advocates physical culture. These six resolutions are the only ones which have the slightest nationalist tinge, and it must be remembered that the first is a Moderate and not a Nationalist resolution. The rest are petitionary resolutions of the ancient type, the last of them compromising a respectable-sized omnibus full of petitions. To our mind, it seems that the Dhulia Nationalists have compromised with a vengeance and if ever there was a Conference framed on non-party lines, this deserves the description. But our excellent old *Moonshine* will not allow anything to be non-party which is not entirely Moderate.

Prescriptive Rights

The first offence of the Conference is that it has not said ditto to the suggestion of the Bombay Presidency Association to postpone the Conference till October by which time the Moderates could have made all arrangements for holding the Congress according to their will and pleasure and would have pleaded that it was too late to make any change. The Association has by prescription been organising Conferences, says the *Indu*, and so to ignore its opinion is Extremism. The idea of an Association in Bombay city having the prescriptive right to organise Conferences and dictate to the Reception Committee, is one of those staggering assumptions which the Bombay Moderate brain puts forth with an appallingly cheerful defiance of common sense, logic and constitutional principles unintelligible to the ordinary man. Might we be allowed to suggest that the early part of the year is now generally accepted as the proper time for a Provincial Conference and that the Bombay Association has no more right to be obeyed in this or any other matter than, say, the Moderate Convention?

The Calcutta Resolutions

The *Indu* proceeds to put forward the remarkable argument that the Conference could have been an united success only if all contentious matter relating to Congress politics had been scrupulously omitted, considering that almost all matters which come before the Congress now involve more or less the contentions as to principles which divide the Congress, this amounts to saying that an united Conference is impossible, — a confession of the country's political incapacity which is redolent of Sir Pherozshah Mehta. The next complaint is that the Moderates did not try to force their creed on the Conference, while the Extremists have unblushingly pushed their hobby of the Calcutta positions. We invite the attention of the country to the practical admission that the Moderates are opposed to the Calcutta resolutions, an admission which may be advantageously compared with the repeated Moderate protestations that there was never any intention of drawing back from the Calcutta positions. Our answer to the contention is that the Calcutta resolutions are in the nature of a compromise by which both parties with their programmes are given scope in the Congress and are therefore not of a party character but the sole possible basis for united work; the creed on the other hand is avowedly of a party character and intended to exclude Nationalists from the Congress. It was for this reason that the Moderates and Nationalists at Dhulia, being sincerely desirous of union, accepted the former and avoided the latter. This is a fact which the Bombay Moderates find it convenient to misrepresent, but it has been clearly recognised both at Pabna and Dhulia; — the Calcutta resolutions are not "Extremist" positions, but a compromise between the parties; as such the Nationalists hold to them and not as a hobby or as their "creed".

Ignoring and Defying

This resolution, says the *Indu*, is an attempt "to ignore and defy the Convention Committee (and commit the Conference to the lines of the Bodas Ghose Committee) the unconstitutionalism of which we exposed the other day." We have unfortunately missed this no doubt luminous exposure, but we are curious to know by what principle of constitutionalism the Convention Committee enjoys any authority over a Provincial Conference for it to defy, or holds any position which it is not at perfect liberty to ignore. What part has a Convention which was avowedly a party Convention excluding over six hundred Congress delegates, in the constitution of the Congress? The Provinces are at liberty to ignore both Committees equally, for neither has at present any constitutional authority or position, if the Congress is alive. If the Congress is dead, there can be no talk of constitution; at most the Convention and the Conference are co-legators and divide the property. The question for a Provincial Conference is not between one committee and another, but between union and division, the death of the Congress or its resuscitation.

The Calcutta Compromise

Finally, the *Indu* after sneering at the Calcutta resolutions as an

Extremist creed, itself charges the Reception Committee with disloyalty to the Calcutta position, because they have adopted the Self-Government resolution without taking on a rider about Legislative Councils and other "steps" to Self-Government. We know it is the position of the Mehta clique that even Self-Government is a far off, almost impracticable dream and that we should in the meanwhile be satisfied with small reforms. The Calcutta Congress fixed Colonial Self-Government as a practical demand, a thing which should be extended to India, but it did not as the *Indu* pretends, fix a far off date for the extension, only knowing that its demand, though perfectly and immediately practical (otherwise the expression "should be extended" has no meaning) would not be granted, it demanded certain reforms as steps towards Colonial Self-Government. The Dhulia Conference does precisely the same though the "steps" are asked for in separate resolutions. The Calcutta Congress, as a compromise, combined petitions with self-help, a resolution for National Education with a prayer for the extension of Government education. The Dhulia Conference does precisely the same. The *Indu* discovers the inconsistency of this position with the air of Newton discovering the law of gravitation. Inconsistent it is, but the Calcutta resolutions are not an essay in logic, they are a compromise between two entirely different programmes, of which the fittest will survive. We have noticed the arguments of the *Indu* at length because it is necessary for the country to realise the sort of shufflings by which it is sought to justify the policy of "divide and serve" on which the Bombay clique has set its heart. If we can save the Congress, we will, but if it is broken, this time at least the responsibility shall rest on the right shoulders.

Bande Mataram, April 8, 1908

The Asiatic Role

THE genius of the Hindu is not for pure action, but for thought and aspiration realised in action, the spirit premeditating before the body obeys the inward command. The life of the Hindu is inward and his outward life aims only at reproducing the motions of his spirit. This intimate relation of his thought and his actions is the secret of his perpetual vitality. His outward life, like that of other nations, is subject to growth and decay, to periods of greatness and periods of decline, but while other nations have a limit and a term, he has none. Whenever death claims his portion, the Hindu race takes refuge in the source of all immortality, plunges itself into the fountain of spirit and comes out renewed for a fresh term of existence. The elixir of national life has been discovered by India alone. This immortality, this great secret of life, she has treasured up for thousands of years, until the world was fit to receive it. The time has now come for her to impart it to the other nations who are now on the verge of decadence and death. The peoples of Europe have carried material life to its farthest expression, the science of bodily existence has been perfected, but they are suffering from diseases which their science is powerless to cure. England with her practical intelligence, France with her clear logical brain, Germany with her speculative genius, Russia with her emotional force, America with her commercial energy have done what they could for human development, but each has reached the limit of her peculiar capacity. Something is wanting which Europe cannot supply. It is at this juncture that Asia has awakened, because the world needed her. Asia is the custodian of the world's peace of mind, the physician of the maladies which Europe generates. She is commissioned to rise from time to time from her ages of self-communion, self-sufficiency, self-absorption and rule the world for a season so that the world may come and sit at her feet to learn the secrets she alone has to give. When the restless spirit of Europe has added a new phase of discovery to the evolution of the science of material life, has regulated politics, rebased society, remodelled law, rediscovered science, the spirit of Asia, calm, contemplative, self-possessed, takes possession of Europe's discovery and corrects its exaggerations, its aberrations by the intuition, the spiritual light she alone can turn upon the world. When Greek and Roman had exhausted themselves, the Arab went out from his desert to take up their unfinished task, revivify the civilisation of the old world and impart the profounder impulses of Asia to the pursuit of knowledge. Asia has always initiated, Europe completed. The strength of Europe is in details, the strength of Asia in synthesis. When Europe has perfected the details of life or thought, she is unable to harmonise them into a perfect symphony and she falls into intellectual heresies, practical extravagances which contradict the facts of life, the limits of human nature and the ultimate truths of existence. It is therefore the office of Asia to take up the work of human evolution when Europe comes to a standstill and loses itself in a clash of vain speculations, barren experiments and helpless struggles to escape from the consequences of her own mistakes. Such a time has now come in the world's history.

In former ages India was a sort of hermitage of thought and peace apart from the world. Separated from the rest of humanity by her peculiar geographical conformation, she worked out her own problems and thought out the secrets of existence as in a quiet Ashram from which the noise of the world was shut out. Her thoughts flashed out over Asia and created civilisations, her sons were the bearers of light to the peoples; philosophies based themselves on stray fragments of her infinite wisdom; sciences arose from the waste of her intellectual production. When the barrier was broken and nations began to surge through the Himalayan gates, the peace of India departed. She passed through centuries of struggle, of ferment in which the civilisations born of her random thoughts returned to her developed and insistent, seeking to impose themselves on the mighty mother of them all. To her they were the reminiscences of her old intellectual experiments laid aside and forgotten. She took them up, re-thought them in a new light and once more made them part of herself. So she dealt with the Greek, so with the Scythian, so with Islam, so now she will deal with the great brood of her returning children, with Christianity, with Buddhism, with European science and materialism, with the fresh speculations born of the world's renewed contact with the source of thought in this ancient cradle of religion, science and philosophy. The vast amount of new matter which she has to absorb, is unprecedented in her history, but to her it is child's play. Her all-embracing intellect, her penetrating intuition, her invincible originality are equal to greater tasks. The period of passivity when she listened to the voices of the outside world is over. No longer will she be content merely to receive and reproduce, even to receive and improve. The genius of Japan lies in imitation and improvement, that of India in origination. The contributions of outside peoples she can only accept as rough material for her immense creative faculty. It was the mission of England to bring this rough material to India, but in the arrogance of her material success she presumed to take upon herself the role of a teacher and treated the Indian people partly as an infant to be instructed, partly as a serf to be schooled to labour for its lords. The farce is played out. England's mission in India is over and it is time for her to recognise the limit of the lease given to her. When it was God's will that she should possess India, the world was amazed at the miraculous ease of the conquest and gave all the credit to the unparalleled genius and virtues of the Engligh people, a fiction which England was not slow to encourage and on which she has traded for over a century. The real truth is suggested in the famous saying that England conquered India in a fit of absence of mind, which is only another way of saying that she did not conquer it at all. It was placed in her hands without her realising what was being done or how it was being done. The necessary conditions were created for her, her path made easy, the instruments given into her hands. The men who worked for her were of comparatively small intellectual stature and with few exceptions did not make and could not have made any mark in European history where no special Providence was at work to supplement the deficiencies of the instruments. The subjugation of India is explicable neither in the ability of the men whose names figure as the protagonists nor in the superior genius of the conquering nation nor in the weakness of the conquered people. It is one of the standing miracles of history. In other words, it was one of those cases in which a particular mission was assigned to a people not otherwise superior to the rest of the world and a special *faustitas* or decreed good fortune set to watch over the fulfilment of the mission. Her mission once over, the angel of the Lord who stood by England in her task and removed opponents and difficulties with the waving of his hand, will no longer shield her. She will stay so long as the destinies of India need her and not a day longer, for it is not by her own strength that she came or is still here, and it is not by her own strength that she can remain. The resurgence of India is begun, it will accomplish itself with her help, if she will, without it if she does not, against it if she opposes.

Love Me or Die

The Editor of the Urdu *Swarajya* has been warned to refrain from seditious writings. The Magistrate in conveying the warning unctuously remarked that "the Government never dissuades righteous criticism, it is only a disaffectionate feeling that it wants to check." The heart of the bureaucracy is evidently in the right place; it is so anxious to be loved that it is ready to chop off the head of anyone who refuses to love it. The bureaucracy has sometimes been compared by editors with exuberant pens to the Emperor Nero, a comparison which it has resented by putting the writer in prison; but it is written in history that Nero suffered precisely from this amiable weakness. He wanted to be loved and anyone who had a "disaffectionate feeling" for him or criticised "unrighteously" his character or his flute-playing or his poetry or his acting, was in instant danger of being taught affection by the sword. Nero also did not want to dissuade "righteous" criticism, but then the judge of the righteousness of the criticism was Nero himself. The love-sick despot is a more difficult kind of animal to tackle than the more ferocious species. "Obey me or perish" is the attitude of the latter, and it is one which can be appreciated if not admired. But "love me or die", is a principle of Government to which human nature cannot so easily accustom itself. It is too ethereal for the grossness of our base terrestrial composition.

Bande Mataram, April 9, 1908

The Work Before Us

THE little that we have done is the first faint shadowing forth of our future activities, nothing more. If we are content with what we have done, even that little will disappear, the movement will be abortive and the country fall back into its former condition. It is therefore necessary to give a new impetus to the movement everywhere, and now that Srijut Bepin Chandra is out of prison, the necessary will no doubt be done. The first work is to revive courage in the hearts of the people. The effect of the recent repression has been not to crush the movement, but to discourage its outward activity. This discouragement must be removed. We cannot allow the movement to be driven inward and become an affair of secret societies and terrorism, as it will inevitably become if the outward expression of it is stopped. The next work is to give a stronger impetus to the boycott, so that the little that we have gained may become the starting-point for fresh victories; the organisation of boycott is the first work to which we should set our hands. The third thing to be done is to spread National Education. A serious effort must be made to take in hand the raising of funds for this branch of national activity, so that the National Council may be in a position both to effect the complete organisation of its scientific, technical and other sides and to extend aid to the increasing number of schools which are springing up all over the country. It is also necessary to bring the existing primary schools under the Council; for this is a work of great importance, and until it is done, the foundations of the new educational edifice will not be secure, since it is the primary schools in which the bulk of the people are educated. If the present institutions will not come into the new system, the country must be covered with a network of new primary schools on national lines, such as the one which is now being projected at Uttarpara, — schools giving a primary literary education along with such technical instruction as will enable the students to earn a livelihood as small artisans. If this is done, the public will flock into the national institutions and the old primary schools will perish.

So much is necessary for the completion of the work for which we have already laid a foundation, but the time has come when we should start actively on fresh lines. The most important of these is arbitration, which will, if successfully carried out, form the basis of our future self-government. Education will give us the necessary training of mind and character for self-government, arbitration will provide a practical field in which our capacities can be tested. In some parts the work has already been begun and with remarkable success, but it is necessary to lay the foundations all over Bengal. The difficulties that lie in its way are not so insuperable as they at first appear; if the lawyer class can be provided with a means of living by the arbitration system, their passive opposition, which is the only real obstacle to be dreaded, can be removed. The existing courts will provide careers for those who wish to earn large fortunes in the legal line, but the host of small practitioners in the mofussil are those who will be affected by the spread of arbitration and some provision must be made in our arbitration schemes by which their field, if restricted, may not be entirely destroyed. This subject is one which demands detailed treatment and it will be the theme of a future article. At present we wish only to emphasise its great importance.

When we have laid the foundations of arbitration, our work is not finished; the positive side of it only has been done. There is another side less palpable, but even more important, and it is the destructive or negative side, the removal of old prepossessions, false beliefs, false ideals from the mind of the people. So long as the least little of faith in the bureaucracy remains in the lowest class of our population, the conditions of success are not complete. The bureaucracy is itself doing much to destroy the ancient faith in its philanthropy, integrity and high motive which was the source of its strength, but this is chiefly in the educated class and the landed aristocracy, both of which, whatever the outward professions, fear or self-interest may dictate, are now thoroughly alienated. The only work which remains to be done so far as these classes are concerned, is to generate faith in the nation, for so far as moderatism still prevails, it is not owing to faith in the bureaucracy but to distrust in the nation. The lower classes have still to be inoculated with the spirit of self-help, separation from the alien and confidence in their own countrymen. To some extent the work has been done, the seed has been sown; Swadeshi is the seedbed of this spirit of self-reliance, this sense of separateness, and, at least among the Hindu community, Swadeshi is deeply rooted in all classes. But this seed has yet to fructify and spring up. The only way in which this can be done is to destroy the barriers between the educated class and the peasantry which English education has created, to restore the old unity of society by mutual service, by love, by self-identification with the mass of our countrymen. The volunteer movement, now in a rudimentary state, has to be developed and perfected so as to form the bridge of communication between the heart of the people and the brain of the educated community. Our propaganda among the masses must consist less in the teaching of ideas than in teaching by acts, less in intellectual conviction than in the appeal to the heart and to the imagination. No time should be lost in taking this work in hand, the days are passing by with great swiftness and bringing us nearer and nearer to the final struggle when the people and the bureaucracy will stand face to face. On that day the masses will weigh down the scale and decide victory or defeat.

Campbell-Bannerman Retires

The resignation of Sir Henry Campbell-Bannerman leaves things for India just where they were, but it is of some importance for England, as it is not unlikely that the transference of leadership to a man of Mr. Asquith's cold, hard and unsympathatic Whiggism may lead to an early disruption of the Liberal majority. For India, of course, that event would mean little or nothing; a Hamilton to a Fowler and a Morley to a Brodrick succeeds, and the only difference made by the retirement of the quondam friend, philosopher and guide of Moderatism into the cool shades of Opposition, will be that we are now suffering from repression with sympathy and will then suffer from repression without sympathy. On the whole we prefer the latter brand; it is more genuine and invigorating.

United Congress*

After several gentlemen's speeches Sj. Aurobindo Ghose rose up at last. He admitted that he had a hand in drafting the resolution but denied the charge of inconsistency on the ground that this new movement, as it is divinely decreed, cannot proceed on the basis of strict consistency of individual conduct from any individual standpoint. The breaking-up of the Congress at Surat was God's will and if it can meet again on a basis of union that would also come from His will. If, again, all our efforts at union fail and the New Party be compelled to face troubles and persecutions, that should also be taken as a divinely appointed destiny. We shall not be eager for compromise to avoid trouble and persecution as sufferings are welcome if it be God's will that we should suffer, so that our Mother India would be saved. But, in the meantime, we are a democratic party: at Pabna, at Dhulia and other places, people wanted a united Congress and it is our duty to try for it if no vital principle is sacrificed to gain that end. This was the Speaker's apology for the attempt at union, though, as he said, his hopes were not high about the success of the attempt. The Congress broke up not over personalities, but for certain definite issues which were: (1) irregularities in the election of the President, (2) the attempt from certain quarters to take advantage of the local majority to recede from the four Calcutta resolutions, (3) the attempt to impose a creed by the help of a local majority with a view to exclude a large and growing party. Under the circumstances it was necessary to oppose the whole thing tooth and nail and Mr. Tilak moved an amendment to have a Congress Continuation Committee and there to proceed with the election of the President. The other party did not give

* A well-attended public meeting was held on Friday, the 10th April, 1908 at the Panti's Math, Calcutta, to discuss the lines on which the Congress postponed *sine die* at Surat may be revived. Dr. Sundari Mohan Das was elected to the Chair.

him any opportunity to carry the amendment and declared the President to be unanimously elected, though many still hold that the election was not valid as the whole Congress could not express any opinion on it. But how to carry out the opinion of the people? We are ready to condone this irregularity if a united Congress is to be held on the basis of the Calcutta resolutions. If the other party does not accept, the responsibility of breaking-up of the Congress and having a party institution in its place will be on their shoulders. Our position is, let us work on our different party lines through our own institutions, but at the same time let us have the united Congress of the whole people.

Bande Mataram, April 10, 1908

The Demand of the Mother

We have lost the faculty of religious fervour in Bengal and are now trying to recover it through the passion for the country, by self-sacrifice, by labour for our fellow-countrymen, by absorption in the idea of the country. When a nation is on the verge of losing the source of its vitality, it tries to recover it by the first means which the environment offers, whether that environment be favourable or not. Bengal has always lived by its emotions; the brain of India, as it has been called, is also the heart of India. The loss of emotional power, of belief, of enthusiasm would dry up the sources from which she derives her strength. The country of Nyaya is also the country of Chaitanya who himself was born in the height of the intellectual development of Bengal as its finest flower and most perfect expression. If now she tries to recover her enthusiasm and perfect power of self-abandonment, it must be through a means which her new environment provides.

This new environment has been responsible for the loss of her springs of vitality; it had turned the Bengalis into a sceptical people prone to swear at and disbelieve in everything great, noble and inspiring. The recovery of her old spirit of enthusiastic faith and aspiration has come about through the sense of political unity which had been slowly developing in the heart of the people as the result of the new environment. That which had supplied the poison, supplied also the cure. If she is to complete the restoration to her true self, the first requisite is that the enthusiasm, the idealism of the new movement should be kept alive. The perfect sense of self-abandonment which Chaitanya felt for Hari, must be felt by Bengal for the Mother. Then only will Bengal be herself and able to fulfil the destiny to which after so many centuries of preparation she has been called.

The great religions of the world have all laid stress on self-abandonment as the source of salvation and the law applies not only to spiritual salvation but to the destinies of a people. Self-abandonment will alone give salvation. He who loses his life shall keep it, and the life of the individual must be the sacrifice for the life of the nation. When the people of Bengal are able to rise to the full height and depth of this idea, they will find the secret of success which till now has escaped them. It is not by patriotic desires that the nation can be liberated, it is not by patriotic work that a nation can be built. For every stone that is added to the National edifice, a life must be given. It is not talk of Swaraj that can bring Swaraj, but it is the living of Swaraj by each man among us that will compel Swaraj to come.

The Kingdom of Heaven is within you; free India is no piece of wood or stone that can be carved into the likeness of a nation but lives in the hearts of those who desire her, and out of these she must be created. We must first ourselves be free in heart before our country can be free. "There is no British jail which can hold me," said the great Upadhyaya before his death, and he died to prove the truth of his words; but his words are true for all of us that aspire to liberate our Mother, whether we prove it by our lives or by our death. When her sons have learned to be free in themselves, free in prison, free under the yoke which they seek to remove, free in life, free in death, when the text of Upadhyaya's words will receive their illuminating commentary in the actions of a people, then the chains will fall off of themselves and outward circumstances be forced to obey the law of our inward life.

How then can we live Swaraj? By abandonment of the idea of self and its replacement by the idea of the nation. As Chaitanya ceased to be Nimai Pandit and became Krishna, became Radha, became Balaram, so every one of us must cease to cherish his separate life and live in the nation. The hope of national regeneration must absorb our minds as the idea of salvation absorbs the minds of the *mumukṣu.* Our *tyāga* must be as complete as the *tyāga* of the nameless ascetic. Our passion to see the face of our free and glorified Mother must be as devouring a madness as the passion of Chaitanya to see the face of Sri Krishna. Our sacrifice for the country must be as enthusiastic and complete as that of Jagai and Madhai who left the rule of a kingdom to follow the Sankirtan of Gauranga. Our offerings on the altar must be as wildly liberal, as remorselessly complete as that of Carthagenian parents who passed their children through the fire to Moloch. If any reservation mars the completeness of our self-abandonment, if any bargaining abridges the fullness of our sacrifice, if any doubt mars the strength of our faith and enthusiasm, if any thought of self pollutes the sanctity of our love, then the Mother will not be satisfied and will continue to withhold her presence. We call her to come, but the call has not yet gone out of the bottom of our hearts. The Mother's feet are on the threshold, but she waits to hear the true cry, the cry that rushes out from the heart, before she will enter. We are still hesitating between ourselves and the country; we would give one anna to the service of the Mother and keep fifteen for ourselves, our wives, our children, our property, our fame and reputation, our safety, our ease. The Mother asks all before she will give herself. Not until Surath Raja offered the blood of his veins did the Mother appear to him and ask him to choose his boon. Not until Shivaji was ready to offer his head at the feet of the Mother, did Bhavani in visible form stay his hand and give him the command to free his people.

Those who have freed nations have first passed through the agony of utter renunciation before their efforts were crowned with success, and those who aspire to free India will first have to pay the price which the Mother demands. The schemes by which we seek to prepare the nation, the scheme of industrial regeneration, the scheme of educational regeneration, the scheme of political regeneration through self-help are subordinate features of the deeper regeneration which the country must go through before it can be free. The Mother asks us for no schemes, no plans, no methods. She herself will provide the schemes, the plans, the methods better than any we can devise. She asks us for our hearts, our lives, nothing less, nothing more. Swadeshi, National Education, the attempt to organise Swaraj are only so many opportunities for self-surrender to her. She will look to see not how much we have tried for Swadeshi, how wisely we have planned for Swaraj, how successfully we have organised education, but how much of ourselves we have given, how much of our substance, how much of our labour, how much of our ease, how much of our safety, how much of our lives.

Regeneration is literally re-birth, and re-birth comes not by the intellect, not by the fullness of the purse, not by policy, not by change of machinery, but by the getting of a new heart, by throwing away all that we were into the fire of sacrifice and being reborn in the Mother. Self-abandonment is the demand made upon us. She asks of us, "How many will live for me? How many will die for me?" and awaits our answer.

Bande Mataram, April 11, 1908

Baruipur Speech*

Sj. Shyamsunder Chakravarti having finished his speech, Srijut Aurobindo Ghose rose to address the audience. He began with an apology for being under the necessity of addressing a Bengali audience in a foreign tongue specially by one like himself who had devoted his life for the Swadeshi movement. He pointed out that through a foreign system of education developing foreign tastes and tendencies he had been de-nationalised like his country and like his country again he is now trying to re-nationalise himself.

Next he referred to the comparative want of the Swadeshi spirit in West Bengal to which Shyamsunder Babu made very polite reference, himself coming from East Bengal. But Sj. Ghose as he belonged to West Bengal had no hesitation in admitting the drawback. This superiority of East Bengal he attributed solely to its privilege of suffering of late from the regulation "lathis" and imprisonment administered by the alien bureaucrat. He offered the same explanation of the increase of the strength of Boycott in Calcutta after the disturbances at the Beadon Square of which the police were the sole authors. The speaker dilated on the great efficacy of suffering in rousing the spirit from slumber by a reference to the parable of two birds in the Upanishads, so often referred to by the late Swami Vivekananda. The parable relates that there was a big tree with many sweet

* A Swadeshi meeting was held at Baruipur, a sub-division of the district of 24 Parganas, on Sunday the 12th April, 1908. Srijuts Bepin Chandra Pal, Sri Aurobindo with a few other prominent nationalist workers of Calcutta were invited on the occasion.

and bitter fruits and two birds sat on the tree, one on the top of it and the other on a lower part. The latter bird looking upwards sees the other in all his glory and richness of plumage and is at times enamoured of him and feels that he is no other than his own highest self. But at other moments when he tastes the sweet fruits of the tree he is so much taken up with their sweetness that he quite forgets his dear and beloved companion. After a while there comes the turn of bitter fruits, the unpleasant taste of which breaks off the spell and he looks at his brilliant companion again. This is evidently a parable concerning the salvation of individual souls who, when they enjoy the sweets of the world, forget to look upwards to the Paramatma who is really none else than their own highest self, and when they forget themselves in this way through the Maya of this world, bitterness comes to dispel the Maya and revive the true self-consciousness. The parable is equally applicable to national *mukti*. We in India fell under the influence of the foreigners' Maya which completely possessed our souls. It was the Maya of the alien rule, the alien civilisation, the powers and capacities of the alien people who happen to rule over us. These were as if so many shackles that put our physical, intellectual and moral life into bondage. We went to school with the aliens, we allowed the aliens to teach us and draw our minds away from all that was great and good in us. We considered ourselves unfit for self-government and political life, we looked to England as our exemplar and took her as our saviour. And all this was Maya and bondage. When this Maya once got its hold on us, put on us shackle after shackle, we had fallen into bondage of the mind by their education, commercial bondage, political bondage, etc., and we believed ourselves to be helpless without them. We helped them to destroy what life there was in India. We were under the protection of their police and we know now what protection they have given us. Nay, we ourselves became the instruments of our bondage. We Bengalis entered the services of foreigners. We brought in the foreigners and established their rule. Fallen as we were, we needed others to protect us, to teach us and even to feed us. All these functions of human life, so utterly was our self-dependence destroyed, we were left unable to fulfil.

It is only through repression and suffering that this Maya can be dispelled, and the bitter fruit of Partition of Bengal administered by Lord Curzon dispelled the illusion. We looked up and saw that the brilliant bird sitting above was none else but ourselves, our real and actual self. Thus we found Swaraj within ourselves and saw that it was in our hands to discover and to realise it.

Some people tell us that we have not the strength to stand upon our own legs without the help of the aliens and we should therefore work in co-operation with and also in opposition to them. But can you depend on God and Maya at the same time? In proportion as you depend on others the bondage of Maya will be upon you. The first thing that a nation must do is to realise the true freedom that lies within and it is only when you understand that free within is free without, you will be really free. It is for this reason that we preach the gospel of unqualified Swaraj and it is for this that Bhupen Dutt and Upadhyaya refused to plead before the alien court. Upadhyaya saw the necessity of realising Swaraj within us and hence he gave himself up to it. He said that he was free and the Britishers could not bind him; his death is a parable to our nation. There is no power so great that can make India subject when we will say that God will make us free. Herein lies the true significance of National Education, Boycott, Swadeshi, Arbitration. Do not be afraid of obstacles in your path, it does not matter how great the forces are that stand in your way, God commands you to be free and you must be free. We ask you to give up the school under the control of the foreign bureaucracy and point out to you National Education, we ask you to keep away from the legal system which prevails in your country as it is a source of financial and moral downfall — another link in the chain of Maya. Do not suffer in bondage and Maya. Let Maya alone and come away. Don't think that anything is impossible when miracles are being worked on every side. If you are true to yourself there is nothing to be afraid of. There is nothing unattainable by truth, love and faith. This is your whole gospel which will work out miracles. Never indulge in equivocations for your ease and safety. Do not invite weakness, stand upright. The light of Swadeshi is growing brighter through every attempt to crush it. People say there is no unity among us. How to create unity? Only through the call of our Mother and the voice of all her sons and not by any other unreal means. The voice is yet weak but it is growing. The might of God is already revealed among us, its work is spreading over the country. Even in West Bengal it has begun its work in Uttarpara and Baruipur. It is not our work but that of something mightier that compels us to go on until all bondage is swept away and India stands free before the world.

April 12, 1908

Peace and Exclusion

The *Bengalee* has a knack of crying "Peace, peace", when not peace but a tactical advantage is in its heart. It has been appealing to us to refrain from party attacks and recriminations while it carries out its policy of excluding the Nationalist Party from the Congress unmolested. The singular nature of this demand has attracted bitter comment and given cause for irritation as well as amusement in the minds of our friends of the Nationalist Party, but it is nothing new on our contemporary's part. Ever since the struggle began between the parties, the *Bengalee* has adopted the *role* of angel of peace in its editorial columns while opening its correspondence columns to the most violent and personal attack on its opponents and has been the champion of a party whose first principle has been to ignore Nationalism when possible, intrigue against it in secret when occasion was favourable and openly exclude it by unconstitutional trickery when secret means would no longer serve. Srijut Surendranath Banerji is the declared editor of this paper and the public connect it and his actions together. We understand that Srijut Surendranath is sincerely anxious for peace and we are ready to take the hand offered to us if it is given in frankness, but he will pardon us for our plain speaking when we say that the past tactics of his paper and his party have not been such as to inspire us with over-abundant confidence. It is by his actions that men judge a party leader and not by his public professions whether on the platform, in print or in private conversation.

Bande Mataram, April 13, 1908

Indian Resurgence and Europe

IN MANY of the European countries in which democracy is at present not fully developed, the monarchy and the people are still in a position of armed neutrality with regard to each other. The people look with distrust on the ruler, the ruler with fear and antipathy on the people. If the ruler takes a step in the direction of absolutism the bomb is ready in the hands of the people to put an end to his life. If the people seem to be inclined towards Republicanism or Socialism the whole energies of the ruler are bent towards the discovery of some means by which the tide of democracy can be kept in check or turned back. When we look to democratic countries we find a similar attitude between capital and labour, property and poverty. Distrust is the atmosphere of modern politics, mutual suspicion and hatred the secret spring of action. Under the fair outside of its material civilisation, a deep-seated moral disease is at work eating into the vitals of European society of which a thousand symptoms strike the eye, from the extreme of bomb-throwing Anarchism to the other extreme of Tolstoy's Utopianism. Is India to be infected with the disease? The present conditions of Government in this country are full of the germs of the occidental malady, and if India is to escape from it, it must be, first, by getting rid of these conditions and secondly, by seeking refuge in its own superior civilisation. The work of Nationalism is therefore twofold. It has to win Swaraj for India so that the present unhealthy conditions of political life, full of the germs of that social and political phthisis which is overtaking Europe, may be entirely and radically cured, and it has to ensure that the Swaraj it brings about shall be a Swadeshi Swaraj and not an importation of the European article. It is for this reason that the movement for Swaraj found its first expression in an outburst of Swadeshi sentiment which directed itself not merely against foreign goods, but against foreign habits, foreign dress and manners, foreign education, and sought to bring the people back to their own civilisation. It was the instinctive protest of Nature against the malady that was eating its way into the national system and threatening to corrupt its blood and disturb the soundness of its organs. If there were some irrational features in the revolt of the people against foreign things, it was the violence of the malady which necessitated the violence of the reaction. The late Upadhyaya was the type and champion of this feature of the National movement. He was never weary of harping on the necessity of stripping from ourselves every rag of borrowed European thought and habits and becoming intensely, uncompromisingly Indian. When we put aside all the mannerisms of that strong personality and seek its kernel, we find that this was his message and the meaning of his life. After himself going through all the phases of Europeanised thought and religion, he returned like his country with a violent rebound to the religion, the thoughts, the habits and the speech of his forefathers. It is the spirit of old Bengal which incarnated itself in him with the strength, courage, passionate adherence to conviction which was the temperament of old Bengal and which modern Bengal had for a period lost. His declaration in Court and his death put a seal upon the meaning of his life and left his name stamped indelibly on the pages of history as a saint and martyr of the new faith. It washed out all human weakness and impurity with the wave of a great spiritual act of devotion and renunciation and left the soul of the man only for posterity to cherish. We have to take up his work and incorporate the essence of it into the accomplished heritage of the nation.

The return to ourselves is the cardinal feature of the national movement. It is national not only in the sense of political self-assertion against the domination of foreigners, but in the sense of a return upon our old national individuality. It is significant that all those who are out of touch with this feature of the movement are losing their position at its head, while those who keep in its forefront are being more and more suffused with the spirit of "Indianity" and overcome with the spell of India, the magic of her thought and civilisation, the overpowering touch of her religion. The highest qualities of head and heart cannot keep the lead for men who have not the saving grace of openness to this passion for India as she was, is and will be. On the other hand, men perhaps of inferior calibre are likely to do better work for the country, who have the power to respond. The secret of this peculiar feature of the movement is to be found in its essential nature and in the purpose which God intends it to serve. If India follows in the footsteps of Europe, accepts her political ideals, social system, economic principles, she will be overcome with the same maladies. Such a consummation is neither for the good of India nor for the good of Europe. If India becomes an intellectual province of Europe, she will never attain to her natural greatness or fulfil the possibilities within her. *Paradharmaḥ bhayāvahaḥ*, to accept the *dharma* of another is perilous; it deprives the man or the nation of its secret of life and vitality and substitutes an unnatural and stunted growth for the free, large and organic development of Nature. Whenever a nation has given up the purpose of its existence, it has been at the cost of its growth. India must remain India if she is to fulfil her destiny. Nor will Europe profit by grafting her civilisation on India, for if India, who is the distinct physician of Europe's maladies, herself falls into the clutches of the disease, the disease will remain uncured and incurable and European civilisation will perish as it perished when Rome declined, first by dry rot within itself and last by irruption from without. The success of the National movement, both as a political and a spiritual movement, is necessary for India and still more necessary for Europe. The whole world is interested in seeing that India becomes free so that India may become herself.

Om Shantih

The impending promotion of John Morley, the philosopher, to the House of Lords is one of the crimes of present day politics. The Radical philosopher, the biographer of Voltaire and Rousseau, the admired bookman of heterodoxy, is to end his days in that privileged preserve of all that is antiquated, anomalous, conservative and unprogressive, that standing negation of democratic principles, that survival of old-world privilege, the House of Lords. Honest John is to end his days as Lord John. It is a fitting reward for the work he has done as Secretary of State for India, the apostasy, the turning of his back on every principle for which he had stood in his books and speeches, the unctuous upholding of tyranny, the final consummation of the self-righteous Pharisee of liberty, the unrepentant oppressor of a rising nationality and a great resurgent civilisation. The culmination suits the beginning as a gargoyle suits a Gothic building; for the life of John Morley is a mass of contradictions, the profession of liberalism running hand in hand with the practice of a bastard Imperialism which did the work of Satan while it mouthed liberal Scripture to justify its sins. Mr. John Morley, the principal spurrer-on of Gladstone when Egypt was enslaved, the Chief Secretary whom the Irish feared and distrusted, the Secretary of State who has begun in India what no Tory statesman could have lightly undertaken, the attempt to stifle Indian aspirations by sheer force and put back the clock of progress from the nineteenth century into the middle ages, could not find a fitter heaven in which to spend his old age than the House of Lords. If anything could add to the just felicity of his translation, it is that there will be no Cottons and Rutherfords to vex his honest soul with irreverent questions. Om Shantih, Shantih, Shantih.

Bande Mataram, April 14, 1908

Conventionalist and Nationalist

IF WE look to the pros and cons of the controversy between Conventionalists and Nationalists, we shall be placed in a better position to understand the real aim of the Moderates in putting the barrier of a creed between themselves and the people. In the first place, a part of the quarrel is over ultimate ideals: the Conventionalists are for the declaration of Colonial Self-Government as the goal of our efforts, the Nationalists for Swaraj without any qualification. Whatever the rights of the controversy, the ideal of the Conventionalists has been accepted in the form of a resolution by the Congress, and as a resolution but not a binding creed it has been submitted to by the Nationalists because it was the will of the majority. A creed is a matter of belief and conscience, a resolution a matter of policy; — and while no conscientious man will accept a creed which he does not believe, he can always submit as a good citizen to the will of the majority in matters of temporary policy. We are not concerned at present with the question whether such submission is imperative in all cases. It is sufficient that the Nationalists while preserving the liberty of every free mind to propagate their own doctrines and get them enforced wherever possible, have submitted to the Colonial Self-Government resolution as a part of the compromise unanimously arrived at in Calcutta. What need was there then of foisting a creed on the Congress? The object of the creed is to exclude the Nationalists, but the exclusion of the Nationalists is itself motived by an ulterior object. It is urged on behalf of the Moderates that it is impossible for them to work with the Nationalists because they are too violent and unruly to be members of an orderly assembly, but this is a plea too flimsy to bear scrutiny. If the Nationalists are sometimes unruly, it is because they are forced to urge their opinions on the Congress when they are deliberately ignored and throttled by the misuse of official authority to secure party ends. If the Nationalists are unruly, the Moderates are autocratic, and it is the autocratic misuse of power which creates the unruliness. Nor is unruliness in a party any good reason for breaking up a great National Assembly and excluding a powerful force from what professes to be the centre of national growth and strength. It is evident that a far more powerful motive is behind the policy of the Conventionalists, and that motive is fear and self-interest. Some are frank enough to confess it, but to put a plausible colour of patriotism on their deeper motives is to pretend that the Congress will be throttled or that by association with men of violent views and actions their work for posterity is hampered and spoiled. In other words, so long as they do not obey the orders of the *Englishman*, the *Madras Mail* and the *Times of India*, and dissociate themselves from the new movement and Nationalism, they will not enjoy the confidence of the bureaucracy or be allowed to approach them with statesmanlike petitions and co-operate with them in the work of prolonging the subjection of their countrymen to foreign absolutism. This loss of position and prestige with the bureaucracy is the ruling motive with the Bombay Moderates, the fear of being involved in the persecution to which the Nationalists willingly expose themselves, is the dominant thought among the respectabilities of Bengal. Another powerful incentive to the hope of getting rid of the Nationalist opposition to their monopoly of influence and control in the country itself when the Nationalists are isolated for the fury of the bureaucracy to wreak on them its vengeance for the awakening of India. "The Nationalists are using us as a shield," the cry goes, "and we refused to be used, in that unheroic capacity." Whether the Nationalists have or have not the courage to face the full fury of bureaucratic persecution and the strength to survive it is a question which will probably be decided before another year is out. The Moderates, at any rate, imagine that they cannot and rejoice over the pleasant expectation of seeing this over-energetic and inconveniently independent party being crushed out of existence by the common adversary of all. It is the spirit of Mir Jafar, the politics of Jagat Sheth repeating themselves in their spiritual descendants.

That these ignoble, but perfectly human and intelligible motives are behind the Conventionalist separatism is further evidenced by the attempt to whittle away the resolution on National Education by the removal of the expression on National lines and National control in order to make it a colourless approval of a mere academic departure. Mr. Gokhale placed his justification in his ardent passion for elegant English, but the resolutions of the Congress are not such literary masterpieces that this particular one should have evoked the dead and gone schoolmaster in Mr. Gokhale's breast. It is clear that the desire of the former was to get rid of the idea of Nationality from the resolution, because the aspiration towards Nationality is offensive to the bureaucracy and to avoid offence to the bureaucracy is, according to Moderate politics, the first condition of political activity in India. The change of a word for the sake of literary elegance was not surely so essential that the Moderates had to prefer breaking the Congress to breaking the rules of English rhetoric. The opposition to the Boycott resolution as originally framed has no root except in fear. No Indian in his heart of hearts can fail to sympathise with the boycott and even when he has not the patriotism or the selflessness to practise it himself; for boycott is the first expression of our national individuality, the first condition for the success of Swadeshi and the standing evidence of National revival. But the boycott is as a red rag to John Bull and the Moderate therefore is anxious to throw away the red rag or at least put it in his pocket so long as he is in the same field with the bull. "Wore horns" is the whole significance of the opposition to boycott, whatever economical or political excuses may be put forward by way of apology. The separatist policy is a policy of fear, selfishness and spite.

Is it possible for a policy of this kind to be a force in the country or for a party actuated by such motives to keep the people in its hands?

Strength against weakness, life against death, aspiration against self-distrust, self-immolation against self-preservation, — this is the real issue between Conventionalist and Nationalist, and it cannot be doubted which will survive.

Bande Mataram, April 18, 1908

The Future and the Nationalists

WHATEVER view we take of the present situation, the first duty of every Nationalist is to take care that the great principles of Nationalism are not infringed by any concession to the party of fear and self-interest which would imperil the future of the movement and the destiny of the nation. All the articles we have written on the Convention have been the expression of a momentary policy dictated by the great and almost universal desire in the country that a split should be avoided. But we should never forget that policy is subordinate to principle. As a democratic party, it is our duty to bow to the will of the majority in all matters which do not break the mould of Nationalism to serve the interests of a moment. Unity is at present a means and not an end in itself. As we have often pointed out, unanimity is not unity but merely an affectation of unity. There is an idea in many minds that our salvation lies in the removal of all differences, religious, social and political, but we may wait for many millenniums before such an Utopia can be reached in this world. Differences of religion, social status and political opinion there must be. Unanimity is a condition only possible to a nation whose heart is numbed and whose intellect has ceased to be active; for diversity is the very condition of activity, its cause and again its result. No one can deny that the differences of opinion which have arisen among us are largely responsible for the extraordinary political activity which has kept India astir for the last two years and set the whole world looking towards the banks of the Ganges in eager expectation of a new birth among the nations. On the other hand, the activity itself has emphasised and increased the differences of opinion both between the parties and in the parties themselves. The only thing we have to see to is that this diversity is not allowed to break up the nation into warring factions, and we are therefore anxious to save, if possible, the Congress from extinction, because the Congress at present is the only ground of unity in diversity, the only field where all can meet to diverge and again meet without loss of principle or violence to conscience. It is a centre into which the different streams of thought and activity in the country can flow and mix with each other, to again separate and work in their own channels till the time to meet and intercommunicate again arrives. The Congress, therefore, provides the point of unity which prevents the diversity of our political activities from dissolving our political life into so many disconnected units.

Unity, as we have said, is a means and not an end. To agree is easy if we are willing to sacrifice our principles, but such agreement is not unity; it is sacrificing the soul of the nation so that an artificial appearance of unanimity may be preserved. No unity can be desirable which is inconsistent with growth or with the march of the people towards the realisation of their great destiny. Growth is the object, unity only one of the means, and if the means can only be had on condition of sacrificing the object, the means and not the object must be sacrificed. If the Convention refuses to associate with the Nationalists except on condition of the latter sacrificing their principles and stultifying their intellectual convictions, the demand for unity can no longer be pressed on the Nationalist Party, which will then be free to take its own course without reference to anything but its own principles and the exigencies of its propaganda. We have done our best to carry out the demand of the people for unity; the refusal comes from the other side and there the responsibility will rest. If the country desires unity, it is for the country to enforce it by refusing to countenance a body claiming to be the Congress and yet taking its stand on the negation of unity. The Nationalists cannot sit as beggars at the doors of the Convention waiting till the doors be opened to them. They are the builders of Indian Nationality, the inheritors of the future, and their work calls them. If the Convention wants at any time in the near future to retrace its steps and become one with the Nationalists, it knows the conditions, but time will increase the difficulty of reunion and the conditions will change as the sacrifices made by the Nationalists for the sake of their cause become greater and their work advances. It is time for us to turn from the attempt to patch up matters with men who are pledged to disruption and concern ourselves with our own proper work.

That work is too heavy for us already, and it will become still more difficult under the new circumstances with an enemy in the house as well as an enemy outside. If we are to face the task with any hope of success, it must be with a much stricter organisation, a general closing up of our ranks and the creation of instruments for united work and mutual co-operation. We have hitherto been able to work in a scattered and desultory fashion, because we were able to use the Congress organisations brought into existence by the demand for practical work and to take part in and give our stamp to existing bodies. The Convention's new District Associations will consist only of men pledged to the creed. Wherever an Association refuses to be bound by the creed, it will be excluded from the Conventionalist Congress and regarded as a Nationalist body. Under these circumstances the country's demand for unity will become impossible of fulfilment and rival organisations will spring into existence in every province and every district, one pledged to association with the bureaucracy, the other to boycott and self-help. If these bodies admit both parties, they will stand apart from any existing organisation. Such a state of things can only be temporary, but it is for a time inevitable if the Convention constitution is carried out. The Nationalists are bound to protect themselves from the attempt to exclude them from political life by organising themselves in such a way that they may become a force in the country which neither bureaucrats nor Loyalists can either ignore or think it an easy task to crush. Organisation, therefore, will be the first difficulty to overcome. When once we have succeeded in organising our present scattered forces, the spirit of progress, once awake, will work for us and through us giving us greater and greater following and strength till the work of building up the nation becomes so evidently ours that the whole country will range itself under our standard. Then and only then will that unity become possible which can create a nation.

Bande Mataram, April 22, 1908

The Wheat and the Chaff

THE result of the Convention meeting at Allahabad is now certain and it seems that after a brief struggle Sir Pherozshah has prevailed. We have done much for reunion, and have striven in vain. The personality of Sir Pherozshah Mehta and the votes of his Bombay henchmen have overborne the feeble patriotism and wavering will of the Bengal Moderates and their Punjab supporters. The Convention has thrown in its lot with Minto and Morley and sacrificed the country at the altar of the bureaucracy and as the Bengal leaders have not dissociated themselves from the Convention, we must hold that the entire Moderate Party have agreed to betray the mandate of their country and the future of their people. For a brief moment God placed the destiny of India in their hands and gave them a free choice whether they would serve Him or self, the country or the bureaucracy. They have chosen, and chosen the worse course. They too have made the great refusal. Whatever may happen henceforth, they must be reckoned as servants of the alien bureaucrat, disguised as patriots to deceive and mislead the people, enemies of Nationalism, foes of Indian independence who prefer the service of a foreign domination to the perils of a struggle for freedom. They have refused to serve the Mother with an undivided heart, they have placed the alien on the throne of her future and dared to think that she will accept a left hand and inferior chair at the side of his seat of empire. Let them serve the master they have chosen and find what wages he will give them for their service. No Nationalist henceforth can consent to seek reconciliation with them or clasp the hand that has sold the country for a foreign hire. A cleavage has been made between those who will suffer for their country and those who have declared that they will have no share in those sufferings, no part or lot in the great struggle of the future. It is well. We need waste no further time in seeking a union with the men who before Surat had resolved on a disruption motived by the desire of bureaucratic favour and the fear of bureaucratic displeasure. The day of compromises is past. Frank, clear and unmistakable, let the great issue stand for the country to decide as between the lovers of freedom and the lovers of servitude, between the men who palter with the demand of the Mother for whole-hearted service and those who have given all to her, between the politicians and the martyrs, between the advocates of a contradiction and the preachers of the unadorned Truth. On the one side the cry is "For India and freedom", on the other "For India and the bureaucracy". Whichever appeals to its heart and its intellect, the country will choose. Of the Conventionalists let us speak no farther. If any of them have it in them to repent, let them repent soon, for the hour of grace that is given them will be short and the punishment swift. Into the secrets of their hearts we cannot pry, and it may be that there are some of them whose will only half consented to the betrayal, or whose intellectual clarity was too small to understand what they were doing. But man's fate is determined by his acts which produce mechanically their inevitable result and they must share the fortune of those with whom they have cast in their lot. Before the world is much older, they will see the fruits of their work and rejoice over them if they can. For Nationalism a new era begins with the 19th of Apirl, 1908. The sharp division that it has created between the two parties will bring the strength of Nationalism, the sincerity of its followers and the validity of its principles to the fiercest test that any cause can undergo. Only that cause is God-created, entrusted with a mission, sure of victory which can stand by itself in a solitude, absolute and supreme, without visible shield or sword, exposed to all that the powers of the world can do to slay it, and yet survive. The powers of the world are the servants of God commissioned to test the purity of His workers, their faith, their courage, their self-devotion, His angels of destruction who put forth their whole strength to uproot the infant faith and scatter its followers, so that the wheat may be sifted from the chaff, the true believers from the half believers, and the new religion grow by suffering to its intended stature. Every religion therefore has to begin with a period of persecution. The religion of Nationalism is already far on in this period and the retreat of the Conventionalists from the field of battle, their distinct repudiation of the new movement and its works, is the first fruit of the persecution. So much chaff has been sifted from the wheat, so many stones have been rejected by the great Builder from His material for the house He is building for our Mother. As time goes on, the test will be fiercer, the sifting more violent and the heavier part of the chaff, if any remains, will follow the lighter. Only the heart that is free from fear, the spirit that is full of faith, the soul that is passionate for realisation will remain for the final test and the last purification. To men of doubtful views and undecided opinions the crisis precipitated by the decision of the Convention Committee will prove a cruel embarrassment. To all who have an emotional preference for the new ideas without a clear understanding of their supreme and urgent necessity, to all who understand the new ideas with their intellects only but have them not in their hearts, to all who, while loving and understanding the new ideas, have not faith to put aside the cloaks of prudence and dissimulation or courage to avow their faith openly before the world, the position is one of great perplexity. God is a hard master and will not be served by halves. All evasions, all subterfuges He cuts away and puts the question plain and loud; and before all mankind, before the friend ready to cut the ties of friendship asunder, before the enemy standing ready with lifted sword to slay the servants of God as soon as they confess their faith, it has to be answered: — "Who is on the Lord's side?" Not once, not twice, but always that question is being put and the answer exacted. If you are unwilling to answer, either you do not believe that it is God's work you are doing and are therefore unfit for it, or you have insufficient faith in His power to get His work done without the help of your diplomacy and cunning, or you are unwilling to meet any plain risks in His service. To serve God under a cover is easy, to stipulate for safety in doing the work is natural to frail human nature, to sympathise and applaud is cheap; but the work demands sterner stuff in the men who will do it and insists on complete service, fearless service and honest service. The waverer must make up his mind either to answer God's question or to give up the work. There is plenty for him to do in a cheap, safe and easy way if he cannot face the risks of self-devotion. He can hold Conferences, enrol himself as a member of the Convention's District Associations, open funds for National purposes, pass resolutions, sign petitions, hold patriotic interviews with Magistrates, Commissioners, Lieutenant-Governors, Governors and even perhaps with a live Viceroy; he can, if he is a barrister, plead in Swadeshi cases; he can take shares in profitable Swadeshi investments and boast himself a great Swadeshi worker, a captain of industry, a solid patriot; he can do real good to the country without peril to himself by subscribing to help National Education. In these and other ways he can satisfy his secret proclivities for the service of his country. But the days when this easy service could pass for Nationalism are numbered. The work now before us is of the sternest kind and requires men of an unflinching sternness to carry it out. The hero, the martyr, the man of iron will and iron heart, the grim fighter whose tough nerves defeat cannot tire out nor danger relax, the born leader in action, the man who cannot sleep or rest while his country is enslaved, the priest of Kali who can tear his heart out of his body and offer it as a bleeding sacrifice on the Mother's altar, the heart of fire and the tongue of flame whose lightest word is an inspiration to self-sacrifice or a spur to action, for these the time is coming, the call will soon go forth. They are already here in the silence, in the darkness slowly maturing themselves, training the muscles of the will, tightening the strings of the heart so that they may be ready when the call comes. Whoever feels the power of service within him, let him make sure of himself while there is yet time; for the present is an hour of easy probation, of light tests in which the punishment of failure is also light, but whoever fails in the day that is coming, will be thrown away not in the rubbish heap as the Conventionalists will be thrown, but into the fire of a great burning. For all who now declare themselves Nationalists the tests will be far severer than that before which the place-hunter, the title-hunter, the popularity-hunter, the politician of mixed motives and crooked ways, the trimmer, the light speaker and ready swearer of the old politics have paled and recoiled so early and so easily. The profession of Nationalism should not be lightly made but with a full sense of what it means and involves. The privilege of taking it is attended with severe pains and penalties for those who take it lightly. If we are few, it matters little, but it is of supreme importance that the stuff of which we are made should be sound. What the Mother needs is hard clear steel for her sword, hard massive granite for her fortress, wood that will not break for the handle of her bow, tough substance and true for the axle of her chariot. For the battle is near and the trumpet ready for the signal.

Bande Mataram, April 23, 1908

Party and the Country

THE uses of party are a secret known only to free nations which value their freedom above all other things. Men of free minds and free habits are too strong of soul to be the slaves of their party feelings and too robust of mind to submit to any demand for the sacrifice of their principles on the altar of expediency. It is only in a servile nation unaccustomed to the habits of freemen that party becomes a master and not an instrument. The strength of mind to rise above personal feeling, the breadth of view which is prepared to tolerate the views of others while fighting resolutely, even aggressively, for one's own, the generosity of sentiment which can clasp the hand of an opponent so long as the claims of patriotism are satisfied, these are qualities that do not grow in the barren soil of servitude or flourish in its vitiated atmosphere. The pains of wounded vanity are as strong in slaves as in children; the pride which will not forgive defeat, the malice which broods over an affront for ever, the narrowness which does not allow good in an opponent or honesty in his opinions, while arrogating all virtues for oneself and one's party, these are the growth of the unhealthy air of slavery. So long as these are present, party is a curse because it becomes faction. And without party self-government is impossible.

The growth of parties immediately before the Swadeshi movement was one of the signs of an approaching awakening in the national mind. When the intellect is stirred and feelings become sincere and acute, parties arise, each passionate for its opinions, eager to carry them out, full of enthusiasm for an imagined ideal. The air becomes vibrant with life, the full blast of hope and endeavour fills the sails of destiny and through a sea sometimes stormy and never quite placid, the ship of a nation's fate plunges forward to its destination. A political life in which there are no parties is political stagnation, death-in-life. It means that the intellect of the nation is torpid, its feelings feeble and flaccid, its aspirations untouched with passion of sincerity, fervour of hope unawakened, love of the country an inoperative sentiment confined to the intellect only and not yet close to the heart. The patriot is consumed with the passion to serve his country, to make her great, free or splendid. His brain is full of plans for the fulfilment of his hopes and he seeks helpers and followers to bring it about, while he tries to disabuse the country of ideas which he believes injurious to his plans. A Mazzini planning the republican freedom of Italy creates the party of New Italy, a Garibaldi filled with the same hope but bent on freedom first and republicanism afterwards forms his Legion of Red Shirts and holds the balance of parties, a Cavour full of grandiose schemes of a Kingdom of Italy leads the old monarchical sentiment of Piedmont and all that gathers round it. These parties fear and distrust each other, but all have one clear and unmistakable purpose, the freedom of Italy, and work for it, each doing something towards the common end which the others could not have done. Thus the purpose of God works itself out and not the purpose of Mazzini, or the purpose of Garibaldi, or the purpose of Cavour. Parties are necessary but they must have a common end overriding their specific differences, the freedom, greatness and splendour of their Motherland. Only one party is inexcusable, inadmissible, not to be parleyed with, the party which is against freedom, the party which seeks to perpetuate national slavery.

In the India of today there are in appearance two parties at issue over the destiny of the country. One puts Swaraj as its goal, the other a modified freedom under the supreme control of a paramount and protecting Britain. Men of both parties try to show that their party is that of the true patriots, the other a faction fatal to the best interests of the country; both claim the lead of the country, the true right to be the representatives of its feelings and in possession of the future. If they were equally patriotic, this opposition would work for the good of the country and not for evil. If both were equally bent on the freedom of their country, they would supply each other's deficiencies, do each what the other is unfit to do and by their mutual rivalry work out the salvation of their country. The Moderate Party contains a certain number of men who are really patriotic and desire the freedom of their country, whatever they may think it prudent to profess in public. If these men formed the whole or the bulk of their party, the present strife of parties would be an unmixed blessing, but unfortunately for the country there is a large and powerful element which is of a very different stamp. The representatives of this clique are the true movers of the Convention and their aims are hardly disguised. They do not believe in the capacity of their people for self-government or in the desirability of freedom for India and, if they subscribe to the formula of self-government, it is avowedly as a distant millennium which is to be kept outside the pale of practical politics. Their political aims are bounded by such changes in the existing system of administration as will give them and their class a greater share in the bureaucratic administration and a safe, easy and profitable road to position, popularity and honours. Patriotism is with them no ideal, no overmastering passion, no duty, but an instrument for advancing certain interests and gaining certain advantages. These men are Loyalists of a baser type, who desire the continuance of the British absolutism out of self-interest and not from any love of it or conviction of its goodness and utility. It is these men who have brought about the Surat fiasco, the Convention, the creed and the Allahabad constitution and the Surendranaths and Gokhales have been tools in their hands. Conventionalism is a factor in our politics which makes for reaction, a revolt against the new ideas and a direct negation of our future. As such it will serve the ends of bureaucracy, tighten the chain and militate against progress; it can never be a factor helping towards our liberation. If the Bengal Moderates cling to the Convention, they too will be no longer a factor in the work of liberation but an enemy and an obstacle like the Italian Moderates who clung to the Austrian domination as necessary to Italy. They are forfeiting their future when they deny the future of their country. If parties are to arise henceforth, it must be among those who are the advocates of freedom and workers for freedom, for they alone can differ without faction and work together for a common end on different lines. Those who make the negation of the country's future the test of admission to their counsels, will themselves be excluded from the counsels of the Power that is shaping that future. Without them, for they are too feeble to be reckoned as an opposing force, that which they deny will accomplish itself.

The "Bengalee" Facing-Both-Ways

We confess we cannot understand the position taken up by the *Bengalee* in the paragraph we quote on another page. The Bengal Moderates at the Convention tried partially but not completely to carry out the country's mandate, but when they were outvoted, they made no protest and have not separated themselves from the action of the Convention. We take it therefore that when the Moderate Convention under the usurped name of the Congress meets at Surat in December, they will take part in it with Dr. Rash Behari Ghose at their head. If so, they sever themselves from the country and forfeit their political future in Bengal, but their position is intelligible. The *Bengalee*, however, talks of reconciliation and the Convention in one breath. It trusts that the path of reconciliation is not yet definitely closed, although the Convention to which Srijut Surendranath belongs has definitely enough adopted an exclusion clause and is going to summon a new-born Congress of its own. It is even bold enough to say that the resolution of the Convention does not preclude reconciliation. We find it difficult to command words which will properly characterise the audacity of this assertion. Does the *Bengalee* imagine that the Nationalists are going to accept a Congress called by the Convention, a Constitution framed by a handful of gentlemen meeting at Allahabad and a creed or "statement of objects" which contradict their fundamental principles? Its appeal to the country to bring about an united Congress stands convicted, coming after such a sentence, as a piece of meaningless vapidity. The *Bengalee* evidently wants to cling to the Convention and yet pose as a champion of reconciliation but this double attitude will not serve. It cannot both have its Convention cake and eat it.

Providence and Perorations

The *Bengalee* cannot bear to be told that the present movement is under the direct guidance of Providence. It regards the proposition as "positively dangerous". It benignly admits that "if properly understood there is an element of vital truth in this proposition", but when preached to "the vulgar" it is likely to work endless mischief. Hush! therefore, do not utter the name of Providence, "for there is no other philosophical doctrine which has done so much to breed and foster the unnatural spirit of difference as this particularly stupid dogma." But tell people that foreign sugar and Liverpool salt contain the blood and bone of cows and pigs, and all the while go on consuming ham and bacon as great delicacies. Talk not of the presence of the divine in political activities, because this "stupid dogma" is calculated to create difference in our camp, but appeal to the Mahomedan's religious aversion to pork and the Hindu's hatred of beef, in the interest of national unity! Keep Providence for rounding the periods of your magnificent perorations, but bring him not down to the realities of your social or political struggles. He is an exceedingly inconvenient guest at the table or the counter.

Bande Mataram, April 24, 1908

The One Thing Needful

A SORT of atavism is at work in the Indian consciousness at the present moment which is drawing it back into the spirit of the fathers of the race who laid the foundations of our being thousands of years ago. Perhaps as a reaction from the excessively outward direction which our life had taken since the European invasion, the spirit of the race has taken refuge in the sources of its past and begun to bathe in the fountains of its being. A reversion such as this is the sole cure for national decay. Every nation has certain sources of vitality which have made it what it is and can always, if drawn upon in time, protect it from disintegration. The secret of its life is to be found in the recesses of its own being.

The root of the past is the source from which the future draws its sap and if the tree is to be saved it must constantly draw from that source for sustenance. The root may be fed from outside, but that food will have to be assimilated and turned to sap in the root before it can nourish the trunk. All nations therefore when they receive anything from outside steep it first in their own individuality before it can form part of their culture and national life. India has always done this with all outside forces which sought to find entry into her silent and meditative being. She has suffused them with her peculiar individuality so completely that their foreign origin is no longer recognisable. If she had done the same with European civilisation, she would have been the first Asiatic nation to rise and show the way to her congeners. But at the time when Europe forced itself upon her, her political life was at its nadir. Exhausted by the long struggle to substitute a new centre of national life for the effete Mogul, she was too weak and void of energy to bring her once robust individuality to bear upon the alien thought of the West. She allowed it to enter her being whole and undigested. The result was a rapid disintegration of her own individuality and a hastening of the process of decay which had set in as a result of the prolonged anarchy of the post-Mogul period. If there had been no reaction, the process would have been soon over and, whatever race finally occupied India, it would not have been the Indian race. For that race would have slowly perished as the Greek, when he parted with the springs of his life, perished and gave way to the Slav, or as the Egyptian perished and gave way to the Berber. This fate has been averted because a great wave of reaction passed over the country and sent a stream of the old life and thought of India beating into the veins of the country and brought it to bear on the foreign matter which was eating up the body of the nation. That process of assimilation has just begun and its effects will not be palpable for many years to come. It will first effect its purpose on the political life of the people, then on its society, last on its literature, thought and speech. The effect on the political life is already visible, but it cannot fulfil itself until the political power is in the hands of the people. No political change can work itself out until the forces of change have taken possession of the government, because it is through the government that the functions of political life work. This is their organ and there can be no other. The possession of the government by the people is therefore the first condition of Indian regeneration. Until this is attained, nothing else can be attained. The new forces will no doubt work quietly on society and on literature, but in an imperfect fashion from which no great results can be anticipated.

Society lives by the proper harmony of its parts and bases that harmony on the centre of power in which the whole community is summed up, the State. If the State is diseased, the community cannot be healthy. If the State is foreign and inorganic, the community cannot live an organic life. If the State be hostile, the community is doomed. The first want of a subject people is the possession of the State, without which it can neither be socially sound nor intellectually great. It was for this reason that Mazzini whose natural tendencies were literary and poetic, turned away from literature and denied his abilities their natural expression with the memorable words, "The art of Italy will flourish on our graves." No great work can be done by a community which is diseased at the centre or deprived of a centre. The hope of social reform divorced from political freedom, unless by social reform we mean the aping of European habits of life and social ideas, is an illogical hope which ignores the nature of social life and the conditions of its well-being. All expectation of moral regeneration which leaves freedom out of the count is a dream. First freedom, then regeneration. This is a truism which we have been obliged to dwell on because there are still remnants of the first delusive teachings which have done so much harm to India by trying to realise social reform without providing the element in which alone any reform is possible.

To recover possession of the State is therefore the first business of the awakened Indian consciousness. If this is so, then it is obvious that the political liberation of India cannot be put off to a distant date as a thing which can be worked out at leisure, with the slow pace of the snail, by creeping degrees of senile caution. It must be done now. It is the first condition of life which must be satisfied if the nation is to survive. On this the whole energies of the people must be concentrated and no other will-o'-the-wisp of social reform, moral regeneration, educational improvement ought to be allowed to interfere with the stupendous, single-souled effort which can alone effect the political salvation of the country. No reasonable reformer ought to be put out by the demand for the precedence being given to political salvation, because it is obvious that the political resurgence of the nation involves and necessitates a regeneration of the society by the great change of spirit and environment which it will bring about. When the whole life of the nation is full of the spirit of freedom and it lives in the great life of the world, then only can the work of the reformer be successful. The preoccupation with politics which seized Bengal after the Partition was a healthy symptom. Recently there has been a tendency in some quarters to revive the old dissipation of energies, to put social reform first, education first or moral regeneration first, and leave freedom to result from these. The mistake should be checked before it gains ground. Whatever reform, social, moral or educational, is necessary to bring about freedom, the effort of the whole people to bring about freedom will automatically effect. More is impossible until freedom itself is attained. No attempt to effect social reform for its own sake has any chance of success, because it will at once reawaken the old bitter struggle between the past and the present which baffled the efforts of the reformers. What the nation needs, it will carry out by the force of its necessity; but it is vain to expect it to dissipate its energies on what is for the moment superfluous. First we must live, afterwards we can learn to live well. The effort to survive must for some years command all our energies and absorb all our time.

Bande Mataram, April 25, 1908

Palli Samiti*

THE resolution on which I have been asked to speak is from one point of view the most important of all that this Conference has passed. As one of the speakers has already said, the village Samiti is the seed of Swaraj. What is Swaraj but the organisation of the independent life of the country into centres of strength which grow out of its conditions and answer to its needs, so as to make a single and organic whole? When a nation is in a natural condition, growing from within and existing from within and in its own strength, then it develops its own centres and correlates them according to its own needs. But as soon as for any reason this natural condition is interrupted and a foreign organism establishes itself in and dominates in the country, then that foreign body draws to itself all the sources of nourishment and the natural centres, deprived of their sustenance, fail and disappear. It is for this reason that foreign rule can never be for the good of a nation, never work for its true progress and life, but must always work towards its disintegration and death. This is no new discovery, no recently invented theory of ours, but an ascertained truth of political science as taught in Europe by Europeans to Europeans. It is there laid down that foreign rule is inorganic and therefore tends to disintegrate the subject body politic by destroying its proper organs and centres of life. If a subject nation is ever to recover and survive, it can only be by reversing the process and establishing its own organic centres of life and strength. We in India had our own instruments of life and growth; we had the self-dependent village; we had the Zemindar as the link between the village units and the central governing body and the central governing body itself was one in which the heart of the nation beat. All these have been either destroyed or crippled by the intrusion of a foreign organism. If we are to survive as a nation we must restore the centres of

* This is a lecture delivered by Sri Aurobindo speaking on the Palli Samiti resolution at Kishoregunj.

strength which are natural and necessary to our growth, and the first of these, the basis of all the rest, the old foundation of Indian life and secret of Indian vitality was the self-dependent and self-sufficient village organism. If we are to organise Swaraj we must base it on the village. But we must at the same time take care to avoid the mistake which did much in the past to retard our national growth. The village must not in our new national life be isolated as well as self-sufficient, but must feel itself bound up with the life of its neighbouring units, living with them in a common group for common purposes. Each group again must feel itself a part of the life of the district, living in the district unity, so each district must not be engrossed in its own separate existence but feel itself a subordinate part of the single life of the province, and the province in its turn of the single life of the country. Such is the plan of reconstruction we have taken in hand, but to make it a healthy growth and not an artificial construction we must begin at the bottom and work up to the apex. The village is the cell of the national body and the cell-life must be healthy and developed for the national body to be healthy and developed. Swaraj begins from the village.

Take another point of view. Swaraj is the organisation of national self-help, national self-dependence. As soon as the foreign organism begins to dominate the body politic, it compels the whole body to look to it as the centre of its activities and neglect its own organs of action till these become atrophied. We in India allowed this tendency of alien domination to affect us so powerfully that we have absolutely lost the habit and for sometime had lost the desire of independent activity and became so dependent and inert that there can be found no example of such helplessness and subservience in history. The whole of our national life was swallowed up by this dependence. Swaraj will only be possible if this habit of subservience is removed and replaced by a habit of self-help. We must take back our life into our own hands and the change must be immediate, complete and drastic. It is no use employing half-measures, for the disease is radical and the cure must be radical also. Our aim must be to revolutionise our habits and leave absolutely no corner of our life and activities in which the habit of dependence is allowed to linger or find refuge for its insidious and destructive working; education, commerce, industry, the administration of justice among ourselves, protection, sanitation, public works, one by one we must take them all back into our hands. Here again the village Samiti is an indispensable instrument, for as this resolution declares, the village Samiti is not to be a mere council for deliberation, but a strong organ of executive work. It is to set up village schools in which our children will grow up as good citizens and patriots to live for their country and not for themselves or for the privilege of dependent life in a dependent nation. It is to take up the work of arbitration by which we shall recover control of the administration of justice, of self-protection, of village sanitation, of small local public works, so that the life of the village may again be self-reliant and self-sufficient, free from the habit of dependence rooted in the soil. Self-help and self-dependence, the first conditions of Swaraj, depend for their organisation on the village Samiti.

Another essential condition of Swaraj is that we should awaken the political sense of the masses. There may have been a time in history when it was enough that a few classes, the ruling classes, the learned classes, at most the trading classes should be awake. But the organisation of the modern nation depends on the awakening of the political sense in the mass. This is the age of the people, the millions, the democracy. If any nation wishes to survive in the modern struggle, if it wishes to recover or maintain Swaraj, it must awaken the people and bring them into the conscious life of the nation, so that every man may feel that in the nation he lives, with the prosperity of the nation he prospers, in the freedom of the nation he is free. This work again depends on the village Samiti. Unless we organise the united life of the village we cannot bridge over the gulf between the educated and the masses. It is here that their lives meet and that they can feel unity. The work of the village Samiti will be to make the masses feel Swaraj in the village, Swaraj in the group of villages, Swaraj in the district, Swaraj in the nation. They cannot immediately rise to the conception of Swaraj in the nation, they must be trained to it through the perception of Swaraj in the village. The political education of the masses is impossible unless you organise the village Samiti.

Swaraj, finally, is impossible without unity. But the unity we need for Swaraj is not a unity of opinion, a unity of speech, a unity of intellectual conviction. Unity is of the heart and springs from love. The foreign organism which has been living on us, lives by the absence of this love, by division, and it perpetuates the condition of its existence by making us look to it as the centre of our lives and away from our Mother and her children. It has set Hindu and Mahomedan at variance by means of this outward outlook; for by regarding it as the fountain of life, however, we are led to look away from our brothers and yearn for what the alien strength can give us. The Hindu first fell a prey to this lure and it was the Mahomedan who was then feared and held down. Now that the Hindu is estranged, the same lure is held out to the Mahomedan and the brother communities kept estranged because they look to the foreigner for the source of prosperity and honours and not to their own Mother. Again, in the old days we did not hear of this distress of the scarcity of water from which the country is suffering now so acutely. It did not exist and could not exist because there was love and the habit of mutual assistance which springs from love. The Zemindar felt that he was one with his tenants and could not justify his existence if they were suffering, so his first thought was to meet their wants and remove their disabilities. But now that we look to a foreign source for everything, this love for our countrymen, this habit of mutual assistance, this sense of mutual duty has disappeared. Each man is for himself and if anything is to be done for our brothers, there is the government to do it and it is no concern of ours. This drying up of the springs of mutual affection is the cause which needs most to be removed and the village Samiti is again the first condition of a better state of things. It will destroy the aloofness, the separateness of our lives and bring us back the sense of community, the habit of mutual assistance and mutual beneficence. It will take up the want of water and remove it. It will introduce arbitration courts and, by healing our family feuds and individual discords, restore the lost sense of brotherhood. It will seek out the sick and give them medical relief. It will meet the want of organisation for famine relief. It will give justice, it will give protection and when all are thus working for the good of all, the old unity of our lives will be restored, the basis of Swaraj will have been laid in the tie which binds together the hearts of our people.

This is therefore no empty resolution, it is the practice of Swaraj to which you are vowing yourselves. Bengal is the leader of Indian regeneration, in Bengal its problems must be worked out and all Bengal is agreed in this — whatever division there may be among us — that the recovery of our self-dependent national life is the aim and end of our national movement. If you are really lovers of Swaraj, if you are not merely swayed by a blind feeling, a cry, but are prepared to work out Swaraj, then the measure of your sincerity shall be judged by the extent to which you carry out this resolution. Before the necessity of these village Samitis was realised there was some excuse for negligence, but now that the whole of Bengal is awakened to the necessity, there is none. You have assembled here from Kishoregunj, from all quarters of the Mymensingh district and on behalf of the people of Mymensingh are about to pass this resolution. If by this time next year you have not practically given effect to it, we shall understand that your desire for Swaraj is a thing not of the heart but of the lips or of the intellect at most. But if by that time Mymensingh is covered with village Samitis in full action, then we shall know that one District at least in Bengal has realised the conditions of Swaraj and when one District has solved the problem, it is only a question of time when over all Bengal and over all India, Swaraj will be realised.

April 26, 1908

New Conditions

A GREAT deal of the work done by us during the last three years has been of a purely preparatory character. The preparation of the national mind was the first necessity. All that the old schools of politics did was to prepare the way for the new thought by giving a full trial to the delusions that then possessed the people and demonstrating their complete futility. Since the awakening of the nation to the misdirection of its energies a fresh delusion has taken possession for a time of the national mind, and this is the idea that a great revolution can be worked out without the sacrifices of which history tells in the case of other nations. There is a general shrinking from the full danger of the struggle, a wish to try by how few sacrifices the work can be accomplished and at how cheap a cost the priceless boon of liberty can be purchased. This reluctance to enter on the real struggle was a necessary and salutary stage of the movement, because the nation, after the long pauperisation of its energies and enervation of its character by a hundred years of dependence and mendicancy, would have been unequal to the sacrifices the real struggle demands. A fresh stage is at hand in which this reluctance can no longer be indulged. A nation cannot afford to haggle with Providence or to buy liberty in the cheapest market from the Dispenser of human fate. The sooner the struggle now commences, the sooner the fate of India is fought out between the forces of progress and reaction, the better for India and for the world. Delay will only waste our strength and give opportunities to the enemy. A band of men is needed who can give up everything for their country, whose sole thought and occupation shall be the stimulation of the movement by whatever means the moment suggests or opportunity allows. If such a band can be got together, then only will real work as distinct from the work of preparation be possible; for the salvation of a country cannot be the work of our leisure moments, the product of our superfluous energy or the result of a selfish life in which the country comes in only for the leavings. Devoted servants of India are needed who will ask for no reward, no ease, no superfluities, but only their bare maintenance and a roof over their heads to enable them to work for her. This attitude of utter self-abandonment is the first condition of success. *Sannyāsa*, utter and inexorable, *tyāga*, unreserved and pitiless, *mumuksutva*, burning and insatiable, must be the stamp of the true servant of India. Academical knowledge, power of debate, laborious study of problems, the habit of ease and luxury at home and slow and tentative work abroad, the attitude of patience and lesiurely self-preparation are not for this era or for this country. An immense and incalculable revolution is at hand and its instruments must be themselves immense in their aspiration, uncalculating in their self-immolation. A sacrifice of which the mightiest *yajña* of old can only be a feeble type and far-off shadow, has to be instituted and the victims of that sacrifice are ourselves, our lives, our property, our hopes, our ambitions, all that is personal and not of God, all that is devoted to our own service and taken from the service of the country. The greatest must fall as victims before the God of the sacrifice is satisfied. Whoever is afraid for himself, afraid for his property, afraid for his kith and kin, afraid for his vanity, self-interest, glory, ease or liberty, had better stand aside from the sacrifice, for at any time the call may come to him to lay down all these upon the altar. If he then refuses, his fate will be worse than that of the fugitive who prefers safety to the struggle, for he will be a recusant doomed to suffer without reward and fall without glory.

The times are thickening already with the shadow of a great darkness. The destruction of the Congress, begun at Surat and accomplished at Allahabad, is the prelude for the outburst of the storm that has long been brewing. Great issues were involved in that historic struggle at Surat of which none of the actors were aware. Only posterity looking back with awe on the sequel, will date the commencement of the real world-shaking earthquake from that slight ruffling of the untroubled surface of the soil. The forces that sent that slight quiver of the earth to the surface are hidden as yet from the eye of contemporary politics or only dimly guessed by a few, but within a brief period they will have declared themselves to the amazement of those who thought that they were only playing a clever tactical game with the lifeless figures of a puppet show. The grim forces that have been moving under the surface will now find the field open to them by the shattering of the keystone of the old political edifice. The efforts of the two parties to replace the Congress by new bodies of a party character are not likely to prosper, for the Moderate Convention will fade into nothingness by its inherent want of vitality, while the Congress of the Nationalists, whatever its destiny, will not be the old Congress but a new and incalculable force, the product of a revolution and perhaps its plaything. The disappearance of the old Congress announces the end of the preparatory stage of the movement, the beginning of a clash of forces whose first full shock will produce chaos. The fair hopes of an orderly and peaceful evolution of self-government, which the first energies of the new movement had fostered, are gone for ever. Revolution, bare and grim, is preparing her battle-field, mowing down the centres of order which were evolving a new cosmos and building up the materials of a gigantic downfall and a mighty new-creation. We could have wished it otherwise, but God's will be done.

Whom to Believe?

The account of the Conference given by the Lucknow *Advocate* which we quote elsewhere makes curious reading. If we are to believe this apparently well-informed source, the reports of the great fight made by the Bengal Moderates are a tissue of exaggerations. There was no fight at all over the question of creed or objects, and indeed the difference of name is so trivial that the legend of this stout fight over a shadow has little verisimilitude. About the question of the subscription to the creed the only difference between the Bengal-Punjab Party and the Bombay-United Provinces Party was whether it should be obligatory to sign the creed or sufficient to swear verbally to it. *That the clause should be binding and express acceptance obligatory as a condition of admission to the Congress, both parties were agreed.* What becomes then of the story of Surendranath's gallant battle for the freedom of election and freedom of conscience in the Congress? It seems that the whole Committee was solid for exclusion. The other point of difference was whether there should be a new Congress called by the Convention or the adjourned Congress resummoned by Dr. Rash Behari Ghose. As this adjourned Congress would in any case be saddled with the creed and the Convention constitution, it would be in effect a new Congress. This subject of quarrel, too, like the others, turns out to be a distinction without a difference. According to the *Advocate*, then, Surendranath's Party and the Mehta Party were in entire agreement, only the Bengal members wanted to call the same things by other names. Not a creed but a statement of objects binding on every delegate; not a written subscription but a verbal oath of allegiance; not a new Congress without the Nationalists, but the old Congress without the Nationalists. If we are to believe the *Advocate*, the Bengal Moderates only succeeded in showing themselves consummate hypocrites and fencers with words. If this account be a libel on them, it should, we think, be authoritatively contradicted. Otherwise, the public will form their own conclusions.

BY THE WAY

The Parable of Sati

Daksha, the great Prajapati, had a daughter, named Sati, whom he loved beyond all his children, and the Rishis wedded her to Mahadeva, the great lord of the Universe. The choice of the Rishis was not pleasing to Daksha, because he was unable to see in Mahadeva anything but a houseless ascetic wandering with the beasts of the field and the demons of the night, a beggar's bowl in his hand, his body smeared with ashes, a tiger's skin for his only robe. His scorn increased the more he came to know of his son-in-law, a Bhang-eating, lazy ne'er-do-weel, with no ascertainable means of livelihood, no home, no property, no degree or other educational qualification, no stake in the world. He cursed the Rishis for fools and evil counsellors, visionaries who saw in this pauper with his bowl and his matted hair the Master of the World. So when he had to offer a great sacrifice, he sent invitations to all the gods, but deliberately excluded his son-in-law. The result was disastrous. Sati, full of grief and indignation at the affront to her lord, gave up her body and disappeared from mortal ken. Then came Mahadeva in his wrath, the mighty One, the destroyer of Universes, and broke Daksha's sacrifice to pieces and shattered the hall of sacrifice and slew Daksha in his hall.

*

There was a Daksha too in India which was called the Indian National Congress. Like Daksha it was a great figure, a Prajapati with numerous offspring, full of dignity, sobriety, wisdom, and much esteemed by the gods. This Daksha too had a daughter whom he loved, the young Indian Nation. When the time for her marriage came, she chose for herself the bridegroom offered to her by the Rishis who declared him to be Mahadeva, the Destiny of India and her fated Lord. It was at sacred Benares that she first saw Mahadeva face to face and betrothed herself to him, but the marriage took place at Calcutta with a fourfold Mantra, Swaraj, Swadeshi, Boycott, National Education, as the sacred formula of union. The marriage did not please Daksha, but the Rishis were importunate and Sati firm, so he was compelled to give way. He cursed the Rishis freely. "What manner of husband is this they have given to my Sati? A homeless beggar, wild and half crazy with the Bhang he has drunk, wandering on the hills in company with the wild beasts and the demons, without culture, enlightenment and education, rude in speech, rough in manners, ill-clad, destitute, with no past, no present and no future! Yet these fanatics call him the Master of the World, an embodiment of the Almighty, and what not!" So he hid his grief and wrath but determined to be revenged. For Mahadeva the Mighty, the Destiny of India, had long wandered in the wilderness with a beggar's bowl in his hand, poor and destitute, an ascetic smeared with ashes and clad in a tiger's skin, with no home in which he could lay down his head. And when he came to the marriage, it was in fearsome guise and in evil company, drunk with the Bhang of a wild inspiration, shouting "Bombom Bande Mataram" at the top of his mighty voice, disreputable in appearance and unfit to associate with polite and cultured gentlemen such as Daksha had hitherto made his friends, poor, shaggy, ill-clad, with no visible means of existence and no tangible prospects in the future; and his companions were a wild company of lathi-bearing National Volunteers and other disquieting phantasms quite out of place in Daksha's tastefully got-up and elegant marriage Pandal. How could Daksha realise that in this uncouth figure was the Destroyer and Creator of an Universe, One who held the fate of India and of the world in his hands? The Rishis only knew it and they were called visionaries and fanatics for their pains.

*

Daksha prepared a great annual sacrifice in the year after the marriage and held it with much pomp, but he determined to exclude Mahadeva the Mighty from the sacrifice and so framed the rules of admission that the undesirable son-in-law might keep away in future. The result is known to everybody. The Destiny of India, whom Daksha tried to exclude, came in wrath and knocked at the gates of the hall of sacrifice and when Daksha's hired men tried to beat him back, he broke into the hall and shattered the sacrifice and slew Daksha in his hall.

*

The story goes that Mahadeva, entreated on behalf of Daksha, restored him to life, but when the head of Daksha was sought for, it could not be found, and so a goat's head was incontinently clapped on the unfortunate Prajapati's shoulders. When the modern Daksha died, there was a similar desire to revive him but the head could not be found. Some said it was lost, others argued in more legal language that it was *functus officio*. Accordingly, these wise men found a goat's head which they called a creed and stuck it on the shoulders of Daksha and put life into his trunk and swore that this goat-headed legless anomaly should in future be called Daksha. Unfortunately, they made the whole thing more grotesque by clapping on the goat's head the wrong way, so that its face was turned backward and, when the crippled monster tried to shove itself along, its progress was retrogression and its advance a retreat. For its eyes were turned to the past and not to the future.

*

Meanwhile, Mahadeva the Mighty wandered over the world carrying the dead body of Sati on his head, dancing a wild dance of ruin which shook the world to its foundations. For Sati had left her old body and men said she was dead. But she was not dead, only withdrawn from the eyes of men, and the gods clove the body of Sati into pieces so that it was scattered all over India, which thing is also a parable; for after the death of the Congress the unity of India which was the daughter of the Congress, must break up into factions and groups. The Convention is already developing parties and in the wild times that are coming the Nationalists also will break up into parties, some of which will make the present designation of extremism as applied to us look an absurdity, and the political life of India will become an anarchy. But not for ever. For Sati will be born again, on the high mountains of mighty endeavour, colossal aspiration, unparalleled self-sacrifice she will be born again, in a better and more beautiful body, and by terrible *tapasyā* she will meet Mahadeva once more and be wedded to him in nobler fashion, with kinder auguries, for a happier and greater future. For this thing is written in the book of God and nothing can prevent it, that Sati shall wed Mahadeva, that the national life of India shall meet and possess its divine and mighty destiny.

Bande Mataram, April 29, 1908

Leaders and a Conscience

We find it difficult not to sympathise with one passage at least on

Mr. Khare's letter to the Dhulia Reception Committee. "Moreover," he says, "I don't know who the leaders are. I for instance cannot specify any such, nor can I give my conscience into the keeping of anyone." We cannot follow Mr. Khare in his ultra-judicial ignorance of the personality of the party leaders, and it is certainly hard on Sir Pherozshah and Mr. Gokhale that a new recruit should so bluntly express his inability to specify them as leaders. But the concluding sentiment is unexceptionable and we think the Dhulia Reception Committee made a mistake in calling on the leaders to unite instead of referring, as the Pabna Conference did, to a definite authority. The time has gone by when a few leaders could play a quiet game among themselves with the destinies of the country. Mr. Khare was once taken for a Nationalist of a sort, and we are glad that he preserves in his new camp so much at least of Nationalist robustness as to keep possession of his own conscience. We Nationalists too, like Mr. Khare, decline to give our conscience into the keeping of anyone, be it a leader or a knot of leaders, or the whole Congress itself in session assembled. For this precise reason we refuse to sign or verbally swear to any creed imposed on us from outside.

An Ostrich in Colootola

Srijut Surendranath's organ is very anxious for union, we wish it were equally passionate for truth. The country has begun to speak out about the Convention and at Dhulia and Chittagong references have been made to the Convention and opinions expressed for an united Congress on the old lines which are of the utmost significance. The *Bengalee* seems to have received precisely the same telegram as we have received from Dhulia and it marks it as sent by its Own Correspondent. Yet the merciless manner in which it has dealt with the telegram of its Own Correspondent is amusing and instructive. The speech of the Dhulia President breaks off abruptly in our contemporary's telegram with a blessing on the National Schools and all the rest of the weighty and trenchant remarks about the Convention and the Continuation Committee are boycotted. But is anything gained by burking facts or burying one's head in the sand in this ostrich fashion? It is an old moderate habit but one which does not improve with age.

·

I Cannot Join

We quote the following from Mr. Khare's letter to the Secretaries of the Dhulia Reception Committee giving his reasons for withdrawing from the Presidentship. "I see resolution No. IV adopted by them. This resolution calls upon the leaders of all the parties in the land to make a united effort to arrange the holding of the next Congress etc. Now having signed the creed *I cannot join those who refuse to sign the creed* (until at all events the creed is formally set aside) in arranging the holding of the National Congress etc." The attitude of Mr. Khare is the attitude of the Bombay and Poona Moderates and Srijut Surendranath had a taste of it at Allahabad. Yet the *Bengalee* still talks smoothly of remaining in the Convention in order to secure a mandate for Dr. Rash Behari Ghose to resummon the adjourned Congress! But Srijut Surendranath was always a sanguine optimist.

BY THE WAY

Colootola Conjures

There are some who believe that passion and conviction are the sign of want of culture. If the language of poetry is used by a political writer, it shows lack of balance. The use of imagination, the presence of inspiration, the full expression of feeling are violent and indecorous. Whatever the depth of emotion felt, whatever the inspiring character of the vision seen, the emotion must be banished, the inspiration killed, otherwise wisdom takes flight. If our politics had been left to these gentlemen, it would have remained the decorous pastime of lawyers and sober educationists, a sort of half-forensic, half-academic debate with the bureaucracy on the merits of its rule. Sobriety, moderation, wisdom would have been satisfied and the nation killed by a surfeit of gentlemanly decorum. Unluckily for the *Bengalee* and its ilk, the days of "modest and sober and mostly unreadable prose", of Colootola "common sense", of the "healthy mind" which was too healthy to think and too sound to be sincere, are gone. The great passions which move mankind, the rude forces which shake the world, the majestic visions which bring life to dead nations have once more become part of our national existence, and in vain Colootola waves its conjuring rod of bad logic, inconsistent sentiment and sober imbecility to quell the phantasms. They are not to be quelled.

Common Sense and Revolutions

The *Bengalee* is scornful of our prophetic visions. The man of common sense who cannot see what lies before his nose, naturally considers the man who can see a prophet or a visionary. Before the French Revolution many travellers visited France, but only one or two were able to see that there existed in the quiet of that country all the conditions that have in history preceded great revolutions. The men who perceived it were not prophets but merely observers, gifted with sympathy and insight. They were, in fact, men of *uncommon* sense. The *Bengalee* and its like are unable to conceive that anything great can happen in India. Formerly it believed that we should go on for several centuries prosing about our political grievances in an ineffective debating society called the National Congress. Even now it believes that the country will remain obedient to the call of what it terms sobriety, and that fate will wait upon the prudence and fears of a few respectable and wealthy gentlemen in Calcutta and Bombay. Its idea of our future is that we should become a big outlying parish of England, and of the means, that we should peddle forever with the details of a bureaucratic administration.

Pace and Solidarity

It is impossible for such minds, — if minds they can be called — to perceive that what is happening is the first stage of a revolution or that the condition of keeping the wilder forces of revolution in harness was the solidarity of the movement. Once that solidarity has been broken, it is the wildest and most rapid forces which will set the pace; there will be no mean resultant of all the forces producing a swift and yet ordered advance. The solidarity of the movement depends on the existence of an united Congress in which the Moderates and Nationalists should form the brake and the motive energy respectively. But the united Congress has been suffocated with a creed at Allahabad and with it the solidarity of the movement and the check on the fiercer forces which have recently given evidences of their existence will disappear. That means if not "the aproaching end of the world" at least the end of that state of the Indian world in which Surendranaths can perorate, Mehtas brew mischief and Colootola daily enjoy its robust digestion of its own sober and modest prose.

*

The *Bengalee* pretends that the Congress, even after Allahabad, is only collapsed and not dead. Its receipe for reviving the patient is that Dr. Ghose should resummon the adjourned Congress. Great Rash Behari has only to send forth his almighty voice, accompanied by a telling literary joke and an appropriate quotation, has only to say with his inimitable gesture and facial expression, "Let there be an united Congress", and, behold, an united Congress! And Mr. Khare's resolution calling a new Congress does not preclude, it seems, Dr. Ghose from resummoning the adjourned Congress! This is the finished product of Colootola's common sense and the healthy mind that flourishes only at Barrackpore.

*

The Voice of Colootola has been lashed into a rage by our article on the Wheat and the Chaff. Unable to wound itself, it engages a correspondent to do the work for it. The exposure of moderate policy which that article made has irritated this gentleman into an outburst of spleen too bitter to be contained, and he foams at the mouth in his fury. "Why should the Nationalists arrogate the right to instruct their elders? What have they done? Who are they? We are the leaders of the people and they are only self-styled leaders. What right have they to be an independent party? They are cowards who dare not act except behind the veil of the Moderates, and are angry because that veil is being withdrawn. Their leaders are ungrateful scoundrels to abuse the party of the barristers who saved them from jail." So the friend of Colootola.

*

A good deal of this epic rage would have been saved if the irate correspondent had taken the trouble to understand the article before writing about it. What we have written about the Moderates, we have written and we do not withdraw one syllable of it. Their action at Allahabad was a betrayal of the country dictated by fear and self-interest. Among those who took part in it, there are prominent men who no more believe in Colonial self-government for India than they believe in the man in the moon. The part they played is especially reprehensible. Others are anxious to put themselves right with the bureaucratic government and hardly take the trouble to conceal their motives. The few who were sincere both in their profession of the creed and in their belief that it is necessary for the country, are too insignificant to be reckoned.

*

What the *Bengalee*'s friend in need has not understood is the latter part of the article in which we pointed out that the amateur kind of Nationalism which has hitherto been the order of the day will no longer serve. The real workers are yet to come.

This part of the homily in which, by the way, the reference to the barristers occurred as addressed to our own party and if anyone has any right to take umbrage at it, it is the Nationalists, barristers or others, and not pseudo-Nationalists like our Colootola critic. The steel for the Mother's sword of which we spoke is not the present Nationalist Party as he imagines, but the rising generation of young men. They are the wheat which will remain. Of the present Nationalist Party much will be winnowed away in the fiercer tests that are coming and rejected as chaff, only a small residue remaining. We do not know whether it was want of patience or want of English which prevented our critic from seeing the drift of the article — probably a combination of these lamentable wants — but if he will take the trouble to reread it with the help of a tutor, he may even yet understand. We did not condemn pleading in Swadeshi cases or taking shares in Swadeshi concerns any more than we condemned subscribing to National School funds. We said that these were safe and petty forms of patriotism and those who could not go beyond them were not the stuff of which the future will be built. And that is, after all, only a truism. Our whole lives are what is demanded of us and not a bit of our leisure or a mite from our purse.

Bande Mataram, April 30, 1908

Ideals Face to Face

A NEW ordeal always brings with it a new awakening. The ordeal of Partition brought with it a great industrial awakening with politics as its undercurrent, a sort of economico-political self-realisation. All that such an awakening could do for the political future of the country has now been done. The ordeal of the Risley Circular brought with it a great educational awakening with politics as its impulse, a sort of politico-educational self-realisation. The ordeal of the Congress split will also bring with it a fresh awakening. This time the awakening will be political with a religious undercurrent. It is time that the nation rose above Swadeshi to Swaraj. It is time that it left the path of self-realisation through disguises and side-issues and flung itself frankly and wholly into the attempt to win Swaraj. The Surat split took place over the side-issue of the President's election, but the Convention's attitude has brushed away all side-issues and brought to the front the question of Swaraj. The future success of the Nationalist Party depends on the boldness with which it takes up the real point at issue and affirms its beliefs. If it hedges, then the Convention will have a sort of sanction for its attitude which will give it a moral force otherwise entirely lacking to its action. The ideal of unqualified Swaraj has a charm for the national mind which is irresistible if it is put before it in the national way by minds imbued with Indian feeling and free from the gross taint of Western materialism. Swaraj as a sort of European ideal, political liberty for the sake of political self-assertion, will not awaken India. Swaraj as the fulfilment of the ancient life of India under modern conditions, the return of the *satyayuga* of national greatness, the resumption by her of her great *role* of teacher and guide, self-liberation of the people for the final fulfilment of the Vedantic ideal in politics, this is the true Swaraj for India. Of all the proud nations of the West there is an end determined. When their limited special work for mankind is done they must decay and disappear. But the function of India is to supply the world with a perennial source of light and renovation. Whenever the first play of energy is exhausted and earth grows old and weary, full of materialism, racked with problems she cannot solve, the function of India is to restore the youth of mankind and assure it of immortality. She sends forth a light from her bosom which floods the earth and the heavens, and mankind bathes in it like St. George in the well of life and recovers strength, hope and vitality for its long pilgrimage. Such a time is now at hand. The world needs India and needs her free. The work she has to do now is to organise life in the terms of Vedanta, and that is a work she cannot do while overshadowed by a foreign power and a foreign civilisation. She cannot do it without taking the management of her own life into her own hands. She must live her own life and not the life of a part or subordinate in a foreign Empire.

All political ideals must have relation to the temperament and past history of the race. The genius of India is separate from that of any other race in the world, and perhaps there is no race in the world whose temperament, culture and ideals are so foreign to her own as those of the practical, hard-headed, Pharisaic, shopkeeping Anglo-Saxon. The culture of the Anglo-Saxon is the very antipodes of Indian culture. The temper of the Anglo-Saxon is the very reverse of the Indian temper. His ideals are of the earth, earthy. His institutions are without warmth, sympathy, human feeling, rigid and accurate like his machinery, meant for immediate and practical gains. The reading of democracy which he has adopted and is trying to introduce first in the colonies because the mother country is still too much shackled by the past, is the most sordid possible, centred on material aims and void of generous idealism. In such a civilisation, as part of such an Empire, India can have no future. If she is to model herself on the Anglo-Saxon type she must first kill everything in her which is her own. If she is to be a province of the British Empire, part of its life, sharing its institutions, governed by its policy, the fate of Greece under Roman dominion will surely be hers. She may share the privileges and obligations of British citizenship, — though the proud Briton who excludes the Indian from his colonies and treats him as a lower creature, will perish rather than concede such an equality, — but she will lose her Indian birthright. She will have to pass a sponge over her past and obliterate it from her life, even if she preserves the empty records of it in her schools. The degradation of a great nation, by the loss of her individuality, her past and her independent future, to the position of a subordinate satellite in a foreign system, is the ideal of the Convention. It is sheer political atheism, the negation of all that we were, are and hope to be. The return of India on her eternal self, the restoration of her splendour, greatness, triumphant Asiatic supremacy is the ideal of Nationalism. Is it doubtful which ideal will be more acceptable to the nation, that which calls on it to murder its instincts, sacrifice its future and deny its past for the advantage of an inglorious security, or that which asks it to fulfil itself by the strenuous reassertion of all that is noble and puissant in the blood it draws from such an heroic ancestry as no other nation can boast?

The ideal creates the means of attaining the ideal, if it is itself true and rooted in the destiny of the race. All that can be said for the Convention's ideal is that it saves the professor of the ideal from the wrath of the bureaucracy. Otherwise it is as grotesquely out of proportion to the strength of the people who profess it as any which the Nationalist can uphold. It has no exciting virtue of divine enthusiasm which can inspire to heroic effort and enable a fallen nation to shake off its weakness, turn cowards into heroes and selfish men into self-denying martyrs of the cause, and yet the effort it demands for realisation is as heroic as anything which the Nationalist expects from the people. The pride of race, the pride of empire, the pride of colour are the three invincible barriers which stand between it and its realisation. What force have the Conventionalists to set against these? Tears and supplications, appeals to British justice and British generosity — nothing else. They are not serious in their ideal and do not really hold it but flaunt it as a counterpoise to the Nationalist ideal so that the country may be deceived into thinking they have an aim and a policy. They have none. A false ideal is always a veil for something else, and the Convention creed is with some a veil for secret hopes of liberty which they dare not avow and with others a veil for the absence of any aim except the hope of securing a few peddling reforms in the existing system of administration.

The future is with the Nationalist ideal because there is no other. But the danger is that the false shadow of an ideal which is now being put forward as a reality will be accepted as a convenient instrument for self-protection against the anger of the bureaucracy. The temptation it holds out is one to which all new faiths are exposed, that which was the chief danger of Christianity in the days of persecution, to which, for a fleeting moment, Mahomed is said to have succumbed when harassed by the Koreish, the temptation of securing a respite from persecution by a false profession which, masking itself as a harmless piece of diplomacy, will really be a fatal stab at the very heart of the new religion. This temptation must be religiously eschewed and the true issue boldly proclaimed if Nationalism is to fulfil its divinely-appointed mission.

Bande Mataram, May 1, 1908

The New Nationalism*

THE nicknames of party warfare have often passed into the accepted terminology used by serious politicians and perpetuated by history, and it is possible that the same immortality may await the designations of Moderates and Extremists by which the two parties now contending for the mind of the nation are commonly known. The forward party is the party of Nationalism; but what is Nationalism? For there is a great deal in a name in spite of Shakespeare. The word has only recently begun to figure as an ordinary term of our politics and it has been brought into vogue by the new, forward or extreme party, which, casting about for a convenient description of themselves, selected the new name as the only one covering in a word their temper and gospel as attached to a political party or school of thought. A name serves not only to show the temper and point of view of the giver, but it helps greatly to colour contemporary ideas about the party it seeks to exalt or disparage. The advanced men whom Anglo-Indian and Moderate unite in branding as Extremists have always repudiated the misleading designators. At first they preferred to call themselves the New School; they now claim the style of Nationalists, a claim which has been angrily objected to on the ground that the rest of the Congress Party are as good Nationalists as the forward party.

The new Nationalism, I said in a former article in this Review, is a negation of the old bourgeois ideals of the nineteenth century. It is an attempt to relegate the dominant bourgeois to his old obscurity, to transform the bourgeois into the Samurai and through him to extend the workings of the Samurai spirit to the whole nation, or to put it more broadly, it is an attempt to create a nation in India by reviving the spirit and action of the ancient Indian character, the strong, great and lofty spirit of old Aryavarta and setting it on fire, and mould the methods and mate-

* This article was produced as an exhibit in the Alipore Conspiracy Case and was first published in the *Hindusthan Standard* of August 14, 1938.

rials of modernity for the freedom, greatness and well-being of an historic and immortal people. This is not, I am well aware, a description under which the ordinary Congress politician will recognise what he knows of desperate Extremism, but it will be well understood by those who are constant readers of the Nationalist journals in Bengal, whether the *Bande Mataram* or *New India* or vernacular journals like the *Yugantar*, the *Nabasakti*, or the *Sandhya*. Whatever their differences of temper or tone, however the methods they recommend may differ in detail, they are united by a common faith and a common spirit, a common faith in the Nationalism which existed in India before it became definite and articulate in Bengal. But it is Bengal that gave it a philosophy, a faith, a method and a battle-cry. India, not an Anglicised and transmogrified nation unrecognisable as India, but an India of the immortal past, India of the clouded but fateful present, India mighty, crowned with the imperial diadem of the future, a common spirit of enthusiasm, hope, desire to demand all things so that our vision of her future may be fulfilled greatly and soon: this is the heart of Nationalism. The ordinary Congress politician's ideas of Nationalism are associated with wasted discussions in committee and Congress, altercations at public meetings, unsparing criticism of successful and eminent respectabilities, sedition trials, National volunteers, East Bengal disturbances, Rawalpindi riots. To him the Nationalist is nothing more than an Extremist, a violent, unreasonable, uncomfortable being whom some malign power has raised up to disturb with his Swaraj and boycott, his lawlessness and his lathis the respectable class and the safety of Congress politics. He finds him increasing in numbers and influence with an alarming rapidity which it is convenient to deny but impossible to ignore; he has no clear idea of the aim and the drift of Extremism, but he imagines it to be its object to drive out the English and make India free by boycott and lathis, and having thus erected a scarecrow to chuck stones at, he thinks himself entitled to dismiss the New Party from his mind as a crowd of enthusiasts who talk nonsense and advocate impossibilities.

Nationalism cannot be so easily dismissed; a force which has shaken the whole of India, trampled the traditions of a century into a refuse of irrecoverable fragments and set the mightiest of modern empires groping in a panic for weapons strong enough to meet a new and surprising danger, must have some secret of strength and therefore of truth in it which is worth knowing. To get at the heart of Nationalism we must first clear away some of the conceptions with which its realities have been clouded. We must know what Nationalism is not, before we ask what it is.

Extremism in the sense of unreasoning violence of spirit and the preference of desperate methods, because they are desperate, is not the heart of Nationalism. The Nationalist does not advocate lawlessness for its own sake; on the contrary, he has deeper respect for the essence of the law than anyone else, because the building up of a nation is his objective and he knows well that without a profound reverence for law a national life cannot persist and attain a sound and healthy development. But he qualifies his respect for legality by the proviso that the law he is called upon to obey is the law of the nation, an outgrowth of the organic existence and part of its Government. A law imposed from outside can command only the obedience of those whose chief demand from life is the safety to their persons and property, or the timid obedience of those who understand the danger of breaking the law. The claim made by it is an utilitarian, not a moral claim. Farther, the Nationalist never loses sight of the truth that law was made for man and not man for law. Its chief function and reason for existence is to safeguard and foster the growth and happy flowering into strength and health of National life. And a law which does not subserve this end or which opposes and contradicts the same, however rigidly it may enforce peace, or order and security, forfeits its claim to respect and obedience. Nationalism refuses to accept law as a fetish or peace and security as an aim in themselves; the only idol of its worship is Nationality and the only aim it in itself recognises is the freedom, power, and well-being of the Nation. It will not prefer violent or strenuous methods simply because they are violent or strenuous, but neither will it cling to mild and peaceful methods simply because they are mild and peaceful. It asks of a method whether it is effective for its purpose, whether it is worthy of a great people struggling to be, whether it is educative of national strength and activity; and these things ascertained, it asks nothing farther. The Nationalist does not love anarchy and suffering for their own sake, but if anarchy and suffering are the necessary passage to the great consummation he seeks, he is ready to bear them himself, to expose others to them till the end is reached. They will embrace suffering of their children, and embrace suffering as a lover and clasp the hand of anarchy like that of a trusted friend. It is not the temper of the Nationalist to take the inevitable grudgingly or to serve or struggle with a half heart. If that is Extremism and fanaticism, he is an Extremist and a fanatic; but not for their own sake, not out of a disordered love for anarchy and turmoil, not in madness and desperation but out of a reasoned conviction and courageous acceptance of the natural love by which a man who aspires to reach a difficult height must climb up the steep rocks and risk life and limb in arduous places, that have decreed that men who desire to live as free men in a free country must not refuse to be ready to pay toll for freedom with their own blood, the blood of their children, and still more, the nation which seeks to grow out of subjection into liberty must consent first to manure the soil with the tears of its women and the bodies of its sons. The Nationalist knows what he asks from fate and he knows the price that fate asks from him in return. Knowing it he is ready to drag the nation with him into the valley of the shadow of death, dark with night and mist and storm, sown thick and crude with perils of strange monsters and perils of morass and fire and flood, holding all danger and misery as nothing because beyond the valleys are the mountains of Beulah, where the nation shall enjoy eternal life. He is ready to lead the chosen people into the desert of long wanderings though he knows that often in the bitterness of its sufferings it will murmur and rebel against his leadership and raise its hand to stone him to death as the author of its misery, for he knows that beyond is the promised land flowing with milk and honey which, the divine voice has told him, those who are faithful will reach and possess. If he embraces anarchy, it is as the way to good government. If he does not shrink from disorder and violent struggle it is because without that disorder there can be no security and without that struggle no peace, except the security of decay and the peace of death. If he has sometimes to disregard the law of man, it is to obey the dictates of his conscience and the law of God.

CONTENTS ARRANGED SUBJECTWISE

CONTENTS ARRANGED SUBJECTWISE

Swaraj, Swadeshi, Boycott, National Education

References to Individuals

BIBLIOGRAPHICAL NOTE

Volume I of the SRI AUROBINDO BIRTH CENTENARY LIBRARY is a compilation of Sri Aurobindo's political writings and speeches of the period 1890 to May 1908. Concerned principally with India's freedom from British rule and the means of attaining it, they cover also the resurgence of Asiatic countries, the necessity of their emergence as representatives of spiritual culture, and other historical and contemporary events or issues.

Sri Aurobindo's preoccupation with India's freedom and renaissance began in his student days at Cambridge where he gave speeches at meetings of the Indian Majlis. Only a few incomplete notes on this subject are found in his manuscripts of 1890-1892.

Soon after his return to India in 1893, Sri Aurobindo contributed a series of unsigned articles to the *Indu Prakash*, a Marathi-English daily of Bombay, at the request of its editor, K. G. Deshpande, his Cambridge friend. The series called "New Lamps for Old" was stopped after a time because the editors were advised that, if the views expressed in their columns were continued, the Government would take action against the paper. The nine articles of this series written during the period 1893-1894 are reproduced here directly from the *Indu Prakash.* Haridas Mukherjee and Uma Mukherjee have included them in their book *Sri Aurobindo's Political Thought* (Calcutta 1958).

From 1894 to 1902 we do not find any political writings, published or unpublished.

From 1902 to 1906 Sri Aurobindo carried on his political work in secret. Some stray notes and unfinished articles found in his manuscripts of that period have been collected in this volume. Of the published writings of this period only *Bhavani Mandir* exists. This was recovered from the Government of West Bengal files and first printed in the *Sri Aurobindo Mandir Annual* in 1956. 'No Compromise', an article which was privately printed and circulated, has not been traced so far.

Only after his return to Bengal in February 1906 could Sri Aurobindo do his political work openly, unhampered by conditions imposed by his Baroda service. In March the same year, under his guidance his brother Barindra Kumar and others started a Bengali weekly, *Yugantar*. Sri Aurobindo wrote a few articles in the earlier issues of this journal and kept a general control over its conduct and policy. It openly preached revolutionary ideals of political freedom and action. We have, however, not been able to find a single copy of this journal.

On August 7, 1906 the *Bande Mataram* was started by Bepin Chandra Pal with Sri Aurobindo's assistance. It was in this journal that Sri Aurobindo gave full expression to his ideas on Independence as India's political goal and discussed the methods of its realisation. Of this journal no complete file is available at present. Only one file is known to be extant, that with the Prabartak Sangha of Chandernagore, and this is incomplete. The file, however, of the *Bande Mataram Weekly*, which began later in June 1907, is available in its entirety. As most of the important editorials, articles and comments published in the *Bande Mataram Daily* were reproduced in this Weekly, the period from June 1907 to September 1908 is well represented. The gaps in the file are most notable in August, November and December 1906 and January 1907. A series of articles on the Calcutta Congress of December 1906, referred to in *The Doctrine of Passive Resistance*, is missing.

After Bepin Chandra Pal left the *Bande Mataram* sometime towards the end of 1906 Sri Aurobindo became its chief editorial writer. The paper had no declared editor. (Sri Aurobindo's name was given in one issue without his knowledge but was withdrawn on his protesting against it.) Sri Aurobindo was the guiding spirit,[1] but there were other contributors of marked literary ability: Shyam Sunder Chakravarty, Bijoy Krishna Chatterjee and Hemendra Prasad Ghosh, and it would have been very difficult to attribute specific *Bande Mataram* editorials to Sri Aurobindo with reasonable certainty were it not that a certain number of them, admittedly small, had been identified by Sri Aurobindo himself. References and allusions in his notes[2] and letters have also been made use of in identifying his writings. A few of the articles selected for inclusion in this volume on the basis of style have been confirmed by notes made by Hemendra Prasad Ghosh in his diary.

The *Bande Mataram* editorials and leading articles were occasionally reproduced in other papers of the time, *e.g.* in the *Maratha* of Poona, and were also translated into several Indian languages. A journal in Marathi, *Vande Mataram*, published by Hari Raghunath Bhagavat from the Vande Mataram Press Poona drew much of its material from its English namesake. The Vande Mataram Press also published in 1909 selections from *Bande Mataram* in three parts. The Swaraj Publishing House, Benares brought out in 1922 a selection from the *Bande Mataram*. Haridas Mukherjee and Uma Mukherjee included some articles in their book *Bande Mataram and Indian Nationalism* (1957). They have also made a comprehensive study and identified over a hundred articles of Sri Aurobindo in their two

[1] R. C. Majumdar in his book *History of the Freedom Movement in India* has quoted the following passage from J. L. Banerji's tribute to Sri Aurobindo.

"Whoever the actual contributor to the *Bande Mataram* might be — the soul, the genius of the paper was Arabinda. The pen might be that of Shyam Sundar or whoever else...but the voice was the voice of Arabinda Ghose...."

[2] See Centenary Volume No. 26, page 28: "Shyam Sunder (Chakravarty) caught up something like Sri Aurobindo's way of writing and later on many took his articles for Sri Aurobindo's."

books, *Sri Aurobindo's Political Thought* (1958) and *Sri Aurobindo and the New Thought in Indian Politics* (1964). But in these books some articles are wrongly attributed to Sri Aurobindo. That they are not by him is revealed by a file of some *Bande Mataram* articles read out to Sri Aurobindo for identification. Similarly *On Nationalism* (1965), published by the Sri Aurobindo Ashram, also contains two articles that are not his.

For the purposes of this volume, all available issues of the *Bande Mataram* were collected in microfilm and photostat copies and their editorial contents studied.

However, even after all the clues and circumstantial evidence have been taken into account, the authorship of some of the writings included here may still be questioned. On the other hand, it may be argued that a few of the articles left out are by Sri Aurobindo. We hope future scholarship will give us a more complete collection made on a surer and ampler basis.

Sri Aurobindo's speeches were brought together in book-form in 1922 by the Prabartak Sangha of Chandernagore. They were reprinted in 1948 by the Arya Publishing House, Calcutta and issued again by the Sri Aurobindo Ashram in 1952 and 1969. The speeches of 1907-1908 and 1909-1910 are arranged chronologically in Volumes 1 and 2.

ISBN 81-7058-469-8

Set of 22 volumes Rs. 3500/-